International Conference on Digital Transformation and Innovation Management (DTIM2025), and ICT, Society, and Human Beings (ICT2025)

Held at the Multi-Conference on Computer Science and Information Systems (MCCSIS 2025)

Lisbon, Portugal
23-25 July 2025

ISBN: 979-8-3313-2769-9

Printed from e-media with permission by:

Curran Associates, Inc.
57 Morehouse Lane
Red Hook, NY 12571

Some format issues inherent in the e-media version may also appear in this print version.

International Association for Development of the Information Society (IADIS)
Rua Sao Sebastiao Da Pedreira
No. 100, 30, 1050-209
Lisbon, Portugal

Phone: 351 21 3151373
Fax: 351 21 3151244

secretariat@iadis.org

Additional copies of this publication are available from:

Curran Associates, Inc.
57 Morehouse Lane
Red Hook, NY 12571 USA
Phone: 845-758-0400
Fax: 845-758-2633
Email: curran@proceedings.com
Web: www.proceedings.com

INTERNATIONAL CONFERENCES ON

DIGITAL TRANSFORMATION AND INNOVATION MANAGEMENT 2025

and

ICT, SOCIETY AND HUMAN BEINGS 2025

part of the

MULTI CONFERENCE ON COMPUTER SCIENCE AND INFORMATION SYSTEMS 2025

PROCEEDINGS OF THE INTERNATIONAL CONFERENCES ON

DIGITAL TRANSFORMATION AND INNOVATION MANAGEMENT 2025

and

ICT, SOCIETY AND HUMAN BEINGS 2025

Lisbon, Portugal

JULY 23 - 25, 2025

Organised by

iadis

international association for development of the information society

As a member of Crossref (a non-profit membership organization for scholarly publishing working with the purpose to make content easy to find, link, cite and assess) each published paper in this book of proceedings will be allocated a DOI (Digital Object Identifier) number for its fast and easy citation and indexation.

Volume Editors:
Pedro Isaías, Paula Miranda and Piet Kommers

Computer Science and Information Systems Series Editors:
Piet Kommers and Pedro Isaías

Associate Editor: Luís Rodrigues

TABLE OF CONTENTS

ICT, SOCIETY AND HUMAN BEINGS

SHORT PAPERS

DIGITAL TRANSFORMATION AND INNOVATION MANAGEMENT

ICT, SOCIETY AND HUMAN BEINGS

REFLECTION PAPER

ICT, SOCIETY AND HUMAN BEINGS

POSTERS

ICT, SOCIETY AND HUMAN BEINGS

FOREWORD

These proceedings contain the papers and posters of the International Conference on Digital Transformation and Innovation Management (DTIM 2025) and of the International Conference on ICT, Society and Human Beings (ICT 2025), which were organised by the International Association for Development of the Information Society, from 23-25 July, 2025. These conferences are part of the Multi Conference on Computer Science and Information Systems 2025, 23-25 July, which had a total of 608 submissions.

In the rapidly evolving landscape of technology and business, the International Conference on Digital Transformation and Innovation Management (DTIM 2025) serves as a premier platform for researchers, academicians, and industry practitioners to converge and explore cutting-edge advancements at the intersection of Information Systems and Management Innovation.

This conference aims to foster a collaborative environment that stimulates insightful discussions and paves the way for novel approaches to digital transformation, emphasizing its deep impact on organizational strategies, operations, and global societal progress.

Submissions were accepted under the following 6 main topics:
- Digital Strategy and Leadership:
- Data Analytics and Business Intelligence:
- Emerging Technologies and Disruptive Innovation:
- E-Commerce and Digital Marketing:
- Sustainable Innovation
- Application Areas

The Network period in the evolution of computer technology is very much based on the convergence and integration of three main technologies; computer technology, tele technology and media technology. Telecommunication technology is playing a more and more dominant role in this convergence, especially internet and web technology. Embedded (ubiquitous) computer technology is making the process invisible, and media technologies converge within itself (multimedia and cross media). The convergence process is enforced all the time by smaller, cheaper, and more powerful components.

ICT and its applications are interacting with environments, roles, and processes which can also be modelled by converging circles. The process of social and psychosocial change and ICT from a global perspective is described graphically in the convergence model in figure 1 (Bradley 2006 Routledge) with concepts and their interrelations. Both "convergence" and "interactions" are important features in the model. Read from the left hand side in the model for the titles of some main tracks of the conference:

- Globalisation and ICT: When technology, economy, norms/values and labour market are converging on a global level, what are the hard questions? When the geographical space in the future will be both global and beyond – including virtual reality (VR) what is the state of art in research? (see the list of key words under ´globalisation´)
- Information and Communication Technology (ICT), next cluster of circles to the left in the figure, what applications contribute to desirable goals in the society?

• When Work Environment, Home Environment, and Public Environment are converging and the work and public issues tend to merge into the private sphere of our homes – what main changes in peoples Life Environment occur?.
• If the Professional Role (Work Life), Private Role (Private Life) and Citizen's Role (Public Life) converge forming a Life Role, what are the main social-psychologial changes?
• Four circles representing Virtual Reality (VR) are marked with dotted lines and are surrounding the set of converging circles. These circles reflect our participation in cyberspace on various levels. To the left part in figure we could talk about Virtual Worlds on the global level. Within the concept of ICT, the steps taken by applied Embedded and ubiquitous technology make technology more hidden to the individual and society as a whole.
Virtual Environments are already a common concept. Finally, we could talk about Virtual Human Roles, which could in more extreme forms be another personality that you play e g avatars. The converging circles are forming a Life Role and new life styles are being shaped.
• Effects on humans become more multi faceted and complex. Research focusing upon the individual is crucial i. e. research on how the use of ICT interacts with and impacts identity, social competence, creativity, integrity, trust, dependency etc. A compass rose (card) for "Effects on Humans" (to the right) is used as a metaphor reminding us of the importance to keep the direction towards desirable human and societal goals and qualities at the development and use of ICT.

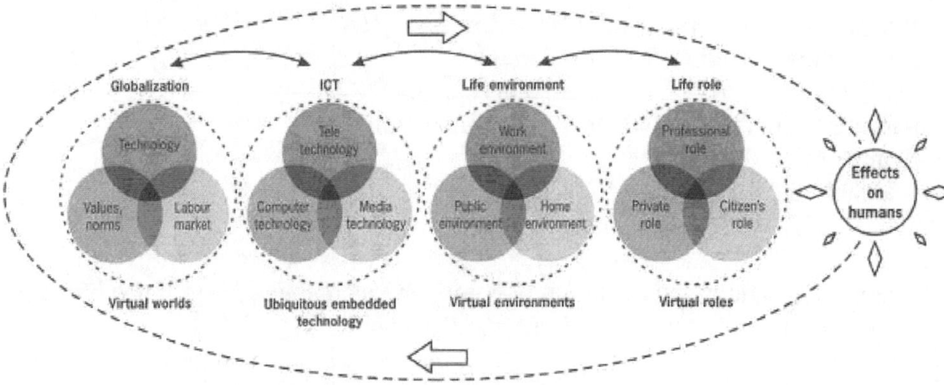

Figure 1. Convergence Model on ICT and Psychosocial Life Environment (Source: Bradley, 2005, 2006)

ICT can provide tools for promoting sustainability (environmental, economic, and social sustainability) but can also be a threat for sustainability. Sustainability as a guiding principle involves system perspective, holism, human aspects, bottom up approach, common good, and equality. A change in focus regarding research and development is taking place. Analysis and design increasingly address both the work process and management connected to the sphere of production life and people's life environment. Analysis and design of ICT and societal systems both at local level and globally become important. What research in the field exists or is needed?

Community research in a broad sense comes to the fore – both physical and virtual communities. There is also a requirement to involve new and additional actors at the deeper and broader integration of ICT in the society (children, elderly, and consumer organisations). Educational programs on Community Informatics and Social Informatics are appearing in many academic institutions. Can a new infrastructure of the society be identified?

The effects of ICT on human beings as well as the interaction between ICT, individuals, and society are all within the focus of this conference. Both analyses of interactions and effects are important. Changes in behaviour, perspectives, values, competencies, human and psychological aspects and feelings are all of interest. Reflections on past, present, and future challenges – especially planning for handling the latter – are encouraged.

Today, computer science and ICT-related disciplines are working more and more together with various behavioural and social sciences including child psychology and developmental psychology. For this reason, the conference pays attention to societal changes, global and more local organisational and institutional changes, changes in values and in lifestyles, as well as individual cognitive effects and changes, motivational and emotional changes. It also appeals to solution-building in terms of desirable goals and actions for reaching a Good Information Society.

In general, all types of research strategies are encouraged, and especially cross-disciplinary and multi-disciplinary studies. Case studies, broader empirical field studies, theoretical analyses, cross-cultural studies, scenarios, ethnographic studies, epistemological analyses may all be presented.

The ICT, Society and Human Beings 2025 conference addresses in detail seven main aspects:
- Globalization and ICT
- Life environment and ICT
- Life role and ICT
- ICT and effects on humans
- Perspectives on ICT
- Desirable goals and ICT
- Actions for reaching the Good Information Society

These conferences received 153 submissions from more than 27 countries. Each submission has been anonymously reviewed by an average of four independent reviewers, to ensure that accepted submissions were of a high standard. Consequently, only 25 full papers were approved which means an acceptance rate of 16%. A few more papers were accepted as short and reflection papers and posters. An extended version of the best papers may be published in the IADIS International Journal on Computer Science and Information Systems (ISSN: 1646-3692), IADIS International Journal on WWW/Internet (ISSN: 1645-7641), and also in other selected journals.

Besides the presentation of full, short and reflection papers and posters, these conferences also included one tutorial presentation by Zhiping Zheng, Vivaport, vivaport.com, USA.

This volume has taken shape as a result of the contributions from a number of individuals. We are grateful to all authors who have submitted their papers to enrich the conference proceedings. We wish to thank all members of the organizing committee, delegates, invitees and guests whose contribution and involvement are crucial for the success of the conference. We are especially grateful to Professor Dr. Piet Kommers, UNESCO Professor of Educational Technology (The Netherlands), for serving as the keynote speaker at MCCSIS 2025.

Last but not least, we hope that everybody enjoyed the presentations, and we invite all participants for next year's edition of these conferences.

Pedro Isaias, Universidade Aberta (Portuguese Open University), Portugal
Paula Miranda, School of Technology, Setubal Polytechnic University, Portugal
DTIM 2025 Program Co-Chairs

Piet Kommers, UNESCO Professor of Educational Technology, The Netherlands
ICT 2025 Program Chair

Piet Kommers, UNESCO Professor of Educational Technology, The Netherlands
Pedro Isaias, Universidade Aberta (Portuguese Open University), Portugal
MCCSIS 2025 General Conference Co-Chairs

July 2025

PROGRAM COMMITTEE

DIGITAL TRANSFORMATION AND INNOVATION 2025
PROGRAM CO-CHAIRS

Pedro Isaias, Universidade Aberta (Portuguese Open University), Portugal
Paula Miranda, School of Technology, Setubal Polytechnic University, Portugal

ICT, SOCIETY AND HUMAN BEINGS 2025
PROGRAM CHAIR

Piet Kommers, UNESCO Professor of Educational Technology, The Netherlands

MCCSIS 2025 GENERAL CONFERENCE CO-CHAIRS

Piet Kommers, UNESCO Professor of Educational Technology, The Netherlands
Pedro Isaias, Universidade Aberta (Portuguese Open University), Portugal

DIGITAL TRANSFORMATION AND INNOVATION 2025

COMMITTEE MEMBERS

Abdul Rahman Abdel Razek, Furtwangen University, Germany
Abeer Alkhwaldi, Mutah University, Jordan
Alessandra Costa, University of Messina, Italy
Amor Jiménez, University of Huelva, Spain
Antonio Cimino, University of Messina, Italy
Antonio Crupi, University of Messina, Italy
Ayse Aslı Bozdag, Bahcesehir University, Turkey
Beata Gavurova, Charles University in Prague, Czech Republic
Budi Setiawan, Indo Global Mandiri University, Indonesia
Chun-nan Lin, National Kaohsiung University of Hospitality and Tourism, Taiwan
Cristina Alcaide Muñoz, University of Granada, Spain
Cristina Mazas, University Eropea del Atlantico, Spain
Daniele Doneddu, Swansea University, United Kingdom
Debora Di Caprio, University of Trento, Italy
Domitilla Magni, Catholic University of the Sacred Heart, Italy
Elvira Ismagilova, Swansea University, United Kingdom
Encarnación Manresa, University of Alicante, Spain
Federica Murmura, University of Urbino Carlo Bo, Italy
Francisco J. Santos-Arteaga, Universidad Complutense de Madrid, Spain
Giada Pierli, University of Urbino Carlo Bo, Italy
Giuseppe Basile, University of Foggia, Italy
Giuseppe Lanfranchi, University of Messina, Italy
Hanlie Smuts, University of Pretoria, South Africa
Hsiao-hui Li, National Kaohsiung University of Science and Technology, Taiwan

ICT, SOCIETY AND HUMAN BEINGS 2025

COMMITTEE MEMBERS

KEYNOTE LECTURE

A.I. FOR STUDENTS' METACOGNITIVE SKILLS AND CREATIVE THINKING

Prof. Dr. Piet Kommers
UNESCO Professor of Educational Technology
The Netherlands

ABSTRACT

Similar to the advancements made in ICT three decades ago, the emergence of AI today signals to educators that the human learning process may be at risk. This keynote lecture will provide an additional perspective on this issue. It is crucial to recognize that the WWW supplies all the information that AI currently presents. The main difference lies in its rhetoric concerning establishing a specific viewpoint. In other words, AI now acts as a powerful catalyst for refining criteria for student assessments, concentrating on discovering unique creative solutions rather than merely elaborating on existing ones. The foundation of creative thinking is metacognition: the awareness of what one already knows, one's preferred thinking style, and an evolving intuition about how learning builds on prior knowledge. This lecture will outline a roadmap for innovative didactic, instructional, and curricular approaches in the future. Previous research into conceptual representations, ontologies, and metaphoric analogies has supported education in expanding the fields of knowledge elicitation and conceptual thinking. Once AI is integrated, we will witness a growing need among young people to navigate complexities, such as sources of information that do not rely on empirical and validated scientific evidence. This keynote will highlight new aspirations that have emerged and how to seamlessly incorporate them into 'standing education' at this very moment. Topics such as teacher education, student selection, and assessment will be discussed.

TUTORIAL

DESIGN AND EVALUATION OF ECOMMERCE CATEGORICAL BROWSING

Zhiping Zheng
Vivaport, vivaport.com, USA

ABSTRACT

E-commerce has grown rapidly, offering numerous advantages over traditional brick-and-mortar stores. A key driver of product discovery on eCommerce platforms is categorical browsing - the process by which users navigate a structured hierarchy of categories and subcategories to discover products, as opposed to using keyword-based search. For well-established eCommerce sites, categorical browsing accounts for 40-70% of total traffic, with some sites seeing even higher numbers. However, many companies treat browsing merely as an extension of search by using category names as search keywords and applying search ranking algorithms, which results in the loss of essential browsing features. This tutorial offers an in-depth exploration of the design and optimization of categorical browsing systems, grounded in real industrial cases from large-scale, high-traffic e-commerce environments across sectors such as fashion, electronics, and general merchandising. These real-world implementations provide actionable insights into managing system complexity, aligning with business objectives, and understanding user behavior at scales. Intended for system architects, product managers, software engineers, data scientists, and students, this session offers practical guidance for building or enhancing categorical browse frameworks to improve user experience, drive product discovery, and boost sales conversion.We cover the depth of technical content and prerequisites, including product data structuring, hierarchical taxonomies, dynamic item collections, and ranking methods (static, personalized, and business-driven). We explore scoring functions using revenue, seasonality, pricing, inventory, and discount signals. In addition, we examine evaluation techniques, from offline simulation to real-time A/B testing and user engagement metrics.

This tutorial will be interactive, featuring hands-on exercises in areas like offline evaluation and simulation, so participants can directly apply key concepts. We'll also dedicate time to audience-driven Q&A, addressing specific challenges and scenarios from participants' own experiences, and providing practical guidance rooted in industry best practices. What makes this tutorial unique is its comprehensive coverage of end-to-end categorical browse design - spanning data modeling, ranking systems, evaluation methods, tuning strategies, SEO, caching, and dynamic faceting - tailored for practitioners across different roles and company sizes. It introduces Empirical Relevance Gain (ERG), a fresh metric designed specifically to evaluate categorical browsing experiences.

ABOUT THE SPEAKER

Zhiping Zheng is a principal/distinguished engineer and data scientist with extensive experience at top-tier eCommerce companies, including Walmart, Target, eBay, Michaels, Macy's, Nike, and Microsoft. He has led the architectural design and development of critical systems, including search engines, browsing platforms, recommendation engines, and many other AI related engineering tools/systems. Zhiping has served as a research scientist and lecturer at several universities as well, focusing on researching and teaching in the fields of Natural Language Processing and Information Retrieval.Recently, Zhiping and a group of collaborators launched a startup focused on partnering with eCommerce companies to create a dynamic digital ecosystem - encouraging collaborative growth, driving innovation, and empowering both businesses and individuals to thrive in a sustainable, forward-looking environment. In parallel, he continues to support organizations in solving long-standing and complex technical problems.

Full Papers

THE IMPACT OF INTEGRATED MARKETING COMMUNICATION AND SUSTAINABILITY-ORIENTED SERVICE INNOVATION ON RETAIL PERFORMANCE: DOES SIZE MATTER?

Antonio Marín-García, Irene Gil-Saura, Maria Eugenia Ruiz-Molina and Mihaela Simona Moise
Universitat de Valencia, Spain

ABSTRACT

In the current retail landscape, competition and evolving consumer expectations have driven companies to innovate in both marketing strategies and service offerings. This study examines the role of Integrated Marketing Communication (IMC) and Sustainability-Oriented Service Innovation (SOSI) in shaping organizational success, comparing their impact across large and small retailers. IMC ensures brand consistency and enhances sustainability awareness, fostering an environment conducive to sustainable service innovation. SOSI, in turn, integrates sustainability and innovative principles into service development, responding to consumer demands and regulatory pressures. Using a structured survey of retail managers from Barcelona, Madrid, and Valencia, this study explores the influence of IMC on SOSI and the subsequent impact on financial and non-financial organizational performance. Findings confirm that IMC significantly enhances SOSI adoption, which in turn positively affects business outcomes. Moreover, the moderating role of retailer type is examined, revealing that small retailers benefit more from SOSI-driven strategies due to their flexibility and customer proximity, whereas large retailers leverage advanced logistics and resources for sustainability initiatives. These insights provide theoretical and managerial implications, emphasizing the need for coherent communication strategies, sustainable innovation investments, and tailored marketing approaches based on retailer type. The study also highlights limitations related to sample scope and suggests future research avenues focusing on emerging technologies and digitalization in sustainable marketing strategies.

KEYWORDS

Integrated Marketing Communication (IMC), Sustainability-Oriented Service Innovation (SOSI), Organizational Performance, Small Retailers, Large Retailers

1. INTRODUCTION

Retailing has undergone a significant transformation in recent decades, driven by growing competition and consumers with increasingly demanding expectations (Erensoy et al., 2024). In this dynamic environment, retail companies must constantly innovate, not only in their product offerings, but also in their services and communication strategies. Integrated Marketing Communication (IMC) has established itself as a key strategy to attract and retain customers, enabling companies to establish stronger and more lasting relationships with their target audience (Bordian et al., 2023). However, in the current context, where sustainability and innovation play a central role in business management, this vision needs to be expanded (Bordian et al., 2024).

In this sense, Sustainability-Oriented Service Innovation (SOSI) emerges as an essential strategic approach within the retail sector (Gil-Saura et al., 2023). Unlike traditional business models, SOSI incorporates sustainability principles in the design and delivery of services, responding to both the growing environmental awareness of consumers and increasingly stringent sustainability regulations (Calabrese et al., 2021).

This study seeks to contribute to knowledge in this area by examining the link between IMC and SOSI, as well as how a sustainability-based corporate culture influences organizational performance, both in financial and non-financial terms. In addition to exploring the relationship between IMC and SOSI and their impact on business performance, this research introduces an additional variable: the type of retailer. Retailing ranges from large retail chains to small independent stores, each with particular characteristics and challenges (Cho et al., 2023). For managers in the sector, understanding these dynamics is critical in formulating effective strategies, but studies addressing this perspective remain limited. In this regard, this research seeks to close that gap by providing useful insights and recommendations for managers to align their marketing strategies with business objectives.

In order to meet these objectives, this paper is structured as follows: after this introduction, the theoretical framework that supports the research and allows the formulation of hypotheses within a conceptual model is developed. Subsequently, the methodology used is detailed and the results obtained are presented. Finally, the main conclusions, both theoretical and practical, are presented, together with the limitations of the study and possible lines of future research.

2. THEORETICAL FRAMEWORK

2.1 Integrated Marketing Communication (IMC)

Integrated Marketing Communication (IMC) is a strategic approach that seeks to effectively align and coordinate all the communication actions of an organization, ensuring that the messages transmitted are consistent and reinforced through different channels (Porcu et al., 2019). This concept, which began to gain relevance in the 1990s, emerged as a response to the need to avoid the dispersion of messages derived from the isolated use of various communication tools (Villanova et al., 2021).

The fundamental purpose of the IMC is to establish and consolidate consistent relationships with different stakeholders, including customers, employees, investors and other stakeholders (Šerić et al., 2015). To achieve this, it strategically integrates all elements of the marketing mix (product, price, distribution and promotion), ensuring that brand communication is clear, homogeneous and aligned with corporate values. For IMC to be truly effective, it is crucial to have strategic planning that includes segmentation of the target audience, selection of the most appropriate communication channels, generation of attractive and relevant content, as well as constant evaluation of the results obtained. This makes it possible to make adjustments in real time and optimize strategies to maximize their impact (Bordian et al., 2023).

2.2 Sustainability-Oriented Service Innovation (SOSI)

Sustainability-Oriented Service Innovation (SOSI) is a concept that arises from the need to integrate innovation and sustainability in the development of products and services, considering environmental, social and economic aspects (Marín-García et al., 2024). According to Calabrese et al. (2018), SOSI is defined as a multidimensional approach that encompasses various service strategies designed to incorporate sustainability in their processes and outcomes. This business perspective is founded on the convergence of three key elements: service innovation (SI), sustainability-focused innovation (SOI), and product-service systems (PSS).

Beyond meeting social and environmental responsibility requirements, SOSI contributes to strengthening business relationships by generating value for both companies and consumers (Calabrese et al., 2021). The implementation of sustainable practices not only improves the connection between suppliers and customers, but also aligns business interests with shared values. This strategic alignment, based on innovation and sustainability, strengthens the corporate image and fosters long-term relationships, promoting a joint commitment towards a more sustainable development (Calabrese et al., 2018).

In summary, the vision of SOSI put forward by Calabrese et al. (2018) is based on the premise that cooperation among different stakeholders generates greater benefits than individual action. In this sense, the present study analyzes SOSI as a multidimensional concept based on the dimensions identified by Wikhamn (2019), which allows for a strategic and balanced integration of sustainability and innovation in the business environment.

2.3 Organizational Performance

Business performance refers to the ability of an organization to efficiently manage its resources with the purpose of achieving previously defined strategic objectives, ensuring its relevance and value for different stakeholders (Liu et al., 2022). This concept has acquired great relevance both in strategic management research and in the formulation of marketing strategies (Marín-García et al., 2024).

Within this field, financial indicators are key tools for evaluating the economic performance and profitability of a company. These include metrics such as return on investment (ROI), sales growth, profitability and market share. Such indicators make it possible to measure the financial stability of an organization and its ability to generate sustainable profits over time.

On the other hand, non-financial indicators reflect aspects of organizational performance that, although not directly related to economic results, are decisive for its long-term success. These include customer loyalty, service quality, competitive advantage and occupancy rate, among other factors. These elements contribute significantly to the consolidation and sustainability of the company in its sector.

2.4 Hypotheses Formulation

2.4.1 Impact of IMC on SOSI

The relationship between Integrated Marketing Communication (IMC) and Sustainability-Oriented Service Innovation (SOSI) is based on the impact of a unified communication strategy on the promotion and adoption of sustainable services within organizations. IMC, by integrating different communication channels and tools to convey a clear and consistent message, contributes to strengthening the perception of sustainability among consumers and employees, thus facilitating an environment conducive to innovation in this area (Aiello et al., 2022).

The combination of these elements generates optimal conditions for the design and implementation of innovative and sustainable services. In this context, and supported by the existing literature, the first hypothesis of this study is put forward:

H1. *Integrated Marketing Communication significantly and positively drives Sustainability-Oriented Service Innovation.*

2.4.2 Impact of SOSI on Organizational Performance

The relationship between sustainable service innovation and organizational performance has been extensively studied in the academic literature (Maletič et al., 2016; Calabrese et al., 2021; Maletič et al., 2021; Marín-García et al., 2024). Recent research has shown that the adoption of innovative sustainability-oriented practices can generate various benefits for an organization's overall performance (Maletič et al., 2014).

Based on these theoretical foundations, the following research hypotheses are established:

H2. Sustainability-Oriented Service Innovation has a significant and positive impact on financial performance.

H3. Sustainability-Oriented Service Innovation has a significant and positive impact on non-financial performance.

2.4.3 Moderating Effect of Retail Type

Several studies point out that the type of retailer can play a fundamental role in the implementation of marketing strategies (Cho et al., 2023). Therefore, it is crucial to analyze how the particularities of each retailer model influence the dynamics of the relationship between suppliers and consumers, as well as organizational outcomes.

On the one hand, large retailers, such as large supermarket chains, tend to have more complex organizational structures and extensive resources, allowing them to develop advanced strategies in marketing and logistics (Delgado-de Miguel et al., 2019).

On the other hand, small retailers, such as neighborhood or specialty stores, are differentiated by their focus on personalized attention and the offer of exclusive products, which are often not available in large supermarkets.

Based on these considerations, the following set of hypotheses is put forward, which forms the fourth research hypothesis:

H4a: *The relationship between IMC and SOSI is moderated by retail type (large retailer vs. small retailer).*

H4b: *The relationship between SOSI and financial performance is moderated by retail type (large distribution vs. small retailer).*

H4c: *The relationship between SOSI and non-financial performance is moderated by retail type (large distribution vs. small retail).*

3. METHODOLOGY

In order to collect the necessary information and test the hypotheses, a structured survey was carried out among managers and directors of retail establishments in Barcelona, Madrid and Valencia. These cities were selected for their economic relevance and representativeness of the Spanish retail sector. The selection of the retail sector was based on the nature of the products marketed and its contribution to the Gross Value Added (GVA) within the Spanish market, consolidating it as one of the key sectors of the national economy. Including multiple metropolitan areas enhances the external validity and generalizability of the results.

The variables analyzed were measured using items extracted and adapted from scales previously validated in the marketing literature. In particular, Integrated Marketing Communication (IMC) was assessed based on the scale proposed by Lee and Park (2007). For Sustainability-Oriented Service Innovation (SOSI), an adapted version of the scale developed by Wikhamn (2019) was used, which conceptualizes SOSI as a multidimensional construct composed of four dimensions: sustainable service innovation, sustainable process innovation, sustainable organizational innovation, and sustainable marketing innovation. On the other hand, organizational performance, both in financial and non-financial terms, was measured following the proposal of Bath and Sharma (2022).

The questionnaires were applied through a digital platform that allowed both computer-assisted personal interviews (CAPI) and computer-assisted telephone interviews (CATI). To minimize social desirability bias, which could skew responses towards socially acceptable practices (particularly regarding sustainability), the questionnaire was designed to ensure anonymity and confidentiality. A total of 200 valid questionnaires were obtained, with equal representation from various sectors, including food, textile/footwear, electronics/appliances and furniture/wood, each contributing 25% of the responses. In terms of type of trade, 57% of the responses were from small retailers, while the remaining 43% came from large retail outlets.

4. RESULTS

4.1 Validation of the Measuring Instrument

In order to evaluate the reliability and validity of the measurement instrument, the PLS-SEM technique was used, calculating a PLS algorithm with a parameter of 300 maximum interactions and a path weighting scheme. PLS-SEM is particularly suitable for exploratory models and theory development, especially when constructs are formative or hierarchical, as is the case with SOSI. In addition, it is robust for small to medium sample sizes and does not require multivariate normality, making it ideal for business field studies like this one.

The results obtained for Cronbach's α are satisfactory, far exceeding 0.7, the minimum required (Churchill, 1979; Nunnally and Bernstein, 1994), and ranging between 0.8 and 0.9, values recommended for more advanced stages of research (Nunnally and Bernstein, 1994). The analysis of composite reliability yields very satisfactory results, well above the minimum required, 0.7 (Chin, 1998). Moreover, all the constructs of the structural model obtain values for the average extracted variance above 0.5, which implies that each construct explains at least 50% of the variance of the assigned indicators (Fornell and Larcker, 1981).

Furthermore, discriminant validity is confirmed, since for all cases the square root of the average variance extracted (AVE) was higher than the estimated correlation between the factors, which appears below the diagonal, according to the Fornell-Larcker (1981) criterion.

4.2 Estimation of the Causal Model

For the analysis of the proposed structural model, the SmartPLS software was again used with full bootstrapping with 5000 subsamples (Ringle, 2015). Figure 1 shows the results of the estimation of the structural model of this research.

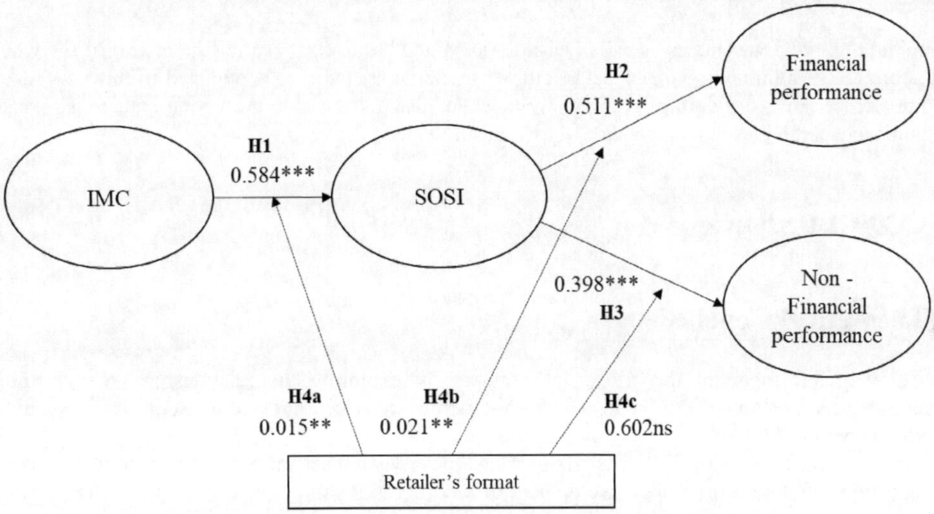

Figure 1. Estimation of causal relationships

Figure 1 presents the results obtained from the PLS-SEM analysis, which allow us to support all the proposed relationships of the causal model. First, it is observed that IMC has a positive and significant impact on SOSI ($\beta1=0.584$, $p<0.01$, H1), suggesting that the implementation of integrated marketing communication strategies is crucial to foster SOSI within retail companies. Secondly, the dynamizing power of SOSI la on the financial performance of organizations is confirmed by obtaining a positive and significant result on the financial performance of companies ($\beta2=0.511$, $p<0.01$, H2). This relationship indicates that sustainable innovations in services contribute significantly to improve profitability and financial performance of organizations. Finally, this study also confirms the relationship between SOSI and non-financial performance ($\beta3=0.398$, $p<0.01$, H3). This result suggests that SOSI can improve indicators of a qualitative nature such as customer loyalty, service quality and competitive advantage. These results are aligned with the research elaborated by Maletič et al. (2021).

4.3 Analysis of the Moderating Effect of the Type of Retail Trade

Finally, in order to test the set of hypotheses that make up H4 of this research, a multigroup analysis was carried out using the PLS-MGA technique. The results shown in Table 1 allow us to affirm that the moderating effect of the type of retail trade on the proposed relationships is statistically significant in most of the relationships.

Table 1. Results of the multigroup analysis

Hypothesis	**Relation**	**Large distribution** *N=86*		**Small distribution** *N=114*		***p*-value**
		Standardised parameter	*t*	*Standardised parameter*	*t*	
H4a	IMC → SOSI	0.339***	3.908	0.604***	8.944	0.015**
H4b	SOSI → Financial performance	0.252ns	1.343	0.553***	6.961	0.021**
H4c	SOSI → Non-financial performance	0.294ns	1.740	0.442***	4.413	0.602ns

*Statistically significant at ***p<0.01; **p<0.05 ns = no non-statistically significant*

Building on previous studies such as Delgado-de Miguel et al. (2019) and Cho et al. (2023), who argue the importance of retaining retailer type-specific characteristics, the results obtained in this paper underline the importance of considering retailer type when designing and evaluating integrated marketing communication strategies in line to a SOSI-based business perspective.

5. CONCLUSIONS

5.1 Theoretical Conclusions

This study offers important theoretical implications by exploring the relationship between Integrated Marketing Communication (IMC), Sustainability-Oriented Service Innovation (SOSI) and organizational outcomes in retailing.

First, it is confirmed that IMC has a significant positive impact on SOSI, suggesting that consistent communication strategies drive the development of a corporate culture where innovation and sustainability are at the forefront.

Second, SOSI is shown to positively influence financial and non-financial performance. The holistic view of innovation and sustainability not only improves the company's image and reputation, but also contributes directly to its profitability and growth.

Finally, the differentiation between types of retailers (large *versus* small retailers) shows that small retailers, despite having fewer resources, can develop a more effective SOSI-based business culture due to their flexibility and proximity to customers.

5.2 Implications for Management

The present study offers several significant practical implications for retail managers and practitioners, providing concrete actions based on the interplay between Integrated Marketing Communication (IMC), Sustainability-Oriented Service Innovation (SOSI) and organizational outcomes.

First, managers must develop coherent and unified communication strategies. To do so, they can implement an integrated communication plan that includes sustainability marketing campaigns across multiple channels such as advertising, sales promotions, public relations, social media and packaging.

Second, it is crucial to invest in sustainable innovations. Managers should allocate resources to research and development of sustainable products and services, including the adoption of green technologies, improvement of internal processes to reduce waste and the use of recyclable materials.

Third, effectively communicating sustainability efforts and achievements to customers and stakeholders is essential. Using databases to segment and customize messages that highlight the company's sustainable initiatives can be very effective.

Fourth, small retailers should leverage their flexibility and proximity to customers to implement sustainable innovations more effectively.

Fifth, large retailers should use their greater resources to lead in sustainability. They can develop and implement large-scale sustainable initiatives, leveraging their logistics capabilities. Investing in fleets of electric vehicles for transporting goods, establishing green distribution centers with renewable energy technologies, and launching global sustainability awareness campaigns are just some of the actions they could implement.

5.3 Limitations and Future Lines of Research

This study has some limitations that should be considered when interpreting the results. First, the sample is limited to managers of retail establishments located in the three main Spanish cities (Barcelona, Madrid and Valencia), which may not be representative of other regions or countries with different economic and cultural contexts. Future research should incorporate these organizational and cultural barriers to offer a more nuanced and balanced perspective for practitioners. Second, the in-person survey methodology, while allowing for greater depth of responses, may also introduce social desirability bias, where managers may have provided responses that they consider more socially acceptable rather than reflecting their actual practice. To address this limitation, the incorporation of mixed methods, combining surveys with in-depth interviews and secondary data analysis, could enrich the understanding of the mechanisms behind the implementation and success of marketing strategies. Third, this study focuses on managers' perceptions and self-assessments of IMC and SOSI. It would be beneficial to supplement these data with objective measures of organizational performance and longitudinal analyses to observe how these relationships evolve over time. The cross-sectional design limits our ability to capture the dynamic nature and long-term evolution of IMC and SOSI. Longitudinal studies would provide deeper insights into how these practices mature over time, adapt to external pressures, and influence organizational performance in the medium and long term. Second. In addition, incorporating financial figures or benchmarking data in future studies would allow for more tangible comparisons and improve the practical applicability of the findings for decision-makers. Finally, future research could further explore the role of emerging technologies and digitization in IMC and SOSI, especially considering the rapid technological advancement and the growing importance of e-commerce in the retail sector.

ACKNOWLEDGEMENT

This research has been developed within the framework of the project Grant PID2020-112660RB-I00 funded by MCIN/ AEI/10.13039/501100011033, and the consolidated research group AICO/2021/144 and CIAICO/2023/069 funded by the Conselleria d'Innovació, Universitats, Ciència i Societat Digital of the Generalitat Valenciana.

REFERENCES

Aiello, G., Dasmi, C. and Nechaeva, O., (2022). Communication of Sustainability in Omnichannel Retailing as a Tool to Increase Brand Engagement: An Abstract" in *Academy of Marketing Science Annual Conference*. Cham, Springer Nature Switzerland, pp. 279-280.

Bhat, D.A.R. and Sharma, V., (2022). Enabling service innovation and firm performance: the role of cocreation and technological innovation in the hospitality industry. *Technology Analysis & Strategic Management,* Vol. 34, N0. 7, pp. 774–786.

Bordian, M., Gil-Saura, I. and Šerić, M., (2023). The impact of value co-creation in sustainable services: understanding generational differences. *Journal of Services Marketing,* Vol. 37, No. 2, pp. 155-167.

Bordian, M. et al, (2024). Boost effect of sustainable practices and relational innovation on value co-creation and brand equity: outcomes of hotel size moderation. *Journal of Marketing Analytics*, pp. 1-17.

Calabrese, A., Forte, G. and Ghiron, N.L., (2018). Fostering sustainability-oriented service innovation (SOSI) through business model renewal: the SOSI tool. *Journal of Cleaner Production,* Vol. 201, pp. 783-791.

Calabrese, A. et al, (2021). How sustainable-orientated service innovation strategies are contributing to the sustainable development goals. *Technological Forecasting and Social Change,* Vol. 169, 120816.

Chin, W.W., (1998). The partial least squares approach to structural equation modelling. *Modern Methods for Business Research,* Vol. 295 No. 2, pp. 295-336.

Cho, J., Chun, H. and Lee, Y., (2023). Productivity dynamics in the retail trade sector: the roles of large modern retailers and small entrants. *Small Business Economics*, Vol. 60, No. 1, pp. 291-313.

Churchill Jr, G. A., (1979). A paradigm for developing better measures of marketing constructs. *Journal of marketing research*, Vol. 16, No. 1, pp. 64-73.

Delgado-de Miguel, J. F. et al., (2019). Proximity trade and urban sustainability: Small retailers' expectations towards local online marketplaces. *Sustainability*, Vol. 11, No. 24, pp. 71-99.

Erensoy, A. et al., (2024). Consumer behavior in immersive virtual reality retail environments: A systematic literature review using the stimuli-organisms-responses (S-O-r) model. *Journal of Consumer Behaviour*. Vol. 23, No. 6, pp. 2781-2811

Fornell, C. and Larcker, D.F., (1981). Evaluating structural equation models with unobservable variables and measurement error. *Journal of Marketing Research*, Vol. 18, No. 1, pp. 39-50.

Gil-Saura, I. et al., (2023). Sustainability-oriented commerce innovation: How does it influence consumer satisfaction? *International Journal of Retail & Distribution Management*, Vol. 51, No. 11, pp. 1477-1496.

Lee, D.H. and Park, C.W. (2007). Conceptualization and measurement of multidimensionality of integrated marketing communications. *Journal of Advertising Research*, Vol. 47, No. 3, pp. 222-236.

Liu, Y. et al., (2022). Relationship between sustainable management activities and financial performance: mediating effects of non-financial performance and moderating effects of institutional environment. *Sustainability*, Vol. 14, No. 3, pp. 11-68.

Maletič, M., Gomišček, B. and Maletič, D., (2021). The missing link: sustainability innovation practices, non-financial performance outcomes and economic performance. *Management Research Review*, Vol. 44, No. 11, pp. 1457-1477.

Maletič, M. et al., (2014). Sustainability exploration and sustainability exploitation: From a literature review towards a conceptual framework. *Journal of Cleaner Production*, Vol. 79, pp. 182-194.

Maletič, M. et al., (2016). Effect of sustainability-oriented innovation practices on the overall organisational performance: An empirical examination. *Total Quality Management & Business Excellence*, Vol. 27, No. 9-10, pp. 1171-1190.

Marín-García, A. et al., (2024). Does ICT contribute to bootstrapping SOSI? Evidence in retailing. *International Journal of Retail & Distribution Management*, Vol. 52, No. 7/8, pp. 737-753.

Nunnally, J.C. and Bernstein, I.H., (1994). *Psychological Theory*. MacGraw-Hill, New York.

Porcu, L. et al., (2019). Analyzing the influence of firm-wide integrated marketing communication on market performance in the hospitality industry. *International Journal of Hospitality Management*, Vol. 80, No. 1, pp. 13–24.

Ringle, C.M., Wende, S. and Becker, J., (2015). *SmartPLS 3. SmartPLS. GmbH*, available at: http://www.Smartpls.com

Šerić, M., Gil-Saura, I. and Ozretić-Došen, Đ. (2015). Insights on integrated marketing communications: implementation and impact in hotel companies. *International Journal of Contemporary Hospitality Management*, Vol. 27, No. 5, pp. 958–979.

Villanova, D. et al., (2021). Retailer marketing communications in the digital age: getting the right message to the right shopper at the right time. *Journal of Retailing*, Vol. 97, No. 1, pp. 116-132.

Wikhamn, W., (2019). Innovation, sustainable HRM and customer satisfaction. *International Journal of Hospitality Management*, Vol. 76, pp. 102-110.

SUSTAINABLE TOURISM USING LARGE LANGUAGE MODEL AGENTS IN REAL-WORLD APPLICATIONS

Po-Chun Chang[1], Yuan-Hsun Liao[1], Hsiao-Hui Li[2] and Yu-Chen Hu[1]
[1]*Department of Computer Science, Tunghai University, Taichung, 407224, Taiwan*
[2]*Department of Maritime Information and Technology, National Kaohsiung University of Science and Technology Kaohsiung, 805301, Taiwan*

ABSTRACT

This paper addresses the growing need for sustainable tourism by introducing a novel AI-Agent framework for optimizing tourism packing. While past research has focused on route planning and sustainability evaluation, limited attention has been given to the challenge of optimizing tourism packages, which involves the complex knapsack problem. The proposed AI-Agent framework gathers real-world data, applies Topology Data Analysis for weight calculation, and utilizes a meta-heuristic approach to optimize item combinations for packing. Two experiments are conducted: the first analyzes weight distribution, revealing a resemblance to the beta distribution, while the second compares meta-heuristic algorithms, finding the genetic algorithm (GA) to be most effective in maximizing total weight. This AI-Agent framework provides efficient solutions for the tourism package problem and lays the foundation for future work in AI-Agent tourism planning.

KEYWORDS

Large Language Model, Meta-Heuristic Algorithm, AI-Agent, Sustainable Tourism, Topology Data Analysis

1. INTRODUCTION

In recent years, sustainable tourism has become a key focus in research (Niñerola, Sánchez-Rebull, & Hernández-Lara, 2019). To promote sustainability, various algorithms have been developed to optimize tourism planning (Liang, Jiao, Du, & Qu, 2021). One approach utilizes hybrid integrated computing algorithms to design travel routes that minimize disruption to ecological systems. Additionally, genetic algorithms and iterated local search are used to balance tourist numbers with environmental impact, ensuring sustainability at each location (Parolo, Ferrarini, & Rossi, 2009). Improvements in genetic algorithms, such as integrating ant colony optimization, have enhanced route planning by addressing issues like premature convergence (Chen & Dai, 2020). Fuzzy logic models are also employed to assess sustainability by evaluating factors like cost, duration, and satisfaction (Tan, Shuai, Jiao, & Shen, 2017). Furthermore, machine learning platforms have been proposed to recommend eco-friendly tourism options. Lastly, system dynamics combined with neural networks help assess tourism sustainability, providing dynamic control strategies. These advancements offer effective tools for achieving environmentally responsible and culturally respectful tourism development.

However, the past technique is less to study the tourism package problem. In the tourism, traveler need to packed the package. The mainly problem is, the different items have multiple weighted, likes prefer level, size, the degree of consumables, etc. This is called knapsack problem, is an NP Hard problem (Pisinger, 2005). In the past technique is focus on the developing algorithms to plan tourist routes, evaluating the sustainability of tourist destinations using fuzzy logic and multicriteria models, and utilizing machine learning platforms and system dynamics methods to asses tourism sustainability and dynamic management (Ruiz-Meza, Brito, & Montoya-Torres, 2021). Leak the topic about deploy the AI to support tourism packing their package (Pillai & Sivathanu, 2020). Moreover, the previous AI Agent packing method involved directly inputting the entire packing list into the LLM request to create a plan that fits the travel mission (Chen, Wu, Zhou, & Tung, 2013). However, without handling data-related tasks, the LLM struggles to provide broad packing suggestions based on the data. Therefore, creating an intelligent AI Agent specifically designed to address packing issues has become an increasingly important topic in recent years (Li et al., 2017).

In this paper proposed the novel framework, aimed to create an AI Agent for helping tourism packing optimize (Doborjeh, Hemmington, Doborjeh, & Kasabov, 2022). The AI-Agent framework (Kurylek, Camara, Nandi, & Markopoulos, 2024) operates by first gathering real-world data. It then uses Topology Data Analysis to calculate the Vietoris–Rips complex (Zomorodian, 2010), which is employed to compute simplices and ultimately determine weights. With the weighted data, a meta-heuristic approach is applied to optimize combinations, with the core problem being a variation of the knapsack problem (Lust & Teghem, 2012). The optimization process selects the best items to organize into packages, and these packages are then used as input for a Large Language Model (Cerf, 2023) to generate a tourism plan. This plan helps in organizing tourism packages that can be used for effective travel planning.

The two experiments conducted in the paper evaluate key aspects of the framework. Experiment 1 focuses on analyzing the distribution of weights, showing that the weighted distribution most closely resembles the flexible and adaptable beta distribution. Experiment 2 evaluates different metaheuristic algorithms for solving the knapsack problem, with the genetic algorithm (GA) achieving the best performance in terms of maximizing the total weight, making it the most suitable method for optimal solutions in this context.

In summary, the paper introduces a powerful AI-Agent framework for tourism packing that leverages real-world data, optimization techniques, and personalized travel plans to offer more efficient solutions. This framework effective solve the tourism package problem.

2. BODY OF PAPER

The introduction sections mention the past issue, the past issue problem, the important of this motivation, the structure of this framework and the experiment result explain. In this section digitally organize the background knowledge of this framework, the framework design and core meaning, and the experiment of this framework.

2.1 Literature Review

To bridge the gap in tourism planning, this framework introduces AI-Agent solutions for sustainable packing. While previous studies focused on route planning and destination sustainability, little attention has been given to optimizing packing decisions. By combining Topological Data Analysis (TDA) and metaheuristics, this approach provides a novel way to improve packing efficiency and sustainability in tourism, offering smarter, more effective solutions for travelers.

2.1.1 Topic Review of Sustainable Tourism

Travel and tourism have a tremendous contribution to our modern economical system (Sofronov, 2018). In order to be accepted globally, a sustainable, desirable and politically appropriate tourism should be developed. Sustainable tourism activates principally cover the environmental, economic, social and cultural aspects of development (Sharma, 2019). In the sustainable tourism develops as quickly as possible, taking into account current accommodation capacity, the local population and environment (Butler, 1991). It must be capable of adding to the array of economic opportunities open to people without adversely affect (Cebula & Vedder, 1972). So, to implement the AI Agent to support tourism be more intelligence sustainably is an important issue. Previously, the focus was on developing algorithms for planning tourist routes, assessing the sustainability of tourist destinations through fuzzy logic and multicriteria models, and applying machine learning platforms and system dynamics methods to evaluate tourism sustainability and dynamic management. However, there is a gap in exploring the use of AI to assist in packing tourism packages (Samala, Katkam, Bellamkonda, & Rodriguez, 2020). Therefore, this paper proposed the state of art AI Agent framework to help tourism more sustainably packing.

2.1.2 Topology Data Analysis

Topology Data Analysis (TDA) seeks to bridge this gap by providing methods based on the idea that data possesses an inherent shape that can be accurately measured to analyze the data (Carlsson, 2020). TDA offers a variety of powerful tools that help quantify the shape and structure of data to address specific questions in various domains (Patania, Vaccarino, & Petri, 2017). The objective of using topological methods is to generate more compact and understandable summaries of complex datasets (Snášel, Nowaková, Xhafa, & Barolli, 2017).

In real-world applications, TDA is used to detect structural changes in time-evolving graphs, such as social networks or communication systems (Munch, 2017). The approach applies topological methods to identify cyclic patterns and anomalies, providing valuable insights into the behavior of complex systems. This framework uses TDA to extract geometric features, which are treated as weighted attributes, and employs the Akaike Information Criterion to assess the quality of the weighted distribution derived from TDA.

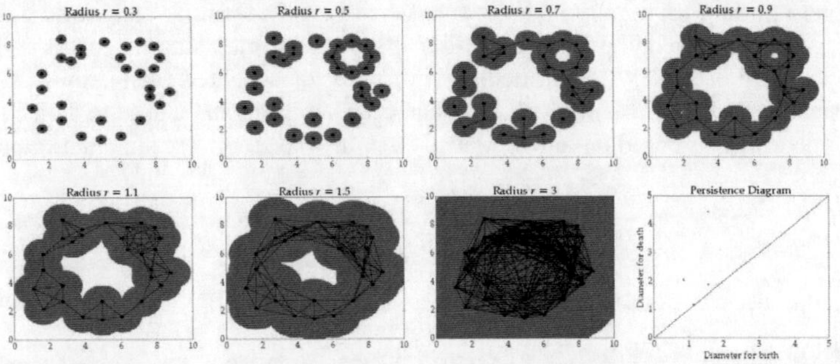

Figure 1. An example of using persistent homology to analyze a point cloud dataset. The Rips complex edges are shown in black, with higher-dimensional simplices implied but not drawn. The persistence diagram summarizes the appearance and disappearance of loops as the Rips complex parameter changes (Munch, 2017)

2.1.3 Meta Heuristic Algorithm

Metaheuristics are stochastic optimization techniques that enhance the performance of traditional heuristic methods (Ma, Wu, Suganthan, Song, & Luo, 2023). These techniques address the issue of local optima and have been effectively applied to solve a wide range of optimization problems (Paquete, Schiavinotto, & Stützle, 2007). The metaheuristic process begins with one or more random initial solutions, which are then improved using random operators throughout the process (Agushaka & Ezugwu, 2022). This design allows the algorithm to escape local optima. Due to this capability, metaheuristics can be applied to various research fields. This framework utilizes metaheuristics to solve the knapsack problem, optimizing the packing solution. In Experiment 2, three different metaheuristic algorithms are compared: Simulated Annealing Algorithm, Genetic Algorithm, and Particle Swarm Algorithm. Metaheuristics have also been used in mechanical engineering design challenges, such as the Robot Gripper Problem, Pressure Vessel Design Problem, and Rolling Element Bearing Problem (Abd Elaziz et al., 2021) (Gupta et al., 2021) (Meng et al., 2021). The framework selects the highest weighted solution as the optimal packing solution and uses it as input for an AI agent, providing intelligent recommendations for tourism tasks.

2.1.4 AI Agents

AI agents are intelligent systems designed to perform tasks autonomously or semi-autonomously on behalf of humans (Zhou et al., 2023). Often powered by Large Language Models (LLMs), these agents can manage complex tasks by breaking them down into smaller sub-tasks and collaborating with other agents when necessary. A real-world example of an AI agent is iAgent. The main goal of iAgent is to improve the intelligence of mobile agents, specifically within wireless sensor networks (WSNs) (Lu et al., 2019). By integrating AI, iAgent enables these agents to learn and adapt, allowing them to make dynamic decisions and plan paths in response to changing environments. This paper presents a framework for tourism packing AI agents. The framework combines Topological Data Analysis (TDA) and metaheuristics to extract the geometry of packing datasets and determine the optimal packing solution. These solutions are then formatted as inputs for the AI agent, as outlined in Table 2. In the tourism context, the agent receives the formatted task and generates the most suitable plan for the traveler. Unlike simply providing a dataset to the AI agent for planning, this innovative framework improves the handling of packing tasks for travelers.

2.2 Tourism AI-Agent Framework Design

The framework input is real world dataset and tourism task. The dataset includes items name and items describe. Tourism task is the tourism goal while tourism, for example, visit the country, working with hub, adventure at the city, etc. The framework output is optimized tourism plan for tourism task. The plan is generated by LLM AI-Agent.

The AI-Agent framework mainly includes five steps. Step 1 is getting real world dataset. Step 2 is using dimension reduction to embedding dataset as 2-dimension point set. Using the Vietoris-Rips complex, which belongs to topological data analysis, to calculate simplexes for weighted calculations. A simplex S is defined as a set of data points, where $S = \{p_1, p_2, \dots, p_k\}$, and each simplex can be used to define the weight $w(p)$ of a data point p. The weight is based on how frequently a point appears in the simplices. Specifically, the weight can be calculated as:

$$w(p) = \sum_{S \in \mathcal{S}} \mathbf{1}_{p \in S} \tag{1}$$

where $\mathcal{S}$ is the set of all simplices, and $\mathbf{1}_{p \in S}$ is an indicator function that is 1 if p is part of the simplex S, and 0 otherwise.

Step 4 is using weighted and meta heuristic algorithm to optimize the combinate problem, the based problem is knapsack problem. The general form of the knapsack problem can be written as:

$$\text{Maximize} \sum_{i=1}^{n} w_i x_i \tag{2}$$

$$\text{subject to} \sum_{i=1}^{n} c_i x_i \leq C, x_i \in \{0,1\} \tag{3}$$

In this scenario, w_i represents the weight of item i, and c_i is its cost. C is the total capacity available, and x_i is a binary variable that indicates whether item i is selected (1) or not (0). The objective is to choose items such that their total weight doesn't exceed C ,while maximizing the total cost based on the selected items.

Step 5 is using the optimized selection index to organize the packages. The packages generated from the optimization process are then fed into a large language model, which uses them to generate a tourism plan.

The core design is step 2 and 3. In step 3 of the AI-Agent framework, the goal is to compute the weighted significance of each data point through the Vietoris–Rips complex. The Vietoris–Rips complex helps calculate the simplices formed by the data points, which represent higher-dimensional analogs of triangles. Each simplex is formed by a combination of points, and the weight of a point is determined by how often it appears in the simplices. The weight of a data point in this context plays a crucial role in its interactions with other data points. If the weight is small, this suggests that the point predominantly interacts with other points that are very similar to itself, as it tends to appear in fewer simplices. On the other hand, if the weight is large, the point has a more balanced interaction with a diverse range of other points, indicating that it is more central and influential in the structure of the dataset. These data points are derived from a dimensionality reduction process, where the goal is to preserve the local structure of the data. In the reduced-dimensional space, points that are closer together are typically more similar to each other (Kasun, Yang, Huang, & Zhang, 2016). Therefore, the weighted significance of a point is closely tied to its proximity to other points in this new space, reflecting its relative similarity and importance in the overall dataset.

2.3 Experiment and Discussion

The sections on the literature review and the tourism AI agent framework design explain the background knowledge of the framework and its design methodology. This section will explain the experimental design. Experiments 1 and 2 aim to quantify the data for the framework, and the results show that this framework is very useful.

2.3.1 Experiment of Weighted Calculate

This experiment is aim for analysis the distribution of weighted. The weighted distribution is aim to similar as beta distribution. When a weight distribution closely resembles a Beta distribution (Nadarajah & Kotz, 2006), it suggests that the weights are distributed in a manner that is both flexible and adaptable to different scenarios. The pointer is Akaike information criterion (AKI) (Larrañaga & Bielza, 2004), if AKI lower, meaning the weighted is more fitting the bate distribute well without being unnecessarily complex. The objective of this experiment is pursuit the lower Akaike information criterion. The process of this experiment is executed framework step 1 to step 3, for getting weighted of each data. To compare different scenarios, two selection methods were compared: one where 25 samples are selected from each of the four categories to form the dataset, and another where 50, 50, 3, and 6 samples are selected from the four categories, respectively, to form the dataset. Named two selection methods as same selection strategy and different selection strategy. This was done to evaluate whether the weight distribution approximates a Beta distribution under both balanced and imbalanced selection conditions.

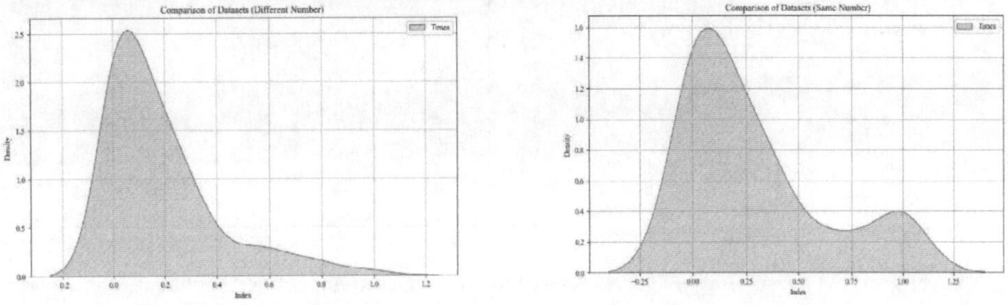

Figure 2. The weighted distribute, left distribute is different selection strategy and same selection strategy

While getting the distribute, the experiment calculates AIC value, using weighted distribution and classification distribution. Table 1 describe the AIC value, the distribution columns is the classification distribution name, different number AIC is the AIC values calculated by different selection strategy weighted and classification distribution, same number AIC is the AIC values calculated by same selection strategy weighted and classification distribution. Sum of AIC is the sum values of different number AIC and same number AIC.

Table 1. The Akaike Information Criterion (AIC) values from different selection strategy and same selection strategy

Distribution	Different Number AIC	Same Number AIC	Sum of AIC
Norm	-25.4163	66.6734	41.2571
Expon	-151.5467	-42.8101	-194.3568
Lognorm	-1152.7319	-1200.3797	-2353.1116
Weibull Min	-617.8960	-1276.0762	-1893.9722
Beta	-1103.7782	-2133.4763	-3237.2545
Pareto	-155.7894	-48.6974	-204. 4868
Logistic	-39.5689	65.2974	25.7283
Cauchy	-36.3273	72.2778	35.9505
Triang	-46.8808	107.0087	60.1279

In the table 1, the minimum sum of AIC is Beta distribution. Therefore, for these classic distributions, the weight distribution generated by this framework most closely resembles the Beta distribution, which aligns with the ideal weight distribution for this framework. This is because when a weight distribution closely resembles a Beta distribution, it suggests that the weights are distributed in a manner that is both flexible and adaptable to different scenarios.

2.3.2 Experiment of Meta Heuristic Optimize and LLM Response

The purpose of this experiment is to use heuristics to determine which algorithm can achieve the maximum total weight for the knapsack problem. In this experiment, the metric is the total weight. The weight here is derived from two strategies: different selection strategy and same selection strategy. Among the approximate optimal solutions calculated by the meta heuristic algorithms, the choice with the largest total weight indicates that, under the allowable knapsack capacity, this selection combination has the highest total weight. The goal of this experiment is to obtain the knapsack selection with the maximum total weight, which will be used as the input for the fifth step (LLM) in the framework, and finally, the LLM output for this knapsack selection will be displayed.

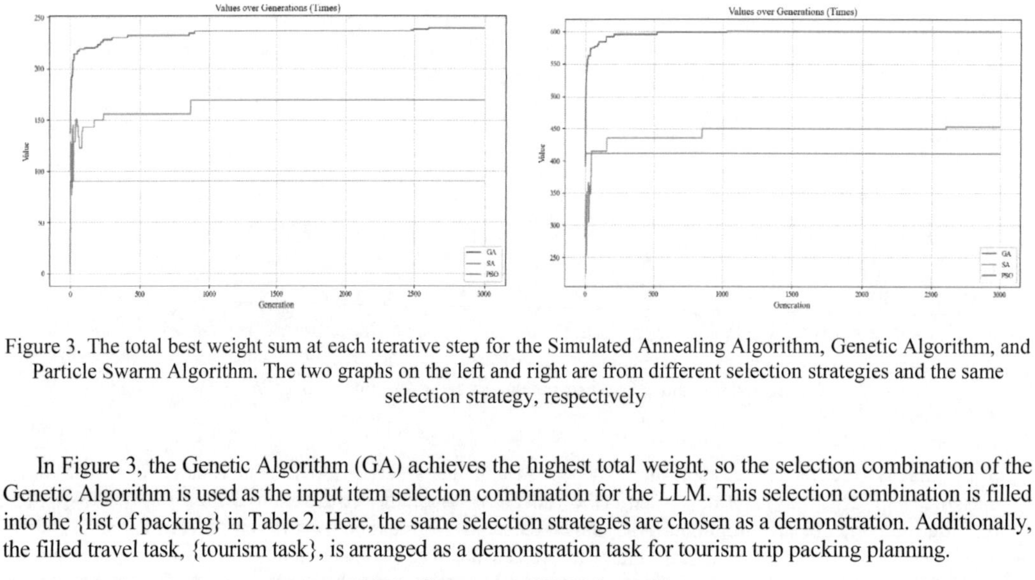

Figure 3. The total best weight sum at each iterative step for the Simulated Annealing Algorithm, Genetic Algorithm, and Particle Swarm Algorithm. The two graphs on the left and right are from different selection strategies and the same selection strategy, respectively

In Figure 3, the Genetic Algorithm (GA) achieves the highest total weight, so the selection combination of the Genetic Algorithm is used as the input item selection combination for the LLM. This selection combination is filled into the {list of packing} in Table 2. Here, the same selection strategies are chosen as a demonstration. Additionally, the filled travel task, {tourism task}, is arranged as a demonstration task for tourism trip packing planning.

Table 2. The prompt of LLM for packing

Tourism Packing Prompt Output Format
You are given a list of items for packing {list_of_packing}. This is the task that tourism want: {tourism_task}. Please using this list of items, to help tourism complete his/her task.

In summary, this experiment applies meta-heuristic algorithms, such as the Simulated Annealing, Genetic Algorithm, and Particle Swarm Algorithm, to solve the knapsack problem and identify the optimal selection combination based on maximum total weight. The Genetic Algorithm was found to yield the highest weight, and its selection combination was used as input for the subsequent LLM step. This combination, along with the tourism task, was then formatted for the LLM to generate packing recommendations for the tourism trip, as shown in Table 2.

3. CONCLUSION

This paper proposes a novel framework for a sustainable tourism packing AI agent. Through this advanced AI agent framework, travelers can receive more tailored packing lists that align with various travel plans. Traditional methods involve directly inputting the entire packing list into the LLM request to generate a plan that matches the travel mission. In contrast, the approach in this framework combines topology data analysis, metaheuristic algorithms, and the knapsack problem to intelligently analyze datasets. This enables the LLM to better capture the data's characteristics, resulting in the creation of more optimal travel plans, making this the state-of-the-art tourism AI agent.

The paper presents two experiments. Experiment 1 aims to analyze the distribution of weights. Experiment 2 focuses on identifying which metaheuristic algorithm can achieve the maximum total weight for the knapsack problem. In Experiment 1, the minimum sum of the AIC for the beta distribution shows that the weighted distribution calculated by this framework most closely resembles the beta distribution. This result is ideal, as the beta distribution is flexible and adaptable to various scenarios. In Experiment 2, the GA algorithm achieves the best performance, regardless of whether the training dataset comes from different selection strategies or the same strategy. Therefore, the GA algorithm is the most suitable method in this framework for obtaining optimal solutions.

The key advantages of this paper are threefold: First, it utilizes real-world data to guide decision-making. Second, it employs topology analysis and metaheuristics for optimization, ensuring efficient and effective packing creation. Third, it leverages a large language model to generate personalized tourism plans, making the system more adaptable to individual needs. In summary, this paper proposes a powerful framework for building a tourism AI agent.

REFERENCES

Abd Elaziz, M., Elsheikh, A. H., Oliva, D., Abualigah, L., Lu, S., & Ewees, A. A. (2021). Advanced metaheuristic techniques for mechanical design problems. *Archives of Computational Methods in Engineering*, 1-22.

Agushaka, J. O., & Ezugwu, A. E. (2022). Initialisation approaches for population-based metaheuristic algorithms: A comprehensive review. *Applied Sciences*, *12*(2), 896.

Butler, R. W. (1991). Tourism, environment, and sustainable development. *Environmental conservation*, *18*(3), 201-209.

Carlsson, G. (2020). Topological methods for data modelling. *Nature Reviews Physics*, *2*(12), 697-708.

Cebula, R., & Vedder, R. (1972). A note on migration, economic opportunity, and the quality of life.

Cerf, V. G. (2023). Large Language Models. *Commun. ACM*, *66*(8), 7.

Chen, G., Wu, S., Zhou, J., & Tung, A. K. (2013). Automatic itinerary planning for traveling services. *IEEE transactions on knowledge and data engineering*, *26*(3), 514-527.

Chen, X., & Dai, Y. (2020, June). Research on an improved ant colony algorithm fusion with genetic algorithm for route planning. In 2020 IEEE 4th Information Technology, Networking, Electronic and Automation Control Conference (ITNEC) (Vol. 1, pp. 1273-1278). IEEE.

Doborjeh, Z., Hemmington, N., Doborjeh, M., & Kasabov, N. (2022). Artificial intelligence: a systematic review of methods and applications in hospitality and tourism. *International Journal of Contemporary Hospitality Management*, *34*(3), 1154-1176.

Gupta, S., Abderazek, H., Yıldız, B. S., Yildiz, A. R., Mirjalili, S., & Sait, S. M. (2021). Comparison of metaheuristic optimization algorithms for solving constrained mechanical design optimization problems. *Expert Systems with Applications*, *183*, 115351.

Kasun, L. L. C., Yang, Y., Huang, G. B., & Zhang, Z. (2016). Dimension reduction with extreme learning machine. *IEEE transactions on Image Processing*, *25*(8), 3906-3918.

Kurylek, B., Camara, A., Nandi, A., & Markopoulos, E. (2024). A Novel Agent-Based Framework for Conversational Data Analysis and Personal AI Systems. *Artificial Intelligence and Social Computing*, *122*, 124-136.

Larrañaga, P., & Bielza, C. (2004). Akaike information criterion. Dictionary of Bioinformatics and Computational Biology.

Li, T. H. S., Liu, C. Y., Kuo, P. H., Fang, N. C., Li, C. H., Cheng, C. W., ... & Chen, C. Y. (2017). A three-dimensional adaptive PSO-based packing algorithm for an IoT-based automated e-fulfillment packaging system. *Ieee Access*, *5*, 9188-9205.

Liang, S., Jiao, T., Du, W., & Qu, S. (2021). An improved ant colony optimization algorithm based on context for tourism route planning. *PLoS One*, *16*(9), e0257317.

Lu, J., Xiao, W., Song, E., Hassan, M. M., Almogren, A., & Altameem, A. (2019). iAgent: when AI meets mobile agent. *IEEE Access*, *7*, 97032-97040.

Lust, T., & Teghem, J. (2012). The multiobjective multidimensional knapsack problem: a survey and a new approach. *International Transactions in Operational Research*, *19*(4), 495-520.

Ma, Z., Wu, G., Suganthan, P. N., Song, A., & Luo, Q. (2023). Performance assessment and exhaustive listing of 500+ nature-inspired metaheuristic algorithms. *Swarm and Evolutionary Computation*, *77*, 101248.

Meng, Z., Li, G., Wang, X., Sait, S. M., & Yıldız, A. R. (2021). A comparative study of metaheuristic algorithms for reliability-based design optimization problems. *Archives of Computational Methods in Engineering*, *28*, 1853-1869.

Munch, E. (2017). A user's guide to topological data analysis. Journal of Learning Analytics, 4(2), 47-61.

Nadarajah, S., & Kotz, S. (2006). The beta exponential distribution. *Reliability engineering & system safety*, 91(6), 689-697.

Niñerola, A., Sánchez-Rebull, M. V., & Hernández-Lara, A. B. (2019). Tourism research on sustainability: A bibliometric analysis. *Sustainability*, *11*(5), 1377.

Paquete, L., Schiavinotto, T., & Stützle, T. (2007). On local optima in multiobjective combinatorial optimization problems. *Annals of Operations Research*, *156*, 83-97.

Parolo, G., Ferrarini, A., & Rossi, G. (2009). Optimization of tourism impacts within protected areas by means of genetic algorithms. *Ecological Modelling*, *220*(8), 1138-1147.

Patania, A., Vaccarino, F., & Petri, G. (2017). Topological analysis of data. *EPJ Data Science*, *6*(1), 1-6.

Pillai, R., & Sivathanu, B. (2020). Adoption of AI-based chatbots for hospitality and tourism. *International Journal of Contemporary Hospitality Management*, *32*(10), 3199-3226.

Pisinger, D. (2005). Where are the hard knapsack problems?. *Computers & Operations Research*, *32*(9), 2271-2284.

Ruiz-Meza, J., Brito, J., & Montoya-Torres, J. R. (2021). Multi-objective fuzzy tourist trip design problem with heterogeneous preferences and sustainable itineraries. *Sustainability*, *13*(17), 9771.

Samala, N., Katkam, B. S., Bellamkonda, R. S., & Rodriguez, R. V. (2020). Impact of AI and robotics in the tourism sector: a critical insight. *Journal of tourism futures*, *8*(1), 73-87.

Sharma, A. (Ed.). (2019). Sustainable tourism development: futuristic approaches. CRC Press.

Snášel, V., Nowaková, J., Xhafa, F., & Barolli, L. (2017). Geometrical and topological approaches to Big Data. *Future Generation Computer Systems*, *67*, 286-296.

Sofronov, B. (2018). The development of the travel and tourism industry in the world. *Annals of Spiru Haret University. Economic Series*, *18*(4), 123-137.

Tan, Y., Shuai, C., Jiao, L., & Shen, L. (2017). An adaptive neuro-fuzzy inference system (ANFIS) approach for measuring country sustainability performance. *Environmental Impact Assessment Review*, *65*, 29-40.

Zhou, S., Xu, F. F., Zhu, H., Zhou, X., Lo, R., Sridhar, A., ... & Neubig, G. (2023). Webarena: A realistic web environment for building autonomous agents. arXiv preprint arXiv:2307.13854.

Zomorodian, A. (2010). Fast construction of the Vietoris-Rips complex. *Computers & Graphics*, *34*(3), 263-271.

THE DIGITAL TRANSFORMATION OF CORPORATE SOCIAL RESPONSIBILITY: A TECH-DRIVEN MODEL FOR EVALUATING SUSTAINABILITY PERFORMANCE

Maria Virginia Sirolli[1], Francesca Igini[1] and Andrea Rocchi[2]
[1]Department of Management, Sapienza University of Rome
Via Castro Laurenziano, 9 (00161) Roma, Italy
[2]Department of Communication and Social Research, Sapienza University of Rome
Via Salaria, 113, (00198) Roma, Italy

ABSTRACT

Corporate Social Responsibility (CSR) has evolved from a reputational tool to a strategic function, yet its evaluation practices remain largely static and retrospective. This paper explores how digital transformation can enhance CSR assessment by integrating real-time data and advanced analytics. Building on Industry 4.0 technologies such as Artificial Intelligence (AI), Internet of Things (IoT), and Big Data, we propose the Tech-CSR Model (TCSR-M)—a conceptual framework structured around three functional dimensions: Enviro (environmental metrics), People (social inclusion and well-being), and Trust (governance and compliance). Designed as a proof-of-concept, the model illustrates how emerging technologies could support a more dynamic, transparent, and continuous approach to sustainability monitoring. The paper highlights both the opportunities and challenges of this transition, emphasising the need for ethical oversight, standardisation, and scalability. While not empirically tested, the TCSR-M provides a foundation for future research and aims to stimulate debate on embedding CSR into the broader agenda of digital transformation.

KEYWORDS

Corporate Social Responsibility, Digital Transformation, Sustainability Assessment

1. INTRODUCTION

Corporate Social Responsibility (CSR) has has shifted from a voluntary initiative to a strategic imperative, reshaping business operations, governance, and stakeholder engagement. Once seen as peripheral - focused on ethics, environment, and social good - CSR now plays a central role in value creation, influencing financial performance, risk management, and legitimacy (European Commission, 2011). In this context, companies are increasingly expected not only to mitigate the negative externalities of their activities but also to proactively contribute to sustainable development (Montiel et al., 2021). Yet, CSR evaluation frameworks remain largely static and retrospective, relying on voluntary disclosure. Tools like the Global Reporting Initiative (GRI) and ESG ratings provide useful guidelines but struggle to capture the complexity and dynamism of sustainability in a digital era. Consequently, many organisations find it difficult to translate sustainability goals into real-time impact.

Digital transformation offers a path forward. Industry 4.0 technologies, such as AI, IoT and Big Data, are reshaping how businesses collect, process, and analyse information, enabling real-time monitoring, predictive modelling, and automated compliance (Bai et al., 2020; Gaur et al., 2023). However, this convergence also introduces new risks, including data privacy issues, algorithmic bias, and the environmental footprint of digital infrastructure (Floridi et al., 2018; Wamba et al., 2021).

This paper proposes the Tech-CSR Model (TCSR-M), a conceptual framework for enhancing CSR evaluation in a data-driven economy. Rather than a prescriptive tool, the model is intended to foster debate, guide future empirical work, and support the integration of CSR into digital transformation strategies.

2. THEORETICAL BACKGROUND

2.1 Traditional Frameworks for Assessing CSR Performance

Initially rooted in ethical responsibility and philanthropic actions (Bowen, 1953), Corporate Social Responsibility has progressively evolved into a strategic paradigm that integrates sustainability, governance, and stakeholder value (Porter & Kramer, 2006; Visser, 2010), paving the way for structured frameworks aimed at evaluating and disclosing CSR performance.

In this context, several frameworks emerged to support its evaluation and disclosure. Although not originally designed for CSR, models such as the Triple Bottom Line (TBL), Global Reporting Initiative (GRI) and Environmental, Social and Governance (ESG) frameworks have become key references for sustainability reporting. The TBL framework, introduced by Elkington (1997), broadened organisational reporting beyond profit to include social and environmental dimensions, promoting the "people, planet, profit" triad. While conceptually influential, TBL has been criticised for lacking operational guidance and offering limited applicability in complex, rapidly evolving contexts. Slaper and Hall (2011) noted the absence of standardised metrics, which hampers comparability and meaningful performance assessment. Milne and Gray (2013) argued that TBL often oversimplifies sustainability, leading to superficial disclosures rather than systemic change. Elkington himself (2018) later acknowledged the model's misinterpretation as an accounting tool rather than a framework for challenging capitalism's trajectory.

Building on TBL, the Global Reporting Initiative (GRI), established in 1997, became the most widely used voluntary sustainability reporting framework. It offers detailed guidance on economic, environmental and social performance, aiming to harmonise reporting practices and enhance consistency and comparability. GRI encourages disclosure of both positive and negative impacts, promoting transparency and accountability. It has also become a valuable source for empirical sustainability research (Bais, Nassimbeni & Orzes, 2024). However, scholars have questioned its transformative potential, warning that highly stylised reports may obscure unsustainable practices (e.g. Tschopp & Nastanski, 2014).

In parallel, ESG frameworks have integrated sustainability into corporate governance and financial markets. Launched in 2004 by the UN Global Compact's "Who Cares Wins" report, ESG structures performance across three pillars: environmental (e.g. resource efficiency, emissions, climate risk), social (e.g. labour practices, human rights, community engagement) and governance (e.g. board structure, ethics, shareholder rights). Once peripheral, ESG is now seen as a strategic driver of reputation, trust, and financial performance. Studies have shown that ESG disclosure can enhance market valuation and reduce financial risk, especially in volatile contexts (Liu & Lin, 2022) Recent regulations - such as the EU Directive 2014/95/EU - have made ESG reporting increasingly mandatory, reflecting rising expectations for transparent, measurable and ethical business conduct (Wei et al., 2024; Eyo-Udo et al., 2024).

2.2 The Evolution of CSR in the Age of Digitalization

The progressive digitalisation of business processes has not only reshaped production and operations, but also transformed the way organisations engage with Corporate Social Responsibility (CSR). This shift marks a transition from symbolic, compliance-based practices to a more data-driven, performance-oriented approach, where emerging technologies play a crucial role in enhancing transparency, accountability, and strategic alignment (Di Vaio et al., 2023).

Artificial Intelligence (AI), the Internet of Things (IoT), and Big Data analytics are key enablers of this transformation, supporting real-time data collection, impact monitoring, and predictive analysis. These tools allow companies to integrate sustainability metrics into daily operations, moving from retrospective reporting to dynamic and proactive CSR management. For example, AI can detect energy inefficiencies, Big Data can map ESG risks across supply chains, and IoT sensors can provide real-time insights on emissions or safety.

Although not inherently sustainable, these technologies offer essential tools for monitoring, evaluation, and optimization - if adopted within a broader framework of responsible innovation. In 2023, global investment in IoT reached \$596 billion, with forecasts exceeding \$4 trillion by 2032 in sectors like manufacturing, agriculture and logistics (Fortune Business Insights, 2024). The Big Data market is projected to surpass \$1.1 trillion, reflecting its growing role in impact measurement (Allied Market Research, 2024). Generative AI alone attracted \$22.4 billion in 2023, nearly nine times the 2022 figure.

As highlighted by Gaur et al. (2023), The convergence of CSR and digitalisation enhances both operational efficiency and stakeholder engagement but also raises challenges such as data privacy, algorithmic bias, and the environmental impact of digital infrastructures. Nevertheless, integrating emerging technologies into CSR is increasingly viewed as a lever for competitiveness, resilience, and sustainable innovation (Khan, Mehmood & Ali, 2024). Despite promising developments, implementation remains at an early stage. While pilot initiatives demonstrate the potential of AI and IoT in sustainability reporting, the absence of real-time indicators and universally accepted standards hinders widespread adoption (Loukides, 2025). Traditional frameworks such as GRI or ESG ratings are only beginning to incorporate digital metrics and often rely on static disclosures that fail to capture the evolving nature of corporate impact.

This evolving scenario presents both opportunities and complexities: emerging technologies offer new pathways for embedding CSR into core strategies but require rethinking measurement systems, ethical safeguards, and institutional accountability. To address these limitations - particularly the static nature of existing models and their disconnect from real-time data - this paper introduces a conceptual model as a proof-of-concept for a more responsive, integrated and data-driven approach to CSR evaluation. The model does not claim to provide a universal solution but aims to foster critical debate and support future empirical developments. Recent contributions underscore that digital transformation now extends beyond technology deployment, encompassing socio-institutional dimensions such as financial literacy, regulatory evolution, and quality of life improvements, while revealing new opportunities and systemic challenges across finance, governance and sustainability (Alhassan et al., 2024).

3. THE TECH-CSR MODEL (TCSR-M): A CONCEPTUAL APPROACH TO DATA-DRIVEN SUSTAINABILITY ASSESSMENT

This section presents the Tech-CSR Model (TCSR-M), a conceptual and exploratory framework designed to illustrate how advanced technologies might support real-time CSR evaluation. Rather than replacing existing standards, the model aims to initiate a broader reflection on how digitalisation can enable a more dynamic, transparent, and data-driven approach to sustainability monitoring.

The TCSR-M is structured around three functional components - (1) Enviro, (2) People and (3) Trust - each aligned with a key dimension of corporate sustainability. These components are not intended as prescriptive categories but as heuristic tools to explore how digital technologies might operationalise CSR evaluation. Enviro focuses on real-time quantification and forecasting of environmental indicators; People examines social inclusion and workforce dynamics; Trust addresses governance, legitimacy and compliance through data-enabled monitoring. Together, these layers provide a conceptual scaffold for rethinking CSR as an integrated, continuous, and technology-enhanced process, rather than a retrospective reporting function.

3.1 Data Infrastructure and Analytical Instruments

The TCSR-M is built around a data-centric architecture that conceptually integrates multiple layers of technology to enable continuous and scalable CSR monitoring. In this model, Internet of Things (IoT) devices, blockchain systems, and data analytics platforms are envisioned as key enablers for capturing, processing and interpreting information related to environmental impact, social dynamics, and governance practices.

IoT sensors and connected devices could, for instance, monitor emissions, resource consumption, or workplace conditions in real time. These data streams would be aggregated in a centralised system, supported by interoperable protocols. Blockchain technologies may enhance traceability and auditability—particularly in supply chain verification and contract execution - while analytics tools such as machine learning (ML) and natural language processing (NLP) would be used to extract insights from both structured and unstructured data, feeding into a dynamic reporting layer with real-time dashboards and role-based access.

3.1.1 Enviro: Environmental Dimension

In the Enviro layer, environmental performance indicators - such as CO_2 emissions, energy efficiency, and resource use - are conceptually assessed through AI-assisted forecasting and optimisation tools (Uddin et al., 2023). In this preliminary formulation, the use of predictive analytics (e.g. regression models, anomaly detection) applied to time-series data from factory and building systems is envisioned as a way to anticipate inefficiencies and detect sustainability risks (Olawumi et al., 2025). Additionally, technologies like RFID could support resource flow monitoring, enabling the construction of KPI-based scoring models that inform environmental strategy in near real time (Bukova et al., 2023).

Table 1 summarises the main indicators envisioned in the Enviro layer, along with their associated technologies, data sources and analytical techniques.

Table 1. Enviro: Environmental Indicators and Analytics

Enviro metric	Envisioned technology stack	Illustrative data source	Data capture frequency	Exploratory analytical techniques
CO_2 Emissions	IoT Sensors, AI Forecasting	Smart meters, exhaust logs	Real-time	Predictive ML, Anomaly Detection
Energy Efficiency	AI Optimization, IoT	Factory systems, BMS	Hourly	Regression, Pattern Recognition
Resource Utilization Index	RFID, Blockchain	Supply chain sensors	Daily	KPI Scoring Model

3.1.2 People: Social Dimension

The People component focuses on human-centred metrics such as workforce safety, employee sentiment, and diversity and inclusion. These indicators would ideally be derived from diverse data sources, including wearable IoT devices, survey platforms and human resources systems (Nguyen et al., 2024). Preliminary analytical approaches may include edge AI for generating alerts on safety incidents, and deep learning NLP models - such as BERT or RoBERTa - to extract sentiment and patterns from employee communications (Deng & Liu, 2025). Furthermore, the use of machine learning techniques like decision trees and bias detection algorithms could support the identification of inclusion trends in recruitment and career advancement (Kondra et al., 2025). Table 2 summarises the main indicators envisioned in the People layer, along with their associated technologies, data sources and analytical techniques.

Table 2. People: Social Indicators and Analytics

People metric	Envisioned technology stack	Illustrative data source	Data capture frequency	Exploratory analytical techniques
Workforce Safety Index	Wearable IoT, Edge AI	Helmets, Health bands	Real-time	Alert System, Threshold Analysis
Sentiment on CSR Initiatives	NLP, Sentiment Analysis	Surveys, Social Media	Weekly	NLP Models (BERT, RoBERTa)
Diversity & Inclusion Score	AI-driven HR Analytics	HR database	Monthly	Decision Trees, Bias Detection

3.1.3 Trust: Governance Dimension

The Trust dimension emphasises compliance monitoring, contract execution, and the detection of governance anomalies. Analytical tools in this domain use a combination of rule-based systems and machine learning models to validate legal compliance and financial integrity (Kalogiannidis et al., 2024). Smart contracts deployed on blockchain platforms are audited using event-triggered analytics (Balogun et al., 2023), while anomaly detection engines—such as autoencoders and random forest classifiers - are applied to time-series and ledger data to detect irregularities or emerging risks (Bakumenko & Elragal, 2022). Table 3 summarises the main indicators envisioned in the Trust layer, along with their associated technologies, data sources and analytical techniques.

Table 3. Trust: Governance Indicators and Analytics

Trust metric	Envisioned technology stack	Illustrative data source	Data capture frequency	Exploratory analytical techniques
Compliance Index	Big Data, Regulatory Ontology	Legal databases, policy records	Monthly	Rule-Based + ML Hybrid
Smart Contract Execution	Blockchain, IoT Integration	Supplier platforms	Event-based	Smart Contract Audit Triggers
Governance Anomaly Detection	AI Auditing, Time-Series ML	Financial and compliance data	Weekly	Autoencoders, Random Forests

4. DISCUSSION

Although the Tech-CSR Model (TCSR-M) has not yet been empirically validated, it offers a conceptual foundation for exploring how emerging technologies can support more accurate, real-time and data-driven CSR evaluation. As a proof of concept, the model is intended as an exploratory architecture rather than a tested prototype. No simulations or pilot implementations have been developed; instead, the framework aims to guide future research on its assumptions and feasibility in real-world settings. Developed in response to the limitations of traditional CSR models - often qualitative, static and disclosure-based - the TCSR-M reframes CSR assessment as a dynamic, continuous process. It unfolds in three phases: (1) defining a conceptual architecture based on three core dimensions aligned with sustainability intelligence; (2) designing a data-centric system to collect information from heterogeneous sources and (3) applying advanced analytics to interpret sustainability metrics. This multi-stage approach shifts CSR from a compliance-based function to an adaptive, evidence-driven practice focused on transparency, responsiveness, and real-time insight. While still theoretical, the model's potential advantages are significant. By integrating IoT, AI, blockchain, and big data analytics, the TCSR-M could enable organisations to monitor CSR-related data more continuously and in greater depth. This may improve responsiveness to inefficiencies, regulatory changes, and stakeholder expectations. A data-driven approach could also strengthen the traceability and credibility of CSR actions, enhancing communication with investors, regulators and the public. Strategically, adopting such a framework could reduce latency in sustainability insights, support informed decision-making and align companies with evolving global standards. Through its emphasis on structured, verifiable and time-sensitive data, the model may also help firms meet the expectations of ESG-focused investors and certification bodies. Importantly, the model does not suggest that all organisations - particularly SMEs - must invest heavily in CSR-specific technologies. However, SMEs may face scalability challenges beyond financial constraints, such as limited access to specialised personnel (e.g. data scientists, sustainability analysts) and outdated IT infrastructures. Regulatory uncertainty and weak internal governance on digital ethics may further hinder adoption. Addressing these issues may require modular, low-code solutions and institutional support, such as shared platforms or sector-specific toolkits. Rather than promoting additional investment, the model recognises that digitalisation is already reshaping most sectors through efficiency, competitiveness and compliance. In this context, the TCSR-M proposes leveraging existing digital infrastructures for more strategic and transparent sustainability management. Nonetheless, implementation poses notable limitations and risks. Technically, integrating AI, IoT and big data into legacy systems requires substantial investment and expertise, raising concerns over accessibility. Modular, open-source adaptations and intermediary platforms may ease adoption in resource-constrained settings. Moreover, automated analytics introduce challenges of fairness and explainability. Poorly designed or unmonitored AI and ML systems may reproduce existing biases, especially in sensitive domains like workforce inclusion or governance. Transparent architectures and human oversight are essential to mitigate these risks. There are also broader systemic limitations. Most CSR frameworks, including GRI and ESG ratings, have only begun integrating digital capabilities and still rely heavily on static disclosures, which inadequately reflect technological complexity and change (Di Vaio et al., 2023; Loukides, 2025). The TCSR-M contributes to this ongoing debate by envisioning CSR as responsive to both the opportunities and governance challenges of the Fourth Industrial Revolution. Finally, the model may raise ethical concerns across its three dimensions. In Enviro, automated monitoring (e.g. energy use or predictive waste analytics) may lead to overreliance on opaque systems and overlook local contexts. In People, wearable IoT for safety or sentiment tracking raises issues around privacy, consent, and surveillance. In Trust, AI-based governance monitoring may perpetuate structural bias if algorithms lack transparency and auditability. These concerns underscore the need for integrated ethical governance to ensure technology strengthens - not undermines - social responsibility, fairness and transparency.

5. CONCLUSION

In an era increasingly defined by the convergence of sustainability goals and digital transformation processes, this paper has explored how emerging technologies may serve as catalysts for more dynamic, transparent, and data-driven approaches to Corporate Social Responsibility (CSR). The limitations of traditional CSR frameworks - typically reliant on static indicators, qualitative evaluations, and retrospective reporting - have underscored the need for new models that align with the logic of real-time monitoring, predictive insight, and operational integration.

Digitalisation, already reshaping business operations across sectors, offers a timely opportunity to reimagine CSR as a core organisational function rather than a symbolic or ancillary activity. Technologies such as Artificial Intelligence (AI), the Internet of Things (IoT), and data analytics can support more responsive and evidence-based sustainability management. Particularly in sectors like agriculture, manufacturing, and logistics - where digital tools are already being adopted to improve efficiency and meet regulatory requirements - CSR frameworks that leverage existing data infrastructures can amplify the value of those investments by linking them to broader social and environmental objectives.

Within this context, the Tech-CSR Model (TCSR-M) has been introduced as a preliminary conceptual framework to stimulate debate and guide future research. Organised around three functional dimensions—Enviro, People, and Trust - the model illustrates how digital technologies might enable a more continuous, scalable, and accountable approach to CSR evaluation. Rather than prescribing solutions, it proposes a starting point for rethinking CSR as an embedded, data-informed practice.The model also raises critical challenges. Issues such as algorithmic bias, data privacy, digital inequality, and the energy impact of advanced infrastructures must be addressed to ensure that technology supports, rather than undermines, corporate responsibility. The risk of performative sustainability - or tech-enabled greenwashing - underscores the need for strong governance and standardised evaluation criteria.To advance beyond conceptualisation, future research should empirically validate the TCSR-M through a multi-phase approach: (1) applying the model to internal data and public sustainability reports; (2) benchmarking it against established CSR and ESG frameworks; and (3) examining links between CSR indicators and outcomes such as financial performance, regulatory compliance, and stakeholder trust. These efforts are essential to assess the model's practical relevance, scalability, and added value. Particular attention should be given to small and medium-sized enterprises (SMEs), which may face resource constraints. However, many SMEs - especially in digitally evolving sectors like agrifood - are already adopting IoT systems, precision tools, and smart logistics to meet operational needs and regulatory demands. In this light, the TCSR-M should not be viewed as a technological burden but as a strategic complement to ongoing digitalisation. By leveraging data already collected for productivity or compliance, organisations can integrate CSR more effectively into existing systems, enhancing transparency and strategic alignment with minimal additional investment.

ACKNOWLEDGEMENT

This research was partially financed by the European Union - Next Generation EU, Mission 4 Component 1 CUP B53C23001650006.

REFERENCES

Alhassan, A. et al., (2024). Digital transformation in financial industry: antecedents of fintech adoption, financial literacy and quality of life. *International Journal of Law and Management*, Vol. ahead-of-print, No. ahead-of-print. https://doi.org/10.1108/IJLMA-11-2023-0249

Allied Market Research, (2024). *Big data analytics market size, share, competitive landscape and trend analysis report, by component, by application, by end user: Global opportunity analysis and industry forecast, 2024–2032*. August. Available at: https://www.alliedmarketresearch.com/big-data-analytics-market-A189561

Alsayegh, M. F., Abdul Rahman, R., & Homayoun, S. (2020). Corporate economic, environmental, and social sustainability performance transformation through ESG disclosure. *Sustainability*, *12*(9), 3910.

Bai, C. et al., (2020). Industry 4.0 technologies assessment: A sustainability perspective. *International Journal of Production Economics*, 229, 107776.

Bais, B., Nassimbeni, G. and Orzes, G., (2024). Global Reporting Initiative: Literature review and research directions. *Journal of Cleaner Production*, 143428.

Bakumenko, A., & Elragal, A. (2022). Detecting anomalies in financial data using machine learning algorithms. *Systems*, *10*(5), 130.

Balogun, E. D., Ogunsola, K. O., & Samuel, A. D. E. B. A. N. J. I. (2023). Blockchain-Enabled Auditing: A Conceptual Model for Financial Transparency, Regulatory Compliance, and Security. *Journal of Blockchain Technology and Financial Innovation*, *11*(2), 97-112.

Billio, M. et al., (2021). Inside the ESG Ratings: (Dis)agreement and performance. *Corporate Social Responsibility and Environmental Management*, 28(5), pp.1426–1445.

Bowen, H.R., (2013). *Social responsibilities of the businessman*. University of Iowa Press, Iowa.

Brown, H.S., de Jong, M. and Levy, D.L., (2009). Building institutions based on information disclosure: Lessons from GRI's sustainability reporting. *Journal of Cleaner Production*, 17(6), pp.571–580. https://doi.org/10.1016/j.jclepro.2008.12.031

Bukova, B., Tengler, J., Brumercikova, E., Brumercik, F., & Kissova, O. (2023). Environmental burden case study of RFID technology in logistics centre. *Sensors*, *23*(3), 1268.

Deng, J., & Liu, Y. (2025). Research on Sentiment Analysis of Online Public Opinion Based on RoBERTa–BiLSTM Attention Model. *Applied Sciences*, *15*(4), 2148.

Elkington, J., (1997). The triple bottom line. *Environmental Management: Readings and Cases*, 2, pp.49–66.

Eyo-Udo, N.L., Odimarha, A.C. and Kolade, O.O., (2024). Ethical supply chain management: balancing profit, social responsibility, and environmental stewardship. *International Journal of Management & Entrepreneurship Research*, 6(4), pp.1069–1077.

Floridi, L. et al., (2018). AI4People—An ethical framework for a good AI society: Opportunities, risks, principles, and recommendations. *Minds and Machines*, 28(4), pp.689–707. https://doi.org/10.1007/s11023-018-9482-5

Fortune Business Insights, (2024). *Big data technology market size, share & COVID-19 impact analysis, by offering (hardware, software, and services), by deployment (on-premises and cloud), by application, by end-user, and regional forecast, 2024–2032*. Available at: https://www.fortunebusinessinsights.com/industry-reports/big-data-technology-market-100144

Gaur, L. et al., (2023). Artificial intelligence for carbon emissions using system of systems theory. *Ecological Informatics*, 76, 102165. https://doi.org/10.1016/j.ecoinf.2023.102165 GRI, 2011. *Sustainability Reporting Guidelines*. Global Reporting Initiative. Available at: https://www.globalreporting.org

Halkos, G. and Nomikos, S., (2021). Corporate social responsibility: Trends in Global Reporting Initiative standards. *Economic Analysis and Policy*, 69, pp.106–117. https://doi.org/10.1016/j.eap.2020.12.006

Kalogiannidis, S., Kalfas, D., Papaevangelou, O., Giannarakis, G., & Chatzitheodoridis, F. (2024). The role of artificial intelligence technology in predictive risk assessment for business continuity: A case study of Greece. Risks, *12*(2), 19. doi:10.3390/risks12020019

Khan, A.N., Mehmood, K. and Ali, A., (2024). Maximizing CSR impact: Leveraging artificial intelligence and process optimization for sustainability performance management. Corporate Social Responsibility and Environmental Management, 31(5), pp.4849–4861. https://doi.org/10.1002/csr.2832

Kondra, S., Medapati, S., Koripalli, M., Nandula, S. R. S. C., & Zink, J. Z. (2025). AI and Diversity, Equity, and Inclusion (DEI): Examining the Potential for AI to Mitigate Bias and Promote Inclusive Communication. *Journal of Artificial intelligence and Machine Learning*, *3*(1), 1-8.

Liu, Y. and Lin, M., (2022). Research on the influence of ESG information disclosure on enterprise financial risk: Taking pharmaceutical industry as an example. *Frontiers in Business, Economics and Management*, 5(3), pp.264–271.

Milne, M.J. and Gray, R., (2013). W(h)ither ecology? The triple bottom line, the Global Reporting Initiative, and corporate sustainability reporting. *Journal of Business Ethics*, 118, pp.13–29.

Montiel, I. et al., (2021). Implementing the United Nations' Sustainable Development Goals in international business. *Journal of International Business Studies*, 52, pp.999–1030. https://doi.org/10.1057/s41267-021-00445-y

Nguyen, T., Nguyen, D. H., Nguyen, Q. T., Tran, K. D., & Tran, K. P. (2024). Human-Centered Edge AI and Wearable Technology for Workplace Health and Safety in Industry 5.0. In *Artificial Intelligence for Safety and Reliability Engineering: Methods, Applications, and Challenges* (pp. 171-183). Cham: Springer Nature Switzerland.

Olawumi, M. A., & Oladapo, B. I. (2025). AI-driven predictive models for sustainability. *Journal of Environmental Management*, *373*, 123472.

Porter, M.E. and Kramer, M.R., (2006). Strategy and society: The link between competitive advantage and corporate social responsibility. *Harvard Business Review*, 84(12), pp.78–92.

Slaper, T.F. and Hall, T.J., (2011). The triple bottom line: What is it and how does it work. *Indiana Business Review*, 86(1), pp.4–8.

Tschopp, D. and Nastanski, M., (2014). The harmonization and convergence of corporate social responsibility reporting standards. *Journal of Business Ethics*, 125, pp.147–162.

Uddin, M. S., Mohamed, O. E. B., & Ebert, J. (2024). Artificial Intelligence-Powered Carbon Emissions Forecasting: Implications for Sustainable Supply Chains and Green Finance. *Energy, Environment, and Economy*, *2*, 1-13.

Visser, W., (2010). *The age of responsibility: CSR 2.0 and the new DNA of business*. Wiley. https://doi.org/10.15209/jbsge.v5i3.185

Wamba, S.F. et al., (2017). Big data analytics and firm performance: Effects of dynamic capabilities. *Journal of Business Research*, 70, pp.356–365. https://doi.org/10.1016/j.jbusres.2016.08.00

Wei, Y., Sit, K.J. and Ekinci, Y., (2024). Customer definitions of moral value for retail brands: A qualitative understanding. *Journal of Retailing and Consumer Services*, 77, 103697.

THE EFFECT OF VALUE CO-CREATION AND SOSI ON BUSINESS PERFORMANCE: DIFFERENCES BETWEEN HOTELS AND RETAIL ESTABLISHMENTS

Mihaela Simona Moise, Irene Gil-Saura, Maria Eugenia Ruiz-Molina and Antonio Marín-García
Universitat de València, Spain

ABSTRACT

The purpose of this study is to analyze how value co-creation with customers can act as a driver of Sustainability-Oriented Service Innovation (SOSI), a new concept that focuses on the connection between service innovation and sustainability, triggering positive effects on business performance. Additionally, the moderating role of the sector type (hospitality vs. retail) in the proposed relationships is examined. To address the stated objectives, an empirical study was conducted through personal surveys with 450 managers from hotels and retail establishments. The evidence underscores the critical role of SOSI in driving business performance, emphasizing the influence of value co-creation on the implementation of sustainable innovative practices within the hospitality and retail sectors. Our findings reveal significant sectoral differences in the impact of value co-creation on SOSI and the effect of non-financial results on financial results. These insights provide hospitality and retail managers with practical guidance on recognizing SOSI as a strategic tool for enhancing business outcomes.

KEYWORDS

Sustainability-Oriented Service Innovation, Value Co-Creation, Business Results, Hotel, Retail Establishments

1. INTRODUCTION

In today's competitive landscape, innovation is widely recognized as a crucial factor for the survival of all types of organizations, including hospitality businesses and retail establishments (Bordian et al., 2024; Gil-Saura et al., 2024). This is because innovative companies can swiftly adapt their service offerings to market changes, enabling them to sustain their competitive advantages (Kumar et al., 2024). In addition, it has also been identified in the literature that sustainability across economic, social, and environmental perspectives represents a crucial factor to achieve a competitive advantage for companies (Bordian et al., 2024). Due to the importance of both innovation and sustainability for companies, in recent years there has been an increase in interest in analyzing how service innovation can promote sustainability to address current economic, social and environmental challenges. Consequently, a new approach known as 'Sustainability-Oriented Service Innovation' (SOSI) has emerged (Calabrese et al., 2018). This concept represents a strategic integration of innovation and sustainability principles across economic, social, and environmental dimensions (Elkington, 1998). Moreover, while the connection between innovation and sustainability has been extensively studied in the manufacturing industry, there has been limited analysis in the service sector (Kumar et al., 2024).

The existing literature suggests that value co-creation is an innovative approach to engage clients and foster positive experiences by actively involving them in co-creation activities (Vargo et al., 2020). However, despite efforts by Vargo et al. (2020) to highlight the significance of expanding knowledge on value co-creation to encompass social and ecological sustainability, there has been limited empirical research on the implementation of value co-creation within a sustainability context (Bordian et al., 2024).

The relationship between innovation and business performance is well-supported in the existing literature. However, many studies that have explored this relationship have focused only on the financial aspects, which are measured through indicators such as sales, economic profitability, or financial profitability (Bhat and Sharma, 2022). However, financial performance alone is insufficient to fully assess the uncertainties arising from changes in the business environment and the potential for achieving corporate sustainability (Galarza et al., 2023). This highlights the need for a more comprehensive measurement of organizational results, incorporating both financial and non-financial aspects in the evaluation (Bhat and Sharma., 2022). Furthermore, despite the increasing significance of innovation and sustainability for service companies, which constantly face changing consumer behavior, empirical studies on the differences between various types of companies remain limited (Huang and Ichikohji, 2023). This study aims to address the differences between the Spanish hotel and retail sectors, given that they represent two key economic activities that significantly contribute to the Spanish society and the economy, accounting for 10% and 7% of total income, respectively.

This article attempts to pursue the following threefold objective: (1) to examine the relationship between value co-creation with customers and SOSI; (2) to evaluate the effect of SOSI on business performance; and (3) to examine the possible differences in the variables relationships depending on sector activity. Through the empirical testing of these relationships, this study aims to bridge significant gaps in the existing literature and offer practical insights for businesses in the hospitality and retail sectors.

2. LITERATURE REVIEW AND HYPOTHESIS

2.1 Sustainability-Oriented Service Innovation (SOSI)

In a highly competitive environment when the subject matter is retaining customers, service innovation becomes essential for meeting the changing needs of consumers and distinguishing themselves from competitors (Liu and Li, 2024). Service innovation refers to the creation of new processes, activities or solutions aimed at enhancing productivity, gaining a competitive edge, and improving customer satisfaction across businesses (Maziliauske, 2024). However, to maximize these benefits, companies must ensure that their innovative services are also sustainable (Gil-Saura et al., 2024). By integrating sustainable practices into their operations, companies can enhance their economic contribution to society, improve stakeholders' well-being, and minimize their environmental footprint, in other words, strive toward comprehensive sustainable development (Kumar et al., 2024). Recognizing the growing importance of both sustainability and innovation for businesses, a recent research focus has emerged, investigating the interaction between these two concepts and analyzing the impact their integration can have on generating value for companies. Based on three main existing research streams: product–service system, service innovation and sustainability-oriented innovation, Calabrese et al. (2018) were the first authors to introduce the term sustainability-oriented service innovation (SOSI). SOSI is an approach that seeks to implement innovative processes, services, or business models to enhance efficiency, address social needs, and minimize environmental impact (Calabrese et al., 2018a). This form of innovation enables managers to adopt novel approaches in service design while aligning sustainability objectives and the principles of the Triple Bottom Line – economic, social and environmental sustainability (Liu and Li, 2024). Recent studies by Gil-Saura et al. (2024) have sought to conceptualize SOSI within the retail sector, incorporating other variables such as brand equity and customer satisfaction. In the hospitality sector, Bordian et al. (2024) defined SOSI as having two subconcepts: relational innovation and sustainable practices. Based on the works of Calabrese et al. (2018) and Wikhamn (2019), in this study SOSI is presented as a multidimensional construct that is composed of four key elements: sustainability-oriented innovation in service, in process, in organisation and in marketing.

2.2 Value Co-Creation

Value co-creation is the process through which stakeholders and companies collaboratively generate value by developing or enhancing products or services (Vargo et al., 2020). It is an experience-driven concept that emphasizes collaboration between the business and the customer (Bhat and Sharma, 2022). Consequently, co-creation involves three key aspects: the customer, the firm, and the interaction between them. The emerging paradigm of Service-Dominant Logic (SDL), applied within the service sector, views value co-creation as a dynamic, interactive process that relies on both the company's efforts and the active involvement of customers in shaping their own consumption experience (Vargo and Lusch, 2008). Traditionally, companies have relied on closed processes to develop new products and services. However, research and practice have increasingly shifted toward a new model of innovation that integrates both external and internal capabilities throughout the innovation process (Sigala, 2016). Technological advancements have given customers access to vast amounts of information, making them more demanding and increasingly seeking personalized services. As a result, companies must actively listen to their customers and involve them in the development of innovative services to meet their expectations (Bordian et al., 2024). Many scholars have reported positive relationship between value co-creation and innovation. Specifically, Bhat and Sharma (2022) further highlight that value co-creation positively influences service innovation, emphasizing the need to integrate customers' ideas and expectations into the design of new services. Therefore, we hypothesize:

H1: Value co-creation with customers is positively related to SOSI.

2.3 Business Performance

Business performance refers to a company's capacity to effectively utilize its available resources to achieve its objectives, ensuring that these outcomes align with stakeholder expectations (Bhat and Sharma, 2022). The majority of previous research has predominantly adopted a financially oriented perspective, emphasizing accounting-based metrics when assessing the influence of innovation on business outcomes (Gök and Peker (2017). These studies often conceptualize business performance as a singular construct, concentrating primarily on narrow indicators such as revenue and return on investment (ROI). However, no single performance measure can comprehensively capture all dimensions of organizational performance (Bhat and Sharma, 2022). For this reason, many companies have long monitored non-financial indicators of business performance, such as product/service quality, customer satisfaction, loyalty, and retention (Galarza et al., 2023). By integrating non-financial indicators, firms gain a more comprehensive view of their performance in relation to innovations (Bhat and Sharma, 2022.

To strengthen their competitive advantage and enhance financial performance, firms must integrate sustainable innovative practices into their service delivery processes, enabling them to adapt and deliver diverse, high-quality customer experiences (Galarza et al., 2023). A firm's sustainable innovation activities can support resource acquisition and reduce average costs by enhancing the efficiency of resource utilization. Consequently, strong sustainable innovation performance strengthens the firm's financial position by generating process-based advantages that, over time, enhance the firm's overall innovation efficiency. Several prior studies have confirmed the link between innovation and firms' financial performance (Maletič et al. 2016; Gök and Peker, 2017; Rajapathirana and Hui, 2018). Based on the prior evidence, we hypothesize the following:

H2: SOSI is positively related to financial results.

Innovation can influence a firm's non-financial performance in various ways. It enables firms to align technological capabilities with market demands, enhance the quality of products and services, attract new customers, expand into new markets, and ultimately strengthen their competitive position in the marketplace. Innovative organizations often implement new processes and methods, which can lead to greater customer satisfaction and loyalty, while also attracting new customers (Gök and Peker, 2017). Customers may also view an innovative firm as offering higher-quality products, which can, in turn, increase demand for its new innovations (Rajapathirana and Hui, 2018). However, a limited number of studies reports a positive association between innovation and non-financial performance. Gök and Peker (2017) verify this link in the manufacturing and service industry firms in Turkey. In a similar vein, Rajapathirana and Hui (2018) highlight that strong innovation performance can generate superior value for customers, which may, in turn, drive improved non-financial results and increased profitability. Following prior findings, we hypothesize as follows:

H3: SOSI is positively related to non-financial results.

Prior studies mostly address the link between innovation and financial performance. However, studies that simultaneously investigate the interrelationships among innovation and financial and non-financial performance are still scarce (Rajapathirana and Hui, 2018). Satisfied and loyal customers contribute to improved financial performance by decreasing price sensitivity, reducing marketing expenses through positive word-of-mouth, lowering transaction costs, and strengthening the firm's reputation (Gök and Peker, 2017). Furthermore, the positive reputation generated by strong non-financial performance allows the firm to attract new customers, ultimately leading to increased profitability (Rajapathirana and Hui, 2018). The benefits of sustainable innovative practices are closely linked to non-financial aspects of business performance, such as greater customer satisfaction and the acquisition of new customers, both of which ultimately lead to increased financial returns (Maletič et al. 2016). Therefore, we posit:

H4: Non-financial results are positively related to financial results.

2.4 Moderating Effect of Industry Type

Research has demonstrated that the characteristics of a business sector can shape the significance of innovation as a key driver of competitive advantage in the market (Jabeen et al., 2023). Moreover, it has been emphasized that collaboration with stakeholders is crucial for all companies seeking to innovate and ensure long-term survival (Jabeen et al., 2023). In the hotel sector, recent research has identified value co-creation and innovation as two essential pillars for enhancing organizational performance (Bhat and Sharma, 2022). Similarly, retail businesses can leverage innovation and collaborate closely with customers to adapt their operations and routines, improving efficiency and achieving significant cost reductions (Maldonado-Guzmán et al., 2018). Therefore, a strong innovation capacity enhances service quality and enables firms to gain competitive advantages, ultimately leading to improved performance outcomes (Jabeen et al., 2023). However, there is a lack of empirical evidence demonstrating the moderating effect of the type of sector on the relationships between these variables. Given that the hotel sector differs from the retail sector, particularly in its emphasis on customer experience, strategy implementation in hotels often requires more intensive collaboration with customers compared to the retail sector. With SOSI as the central construct, this study seeks to examine whether type of sector, specifically the hotel or retail sectors, accounts for differences in managers' perceptions of value co-creation with customers, SOSI, and business performance. Based on this discussion, the following hypothesis is proposed:

H5(a-d): The intensity of the relationships between value co-creation with customers, SOSI, and business results varies depending on the sector to which the company belongs (hotel or retail).

The proposed model that relates to the different constructs is shown in Figure 1.

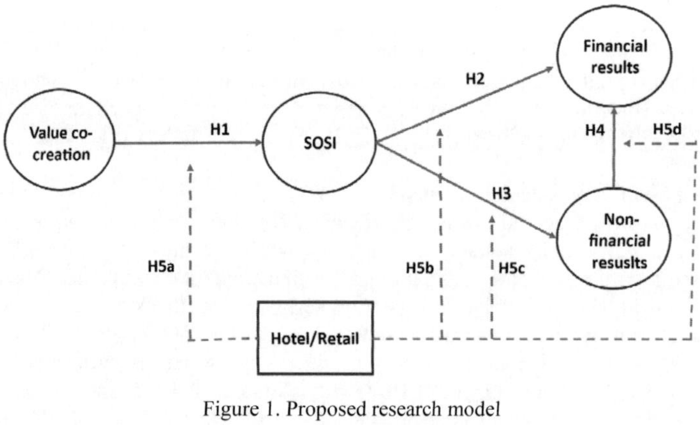

Figure 1. Proposed research model

3. METHODOLOGY

All variables in the study were measured through items adapted from a review of various previous studies. A 7-point Likert scale was used for all items, ranging from 1 ('strongly disagree') to 7 ('strongly agree'). The items related to value co-creation with customers have been adapted from the scale proposed by O'Cass and Ngo (2012). To measure SOSI, 12 items adapted from Wikhamn (2019) were used, grouped into four dimensions. Finally, business performance was assessed using four items measuring financial results and four items measuring non-financial results, based on Bhat and Sharma (2022). Data collection involved face-to-face personal interviews with 450 managers or supervisors from hotel and retail establishments in Barcelona, Madrid, and Valencia. The administration process was supported by an electronic structured questionnaire integrated into a survey platform, allowing for using CAPI (Computer-Assisted Personal Interviewing) and CATI (Computer-Assisted Telephone Interviewing) methods. Data collection took place between February and June 2023, resulting in a final sample of 450 valid questionnaires. Regarding the sample distribution, out of the 450 questionnaires collected, 250 corresponded to the hotel sector, and 200 to the retail sector. Among the hotels, 78.4% were family-run, while the remaining 21.6% belonged to a hotel chain. As for the retail establishments, data was gathered from businesses in the food, textile/footwear, electronics/household appliances, and furniture/wood sectors, with each sector representing 25% of the retail sample.

4. ANALYSIS OF THE RESULTS

To test the hypotheses proposed in the theoretical model, a two-stage analytical procedure was applied. First, the measurement instrument was assessed through confirmatory factor analysis (CFA) to evaluate the validity and reliability of the measurement scales. Second, the structural model was estimated using Partial Least Squares Structural Equation Modeling (PLS-SEM) with the SmartPLS 4.0.9.6 software. The decision to use PLS-SEM is based on several reasons: a) the non-normal distribution of all measurement variables; b) the presence of composites in both Mode A and Mode B; and c) the complexity of the model, given its multidimensional structure, which includes both first- and second-order constructs (Hair et al., 2016).

For the reflective constructs, the CFA results confirm the reliability of all scales, as the composite reliability (CR) and Cronbach's alpha (CA) values exceed the recommended threshold of 0.7 for all constructs (see Table 1). Convergent validity was assessed by analyzing item loadings and the average variance extracted (AVE). Three items related to SOSI were removed due to loadings below 0.5. All remaining loadings are statistically significant and exceed 0.6. Furthermore, the AVE values for all variables surpass the critical threshold of 0.5, as recommended in the literature (Hair et al., 2016). These results confirm both the reliability of the scales and the convergent validity of the proposed variables (see Table 1). The square root of the AVE for each construct exceeds the highest correlation with any other construct in the model, confirming the discriminant validity of the measurement model (Fornell and Larker, 1981).

Subsequently, a new model was developed, incorporating two second-order construct sustainability-oriented service innovation (SOSI). As this construct was estimated in Mode B, its measurement was assessed using the variance inflation factor (VIF) and indicator weightings. The VIF values for all indicators are below the upper threshold of 3.3 and the weightings are statistically significant at the 1% confidence level.

After verifying the psychometric properties of the measurement instrument, standardized path coefficients (β) were estimated using the bootstrapping technique with 10,000 subsamples. For the total sample, as shown in Table 2, all path coefficients were significant and aligned with the hypothesized directions. In line with hypothesis H5, we anticipated significant differences in the strength of relationships between constructs depending on the sector (hotels vs. retail). To test this hypothesis, a multi-group analysis was conducted by dividing the dataset into two subgroups: hotels and retail establishments. The model was estimated separately for each group using MGA analysis, and path coefficients were obtained through bootstrapping. The results of the multi-group analysis, shown in Table 2, reveal significant sector moderation in two relationships within the structural model: specifically, between value co-creation with customers and SOSI as well as between non-financial and financial results.

Table 1. Measurement model for Mode A composites

Factor	Item	Loadings	CA	CR	AVE
Value co-creation	COC1	0.880	0.928	0.943	0.735
	COC2	0.820			
	COC3	0.869			
	COC4	0.830			
	COC5	0.871			
	COC6	0.872			
Sustainability-oriented innovation in service design (SOSI 1)	SOSI 1.1	0.872	0.731	0.881	0.788
	SOSI 1.3	0.902			
Sustainability-oriented innovation in process (SOSI 2)	SOSI 2.1	0.886	0.759	0.892	0.805
	SOSI 2.3	0.909			
Sustainability-oriented innovation in organization (SOSI 3)	SOSI 3.1	0.876	0.723	0.878	0.783
	SOSI 3.3	0.894			
Sustainability-oriented innovation in marketing (SOSI 4)	SOSI 4.1	0.868	0.769	0.858	0.752
	SOSI 4.3	0.866			
Financial results	FR1	0.872	0.858	0.904	0.702
	FR2	0.906			
	FR3	0.868			
	FR4	0.804			
Non-financial results	NFR1	0.811	0.839	0.892	0.672
	NFR2	0.841			
	NFR3	0.813			
	NFR4	0.820			

CA= Cronbach's alpha; CR= Composite Reliability; AVE= Average Variance Extracted; *p<0,01

Table 2. Path analysis

Hypotheses	Total sample		Hotels vs. Retail				
			Hotels		Retail		p value differ.
	β	p value	β	p value	β	p value	
Value co-creation - SOSI	0.597	0.000	0.740	0.000	0.274	0.000	0.000
SOSI – Financial results	0.273	0.000	0.272	0.000	0.294	0.000	0.382
SOSI – Non-financial results	0.632	0.000	0.669	0.000	0.645	0.000	0.134
Non-fin. results – Financial results	0.625	0.000	0.626	0.000	0.528	0.000	0.002

β= standardized path coefficient

5. CONCLUSION

From a theoretical standpoint and in response to recent calls for research on sustainability and service innovation (Calabrese et al., 2018; Vargo et al., 2020), the findings of this study make several key contributions to the existing body of knowledge. Firstly, the results allow us to continue advancing in the gap highlighted by Calabrese et al. (2018) and Kumar et al., (2024) completing the body of knowledge related to conceptualization of sustainability-oriented service innovation (SOSI) in the service sector. Our analysis confirmed the multidimensional nature of SOSI, demonstrating that sustainable innovative practices are crucial for driving sustainability-related service innovation. Secondly, and in response to the research call by Vargo et al. (2020) encouraging studies on Service-Dominant Logic within the context of sustainability, this study confirms the role of value co-creation with customers as key antecedents of SOSI. These findings align with previous research (Bordian et al., 2024; Bhat and Sharma, 2022), which highlights that collaboration between service companies and external stakeholders plays a crucial role in implementing sustainable innovative practices. More precisely, our results reaffirm the significance of collaborating with customers to develop sustainable innovative practices that meet their needs. Thirdly, this study contributes to the literature by incorporating both financial and non-financial performance dimensions into our model. The results indicate that sustainability-oriented service innovations contribute to enhancing business performance. Specifically, innovations focused on sustainability across services, processes, organization, and marketing (Calabrese et al.,

2018a; Wikhamn, 2019) facilitate the development of new services in sectors such as hospitality and retail. This, in turn, leads to improvements in both financial and non-financial performance, thereby confirming and expanding upon prior research (Gök and Peker, 2017; Rajapathirana and Hui, 2018; Bhat and Sharma, 2022). Given the constant shifts in markets and the growing integration of sustainable management practices into daily business operations, distinguishing between these two performance measures offers a more comprehensive and nuanced evaluation of a company's activities, providing a more realistic understanding of its overall performance. Finally, this study validates the moderating effect of the sector type (hotel vs. retail) on the proposed relationships. Specifically, the findings reveal differences between the hotels and retailers in the relationships between value co-creation with consumers and SOSI, as well as between non-financial and financial performance. These relationships are found to be stronger within the hotel sector. One possible explanation for this phenomenon could be the inherent characteristics of the tourism industry, particularly the hotel sector, which emphasizes client relationships. In the hotel sector, non-financial outcomes, such as customer satisfaction or service quality, tend to have a stronger and more direct impact on financial performance. This is because the hotel industry heavily relies on customer experiences, reviews, and loyalty, which can quickly translate into increased bookings, higher occupancy rates, and revenue growth. Positive non-financial indicators often lead to repeat customers and word-of-mouth recommendations, which are crucial for hotel success. In contrast, in the retail sector, the connection between non-financial and financial results is often less direct and more complex. While customer satisfaction and operational efficiency are still important, retail performance can be influenced more heavily by factors like pricing strategies, product assortment, inventory management, and market competition. Non-financial improvements may take longer to translate into financial gains, as retail sales can fluctuate based on external factors like seasonality, promotions, or competitor actions.

From a practical standpoint, this study offers valuable insights for hotel and retail managers to enhance their understanding and promotion of sustainable innovative practices. The adoption of sustainable innovative practices enhances these businesses' capacity to tackle current challenges while also preparing them to adapt to future changes and developments. Achieving this requires cultivating a SOSI culture among employees. Furthermore, digital technologies such as artificial intelligence and data analytics can play a crucial role in SOSI, enabling companies to develop more efficient, greener and customer-centric solutions. Specifically, these technologies can optimize energy consumption in hotels and retail stores and prevent excess inventory and waste by forecasting demand and optimizing supply chains. Integrating technological tools would enable the restructuring of internal processes, significantly enhancing operational efficiency, an essential factor for swiftly adapting to market changes and ensuring the company's long-term success and sustainability. Moreover, companies rely on external information to develop specific competencies that enable them to identify new opportunities. In particular, the adoption of sustainable innovative practices necessitates both the exploration and utilization of external knowledge sources through collaboration with external stakeholders. Integrating this external insight with the organization's internal knowledge can foster the development of new resources and capabilities, ultimately enhancing the effectiveness of innovation processes.

Finally, it is important to acknowledge certain limitations of this study, which may serve as avenues for future research. First, the way SOSI was measured represents a limitation of the present work. Therefore, future research could focus on developing a more robust and specific scale that better captures the various dimensions of SOSI. Secondly, as our study is built upon cross-sectional data, longitudinal data could be further used to gain a better understanding of the causal associations related to present study constructs. Thirdly, our research represents only hotel and retail sectors, and one country (Spain) as a framework. Therefore, future studies can reproduce the projected relationships among dissimilar contexts and countries to offer higher generalisability of the findings. Furthermore, the analysis could incorporate additional variables such as customer orientation or the degree of innovativeness, as antecedents, and the satisfaction of its internal and external stakeholders, as consequences, thus expanding the analysis of SOSI by relating it to other constructs that make it possible to enrich and strengthen the research with other approaches.

ACKNOWLEDGEMENT

This research has been developed within the framework of the project Grant PID2020-112660RB-I00 funded by MCIN/ AEI/10.13039/501100011033, and the consolidated research group AICO/2021/144 and CIAICO/2023/069 funded by the Conselleria d'Innovació, Universitats, Ciència i Societat Digital of the Generalitat Valenciana.

REFERENCES

Bhat, D.A.R. and Sharma, V. (2022). Enabling service innovation and firm performance: the role of co-creation and technological innovation in the hospitality industry. *Technology Analysis & Strategic Management,* Vol. 34, No. 7, pp.774-786.

Bordian, M. et al. (2024). Sustainability-oriented service innovation and customer satisfaction in hospitality: Assessing the impact of value co-creation, ecological knowledge and gender. *Journal of Vacation Marketing*, 13567667241261395.

Calabrese, A. et al. (2018). "Sustainability-oriented service innovation: An emerging research field", *Journal of cleaner production*, Vol. 193, pp.533-548.

Elkington, J. (1998). Partnerships from cannibals with forks: The triple bottom line of 21st-century business. *Environmental quality management*, Vol. 8, No. 1, pp.37-51.

Fornell, C. and Larcker, D.F. (1981). Evaluating structural equation models with unobservable variables and measurement error. *Journal of marketing research,* Vol. 18, No. 1, pp.39-50

Galarza, I.S. et al. (2023). Innovation in the tourism sector, organizational learning and performance. *Academia Revista Latinoamericana de Administración*, Vol. 36, No. 4, pp.463-486.

Gil-Saura, I. et al. (2024). Sustainability-oriented innovation in retailing. *Psychology & Marketing*, Vol. 41, No. 2, pp. 240-253.

Gök, O. and Peker, S. (2017). Understanding the links among innovation performance, market performance and financial performance. *Review of managerial science*, Vol. 11, pp.605-631.

Hair Jr, J.F. et al. (2016). A primer on partial least squares structural equation modeling (PLS-SEM). Sage publications. *Thousand Oaks, CA, USA*.

Huang, W. and Ichikohji, T. (2023). A review and analysis of the business model innovation literature. *Heliyon*, Vol. 9, e17895.

Jabeen, F. et al. (2023). The role of open innovation in fostering SMEs' business model innovation during the COVID-19 pandemic. *Journal of knowledge management*, Vol. 27, No. 6, pp.1562-1582

Kumar, R. et al. (2024). Service innovation research: a bibliometric analysis using VOSviewer. *Competitiveness Review: An International Business Journal*, Vol. 34, No. 4, pp.736-760.

Liu, X. and Li, M.Y. (2024). Sustainable service product design method: Focus on customer demands and triple bottom line. *Journal of Retailing and Consumer Services*, Vol. 80, 103935.

Maldonado-Guzmán, G. et al. (2018). Innovation capabilities and performance: are they truly linked in SMEs?. *International Journal of Innovation Science*, Vol. 11, No. 1, pp.48-62

Maletič, M. et al. (2016). Effect of sustainability-oriented innovation practices on the overall organisational performance: An empirical examination. *Total Quality Management & Business Excellence*, Vol. 27, No. 9-10, pp.1171-1190

Maziliauske, E. (2024). Innovation for sustainability through co-creation by small and medium-sized tourism enterprises (SMEs): Socio-cultural sustainability benefits to rural destinations. *Tourism Management Perspectives*, Vol. 50, 101201.

O'cass, A. and Ngo, L.V. (2012). Creating superior customer value for B2B firms through supplier firm capabilities. *Industrial Marketing Management*, Vol. 41, No. 1, pp.125-135.

Rajapathirana, R.J. and Hui, Y. (2018). Relationship between innovation capability, innovation type, and firm performance. *Journal of Innovation & Knowledge*, Vol. 3, No. 1, pp.44-55.

Sigala, M. (2016). Learning with the market: A market approach and framework for developing social entrepreneurship in tourism and hospitality. *International Journal of Contemporary Hospitality Management*, Vol. 28, No. 6, pp. 1245-1286.

Vargo, S.L. and Lusch, R.F. (2008). Service-dominant logic: continuing the evolution. *Journal of the Academy of marketing Science*, Vol. 36, pp.1-10.

Vargo, S.L. et al. (2020). *Service-dominant logic: foundations and applications*. In: Bridges E and Fowler K (ed) The Routledge Handbook of Service Research Insights and Ideas. New York: Routledge, pp.3–23.

Wikhamn, W. (2019). Innovation, sustainable HRM and customer satisfaction. *International Journal of Hospitality Management*, Vol. 76, pp.102-110.

SOCIAL MEDIA MARKETING INNOVATIONS IN ROMANIAN ELECTORAL CAMPAIGNS: THE CASE OF THE 2024 PRESIDENTIAL ELECTIONS

Stelian Brad[1] and Bianca-Simina Deac[2]
[1]*Faculty of Industrial Engineering, Robotics and Production Management, Technical University of Cluj-Napoca*
[2]*Faculty of Industrial Engineering, Robotics and Production Management, Technical University of Cluj-Napoca, Doctoral School, PhD Candidate*
Bulevardul Muncii 103-105, Cluj-Napoca, 400641, Romania

ABSTRACT

The 2024 Romanian presidential elections marked a watershed in political marketing, showcasing how social media platforms transformed campaign strategies, voter engagement, and even electoral outcomes. This paper analyzes the innovative digital marketing techniques employed during the campaign, focusing on algorithmic amplification, micro-targeting, influencer campaigns, and AI-driven content. It examines how these digital strategies influenced voter behavior and election integrity, with particular attention to the unprecedented annulment of the first-round results due to confirmed online manipulation. The study underscores the evolving relationship between social media and democratic processes, identifying both the opportunities and challenges presented by digital campaign innovations. With approximately 13.3 million active social media users in Romania (67.4% of the population) as of 2024, platforms like Facebook (around 9–10 million users) and TikTok (8.97 million users) became crucial battlegrounds for political influence. TikTok – a relatively new platform in the political arena – nearly matched Facebook in user numbers and significantly outperformed it in terms of engagement, with users spending an average of 32.5 hours per month on TikTok compared to 13 hours on Facebook. The most notable case study emerged around independent candidate Călin Georgescu, who achieved a surprising first-round victory (22.94% of votes) despite minimal traditional campaign spending, by leveraging TikTok's viral mechanics to amplify his nationalist and anti-Western message. The findings highlight an urgent need for regulatory frameworks to address the unique challenges of digital campaign innovations – including enhanced transparency for online political content, strengthened digital monitoring by electoral authorities, and platform-specific regulations – to ensure that future elections harness these tools without undermining democratic integrity.

KEYWORDS

Social Media Marketing, Electoral Campaigns, Digital Innovation, Political Communication, Voter Behavior

1. INTRODUCTION

Romania's 2024 presidential election took place during an exceptionally intense "super electoral year," with local, European Parliament, general, and presidential elections all scheduled within months of each other. This crowded calendar provided a unique context for examining how political marketing strategies have evolved in the digital era. This evolution aligns with broader trends of digital transformation and e-governance in politics, as public institutions increasingly leverage social media and other technologies to engage citizens. The presidential race became a focal point for innovative social media marketing practices that transformed the political landscape. It also raised critical questions about electoral integrity, culminating in an unprecedented development: for the first time in Romania's post-1989 democracy, the Constitutional Court annulled the first-round election results due to confirmed evidence of widespread online manipulation (for example, the discovery of thousands of coordinated fake accounts disseminating disinformation). Traditional media channels that dominated Romanian campaigns for decades have been steadily losing ground to digital platforms. Recent data indicate that only about 15% of young Romanians under 30 follow electoral content on television, while over 70% are exposed to political content via social media (primarily TikTok and

Facebook). This generational shift has forced political actors to adapt their communication strategies and invest heavily in new digital approaches.

The significance of social media in Romanian campaigns reached new heights in 2024. The country was home to roughly **13.3 million social network users (67.4% of the population) as of January 2024**. Facebook remained the single largest platform, with an estimated 9–10 million Romanian users, but its growth had plateaued; in early 2019 there were 9.8 million Facebook users, and by 2024 the local user base was around 9–11 million (depending on measurement) – indicating little increase. In contrast, **TikTok's popularity skyrocketed**. In February 2019, there were only about 175,000 TikTok users in Romania; by the start of 2024, that figure had ballooned to **8.97 million users**. TikTok – which did not even exist in 2014 – thus caught up to Facebook's scale within just a few years.

TikTok not only matched Facebook in user numbers but far surpassed it in engagement, with users spending around 32.5 hours monthly compared to Facebook's 13 hours. Social media also reshaped political communication, shifting from traditional one-way broadcasts to peer-driven, dialogic interactions—especially among younger users—where political messages spread organically through shares and debates.

Yet, message framing remained central to political success (Silverstein, 2011). Candidates in Romania's 2024 election strategically tailored content to social media, reflecting a shift toward digital campaigning. We applied a multi-platform, data-driven approach, collecting high-impact content and engagement metrics from TikTok, Facebook, and YouTube via platform APIs and analytics tools, capturing viral videos (over 100,000 views), trending posts, and popular hashtags. Official voter statistics from the Central Electoral Bureau and credible investigative reports (e.g., on bots and misinformation) provided additional context, while Google Trends data measured shifts in public interest. This comprehensive dataset enabled analysis of the election's most influential digital strategies.

1.1 Research Questions and Hypotheses

This study seeks to answer two central research questions:

(1) **What innovative digital campaign strategies proved most influential in shaping voter behavior and electoral outcomes during Romania's 2024 presidential election?**

(2) **How did the use of these innovative strategies impact electoral integrity and public perceptions of the legitimacy of the electoral process?**

Specifically, we investigate how innovative social media marketing techniques—particularly algorithmically amplified, AI-enhanced, and influencer-driven campaigns—shaped voter engagement and potentially affected electoral integrity. We hypothesize that these digital tactics significantly influenced voter behavior, offering disproportionate advantages to campaigns adept at platform-specific strategies, especially those leveraging TikTok's viral mechanics.

We focus specifically on the 2024 Romanian presidential election due to its unprecedented context: it was the first instance in Romania's post-1989 democracy—and within the European Union—where election results were annulled following confirmed online manipulation, involving coordinated fake accounts and widespread disinformation. This unique situation provides an exceptional opportunity to analyze both the advantages and challenges of social media marketing in contemporary electoral contexts. Insights gained from this analysis aim to enhance understanding of digital political marketing dynamics and electoral integrity challenges, contributing valuable knowledge relevant both to Romania and to democracies worldwide.

2. METHODOLOGY

This study employs a multi-platform, data-driven case study approach focused on the 2024 Romanian presidential campaign. The research design integrates both quantitative and qualitative methods, drawing data from major social media platforms (TikTok, Facebook, YouTube), official electoral reports from the Romanian Central Electoral Bureau, investigative journalism outputs, and Google Trends analytics.

Our primary objective was to identify and analyze grassroots engagement and key issues of public salience as manifested through online activities. The analytical framework explicitly aligns with the principle of **vox populi, vox dei** (Latin for "the voice of the people is the voice of God"). According to this principle, the analysis assumes that genuine voter concerns and public sentiment can be reliably inferred from measurable online behaviors and trends. Specifically, Google Trends data were employed to detect shifts in public interest for key campaign issues and candidates, while the analysis of viral hashtags and highly engaged social media content served as direct indicators of grassroots mobilization. For each data source, we identified its role in capturing this "voice of the people." Social media platforms like TikTok, Facebook, and YouTube provided engagement metrics (e.g., likes, shares, views) that revealed which campaign messages resonated most widely with voters. Official electoral reports (voter turnout and vote counts) offered a ground-truth benchmark of the electorate's voice as expressed through ballots. Investigative journalism outputs (including fact-check reports) documented citizen-driven narratives and exposed instances of online manipulation, reflecting underlying public concerns. Finally, Google Trends analytics quantified shifts in collective attention on key issues or candidates over time. Together, these channels operationalized vox populi, vox dei by translating the electorate's digital footprints and formal votes into measurable indicators of public sentiment and engagement.

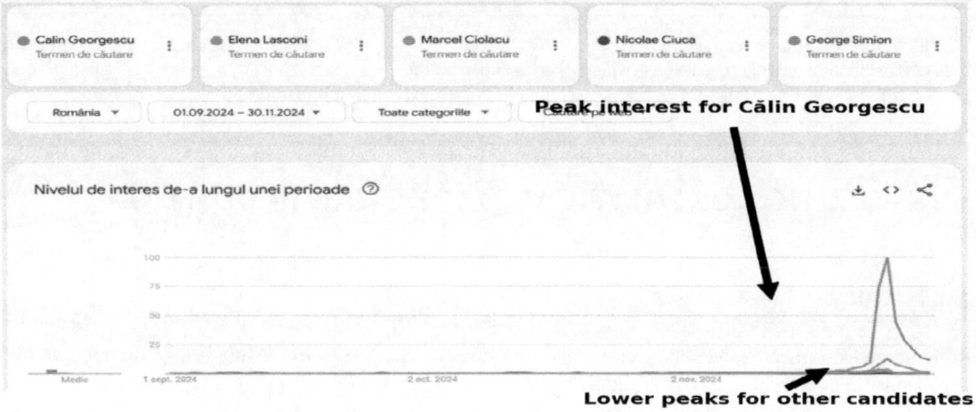

Figure 1. Google Trends comparative analysis (September–November 2024)

The combination and cross-validation (triangulation) of digital engagement metrics with traditional electoral data (official voter turnout statistics, election results, and polling data) allowed us to distinguish between authentic public interest and orchestrated digital manipulation. This transparent, mixed-method approach ensured findings that are both rigorously evidence-based and contextually informed.

Table 1. Overview of Data Sources and Analytical Use

Data source	Type of data collected	Selection criteria	Analytical purpose	Tools used
TikTok	Video content, hashtags, views, shares, comments	Videos with 100,000+ views; trending election hashtags	Measure virality, grassroots engagement, message framing	TikTok API, manual collection
Facebook	Posts, image macros, video shares, user engagement	Top 10 shared posts per week; meme frequency	Assess messaging strategy, polarizing content, demographic reach	Facebook API, CrowdTangle
YouTube	Long-form videos, vlogs, speeches, influencer commentary	Candidate channels, election playlists, 50k+ views	Analyze content depth, candidate branding	YouTube Analytics, manual review
Google Trends	Search volume for keywords (candidate names, campaign topics)	Daily trend spikes from Aug–Nov 2024	Track public interest, align attention with campaign phases	Google Trends interface

Data source	Type of data collected	Selection criteria	Analytical purpose	Tools used
Election Reports	Turnout rates, vote shares, regional breakdowns	Official 1st and 2nd round datasets from Central Electoral Bureau	Validate digital impact with real-world voting patterns	Electoral Bureau datasets (CSV)
News Investigations	Articles on online manipulation, bot networks, platform violations	Reports from verified sources (e.g., RFE/RL, EDMO, Funky ONG)	Support manipulation claims, enrich contextual interpretation	Media monitoring, source validation
Telegram & WhatsApp	Forwarded content, group messaging patterns (where accessible)	Monitoring influencer-linked Telegram groups	Understand private peer-to-peer mobilization	Manual tracking, qualitative logs

3. EVOLUTION OF POLITICAL MARKETING IN ROMANIA

3.1 History

Romanian election campaigns have evolved dramatically since the 1990s. After 1989's democratic transition, **traditional media** (TV, radio, print) and in-person tactics dominated campaigning for two decades. The **late 2000s** saw the first steps into digital politics (e.g., some online forums in 2008), and by **2014** social media played a pivotal role – exemplified by Klaus Iohannis's upset 2014 victory, often attributed to effective **Facebook mobilization** of young voters. By the **late 2010s**, virtually all major parties had embraced online platforms (Facebook and others) as campaign staples, even as **television** remained important for older and rural demographics. In short, Romania's political marketing shifted from a TV-centric model to a hybrid approach by 2020, setting the stage for the fully **digital campaign era** of 2024.

3.2 Transition from Traditional to Digital Campaigning

Traditional methods rapidly lost ground to digital tactics due to cost and reach advantages of online media. Expensive **TV ads** (costing thousands of euros for a 30-second spot) were increasingly hard to justify when a **targeted Facebook or YouTube ad** could reach a similar audience for a few dozen euros. Likewise, a physical rally might gather a few hundred people, whereas **live-streamed events** on social media could draw tens of thousands. The gap was most pronounced among young voters: in 2024 only ~18% of under-30s watched televised debates, yet over 70% consumed political content on TikTok. Accordingly, campaign **ad budgets** shifted dramatically from 2014 to 2024 – TV's share fell from ~70% to just ~52%, while digital ads grew to ~36%. Parties redirected spending from billboards and TV into Facebook, YouTube, and especially TikTok, mirroring where voters' attention had moved.

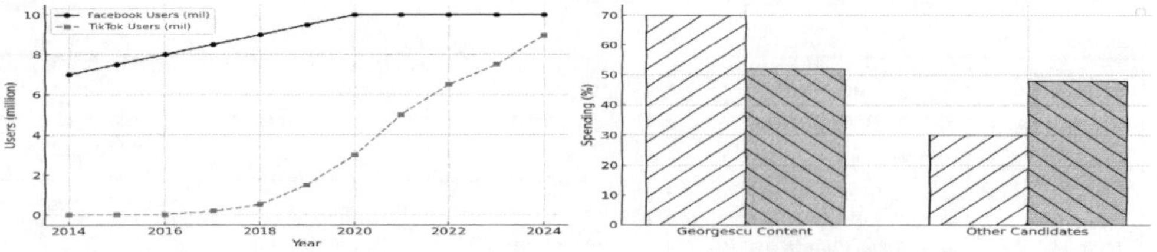

Figure 2. Voter turnout by age group (2014 vs. 2019 vs. 2024)

Social media platforms evolved rapidly between 2019 and 2024, reshaping Romanian political campaigns. While Facebook remained the largest network (9–10 million users), it stagnated and lost ground among youth. In contrast, TikTok surged to 8.97 million users—nearly half of Romania's adult population—with far higher engagement, making it a must-use platform for reaching younger voters. YouTube (10–11 million users) also played a major role, while Instagram, WhatsApp, and Telegram served as secondary channels. Successful campaigns became "platform-fluid," tailoring content to each outlet's style and audience.

At the same time, Romania's generational turnout gap persisted. Youth participation remained low despite improvement: around 50% of 18–34-year-olds voted in 2024, still trailing older age groups. This gap pushed campaigns to double down on digital outreach, with social media seen as the best way to engage and mobilize younger voters.

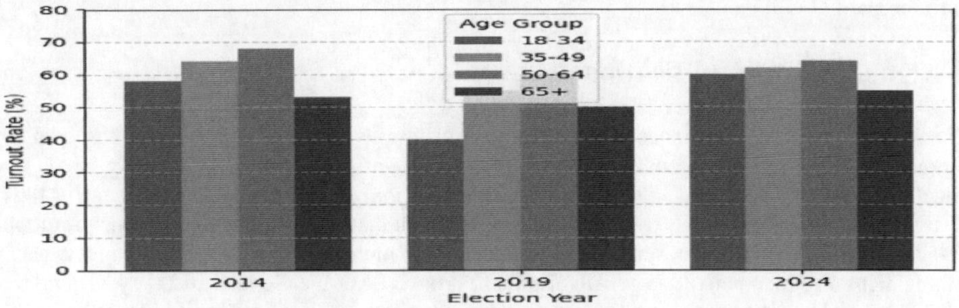

Figure 3. Voter turnout by age group (2014 vs. 2019 vs. 2024)

By 2024, the Romanian electorate was highly digitized, but demographics still influenced where and how people engaged with campaigns. Facebook remained important for reaching middle-aged and older voters (especially in rural areas and small towns where Facebook and WhatsApp are popular), while TikTok became indispensable for targeting the under-30 demographic. This evolution set the stage for the innovative strategies observed in the 2024 presidential contest, where candidates pushed the limits of what could be done with social media marketing in politics.

4. THEORETICAL FRAMEWORK AND RESEARCH GAP

Social media-driven political marketing can be understood in the context of broader digital transformation and e-governance theories. Prior studies have examined how digital technologies influence governance and citizen engagement (Alareeni, 2025; ICITST, 2017; IEEE, 2019). In the Romanian setting specifically, research on online campaigning exists – for example, **Cambridge Core (2020)** analyzed the Social Democrats' online marketing strategies in a previous election – but no study to date has addressed the *combined impact* of algorithmic amplification, influencer-driven outreach, and AI-generated content within a single election. This is the identified **research gap**: we lack understanding of how these innovative tools, in tandem, shape electoral outcomes and voter behavior in emerging digital democracies. Our work also draws on the concept **"Vox Populi, Vox Dei,"** which posits that the will of the people can be gauged through aggregate public expressions. Puhr and Müllner (2024) provide a foundation for this idea by demonstrating that Google Trends data can serve as a proxy for grassroots socio-political sentiment. Building on this theoretical notion, we treat digital engagement metrics as a reflection of the electorate's voice in our analysis.

Case Study Approach – Justification: We adopt a case study methodology focused on the 2024 Romanian presidential election as a critical case. This approach is justified because the 2024 election presented an unprecedented convergence of factors (including the first-round result being annulled due to online manipulation) that make it an *extreme* case of digital campaign innovation. Studying a single, information-rich case in depth allows for insight into causal mechanisms and context-specific dynamics that broad surveys or multi-case studies might overlook. By examining this unique event, we can explore how and why novel campaign tactics succeeded or failed under real-world conditions, generating findings that can inform theory and practice in digital political marketing.

5. SOCIAL MEDIA MARKETING INNOVATIONS IN CAMPAIGN

The 2024 presidential campaign in Romania featured several novel digital marketing tactics that had not been seen in prior elections. We identify four major categories of innovation: (1) Algorithmic Amplification, where campaigns exploited platform algorithms to boost content reach; (2) Micro-targeting and Influencer Strategies, involving precision audience segmentation and partnership with social media influencers; (3) AI Tools and Automated Campaigning, including the use of bots and AI-generated content to augment campaign efforts; and (4) Platform Comparisons and Figures, highlighting how different social networks performed and the comparative data from the campaign. In practice, these areas overlap – for example, micro-targeted content often leveraged algorithmic trends, and AI-driven bots were used to amplify messages – but we discuss each in turn for clarity.

5.1 Algorithmic Amplification

Social media content is heavily shaped by platform algorithms, which recommend posts based on engagement. In Romania's 2024 election, campaigns—especially Georgescu's team—strategically exploited these systems, particularly TikTok's "For You" algorithm. By using emotionally charged, polarizing content ("us vs. them" narratives, anti-elite claims), they triggered high engagement that led to further algorithmic promotion. Internal analysis confirmed that extreme, sensational content spread more widely than moderate messages.

Campaigns also manipulated search algorithms. Through SEO and Google Ads, they ensured that searches like "2024 social benefits" led to partisan websites posing as news sources. These narratives were reinforced across platforms—via Facebook ads, TikTok videos, and Google results—creating the illusion of consensus. This coordinated strategy blurred the line between genuine public sentiment and engineered virality, revealing how algorithmic loopholes were weaponized to shape voter perception.

5.2 Micro-Targeting and Influencer Strategies

Campaigns in 2024 made **unprecedented use of micro-targeting**, tailoring messages to specific groups and leveraging social media influencers to expand reach. For example, **young voters** were targeted on TikTok and Instagram with anti-establishment memes and relatable content, while **older voters** received stability-and-tradition messaging on Facebook and WhatsApp. Messages were also geo-tailored: rural audiences saw pledges for agricultural support and local development, whereas **urban voters** heard promises of tech jobs, transparency, and pro-EU reforms – each region's content focusing on its unique concerns. The **diaspora** was courted via nationalist-themed posts on platforms like Telegram and TikTok (e.g. slogans like *#RomaniaPentruRomâni*, "Romania for Romanians"), contributing to a record diaspora turnout. In addition, campaigns **partnered with social media influencers** to humanize and amplify their message. Notably, independent candidate Călin Georgescu paid dozens of popular TikTok creators to covertly promote his nationalist platform, generating huge organic-style buzz among young users. This influencer tactic, combined with a coordinated hashtag campaign (#CălinGeorgescu accumulating ~784 million TikTok views), propelled Georgescu's once-obscure candidacy into the spotlight. **Although effective**, such methods raised ethical questions, as paid political endorsements went undisclosed and orchestrated virality blurred the line between genuine grassroots trends and astroturfing.

By combining these innovative strategies—age-specific messaging, geographic targeting, diaspora mobilization, and influencer-driven outreach—campaigns in Romania's 2024 elections demonstrated the transformative potential of digital platforms while also highlighting critical challenges related to transparency and electoral integrity.

In the case of Georgescu, the influencer push coincided with a **highly coordinated hashtag campaign** by his supporters. Pro-Georgescu activists and bot accounts flooded TikTok with content tagged with slogans like *#CălinGeorgescu* and *#RenaștereaRomâniei* ("Romania's Rebirth"). This wasn't an organic trend but a planned effort to dominate the narrative on TikTok. By election day, the primary hashtag **#CălinGeorgescu** had amassed over **51,700 videos** and **783.7 million views** on TikTok – more than half of the total ~1.4 billion views across top election-related hashtags. **Figure 3** illustrates how Georgescu's tag dwarfed others in share of views. Through savvy micro-targeting and an army of aligned influencers (both authentic and fake), his campaign managed to set the agenda on TikTok, making his once-obscure candidacy the most talked-about online. This online popularity translated into real votes: Georgescu shocked observers by winning **22.94%** in the first-round vote, the highest of any candidate, despite minimal spending on conventional advertising.

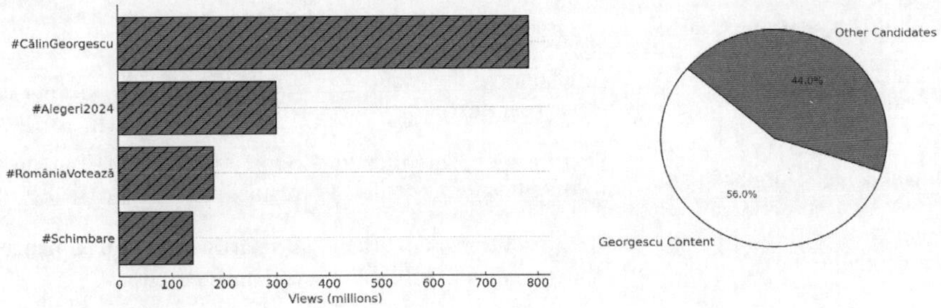

Figure 4. TikTok hashtag virality and content views for Georgescu's campaign (2024 Romanian presidential election)

5.3 AI Tools and Automated Campaigning

Campaigners in 2024 also began integrating artificial intelligence (AI) and automation into their digital operations. Although still emerging, AI-driven tools contributed to content creation, message targeting, and the overall amplification of campaign narratives, as described below:

- **Bot networks**: Over 25,000 fake TikTok accounts helped boost Georgescu's content in 2024, according to Romanian intelligence. These bots liked, shared, and commented on videos to trigger TikTok's algorithm, creating the illusion of grassroots support ("astroturfing") and encouraging real users to engage. Similar, smaller bot activity was found on Facebook and Twitter. While bots have been used globally, 2024 marked Romania's first large-scale use of AI-assisted political bots—possibly involving foreign actors.
- **AI-generated content**: Although no deepfake scandal emerged, some campaigns used AI to generate rapid content variations—e.g., testing different slogans or subtitling videos. At least one campaign developed a basic AI chatbot for answering voter questions on Messenger. Some Twitter accounts even posted algorithm-generated text to bypass spam filters. While more advanced AI manipulation didn't fully materialize, signs of automated messaging were clear.
- **AI targeting and data analytics**: Campaigns used machine learning to enhance micro-targeting, analyzing social media data to identify persuadable voters and tailor messages accordingly (e.g., nationalist vs. economic themes). This allowed for more precise targeting on platforms like Facebook. However, the practice raised concerns about privacy and transparency—delivering personalized content without users fully understanding how or why they were being targeted.

AI tools significantly increased the speed and reach of the 2024 campaigns, enabling real-time trend responses and widespread tailored messaging, often through automated accounts. This blurred the line between genuine engagement and artificial amplification, challenging regulators and highlighting vulnerabilities in oversight. The campaign illustrated how even modestly funded candidates could leverage AI-driven tactics to nearly secure electoral success, underscoring the need for stronger regulatory preparedness.

5.4 Platform Comparisons and Campaign Metrics

By 2024, TikTok and Facebook dominated Romania's political social media landscape. Facebook plateaued at 9–10 million users, while TikTok grew rapidly to about 9 million, with user engagement over twice as high. This made TikTok especially potent for youth outreach and message amplification.

Table 2. Facebook vs. TikTok reach, engagement, and cost metrics in the 2024 campaign

Metric (2024)	Facebook	TikTok
User base (Romania)	~9–10 million (plateaued growth)	~9 million (rapid growth since ~0.2 million in 2019)
Avg. monthly time per user	~13 hours	~32.5 hours
Typical reach of top content	Few hundred thousand views (per post)	Several million views (per video)
Predominant content format	Text/image posts (often in Groups/Pages)	Short-form videos (trending challenges, memes)
Core user demographics	Mainly 35+ years old (incl. many rural users)	Primarily under-30 audience (urban-focused)
Approx. cost per impression	~€0.05	~€0.01

From this comparison, it is evident that TikTok achieved near parity with Facebook in total users but far outstripped Facebook in engagement and virality. **Contextual interpretation:** TikTok's average user spent roughly 2.5 times longer on the app than Facebook's average user, and TikTok content was much more likely to "go viral" (reaching millions) compared to Facebook posts. Additionally, TikTok proved far more cost-effective for campaign messaging, delivering impressions at around one-fifth the cost of Facebook. These contrasts illustrate how TikTok became an especially influential platform in 2024, particularly for reaching young voters at scale, whereas Facebook — while still massive in reach — offered more incremental growth and tended to engage an older segment of the electorate.

Metrics highlighted TikTok's cost-efficiency: based on advertising data, content impressions on TikTok cost roughly €0.01 each, versus ~€0.05 on Facebook. To evaluate campaign effectiveness, we estimated Călin Georgescu's **cost-per-vote** on each medium by dividing his campaign spending by the number of votes gained. This analysis revealed that Georgescu effectively spent only about 0.2 lei ($0.04) per vote through TikTok outreach. By contrast, traditional television advertising cost on the order of 5 lei ($1+) per vote acquired. In other words, TikTok was nearly **100× more cost-effective** than TV for Georgescu – a remarkable advantage for an underfunded candidate. We also measured **virality** using social media analytics: for instance, the virality of Georgescu's campaign was evident in the TikTok hashtag #CălinGeorgescu, which amassed over 780 million views during the campaign. Such metrics (e.g., hashtag view counts, share/like totals, and growth in follower numbers) were used as quantitative indicators of online buzz and public engagement. These tools and measures enabled us to link digital metrics to real-world impact – in Georgescu's case, showing how unprecedented online traction translated into a surprisingly strong electoral performance (22.94% of first-round votes).

The 2024 presidential contenders in Romania each adapted their message to fit the distinct formats and audiences of major social media channels. With TikTok's rapid ascent (≈8.9 million national users) rivaling Facebook's reach (~10 million), and other platforms offering unique engagement modes, tailored strategies emerged for each network:

- **TikTok (Short-Form Virality):** All three candidates capitalized on TikTok's algorithmic boost for short, viral videos targeting younger voters. George Simion sustained a dominant TikTok presence, amassing ~589,800 followers and **≈240.6 million** total views on his campaign's main. Elena Lasconi's team, while her official account had only ~73k followers, achieved **≈123 million** cumulative TikTok views by leveraging content from affiliated youth accounts and constant organic grow. The most explosive TikTok growth, however, came from Călin Georgescu – in just two months he garnered roughly **145 million** video views, a sudden surge that **exceeded the entire 11-month TikTok visibility of establishment figures like Mircea Geoană**. Georgescu's follower count quadrupled from just 31.8k in September to about 154.9k by November 2024, indicating a coordinated blitz. His TikTok campaign centered obsessively on a single branded hashtag (#CălinGeorgescu), which generated on the order of 150 million views – an unusually concentrated pattern suggesting paid promotion, since organic virality is typically spread across diverse trends (even Simion's engagement was split among multiple hashtags like **#GeorgeSimion**, **#GeorgeSimionPresedinte**, etc.). Georgescu's strategists also orchestrated influencer-driven trends, such as the **#echilibruşiverticalitate** campaign ("balance and uprightness"), wherein lifestyle influencers recited a copy-paste script implicitly praising Georgescu without naming him – a tactic that alone netted about **2.4 million** views. These short-form video barrages made TikTok a kingmaking platform for visibility, especially for Georgescu's otherwise underdog campaign.

- **Facebook (Memetic Outreach and Attack Ads):** Facebook remained crucial for reaching broad and older demographics (around ten million Romanian users), and content here was tailored for shareability and emotional impact. Campaign teams crafted **image macros, memes, and provocative ads** that supporters could rapidly share in networks and groups. The far-right AUR movement under Simion, in particular, excelled at flooding Facebook with highly engaging content – Simion himself **live-streamed "crises" nightly and flooded Facebook groups with video clips each morning** to dominate the feed. Negative campaigning took on meme-like forms: even the typically progressive Lasconi resorted to circulating doctored photos to discredit a rival (prompting complaints about "false photos" and fake news). Georgescu's online promoters likewise ensured his messages proliferated on Facebook alongside other networks. In essence, Facebook served as a battleground for viral propaganda and attack messaging, where catchy visuals and sensational headlines – often in meme format – were used to mobilize supporters and tarnish opponents.
- **YouTube (Long-Form Explainers):** As a video platform favoring longer content, YouTube was used for in-depth communication and credibility-building. Candidates and their supporters produced **long-form videos** – from full speeches and interviews to policy explainers – to delve into complex issues that couldn't be conveyed in short clips. For example, Lasconi's campaign shared extended weekly vlogs and sit-down discussions outlining her policy plans (appealing to educated urban voters seeking substance), while Simion's team uploaded recordings of rallies and fiery speeches to reinforce his messaging beyond the rallies themselves. Georgescu's camp and allied influencers also posted lengthy commentary videos on YouTube to legitimize his sudden rise, complementing the TikTok blitz. Notably, investigators later found **pro-Georgescu content had proliferated on YouTube (along with TikTok and Facebook)** through suspiciously well-funded channels underscoring that even this long-form arena was deliberately seeded with tailored narratives. Overall, YouTube allowed candidates to **present detailed narratives and build an archive of campaign material** for voters who sought more than fleeting clips.
- **Instagram (Curated Authenticity):** On Instagram, where visuals and personal branding reign, candidates cultivated an image of authenticity through carefully curated posts. This platform skews toward younger, urban audiences and demands a relatable, lifestyle-oriented approach. Lasconi, a former TV personality, exemplified this by sharing behind-the-scenes photos, family moments, and snapshots wearing traditional Romanian attire (the **national** blouse and a cross necklace) to signal both modern credibility and traditional values – reinforcing her "approachable yet principled" persona. Simion's social media team likewise took advantage of Instagram's low attention-span feed, posting a steady stream of patriotic imagery, rally photos, and informal selfies to humanize the firebrand image. As one analyst noted, **Simion was highly active on fast-scrolling platforms like Instagram and TikTok that deliver quick-hit images and messages without demanding much viewer attention.** By using Instagram Stories and interactive polls, candidates like Simion and Lasconi invited supporters into their daily campaign life, strengthening parasocial bonds. In sum, Instagram functioned as a **personal PR channel** – projecting authenticity, youthfulness, and humanizing details to complement the political messaging on other networks.

- **WhatsApp and Private Messaging (Peer-to-Peer Mobilization):** Campaigns leveraged **encrypted messaging apps** like **WhatsApp** and **Telegram** to conduct **grassroots mobilization** and spread **rumors discreetly**. Supporters, especially from **diaspora communities**, used **trusted private groups** to share **campaign content** and reminders, benefiting from the peer legitimacy of forwarded messages. **Georgescu's rapid rise** was notably supported by **coordinated Telegram groups**, enhancing his visibility through **covert digital networks** linked to **TikTok campaigns**. In 2024, all candidates exploited this effective **peer-to-peer digital strategy**, integrating it within their broader, tailored **platform-specific campaign approaches.**

6. IMPACT ON ELECTORAL INTEGRITY: POLICY IMPLICATIONS AND ETHICAL CHALLENGES

Despite the many advantages digital marketing brought to the 2024 election, it also tested the limits of Romania's electoral integrity in three key areas:

- **Fragmented public sphere**: Micro-targeting and algorithm-driven feeds led voters to consume vastly different political messages, undermining shared democratic discourse. Social media's preference for content aligned with user tastes created echo chambers, polarizing public discourse along age, location, and interest lines.
- **Distortion of truth and agenda:** Heavy reliance on polarizing, meme-centric posts limited thoughtful policy debate. Bots and paid influencers artificially amplified certain candidates, confusing voters and journalists about genuine support levels. Campaigns prioritized virality over substance, sidelining complex issues and skewing the political agenda based on algorithmic performance rather than real priorities.
- **Misinformation surge:** Fake or manipulated content proliferated faster than in any prior election, aided by deepfake technology and automated posting. Platforms struggled to keep up with content removal, and fact-checkers could not match the speed of misinformation spread, threatening voters' ability to make informed decisions.

These factors severely eroded trust and legitimacy, leading Romania's Constitutional Court to annul the first-round results due to extensive online manipulation, undermining public confidence and voter turnout in the subsequent re-run. The 2024 election also exposed regulatory inadequacies, as traditional election laws and authorities struggled with real-time, decentralized digital campaigning. Despite enhanced platform vigilance and the EU's Digital Services Act, regulators often detected unethical practices too late to prevent electoral impact.

6.1 Policy Implications and Ethical Challenges

The 2024 Romanian election fiasco serves as a cautionary tale that policy and ethical frameworks must urgently catch up with digital campaign realities. Several key implications and challenges emerge:

- **Modernizing electoral laws**: Rules must cover online ads and influencer content, requiring clear labeling and transparency in digital spending (e.g., on bots or consultants). Romania should go beyond EU frameworks like the DSA with real-time ad disclosures and social media archives accessible to regulators.
- **Platform accountability**: Social media companies must adopt stricter protocols during elections—boosting fact-checking, monitoring coordination, and allowing independent audits of algorithmic amplification. They must act as responsible public actors, not neutral tech providers.
- **Ethical AI and data use**: AI-driven micro-targeting raises concerns about privacy and consent. Tools should be built with "privacy-by-design," limit sensitive targeting, and let users see why they're shown ads. Campaigns should avoid bots and respect "data dignity," treating user data ethically.
- **Collaborative oversight**: Regulators, platforms, NGOs, researchers, and parties should coordinate via codes of conduct and task forces. Campaign transparency on digital tactics and voter data usage is key for watchdog monitoring.

- **Digital literacy**: Long-term solutions lie in education. Romania should expand media literacy programs to help citizens recognize manipulation, false trends, and misinformation.

Beyond these measures, we have expanded our analysis to include concrete solutions and ethical considerations: In crafting remedies, it is crucial to balance security and liberty. **Stricter regulations and oversight** of online campaigning must be implemented (to swiftly remove false content and penalize fraud) *without* unduly stifling free political discourse. For example, an independent *Electoral Digital Oversight Committee* could be established to monitor social media campaigns in real time, ensuring transparency in political ads and flagging coordinated fake news attacks. **Ethical frameworks** should guide the use of technology in campaigns: stakeholders must agree on norms for truthfulness, fairness, and accountability in using AI and micro-targeting (Brodny & Tutak, 2025). Recent research highlights a data privacy dilemma in AI-driven marketing (Saura et al., 2024), so campaigns and platforms should adopt privacy-by-design approaches – protecting user data and obtaining consent for political targeting. Internationally, Romania can contribute to or adopt emerging **codes of ethics** for digital elections, learning from best practices in other e-governance contexts. In summary, our revised integrity section not only enumerates policy fixes (modernizing laws, platform accountability, etc.) but also delves deeper into the ethical imperatives behind them. By pairing technological solutions with ethical guidelines, we argue that Romania and other democracies can better safeguard electoral integrity in the digital age.

7. CONCLUSION

The 2024 Romanian presidential election provides a vivid case study of both the power and the peril of social media marketing innovations in politics. On one hand, digital platforms dramatically enhanced the reach and cost-effectiveness of campaign communication, enabling candidates to engage voters – especially young voters – in ways unimaginable just a decade ago. A relatively unknown outsider candidate was able to build a mass following and shape the national debate primarily through social media, demonstrating the democratizing potential of these tools. The use of micro-targeting, viral video messaging, and influencer engagement showed that creative digital strategies can energize parts of the electorate that are often hard to reach, potentially increasing political participation.

On the other hand, these same innovations introduced new vulnerabilities into the democratic process. The election revealed how the fragmentation of the information space can undermine a shared reality among voters, how the viral spread of disinformation can drown out facts, and how clandestine digital tactics (bots, fake accounts, opaque ads) can even call an election's validity into question. The annulment of the first round – effectively a do-over of the election – was a dramatic intervention that underscored the severity of the threats involved. Democracy's core legitimacy rests on voters trusting the process and outcome; when that trust is shaken by perceptions of online manipulation, the consequences are dire.

For policymakers, electoral authorities, and civil society in Romania and beyond, the 2024 experience is a wake-up call. It underscores an **urgent need to modernize regulatory and oversight frameworks** for the digital campaign era. Encouragingly, there were signs of resilience: institutions like the courts did step in when things went off the rails, and public debate in Romania has since turned to how to better regulate political campaigning online. Looking ahead, the challenge will be to strike the right balance between allowing healthy digital innovation in campaigns and enforcing ethical guardrails. Social media and AI will only become more influential in future elections, so the solutions pioneered (or the mistakes made) in Romania could inform approaches elsewhere.

Ultimately, safeguarding democracy in the digital age will require that the **spirit of innovation be matched by an equal commitment to ethics and transparency**. Campaigns that creatively use social media should also embrace norms of truthfulness and accountability. Platforms that profit from political advertising must accept greater responsibility for its impacts. And voters themselves must be vigilant and discerning in navigating the online political arena. By integrating technological innovation with democratic values – encouraging genuine dialogue and community-building even as data-driven tactics are employed – elections can remain not just contests of marketing prowess, but a true contest of ideas and wills among an informed public. The Romanian case shows what is at stake, and it offers lessons that, if heeded, can help ensure that **digital political marketing strengthens rather than undermines democracy**.

REFERENCES

Alareeni, B. (2025). The role of government policy in enabling secure e-government and digital transformation. În B. Alareeni (Ed.), Big Data in Finance: Transforming the Financial Landscape (Studies in Big Data, vol. 164, pp. 205–212). Cham: Springer. https://doi.org/10.1007/978-3-031-75095-3_16

Alkhwaldi, A., Kamala, M., & Qahwaji, R. (2017). From e-government to cloud-government: Challenges of Jordanian citizens' acceptance for public services. În *Proceedings of the 2017 12th International Conference for Internet Technology and Secured Transactions (ICITST)* (pp. 298–304). Cambridge, UK: IEEE. https://doi.org/10.23919/ICITST.2017.8356405

Alkhwaldi, A., Kamala, M., & Qahwaji, R. (2019). Security perceptions in cloud-based e-government services: Integration between citizens' and IT-staff perspectives. În *Proceedings of the 12th International Conference on Global Security, Safety and Sustainability (ICGS3 2019)* (pp. 1–9). London, UK: IEEE.

AP News, (2024). AI-created election disinformation is deceiving the world. *AP News*. [online] Available at: https://apnews.com/article/artificial-intelligence-elections-disinformation-chatgpt

Botan, M., (2024). Algorithmic Influence on Elections: Insights from Romania's Case Study. *European Digital Media Observatory*. [online] Available at: https://edmo.eu/blog/algorithmic-influence-on-elections-insights-from-romanias-case-study/

Brito, K., Silva Filho, R.L.C. and Adeodato, P.J.L., (2024). Stop trying to predict elections only with Twitter – There are other data sources and technical issues to be improved. *Government Information Quarterly*, 41, p.101899.

Brodny, J. and Tutak, M., (2025). Stakeholder interactions and ethical imperatives in big data and AI development. *Journal of Open Innovation: Technology, Market and Complexity*, 11, p.100491.

Carlugeta, S. and Wesolowsky, T., (2024). How TikTok fueled the rise of Romania's far-right presidential candidate Georgescu. *Radio Free Europe/Radio Liberty*. [online] Available at: https://rferl.org

Context Global, (2024). *Social Media and Presidential Elections in Romania 2024*. Academic research report.

Expert Forum, (2025). *2024: Romania's Struggle with Systemic Risks in Digital Services Act Implementation*. [online] Available at: https://expertforum.ro/en

Funky.ong, (2024). *Undermining Democracy: The Weaponization of Social Media in Romania's 2024 Elections*. [online] Available at: https://funky.ong

Oancia, M., (2024). Rise of unknown Romanian presidential candidate preceded by Telegram and TikTok engagement spikes. *DFRLab (Atlantic Council)*. [online] Available at: https://www.linkedin.com/pulse/power-tiktok-ai-digital-systems-transforming-romanias-manuel-oancia-tvake

Pace, S., Buzzanca, S. and Fratocchi, L., (2016). The structure of conversations on social networks: Between dialogic and dialectic threads. *International Journal of Information Management*, 36(6), pp.1144–1151.

Puhr, H. and Müllner, J., (2024). Vox populi, vox dei: A concept and measure for grassroots socio-political risk using Google Trends. *Journal of International Management*, 30, p.101096.

Romania Journal, (2024). Less Romanian Social Media Users in 2024. *Romania Journal*. [online] Available at: https://www.romaniajournal.ro

Romania-Insider, (2024). Social media use in Romania in slight decline, TikTok to rise and surpass Facebook. *Romania Insider*. [online] Available at: https://www.romania-insider.com

Saura, J.R., Škare, V. and Dženopoljac, D., (2024). Is AI-based digital marketing ethical? Assessing a new data privacy paradox. *Journal of Innovation & Knowledge*, 9, p.100597.

Silverstein, M., (2011). The "message" in the (political) battle. *Language & Communication*, 31(3), pp.203–216.

Šlerka, J. and Stănoiu, I., (2024). How TikTok almost won the presidency for Romania's far-right candidate. *VSquare/Context.ro*. [online] Available at: https://vsquare.org/romania-tiktok-campaign-presidential-election-far-right-candidate-russia/

Social Sciences and Education Research Review, (2024). The Impact of Social Media on Romania's 2024 Elections. *Social Sciences and Education Research Review*, issue unspecified.

Tech Informed, (2024). Romania's Election Hit by Cyberattacks and Misinformation. *Tech Informed*. [online] Available at: https://techinformed.com

Tuya Digital, (2024). Social Media in Romania: Statistics and Reports. *TuyaDigital.com*. [online] Available at: https://tuyadigital.com/social-media-romania/

REDEFINING MARKETING IN THE DIGITAL AGE: AN ETHICAL IMPERATIVE FOR RESPONSIBLE AGILITY

Nada Soudi[1], Lina Soudi[2] and Siham Bennani[1]
[1]*Institut Supérieur du Commerce et d'Administration des Entreprises (ISCAE), Morocco*
[2]*Laboratory LARSEMO, Ecole Supérieure des Sciences Economiques et de Management (ESSEM), Morocco*

ABSTRACT

The digital revolution has transformed marketing dynamics generating significant ethical challenges. This research investigates this intersection, focusing on consumer behavioral and attitudinal shifts, ethical marketing principles, and strategies for responsible management that enable responsible agility in the digital age. Through a mixed-methods approach, marketing practitioner's views and quantitative consumer perception data are combined to provide a comprehensive view of this evolving landscape. Key findings highlight the necessity for brands to adapt their strategies, lead with ethical thinking, and incorporate societal and environmental values into business to attain long-term relevance. New consumers are better educated and therefore must observe transparency, authenticity, and accountability traits within a brand so that it can evolve successfully. Analysis of data reveals how ethical challenges impact company growth, emphasizing the necessity of considering both ethical impact and strategic actions. This work argues for rethinking marketing as a thoughtful, ethical and value-driven practice. This model puts power back in the hands of the consumer, creates trust, and puts brands in a better position to weather future disruption. Future researchers would do well to investigate certain practices to be brought into this model to enable long-term agility. With these core principles, marketing can better serve everyone's interests, towards a better future.

KEYWORDS

Digital Transformation, Marketing, Ethics, Adaptation, Changes

1. INTRODUCTION

Marketing has been significantly transformed by relentless exposure to digital technologies. The opportunity for unprecedented reach, personalization, and efficiency is vast; however, this change is not risk-free. Ethical considerations are no longer secondary agenda items but are instead core challenges requiring marketers attention, as well as scholars (Batra & Keller, 2016). This article addresses this juncture directly, examining the behavior and attitudes of consumers toward digital technology, while delving into marketing ethical principles and strategies for ethical marketing management in a digital era. The research is informed by abroad understanding of the impacts resulting from the digital revolution (Roberts & Zahay, 2013), and it examines them through a mixed-methods approach using qualitative analysis from practitioners and consumers. Our research relies on a detailed inspection of how brands have evolved, specifically with a focus on untangling the "Digital Effect" by comparing brand strategies with and without digital technologies to determine the actual impact of the digital revolution. This inspection also includes a critical analysis of how societal and environmental concerns are being embedded within models of business and communication. In addition, it tries to uncover how ethical practices are viewed by consumers and how challenges are posed by marketing experts to balance ethics with performance. Lastly, it tries to understand how marketing and consumer ethics are intertwined by examining how ethical marketing behavior depends on consumer ethical values. The key findings indicate the imperative for brands to accommodate a more digital world by fundamentally reshaping how they approach strategy (Lemon &Verhoef, 2016). A prosperous, long-term strategy also requires conscientiously fulfilling ever-changing modern consumer expectations, who are currently better informed, more empowered than ever. Brands must provide utmost importance to societal and environmental concerns and values if they want to create and preserve consumer trust, loyalty, and credibility. This research makes a contribution to knowledge by giving a systematic review of how digital transformation, consumer behavior, and ethics intersect. The suggested analyses provide tangible information for organizations, along with directions for how organizations can flourish in the era of the consumer's dynamic nature. Through a convergence of this work, this research assists in creating a more informed conversation about how consumers, along with other stakeholders, change to match how the new digital age becomes part of the norm (Schilit et al., 2015).

2. LITERATURE REVIEW

This literature review synthesizes key research on the profound influence of digital technologies on marketing, consumer behavior, and the evolving landscape of marketing ethics. It draws upon existing scholarship to establish a foundation for understanding the transformations detailed in the provided thesis and highlights areas where further investigation is needed.

2.1 The Digital Transformation of Marketing: A Paradigm Shift

Historically, marketing was concerned with a one-way process to deliver products and services to consumers (Kotler & Armstrong, 2014). The paradigm was shaken by digital technologies, however, creating a dynamic, multi-way flow of information and influence (Roberts &Zahay, 2013). Internet access and e-commerce proliferation have given consumers unparalleled access to information, choice, and interaction opportunities (ITU, 2019). This change indicates more than new means; it is a transformation in the nature of marketing itself (Dutot et al., 2016). Digital transformation dissolved traditional distinctions among marketing, sales, and customer service, forcing organizations toward a unified, customer-focused strategy (Lemon & Verhoef, 2016). Social media, content marketing, search engine optimization, and mobile marketing are now core parts of any integrated marketing strategy (Strauss & Frost, 2014). In addition, digital technologies allow organizations to deliver customized experiences, reach narrowly targeted audiences with precision accuracy, and track outcomes at unprecedented levels (Wedel &Kannan, 2016). But with new benefits from digital marketing come new challenges and complications. "Big data" and algorithmic decision capabilities create concerns related to data privacy, security, and transparency (Martin et al., 2017). The spread of false news, misinformation, and online abuse can harm brand image and lead to a loss of trust (Kahr et al., 2016).

2.2 The Evolution of Consumer Behavior in the Digital Age

Not only have digital technologies transformed how marketers conduct business, but also how consumers behave, think, and feel. The constantly connected, constantly "on" nature of the digital environment has produced a generation of customer who expects instant gratification, a tailored experience, and frictionless interactions (Bryn Jolfsson et al., 2013). This "digital native" cohort carries certain distinct qualities that necessitate revisiting conventional marketing strategies (Barton et al., 2014). Consumers are more informed, empowered, and demanding than ever before (Liu et al., 2018).They search for information actively, compare prices, read reviews, and participate in social media discussions with brands. They want brands to be transparent, authentic, and responsive to customer needs (Gilovich et al., 2015). In addition, with growing societal pressures, consumers are more concerned with ethical considerations, including data privacy, environmental responsibility, and social responsibility (Laczniak& Murphy, 1993). They are more likely to patronize a brand if it is aligned with their values and tend to boycott the otherwise (Du et al., 2006). This change in consumer behavior creates both opportunity and challenge for marketers. On one level, it makes targeted, personalized, and compelling marketing possible (Fuchs &Schreier, 2011). On another level, it necessitates being more responsive, honest, and ethical in practice (Goodpaster, 1991).

2.3 Marketing Ethics in the Digital Age

As a result of digital marketing, there exists today a nuanced ethical environment, bringing within new challenges to marketers and customers alike (Smith and Quelch, 1993). Utilitarianism and deontology, traditional ethical structures, offer a grounding for ethical decision making, yet might not necessarily cover the distinctive nuances of the digital age (Ferrell & Ferrell, 2008). Among the most critical ethical dilemmas is data privacy (Acquisti et al., 2013). Companies gather a wealth of information about consumers without their consent or even knowledge. The data can be leveraged to tailor ads to consumers, however, it can also be employed in more sinister ways, including price discrimination, manipulation, and monitoring (Martin et al., 2017). Another topic of concern in terms of ethical considerations are algorithmic decision-making (O'Neil, 2016).Algorithms are not necessarily unbiased, are not transparent, and are not easily comprehensible, resulting in discriminatory or unjust conclusions. Transparency is also a critical ethical concern (Grimmelikhuijsen & Meijer, 2012). The consumer is not necessarily informed about how data are collected, processed, and shared. They do not necessarily know about the algorithm behind it. Transparency can erode trust, and reduce consumer autonomy (Venable et al., 2005). Additionally, the internet environment has brought unprecedented opportunities for manipulated and fraudulent advertising tactics (Darke & Ritchie, 2007). Social media personalities can be compensated to endorse products without revealing their affiliation with a brand. Native advertising can distort editorial content and advertisements. These tactics can deceive consumers and erode their capacity to make knowledgeable choices.

2.4 Towards Responsible Marketing Management

To respond to this new challenge in ethics, academia and practitioners alike have advocated for a new marketing management philosophy focused on responsibility, accountability, and ethical decision making (P.E. Murphy, 1999). This form of marketing approach, sometimes also known as "responsible marketing," transcends complying with legislation alone and aims to generate value for all stakeholders, from customers, employees, to the community and environment (Laczniak & Murphy, 2019). Responsible marketing calls on organizations to be open about collecting and using data, providing consumers with control over data, and not using misleading and manipulative marketing practices. It also calls on organizations to be socially and environmentally responsible, and to conduct sustainable and ethical business (Maignan & Ferrell, 2004). We will present useful learning in how to use digital effectively while being responsible. The conclusions underscore how marketing strategies need to align with consumer values, ethics must be paramount in decision-making, and building quality, open relationships with stakeholders.

3. METHODOLOGY

This research article employs a mixed-methods approach, combining qualitative interviews and a quantitative survey, to gain a comprehensive understanding of the ethical considerations in digital marketing. This methodology allows for both the exploration of nuanced perspectives and the generalize ability of findings to a wider population.

3.1 Qualitative Phase: Exploring the Landscape Through Expert Interviews

A qualitative investigation was carried out in order to investigate marketing professionals lived experiences and views concerning ethical considerations when using digital technologies. The phase purposed to: (1) uncover major ethical dilemmas, (2) discern how practitioners handle them, and (3) develop hypotheses to inform the next quantitative phase. Purposive sampling was employed to obtain participants with heterogeneous backgrounds and marketing expertise. Ten marketing experts were interviewed. The participants came from a variety of sectors and organization sizes. Semi-structured interviews were carried out, enabling flexible and thorough probing of salient topics. The interview schedule addressed topics like:

- Attitudes toward how digital marketing influences consumer behavior.
- Recognition of ethical challenges faced in their practice.

- Methods adopted to address ethical dilemmas.
- Perspectives towards responsible marketing management in today's digital era.

3.2 Quantitative Phase: Measuring Consumer Perceptions and Attitudes

A quantitative survey was administered online to a broader sample to assess consumer perceptions of marketing ethics and to test hypotheses generated from the qualitative phase. The survey instrument was developed based on the literature review and the insights from the qualitative interviews. The target population consisted of adult consumers with experience using digital technologies. A convenience sampling method was utilized to recruit participants through online platforms, resulting in a sample of 1773 respondents. This large sample size increased the ability to obtain statistically significant conclusions and findings. In conclusion, the mixed-methods approach provides a rich understanding of the ethical dimension.

4. RESULTS: IMPLICATIONS FROM QUALITATIVE AND QUANTITATIVE DATA

This section presents findings from qualitative interviews and quantitative survey, identifying principal themes and statistical findings which mirror the convergence of digital transformation, consumer behavior, and marketing ethics.

4.1 Qualitative Findings: Explaining Ethical Concerns within Online Marketing

The qualitative interviews generated detailed, rich data from marketing practitioners in relation to the ethical concerns entailed in digital marketing practices. The thematic analysis and revealed several overarching concepts, each resonating with key tensions and considerations for practionners. Data privacy was the most frequently presented ethical dilemma. Members once more expressed concern over collection storage, and use of consumer data, referring to the intrinsic tension between personalization efforts and basic right to privacy. The participants also acknowledged the strong persuasive power through online advertising techniques, by means of strategic and focused advertisements social media power as key examples. They also envisioned potential for the same techniques to be employed for manipulative purposes or for misleading purposes. It was emphatically argued that a need exists for more transparency in marketing practices.

The interviewed respondents communicated the belief consumers need to be informed about how their data are managed and need to have substantial management of their digital lives. According to a brand strategist at a consulting company, "Transparency is key… Consumers are likely to trust more those companies who are willing to Transparent about their practices."Throughout, participants repeatedly mentioned about the importance requirement for branding to be done authentically in communication and practice. There was a general perception that buyers are becoming increasingly suspicious of hype-oriented or artificial advertising. They are more likely to connect with those brands with real values transparency. Interviewees expressed awareness of an evolving power dynamic between brands and consumers. The access facilitated by online sites enables motivates consumers to give their opinion, thereby building brand impressions and purchases decisions. This balance requires brands to get engaged in substantial discourse rather than simply spread information. Much as respondents admired unprecedented access to information and analytical capabilities through new technologies including artificial intelligence as they were thinking about learning, they also thought about ethics. They said, nevertheless, turning to unfair business practices would gain them a competitive edge, but this the advantage was not a genuine one. A notable sentiment shared by several interviewees was the growing sense that the traditional model of marketing is increasingly irrelevant in the face of the digital revolution. All participants concurred with a perception that historically promotion and product sales, so frequently to the detriment of the consumer, needs and desires, a discredited & unfeasible approach. These insights collectively underscore the complex ethical landscape facing marketing professionals in the digital age, revealing the need for a more nuanced, ethical, and consumer-centric approach, all while giving great emphasis on the integration of regulation efforts.

4.2 Quantitative Findings: Unveiling Consumer Perceptions and Attitudes

Quantitative survey findings supplied detailed information concerning consumer opinion marketing ethics and their relationships to major variables. In particular, the survey revealed the intricate relationship with ethical opinions, brand loyalty, economic motivators, and long term development in the new digital age, and most importantly, key pieces out of the data.

Strong Consumer Valuation of Ethics: A resounding majority of respondents, 82 percent, agreed to a very large extent that they thought brands must return to review their marketing strategies again, further underscoring a significant link between consumers and how they perceive the brand. Moreover, a large percentage of survey the participants (85 percent) overwhelmingly expressed a view that it was highly crucial for all businesses to follow ethical policies. These robust agreements uncover more than a rudimentary preference evident in the strong value put upon ethics in decision making in new, quickly areas for development

Satisfaction in terms of Ethical Expectations: Statistical tests revealed a strong connection between ethical considerations and consumer satisfaction. A share of consumers showed more confidence towards companies, services, and products took ethics into account. With those values shifting, how people engage with these Brands will be encouraged to prioritize that which they see as fair and just.

The Significance of Data Transparency in Establishing Trust: Customers who were aware of the practices and processes grounded in ethics contained more trust than compared to the consumers who believed there was lack of transparency. The great value placed in data transparency has had a vast influence on enhancing ethical practices.

Brand Reputation as a Significant Force: Most people believed that reputation had a significant role. Most respondents of this survey who believed to have ethics also had qualities, thoughts, and more associated with their reputation. Briefly speaking, perceived ethics by consumers can affect brand loyalty.

A Significant Departure: Consumers demonstrated how they preferred tailored and personalized services, yet did not substantially impact how actual management behaved, thereby leaving open ethical considerations. The most significant factor was found to be company brand.

4.3 Bridging Qualitative and Quantitative Findings: Integrated Insights

Qualitative and quantitative results merge to create a compelling description of the ethical. There are challenges and opportunities within digital marketing. The qualitative interviews are rich contextual appreciation for the complexity at hand, while quantitative data provide statistical justification for the need for ethical considerations in consumer choice and brand loyalty. The findings indicate a need to respond to ethical practices from the viewpoint of economic drivers, and performance, as well. Both pairs of findings highlight the need for transparency, genuineness, and ethics interact with each other according to a prior, mutually agreed contract. Emphasize the importance of marketers paying attention to the risk of manipulation and deception in digital marketing strategies.

5. DISCUSSION: ETHICS IN THE DIGITAL MARKETING ERA

The data highlighted above offer a compelling reference point for exploring marketing ethics and responsible business practices in a fast-changing digital world. These findings underscore the need for companies to move toward a new dynamic where Consumers are empowered yet discerning, and ethical factors hold more influence than ever control over buying choices. This segment explores the consequences of such findings, proposes a model for responsible marketing management, and identifies areas of fruitful future investigation.

5.1 The Need for Responsible Agility

Finding that a vast majority of consumers value ethical behavior, even at to the detriment of profit, sends a direct message to marketing society: ethical considerations are now "must-haves" rather than "nice-to-haves" if one desires long-term success. This aligns with wider social trends toward sustainability, responsibility, and purpose (Porter & Kramer Kramer, 2011). Companies can now longer prioritize profits at the expense of people and the environment. There exists a positive correlation between ethical views, customer satisfaction, and brand loyalty. It even further strengthens this requirement. Clients will be more satisfied with and devoted to brands they hold to be ethical. That is, being ethical is not only the right thing to do, but it is also good for business. This ethical transformation requires a change in attitude. Marketers must move to move away from a short-term focus on financial returns to a more broad, holistic approach of value-creation (Freeman, 1984). This means considering the impact of their actions on all stakeholders, including consumers, employees, communities, and the environment. It also means being transparent about their practices, taking responsibility for their mistakes, and actively seeking to improve their ethical performance.

5.2 A Responsible Marketing Management in a Time of Digitalization

Based upon findings from this study and current literature, a solid framework for responsible marketing practice in today's digital era must incorporate a variety of essential components. Foremost among them is a steadfast commitment to openness in operations so that each brand actions are in line with broadly accepted ethical principles made publicly available easily understandable. Second, data privacy as a fundamental right of each person consumer sovereignty is paramount, requiring affirmative action to protect this right at any cost, including obtaining informed consent, implementing strong security practices, and complying with applicable data protection law. Thirdly, creating authentic brand behavior and messaging vital, allowing consumers to easily spot the key values upon which the brand bases its decisions consistency between articulated values and observed practices. Finally, the selection and deployment of AI tools and algorithms must be carefully scrutinized to ensure that they do not perpetuate bias or create other unethical outcomes for any segment of the user base, demanding ongoing monitoring and evaluation. These interwoven elements collectively form a framework for ethical and responsible marketing in the digital age.

5.3 Bridging this Gap: Steps for Marketers

The qualitative interviews provide valuable insights into how marketers can implement these principles in practice. Although, Companies need to invest in data privacy and security initiating aggressive measures to protect consumer data from unauthorized access, use, disclosure. They need to be transparent in how they gather data and use it, showing consumers have control over their data. The businesses need to develop and use artificial intelligence algorithms in a responsible and responsibly, so they remain fair, transparent, and are held accountable. This entails with utmost care for data bias, algorithm development, and human review. The organizations need to promote a culture of ethical decision-making throughout the marketing department, providing workers with training, resources, and assistance in making ethical choices. This would include building sound ethical policies, introducing systems for reporting inappropriate conduct, and compensating ethical Behavior. Businesses need also to engage closely with consumers, people, communities, and stakeholders to understand their concerns and incorporate feedback to marketing decisions. It consists of building trust, creating open communication, and responsiveness to stakeholders'needs. The new brand development model can be summarized in the following illustration:

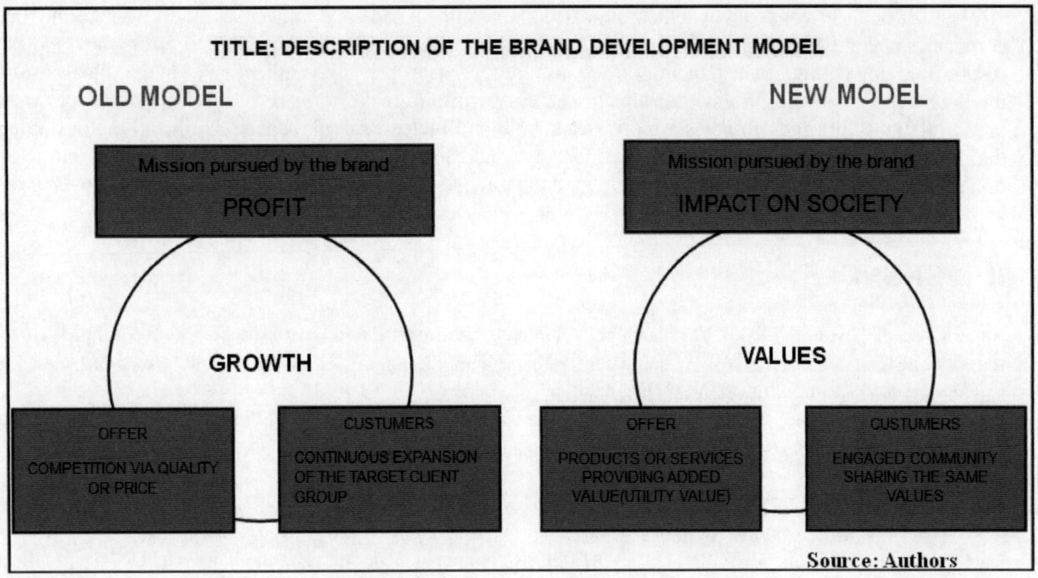

Figure 1.

The old business model focused mainly on profit, competition through quality or price, and expanding the customer base. However, today's challenges and societal expectations require companies to adopt a new approach. The new model emphasizes having a positive societal impact, sharing core values with customers, and creating added value through meaningful products or services. Moving to this new approach is essential for companies to stay relevant, build stronger relationships with their customers, and contribute positively to society. This transition is crucial for adapting to the evolving market and social demands.

5.4 Limitations and Future Research Directions

This study, like any other, also possesses certain constraints, and those need to be mentioned. The reliance availability of data is one of this study's limits. Future research must explore how businesses can better incorporate AI into their ethical approaches, and how their models would vary. Despite these limitations, this research provides valuable insights into the challenges and opportunities of marketing ethics in the digital age. The findings highlight the need for a new approach to marketing management that emphasizes responsibility, transparency, and ethical decision-making. By embracing these principles, brands can build trust with consumers, foster long-term relationships, and create a more sustainable and equitable digital future.

6. CONCLUSION

The digital revolution has transformed marketing dynamics greatly, providing both vast potential as well as severe ethical challenges. This research explained interrelated concepts, with a particular concentration on consumer behavioral and attitude development within digital era, philosophies of ethical marketing, and marketing strategies for responsibility management. The mixed-methods approach, integrating qualitative data from marketing experts' opinions and consumer sentiment statistical data, presented a complete insight into a transforming environment. The key findings necessitate a call for a shift in strategy by brands, stressing the importance of drivers, integrating environmental and social considerations into core business (Bhattacharya et al., 2008). In addition to ethical conduct, agility also characterizes the online environment. Brands must create organizational structures and decision-making models that allow them to stay abreast of change without sacrificing a commitment to core values. Consumers are well-informed, empowered, and discerning, demanding more openness, sincerity, accountability by the companies they like to shop at (Laczniak& Murphy,

1993). Consumers wondered whether ethical considerations had any impact at all. It was found that a company's operations must consider ethical impact as well as economic impact. This requires a new model for responsible marketing management, one transparency, data privacy, authenticity, and ethical artificial intelligence. This would provide consumers enables people to make informed decisions, reinforces trust in brand relationships, and promotes a more sustainable and inclusive digital space. Ultimately, going into the digital age is not a choice, but a necessity for any brand looking to gain credibility. This research helps in establishing a link between consumer behavior and value, to enable additional discourse and discovery.

REFERENCES

Audi, R., & Murphy, P. E. (2006). The many faces of integrity. *Business Ethics Quarterly*, Vol. 16, No. 1, pp. 3-21.

Batra, R., & Keller, K. L. (2016). Integrating marketing communications: New findings, new lessons, and new ideas. *Journal of Marketing*, Vol. 80, No. 6, pp.122-145.

Berzon, J., Shifflett, K., & Scheck, J. (2019). Amazon Has Thousands of Banned, Unsafe Products. *The Wall Street Journal*.

Darke, P. R., & Ritchie, R. J. B. (2007). The defensive consumer: Advertising deception, defensive processing, and distrust. *Journal of Marketing Research*, Vol. 44, No. 1, pp. 114-127.

Deng, X., & Xu, Y. (2017). Consumers responses to corporate social responsibility initiatives: the mediating role of consumer-company identification. *Journal of Business Ethics*, Vol. 142, No. 3, pp. 515-526.

Dutot, V., Galvez, E.L. and Versailles, D.W. (2016). CSR communications strategies through social media and influence on e-reputation: an exploratory study. *Management Decision*, Vol. 54, No.2, pp. 363-389.

Ferrell, O.C. and L. Ferrell (2008). A macromarketing ethics framework: stakeholder orientation and distributive justice. *Journal of Macromarketing*, Vol. 28, No. 1, p.12

Fritze, M. P., Marchand, A., Eisingerich, A. B., &Benkenstein, M. (2020), Access-based services as substitutes for material possessions: The role of psychological ownership. *Journal of Service Research*, Vol. 23, No. 3, pp. 368–385.

Fuchs, C., & Schreier, M. (2011). Customer empowerment in new product development. *Journal of Product Innovation Management*, Vol. 28, No. 1, pp.17-32.

Grimmelikhuijsen, S.G. and Meijer, A.J. (2012). Effects of transparency on the perceived trustworthiness of a government organization: Evidence from an online experiment. *Journal of Public Administration Research and Theory*, Vol. 24, No. 1, pp. 137–157

Haase, M., &Kleinaltenkamp, M. (2011). Property Rights Design and Market Process: Implications for Market Theory, Marketing Theory, and SD Logic. *Journal of Macromarketing*, Vol. 31, No. 2, pp.148-59

Helm, S. V., Ligon, V., Stovall, T., & Van Riper, S. (2018). Consumer Interpretations of Digital Ownership in the Book Market. *Electronic Markets*, Vol. 28, No. 2, pp. 177–89.

Kahr, A., Nyffenegger, B., Krohmer, H. and Hoyer, W.D. (2016), When hostile consumers wreak havoc on your brand: the phenomenon of consumer brand sabotage. *Journal of Marketing*, Vol. 80, pp. 25-41.

Kotler, P., & Armstrong, G. (2014). *Principles of marketing*. Pearson Education.

Laczniak et Murphy (2012). Stakeholder Theory and Marketing: Moving from a Firm-Centric to a Societal Perspective Published version. *Journal of Public Policy & Marketing*, Vol. 31, No. 2, pp. 284-292.

Lemon, K. N., & Verhoef, P. C. (2016). Understanding customer experience throughout the customer journey. *Journal of Marketing*, Vol. 80, No. 6, pp. 69-96

Liu, A. X., Steenkamp, J. B. E. M., & Zhang, J. (2018). Agglomeration as Driver of the Volume of Electronic Word of Mouth in Restaurant Industry. *Journal of Marketing Research*, Vol. 55, No. 4, pp. 507–523

Maignan, I., & Ferrell, O. C. (2004). Corporate social responsibility and marketing: An integrative framework. *Academy of Marketing Science Journal*, Vol. 32, No. 1, pp. 3-19

Naylor, G. (2016). Complaining complimenting and word-of-mouth in the digital age: typology and terms. *Journal of Consumer Satisfaction, Dissatisfaction and Complaining Behavior*, Vol. 29, pp. 131-142.

Roberts, M.L. and Zahay, D. (2013). *Internet Marketing: integrating Online and Offline Strategies*. 3rd ed., Cengage Learning, South-Western.

Sicari, S., Rizzardi, A., Grieco, L. A., & Coen-Porisini, A. (2015). Security, privacy and trust in Internet of Things: The road ahead. *Computer Networks*, Vol. 76, pp.146–164.

LITERATURE REVIEW ON APPLICATIONS OF ACTOR NETWORK THEORY IN DIGITAL PLATFORM RESEARCH

Shu-Chun Liao and Tzu-Chuan Chou
Department of Information Management, National Taiwan University of Science and Technology
43, Sec.4, Keelung Rd., Taipei, Taiwan, R.O.C.

ABSTRACT

When digital platforms can be viewed as non-human actors, actor network theory (ANT) is an appropriate research approach to investigate interactions between digital platforms and their stakeholders. This paper conducts a systematic literature review to explore how ANT has been applied in digital platform research. This paper makes an academic contribution through demonstrating the research trajectory and themes governing applying ANT in digital platform research and provides practical implications through conceptualizing a framework to explain how digital platform operators persuade potential users to enroll in the platform. Future research to validate or test the applicability of the proposed framework in a real-world case is suggested.

KEYWORDS

Digital Platforms, Actor Network Theory, Translation, ANT

1. INTRODUCTION

Digital platforms contribute to the digital transformation of an organization, an ecosystem surrounding them, or an industry or market where digital platforms are located, especially when the technology is disruptive. For instance, small and medium-sized enterprises with limited resources can leverage features, functions, and services of third-party digital platforms (e.g., Alibaba, an e-commerce platform) to enhance digital transformation capabilities (Li *et al.*, 2018). Therefore, such a contribution makes digital platforms a meaningful research topic. Ultimately, the success of a digital platform depends on its interactions with its users. Mlcúchová (2022) highlighted that one of the main attributes of digital platforms is network effects or network externalities. The more users of a platform there are, the greater the network externalities, and the more attractiveness of a platform to its users (Mlcúchová, 2022). Thus, how a digital platform operator recruits relevant stakeholders and ensures their faithful alliance is of vital importance.

The Actor-Network Theory (ANT) as a research tool allows researchers to examine sociotechnical interactions among various actors (including humans and non-humans) (Booth *et al.*, 2016). While digital platforms can be viewed as non-human actors, ANT is an appropriate research approach to investigate interactions between digital platforms and their stakeholders. We conducted a systematic literature review with reference to the research approach proposed by Okoli (2015), aiming to 1) explore how ANT has been applied in digital platform research, and 2) construct a framework on how digital platform operators persuade users to enroll in their platforms based on the results of the literature review. This paper makes an academic contribution by demonstrating the research trajectory and themes that adopt ANT in digital platform research. Moreover, this paper provides practical implications for digital platform operators in creating and expanding the network externalities of platforms.

2. CONTEXT AND THEORETICAL BACKGROUND

2.1 Digital Platforms

The term "platform" has been used and discussed in many perspectives, including an economic one which conceptualizes platforms as two-sided or multi-sided markets (Gawer, 2014). There are other viewpoints, of course, including the following: an engineering design perspective which views digital platforms as a design pattern or a deliberately designed modular technological architecture (Gawer, 2014); a business model perspective which views digital platforms as a technology-driven model in which digital technologies are used to connect different entities in the market (e.g., people, organizations, resources and so forth) to capture, create, exchange or deliver values (Gatautis, 2017; Hauke-Lopes *et al.*, 2022). With reference to previous research, we define digital platforms from an inclusive perspective as a technology-modular-based business model which connects at least one group of users and integrates digital technologies to create, exchange, or deliver values.

Based on the research of Mlcúchová (2022) and Madanaguli *et al.* (2023), we classified digital platforms into two main types. One is internal platforms, which are generally systems for internal use (e.g., spare parts monitoring or tracking) within an organization (Madanaguli *et al.*, 2023); the other is external platforms, which are systems for external use. For instance, a transaction platform plays a role as an intermediary, facilitating interactions, exchanges, or transactions between enterprises or end customers (Mlcúchová, 2022).

2.2 Actor Network Theory

ANT is a research methodology which examines motivations and actions of actors who form elements of an interests-aligned network (Walsham, 1997) and narrates how relations/associations are assembled and transformed or not (Law, 2008). An actor-network is a heterogeneous network of aligned interests of human and non-human actors (Sarker *et al.*, 2006). Actors are not only influenced by the network where they are located but also influence other actors whom they interact with (Law and Callon, 1992).

The main focus of ANT is to investigate the creation of network (Kinder *et al.*, 2019; Lunde, 2024), which is a four-moment translation process (see Table 1 for descriptions of four moments). The translation process allows the focal actor to align relevant actors' interests with his and keep them faithful to him (Sarker et al., 2006). The creation of an obligatory passage point (OPP) is critical to the alignment of interests. OPP is a space created by the focal actor to negotiate and persuade relevant actors to accept a shared interest and enroll in the proposed network (Sarker, Sarker et al. 2006, Kwofie, Tetteh et al. 2020, Minniti and Magaudda 2024). On the other hand, with reference to Callon's works, Bruno Latour (2005) introduced two new concepts, namely intermediaries and mediators, which are means for the creation of the network (Vitale, 2023). Intermediaries are "*what transports meaning or force without transformation*", and mediators are something that "transform, translate, distort, and modify the meaning or the elements they are supposed to carry" as defined by Bruno Latour (Vitale, 2023).

Table 1. Four moments of translation and their descriptions

Moments	Descriptions
Problematization	The focal factor identifies problems, relevant actors and their interests, as well as defines the OPP to render itself indispensable (Sarker et al., 2006)
Interessement	The focal actor takes actions developed in in the "problematization" process to convince relevant actors to accept his proposal (Sarker *et al.*, 2006; Kwofie *et al.*, 2020).
Enrollment	The focal actor successfully persuades relevant actors to accept his proposal and inscription occurs (Sarker *et al.*, 2006; Ekklesia, 2024). Inscription implies that actors' commitments are recorded into shared systems, e.g., software manuals, security systems and so forth (Sarker *et al.*, 2006).
Mobilization	The focal factors and relevant actors as well as their representatives perform upon their commitments (Callon, 1984; Ekklesia, 2024).

3. RESEARCH METHOD

We conducted a literature review based on a systematic literature review approach proposed by Okoli (2015) and Eshraghian and Hafezieh (2017). Systematic reviews aim to bring evidence together to answer pre-defined research questions and to synthesize and summarize existing knowledge (Aromataris and Pearson, 2014; Pollock and Berge, 2018). This approach fits our research aims mentioned in the introduction section. The research steps and main tasks are shown in Table 2.

Table 2. Literature review and research steps as well as main tasks

Step 1 : Planning	Step 2: Selection	Step 3: Analyzation	Step 4: Writing the review
• Establishing purposes of the literature review. • Identifying research questions. • Developing search strategies (search terms, database, search criteria etc.).	• Searching and selecting literature based on research strategies. • Finalizing applicable literature.	• Extracting data from applicable literature in line with research purposes and questions. • Analyzing and synthesizing data in a descriptive and thematic approach.	• Extracting data from applicable literature in line with research purposes and questions. • Analyzing and synthesizing data in a descriptive and thematic approach.

3.1 Planning

To have a comprehensive understanding of past research, we used "actor network theory" and "platform" as search terms and did not impose limits on the year of publications and research methods. The inclusion and exclusion criteria are shown in Table 3.

Table 3. Search criteria

Criteria	Descriptions
Inclusion criteria	• Literature applying ANT alone or applying ANT with other theories in digital platform research.
Exclusion criteria	• Literature whose case objects did not fall into the scope of digital platforms defined by this paper. • Literature which mentioned ANT but did not apply them to examine or analyze empirical phenomena in which platforms are viewed as an IT artifact (non-human actor). • Literature which did not take IT artifacts as the main actors in the network. • Literature whose research focus, questions and purposes were not highly related to digital platforms. • Non-English literature.

3.2 Selection

We collected literature through consulting Scopus and Web of Science (WOS) databases. The search, looking for "actor network theory" and "platform" in the title, abstract, keywords of articles, reviews, book chapters, and conference proceedings, encompassed information from the beginning of the databases to March 4, 2025. The search yielded 277 studies (175 studies from Scopus and 102 studies from WOS, while 21 studies were overlaps). We first screened the abstracts and titles of these studies, finding that 53 studies may fit the search criteria (see Table 3). We further read these 53 studies, finding that 27 studies fully met the search criteria as applicable literature.

3.3 Analyzation

3.3.1 Descriptive Results

Among these 27 studies, 13 studies were journal articles, nine studies were conference papers, and five studies were book chapters. The publishing years of these studies were from 2007 to 2025. Over 50% of the studies were published after 2021, while 22% (six studies) were published in 2023, and 15% (four studies) were published in 2024. We further classified these 27 studies into three research groups based on their research themes and foci (see Table 4 and Figure 1).

Table 4. Research themes and focus, case objects (types of digital platforms), and ANT applied

Group	Themes	Focus	Case objects	ANT applied
1	Implementation, diffusion or expansion of digital platforms and their ecosystems (12*)	• Development, acceptance or inscription of digital platforms (4) • Factors that influence the success of implementing digital platforms (8)	• Internal platform (7) • External platform (5)	• Concepts of actors (12) • The "four-moment translation" process (7)
2	Influences or impacts of digital platforms on other actors (9)	• Impacts made or benefits offered by digital platforms (9)	• External platform (6) • Internal platform (3)	• Concepts of actors (8) • Concepts of intermediary, mediator, and mediation (3) • The "four-moment translation" process (1)
3	• Governance or management of digital platforms (3) • Technology affordance (2) • User influence measurement (1)		• External platform (6)	• Concepts of actors (6)

*Numbers of studies.

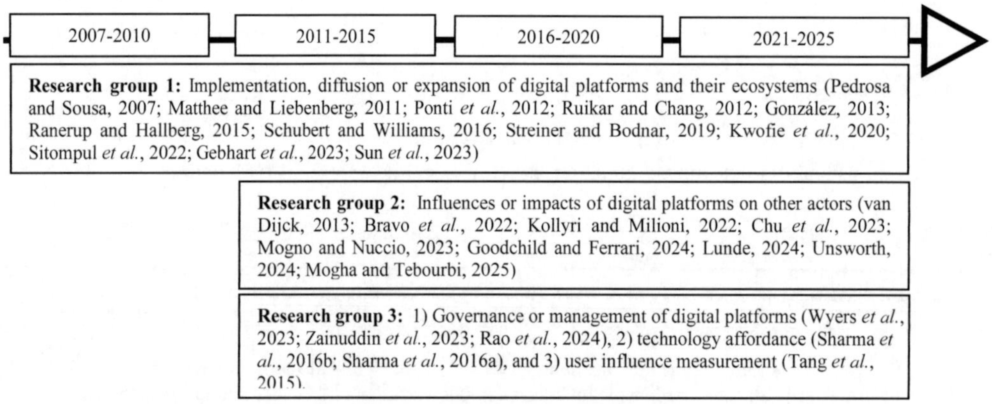

Figure 1. Research trajectory and themes

3.3.2 Thematic Results

We classified applicable studies into three search groups based on research themes and foci (see Table 4 and Figure 1). The "four-moment translation" process from ANT was largely applied in the first research group to analyze factors that contribute to or fail the enrollment of relevant actors into digital platforms and their ecosystems (see Table 5).

Table 5. Factors influencing the four-moment translation process

Moments	Success or failure factors
Problematization	**Success factors** • Clearly categorizing issues as threats or opportunities for initiating the next moment of the translation process, e.g., identifying customers' pain point problems as opportunities (Sun *et al.*, 2023) **Failure factors** • Failing to identify actors, e.g. main actors (Pedrosa and Sousa, 2007; Afarikumah and Kwankam, 2013; Kwofie *et al.*, 2020), and therefore not bringing them on board to address technical or non-technical issues (Kwofie *et al.*, 2020). • Unclear or missing IT platform architectures (Gebhart *et al.*, 2023) • Failing to cope with institutions, e.g., policies or regulations (Gebhart *et al.*, 2023). • Unclarity of the necessities of implementing digital platforms or proposed solutions (Pedrosa and Sousa, 2007; Kwofie *et al.*, 2020) as well as the extent of implementing proposed solutions (Afarikumah and Kwankam, 2013). • Limited support from management (Afarikumah and Kwankam, 2013) or lack of leadership (Gebhart *et al.*, 2023).

Interessement	**Success factors** • Perceived ease of use and positive usefulness of digital platforms (Sitompul *et al.*, 2022) • The design of incentives attracting relevant actors to join the network (Sun *et al.*, 2023). • Actions that can earn users' recognition and impose a digital platform as an OPP, e.g., utilizing a clearer identity for an internal digital platform to effectively communicate the purpose of implementing the platform (Schubert and Williams, 2016). **Failure factors** • Inadequate communication among actors and inappropriate communication channel adopted (Kwofie *et al.*, 2020). • Lack of relevant actors' trust (Gebhart *et al.*, 2023), especially when relevant actors are not familiar with the focal actor (Sun *et al.*, 2023) • Difficulties for relevant actors to appropriate technologies (Gebhart *et al.*, 2023)
Enrollment	**Success factors** • Not merely focusing on a technical inscription, but also adopting a more service-oriented inscription approach (Schubert and Williams, 2016). • Actor linkage which offers resources for achieving the goals set by the focal actor, e.g., using emotional connections or reputational influence as a form of enrollment (Sun *et al.*, 2023).
Mobilization	**Success factors** • The commitment and belief of the core group to promote the vision through media, press or other channels for implementing a digital platform (Schubert and Williams, 2016). • Actions that can earn social recognition and empower relevant actors, e.g., psychological empowerment through interaction and communication, resource empowerment through information sharing and so forth (Sun *et al.*, 2023). • Actions that can expand the focal actor's voice in concerned communities or industries, e.g., establishing or reconstructing quality standards (Sun *et al.*, 2023). **Failure factors** • Lack of spokesmen to represent the needs and opinions of actor groups (Pedrosa and Sousa, 2007; Afarikumah and Kwankam, 2013; Kwofie *et al.*, 2020)

The second research group focused on "influences or impacts of digital platforms on other actors", e.g., how digital platforms influence their users' subjectivities or decisions (Kollyri and Milioni, 2022; Lunde, 2024; Unsworth, 2024), or shape the practices, norms or culture (van Dijck, 2013; Kollyri and Milioni, 2022; Goodchild and Ferrari, 2024). Though the four-moment translation process was applied in this research group (Chu *et al.*, 2023), it was not applied in this research group as much as it was applied in the first research group. Other concepts from ANT were applied. For instance, Goodchild and Ferrari (2024) drew on the concept of intermediary and mediator from ANT to examine how online property platforms influenced UK housing market practices, including practices of searching for a house and conducting property transactions. Unsworth (2024) drew on the concept of "technical mediation" from ANT to investigate how a collaborative technology, namely Google Classroom, influenced and shaped teachers' classroom practices.

The third group included three themes. The first one was research on governance or management of digital platforms, which highlighted the responsibilities of digital platform operators, e.g., responsibility to protect personal data (Wyers *et al.*, 2023). The second one was research on technology affordance, which adopted ANT as a research approach to investigate the creation and actualization of social media technology affordances (Sharma *et al.*, 2016b; Sharma *et al.*, 2016a). The third one was research on user influence measurement, which incorporated ANT to construct a framework to measure user influence in social medial platforms (e.g., Sina Weibo) (Tang *et al.*, 2015).

4. DISCUSSION

In the context of digital platforms, translation is an ongoing process in which a platform operator recruits potential users to enroll in the platform and keep existing users active on the platform. We found that the four-moment translation process has been widely applied in analyzing how digital platforms or their ecosystems are established and expanded (see Table 5), how digital platforms influence other actors (Chu *et al.*, 2023), and how digital platform affordances are actualized or created (Sharma *et al.*, 2016b; Sharma *et al.*, 2016a). Moreover, strategies deployed by the focal actor will influence actions taken to attract potential users to join the platform (Sun *et al.*, 2023; Goodchild and Ferrari, 2024). For instance, online property platforms acting as intermediaries will focus on matchmaking functions, standardize the information and pass the enquiries to agents, but those acting as mediators will change and rework the meaning of the content, aiming to promote the demand of actors for moving to more attractive and comfortable properties (Goodchild and Ferrari, 2024). As such, with reference to the results of the literature review, we constructed a framework to describe how digital platform operators persuade potential users to register with their digital platforms based on the four-moment translation process from ANT (see Figure 2).

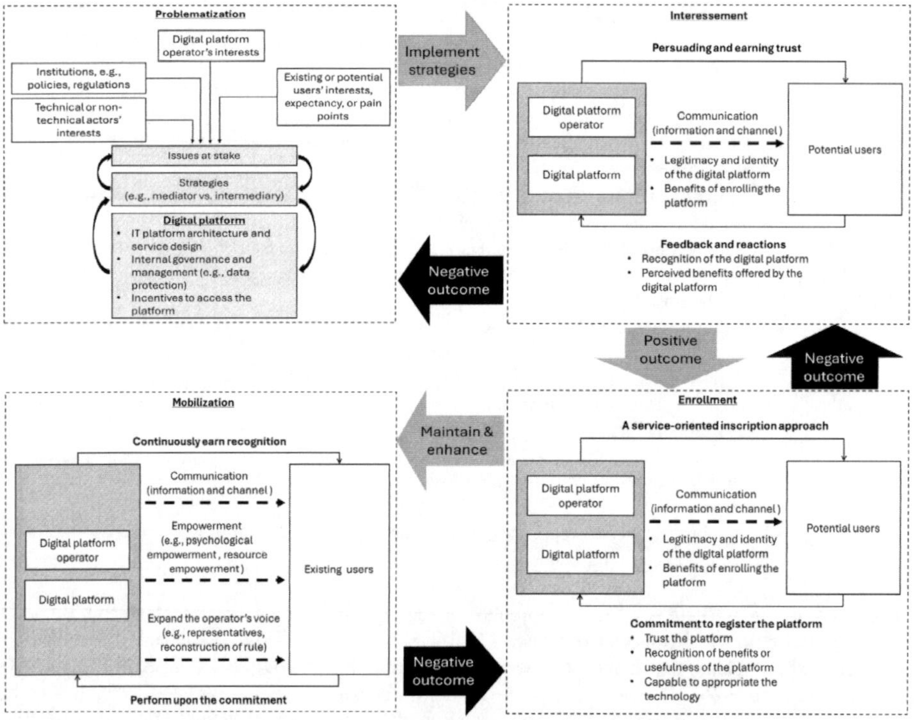

Figure 2. Framework on the creation of the digital platform's actor network

The proposed framework (see Figure 2) inspires digital platform operators, but further empirical research is needed to validate and test its applicability in the real world. Future research may start from the perspective of digital platform operators, focusing on how operators create or maintain a digital platform's actor-network, especially how operators impose the digital platform as an OPP to have potential users adopt solutions provided by the platform. On the other hand, ANT as a research methodology allowing researchers to investigate situations has high levels of description power, but it has less predictive power (Booth et al. 2016; Pollack et al. 2013). Researchers therefore have suggested that combining other theoretical perspectives with the ANT lens is a good approach to mitigate ANT's weakness (Booth et al. 2016). As such, future research may combine other theoretical perspectives while applying the proposed framework (see Figure 2) in real-world cases.

5. CONCLUSION AND RESEARCH LIMITATIONS

Based on a systematic literature review, we answered two research questions. This paper makes an academic contribution through providing a comprehensive picture of existing studies regarding applying ANT in digital platform research. Table 1 and Figure 2 show the main research trajectory and themes. Moreover, the implications of practice, insights, or suggestions on how to recruit potential users or keep existing users on board the digital platform can be explored through literature reviews. With reference to the results of the literature review, we constructed a framework to describe how digital platform operators negotiate and align their interest with potential or existing users based on the four-moment translation process from ANT (see Figure 2). This framework inspires those who adopt digital platforms as a business model and digital platform operators in establishing, running and expanding a digital platform and its ecosystem.

This paper has its limitations. First, the review was limited to English studies, which may ignore important findings in non-English literature. Second, the selection of applicable studies and analyses is subject to authors' subjective interpretations, which may lead to bias in research results. Third, the proposed framework (see Figure 2) is conceptualized based on existing literature, which may mitigate its originality or innovation. Fourth, the framework is conceptional and lacks empirical validation. Future empirical research to validate and test its applicability is needed.

REFERENCES

Afarikumah, E. and Kwankam, S.Y. (2013). Deploying actor-network theory to analyse telemedicine implementation in Ghana, *Science,* 1 (2), pp. 77-84.

Aromataris, E. and Pearson, A. (2014). The systematic review: an overview, *AJN The American Journal of Nursing,* 114 (3), pp. 53-58.

Booth, R.G. *et al.* (2016). Actor-Network Theory as a sociotechnical lens to explore the relationship of nurses and technology in practice: methodological considerations for nursing research, *Nursing Inquiry,* 23 (2), pp. 109-120.

Bravo, R. *et al.* (2022). How does a pandemic disrupt the benefits of eCommerce? A case study of small and medium enterprises in the US, *Journal of Theoretical and Applied Electronic Commerce Research,* 17 (2), pp. 522-557.

Callon, M. (1984). Some elements of a sociology of translation: domestication of the scallops and the fishermen of St Brieuc Bay, *The sociological review,* 32 (1_suppl), pp. 196-233.

Chu, H. *et al.* (2023). Placing the platform economy: The emerging, developing and upgrading of Taobao villages as a platform-based place making phenomenon in China, *Cambridge Journal of Regions, Economy and Society, 16*(2), pp. 319-334.

Ekklesia, J.M. (2024). Understanding digital consumer culture in Indonesia: a case study on youth community in Jakarta using an actor-network theory approach, *Young Consumers,* pp.

Eshraghian, F. and Hafezieh, N. (2017). Affordance theory in social media research: systematic review and synthesis of the literature. *25th European Conference on Information Systems (ECIS 2017),* 2017.

Gatautis, R. (2017). The Rise of the Platforms: Business Model Innovation Perspectives, *Inzinerine Ekonomika-Engineering Economics,* 28 (5), pp. 585-591.

Gawer, A. (2014). Bridging differing perspectives on technological platforms: Toward an integrative framework, *Research Policy,* 43 (7), pp. 1239-1249.

Gebhart, J., Schlick, S. and Marvell, A. (2023). Analysing Barriers in the Business Ecosystem of European MaaS Providers: An Actor-Network Approach. *In:* Gerber, A. and Hinkelmann, K., eds. *EPiC Series in Computing,* 2023. EasyChair, pp.68-81.

González, R.A. (2013). *ScienTI information system Central artifact of the National System of Science and Technology.*

Goodchild, B. and Ferrari, E. (2024). Intermediaries and mediators: an actor-network understanding of online property platforms, *Housing Studies,* 39 (1), pp. 102-123.

Hauke-Lopes, A., Wieczerzycki, M. and Ratajczak-Mrozek, M. (2022). Extra-industry imitation of digital platform business models, *Entrepreneurial Business and Economics Review,* 10 (4), pp. 91-105.

Kinder, E., Jarrahi, M.H. and Sutherland, W. (2019). Gig Platforms, Tensions, Alliances and Ecosystems: An Actor-Network Perspective, *Proc. ACM Hum.-Comput. Interact.,* 3 (CSCW), pp. Article 212.

Kollyri, L. and Milioni, D.L. (2022). "Spectacular" User Subjectivities on Instagram: A Discursive Interface Analysis, *International Journal of Communication,* 16 pp. 5358-5380.

Kwofie, B., Tetteh, E.D. and Coffie, C.P.K. (2020). Institutional E-Learning Implementation: An Actor-Network Theory (ANT) Perspective. In: Williams, I. (ed.) *Contemporary Applications of Actor Network Theory.* Singapore: Springer Nature Singapore, pp. 99-119.

Law, J. (2008). Actor network theory and material semiotics, *The new Blackwell companion to social theory,* pp. 141-158.

Law, J. and Callon, M. (1992). The life and death of an aircraft: a network analysis of technical change, *Shaping technology/building society: Studies in sociotechnical change,* pp. 21-52.

Li, L. *et al.* (2018). Digital transformation by SME entrepreneurs: A capability perspective, *Information Systems Journal,* 28 (6), pp. 1129-1157.

Lunde, I.M. (2024). Learning analytics as modes of anticipation: enacting time in actor-networks, *Scandinavian Journal of Educational Research,* 68 (2), pp. 218-232.

Madanaguli, A. *et al.* (2023). Literature review on industrial digital platforms: A business model perspective and suggestions for future research, *Technological Forecasting and Social Change,* 194 pp. 17.

Matthee, M. and Liebenberg, J. (2011). The ties that bind: a case of establishing a mobile post-training support network, *International Journal of Mobile Learning and Organisation,* 5 (2), pp. 175-191.

Mlcúchová, M. (2022). A Review of Platform Business Models, *Scientific Papers of the University of Pardubice-Series D-Faculty of Economics and Administration,* 30 (1), pp.

Mogha, V. and Tebourbi, N. (2025). Digital platform to scale initiatives for community engagement and social impact: a case study in the Indian plastic recycling industry, *Journal of Asia Business Studies,* pp.

Mogno, S. and Nuccio, M. (2023). Platform-Enabled Business Models in the Arts: The Impact of Digital Transformation on Visual Arts Networks. In: Moretti, A. and Balzarin, L. (eds.) *New Perspectives in Network Studies: A Multidisciplinary Approach.* Cham: Springer International Publishing, pp. 63-89.

Okoli, C. (2015). A guide to conducting a standalone systematic literature review, *Communications of the Association for Information Systems,* 37 pp.

Pedrosa, I. and Sousa, C. (2007). The actor-network theory and moodle in an high school community - A strategical tool and a life-long learning approach. *IADIS International Conference on Cognition and Exploratory Learning in Digital Age, CELDA 2007,* 2007. pp.367-372.

Pollock, A. and Berge, E. (2018). How to do a systematic review, *International Journal of Stroke,* 13 (2), pp. 138-156.

Ponti, M., Renzi, S. and Klobas, J.E. (2012). A wiki for informal learning among social workers in a local health authority. *Wiki Supporting Formal and Informal Learning.* pp. 199-219.

Ranerup, A. and Hallberg, I. (2015). Actors and intentions in the development process of a mobile phone platform for self-management of hypertension, *Informatics for Health and Social Care,* 40 (4), pp. 299-318.

Rao, Z., Liu, S. and Xiao, P. (2024). Under the iceberg of "one-stop": explore multi-actor engagement in one-stop digital cultural platforms through actor-network and commons theories, *Aslib Journal of Information Management,* pp.

Ruikar, S. and Chang, P.C. (2012). Achieving network stability through convergence case study of an e-Government project using actor network theory. *Proceedings of the Annual Hawaii International Conference on System Sciences,* 2012. IEEE Computer Society, pp.2593-2602.

Sarker, S., Sarker, S. and Sidorova, A. (2006). Understanding business process change failure: An actor-network perspective, *Journal of Management Information Systems,* 23 (1), pp. 51-86.

Schubert, P. and Williams, S.P. (2016). The Case of UniConnect-The Shaping of an Academic Collaboration Platform. *MKWI,* 2016. pp.327-338.

Sharma, D., Saha, B. and Sarkar, U.K. (2016a). Affordance lost, affordance regained, and affordance surrendered: The becoming of reachability on social media platforms. *In:* Kavanagh, D. *et al.*, eds. *IFIP Advances in Information and Communication Technology,* 2016a. Springer New York LLC, pp.73-89.

Sharma, D., Saha, B. and Sarkar, U.K. (2016b). Bridging the distance: The agencement of complex affordances on social media platforms. *2016 International Conference on Information Systems, ICIS 2016,* 2016b. Association for Information Systems.

Sitompul, T. *et al.* (2022). Journey on Flattening the Curve: The Actors and Networks of Indonesian Contact Tracing System. *In:* Zheng, Y., Abbott, P. and Robles-Flores, J.A., eds. *IFIP Advances in Information and Communication Technology,* 2022. Springer Science and Business Media Deutschland GmbH, pp.144-155.

Streiner, S.C. and Bodnar, C.A. (2019). Building a local curricular diffusion model based on a gamified homework platform in first year engineering: A case study, *Advances in Engineering Education,* 7 (3), pp.

Sun, Q. *et al.* (2023). How to build business ecosystems for e-waste online recycling platforms: A comparative study of two typical cases in China, *Technological Forecasting and Social Change,* 190 pp. 122440.

Tang, B. *et al.* (2015). Measuring domain-specific user influence in microblogs: An Actor-Network Theory based approach. *In:* Guerrieri, A. *et al.*, eds. *Proceedings of the 2015 IEEE 19th International Conference on Computer Supported Cooperative Work in Design, CSCWD 2015,* 2015. Institute of Electrical and Electronics Engineers Inc., pp.314-319.

Unsworth, R. (2024). Teaching through the cloud: An ethnography of the role of cloud-based collaborative technologies in the formation of teachers' classroom practices, *Anthropology & Education Quarterly,* 55 (1), pp. 24-42.

van Dijck, J. (2013). Facebook and the engineering of connectivity:A multi-layered approach to social media platforms, *Convergence,* 19 (2), pp. 141-155.

Vitale, G. (2023). Theoretical Framework: The Actor-Network Theory (ANT). *Understanding Supply Chain Digitalization Through Actor-Network Theory: The Interplay Between Blockchain, Accounting and Management Control.* Cham: Springer Nature Switzerland, pp. 23-45.

Walsham, G. (1997). Actor-Network Theory and IS Research: Current Status and Future Prospects. In: Lee, A.S., Liebenau, J. and DeGross, J.I. (eds.) *Information Systems and Qualitative Research: Proceedings of the IFIP TC8 WG 8.2 International Conference on Information Systems and Qualitative Research, 31st May–3rd June 1997, Philadelphia, Pennsylvania, USA.* Boston, MA: Springer US, pp. 466-480.

Wyers, K. *et al.* (2023). Identity Platforms and Anti-LGBTQ+ Legislation: Implications for Safeguarding Personal Data. *In:* Jones, M.R. *et al.*, eds. *IFIP Advances in Information and Communication Technology,* 2023. Springer Science and Business Media Deutschland GmbH, pp.209-217.

Zainuddin, S.A. *et al.* (2023). An Application of Actor Network Theory (ANT) in Business-to-Business Procurement Platform. In: Mansour, N. and Bujosa Vadell, L.M. (eds.) *Finance, Accounting and Law in the Digital Age: The Impact of Technology and Innovation in the Financial Services Sector.* Cham: Springer International Publishing, pp. 715-725.

TOWARDS DATA-DRIVEN ACADEMIC GOVERNANCE: CASE STUDIES AT ISIPA

Martin Ekanda, Efrem Mbaki, Antal Bulanza, Patmos Nembalemba and Gloire Soke
Institut Supérieur d'Informatique, Programmation et Analyse (ISIPA),
N° 7518, Avenue Shaumba Kinshasa / Gombe
Democratic Republic of Congo

ABSTRACT

This article presents the application of the Data-Driven approach at ISIPA (Institut Supérieur d'Informatique, Programmation et d'Analyse) in the Democratic Republic of Congo. It shows how the systematic exploitation of data improves academic management, the quality of teaching and the performance of research. The project, already in an advanced phase, aims to build a pool of scientific data including ISIPA's academic productions, such as dissertations, internship reports, theses and scientific articles. The infrastructure is based on internationally recognized practices: user portal, metadata management, secure storage, advanced search engine, analysis tools and access control, in compliance with the FAIR (Findable, Accessible, Interoperable, Reusable) principles and OpenAIRE recommendations. In the sub-Saharan university context, particularly in Congo, this implementation represents a major step forward in the optimization of sustainable and efficient management of scientific data.

KEYWORDS

Data-Driven, FAIR Principles, ISIPA, OpenAIRE, Scientific Data

1. INTRODUCTION

The data-driven approach consists of basing one's decision-making process on the data collected, analyzed and used. With the fall in the price of computer media (hard disk or database) and the ability of companies and administrations to capture information through the many multimedia channels, the data-driven approach is increasingly used in the improvement of business processes, human resources management and the improvement of professional results.For example, companies leverage customer data to personalize their services, predict market trends, and improve customer satisfaction. Similarly, in the public sector, governments are using data to optimize the management of public services, improve decision-making processes, and enhance transparency and accountability (Harris et al., 2020). In recent years, several large-scale technology companies, such as Google and Amazon, have taken advantage of this approach to adjust their business and product development strategies (Smith, 2021).

In higher education and university institutions, the data-oriented approach is also one of the strategic levers. It allows for more precise and efficient management of academic and scientific resources insofar as universities and colleges use the use of data to optimize student performance, monitor the organization of teaching, evaluate the quality of teaching, optimize the planning of research projects or to allocate human and material resources more rationally. In this context, the data-driven approach promotes and improves coordination between the different intra- and inter-institutional entities by strengthening collaboration through data sharing and interoperability. Institutions such as the University of Oxford and MIT have already incorporated data-driven strategies to assess the impact of their research and teaching programs (Jones et al., 2020). The table below provides a comparison of the use of the Data-Driven approach in the entrepreneurial and academic contexts.

Table 1. Comparison of Data-Driven use in entrepreneurship and academia

Criterion	Data-driven business	Data-driven university
Main objective	Make strategic decisions to improve economic performance	Optimizing teaching, research and institutional management
Data Origin	Business Activities: Sales, Marketing, Finance, Operations, HR	Academic activities: students, teachers, research, administrative services
Actors involved	Executives, Team Leaders, Sales and Operations Managers	Academic Leaders, Teachers, Students, Administrative Staff
Areas of application	Market analysis, business forecasting, cost management	Tracking student success, personalizing learning paths
Tools used	CRM, ERP, predictive tools, business intelligence platforms	LMS, educational dashboards, research management systems
Decisions taken	Product launches, adjustment of sales campaigns	Review of programmes, awarding of scholarships based on data
Expected benefits	Sustainable growth, competitive advantage, increased customer satisfaction	Better academic achievement, scientific excellence, institutional effectiveness
Constraints to be overcome	Securing business data, internal resistance to change	Respect for student privacy, progressive integration of technologies
Level of interconnection	Real-time integration of internal systems and customer interactions	Smooth articulation between educational, administrative and scientific systems

In the Democratic Republic of Congo, ISIPA (Institut Supérieur Pédagogique et d'Informatique de Kinshasa) is committed to this digital transformation by adopting the Data-Driven approach. This commitment aims to make ISIPA a model of innovation in higher education in Africa. The project, which is already underway, consists of creating a digital infrastructure that allows academic and scientific data to be optimally managed. ISIPA aims to maximize the impact of its research while improving the quality of teaching and the efficiency of administration. This project is based on the FAIR principles, in particular the accessibility, interoperability and reuse of data produced by ISIPA students and researchers (dissertations, theses, internship reports, scientific articles, etc.) (Wilkinson et al., 2016).

ISIPA, through this approach, serves as a laboratory for the application of these principles in an African context where data management and digital transformation are major challenges, but also opportunities for growth for higher education institutions. This ambitious project, although facing challenges related to infrastructure and resources, shows how an institution can leverage the use of data to boost research, pedagogy and administration, drawing on international best practices (Mays et al., 2020). In addition, this project is intended to be a model of success in a developing academic context, where data can play a key role in the growth and sustainability of African educational institutions.

2. METHODOLOGY

The methodology adopted for the design and implementation of ISIPA's institutional reservoir of scientific data is based on a qualitative and exploratory approach, based on a constructivist epistemology. This approach aimed to understand the social, organizational and technological dynamics influencing the transition to academic data governance in a developing African context (OECD, 2023).

As a first step, an in-depth literature review was carried out to identify international best practices in the management and valorization of scientific data. This review drew on major references, including the FAIR (Findable, Accessible, Interoperable, Reusable) principles formulated by Wilkinson et al. (2016), the OpenAIRE recommendations for open research infrastructures (OpenAIRE, 2023), as well as empirical studies on academic data ecosystems (Tenopir et al., 2015). Operational guides related to data management plans (DMPs), metadata, and institutional repositories were also incorporated into the analysis (Michener, 2015).

This documentary database has made it possible to define a normative reference framework adapted to the institutional reality of ISIPA.

In parallel with this theoretical analysis, a field survey was conducted to anchor the project in the needs and expectations of internal stakeholders. Semi-structured interviews were conducted between [insert months] 2025, with a reasoned sample comprising 32 teacher-researchers from the departments of computer science, management and electronics, 6 administrative agents from the research, documentation and computer services, as well as 230 students enrolled in bachelor's and master's cycles, engaged in scientific projects or practical work. The interviews, conducted in French or Lingala depending on the participants' language preferences, collected qualitative data on perceptions, barriers, needs and expectations related to the management and reuse of academic data at ISIPA (Kvale & Brinkmann, 2009).

The data collected was the subject of a thematic content analysis, carried out using the NVivo software (Lumivero, 2023). The codes were generated inductively, then grouped into analytical categories in order to bring out the main issues of the project. This analysis highlighted several challenges (technical, organizational, cultural), but also potential levers such as continuous training, the establishment of incentives for the valorization of data or the implementation of user-friendly tools. A triangulation of the data was carried out by cross-validation between the different groups interviewed and by comparing the empirical results with good practices from the literature. This methodology, which is both rigorous and participatory, aims to ensure that the proposed digital architecture is not only technically sound, but also socially acceptable, strategically relevant and sustainably integrated into ISIPA's governance practices.

3. STATE OF THE ART

The Data-Driven approach has emerged as a major strategic lever in various sectors, including in higher education, where its adoption is profoundly transforming academic management, teaching, research and innovation. This approach is based on the collection, analysis and exploitation of scientific, pedagogical and administrative data to optimize institutional processes, improve decision-making and boost the performance of universities and higher education institutions. In this regard, the FAIR (Findable, Accessible, Interoperable, Reusable) principles defined by Wilkinson et al. (2016) play a central role, facilitating the accessibility, interoperability and reuse of scientific data. These principles are now at the heart of data management strategies in universities, encouraging archiving, openness, and sharing of data to foster collaboration on a global scale. Repositories such as Zenodo or OpenAIRE have structured this management and allowed for increased transparency in the availability of data, facilitating their reuse by other researchers or institutions (Borgman, 2018). In universities and higher education institutions, the choice of a data-driven approach is based on the strategic desire to integrate advanced digital technologies to manage, store and protect large volumes of data in order to actively contribute to better decision-making at all levels of the institution. Also, the intelligent use of data opens the door to an optimization of educational and administrative processes. In other words, institutions manage to streamline the management of programs, human and material resources, while automating certain repetitive tasks. Under these conditions, the analysis of academic data also allows for individualized follow-up of students, identifying specific difficulties and adjusting pedagogical approaches according to the real needs of learners. The collection of technical data, such as historical network traffic or server logs, also plays a crucial role in optimizing digital infrastructures. This data makes it possible to anticipate malfunctions, monitor system performance and strengthen cybersecurity (Caldwell et al., 2020). Thus, this approach optimizes the governance of institutions in the sense that it allows for better coordination between the different internal entities and strengthens collaboration with other institutions through secure and structured data sharing. Data-driven digital transformation is thus becoming a strategic lever for improving the quality of teaching, research and university management as a whole.

Similarly, feedback on teachers and courses provides a solid basis for adjusting teaching practices and optimizing the quality of teaching. This data also facilitates human resources and program management, enabling more informed and targeted decision-making. The use of data also improves the real-time evaluation of instructional strategies, and the measurement of the impact of learning methods on student outcomes (Baker, Jones, & Taylor, 2020). It is almost impossible to dissociate data from scientific research. Indeed, regardless of the field, data plays a key role in scientific research as it fosters collaboration among researchers at the local, regional, national and even global levels. Indeed, open access to raw or experimental data, research results and scientific publications via dedicated platforms improves intellectual profitability and allows other scientists to validate the results obtained. In addition, sharing open data limits duplication of research efforts, which drives innovation. Similarly, the adoption of data management plans and structured archiving methods ensures sustainable and consistent management of scientific resources, facilitating their future reuse. This approach not only improves the quality of research, but also its visibility and impact in the scientific community (Sullivan & Millar, 2019). However, it should be stressed that the introduction of the data-driven approach in academia raises some major challenges.

Perhaps the most important is the management of data security, especially with regard to sensitive or personal information. Compliance with regulations such as GDPR (General Data Protection Regulation) in Europe has highlighted the critical importance of data security (Hodson, 2018). The management of access rights to information must be rigorously regulated to guarantee their confidentiality. In addition, the quality of the data remains a key issue: the information collected must be reliable and relevant so that it can truly feed strategic decisions. At the same time, the lack of data management skills among academic and administrative teams is a barrier to the adoption of these practices. Hence the importance of continuous training of staff to ensure effective data management and optimal use (Brinkman, 2020). The interoperability of data management systems is also a major challenge. Although many universities are implementing local solutions for data management, the exchange of information between institutions or researchers requires open and compatible systems. Cloud computing technologies and decentralized architectures are suitable solutions to meet these needs. However, their integration can lead to technical difficulties related to the compatibility of data systems and formats (Sullivan & Millar, 2019). In short, the Data-Driven approach in higher education offers considerable opportunities to improve academic management, optimize scientific research and stimulate innovation. However, its implementation requires a significant investment in infrastructure, data management, team training, and compliance with security and privacy standards. International best practices, such as those enacted by the FAIR principles and supported by platforms such as OpenAIRE, offer strong references to support institutions in their transition to more open and collaborative data management (Wilkinson et al., 2016). The ISIPA project, currently underway, is a concrete example of the implementation of a Data-Driven data management architecture, aimed at strengthening the institution's capacities in terms of scientific research and technological innovation.

In a desire to align with international standards, in particular the FAIR principles, ISIPA designs and develops a modern data management infrastructure. With a dual objective of optimizing data-based decision-making while facilitating the reuse of existing data, this initiative aims to centralize all academic productions generated within the institution, including dissertations, reports (daily, weekly, monthly, semester and annual), student internship reports and those of the Competence Center, or the students' tutored projects. Apart from responding to internal needs, this approach is part of an open science approach. By making its academic resources accessible, ISIPA fosters collaboration with other researchers and institutions, both nationally and internationally. The infrastructure in place is flexible, scalable and compliant with data management best practices. It allows unified and simplified access to educational, scientific and administrative resources. By integrating advanced metadata modules as well as a search engine based on semantic indexing, the university community as a whole can perform simple or complex queries, thus increasing the visibility and value of the data produced by the institution. In addition, ISIPA uses data from its own digital infrastructures, such as laboratory logs or data generated by the data center. All this information not only helps to optimize IT resources, but also to improve administrative processes. Thus, by adopting a data-driven approach, ISIPA is moving in the right direction and as a pioneer of digital transformation in the Congolese university context. More specifically, with this project to create a data pool for the implementation of the data-driven approach within ISIPA represents an inspiring model for the intelligent integration of data in African higher education, contributing to sustainably advancing the quality and impact of research and training in DR Congo. This project positions ISIPA as a key player in technological innovation and scientific research in the region.

4. PROGRESSIVE CONSTRUCTION OF A DATA-DRIVEN ECOSYSTEM

After consolidating the foundations of the data-driven approach, ISIPA is starting the gradual development of an integrated data management ecosystem to guide its decisions. As mentioned above, this project is based on several axes, including the collection, processing and analysis of information, while making data at the heart of the institution's essential missions, namely teaching, research and governance. Figure 1, below, illustrates this evolution, which is essentially based on three complementary pillars. The first concerns the strengthening of academic follow-up, through better control of student careers and continuous improvement of educational quality. The second pillar concerns the promotion of internal scientific productions, in order to promote the work carried out within the institution and to facilitate access and dissemination. Finally, the third axis concerns support for strategic decision-making, thanks to reliable and structured data to inform organizational, budgetary and prospective choices. By combining these three dimensions, ISIPA affirms its commitment to establishing data-driven governance and to anchor digital innovation in higher education in the long term.

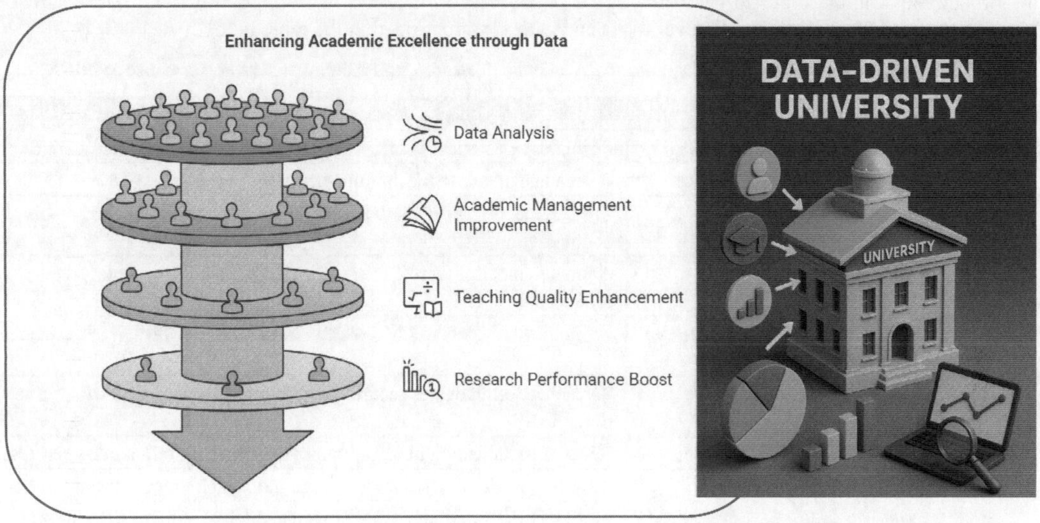

Figure 1. Enhancing Academic Excellence through Data

4.1 Dynamic and Individualized Academic Follow-Up

As part of its digital transformation, ISIPA has strengthened the academic follow-up of students by adopting advanced analysis tools. From now on, data relating to grades, attendance and participation are centralized in a unified system, allowing a quick and accurate diagnosis of educational needs. This integration facilitates a more detailed reading of individual courses and supports responsive learning management. Unlike the old system, which was limited to descriptive analyses after the fact, the new analysis environment allows for a predictive approach. Thanks to dynamic indicators, it is now possible to anticipate academic difficulties, detect potential for excellence and adapt support strategies in real time. This development is a major lever for improving the quality of teaching and promoting the success of each student.

4.2 Strategic Capitalization on Scientific Resources

ISIPA has set up a centralized platform for the archiving and exploitation of its academic resources with the idea of strengthening research activities and systematically structuring scientific production. Now, each data type is associated with a metadata repository. This system improves the traceability of scientific productions, promotes their reuse and facilitates thematic research in the context of various projects. Through this approach, ISIPA maximizes the value of its internal knowledge base, encourages increased collaboration between researchers and strengthens the scientific visibility of the institution. By launching this initiative, ISIPA is part of a dynamic of continuous scientific production, oriented towards innovation, collaboration and academic excellence.

4.3 Discreet but Powerful Support for Strategic Decisions

The Data-Driven orientation within ISIPA is no longer limited to day-to-day administrative management; It now plays a decisive role in supporting major strategic decisions. Rather than simply producing descriptive dashboards, the institution has developed forward-looking performance indicators, designed to monitor and anticipate the achievement of its institutional objectives such as improving the quality of teaching, scientific development and societal impact. Thanks to these advanced analytics tools, it becomes possible to visualize key trends—such as workforce growth, skills development, or the emergence of new projects—and to proactively realign strategic priorities based on observed outcomes. To support this approach, ISIPA has implemented the monitoring of several key indicators, summarized in the table below:

Table 2. Key Indicators for Monitoring Academic, Research, and Administrative Performance at ISIPA

No.	Indicator	Description
1	Academic Success Rate	Percentage of students successfully passing their exams or academic year.
2	Student Retention Rate	Percentage of students continuing their studies year-over-year.
3	Student Skills Progression	Measurement of the evolution of students' key competencies through continuous assessment.
4	Scientific Production	Annual number of theses, scientific articles, patents, or prototypes produced.
5	Digital Learning Resource Usage Rate	Frequency of access to LMS platforms and digital educational resources.
6	Graduate Employment Rate	Percentage of graduates securing employment in their field within a set timeframe.
7	Faculty Research Engagement	Level of participation in research projects, publications, and conferences.
8	Student Satisfaction Index	Results from satisfaction surveys regarding teaching quality and services.
9	Average Administrative Processing Time	Average time required to process student and administrative requests.
10	External Research Funding Rate	Proportion of external funding secured relative to the total research budget.

This structured system of indicators provides ISIPA's management with rapid, informed decision-making capabilities, thereby strengthening the institution's agility and resilience in a constantly evolving academic environment.

5. CHALLENGES AND RISKS OF THE DATA-DRIVEN APPROACH

The adoption of the data-driven approach within ISIPA has been accompanied by multiple challenges. One of the main obstacles encountered was the technical complexity of the project. The need to collect, centralize and analyze data from various systems has required not only the acquisition of advanced technologies, but also a considerable strengthening of internal data governance skills. The institution has made significant investments, both in terms of physical infrastructure and the ongoing training of its staff, to ensure the performance and sustainability of the initiative. As Bihani et al. (2020) point out, such a transition to data-driven management requires a robust technological base, combined with targeted skills development to ensure the quality of the analyses produced. In addition to these technical requirements, there is a major cybersecurity issue. Nothing is left to chance when it comes to the protection of sensitive data. Strict arrangements are made for the management of confidential data such as students' personal information, academic results and scientific productions. In this sense, ISIPA has put in place a set of strict security measures such as systematic data encryption, strict access restrictions and the adoption of protocols in line with international privacy standards. The primary objective of these provisions is to create a trusted digital environment in which innovation is accompanied by a strong ethical responsibility. As such, the literature highlights the importance of these measures in the management of sensitive data (Smith & Johnson, 2019). In addition, it should also be stressed that the technical architecture of the institutional system deserves to be treated with the utmost seriousness insofar as the scientific data pool is based on the open-source platform DSpace 7, recognized for its modularity and scalability. It has been integrated with existing academic systems – such as the student management system, the research project database and the library's documentation system – through standardized application programming interfaces (APIs) and automated synchronisation mechanisms. To ensure scalability, the entire infrastructure was containerized using Docker and hosted in a hybrid cloud environment, combining on-premises resources and secure hosting through a regional provider. This configuration ensures high availability of the service and paves the way for gradual integration with national and international open infrastructures (OpenAIRE, 2023).

Finally, a structured impact evaluation is underway to measure the concrete effects of this transformation. The first results are encouraging: the adoption rate exceeds 65% among teacher-researchers and 48% among master's students, who have already submitted at least one scientific paper. In addition, the visibility of the institution's academic output has improved significantly, with a 37% increase in the number of publications indexed on platforms such as Google Scholar or AJOL (African Journals Online), compared to the previous year. Longitudinal analyses are planned to better assess the contribution of the reservoir to research performance, the development of scientific partnerships, and the strategic reuse of data from a management and valorization perspective (OECD, 2023; Tenopir et al., 2020).

6. CONCLUSION

The integration of a Data-Driven approach within ISIPA marks a significant turning point in the way data is managed, analyzed and exploited within the institution. The adoption of this strategy not only makes it possible to personalize and improve the academic follow-up of students, but also to optimize strategic decision-making processes and enhance scientific resources. However, this transition to data-driven management is not without its challenges. To make this transition to data-driven management a success, ISIPA has acquired a robust and modern data center and laboratory. Practical work rooms and business processes have also undergone huge transformations with a clear objective: to capture as much data as possible, to protect sensitive data and to create an environment conducive to innovation and academic excellence. By working in this direction, administrators, teachers and students can rely on reliable information, available in real time, to better teach, learn and make informed decisions. However, it should be noted that this process of digitization towards the data-driven approach requires constant attention. It would also be necessary to monitor the financial and human resources required to take into account the evolution of business processes and the volume of data available. In conclusion, this initiative offers an interesting model for other educational institutions wishing to undertake a similar transformation, highlighting the importance of strategic and secure data management in improving the quality of higher education.

REFERENCES

Bihani, P., Pandey, R., & Maheshwari, R. (2020). Building a Data-Driven Organization: Tools, Skills, and Strategies. *International Journal of Computer Applications*, *176*(27), 25–30.

Borgman, C. L. (2018). Big data, little data, no data: Scholarship in the networked world. MIT Press.

Brinkman, R. (2020). Cross-institutional data sharing in universities: Challenges and frameworks for integration. *International Journal of Data Management*, *34*(4), 51-67.

Brynjolfsson, E., & McAfee, A. (2014). The Second Machine Age: Work, Progress, and Prosperity in a Time of Brilliant Technologies. W. W. Norton & Company.

Caldwell, M., et al. (2020). Using learning analytics to enhance student success in higher education. *Higher Education Research & Development*, *39*(6), 1090-1103.

Chen, M., Mao, S., & Liu, Y. (2012). Big Data: A Survey. *Mobile Networks and Applications*, *19*(1), 171-209.

Harris, M., Smith, J., & Pires, R. (2020). Data-Driven Decisions in Higher Education: Enhancing Performance and Innovation. *Journal of Educational Technology*, *58*(3), 45-56.

Hodson, R. (2018). The transition to open science: Implications for universities and research institutions. *Open Science Review*, 5(3), 23-35.

ISIPA. (2025). Higher Institute of Pedagogy and Computer Science of Kinshasa. Retrieved from https://www.isipa.cd.

Jones, M., Taylor, K., & Patel, R. (2020). Leveraging Data for Academic and Research Excellence: Insights from Top Universities. *Journal of Higher Education*, *34*(2), 72-89.

Kitchin, R. (2014). Big Data and Human Geography: Opportunities, Challenges and Controversies. *Progress in Human Geography*, *38*(1), 131-146.

Kvale, S., & Brinkmann, S. (2009). InterViews: Learning the craft of qualitative research interviewing (2nd ed.). Sage Publications.

Lumivero. (2023). NVivo: Leading qualitative data analysis software. https://lumivero.com/products/nvivo/

Mayer-Schönberger, V., & Cukier, K. (2013). Big Data: A Revolution That Will Transform How We Live, Work, and Think. Houghton Mifflin Harcourt.

Mays, G., Johnson, R., & Richards, B. (2020). Exploring the Role of Data in African Higher Education Institutions. *Journal of African Educational Development*, *15*(2), 100-118.

Mays, T., Kamau, S., & Balaba, K. (2020). Big Data and Its Applications in African Universities: Opportunities and Challenges. *African Journal of Higher Education*, *25*(1), 12-28.

Michener, W. K. (2015). Ten simple rules for creating a good data management plan. *PLoS Computational Biology*, *11*(10), e1004525.

OECD. (2023). National strategy for data management based on the FAIR principles. https://www.oecd.org/en/publications/access-to-public-research-data-toolkit_a12e8998-en/national-strategy-for-data-management-based-on-the-fair-principles_d3da5ac3-en.html

OECD. (2023). The Promise and Pitfalls of Data-Driven Research Systems. https://www.oecd.org/science/data-driven-research-systems

OpenAIRE. (2023). OpenAIRE Guidelines for Institutional Repositories. https://guidelines.openaire.eu

Smith, J., & Johnson, K. (2019). Data security in education: Policy and practice in digital environments. *Journal of Educational Technology & Society*, *22*(4), 35–46.

Sullivan, C., & Millar, S. (2019). Data management and open research in higher education: Practices and challenges. *Journal of Open Research*, *7*(2), 113-125.

Tenopir, C., et al. (2015). Data sharing by scientists: Practices and perceptions. *PLoS ONE*, *10*(6), e0134826.

Tenopir, C., Sandusky, R. J., Allard, S., & Birch, B. (2020). Research data sharing: Practices and perceptions of scientists. *PLoS ONE*, *15*(12), e0243023.

Wilkinson, M. D., et al. (2016). The FAIR guiding principles for scientific data management and stewardship. *Scientific Data*, 3, 160018.

Zhao, L., & Liu, Y. (2021). Embracing the Big Data Revolution: Opportunities and Challenges for Academic Institutions. *International Journal of Educational Data Mining*, *14*(2), 56-70.

GOVERNANCE STRUCTURING FOR BOT LAB AT SENAC UNIVERSITY CENTER: PLANNING, IMPLEMENTATION AND OPERATIONALIZATION

Nilo Sergio Maziero Petrin, Julio Pedro de Siqueira Júnior and Rômulo Francisco de Souza Maia
SENAC University Center, Brazil

ABSTRACT

With the advent of business process automation, organizations' workforce can stop performing repetitive tasks and start performing more analytical activities with greater added value. Aware of current market demands, Centro Universitário SENAC, São Paulo, Brasil, created Bot Lab, its Business Process Automation Laboratory. This article proposes a framework for the governance of the laboratory's processes, to guide the organization and standardization of services offered to faculty and students who will benefit from it. The framework incorporates widely adopted best practices recommended by the methodologies currently used for project management, business process management, quality management, risk analysis and other relevant activities that will be applied. By providing organized support and control of the activities over a user-friendly service catalog, we aim to maximize laboratory performance and improve the learning experience, while leveraging innovative digital methods and tools to their fullest potential.

KEYWORDS

BPM – Business Process Management, Business Process Automation, RPA (Robotic Process Automation), Bot Lab, IT Governance

1. INTRODUCTION

1.1 Contextualization

Technological hyperdevelopment and its immediate, often disruptive, impacts generate a value competitive advantage for institutions that adapt swiftly. Understanding these changes, participating in an evolutionary way to remain updated and relevant, becomes fundamental the development of professionals prepared for the contemporary market. Process automation and business process management are part of the so-called digital transformation and are among the innovations that have revolutionized previous ways of performing repetitive activities. Mature governance combined with the application of best practices will allow the development and automation of process flows, assignment of roles and responsibilities, use of standardized forms, accountability, measurement of continuous improvement, increasing the satisfaction of your current audience and potential users.

Recognizing these changes, the SENAC University Center established a Bot Lab in 2023 to train faculty and students in automation and BPM (ITFORUM, 2023). However, to ensure an efficient and effective utilization of this facility, a governance model must provide clear policies, guidelines, standards, and goals. Such a model fosters alignment, accountability, and continuous improvement, enabling the institution to attract new partnerships and students and better serve its academic community.

1.2 Objective

The main objective of this research project is to identify, analyze and implement a process governance framework that supports both academic and professional development in SENAC's Bot Lab. The framework includes policies, guidelines, processes, and activities tailored to the needs of faculty and students. To achieve this overarching objective, we have defined three specific aims:

a) Research and identify existing governance models that can be applied to the Bot Lab context.

b) Develop governance guidelines that align with institutional policies and industry the best practices in IT and process governance.

c) Propose and refine a process flow framework that can be adopted for the Bot Lab.

1.3 Methodology

Research methodology involves systematic methods and procedures for observation, data collection, their analysis and solution implementation, with the aim of reaching conclusions and/or evidence, and can be used in different areas of knowledge (Almeida, 2021). Given the objectives of our work, the methodology that is best applied is exploratory research. Exploratory research aims to provide a greater understanding of the problem in question, helping to clarify and detail it (Silva, 2004). It includes bibliographical research, interviews with experts or people with experience in the topic studied, and carrying out case studies (Gil, 2010).

- Literature Review: We examined books, academic journals, and credible web sources on governance, Labs management standards, Project Management and BPM best practices guides.
- Exploratory Approach: Meetings and interviews were held with the Bot Lab coordinator and scientific initiation students to identify operational challenges and gather input on potential governance structures.
- Applied Focus: The framework is intended to solve a specific real-world challenge—managing the Bot Lab effectively—drawing on proven tools.

1.4 Organization

This manuscript is structured as follows: Chapter 1 introduces the context, research problem, objectives, and methodology. Chapter 2 provides a literature review, focusing on the main concepts and best practices for Bot Lab governance. Chapter 3 presents the proposed Bot Lab governance framework in detail. Chapter 4 discusses the applicability and potential challenges of implementing this framework. Chapter 5 offers concluding remarks and outlines future work, including the development of a comprehensive service catalog for the Bot Lab.

2. LITERATURE REVIEW

Our framework for Bot Lab is designed to enable the efficient and controlled intake of requests, process oversight, and service delivery, fostering an environment conducive to both academic and practical activities in process automation. Drawing on industry's best practices and widely accepted standards, this section synthesizes essential concepts that support the governance model.

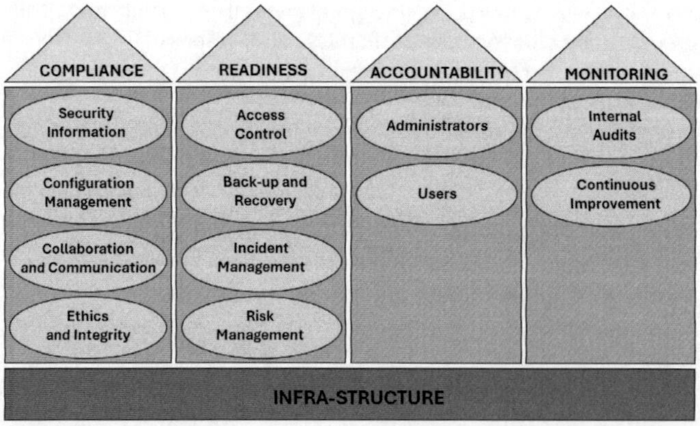

Prepared by the authors.

Figure 1. Pillars and macroprocesses defined for Bot Lab Management

2.1 Initial Surveys and Exploratory Research

Meetings and interviews conducted by SENAC's research and scientific initiation students with the Bot Lab coordinator provided preliminary insights into the lab's existing structure and operational needs. Four foundations pillars emerged: compliance; readiness; accountability; monitoring and control. These pillars reflect key concerns in IT governance (COBIT, ITIL, ISO 38500) and BPM (ABPMP Brasil, 2013). Figure 1 illustrates the macroprocesses associated with each pillar, serving as the organizational basis for detailed processes and subprocesses.

2.1.1 Compliance

Compliance addresses how the Bot Lab adheres to institutional and external regulations, including: security information; configuration management; collaboration and communication; ethics and integrity, as follows:

Security Information

According to the NBR ISO/IEC 27002 standard (ABNT, 2022), responsibilities for information security must be assigned in accordance with established policies, ensuring adequate protection of assets and effective execution of security processes. Information security is structured based on 3 subjects: confidentiality, integrity, and authenticity. Organizations must develop and follow information security policies and guidelines to ensure that these subjects are respected.

In terms of confidentiality, access should be restricted to authorized individuals only, protecting data at all stages of its life cycle. Authorized users should have access whenever necessary, and only to information for which they are authorized by the owner of the information, thus avoiding losses in programmed processes and keeping the information within the limits of its use. As for integrity, it is essential that the storage, processing, retrieval, and transmission of this information preserve its accuracy and meaning. To ensure authenticity, validation procedures, encryption, and other methods that prevent modification of the original information are used.

Configuration Management

According to the NBR ISO/IEC27002 standard (ABNT, 2022), configuration management comprises the procedures for controlling software installations in operating systems, so that they are carried out in compliance with good practices so that they are healthy and attempt to prevent attacks. The main guidelines should:

- Keep operating system and application software versions up to date.
- New application software that requires installation must be approved after analyzing the security aspects and impact on computer performance.
- Follow a strategy to return to the initial operating system condition or return to previous conditions.
- A registration system that stores the procedures adopted for each configuration operation, as well as the actions performed, is recommended.

Other relevant bibliographies are added to Change Management, Problem Management, and Incident Management from ITIL - Information Technology Infrastructure Library (AXELOS, 2019); to IT Planning and Governance (ISACA, 2012) through COBIT 5; and to the recommendations of the Information Technology Service Management Forum (ITSMF, 2006).

Collaboration and Communication

According to PMBOK® (PMI, 2021), communications management must begin with the identification of stakeholders who will be sources and receivers of information, then planning is carried out to ensure that communications will function properly from generation to collect, distribute, storage, retrieval, and organize. Communications planning must identify the information needs of each stakeholder, followed using tools and techniques that will ensure the quality of the content, completed by the distribution and management of documents, which will make communications available.

Ethics and Integrity

SENAC University Center has a Code of Ethics and Professional Conduct containing guidelines on the values, principles and conduct to be adopted and practiced by everyone within the institution.

The document is organized into general conduct, interpersonal relationships, relationships with customers, society, suppliers, partners, and the environment (SENAC, 2022).

2.1.2 Readiness

The theoretical bases for readiness for operational procedures can be divided into access control; data backup and restoration; incident management; risk assessment. To support these topics, the ABNT NBR ISO/IEC 27002 standard (ABNT, 2022) and the Project Management Body of Knowledge (PMI, 2021) were used.

Access Control

Access control seeks to detail guidelines for matters related to security, starting with physical access, which occurs by obtaining the laboratory key from the key center on the SENAC University Center campus, accompanied by their respective withdrawal and return records. In the laboratory there may be access via software, to the network, to the operating system, to information and to the application, as well as management of access and user responsibilities, following recommendations from (ABNT, 2022). An example of how to control access is to control data that can be accessed by a specific user and who can read, write, execute, and delete it.

Backup Storage and Data Restoration

The objective of backup is to protect the system against data loss, so that backup copies of information, software and images are constantly made and reviewed frequently following recommendations from (ABNT, 2022). The backup policy should define copy requirements across the organization, covering protection, retention, and ensuring that adequate resources are available for recovery after disasters or failures. Additionally, remote storage of copies, protection of information, and accurate records of backups and restoration procedures are necessary.

Incident Management

For the Information Technology Infrastructure Library – ITIL, an incident is understood as any event that is not part of the normal operation of a service and that results, or may result, in suspension or decline in the quality of the service (AXELOS, 2019). According to the NBR ISO/IEC27002 standard, information security incident management must be consistent and effective, communicating about the weaknesses and events that occurred in the incident (ABNT, 2022). In addition, ITIL also deals with problem management, which aims to identify and resolve the main causes of incidents, and change management, which executes changes with control and minimized risk. Guidelines for incident management should include incident response planning, monitoring, detection, and analysis procedures, as well as an incident management structure, with records of the events and procedures involved. To notify incidents, forms must be prepared containing the classification and details of the event, as well as the procedures adopted in response to the incident.

Risk Management

According to PMBOK® (PMI, 2021), risk is a condition of uncertainty that can be predicted and that, if it occurs, can affect the progress of a project's objectives and activities. Risks can be classified as those that have a negative impact, which indicate threats and can cause delays, cost increases and other abnormalities, and those that have a positive impact, which generate opportunities and benefits, such as delivery made ahead of schedule or savings in project costs. Risk assessment and management begins with identifying the risks inherent to the project or activity. The sources of the risks are identified and a qualitative analysis is prepared that evaluates the priority levels that each risk will have, and a quantitative analysis, which will provide objective data that demonstrate the impacts of the risks if they occur, defining responses to the risks, those responsible and deadlines.

2.1.3 Accountability

Staff and user responsibilities are covered in this section.

Administrators

To define roles and responsibilities, a tool recommended by PMBOK® is the RACI matrix, which allows team members to associate their responsibilities, facilitating monitoring and communication (PMI, 2021). The RACI matrix is an acronym in English, composed of the initials: Responsible, Accountable, Consulted, and Informed. To assemble the matrix, we build the horizontal lines with tasks or activities, and the vertical columns are filled with the names of the team members or their roles. After that, apply the letters "R, A, C, I" to identify the relationship between the tasks and each team member.

Laboratory Users

Laboratory users must have their responsibilities defined according to each activity in which they are participating (courses, training, scientific research, etc.) respecting the access control guidelines and the institution's code of ethics.

2.1.4 Monitoring and Control

This topic explores aspects of quality, including internal audits and continuous improvement, based on the ABNT ISO 9001 standard (ABNT, 2015).

Internal Audits

Auditing is a process that estimates the degree or level to which an organization's activities or procedures correspond to pre-established criteria. Internal audits, according to ISO 9001:2015, must be carried out at planned intervals and with the aim of gathering information to monitor established quality guidelines (ABNT, 2015). To carry out audits, in addition to frequency, methods, responsibilities, criteria and scope must be defined, to establish the objective of the audit and consequently the criteria for analyzing its results. After carrying out the audits, their results are reported to higher authorities and, if applicable, corrective actions are taken. All information involved in the audit process must be retained and stored to serve as proof of audit performance and as a knowledge base for the quality program.

Continuous Improvement

In the context of the ISO 9001:2015 standard, the organization must always seek continuous improvement of processes, aiming at the adequacy, efficiency, and effectiveness of the quality system. As a tool for implementing continuous improvement, the PDCA cycle can be used (Plan – Do – Check – Act). Starting with planning that defines objectives and expected results, followed by implementation, and then monitoring and analysis, the PDCA cycle ends with actions to improve process performance (ABNT, 2015).

2.2 Process Management

Business Process Management (BPM – Business Process Management) is the way of visualizing operations with a focus on the work performed to deliver a product or service, regardless of the functional areas involved. It starts at a higher level, which is subdivided into subprocesses, which are carried out through activities and tasks, as recommended by the CBOK (ABPMP Brasil, 2013).

2.2.1 Architecture, Mapping and Classification of Processes

Process Architecture aims to standardize, classify and group transversal processes according to affinity and origin criteria, to provide a form of organization and visualization. Mapping with BPMN notation can start with macroprocesses, followed by processes, activities, and tasks. It is also possible to start with an AS IS operational model (Usirono, 2015). For process nomenclature, the PCF framework (Process Classification Framework) from the American Productivity & Quality Center organization (APQC, 2019) is a good starting point. This classification provides naming standards and structures that can be used to create an initial process model (ABPMP Brasil, 2013).

2.2.2 Performance Management

The main objective of structuring governance is to maintain good functioning and constant evolution, focused on clear and defined processes (ISACA, 2022). The ISO 38500 standard presents the basic principles of responsibility, strategy, procurement, compliance, and human behavior. Another challenge is monitoring these processes, which can be done using performance and compliance indicators, which will provide at any time the current state of activity compliance and achievement of goals (Usirono, 2015).

2.3 Proposed Framework Design

2.3.1 The Framework

A framework is the representation of a process or sets of processes in a structured way, which groups knowledge, theories, and best practices, facilitating understanding, learning and adoption of the processes involved (Usirono, 2015). For grouping and orchestrating processes, and assembling the framework structure, BPM works with processes running end-of-the-end, organized into activities that pass through multiple business functions, offering a structured view of the processes (Baldam, *et al.*, 2014).

For this purpose, the CBOK process management best practices guide, from ABPMP, recommends a structure, in which the vertical columns represent the functional areas of the business and horizontally we have the business processes that, from the initial input, are subdivided into activities distributed among the various business functions, until the process is completed with the output.

Using this recommendation as a model, the Bot Lab's governance framework was created, as shown in Figure 2. For each functional (horizontal) macroprocess, standards and procedures must be established relating to each support pillar for Bot Lab governance. In each vertically represented pillar, subprocesses are established, which must follow the best practices highlighted in the literature review above.

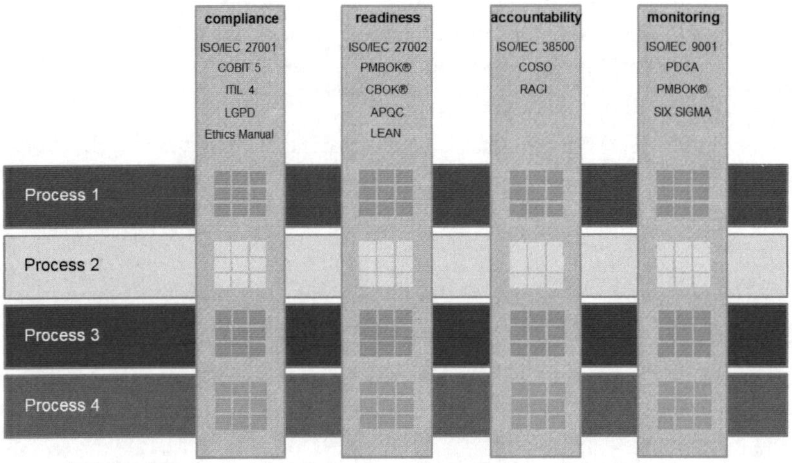

Prepared by the authors

Figure 2. Proposed Framework for Bot Lab Process Governance

3. APPLICATION

The creation of processes and services using the Bot Lab framework allows the elaboration of processes in an orderly and complete manner, as well as performance metrics (Usirono, 2015). The Process and Subprocess fields must be filled in with the respective names chosen for identification. An indicator field must contain a formula or method for measuring success or failure in the execution of the process, being able to measure effectiveness and efficiency. An Owner field can be created using responsibility roles, for this you can use the RACI matrix. In the lines of activities, the tasks involved in the execution of the process will be described in a unitary manner, and its respective functional area will then be defined for each task, which may include internal sectors of the laboratory or external sectors, such as, for example, different sectors of SENAC. For each activity, the solution will be defined that will correspond to the task to be performed, created in accordance with the standards, practices and tools available in the theoretical framework, allowing each activity to be created in detail with its respective actions, which once carried out, will complete the task.

During 2024, four training sessions were carried out at basic and intermediate levels, with the aim of making participants competent in using process automation and business management tools. These training courses were aimed at students, teachers, and employees of the institution, providing a practical and applied learning environment, conducted by (ANYWHERE AUTOMATION, 2023). In total, the training reached an average of 120 participants, contributing to the development of technical and strategic skills essential for digital transformation and innovation in organizational processes.

A scientific initiation project is scheduled for 2025, which will have the support of 3 professors and will create a catalog of services for the use of the laboratory. Performance indicators can be improved as processes mature. We can mention some examples as follows: level of user's satisfaction; number of incidents; response time for the demands; number of automations executed by then users, etc.

4. DISCUSSION

This work provides a model for the future construction of processes and the Bot Lab service catalog, as well as overcoming the difficulties faced in the first year of using the laboratory, we can map challenges and mitigation strategies in order to solve some issues, such as: lack of defined processes and forms; manual access and activity controls; lack of setup tools to reestablish the current status of databases and processes when starting a new training class; automatic recording of operations to audit trails; automation of routine activities. Thus, once the needs and theoretical bases that contain the solutions to these problems have been mapped, the next step is to create a list of activities that meets each item of the governance pillars, using best market practices as a reference.

With the processes mapped, the subprocesses and their activities are described, these can be organized to use functional resources and best practices and tools, as shown in Figure 2 – Framework for creating Bot Lab processes. In this figure, each vertical pillar represents a governance area, while the processes are represented by horizontal rectangles that can be subdivided into subprocesses, which are composed of multiple activities distributed among the governance pillars. Thus, interdisciplinary processes are created focused on the delivery of products or services, which can be managed by a person responsible, who interacts and covers the various areas of governance.

The framework represents the set of best practices, techniques and process management tools and is organized into vertical pillars representing the functional areas (Usirono, 2015). The processes are organized in a horizontal position, or in an overturned manner, with a focus on the execution of the processes by a single agent or owner, making the structure process-oriented (Lavorienti, 2011). Each process can have one or more subprocesses, which, in turn, are subdivided into activities, which are the stages of lesser granularity. The activities represent the specific tasks that make up each subprocess, and use components from functional areas, internal or external to the laboratory, but independently, providing the agent or process owner with the flexibility to direct and make the process more agile and efficient.

In a university context, research, teaching and extension needs require flexibility and balanced governance. The framework meets both corporate management aspects (efficiency, security, control) and academic needs (experimentation, innovation, student training).

5. FINAL CONSIDERATIONS

The Bot Lab, recently opened on the Santo Amaro campus of SENAC University Center, needs a governance model to be created for its operation. Based on the data collected from the professor responsible for the laboratory, the theoretical framework was surveyed, and a framework was developed that provides a method for building the governance elements. The governance model of this functional framework, developed based on the best practices and tools on the market, will allow the creation and management of Bot Lab processes and services, in addition to structuring administration, and can be the basis for the creation of a service catalog, which will enable the governance of the laboratory and the satisfaction of its users, as follows:

i) process flow designs to meet each planned service.
ii) request and control forms, with provision of a catalog of academic services.
iii) automation of processes and incorporation of forms into established flows.
iv) validation and operationalization of the model.

This framework can be replicated in others Bot Labs and Universities and constitutes a practical model that ensure a governance of processes on academic's lab environments.

ACKNOWLEDGEMENT

We are grateful to the SENAC University Center, Santo Amaro campus, for providing a conducive environment and essential support for successfully implementing the proposed framework. Furthermore, we thank the students who dedicated themselves and participated in the experiments applying the methodology proposed in this work. This work shows the spirit of learning and innovation that characterizes our institution but also highlights the dedication and enthusiasm of our students. We will continue to explore the ever-evolving challenges and frontiers towards the best practices for the governance of Bot Lab.

REFERENCES

ABPMP Brasil (2013). BPM CBOK: Guia para o Gerenciamento de Processos de Negócio Corpo Comum de Conhecimento ABPMP BPM CBOK V3.0.

Almeida, Ítalo D'artagnan (2021). Metodologia do trabalho científico. Recife: Ed. UFPE. Disponível em: https://repositorio.ufpe.br/bitstream/123456789/49435/1/METODOLOGIA%20DO%20TRABALHO%20CIENT%C3%8DFICO.pdf. Accessed 04 nov. 2024.

APQC (2019). American Productivity & Quality Center. Process Classification Framework (PCF). Houston: APQC. Disponível em: https://www.apqc.org/process-frameworks. Accessed 12 nov. 2024.

ABNT (2015). Associação Brasileira De Normas Técnicas. NBR ISO 9001:2015: Sistemas de gestão de qualidade - Requisitos. Rio de Janeiro.

ABNT (2022). Associação Brasileira De Normas Técnicas. NBR ISO/IEC 27002:2022: Segurança da informação, segurança cibernética e proteção à privacidade - Controles de segurança da informação. Rio de Janeiro.

AUTOMATION ANYWHERE (2023). Free RPA Community Edition: for small businesses, developers, and students. Available at https://www.automationanywhere.com/br/lp/community-edition-old Acessado em 16-08-2023.

AXELOS (2019). ITIL® Foundation: ITIL 4 Edition. Londres, AXELOS Limited.

Baldam, Rozenfeld, Vale (2014). Gerenciamento de Processos de Negócio – BPM: Uma referência para aplicação prática. Elsevier.

Gil, A. C.(2010). *Como elaborar projetos de pesquisa*. 5. ed. São Paulo: Atlas.

ITFORUM (2023). *Automation Anywhere e Senac inauguram centro de inovação em São Paulo*. Available at: https://itforum.com.br/noticias/automation-anywhere-senac-inovacao/ . Published 21-06-2023. Accessed 16-08-2023.

ITSMF. ISO/IEC 20000 (2006). *The IT Service Management Forum: A Pocket Guide*. ISBN-10 9077212795.

ISACA (2012). *COBIT 5. A Business Framework for the Governance and Management of Enterprise IT*. ISACA. ISBN-13 978-1604202373.

ISACA (2022). *Effective IT Governance at Your Fingertips*. Available at https://www.isaca.org/resources/cobit . Accessed 16-08-2023.

Lavorienti, M. S. (2011). *O tombamento da gestão empresarial por meio de processos*. Blog do BPM, 2 mar. 2011. Available at: https://blogdobpm.blogspot.com/2011/03/o-tombamento-da-gestao-empresarial-por.html. Accessed 29 out. 2024.

Muniz, A., et al. (2022). *Jornada RPA e Hiperautomação: Como acelerar a transformação digital somando tecnologia e processos inteligentes*. Rio de Janeiro: Editora Brasport.

PMI (2021). Project Management Institute. Guia do Conhecimento em Gerenciamento de Projetos (Guia PMBOK). 7 ed. Pennsylvania: Project Management Institute, Philadelphia.

SENAC (2022). *Código de Ética e Conduta Profissional*. São Paulo.

Silva, C. R. O. (2004). *Metodologia do Trabalho Científico*. Centro Federal de Educação Tecnológica do Ceará. Fortaleza.

Usirono, C. H. (2015). *Escritório de Processos: BPMO – Business Process Management Office*. Brasport.

THE USABILITY OF AND USER EXPERIENCE WITH ELECTRONIC GAMING MACHINES AT CASINOS: EVALUATION OVER THE PAST TWO YEARS

Victor K. Y. Chan
Macao Polytechnic University
Rua de Luis Gonzaga Gomes, Macao, China

ABSTRACT

This article seeks to not only evaluate gamblers'/users' perception of electronic gaming machines' (EGMs') usability and user experience but also compare such evaluations over the period between the years 2022 and 2024 with a view to tracking how gamblers'/users' perception of EGMs' usability and user experience evolved over such a period of casinos' digital transformation. Such evaluations were based on the backbone constructs of the technology acceptance model (TAM) and the extended unified theory of acceptance and use of technology (UTAUT2) alongside the additional construct "trust" as they were commonly operationalized in the literature. Such constructs as "perceived ease of use" (EOU), "perceived usefulness" (PU), "perceived risk" (RISK), "attitude" (ATTD), "social influence" (SI), "innovativeness" (INNOVA), "stress to use a technology" (STRESS), and "trust" (TR) in respect of EGMs were rated by n = 693 respondents in a questionnaire survey conducted in phase 1 (in late 2022) in Macao and similarly by n = 179 respondents in phase 2 (in late 2024). Paired-samples t-tests were employed to pairwise compare the ratings of these constructs independently in each of the two phases. It was found in phase 2 that, of all these constructs, EOU, INNOVA, STRESS registered the highest population mean construct ratings whilst RISK and TR the lowest. These findings are in partial contrast to the counterparts in phase 1 when RISK's population mean rating was the lowest and ATTD's the highest. In essence, these findings reiterate the 2022 advice that risk prevention be prioritized for amelioration, and recommend that gamblers' trust in EGMs be so prioritized in addition by 2024. Also, the findings, in effect, further advocate keeping up gamblers'/users' perceived ease of use, self-evaluated innovativeness, and mitigation of perceived stress in using EGMs by 2024 as opposed to maintaining gamblers'/users' attitude toward EGMs back in 2022. As EGMs emulate mechanical slot machines and typify electronic gambling equipment at casinos, such findings epitomize one major aspect of the outcomes of digital transformation at casinos, which are generally regarded as a tendentious leisure industry and thus seldom studied in the information systems literature.

KEYWORDS

Usability, User Experience, Electronic Gaming Machines, Casino, Evolution, Digital Transformation

1. INTRODUCTION

1.1 Casinos' Digital Transformation and Electronic Gaming Machines

Despite its fundamental purpose for gamblers' leisure, casinos are popularly regarded as a tendentious, non-mainstream entertainment industry (Chan and Lei, 2024; Marfels, 2001). Casinos' digital transformation has been almost a virgin land that has barely been studied. For example, though instrumental in their digital transformation, casinos' electronic gambling equipment is highly specialized information systems specific to the industry, and far less often investigated in extant literature on usability and user experience than those applicable to other industries or those generic information or electronic systems. Therefore, Liu et al (2021) was keenly in favor of further study into "the acceptance level of customers (gamblers) regarding advanced technology on the casino floor."

Of the limited researches (Chan and Lei, 2024), Nisbet (2006) analyzed the attributes of gambling technologies that affect consumer (gambler) intention to use card-based gambling in Australia by means of a modified version of the technology acceptance model (TAM) and a kindred 23-item questionnaire administered to 134 patrons (gamblers) of two gambling venues. Structural equation modelling affirmed that "usefulness" is a significant predictor of "intention to use" card-based gambling systems, and that "ease-of-use" also exerted a positive effect on "intention to use" the technologies.

To an extent, slot machines' evolution epitomizes at least one major aspect of Casinos' digital transformation as the machines morphed from their mechanical operation to their electronic counterpart, known commonly as electronic gaming machines (EGMs) and by now dominating casino floors (Chan and Lei, 2024; Liu et al, 2021; Cummings and Brewer, 1994). Whereas they were historically the forerunner of electronic gambling equipment at casinos, they themselves have undergone metamorphosis over the years. Today, modern EGMs are often characterized by their advanced designs like curved and touch screens (Chan and Lei, 2024; Liu et al, 2021). Financially, they are the most profitable game in casinos across quite some locales worldwide (Chan and Lei, 2024; Turner and Horbay, 2004). EGMs are believed to engender immersion in the form of what is called "slot machine zone" or a "trance-like" state typified by gamblers' diminished attention to time passing and gambling-irrelevant events during their use (Chan and Lei, 2024; Murch and Clark, 2021). In lay terms, EGMs are so enchanting that gamblers may be unconscious of the passage of time and the reality in the environs. Whilst there are probably myriad perspectives underlying such enticement, the usability and user experience perspectives per se of EGMs, being information systems, may deserve more thorough analysis than what is currently in the literature.

1.2 Technology Acceptance Model and Unified Theory of Acceptance and Use of Technology

Albeit the TAM has been conventionally, if not classically, applied for decades to uncover the factors conducive to users' acceptance of information technologies and systems, its factors may be regarded as insufficient to encompass all aspects of such acceptance. For instance, it did not embrace such factors/constructs as facilitating conditions, social influence, etc. (Chan and Lei, 2024; Dwivedi et al, 2019), so the unified theory of acceptance and use of technology (UTAUT) (Chan and Lei, 2024; Dwivedi et al, 2019) was subsequently put forward as an alternative with elevated compendiousness. As the name implies, the extended unified theory of acceptance and use of technology (UTAUT2) further extends UTAUT by incorporating the factors/constructs of hedonic motivation, price and habit (Chan and Lei, 2024; Singh et al, 2020). This theoretical extension has thus far been applied to profuse information technologies and systems in identifying the determinants of users' acceptance of them. For example, in the context of mobile payment, Oliveira et al (2016) found factors like "compatibility," "perceived technology security," "performance expectations," "innovativeness," and "social influence" to have significant direct and indirect effects on the adoption of mobile payment and the "intention to recommend" this technology (Chan and Lei, 2024). The relevance of customers' "intention to recommend" mobile payment technology in social networks and other means of communication was also verified, justifying its inclusion in social marketing campaigns and in future technology adoption studies (Chan and Lei, 2024). Specifically in the realm of mobile wallets, Singh et al. (2020) attested that "ease of use," "usefulness," "perceived risk," and "attitude" exerted significant effects on users' "intention to use" mobile wallets, which in turn influenced users' "perceived satisfaction" and "recommendation to use" mobile wallet services (Chan and Lei, 2024). They also affirmed the significant moderating effects of "stress to use" and "social influence" on users' "perceived satisfaction" and "recommendation to use" mobile wallet services (Chan and Lei, 2024).

1.3 The Current Study

Among the scant literature on the related realm, Chan and Lei (2024) evaluate gamblers'/users' perception of EGMs' usability and user experience in perspectives represented by the TAM's and the UTAUT2's factors/constructs and the additional construct "trust" (Alalwan et al, 2017). Given the temporality of perceived usability of and/or user experience with information systems having long been established (Karapanos et al, 2009), this article attempts to track the aforesaid gamblers'/users' perception of EGMs' usability and user experience over time from the time point in late 2022 to that in late 2024 in order to reveal how such usability and user experience evolved over the two years as an indicator of how this single aspect of casinos' digital transformation transpired progressively over the period. Dual cross-sectional research design was adopted to compare the usability and user experience as gauged by the TAM's and the UTAUT2's factors/constructs and the additional construct "trust" in 2022 with those in 2024. In essence, the comparison charted the "teething" over the two years as to the adaptation of the gamblers/users to the EGMs, which themselves were undergoing continual development, after decades of mechanical slot machines in operation. Equivalently, it charted the human aspects of casinos' digital transformation of one of their mainstream games (Browne et al, 2023). Specifically, the comparison identifies any improvement or deterioration over the two years in gamblers'/users' perceived usability and/or user experience as per any of the aforementioned factors/constructs.

2. METHODOLOGY

2.1 Materials

The data samples of this study were collected in a survey in two phases, respectively, in late 2022 and late 2024. Both administered basically the same questionnaire in Macao (also spelt as "Macau"), which was on average regarded as the world's largest gambling city in more than a decade (Metaxas and Folinas, 2021). Data collection was part of students' coursework in a course on system analysis and design, phase 1 being in the academic year 2022/2023 and phase 2 in 2024/2025. The questionnaire was compiled by the author who was the professor in charge of the course. The questionnaire sought to measure the constructs of the TAM and the UTAUT2, namely, the "perceived ease of use" (EOU), the "perceived usefulness" (PU), the "perceived risk" (RISK), the "attitude" (ATTD), the "social influence" (SI), the "intention to use" (INTU), the "innovativeness" (INNOVA), the "stress to use a technology" (STRESS), the "perceived satisfaction" (SATISFN), and the "recommendation to use" (RECOMD), together with the additional construct "trust" (TR) (as borrowed from Alalwan et al., 2017) in connection with gamblers'/users' perception of EGMs' usability and user experience. In particular, each of these constructs was operationalized by a few observed variables, each being measured by one question in the questionnaire on a scale of 1 to 7, with 1 strongly disagreeing to the question (in the form of a statement) and 7 strongly agreeing to the question. In other words, the rating of each question by each respondent became the corresponding observed variable's value for the respondent. Such operationalization of the TAM's and the UTAUT2's constructs and the additional construct "trust" almost exactly adhered to the extant literature, e.g., Singh et al (2020) and Alalwan et al. (2017) respectively.

In each phase, a few copies of the questionnaire were posted online on the Tencent Wenjuan survey platform, each copy being accessible through its corresponding Internet domain names and access QR codes. Each team of students picked one distinct copy and invited by e-mail, instant messaging or otherwise appropriate acquaintances of theirs to respond to the questionnaire copy through the corresponding Internet domain names or access QR codes. Each team then wrote an essay on the way they invited respondents, the total number of invitations, etc. alongside some descriptive statistics and analysis of the data so collected. The essay was graded as part of the students' coursework assessment for some bonus marks on top of the basic marks for the rest of the coursework.

The respondents were all aged 16 years or above. This age of 16 years aimed to include respondents having gambled outside of Macao where the legal age for gambling casino was a few years higher. At the beginning of the questionnaire, they were well informed of the survey's purpose, the authors' and thus the students' university, the university's contacts, the questionnaire's anonymity, the strict confidentiality of the response data, their being totally voluntary in responding and their absolute right to terminate at any time when responding. Also, right before the questions, the questionnaire illustrated by means of a photograph of a typical EGM at a casino what "EGM" referred to. The data collected by all the teams in each phase were pooled to form a sample of $n = 693$ respondents in phase 1 (in 2022) and $n = 179$ respondents in phase 2 (in 2024).

2.2 Methods

The analysis only included the TAM and the UTAUT2 constructs that usually acted as independent or moderating variables in the TAM and the UTAUT2 modelling, namely, EOU, PU, RISK, ATTD, SI, INNOVA, and STRESS, together with TR. In other words, constructs that usually took the role of dependent variables, such as INTU, SATISFN, and RECOMD, were excluded because these three constructs were usually to indicate results from the effects exerted by the independent and moderating variables above but not any users' evaluative perception of usability of and user experience with any information technology or system (e.g., EGMs in the present study). For each of all these TAM/UTAUT2 constructs included and the construct TR, the questionnaire questions for operationalization were occasionally framed in opposite directions within the construct such that a high rating for a particular question (i.e., for a particular observed variable) could mean good usability and user experience but bad usability and user experience for another question. Such ratings (i.e., such corresponding observed variables' values) accorded by each respondent were harmonized in a way such that a respondent's high rating for any question unilaterally corresponded to favorable evaluation of usability and user experience. Then, for each construct and each respondent, the corresponding harmonized ratings were averaged to yield a construct score. Then, for each phase, a paired samples *t*-test (two-tailed) was applied to the construct scores of each pair of these constructs over all respondents so as to find the constructs with construct scores systematically lower (or higher) than those of all other constructs in the phase. These constructs so found in each phase were the usability and user experience perspectives of the EGMs that disappointed the gamblers' most (or those that gamblers/users found most satisfactory) in the phase. Such *t*-test (two-tailed) findings in the two phases were juxtaposed correspondingly to discern any variation over the two years in between.

3. RESULTS

For each of the two phases, Table 1 depicts the results from the paired samples *t*-tests (two-tailed) applied to the construct scores of each construct pair over all respondents. Also included therein are the sample mean difference in the construct scores in each pair, the 95% confidence interval for the population mean difference, the *t*-statistic, its degrees of freedom, and its *p*-value. The results for phase 1 are from Chan and Lei (2024) and included for comparison purposes. If one is to interpret the *t*-statistics in the table as those for one-tailed *t*-tests (for example, to test for positivity or negativity of the population mean differences in the construct scores in each construct pair), the *p*-values enumerated therein should be halved before treating them as *p*-values for the corresponding one-tailed *t*-tests.

Table 1. Results from the paired samples *t*-tests (two-tailed) and others for each of the two phases (in 2022 and 2024), those for phase 1 being from Chan and Lei (2024)

Difference in the construct scores in each construct pair	Phase 1 (in 2022)			Phase 2 (in 2024)		
	Sample mean	95% confidence interval	*t* (degrees of freedom), *p*-value	Sample mean	95% confidence interval	*t* (degrees of freedom), *p*-value
EOU – PU	−0.0437	−0.1172 to 0.0299	−1.165(692), 0.2450	0.2388	0.0520 to 0.4256	2.523(178), .013*
EOU – RISK	0.9275	0.7345 to 1.1205	9.436(692), 0.0000**	0.6453	0.2846 to 1.0059	3.531(178), .001**
EOU – ATTD	−0.1331	−0.2227 to −0.0436	−2.919(692), 0.0040**	−0.0629	−0.2585 to 0.1328	−.634(178), .527
EOU – SI	0.1461	0.0509 to 0.2413	3.014(692), 0.0030**	0.2081	−0.0032 to 0.4194	1.943(178), .054
EOU – INNOVA	0.6645	0.4537 to 0.8753	6.19(692), 0.0000**	−0.2495	−0.5286 to 0.0296	−1.764(178), .079
EOU – STRESS	0.6183	0.4226 to 0.8140	6.203(692), 0.0000**	−0.2439	−0.5808 to 0.0929	−1.429(178), .155
EOU – TR	−0.0178	−0.1097 to 0.0741	−0.38(692), 0.7040	0.5764	0.3411 to 0.8116	4.834(178), .000**
PU – RISK	0.9711	0.7742 to 1.1681	9.68(692), 0.0000**	0.4064	0.0321 to 0.7808	2.143(178), .034*
PU – ATTD	−0.0895	−0.1713 to −0.0076	−2.146(692), 0.0320**	−0.3017	−0.4918 to −0.1116	−3.131(178), .002**
PU – SI	0.1898	0.0984 to 0.2811	4.079(692), 0.0000**	−0.0307	−0.2433 to 0.1818	−.285(178), .776

PU – INNOVA	0.7082	0.4934 to 0.9229	6.473(692), 0.0000**	−0.4884	−0.7714 to −0.2053	−3.405(178), .001**
PU – STRESS	0.6620	0.4630 to 0.8610	6.532(692), 0.0000**	−0.4828	−0.8406 to −0.1249	−2.662(178), .008**
PU – TR	0.0259	−0.0668 to 0.1185	0.548(692), 0.5840	0.3375	0.0964 to 0.5786	2.763(178), .006**
RISK – ATTD	−1.0606	−1.2521 to −0.8691	−10.876(692), 0.0000**	−0.7081	−1.0640 to −0.3522	−3.926(178), .000**
RISK – SI	−0.7814	−0.9354 to −0.6274	−9.96(692), 0.0000**	−0.4372	−0.7222 to −0.1521	−3.027(178), .003**
RISK – INNOVA	−0.2630	−0.3895 to −0.1365	−4.081(692), 0.0000**	−0.8948	−1.1631 to −0.6265	−6.581(178), .000**
RISK – STRESS	−0.3092	−0.4146 to −0.2037	−5.758(692), 0.0000**	−0.8892	−1.1467 to −0.6317	−6.815(178), .000**
RISK – TR	−0.9453	−1.1289 to −0.7617	−10.108(692), 0.0000**	−0.0689	−0.3810 to 0.2432	−.436(178), .664
ATTD – SI	0.2792	0.1938 to 0.3646	6.419(692), 0.0000**	0.2710	0.0822 to 0.4597	2.833(178), .005**
ATTD – INNOVA	0.7976	0.5920 to 1.0033	7.616(692), 0.0000**	−0.1867	−0.4680 to 0.0946	−1.310(178), .192
ATTD – STRESS	0.7514	0.5606 to 0.9423	7.73(692), 0.0000**	−0.1811	−0.5220 to 0.1598	−1.048(178), .296
ATTD – TR	0.1153	0.0311 to 0.1995	2.69(692), 0.0070**	0.6392	0.4189 to 0.8595	5.725(178), .000**
SI – INNOVA	0.5184	0.3408 to 0.6960	5.731(692), 0.0000**	−0.4576	−0.6714 to −0.2439	−4.225(178), .000**
SI – STRESS	0.4722	0.3137 to 0.6307	5.849(692), 0.0000**	−0.4520	−0.7420 to −0.1621	−3.077(178), .002**
SI – TR	−0.1639	−0.2557 to −0.0721	−3.505(692), 0.0000**	0.3682	0.1786 to 0.5579	3.832(178), .000**
INNOVA – STRESS	−0.0462	−0.1611 to 0.0688	−0.789(692), 0.4310	0.0056	−0.2149 to 0.2261	.050(178), .960
INNOVA – TR	−0.6823	−0.8944 to −0.4702	−6.316(692), 0.0000**	0.8259	0.5338 to 1.1180	5.580(178), .000**
STRESS – TR	−0.6361	−0.8331 to −0.4391	−6.34(692), 0.0000**	0.8203	0.4710 to 1.1696	4.634(178), .000**

** $p < 0.01$
* $p < 0.05$
If one is to interpret the above *t*-statistics as those for one-tailed *t*-tests (for example, to test for positivity or negativity of the mean differences in the construct scores in each construct pair), the *p*-values above should be halved before treating them as *p*-values for the corresponding one-tailed *t*-tests.

From Table 1 and pinpointing the transition of the construct scores from phase 1 (in 2022) to phase 2 (in 2024), the following findings can be drawn:

- For phase 2, the population mean difference between EOU's and PU's construct scores and that between EOU's and TR's construct scores were positive and differed from zero at the 5% and 1% significance level (i.e., $p < 0.05$ and $p < 0.01$) respectively. This is in contrast to phase 1 when such mean differences gave rise to no statistical significance.
- On the contrary, for phase 2, the mean difference between EOU's and ATTD's construct scores, that between EOU's and SI's construct scores, that between EOU's and INNOVA's construct scores, and that between EOU's and STRESS's construct scores did not result in any statistical significance as opposed to their counterparts for phase 1.
- From phase 1 to phase 2, the mean difference between PU's and SI's construct scores no longer ended up with statistical significance, and it drifted from positivity to negativity.
- In contrast, for phase 2, the population mean difference between PU's and INNOVA's construct scores and that between PU's and STRESS's construct scores were negative and differed from zero at the 1% significance level (i.e., $p < 0.01$). However, for phase 1, such mean differences were positive and differed from zero at the 1% significance level (i.e., $p < 0.01$).

- For phase 2, the population mean difference between PU's and TR's construct scores was positive and differed from zero at the 1% significance level (i.e., $p < 0.01$). This is at odds with phase 1 when such a mean difference gave rise to no statistical significance.
- From phase 1 to phase 2, the mean difference between RISK's and TR's construct scores no longer resulted in statistical significance though still negative.
- From phase 1 to phase 2, the mean difference between ATTD's and INNOVA's construct scores and that between ATTD's and STRESS's construct scores no longer ended up with statistical significance, and they drifted from positivity to negativity.
- From phase 1 to phase 2, the population mean difference between SI's and INNOVA's construct scores and that between SI's and STRESS's construct scores changed from positivity to negativity though remaining statistically significant at the 1% significance level (i.e., $p < 0.01$) whereas the population mean difference between SI's and TR's construct scores, that between INNOVA's and TR's construct scores, and that between STRESS's and TR's construct scores changed from negativity to positivity though remaining statistically significant at the 1% significance level (i.e., $p < 0.01$).
- From phase 1 to phase 2, the population mean difference between EOU's and RISK's construct scores, that between PU's and RISK's construct scores, that between ATTD's and SI's construct scores, and that between ATTD's and TR's construct scores remained positive and statistically significant at the either 1% or 5% significance level (i.e., either $p < 0.01$ or $p < 0.05$) whilst the population mean difference between PU's and ATTD's construct scores, that between RISK's and ATTD's construct scores, that between RISK's and SI's construct scores, that between RISK's and INNOVA's construct scores, and that between RISK's and STRESS's construct scores remained negative and statistically significant at the 1% significance level (i.e., $p < 0.01$).

In summary, there are quite some concordance and discordance between phase 1's (2022's) and phase 2's (2024's) pairwise construct score differences.

4. CONCLUSION AND DISCUSSION

In view of the temporality of perceived usability of and/or user experience with information systems, this article seeks to chart gamblers'/users' perception of EGMs' usability and user experience over the period from the time point of phase 1 (in 2022) to that of phase 2 (in 2024) so as to unravel how such usability and user experience evolved over such a period of casinos' digital transformation. Dual cross-sectional research design was implemented to compare the usability and user experience as measured by the TAM's and the UTAUT2's factors/constructs and the additional construct "trust" in 2022 with those in 2024. Nuanced statistical findings are enumerated in Table 1, which juxtaposes those for 2022 and those for 2024.

Deducing from the findings in the last section, for the population mean construct scores of all constructs analyzed, phase 2 (in 2024) found that EOU > PU ($p < 0.05$), EOU > RISK ($p < 0.01$), EOU > TR ($p < 0.01$), PU > RISK ($p < 0.05$), PU < ATTD ($p < 0.01$), PU < INNOVA ($p < 0.01$), PU < STRESS ($p < 0.01$), PU > TR ($p < 0.01$), RISK < ATTD ($p < 0.01$), RISK < SI ($p < 0.01$), RISK < INNOVA ($p < 0.01$), RISK < STRESS ($p < 0.01$), ATTD > SI ($p < 0.01$), ATTD > TR ($p < 0.01$), SI < INNOVA ($p < 0.01$), SI < STRESS ($p < 0.01$), SI > TR ($p < 0.01$), INNOVA > TR ($p < 0.01$), and STRESS > TR ($p < 0.01$), implying that EOU, INNOVA, STRESS registered the highest population mean construct scores whilst RISK and TR the lowest. These findings are in partial contrast to the counterparts of phase 1 (in 2022) when RISK's population mean construct score was the lowest and ATTD's the highest (Chan and Lei, 2024). On the one hand, relative to other perspectives of gamblers' perceived usability of and user experience with the then existing EGMs' designs, mitigation or prevention of gamblers' "perceived risk" (or its presentation to the gamblers) remained as the most dissatisfactory perspective over the duration from phase 1 (in 2022) to phase 2 (in 2024), noting that RISK denotes mitigation or prevention of gamblers' "perceived risk" upon rating harmonization. On the other hand, gamblers' trust in EGMs, albeit superior to mitigation or prevention gamblers' "perceived risk" in phase 1 (in 2022), "raced to the bottom" with mitigation or prevention of gamblers' "perceived risk" in phase 2 (in 2024). Also, whereas gamblers' attitude toward EGMs was most laudable in phase 1 (in 2022), it was leapfrogged in phase 2 (in 2024) by gamblers' perceived ease of use, self-evaluated innovativeness, and mitigation of perceived stress (as what STRESS denoted, upon rating harmonization) in using EGMs.

In essence, not only do these findings of phase 2 (in 2024) reiterate the advice of phase 1 (in 2022) that risk prevention be prioritized for amelioration, but also they suggest that gamblers' trust in EGMs be additionally so prioritized in phase 2 (in 2024). Also, these findings, in effect, further advocate keeping up gamblers' perceived ease of use, self-evaluated innovativeness, and mitigation of perceived stress in using EGMs. In other words, in the course of casinos' digital transformation, EGMs, as quintessential and mainstream electronic gambling equipment, underwent drifts and evolution in terms of gamblers'/users' perception of EGMs' usability and user experience. Correspondingly, the practical implication is that casinos' almost sole need for improvement in risk prevention in 2022 was additionally diversified into improvement in gamblers' trust in EGMs by 2024.

This study is not without its critics. First, EGMs' designs vary tremendously across different casinos and across brands and versions. This study's data sample collected was only generically representative of the usability of and user experience with, as perceived by gamblers/users, the various EGM brands and versions installed in the casinos across Macao as of the points in time during the data collection in phase 1 (in 2022) and phase 2 (in 2024). It would have been better off collecting and analyzing data specific to each distinct EGM brand and version of each casino operator, of course, at a far higher cost than that of this study. Second, this study's data sample was self-reported and self-evaluated based on respondents' memory of their perception when inside casinos some time back. The truthfulness of the data would have been higher if they had been collected right inside or at least around the exits of casinos where respondents were likely to recollect fresh memory of their perception when gambling on EGMs. Third, the sample size for phase 2 (in 2024) was substantially smaller than that for phase 1 (in 2022). Though not absolutely necessary in statistics, if the sample size for phase 2 (in 2024) had been comparable to that for phase 1 (in 2022), quite some statistical significance in the paired samples *t*-tests in phase 2 (in 2024) would have been manifested readily even if it might have otherwise been obscure in case of a much smaller sample size. Stated differently, the smaller sample size for phase 2 (in 2024) might have debilitated the *t*-tests' statistical power. In addition, the smaller sample size might have amplified the *t*-tests' errors in case the sample did not conform perfectly to normality. Four, this study sought to track how gamblers'/users' perception of EGMs' usability and user experience evolved over such a period of casinos' digital transformation but did not aim to demystify the causes of such evolution, which were left to future researches. Fifth, this study basically drew on data samples from Macao alone. Therefore, the author suggests extension to countries or regions elsewhere for generalization.

REFERENCES

Alalwan, A. A. et al. (2017). Factors Influencing Adoption of Mobile Banking by Jordanian Bank Customers: Extending UTAUT2 with Trust. *In International Journal of Information Management*, Vol. 37, No. 3, pp: 99–110. https://doi.org/10.1016/j.ijinfomgt.2017.01.002

Browne, M. et al. (2023). Unambiguous Evidence That over Half of Gambling Problems in Australia Are Caused by Electronic Gambling Machines: Results from a Large-Scale Composite Population Study. *In Journal of Behavioral Addictions*, Vol. 12, No. 1, pp. 182–193. https://doi.org/10.1556/2006.2022.00083

Chan, V. K. Y. and Lei, H. M. (2024). Evaluating the Usability of and User Experience with Electronic Gaming Machines at Casinos. *In Procedia Computer Science*, Vol. 239, pp. 846–851. https://www.sciencedirect.com/science/article/pii/S1877050924014868

Cummings, L. E. and Brewer, K. P. (1994). An Evolutionary View of the Critical Functions of Slot Machine Technology. *In UNLV Gaming Research & Review Journal*, Vol. 1, No. 2, pp. 67–78.

Dwivedi, Y. K. et al. (2019). Re-examining the Unified Theory of Acceptance and Use of Technology (UTAUT): Towards a Revised Theoretical Model. *In Information Systems Frontiers*; Vol. 21, pp. 719–734. https://doi.org/10.1007/s10796-017-9774-y

Karapanos, E. et al. (2009). User Experience over Time: An Initial Framework. *Proceedings of the SIGCHI Conference on Human Factors in Computing Systems (CHI '09).* Boston, USA, pp. 729–738. https://doi.org/10.1145/1518701.1518814

Liu, M. T. et al. (2021). The Application of Digital Technology in Gambling Industry. *In Asia Pacific Journal of Marketing and Logistics*, Vol. 33, No. 7, pp.1685–1705. https://doi.org/10.1108/APJML-11-2020-0778.

Marfels, C. (2001). Is Gambling Rational? The Utility Aspect of Gambling. *In Gaming Law Review*, Vol. 5, No. 5, pp. 459–466. https://doi.org/10.1089/109218801753204423.

Metaxas, T. and Folinas, S. (2021). Gambling Tourism and Economic Development: Some Lessons from Macao. *In Journal of Economics, Finance and Management Studies*, Vol. 4, No. 3, pp. 156–165. https://doi.org/10.47191/jefms/v4-i3-07.

Murch, W. S. and Clark, L. (2021). Understanding the Slot Machine Zone. *In Current Addiction Reports*, Vol. 8, pp: 214–224. https://doi.org/10.1007/s40429-021-00371-x

Nisbet, S. L. (2006). Modelling Consumer Intention to Use Gambling Technologies: An Innovative Approach. *In Behaviour & Information Technology*, Vol. 25, No. 3, pp. 221–231. https://doi.org/10.1080/01449290500167840

Oliveira, T. et al. (2016). Mobile Payment: Understanding the Determinants of Customer Adoption and Intention to Recommend the Technology. *In Computers in Human Behavior*, Vol. 61, pp. 404–414. https://doi.org/10.1016/j.chb.2016.03.030

Singh, N. et al. (2020). Determining Factors in the Adoption and Recommendation of Mobile Wallet Services in India: Analysis of the Effect of Innovativeness, Stress to Use and Social Influence. *In International Journal of Information Management*, Vol. 50, pp. 191–205. https://doi.org/10.1016/j.ijinfomgt.2019.05.022

Turner, N. and Horbay, R. (2004). How Do Slot Machines and Other Electronic Gambling Machines Actually Work? *In Journal of Gambling Issues*, pp. 1–36. https://doi.org/10.4309/jgi.2004.11.21

DEVELOPING A MODEL FOR THE ACCEPTANCE OF PROJECT MANAGEMENT TOOLS IN ORGANIZATIONS

Sevgi Özkan Yıldırım and Ezgi Erkaş
Middle East Technical University
Ankara, Turkey

ABSTRACT

The acceptance of project management tools plays a pivotal role in project success. This study employs a systematic literature review to identify and analyze factors influencing tool adoption. A total of 22 papers were reviewed, of which 13 were selected for their inclusion of meaningful factors relevant to the study.. The factors were categorized into key themes, including usability, organizational The study utilized qualitative and quantitative methods, including participant feedback, statistical analyses, and literature reviews, to synthesize findings. It highlights the interconnectedness of factors like information quality and perceived usefulness. Proposed hypotheses and actionable insights guide future research and practice, emphasizing user-centered design and organizational alignment. While offering a structured framework for analyzing tool acceptance, the study underscores the need for empirical validation and further exploration of context specific and unclassified factors.

KEYWORDS

Acceptance, Project Management Tools, Project Management Software, Adoption, Technology Acceptance

1. INTRODUCTION

Project management is a cornerstone of organizational success, ensuring that initiatives are delivered on time, within budget, and to the required quality standards. As organizations increasingly embrace complex and multifaceted projects, the need for efficient project management practices has never been greater. Central to these practices are project management tools, which serve as indispensable enablers for planning, monitoring, and controlling project activities.

The role of project management tools extends beyond mere task scheduling; they facilitate collaboration, enhance communication, and provide actionable insights through data analytics and reporting. Tools such as Jira, Trello, Microsoft Project, and Asana have become integral to modern project management, offering features that cater to diverse organizational needs. By enabling teams to track progress, manage resources, and identify potential risks, these tools significantly contribute to the success of projects across various industries.

Despite their evident benefits, the adoption and effective use of project management tools can be challenging. Factors such as user acceptance, organizational culture, and perceived ease of use often influence the integration of these tools into project workflows. Understanding these dynamics is essential for organizations seeking to leverage project management tools to their full potential.

This paper explores the acceptance of project management tools, focusing on the factors that drive or hinder their adoption in organizational settings. By examining existing theories and empirical studies, it aims to provide insights into how organizations can optimize the use of these tools to achieve project success.

2. RESEARCH METHODOLOGY

This study follows the Kitchenham methodology for conducting a systematic literature review (SLR), a widely recognized approach in software engineering and technology adoption research. The Kitchenham method provides a structured framework for identifying, analyzing, and synthesizing relevant literature, ensuring the rigor and reliability of the review process.

A. Planning the Review

The review began with the formulation of clear research questions to guide the study, focusing on identifying factors influencing the acceptance of project management tools. A review protocol was established, detailing the search strategy, inclusion and exclusion criteria, and methods for data extraction and synthesis.

B. Conducting the Search

The search process involved using predefined keywords, including acceptance, adoption, project management tools, and project management software. These keywords were strategically combined to refine the search and maximize the retrieval of relevant studies, with queries such as "Acceptance of Project Management Tools" and "Adoption of Project Management Software." Searches were conducted in three major academic databases: Scopus, Web of Science and Google Scholar.

C. Inclusion and Exclusion Criteria

The inclusion and exclusion criteria were carefully designed to ensure the relevance and quality of the studies selected for this review. The initial search yielded a total of 4,201 results across Google Scholar, Scopus, and Web of Science. To refine this large pool, only studies that included the keywords acceptance, adoption, project management tools, or project management software in their title, abstract, or keyword sections were considered. Papers failing to meet this criterion were excluded in the first screening phase. Subsequently, abstracts and introductions were reviewed to assess the alignment of the study's objectives with the research questions. Studies not addressing factors related to the acceptance or adoption of project management tools were excluded. The remaining papers underwent a full-text review to ensure they provided meaningful empirical or theoretical insights. Only peer reviewed journal articles and reputable conference proceedings were retained to guarantee the quality and reliability of the findings. Through this rigorous process, the initial pool was narrowed down to 22 studies. Further filtering based on the inclusion of meaningful factors relevant to the study's objectives resulted in 13 papers being selected for detailed analysis. These final selections provided the foundation for identifying and categorizing the factors influencing project management tool acceptance.

D. Data Extraction and Synthesis

Relevant data were systematically extracted from the selected papers, focusing on the factors influencing tool acceptance, research methodologies used, and significant findings. The extracted data were categorized into thematic groups, such as usability, organizational readiness, technical aspects, project characteristics, resource constraints, and awareness, enabling a structured analysis of recurring patterns and relationships.

E. Most Frequently Used Methodology in the Literature

Survey-based empirical studies emerged as the most frequently used research methodology among the reviewed literature. These studies employed quantitative techniques to gather data from project management professionals and applied statistical methods, such as regression analysis and factor analysis, to validate their findings. So, by adhering to the Kitchenham methodology, this study ensures a systematic and unbiased review process. The inclusion and exclusion criteria, coupled with rigorous data extraction and synthesis, provide a solid foundation for understanding the factors influencing project management tool acceptance. This structured approach also lays the groundwork for actionable insights and future research directions.

3. RESULTS

3.1 Trend in the Field Based on Years

The evolution of research on the acceptance and adoption of project management tools can be categorized into three distinct periods. The early phase (2000–2008) marks the foundational work in this field. Seminal studies like Venkatesh and Davis (2000) introduced the theoretical rly indicate advantages, limitations and possible applications. frameworks, such as the Technology Acceptance Model (TAM), which served as a basis for future research. During this period, researchers focused on practical factors influencing tool adoption, with notable contributions such as Liberatore and Pollack-Johnson (2003), which examined selection criteria for project management software, and Hernández et al. (2008), which extended TAM to include IT decision-makers' roles. This period highlights an initial interest in understanding adoption drivers from both organizational and technological perspectives.

The second phase (2009–2017) saw a significant expansion in the scope and application of technology acceptance research. Studies during this time delved into diverse domains and specific contexts, such as public organizations (Fitsilis and Chalatsis, 2014) and building information modeling in construction projects (Howard et al., 2017). Researchers increasingly integrated advanced frameworks, like the Unified Theory of Acceptance and Use of Technology (UTAUT), to address individual and organizational perceptions. This period reflects a maturing of the research focus, with a growing emphasis on domainspecific applications and practical adoption barriers.

The most recent phase (2018–present) is characterized by a strong emphasis on digitalization and emerging technologies. With advancements in cloud computing, blockchain, and digital transformation, studies such as Bajwa and Deichmann (2018) explored the acceptance of cloudbased project management tools, while Amoah and Oh (2021) investigated blockchain adoption in project management. More recent works, such as Vărzaru (2022), introduced empirical frameworks for assessing the acceptance of digital technologies in project management. This phase highlights a shift toward integrating cutting-edge technologies and assessing their implications for project management practices. Across all periods, there has been a consistent focus on practical outcomes, with studies addressing adoption barriers, usability, and the alignment of project management tools with organizational needs. Key peaks in publication activity occurred in 2008, with notable works on extending TAM and its application, and in 2022, driven by the rising importance of digital tools and technologies. These trends underline the dynamic evolution of research in this field, from foundational theoretical explorations to the integration of advanced digital frameworks in recent years (Figure 1)

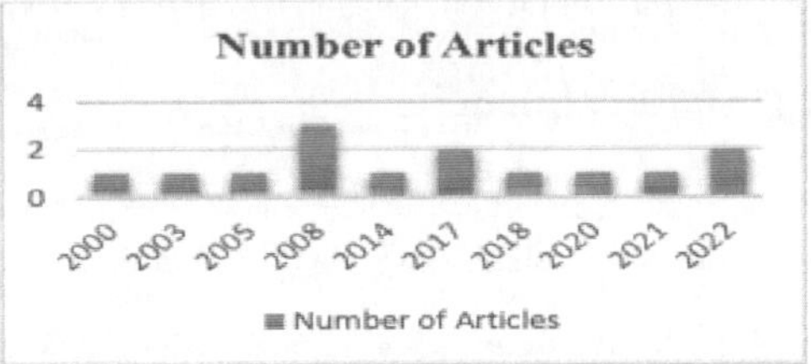

Figure 1. Total number of articles per year

3.2 How Factors Were Concluded

The factors influencing the acceptance of project management tools were derived from various methodological approaches across the reviewed papers. These methods ensured a comprehensive and evidence based understanding of the dynamics at play. The following summarizes the approaches used to conclude these factors.

3.2.1 Field Studies and Participant Feedback

Several studies utilized qualitative methods, including field research and semi structured interviews, to gather insights directly from stakeholders. These methods captured diverse perspectives on the challenges of adopting project management tools, particularly in local government organizations and other structured environments. Participants evaluated factors based on their occurrence frequency and importance, which allowed researchers to identify critical barriers and facilitators of acceptance.

3.2.2 Empirical and Statistical Analysis

Quantitative methodologies were prevalent, with many studies employing surveys targeting large samples of project management professionals. Techniques such as regression analysis, factor analysis, and structural equation modeling were used to validate hypotheses and examine relationships among factors. These statistical approaches highlighted the significance of constructs like perceived usefulness, ease of use, and information quality in influencing acceptance.

3.2.3 Literature Reviews and Theoretical Frameworks

Many studies were grounded in established theoretical models, such as the Technology Acceptance Model (TAM). These frameworks provided a conceptual basis for identifying and categorizing factors. Literature reviews were also instrumental in contextualizing findings within the broader body of knowledge, ensuring that identified factors were aligned with existing research while addressing previously unexplored gaps.

3.2.4 Categorization and Synthesis of Findings

To enhance clarity, researchers categorized factors into themes, such as usability, organizational readiness, and project-specific characteristics. Some studies employed advanced statistical techniques, such as reliability testing and path coefficient analysis, to ensure the validity of the conclusions. This process facilitated a deeper understanding of how different factors interact to influence acceptance.

3.2.5 Prototyping and Practical Testing

A few studies incorporated practical elements, such as the development and testing of prototypes. These efforts provided firsthand insights into operational dynamics and allowed researchers to observe how users interacted with project management tools in real-world scenarios. The combination of qualitative, quantitative, and practical approaches allowed for a robust identification of factors. Methods such as participant feedback, hypothesis testing, and statistical validation ensured that the conclusions were both theoretically sound and practically relevant. These methodologies collectively offer a comprehensive perspective on the multifaceted nature of project management tool acceptance.

3.3 Factor Grouping and Frequencies

The factors influencing the acceptance of project management tools were extracted and grouped into several categories based on their thematic alignment. These categories aim to provide a comprehensive understanding of the diverse considerations outlined in the literature. The factors were grouped into seven primary categories, with their respective frequencies summarized in Table 1.

Table 1. Factor Grouping

Group	Frequency	Group	Frequency
Organizational Factors	5	Awareness and Knowledge	4
Project Characteristics	5	Resource Constraints	3
Usability	4	Technical Factors	3
User and Environmental Influences	4	Other	34

3.4 Key Observations

The grouping of factors reflects both general and context-specific elements influencing project management tool acceptance. The majority of factors fell into broad categories such as organizational aspects, usability, and technical concerns, while a significant portion remained in the "Other" category, indicating the nuanced nature of these influences.

3.4.1 Organizational Factors

Organizational dynamics play a significant role, with factors such as "Organization Size," "Human Resources Management," "Coordination Deficiencies," and "Training and Support" emphasizing the internal readiness and alignment of teams. These factors suggest that effective leadership, clear communication, and adequate training are critical prerequisites for successful tool adoption.

3.4.2 Project Characteristics

Projects vary in size, complexity, and maturity, influencing the tools required for management. Factors such as "Project Complexity," "Project Size," and "Project Management Maturity" highlight the importance of tailoring tool selection to the specific needs of projects. Larger or more complex projects typically demand more robust and feature-rich tools. Usability: Ease of use remains one of the most influential categories, with factors like "Ease of Use," "Usage Degree," "Compatibility," and "Innovativeness." This grouping demonstrates that the user friendliness of a tool and its ability to integrate seamlessly with existing workflows are central to its acceptance.

3.4.3 User and Environmental Influences

This category encompasses factors such as "User Characteristics," "Image," "External Influences," and "Reallife Applications." The findings suggest that individual and contextual variables, including user preferences and societal trends, significantly affect adoption decisions.

3.4.4 Awareness and Knowledge

Knowledge related factors, including "Training Level," "User Training Level," and "Education Level and Experience," underscore the role of awareness and preparation in tool adoption. These findings indicate that organizations must invest in comprehensive training programs to increase tool usage and effectiveness.

3.4.5 Resource Constraints

Factors like "Adjustment Problems," "Adjustment Challenges," and "Demographic Factors" represent the barriers and limitations faced during tool implementation. Resource constraints, both human and financial, appear to significantly hinder adoption. Technical Factors: Trust in the technology itself emerges as a critical concern. Factors such as "Trust and Security," "Perceived Information Quality," and "Information Quality" emphasize the need for tools to deliver reliable, secure, and transparent solutions.

3.4.6 Unclassified Factors

A notable subset of factors could not be grouped under existing categories due to their unique or context specific nature. These include "Complexity," "Individual Differences," "Adjustment Challenges," "User Training Level," "Image," and "Real-life Applications." The high frequency of unclassified factors suggests that the landscape of project management tool acceptance is complex and multifaceted, with nuances that require further exploration.

4. THE CONCEPTUAL RESEARCH MODEL

Based on the findings, the following hypotheses are proposed for further investigation (Figure 2):

H1: Usability positively impacts the acceptance of project management tools. Factors like ease of use, compatibility, and innovativeness are expected to enhance user satisfaction and tool adoption.

H2: Organizational readiness significantly influences the adoption of project management tools.

This includes aspects like management commitment, training support, and effective communication.

H3: Awareness and knowledge about project management tools positively correlate with their successful implementation. Comprehensive training and higher education levels are hypothesized to increase acceptance.

H4: Resource constraints negatively affect the adoption of project management tools. Limited resources, including time, budget, and human capacity, are expected to act as barriers.

H5: Trust and perceived information quality in a tool positively influence its adoption. Tools that demonstrate high levels of security, transparency, and reliability are more likely to be embraced.

H6: Project characteristics moderate the relationship between usability and tool acceptance. Larger and more complex projects may require tools with higher functionality, emphasizing usability. These hypotheses align with the observed frequencies and thematic groupings, providing a foundation for future empirical testing.

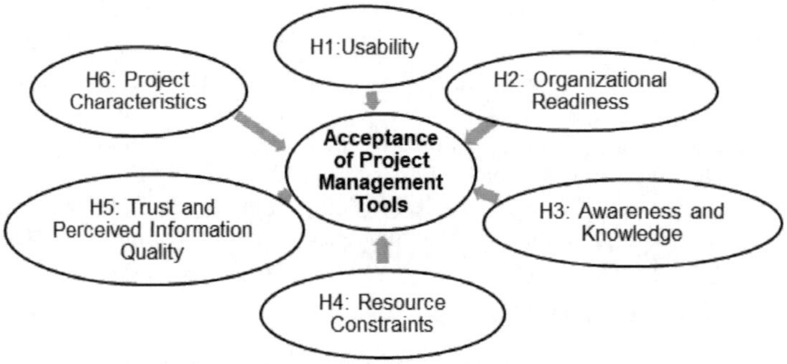

Figure 2. Conceptual Model for Project Management Tools Acceptance

5. DISCUSSION AND CONCLUSION

This study offers a comprehensive analysis of the factors influencing the acceptance of project management tools, synthesizing findings from existing literature. The factors were categorized into key groups, including usability, organizational readiness, technical factors, project characteristics, resource constraints, and awareness. The results emphasize the multifaceted nature of tool acceptance and the need for a holistic approach when designing and implementing such tools.

Usability emerged as one of the most significant categories, highlighting the importance of ease of use, compatibility, and innovative features. Tools that are intuitive and seamlessly integrate with existing workflows are more likely to be adopted by users. This finding aligns with the broader literature on technology acceptance, which consistently emphasizes user-friendliness as a critical determinant.

Organizational factors, such as management commitment, training support, and coordination, were also prominent. These findings suggest that organizations play a crucial role in facilitating tool adoption by fostering an environment conducive to technological change. Additionally, project-specific characteristics, such as size and complexity, further underline the importance of tailoring tools to meet the unique demands of each project. A notable finding was the presence of unclassified factors, such as "Complexity," "User Characteristics," and "Real-life Applications." These unique and context dependent elements suggest that the landscape of project management tool acceptance is highly nuanced. Future research should focus on exploring these factors to provide a deeper understanding of their influence. This study contributes to both theory and practice by providing a structured framework for analyzing tool acceptance and proposing hypotheses for further research. The findings offer actionable insights for practitioners, such as prioritizing user-centered design, investing in training programs, and aligning organizational processes to support adoption. However, the study is not without limitations. The qualitative nature of the analysis, the generalization of factors across contexts, and the static approach to understanding adoption patterns suggest that additional empirical and longitudinal research is needed. Despite these limitations, the study lays a solid foundation for understanding the factors influencing project management tool acceptance and offers valuable directions for future work.

5.1 Contributions of This Study

This study makes several meaningful contributions to the field of project management and technology adoption. First, it offers a structured framework for categorizing and analyzing the factors influencing the acceptance of project management tools. This framework provides a clear foundation for both researchers and practitioners seeking to understand and address these factors. Second, the study identifies key themes, such as usability, organizational readiness, and technical factors, that are critical to successful tool adoption. By highlighting these areas, the study provides actionable insights for organizations aiming to improve their adoption strategies. For instance, the findings emphasize the importance of user-centered design, comprehensive training programs, and organizational alignment to enhance the likelihood of tool acceptance. Third, the study's proposed hypotheses serve as a roadmap for future research. They guide empirical investigations into the relationships between specific factors and tool adoption, thereby advancing theoretical understanding in this domain. Finally, the study contributes to practice by equipping decision-makers with the knowledge to evaluate and implement project management tools effectively. By addressing the identified factors, organizations can optimize tool adoption, improve project outcomes, and ultimately enhance organizational efficiency.

5.2 Suggestions for Future Work

The findings of this study highlight several areas for further research. First, future studies should empirically validate the proposed hypotheses to confirm the relationships between the identified factors and the acceptance of project management tools. Quantitative methods, such as surveys and experiments, can provide robust evidence for these relationships. Second, the significant number of unclassified factors, such as "Complexity" and "User Characteristics," points to the need for more in-depth exploration of these unique influences. Researchers should investigate these factors in greater detail to uncover their specific roles and interactions in the adoption process. Third, context-specific studies are essential to understand how adoption factors vary across industries, organizational sizes, and cultural settings. Such studies can help refine the framework presented in this research and enhance its applicability to diverse scenarios. Additionally, longitudinal research would provide valuable insights into how adoption patterns evolve over time. Tracking the implementation and usage of project management tools over extended periods can reveal dynamic trends and the impact of changes in organizational and technological contexts. Finally, as technologies such as artificial intelligence and blockchain continue to advance, future research should explore their implications for project management tools. Understanding how these emerging technologies affect usability, security, and functionality will be critical for designing tools that align with future needs.

5.3 Limitations of This Study

While this study provides valuable insights, several limitations should be acknowledged. First, the research is based on a qualitative analysis of factors identified in the literature. Without empirical validation, the relationships between these factors and tool acceptance remain theoretical. Future studies should test these findings using quantitative methods to establish causal relationships. Second, the study's grouping of factors may oversimplify the nuanced nature of project management tool adoption. The diversity of organizational contexts, user preferences, and project types means that some factors may behave differently depending on the setting. This limitation highlights the importance of conducting context-specific research to refine the proposed framework. Third, the study does not account for the dynamic nature of adoption. Factors influencing tool acceptance may evolve as technologies and organizational processes change. Longitudinal studies are needed to capture these temporal dynamics and provide a more comprehensive understanding of the adoption process. Finally, a significant portion of factors remained unclassified, indicating that the framework does not fully capture the complexity of tool acceptance. Further exploration of these factors is necessary to address this gap. Despite these limitations, the study offers a strong foundation for future research and practical application in the field of project management.

REFERENCES

Abd El Halim, H. (2020). Project Management (PM) Tools: Awareness, Acceptance of Learning and Use, User Selected Tools, and Usage Degree in Egypt: The Case Study of College of Management and Technology (CMT).

Ali, A. S. B., & Money, W. H. (2005). A study of project management system acceptance. Proceedings of the 38th Hawaii International Conference on System Sciences. IEEE. https://doi.org/10.1109/HICSS.2005 .11

Amoah, E., & Oh, J.-Y. (2021). Blockchain adoption in project management. *Issues in Information Systems*, *22*(4), 143- 156. https://doi.org/10.48009/4_iis_2021_ 152-167

B. Kitchenham, "Procedures for Performing Systematic Reviews. Technical Report TR/SE0401," Computer Science Department, Keele University, National ICT Australia Ltd, Tech. Rep. 0400011T.1, 2004.

Bach, M. P., et al. (2022). "An extension of the technology acceptance model for business intelligence systems: project management maturity perspective." *International Journal of Information Systems and Project Management 5*(2): 5- 21.

Bajwa, A., & Deichmann, R. (2018). How Digitalization influences Project Management Acceptance of Cloudbased Project Management Tools.

Bani Ali, A. S., et al. (2008). "Impact of Organizational and Project Factors on Acceptance and Usage of Project Management Software and Perceived Project Success." *Project Management Journal 39*(2): 5-33.

Dasig, D. D. Jr., & Mojica, G. (2017). An evaluative study on project management tools for managing engineering projects. *Ascendens Asia Journal of Multidisciplinary Research Conference Proceedings*, *1*(1), 22-23.

Fitsilis, P. and T. Chalatsis (2014). "Adoption of Project Management Practices in Public Organizations." *iBusiness 06*(03): 131-142.

Hart, A. (2021). "Virtual Project Teams Acceptance of Communication Tools: A Qualitative Delphi Study", Capella University ProQuest Dissertations & Theses.

Hart, A. (2023). "Virtual Project Teams Acceptance of Communication Tools: A Qualitative Delphi Study", Capella University ProQuest Dissertations & Theses, 2021 "Towards a technology acceptance methodology for Industry 4.0," Procedia Computer Science.

Hernández, B., et al. (2008). "Extending the technology acceptance model to include the IT decision-maker: A study of business management software." *Technovation 28*(3): 112-121.

Howard, R., et al. (2017). "Addressing individual perceptions: An application of the unified theory of acceptance and use of technology to building information modelling." *International Journal of Project Management 35*(2): 107-120.

Karmin Gray, Frank Ulbrich, "Ambiguity acceptance and translation skills in the project management literature", International Journal of Managing Projects in Business, 2017

Kunal Mohan, "Understanding the Acceptance and Usage of IT Project Management Methodologies: Towards a Conceptual Model supported by Case Studies" European Business School (EBS), 2010

Liberatore, M. J. and B. Pollack Johnson (2003). "Factors influencing the usage and selection of project management software." *IEEE Transactions on Engineering Management 50*(2): 164-174.

Lo-Fo-Wong, Kevin (2023). "Acceptance of standardized construction management processes: Project managers' acceptance in a change towards Standard Operating Procedures in construction".

Mohan, K. (2012). "Understanding the Acceptance and Usage of Project Management Methodologies", EBS Business School, 2012

Sietse Overbeek & Remko Helms , "Describing Criteria for Selecting a Scrum Tool Using the Technology Acceptance Model", Asian Conference on Intelligent Information and Database Systems, 2017

Stergiou, G., & Kavakli, E., & Kotis, K. (2012). Management Methodologies", EBS Business School, 2012

Vărzaru, A. A. (2022). "An Empirical Framework for Assessing the Digital Technologies Users' Acceptance in Project Management." *Electronics 11*(23).

Venkatesh, V. and F. D. Davis (2000). "A Theoretical Extension of the Technology Acceptance Model: Four Longitudinal Field Studies." *Management Science 46*(2): 186-204.

Xelhuantzi, S. S., & González, J. C. (2024). Project management and sensory acceptance in ready-to-Use bakery products: A systematic literature review. *Saudi Journal of Engineering and Technology*, *09*(07), 312-322.

AN APPROACH TO TEXTILE INDUSTRIAL EQUIPMENT MAINTENANCE ASSISTANCE USING AN AUGMENTED REALITY APPLICATION

João Miranda[1], Nuno Dinis[2], Luís Romero[1] and Pedro Miguel Faria[1]
[1]*Instituto Politécnico de Viana do Castelo, Portugal*
[2]*Riopele, Vila Nova de Famalicão, Portugal*

ABSTRACT

Industries are increasingly striving for digitalization to integrate predictive maintenance systems into their equipment. However, these interventions are becoming more challenging due to the growing complexity of industrial machinery. In response, technologies such as Augmented Reality (AR) have emerged as valuable tools, providing real-time support and guidance to operators during maintenance processes. This paper presents the development and implementation of a prototype AR application designed to assist in the maintenance of equipment within a real textile factory. The primary goal is to enable operators to use the application for training purposes, as an interactive guide during actual maintenance procedures, and/or to access real-time equipment data. The ongoing development of this project has demonstrated the potential of AR applications to enhance industrial data visualization, improve operator training, and streamline maintenance tasks. The findings in this work contribute to the broader digital transformation of the manufacturing sector and lay the groundwork for future advancements in AR assisted maintenance across various industries.

KEYWORDS

Augmented Reality, Textile Industry, Equipment Maintenance, Digital Twin, Mobile Application

1. INTRODUCTION

In recent years, we have witnessed a rapid advancement in information technologies, which has motivated a strong initiative for modernization within industries. These innovations are fundamental to the transformation of the industry, promoting efficiency and innovation. The intelligent adoption of these technologies not only optimizes processes and reduces costs but also facilitates logistics, making it essential to boost companies' competitiveness. Among these innovations, Augmented Reality has emerged as a powerful tool for modernizing industrial processes. According to the authors of (Caiza and Sanz, 2022), AR functions as an intuitive link between the physical and digital worlds, facilitating the interpretation and interaction with data. The ability to overlay digital information into the physical environment in real-time (Gong, L. et al., 2021) makes this technology particularly useful in applications aimed at industrial maintenance, inspection, and training. The application of AR in industrial equipment maintenance enables more efficient assistance, reducing diagnostic and failure correction times (Zhu, Z. et al., X., 2019). Technicians can visualize detailed instructions directly on machines, access operational information, and receive step-by-step guidance, improving intervention accuracy and minimizing errors. Additionally, the technology contributes to reducing equipment downtime, positively impacting productivity and operational costs. In this context, this paper presents the development of an Augmented Reality application designed to assist in the maintenance of spinning machinery, implemented in a real industrial factory. This application is powered by real-time machine data and, in addition to maintenance support, allows users to access relevant machine information. To achieve this, an initial study was conducted by selecting relevant IEEE studies, followed by an analysis of key concepts. Finally, this paper presents the work developed in this field, evaluating the potential of the tools used and providing valuable insights for optimizing industrial equipment operation and maintenance.

2. RELATED WORK

In this section, a study of related works is conducted, beginning with the selection of nine studies for analysis. Each study is first summarized, followed by a comparative analysis of the technologies and approaches employed in these works and in this project.

In (Paripooranan, C.S. et al., 2020), the authors propose an integrated application within a Digital Twin system for a 3D printer, controlled via Augmented Reality. The application displays key printer parameters, such as print head coordinates, temperatures, and real-time printing progress, while allowing the user to control essential functions. Bidirectional communication is achieved through MQTT and HTTP protocols. The app was developed using Unity (Unity Technologies, 2023) and Vuforia (PTC, 2024), with the printer's CAD model created in Autodesk Fusion 360, and data communication managed via Node-RED. The approach is considered adaptable to other industrial devices with different 3D CAD models.

An Augmented Reality-based system has been proposed to support industrial maintenance procedures in an automotive component production unit, aligning with Industry 4.0 principles (Alves, F. et al., 2020) (Cachada, A. et al., 2019). The system uses Unity, with its support for 2D and 3D development, and integrates the Vuforia SDK to implement a marker-based AR system. Unity was chosen for its ability to create lightweight, fast, multiplatform applications using C#. The system combines AR interaction, guiding operators through maintenance tasks with support from texts, videos, and 3D models, along with a MySQL database for collecting operational data. The application works on both mobile devices and smart glasses, specifically Microsoft HoloLens for hands-free use. Vuforia enables target image tracking to trigger maintenance procedures. The system offers two modes: training mode, allowing operators to practice steps before performing tasks on real machines, and execution mode, which provides real-time guidance and visual assistance to ensure correct task completion.

The article by Hong-Yi Pai (Pai, H.Y., 2020) addresses the challenges in aircraft maintenance training due to complex procedures, such as the Airbus A330 braking system. To tackle this, a mobile learning (M-learning) system was developed to simulate the installation and disassembly of brake components using ARKit (Apple Inc., 2025), 3D animations, and contextual guidance. Currently a prototype, the system aims to evaluate its effectiveness through user feedback.

A low-cost control and maintenance system for a stone counter, designed for small businesses, is presented in (Fernandez, F. et al., 2021). The system was developed using Unity, Vuforia, and an SQLite database, with an Atmega328p microcontroller managing sensors and actuators. It enables real-time monitoring and maintenance operations through AR features, including labels and explanatory texts. Bluetooth was implemented for communication between the microcontroller and the application. Testing demonstrated an 80% reduction in operation time and a counting accuracy with an error of less than 1%. The high number of components and the structural complexities involved in the assembly and maintenance of avionics equipment have traditionally required operators to possess a high level of expertise. To address this challenge (Xue, Z. et al., 2024) presented an augmented reality based assisted guidance system. To overcome difficulties such as confined spaces and hidden assembly areas, the authors propose an AR-based guidance method that employs a multimodal anti-occlusion tracking algorithm to determine the position of each component and display assembly information directly onto the real parts. Furthermore, an assembly step identification method was developed to reduce the need for user interaction. The system was subsequently evaluated based on various criteria, including ease of learning, with results demonstrating a significant improvement in training efficiency for maintenance tasks compared to traditional methods.

The article by Knopp, Klimant, and Allmacher (Knopp, S. et al., 2019) examines the use of Augmented Reality with Microsoft HoloLens for guiding the assembly and disassembly of modular concrete molds. The system employs a marker-based approach for reliable tracking in challenging environments and a hands-free, gesture-driven interface. It also supports real-time streaming for remote assistance, allowing experts to view the worker's perspective. Tests showed a 30% reduction in maintenance time, primarily by minimizing downtime.

To enhance equipment maintenance in Industry 5.0, (Dourado, I.L. et al., 2024) developed an AR application for maintaining a Programmable Logic Controller (PLC) system. Designed for AR glasses, the application features an intuitive interface that provides real-time assistance to maintenance technicians, optimizing processes and reducing errors. To this end, technologies such as image recognition, gesture-based interfaces, and voice commands were employed. Finally, the application's usability was assessed through usability questionnaires, cognitive load analysis, and physiological measurements. The results were positive, highlighting this tool as a promising solution for Industry 5.0.

Hsu and Chuang (Hsu, H.H. and Chuang, C.Y., 2022) propose an AR application for equipment maintenance and employee training in a factory, developed with Unity 3D and Vuforia SDK for Android devices. The app offers visual instructions through 3D models and videos, aiding less experienced workers with preventive maintenance. It enhances efficiency, reduces costs, minimizes errors, and helps monitor machine performance, optimize processes, and improve resource allocation.

In (Rodrigues, A. et al., 2021), the authors present an AR application for urban maintenance workers, addressing issues like outdated or missing equipment manuals. The mobile app tracks equipment and provides real-time data and step-by-step instructions, while a desktop app called "Archer" manages the instructions. The system uses AR checkpoints to ensure stable tracking, even with equipment changes, by employing Raycasts to determine optimal checkpoint locations. Tests demonstrated high accuracy and usability, showcasing AR's potential to enhance efficiency and reduce errors in urban maintenance tasks. Overall, the studies highlighted in Table 1 demonstrate the potential of Augmented Reality in optimizing industrial processes, from predictive maintenance to technician training.

Table 1. Comparative analysis of technologies and approaches in related studies

System	Platform	Field of Application	Media Used
(Paripooranan, C.S. et al., 2020)	Smartphone & Tablet	3D Printer	3D Animation / Text
(Alves, F. et al., 2020) (Cachada, A. et al., 2019)	Smartphone & Tablet / HoloLens	Manufacturing Industry	3D Animation / Image / Text
(Pai, H.Y., 2020)	Smartphone & Tablet	Aircraft Maintenance	3D Animation / Text
(Fernandez, F. et al., 2021)	Smartphone & Tablet	Stone Counter	Text
(Xue, Z. et al., 2024)	HoloLens	Avionics Equipment	3D Animation / Image / Text
(Knopp, S. et al., 2019)	HoloLens	Modular Mold	Text
(Dourado, I.L. et al., 2024)	Meta Quest Pro	PLC System	3D Animation / Image / Text
(Hsu, H.H. and Chuang, C.Y., 2022)	Smartphone & Tablet	Manufacturing Industry	Image / Video / Text
(Rodrigues, A. et al., 2021)	Smartphone & Tablet	Urban Maintenance	3D Animation / Text

The studies are evaluated based on the platform used, the field of application, and the media format. The analysis indicates that mobile devices, such as smartphones and tablets, are the most utilized platforms, emphasizing their practicality in industrial settings. Regarding the field of application, each study explores different aspects of AR integration, highlighting its versatility across various domains. In terms of media formats, the most frequently used types are 3D animation, images, and text, reinforcing their effectiveness in delivering maintenance instructions and technical guidance. Although challenges such as technological integration persist, the continuous advancement of AR suggests a future where efficiency, innovation, and adaptability will play a crucial role in industrial modernization. In contrast to the reviewed studies, the application developed in this project stands out as it is specifically designed for the textile industry, unlike other works that focus on manufacturing or maintenance in different sectors. It utilizes smartphones and tablets as its primary platform and, at the moment, employs videos, images, and text as media formats. This tailored approach aims to improve maintenance procedures and facilitate knowledge transfer within the textile sector.

3. SYSTEM ARCHITECTURE PROPOSAL

This project is a continuation of the study presented in (Miranda, J. et al., 2024), where a small prototype of an augmented reality application for a digital twin system was developed. For this approach, the objective is to develop an application for a real-world factory. Therefore, all decision-making processes were previously approved and encouraged by the factory's representatives. To achieve this goal, the project focuses on the spinning section of the factory, where 12 pre-defined spinning machines will be used. However, the application is designed to be scalable, allowing for the integration of additional machines in the future. This ensures system flexibility while enhancing maintenance procedures and data visualization. This section describes the current system architecture being developed for equipment maintenance and real-time data visualization of various spinning machines in a factory. The architecture designed for this purpose is illustrated in Figure 1.

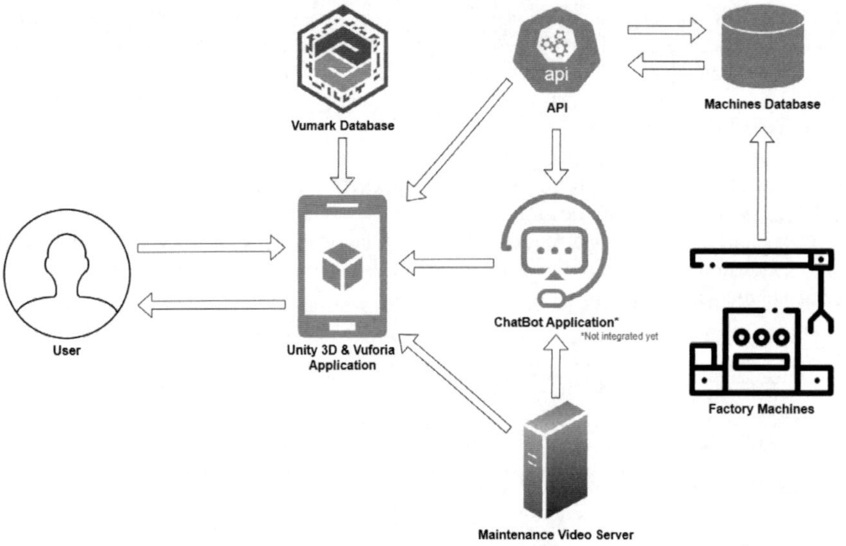

Figure 1. System architecture

Unity 3D & Vuforia

To ensure a user-friendly interface, the Unity game engine was used during application development, enabling the creation of lightweight, fast, and compact 3D applications. In conjunction with Unity, the Vuforia SDK was integrated to enhance Augmented Reality functionalities, enabling object recognition, tracking, and the overlay of digital content onto real-world components.

Vumark Database

The application utilizes Vuforia for image target detection (Vumarks), which are stored in a dedicated database provided by Vuforia and subsequently trigger the Augmented Reality content. The constructed database supports up to 999 different Vumarks and allows the user to generate a new Vumark instantly. Each Vumark is associated with a unique ID corresponding to the ID of a real machine in the factory.

Machines Database

All machine data used by the application is retrieved from an API provided by the factory itself, which gathers data from sensors present in the different machines. The application establishes real-time connections with the API to deliver various data.

Maintenance Videos Server

To facilitate machine maintenance, real-life videos of operators performing maintenance steps and procedures in the factory are used. These videos are then stored on an online server and accessed by the application as needed.

ChatBot Application

In parallel, a chatbot application is under development. This AI-powered system leverages the machine database to provide accurate and timely responses to user inquiries. Once completed, it will be seamlessly integrated into the augmented reality system.

Output

The application architecture was designed to integrate functionalities that allow operators to view machine details, search for events and/or production data for each machine, and access videos of maintenance procedures. Additionally, the architecture is prepared for the integration of chatbot components, enabling quick and dynamic responses through text and audio inputs.

The proposed architecture enables the integration of an augmented reality system for industrial maintenance and real-time machine data visualization. By leveraging Unity 3D, Vuforia, factory-provided API and the maintenance videos server, the application aims to enhance operational efficiency by offering intuitive access to machine data, maintenance videos, and chatbot support. The implemented architecture is designed to be scalable, allowing for future expansions such as the integration of the chatbot. Ultimately, this architecture aims to improve and optimize factory processes by reducing decision-making time and enhancing maintenance operator training.

4. SYSTEM DEVELOPMENT

The developed AR application is mobile-based, and its development was carried out using the Unity game engine. Unity is a powerful engine that enables the creation of 2D and 3D applications for multiple platforms and offers a primary scripting API in C# for programming purposes. Through Unity, it was possible to develop the entire user interface of the application and, via scripting, establish the necessary connections with the API provided by the textile industry and the online server hosting the maintenance videos. These videos were initially recorded by us, according to the required maintenance processes, and were later stored on the online server for convenient access when needed.

For the integration of augmented reality components, the Vuforia Software Development Kit (SDK) was used. Vuforia enables the development of AR applications based on a marker-based tracking system, where a set of standardized target images is defined. These target images are detected by the application, with each one corresponding to a specific machine in the factory. The marks were created using Adobe Illustrator and later integrated into a Vuforia database, before being imported into the Unity environment as Vumarks. The overall structure of the developed system and its current functional output is illustrated in Figure 2.

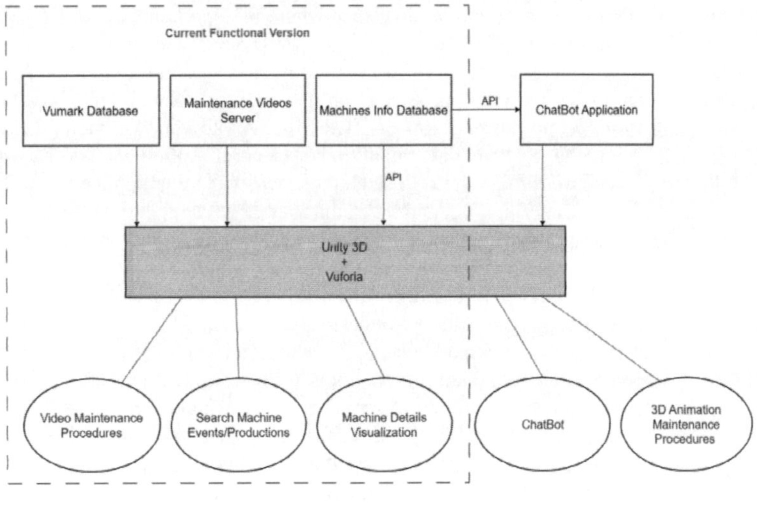

Figure 2. Schematic of the developed system and current output

To use the application, the factory operator must scan a marker using the camera of a smartphone or tablet. Once detected, a menu specific to the machine will appear, offering four options: "Maintenance," "Production," "Events," and "General". Selecting the “Maintenance” option opens a submenu where the operator can choose from six maintenance procedures: Upper Folding, Lower Folding, Ruler Replacement, PLC Configuration, Cleaning, and Long Fiber Pad Assembly. Upon selection, a video player will appear, presenting one or more instructional videos related to the chosen maintenance task, as shown in Figure 3.

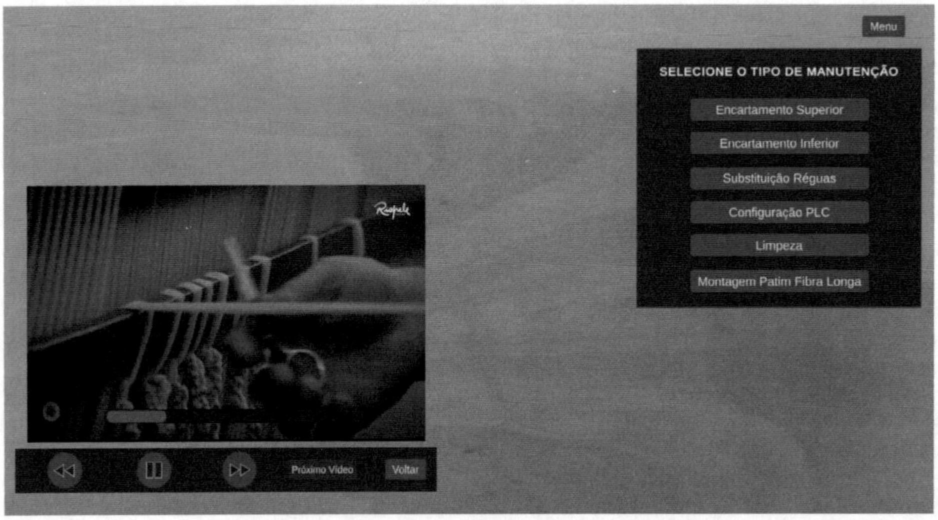

Figure 3. Schematic of the developed system and current output

Within the video player, the user can pause, play, and skip forward or backward by 10 seconds. If the maintenance procedure includes more than one video, the user can also navigate to the next or previous video as wanted. Additionally, at any moment, a new maintenance procedure can be quickly selected from the menu. The “Production” option provides access to an interface where the operator can view production-related data for the selected machine within a user-defined time range, displayed in a dynamic table format. If the number of results is extensive, a scroll bar is provided to allow smoother navigation for the user. Available information includes the order number, batch number, and total quantity produced. The “Events” option follows a similar structure to the “Production” menu but provides detailed insights into various machine events, such as event name, date, event status, and other relevant data. Finally, the “General” option displays a card with key machine information, following a standard format already used by the factory in other applications. This section presents details such as twist direction, material type, and batch number.

Through this system, operators are expected to access information about spinning machines quickly and efficiently, as well as receive rapid training on the associated maintenance procedures. The use of markers enables fast selection of the desired machine without the need to leave the machine section. The entire machine data retrieval system was developed based on a standard already adopted by the factory in other applications, ensuring a seamless and familiar user experience for the operators. The incorporation of instructional videos as training aids and support during maintenance procedures allows for quick execution of a wide range of tasks, helping to reduce troubleshooting time and minimize machine and component downtime.

Integration of future functionalities will further enhance the application's capabilities. Through the chatbot, users will be able to quickly retrieve comprehensive information about any spinning machine. Moreover, it will allow users to compare machines, predict data trends, and search for in-depth maintenance details contained in the machine manuals. The integration of 3D animations into maintenance processes can complement the training videos by providing enhanced visual references and a more intuitive understanding of the procedures, showing different angles and revealing additional details.

5. TESTS AND RESULTS

To validate the developed application, a qualitative questionnaire was conducted in an industrial environment and administered to actual factory employees who perform critical roles in equipment operation and maintenance. Among the participants were the General Maintenance Manager, a Maintenance Area Manager, a Computer Engineer, and an Industrial Engineer. The sample consisted of four male individuals: two aged between 37–50 years and two between 50–65 years, all holding higher education degrees.

All participants unanimously found the proposed tasks easy to perform, highlighting the intuitiveness of marker recognition and the speed and accuracy of both voice and touch commands. Furthermore, they expressed overall satisfaction with the experience of using the Augmented Reality application, emphasizing positive aspects such as:

- Application fluidity;
- The training component;
- Ease and practicality of accessing machine data;

In addition to these comments, participants also provided suggestions for potential future improvements, including:

- A more appealing design;
- Enhanced interaction in the "Productions" and "Events" menus;

Lastly, the questionnaire incorporated the SUS (System Usability Scale) evaluation method (Sauro, J., 2017), which resulted in an overall score of 85 points, a value that indicates an excellent level of usability and strong user acceptance.

6. CONCLUSIONS AND FUTURE WORK

As earlier mentioned, this project is a continuation of a previous study. Accordingly, in addition to the existing conceptual review, a new, more focused study of related works was conducted, specifically examining articles on augmented reality and industrial maintenance. Finally, an application was developed that not only follows similar standards to the previously referenced studies but also meets the specific objectives of the real-world factory for which it is intended. The primary objective of this application is to optimize industrial maintenance processes and enhance information retrieval in a factory environment. This study explores the integration of augmented reality, an emerging technology, into the field of maintenance, with a particular focus on industrial textile machinery. The developed system has shown promising progress in optimizing maintenance processes and enabling real-time data access, as evidenced by the feedback obtained from factory employees. The results highlighted several positive aspects of using this technology, particularly its practicality in data visualization and its significant contribution to the training of operators. These findings underscore the successful implementation of the system and the high level of satisfaction expressed by the application's users. The integration of this type of technology is expected to enhance factories' ability to respond to equipment maintenance needs, reducing downtime and increasing operational efficiency.

In summary, this project has demonstrated the potential of an augmented reality application while establishing a foundation for further research and similar developments in the field of industrial maintenance. The initial state of the developed application is promising. However, to make it more comprehensive, further expansion will be necessary. In parallel with this application, an intelligent chatbot is being developed, leveraging machine data and maintenance PDFs to instantly respond to user queries via both text and voice. At present, however, this chatbot is only available as a web-based version. Integrating it into the augmented reality application will be essential to enhance functionality and further improve the level of support provided to factory operators. Additionally, a potential expansion could involve integrating additional support tools beyond the existing maintenance videos. This may include incorporating 3D models in AR, precisely overlaid onto the real components of the textile machines. To enable the inclusion of 3D animations, it is also essential to utilize 3D models of the objects for their detection. Suggestions provided by factory employees should also be carefully evaluated and considered for future implementations. Finally, exploring other types of devices, such as augmented reality glasses, should be considered to further enhance the application's practicality and ease of use, as well as to incorporate some of the improvements suggested by the factory employees.

ACKNOWLEDGEMENT

This work received financial support from the integrated project Pacto Mobilizador TEXP@CT – Innovation Pact for the Digitization of Textiles and Apparel (TC-C12-i01, Sustainable Bioeconomy No. 02/C12-i01/202), promoted by the Recovery and Resilience Plan (PRR), Next Generation EU, for the period 2021-2026.

REFERENCES

Alves, F. et al. (2020). Deployment of a Smart and Predictive Maintenance System in an Industrial Case Study. Proceedings of the IEEE 29th International Symposium on Industrial Electronics (ISIE), Delft, Netherlands, pp. 493-498.

Apple Inc. (2025). ARKit. Version 6. Available at: https://developer.apple.com/augmented-reality/arkit/.

Cachada, A. et al. (2019). Using AR Interfaces to Support Industrial Maintenance Procedures. Proceedings of the 45th Annual Conference of the IEEE Industrial Electronics Society (IECON), Lisbon, Portugal, pp. 3795-3800.

Caiza, G. and Sanz, R. (2022). Digital Twin for Monitoring an Industrial Process Using Augmented Reality. Proceedings of the 17th Iberian Conference on Information Systems and Technologies (CISTI), Madrid, Spain, pp. 1-5.

Dourado, I.L. et al. (2024). A Wearable AR System for Maintenance in Industry 5.0: Assessing Mental Workload and Usability. Proceedings of the 29th International Conference on Automation and Computing (ICAC), Exeter, UK, pp. 1-6.

Fernandez, F. et al. (2021). Control and Maintenance System with Augmented Reality for a Stone Counter. Proceedings of the 8th International Conference on Internet of Things: Systems, Management and Security (IOTSMS), Barcelona, Spain, pp. 1-5.

Gong, L. et al. (2021). A Framework for Extended Reality System Development in Manufacturing. IEEE Access, 9, pp. 24796-24813.

Hsu, H. H. and Chuang, C. Y. (2022). Application of Augmented Reality for Equipment Maintenance and Employee Training in Manufacturing Plant. Proceedings of the IEEE 4th Eurasia Conference on Biomedical Engineering, Healthcare and Sustainability (ECBIOS), Tainan, Taiwan, pp. 136-139.

Knopp, S. et al. (2019). Industrial Use Case - AR Guidance using HoloLens for Assembly and Disassembly of a Modular Mold, with Live Streaming for Collaborative Support. Proceedings of the IEEE International Symposium on Mixed and Augmented Reality Adjunct (ISMAR-Adjunct), Beijing, China, pp. 134-135.

Miranda, J. et al. (2024). Revolutionizing Industrial Maintenance: Virtual and Augmented Reality Meets Digital Twin. Proceedings of the 19th Iberian Conference on Information Systems and Technologies (CISTI), Salamanca, Spain, pp. 1-6.

Pai, H. Y. (2020). Mixed Reality of Augmented Reality in Mobile Learning for Aircraft Maintenance. Proceedings of the IEEE Eurasia Conference on IoT, Communication and Engineering (ECICE), Tainan, Taiwan, pp. 1-4.

Paripooranan, C. S. et al. (2020). An Implementation of AR Enabled Digital Twins for 3-D Printing. Proceedings of the IEEE International Symposium on Smart Electronic Systems (iSES), Chennai, India, pp. 155-160.

PTC. (2024). Vuforia. Version 2024. Available at: https://www.ptc.com/en/products/vuforia.

Rodrigues, A. et al. (2021). Mobile Augmented Reality as a Field-Assistance Tool in Urban Maintenance. Proceedings of the IEEE International Symposium on Mixed and Augmented Reality Adjunct (ISMAR-Adjunct), Bari, Italy, pp. 268-273.

Sauro, J. (2017). Recent Advances with the System Usability Scale. Available at: https://measuringu.com/sus-advances/.

Unity Technologies. (2023). Unity. Version 2022.3.18f1. Available at: https://unity3d.com/unity/.

Xue, Z. et al. (2024). AR-Assisted Guidance for Assembly and Maintenance of Avionics Equipment. Applied Sciences, 14(3), p.1137.

Zhu, Z. et al. (2019). Visualization of the Digital Twin Data in Manufacturing by Using Augmented Reality. Procedia CIRP, 81, pp. 898-903.

TWO YEARS ON, BENCHMARKING OF USABILITY AND USER EXPERIENCE: ELECTRONIC TABLE GAMES AGAINST ELECTRONIC GAMING MACHINES AT CASINOS

Victor K. Y. Chan
Macao Polytechnic University
Rua de Luis Gonzaga Gomes, Macao, China

ABSTRACT

Electronic gaming machines (EGMs), which emulated mechanical slot machines, were basically the first category of electronic gambling equipment ever at casinos and thus have epitomize such equipment. Admittedly, usability and user experience evaluation of EGMs, as information systems, can often be regarded as a baseline against which analogous evaluation of other less dated electronic gambling equipment, also as information systems, can be benchmarked. Another commonplace category of electronic gambling equipment is electronic table games (ETGs), which are electronic versions of myriad standardized, traditional table games and are considered as a newer generation of equipment than EGMs. Both these EGMs and ETGs play a substantive role in the digital transformation of the casino industry. This article dwells on not only benchmarking gamblers'/users' perceived usability of and user experience with ETGs against those of and with EGMs but also comparing such benchmarking in late 2022 with that in late 2024 in order to track the evolution of such benchmarking over the two years of casinos' digital transformation in between. Upon operationalizing the major constructs of the technology acceptance model (TAM) and the extended unified theory of acceptance and use of technology (UTAUT2) as well as the additional construct "trust" as per the mainstream literature, gamblers'/users' perceived usability of and user experience with ETGs and EGMs were gauged by such constructs as "perceived ease of use," "perceived usefulness," "perceived risk," "attitude," "social influence," "innovativeness," "stress to use a technology," and "trust." These constructs of ETGs and EGMs were rated in a questionnaire survey in Macao by $n = 693$ respondents in late 2022 and $n = 179$ in late 2024. A paired-samples t-test was conducted to contrast ETGs' and EGMs' construct scores of each construct derived from the ratings. reviewed It was found that mitigation or prevention of gamblers'/users' "perceived risk" was the only construct for which ETGs' mean construct score outperformed vis-à-vis EGMs' in both 2022 and 2024 ($p < 0.01$). Also, for the construct of "attitude" toward ETGs versus EGMs, ETGs' mean construct score surpassed EGMs' solely in 2022 ($p < 0.05$) but not any more in 2024. Additionally, for the construct of mitigation of "stress" to use ETGs versus EGMs, ETGs' mean construct score underperformed vis-à-vis EGMs' solely in 2024 ($p < 0.05$) but not any earlier in 2022. Furthermore, the mitigation or prevention of gamblers'/users' "perceived risk" was the only construct for which ETGs' versus EGMs' construct score in 2024 improved with respect to that in 2022 ($p < 0.01$). The overall implication was that there were drift and evolution of gamblers'/users' perceived usability of and user experience with ETGs versus EGMs over the two years between 2022 and 2024. This article advises that further research be undertaken to investigate the underlying reason for the above drift and evolution.

KEYWORDS

Usability, User Experience, Benchmarking, Electronic Table Games, Electronic Gaming Machines, Digital Transformation

1. INTRODUCTION

Electronic gaming machines (EGMs), which emulate mechanical slot machines, are often the most profitable game in casinos across various locales globally (Chan, 2024; Turner and Horbay, 2004) and the pioneer and the most emblematic category of electronic gambling equipment at casinos. EGMs epitomize the digital transformation of casinos as manifested by such machines' metamorphosis from mechanical operation into electronic operation (Chan, 2024; Dowling et al, 2005). They have been in the vanguard likely because their single gambling mode, chiefly for slot games (Chan, 2024; Dowling et al, 2005; Liu et al, 2021; Thomas et al, 2009), is conducive to their comparatively simple development and their low risk of failure in their deployment.

Therefore, for the purpose of usability and user experience evaluation, EGMs (as information systems) can often act as a baseline against which analogous evaluation of other electronic gambling equipment (also as information systems) can be benchmarked. Such "other" electronic gambling equipment is usually machines introduced years or even decades later that EGMs. It is noteworthy that the terminology "EGM" may refer to slightly different ranges of electronic gambling equipment dependent on the contexts and/or the locales. Whereas the terminology may broadly cover all electronic machines for slot games, video poker, video blackjack, keno, and so forth in some settings (Chan, 2024; Dowling et al, 2005; Thomas et al, 2009), it may be also exclusively synonymous with those for slot games on other occasions (Chan, 2024; Liu et al, 2021). This article tends to adhere to the latter in narrowing this terminology's coverage.

Another commonplace category of electronic gambling equipment is electronic table games (ETGs), which are electronic versions of myriad standardized, traditional table games like baccarat, sic-bo, craps, roulette, blackjack, poker, Texas hold'em poker, and keno and are considered as a newer generation of equipment than EGMs (Chan, 2024). Sometimes, the terminology "ETGs" also includes livestream table games, which are known as stadium style ETGs and first appeared in Asian casinos around 2000 and subsequently elsewhere in the world. Such stadium style ETGs may also deploy intelligent robot dealers. (Chan, 2024; Liu et al, 2021) Also, Game Source Entertainment, a company dedicated to online gambling platforms, developed mobile ETGs on tablets which were the size of an iPad and offered in a Macao casino (Chan, 2024; Liu et al, 2021). In comparison to traditional table games, ETGs can cut back on labor costs and provide similar gambling experience to mass-market players who prefer a lower minimum bet. They can also almost obviate human errors, staff dishonesty and increase game speed. Their another merit is that ETGs do not take up any table license in, for instance, Macao and probably other jurisdictions legalizing gambling while presenting a modernistic gambling experience to table game players. (Chan, 2024; Liu et al, 2021)

This article dwells on not only benchmarking gamblers'/users' perceived usability of and user experience with ETGs against those of and with EGMs but also comparing such benchmarking in late 2022 with that in late 2024 in order to track the evolution of such benchmarking over the two years of casinos' digital transformation in between. Such comparison and tracking of the evolution were inspired by the temporality of perceived usability of and/or user experience with information systems, which had long been affirmed (Karapanos et al, 2009), and the need to unravel such temporality. Appertaining to the author's motivation behind studying usability of and user experience with ETGs versus EGMs, Liu et al. (2021) strongly proposed further investigation into "the acceptance level of customers (gamblers) regarding advanced technology on the casino floor." In other words, usability of and user experience with such electronic gambling equipment as ETGs and EGMs is conceived of as a determinant in the further development of information system- or information technology-based gaming equipment in the digital transformation of the casino industry.

To benchmark gamblers'/users' perceived usability of and user experience with ETGs against those of and with EGMs, this article primarily adopts the technology acceptance model (TAM) and the extended unified theory of acceptance and use of technology (UTAUT2). As such, the TAM and the UTAUT2 are first briefly introduced in this paragraph, as principally adapted from Chan (2024). In fact, the TAM has virtually been the de facto instrument for decades to predict users' intention to use or acceptance of particular information technologies or information systems. For example, in the domain of electronic gambling equipment, Nisbet (2006) modelled consumers' (gamblers') intention to use gambling technologies for card-based games by means of a modified version of TAM and a related questionnaire administered to 134 patrons of two gambling venues. Structural equation modelling revealed that "usefulness" was a significant predictor of 'intention to use' card-based gambling systems and that "ease-of-use" also had a positive effect on "intention to use" the technologies. Despite TAM's prowess, the unified theory of acceptance and use of technology (UTAUT) redresses TAM's weakness in comprehensiveness by incorporating such factors/constructs as facilitating conditions, social influence, etc. in the prediction of users' intention to use or acceptance of information technologies and information systems (Dwivedi et al, 2019). The extended unified theory of acceptance and use of technology (UTAUT2), as its name implies, further extends the UTAUT by the additional factors/constructs of hedonic motivation, price and habit (Singh et al, 2020). The UTAUT2 has been applied to information technologies and information systems in numerous business domains to predict users' intention to use and acceptance. For mobile payment, Oliveira et al. (2016) found factors like "compatibility," "perceived technology security," "performance expectations," "innovativeness," and "social influence" to have significant direct and indirect effects over the adoption of mobile payment and the "intention to recommend" this technology. The relevance of customers' "intention to recommend" mobile payment technology in social networks and other means of communication was also confirmed, supporting the recommendation to include it in social marketing campaigns and in future technology adoption studies. As for mobile wallets, as a category of mobile payment, Singh et al. (2020) discovered that "ease of use," "usefulness," "perceived risk," and "attitude" exerted significant effects on users' "intention to use" mobile wallets, which further influenced users' "perceived satisfaction" and "recommendation to use" mobile wallet services. They also determined the significant moderating effects of "stress to use" and "social influence" on users' "perceived satisfaction" and "recommendation to use" mobile wallet services. Regrettably, in spite of these examples of the UTAUT2's use, the author could hardly find any of its application to the casino industry except that in Chan (2024). As a matter of fact, this study, as with Chan (2024), employed the TAM and the UTAUT2 for a "niche" purpose as opposed to their mainstream purpose to predict users' intention to use or acceptance of particular information technologies or information systems. To this end, the TAM and the UTAUT2's factors/constructs were harnessed as perspectives of gamblers' perceived usability and user experience in order to benchmark ETGs against EGMs instead of serving as a theoretical framework to attest to any causality as to how such factors/constructs predict users' intention to use or acceptance of ETGs or EGMs. To complement the TAM's and the UTAUT2's constructs, the additional construct "trust" as proposed by Alalwan et al. (2017) was incorporated as another perspective for a similar benchmarking purpose in consideration of Alalwan et al.'s (2017) investigation into mobile banking being rather analogous to this study on ETGs and EGMs at least because both the underlying banking and the gambling industries concerned large volumes of financial transactions of appreciable amounts and thus necessitated "trust" from the industries' "users." This way, this study measured these constructs in respect of gamblers' perceived usability and user experience with ETGs versus those of more long-standing EGMs as a baseline, i.e., on a scale relative to those of EGMs, so as to realize benchmarking gamblers' perceived usability of and user experience with ETGs against those of and with EGMs. Given that this study attempted to compare such benchmarking in late 2022 with that in late 2024 in order to track the evolution of such benchmarking over the two years of casinos' digital transformation in between, it used a multiple cross-sectional research design, or only a dual cross-sectional research design, to conduct such benchmarking (or such measurement) twice at the two points in time above. Such tracking revealed what the industry achieved in the development, enhancement, and upgrades of ETGs as compared with those of well-established and long-standing EGMs as a baseline. It is noteworthy that analyses with respect to baselines are not only common and typical but also traditional (Assmann et al, 2000).

2. METHODOLOGY

2.1 Materials

The methodology of this article's study was in essence a dual cross-sectional research design version of Chan's (2024), which corresponded to phase 1 (in late 2022) of this study' methodology. Each of the two data samples of this study was collected in a questionnaire survey conducted, respectively, in phase 1 (in late 2022) and phase 2 (in late 2024) in Macao (also spelt as "Macau"), which was arguably regarded as one of the world's largest gambling cities (Metaxas and Folinas, 2021). Therefore, the first sample was exactly that of Chan (2024). In each phase, students were tasked with the data collection as part of their coursework in a course on system analysis and design. The author was the professor in charge of the course, and prepared a questionnaire. The questionnaire was designed to gauge gamblers'/users' perceived usability of and user experience with both ETGs and EGMs in the perspectives corresponding to the constructs of the TAM and the UTAUT2 (Singh et al, 2020) and the additional construct "trust" (TR) (Alalwan et al, 2017). The TAM's and the UTAUT2's constructs were the "perceived ease of use" (EOU), the "perceived usefulness" (PU), the "perceived risk" (RISK), the "attitude" (ATTD), the "social influence" (SI), the "intention to use" (INTU), the "innovativeness" (INNOVA), the "stress to use a technology" (STRESS), the "perceived satisfaction" (SATISFN), and the "recommendation to use" (RECOMD). The questionnaire operationalized each of these constructs using a few observed variables, each of which in turn corresponded to a questionnaire question for the respondent to rate on a scale of 1 to 7, with 1 strongly disagreeing to the question (in the form of a statement) and 7 strongly agreeing to the question. For each respondent, each observed variable took on a value equal to his/her rating of the corresponding question. The questionnaire questions for such operationalization of the TAM/UTAUT2 constructs and the additional construct "trust" were adapted from those of Singh et al (2020) and Alalwan et al (2017) but substituting wordings of mobile wallet and mobile banking with those of ETGs and EGMs.

In each phase, the author posted several copies of the questionnaire online on the Tencent Wenjuan survey platform. The platform attached Internet domain names and access QR codes to each questionnaire copy so that potential respondents could access any copy through the corresponding Internet domain names or the corresponding access QR codes. Each team of students opted for one distinct copy and thus the corresponding Internet domain names and the corresponding access QR codes. The students invited their acquaintances by e-mail, instant messaging, or otherwise to respond to the questionnaire copy via such corresponding Internet domain names and access QR codes. Finally, each team submitted a report section on how they invited respondents, how many invitations were issued, etc. The report section might also depict some descriptive statistics and analysis of the collected data sample, and was graded and counted toward the students' coursework marks.

There was a prerequisite that the respondents be aged at least 16 years. Despite the legal age for gambling casino in Macao being a few years higher, this age of 16 years intended not to miss out respondents having gambled elsewhere. The questionnaire's preamble informed the respondents of the survey's objectives, the author's and thus the students' affiliation and its contacts, the anonymity of the questionnaire, the stringent confidentiality of respondents' responses, the absolutely voluntary nature of respondents' responses, and the respondents' inviolable right to terminate their responses at any time. Also, prior to the questions, the questionnaire elucidated what an ETG and an EGM at a casino were with a typical photograph of each of them.

Pooling the data collected by three and four teams respectively, the final sample for phase 1 (in 2022) comprised $n = 693$ respondents and that for phase 2 (in 2024) consisted of $n = 179$ respondents.

2.2 Methods

In consideration of this article's focus on the perceived usability of and user experience with ETGs versus EGMs as information systems, the analysis only targeted the TAM/UTAUT2 constructs that were conventionally independent (i.e., antecedent-like) or moderating variables in TAM/UTAUT2 modelling, i.e., EOU, PU, RISK, ATTD, SI, INNOVA, and STRESS, together with the additional construct TR. In other words, constructs that usually played the roles of dependent (i.e., consequent-like) variables, namely, INTU, SATISFN, and RECOMD, were excluded because these three constructs were to gauge resultant effects (i.e., consequents) as opposed to causes (i.e., antecedent) as measured by the independent and moderating variables above. Each of these TAM/UTAUT2 constructs targeted and the additional construct TR was operationalized in ways where the corresponding questionnaire questions were occasionally structured in opposite directions. Stated differently, a high rating could correspond to favorable usability and user experience in some questions but unfavorable in some other questions. Such ratings as awarded by each respondent were unified such that a high rating of any question cohesively meant favorable usability and user experience as perceived by the respondent. Subsequently, the unified ratings (i.e., the underlying observed variables' unified values) from each respondent for each construct were averaged to give a construct score for the construct as accorded by the respondent.

Paired samples *t*-tests (two-tailed) were conducted to contrast ETGs' and EGMs' construct scores of each construct targeted in this study over all respondents in each of the two samples so as to find the constructs of which ETGs' construct scores were inferior (or superior) to EGMs' in each phase, i.e. to benchmark ETG's construct scores against EGMs' in each phase. These constructs so found were indicative of the perceived usability and user experience perspectives of existing ETGs that lagged behind (or surpassed) existing EGMs' benchmarking baseline. This study then moved on to juxtaposing such benchmarking in phase 1 (in 2022) with that in phase 2 (in 2024) in a bid to compare and track the evolution of such benchmarking over the two years of casinos' digital transformation in between. In addition, independent samples *t*-tests (two-tailed) were applied to the phase 1 (in 2022) sample and the phase 2 (in 2024) sample for the difference between ETGs' and EGMs' construct scores of each construct targeted in the study across all respondents in the two samples. This unraveled such drift and evolution of such benchmarking from phase 1 (in 2022) to phase 2 (in 2024).

3. RESULTS

For each of the two samples, Table 1 enumerates the results from the paired samples *t*-tests (two-tailed) conducted to contrast ETGs' and EGMs' construct scores of each construct targeted in the study across all respondents in each sample, inclusive of the sample mean difference between ETGs' and EGMs' construct scores, the 95% confidence interval for the population mean difference, the *t*-statistic, its degrees of freedom, and its *p*-value. Please note that each *t*-statistic therein tested the hypothesis that the population mean difference in the construct scores of the corresponding construct between ETGs and EGMs differed from zero (i.e., two-tailed). The data for phase 1 (in 2022) are from Chan (2024). Also, if one is to interpret the *t*-statistics in the table as those for one-tailed *t*-tests (for example, to test for positivity or negativity of the differences in the population mean differences in ETGs' and EGMs' construct scores between the two phases), the *p*-values stated therein should be halved before treating them as *p*-values for the corresponding one-tailed *t*-tests.

Table 1. Results from the paired samples *t*-tests (two-tailed) for both phase 1 (in 2022) and phase 2 (in 2024), those for phase 1 being from Chan (2024)

Construct	Sample mean differences between ETGs' and EGMs' construct scores in phases 1 and 2, respectively	95% confidence intervals for the population mean differences in phase 1 and 2, respectively	*t* (degrees of freedom), *p*-value
EOU	0.0382 -0.0335	-0.0244 to 0.1009 -0.1464 to 0.0794	1.199(692), 0.231 -0.586(178), 0.559
PU	0.0206 0.0084	-0.0364 to 0.0775 -0.1050 to 0.1217	0.709(692), 0.478 0.146(178), 0.884
RISK	0.0844 0.7654	0.0254 to 0.1435 0.6287 to 0.9021	2.807(692), 0.005** 11.049(178), 0.000**
ATTD	0.0844 -0.0028	0.0204 to 0.1484 -0.1065 to 0.1009	2.591(692), 0.010* -0.053(178), 0.958
SI	-0.0242 -0.0224	-0.0823 to 0.0340 -0.1340 to 0.0893	-0.816(692), 0.415 -0.395(178), 0.693
INNOVA	0.0635 0.0150	-0.0585 to 0.1855 -0.0540 to 0.0830	1.022(692), 0.307 0.429(178), 0.668
STRESS	-0.0390 -0.1508	-0.1152 to 0.0372 -0.2858 to -0.0159	-1.004(692), 0.316 -2.206(178), 0.029*
TR	-0.0055 0.0372	-0.0570 to 0.0460 -0.0525 to 0.1270	-0.211(692), 0.833 0.819(178), 0.414

* $p < 0.05$
** $p < 0.01$
If one is to interpret the *t*-statistics in the table as those for one-tailed *t*-tests (for example, to test for positivity or negativity of the differences in the population mean differences in ETGs' and EGMs' construct scores between the two phases), the *p*-values stated here should be halved before treating them as *p*-values for the corresponding one-tailed *t*-tests.

Upon rating unification, RISK denotes mitigation or prevention of gamblers'/users' "perceived risk," and it was the only construct for which ETGs' mean construct score outperformed vis-à-vis EGMs' in both phase 1 (in 2022) and phase 2 (in 2024) with statistical significance. This was manifested by the findings that the sample mean differences between ETGs' and EGMs' construct scores in both phase 1 (in 2022) and phase 2 (in 2024) were positive and had the corresponding 95% confidence intervals not spanning zero, and the corresponding two-tailed *t*-tests (degrees of freedom or df = 692 and 178 respectively) had *p*-values less than 1%, so the corresponding population mean differences were positive and differed from zero at the 1% significance level (i.e., $p < 0.01$). In contrast, for the construct ATTD, i.e., "attitude" toward ETGs versus EGMs, ETGs' mean construct score surpassed EGMs' solely in phase 1 (in 2022) with statistical significance but no more in phase 2 (in 2024). This was ascertained by the findings that the sample mean difference between ETGs' and EGMs' construct scores in phase 1 (in 2022) was positive and had the corresponding 95% confidence interval not spanning zero, and the corresponding two-tailed *t*-test (df = 692) had a *p*-value less than 5%, so the corresponding population mean difference was positive and differed from zero at the 5% significance level (i.e., $p < 0.05$) but these findings were no longer true of phase 2 (in 2024). On the contrary, for the construct STRESS, i.e., mitigation of "stress" to use ETGs versus EGMs, ETGs' mean construct score underperformed vis-à-vis EGMs' solely in phase 2 (in 2024) with statistical significance but not in phase 1 (in 2022). This was attested by the findings that the sample mean difference between ETGs' and EGMs' construct scores in phase 2 (in 2024) was negative and had the corresponding 95% confidence interval not spanning zero, and the corresponding two-tailed *t*-test (df = 178) had a *p*-value less than 5%, so the corresponding population mean difference was negative and differed from zero at the 5% significance level (i.e., $p < 0.05$) but these findings were not true of phase 1 (in 2022).

Table 2 delineates the results from the independent samples *t*-tests (two-tailed) applied to the phase 1 (in 2022) sample and the phase 2 (in 2024) sample for the difference between ETGs' and EGMs' construct scores of each construct targeted in the study across all respondents in the two samples, inclusive of the sample mean difference between the two samples in such a difference between ETGs' and EGMs' construct scores of each construct, the 95% confidence interval for the population mean difference between the two corresponding populations, the *t*-statistic, its degrees of freedom and its *p*-value. If one is to interpret the *t*-statistics in the table as those for one-tailed *t*-tests (for example, to test for positivity or negativity of the population mean differences between the phase 1 sample and the phase 2 sample in the difference between ETGs' and EGMs' construct scores), the *p*-values stated therein should be halved before treating them as p-values for the corresponding one-tailed *t*-tests.

Table 2. Results from the independent samples *t*-tests (two-tailed)

Construct	Sample mean difference between the phase 1 sample and the phase 2 sample in the difference between ETGs' and EGMs' construct scores	95% confidence interval for the population mean difference between the phase 1 population and the phase 2 population for the difference between ETGs' and EGMs' construct scores	*t* (degrees of freedom), *p*-value
EOU	0.07176	-0.05715 to 0.20067	1.095(298.448), 0.274
PU	0.01218	-0.11448 to 0.13884	0.189(275.671), 0.850
RISK	-0.68095	-0.82968 to -0.53221	-9.017(249.137), 0.000**
ATTD	0.08721	-0.03443 to 0.20885	1.41(328.636), 0.159
SI	-0.00182	-0.1275 to 0.12385	-0.029(283.634), 0.977
INNOVA	0.04859	-0.0911 to 0.18829	0.683(864.094), 0.495
STRESS	0.11188	-0.04282 to 0.26657	1.423(303.08), 0.156
TR	-0.04278	-0.14606 to 0.0605	-0.815(307.406), 0.416

** $p < 0.01$

If one is to interpret the *t*-statistics in the table as those for one-tailed *t*-tests (for example, to test for positivity or negativity of the population mean differences between the phase 1 sample and the phase 2 sample in the difference between ETGs' and EGMs' construct scores), the *p*-values stated here should be halved before treating them as *p*-values for the corresponding one-tailed *t*-tests.

RISK, i.e., mitigation or prevention of gamblers'/users' "perceived risk," was the only construct for which ETGs' versus EGMs' mean construct score in phase 2 (in 2024) improved with respect to that in phase 1 (in 2022) with statistical significance. This was confirmed by the findings that the sample mean difference between the phase 1 (in 2022) sample and the phase 2 (in 2024) sample in the difference between ETGs' and EGMs' construct scores was negative and had the corresponding 95% confidence intervals not spanning zero, and the corresponding two-tailed *t*-test (df = 249.137) had a *p*-value less than 1%, so the corresponding population mean difference was negative and differed from zero at the 1% significance level (i.e., $p < 0.01$).

4. CONCLUSION AND DISCUSSION

In view of the temporality of perceived usability of and user experience with information systems, this article attempts to chart the drift and evolution of the benchmarking of gamblers'/users' perceived usability of and user experience with ETGs against those of and with EGMs over the two years of casinos' digital transformation from late 2022 to late 2024. Multiple (or, more exactly, dual) cross-sectional research design was employed to compare the gamblers'/users' usability of and user experience with both ETGs and EGMs as measured by the TAM's and the UTAUT2's factors/constructs and the additional construct "trust" in 2022 with those in 2024. Detailed statistical findings are presented in Table 1 and Table 2, which not only juxtapose the benchmarking for 2022 and that for 2024 but also factors/construct(s) with statistically significant variation over the two years in between.

It was found that of all these constructs, mitigation or prevention of gamblers'/users' "perceived risk" was the only construct for which ETGs' mean construct score outperformed vis-à-vis EGMs' in both phase 1 (in 2022) and phase 2 (in 2024) with statistical significance where EGMs were usually treated as a baseline for such benchmarking. In contrast, for the construct of "attitude" toward ETGs versus EGMs, ETGs' mean construct score surpassed EGMs' solely in phase 1 (in 2022) with statistical significance but not any more in 2024. On the contrary, for the construct of mitigation of "stress" to use ETGs versus EGMs, ETGs' mean construct score underperformed vis-à-vis EGMs' solely in phase 2 (in 2024) with statistical significance but not any earlier in phase 1 (in 2022). The implication is that among the various perspectives of gamblers'/users' perceived usability and user experience, only the mitigation or prevention of gamblers'/users' "perceived risk" for ETGs consistently defeated that for EGMs whereas the superiority of the "attitude" toward ETGs over the "attitude" toward EGMs in phase 1 (in 2022) failed to be defended in phase 2 (in 2024). In addition, the mitigation of "stress" to use ETGs versus EGMs deteriorated to realize a disadvantage only in phase 2 (in 2024) but not any earlier in phase 1 (in 2022). In other words, there were drift and evolution of gamblers'/users' perceived usability of and user experience with ETGs versus EGMs over the two years between the two phases in 2022 and 2024 at least in the perspectives of the "attitude" toward ETGs versus EGMs and the mitigation of "stress" to use ETGs versus EGMs. In addition, the mitigation or prevention of gamblers'/users' "perceived risk" was the only construct for which ETGs' construct score versus EGMs' in phase 2 (in 2024) improved with respect to that in phase 1 (in 2022) with statistical significance. In other words, there were additional drift and evolution of gamblers'/users' perceived usability of and user experience with ETGs versus EGMs over the two years in that the lead taken by ETGs' mitigation or prevention of gamblers'/users' "perceived risk" versus EGMs' was enlarged.

Meanwhile, this article is not able to conjecture why gamblers'/users' perceived usability of and user experience with ETGs versus EGMs over the two years exhibited the above drift and evolution, not to mention any scientific rationale for any conjecture. In fact, these are beyond the article's scope. This said, it is at least safe to advise that casinos keep up ETGs' mitigation or prevention of gamblers'/users' "perceived risk" versus EGMs' and that casinos step up the amelioration of the "attitude" toward ETGs versus EGMs and the mitigation of "stress" to use ETGs versus EGMs. Such advice may stand out as the major practical contribution of this article, at least for casino operators. This article also recommends that further research be undertaken to investigate the underlying reason for the above drift and evolution of gamblers'/users' perceived usability of and user experience with ETGs versus EGMs.

This study is not without its critics. First, ETGs' and EGMs' designs vary rather drastically across different casinos and across ETGs' and EGMs' brands and versions. This study's data samples collected were only generically reflective of gamblers'/users' usability of and user experience with the variety of ETG and EGM brands and versions installed in the casinos across Macao as of the points in time during the data collection in phase 1 (in 2022) and phase 2 (in 2024). Nuanced data collection and subsequent analysis pinpointing each individual ETG and EGM brand and version of each casino operator could have rendered the study much more refined though needless to say at a far higher cost than that of this study. Second, this study's data samples were self-reported, self-evaluated, and in accordance with respondents' recollection of their perception while gambling on ETGs and EGMs at casinos some time ago. The fidelity of the data samples to respondents' perception could have been improved by conducting data collection right inside or at least around the exits of casinos where respondents' memory of their perception during gambling on ETGs and EGMs was likely fresh. Third, the data sample size for phase 2 (in 2024) was appreciably smaller than that for phase 1 (in 2022). Though not absolutely necessary in statistics, if the sample size for phase 2 (in 2024) had been comparable to that for phase 1 (in 2022), statistical significance in the paired samples t-tests in phase 2 would have been uncovered even if it was otherwise obscure in this study's phase 2 with a much smaller sample size. In other words, the smaller sample size for phase 2 (in 2024) might have weakened the t-tests' statistical power. Also, the smaller sample size might have rendered the t-tests more prone to errors resulting from the sample's non-normality, if any. Four, this study aimed to track how gamblers'/users' perceived usability of and user experience with ETGs versus EGMs evolved over the past two years of casinos' digital transformation but did not intend to fathom the reasons and mechanisms underlying such evolution, which were left to future researches. Fifth, this study was basically confined to Macao while extension to other locales worldwide may be able to enrich and generalize the findings.

REFERENCES

Alalwan, A. A. et al. (2017). Factors Influencing Adoption of Mobile Banking by Jordanian Bank Customers: Extending UTAUT2 with Trust. *In International Journal of Information Management*, Vol. 37, No. 3, pp: 99–110. https://doi.org/10.1016/j.ijinfomgt.2017.01.002

Assmann, S. F. et al. (2000). Subgroup Analysis and Other (Mis)uses of Baseline Data in Clinical Trials. *In Lancet*, Vol. 355, pp. 1064–1069. https://doi.org/10.1016/S0140-6736(00)02039-0

Chan, V. K. Y. (2024). Benchmarking of Usability and User Experience: Electronic Table Games against Electronic Gaming Machines at Casinos. *In Procedia Computer Science*, Vol. 239, pp. 852–859. https://doi.org/10.1016/j.procs.2024.06.244

Dowling, N. et al. (2005). Electronic Gaming Machines: Are They the "Crack-Cocaine" of Gambling? *In Addiction*, Vol. 100, No. 1, pp. 33–45. https://doi.org/10.1111/j.1360-0443.2005.00962.x

Dwivedi, Y. K. et al. (2019). Re-examining the Unified Theory of Acceptance and Use of Technology (UTAUT): Towards a Revised Theoretical Model. *In Information Systems Frontiers*, Vol. 21, pp. 719–734. https://doi.org/10.1007/s10796-017-9774-y

Karapanos, E. et al. (2009). User Experience over Time: An Initial Framework. *Proceedings of the SIGCHI Conference on Human Factors in Computing Systems (CHI '09)*. Boston, USA, pp. 729–738. https://doi.org/10.1145/1518701.1518814

Liu, M. T. et al. (2021). The Application of Digital Technology in Gambling Industry. *In Asia Pacific Journal of Marketing and Logistics*, Vol. 33, No. 7, pp.1685–1705. https://doi.org/10.1108/APJML-11-2020-0778

Metaxas, T. and Folinas, S. (2021). Gambling Tourism and Economic Development: Some Lessons from Macao. Journal of Economics, Finance and Management Studies, Vol. 4, No. 3, pp. 156–165. https://doi.org/10.47191/jefms/v4-i3-07

Nisbet, S. L. (2006). Modelling Consumer Intention to Use Gambling Technologies: An Innovative Approach. *In Behaviour & Information Technology*, Vol. 25, No. 3, pp. 221–231. https://doi.org/10.1080/01449290500167840

Oliveira, T. et al. (2016). Mobile payment: Understanding the Determinants of Customer Adoption and Intention to Recommend the Technology. *In Computers in Human Behavior*, Vol. 61, pp. 404–414. https://doi.org/10.1016/j.chb.2016.03.030

Singh, N. et al. (2020). Determining Factors in the Adoption and Recommendation of Mobile Wallet Services in India: Analysis of the Effect of Innovativeness, Stress to Use and Social Influence. *In International Journal of Information Management*, Vol. 50, pp. 191–205. https://doi.org/10.1016/j.ijinfomgt.2019.05.022

Thomas, A. C. et al. (2009). Electronic Gaming Machine Gambling: Measuring Motivation. *In Journal of Gambling Studies*, Vol. 25, No. 3, pp. 343–355. https://doi.org/10.1007/s10899-009-9133-0

Turner, N. and Horbay, R. (2004). How Do Slot Machines and Other Electronic Gambling Machines Actually Work? *In Journal of Gambling Issues*, pp. 1–36. https://doi.org/10.4309/jgi.2004.11.21

DEEP LEARNING MODELS FOR BITCOIN PRICE PREDICTION ACROSS MULTIPLE HORIZONS

Sirine El Hadj, Fahmi Ben Rejab and Kaouhter Nouira
Université de Tunis, ISGT, LR99ES04 BESTMOD, Tunis, Tunisia

ABSTRACT

In the intervening years, significant advances have been made in cryptocurrency prediction. Because of the volatility and dynamism of prices, any prediction about the price of cryptocurrencies is complicated. Several thousand cryptocurrencies are currently on the market worldwide. This paper proposes two deep learning models and a hybrid model designed for bitcoin price prediction. According to the RMSE and MAPE, these models provide excellent predictions. The results confirm that the hybrid model outperforms the GRU model and Bi-LSTM model in predicting bitcoin. The hybrid model shows the best prediction for bitcoin (BTC), with an average MAPE of 5.85%. The Bi-LSTM is 6.18%. GRU 6.25%. The three models outlined in this paper yield accurate results on the basis of the real price of the BTC.

KEYWORDS

Bitcoin Prediction, Deep Learning, Cryptocurrency, Machine learning, Hybrid Model

1. INTRODUCTION

Today, bitcoin is the most famous and valuable cryptocurrency (Wang et al, 2024) and was created by Nakamoto (2008) on the basis of blockchain technology. There are approximately 9825 cryptocurrencies according to coinmarketcaps[1]. At the beginning of 2025, bitcoin exceeds $100,000. On 01/27/2025, 1 bitcoin is valued at $102,680.3. For the same day, 1 Ethereum is worth $3,235.85 and is ranked 2nd directly after bitcoin. 1 Solana is the equivalent of $240.88. One doge coin is equal to $0.3363. All this price information is available on a coin market cap. Various studies on predicting the price of cryptocurrencies, particularly BTCs, have employed different methods. To address cryptocurrency prices that exhibit enormous fluctuations and nonstationarity, a major branch of research based on deep learning models was applied. The value of cryptocurrencies depends mainly on many factors, such as historical data, blockchain data and market data. Motivated by the existing state-of-the-art methods and to predict the bitcoin price effectively, we work on real data. We then compared the hybrid model and the deep learning models. We used the MAPE and RMSE metrics to ensure optimum evaluation.

2. RELATED WORKS

Patel et al. (2020) revealed that the LSTM-GRU model predicted the price of cryptocurrencies with excellent accuracy. Hamayel et al. (2021) presented three RNN algorithms for predicting the values of cryptocurrencies, including LTC, BTC, and ETH. The models provide outstanding predictions on the basis of the MAPE. The results demonstrated that the GRU outperformed Bi-LSTM and LSTM. Rafi et al. (2023) recently revealed that the MDI approach using Bi-LSTM performed best. A recent study by Jakubik et al. (2023) revealed that the predictions of LSTM surpass those of random forest and CNN models. The results demonstrate that the proposed scheme significantly predicts prices, revealing that the GRU-LSTM model can predict the prices of several cryptocurrencies. Tanwar et al. (2021) confirmed that the LSTM-GRU generated greater forecast accuracy than other models did. Awoke et al. (2021) employed a deep learning model based on LSTM and a

[1]coinmarketcap.com

GRU to predict the price of bitcoin. Nithyakani et al. (2021) confirmed that the Bi-LSTM model was able to track the test dataset and can help decision makers in bitcoin price prediction. To predict the bitcoin price, Mudassir et al. (2020) applied four types of machine learning models: ANN, SANN, SVM and LSTM. The LSTM performed the best. The shallow Bi-LSTM method proposed by Modi et al. (2023) outperforms the LR, SVR and LSTM methods. In the paper by Hansun et al. (2022), the GRU outperformed Bi-LSTM and LSTM (Table 1).

Table 1. Related work

Category	Author	Year	Dataset	Model
Hybrid model	Patel et al (2020)	2020	LTC, XMR	LSTM-GRU model
Hybrid model	Tanwar et al (2021)	2021	LTC, Zcash	LSTM-GRU model
Hybrid model	Awoke et al (2021)	2021	BTC	LSTM-GRU model
Deep learning	Hamayel et al (2021)	2021	BTC, ETH, LTC	LSTM, GRU, Bi-LSTM
Deep learning	Nithyakani et al (2021)	2021	BTC	Bi-LSTM model
Deep learning	Rafi et al (2023)	2023	BTC, ETH	Bi-LSTM model
ML	Mudassir et al (2020)	2020	BTC	LSTM, ANN, SANN, SVM
ML	Hansun et al (2022)	2022	BTC, ETH, BNB, ADA, USDT	Bi-LSTM, LSTM, GRU
ML	Jakubik et al (2023)	2023	BTC	LSTM, RF, CNN
ML	Modi et al (2023)	2023	BTC	Bi-LSTM, LSTM, Shallow Bi-LSTM, LR, SVR

3. METHODOLOGY

3.1 Bi-LSTM

The Bi-LSTM is a combination of two independent LSTM architectures in which information is learned forward and backwards to generate a network with sequences of input data (Kwak et al, 2020). The target signal forecast is called the composite output. This method has proven very useful. Equations (1) and (2) are used to calculate the direct function of the bi-LSTM with inputs of L units and H as the number of hidden units (Hamayel and Owda, 2021).

$$a_h^t = \sum_{l=1}^{L} x_l^t w_{lh} + \sum_{h',t>0}^{H} b_{h'}^{t-1} w_{h'h} \quad (1)$$
$$a_h^t = \theta_h(a_h^t) \quad (2)$$

3.2 GRU

Gated recurrent neural networks (GRNNs) have shown their efficiency across a number of applications on the basis of sequential or temporal data (Hamayel and Owda, 2021). The following are the transition functions in the GRU's hidden units. The model includes W, V, and b as weights, and biases are learned during training. All the weights are shared across time steps. (.) represents element-by-element multiplication. k is the dimension of the hidden vectors to be chosen as a hyperparameter (Su et al, 2019; Hamayel and Owda, 2021).

$$z_t = \sigma(W^z x_t + V^z h_{t-1} + b^z) \quad (3)$$
$$r_t = \sigma(W^r x_t + V^r h_{t-1} + b^r) \quad (4)$$

$$\bar{h}_t = \tanh(W^c x_t + V^c (r_t . h_{t-1})) \quad (5)$$

$$h_t = (1 - z_t) . h_{t-1} + z_t . \bar{h}_t \quad (6)$$

3.3 Bi-LSTM-GRU

Considering the advantages of Bi-LSTM and the GRU and according to Raju et al. (2023), we propose the Bi-LSTM-GRU model. Combining Bi-LSTM and the GRU allows us to analyse a sequence in both directions with the rapidity of the GRU. Starting with Bi-LSTM, which reads the time series. The GRU then converts this bidirectional representation into a low-dimensional vector, limiting the number of parameters and offering an ideal compromise between expressiveness and rapidity. This architecture eliminates short-term variations before the final prediction phase, which considerably reduces noise and improves forecast accuracy. The methodology comprises the following sequential steps:

Preprocessing Load BTC price data and set the date as the index Normalise values between 0 and 1 using MinMaxScaler
Sequence Construction Use a sliding window of 60 days (look_back = 60) Build X (60-day history) and y (next-day price) arrays
Train/Test Split 80% of sequences for training, 20% for validation
Model Architecture Bidirectional LSTM *with 10 units, returning full sequences* Dropout *layer with rate 0.1* GRU *with 10 units, returning only the last state* Dropout *layer with rate 0.1* Dense *output layer with 1 unit*
Training 100 epochs, batch size of 32 Monitor training and validation loss
Prediction Generate predictions on the test set and invert the normalisation Forecast the next 60 days iteratively using a rolling window

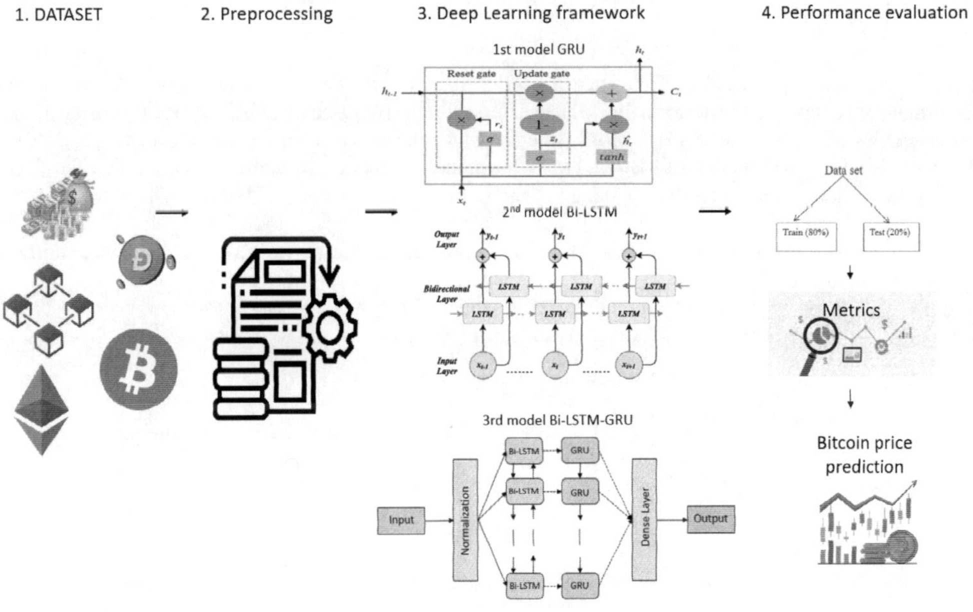

Figure 1. Framework of the proposed methodology

4. SIMULATION RESULTS AND ANALYSIS

4.1 Dataset Preparation Method

Data processing involves gathering, combining, organising and structuring information, which can then be interpreted as data visualisation, analysis and exploration via deep learning (Figure 1). It is crucial to provide accurate information for the questions we are aiming to address. In this section, we present the details of the dataset used for this research consists of daily price values collected from several website databases. The database that we created includes Bitcoin blockchain information from 2013-01-01 to 2024-11-11. Cryptocurrency market data relating to Bitcoin, Tether (USDT), Solana (SOL), Binance coin (BNB), Ripple (XRP), and Doge coin (DOGE) from 2013-01-01 to 2024-10-31. US Data Market from 2013-01-01 to 2024-11-12. European Data Market from 2013-01-01 to 2024-11-12. Asian Data Market from 2013-01-01 to 2024-11-12. Rates from 2013-01-01 to 2024-11-12. Commodities from 2013-01-01 to 2024-11-12. Currencies from 2013-01-01 to 2024-11-12. Cryptocurrency Energy Consumption and Carbon Emissions Indicators from **Bitcoin** 2017–02–10 to 2024–11–13. **Ethereum** 2017-05-20 to 2024-11-13. **Dogecoin** 2021-01-01 to 2024-11-13.

4.2 Results and Discussion

A Bi-LSTM-GRU architecture provides enriched bidirectional context by processing each sequence in both the past and the future, allowing the model to capture information both before and after each time step. The internal gates of LSTMs and GRUs mitigate the vanishing gradient effect, enhancing the ability to retain dependencies over 60 time steps while maintaining learning stability. Compared with two bidirectional LSTMs, replacing a GRU after the Bi-LSTM lightens the model slightly reduces the computational cost while retaining high expressivity. Finally, adding a dropout of 0.1 after each block regularises the training and makes the system more resilient to noise and strong fluctuations in the financial series. While the model has performance limitations, the model requires a high volume of data. With limited historical data, the model risks capturing real dynamics ineffectively. High sensitivity to hyperparameters, the choice of look_back, the number of units, the dropout rate, etc., has a major impact on performance.

4.3 Performance Measures

We applied standard metrics for comparing time series models to measure their short- and long-term predictive performance. To validate the performance of these three models, we used the MAPE (mean absolute percentage error) and RMSE (root mean square error) as performance measures. These error values are obtained via the Bi-LSTM model, GRU model and Bi-LSTM-GRU model (Table 2). In addition, we studied the impact of varying the window size on the performance of the model for a constant seed value. The window size is the number of lag days used to generate input features for the models. These window sizes were 1, 5, 7, 12 and 15 days. The results are shown in Table 2. The analysis of the predictive results over different time horizons reveals that the hybrid Bi-LSTM-GRU model outperforms the other architectures (Bi-LSTM model and GRU model), with lower average RMSE and MAPE values. This model demonstrates a better capacity for generalisation and greater stability, especially in short- and medium-term forecasts.

Table 2. Comparison of the RMSE and MAPE values

Window Size	Number of Days Ahead	Bi-LSTM		GRU		Bi-LSTM + GRU	
		RMSE	MAPE(%)	RMSE	MAPE(%)	RMSE	MAPE(%)
1	1	3150	5,1	3193	5,29	3085	4,88
5	3	3554	5,7	3577,83	5,91	3447,46	5,42
7	5	3854	5,9	3863,83	6,09	3717,46	5,58
12	7	4325	6,7	4302,18	6,93	4128,1	6,29
15	15	5250	6,5	5195	6,55	4975	6,08

Figure 2 shows the GRU model used to predict the Bitcoin price. In blue, the historical data correspond to the progression of the BTC price from 2015 until the end of the learning period. In red, the test data concern actual prices. In orange, the predictions for the same period show that the model is capable of capturing trends and general market volatility. Although there are some deviations in areas of high volatility, overall, the model is able to track market dynamics. Finally, the future forecasts in green extend the acquired trends and forecast an upwards phase followed by a correction. According to these results, the GRU architecture is suitable for time series analysis, but future forecasts should be interpreted with caution, given that financial markets involve a degree of uncertainty. Figure 3 shows the performance of the Bi-LSTM model applied to bitcoin price prediction. The historical data used for training are shown in blue, while the actual values from the test period are in red. The model's predictions on the test data appear in orange, indicating correct adherence. The general trends are well followed, but there are considerable deviations at certain stages, mainly during periods of high market volatility, suggesting that the Bi-LSTM model alone may be limited in its ability to generalise unexpected or rapid movements. Future forecasts (in green) show a sharp fall in the bitcoin price. In summary, Bi-LSTM provides a good understanding of the temporal context of the data. Figure 4 shows the results of bitcoin price prediction by an optimised hybrid Bi-LSTM-GRU model. In blue, the historical data represent the prices used to train the model, and in red, the actual prices during the test phase. The orange curve corresponds to the model's predictions on the test data and shows a remarkable correspondence with actual prices, particularly in regions of high volatility. This shows the model's excellent ability to generalise, as it is faithful to the market trend without overadjustment. In green, future predictions extend the recent uptrend before stabilising, reflecting a controlled projection of market movement. Owing to the combination of Bi-LSTM, which captures temporal relationships in both directions, and the GRU, which optimises efficiency and memory, the model is powerful, stable and efficient for multihorizon bitcoin price forecasting.

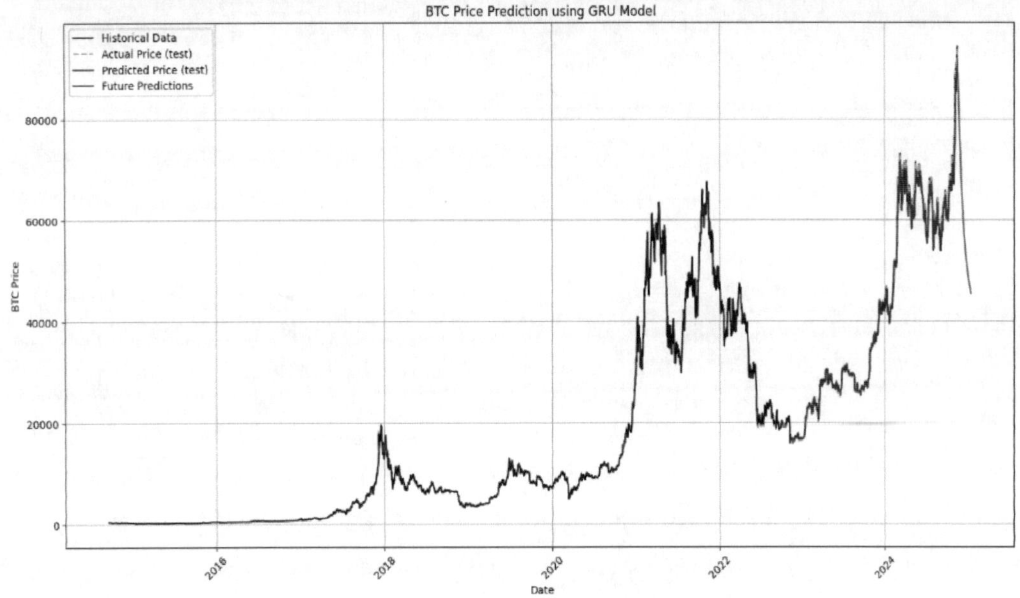

Figure 2. Actual price BTC vs Predicted price BTC via GRU

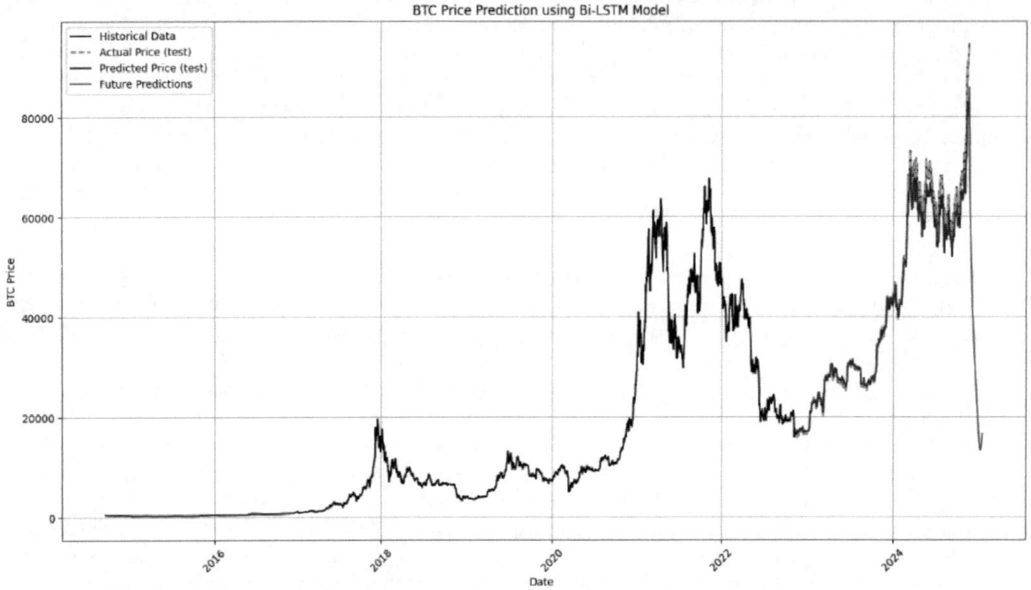

Figure 3. Actual price BTC vs Predicted price BTC via Bi-LSTM

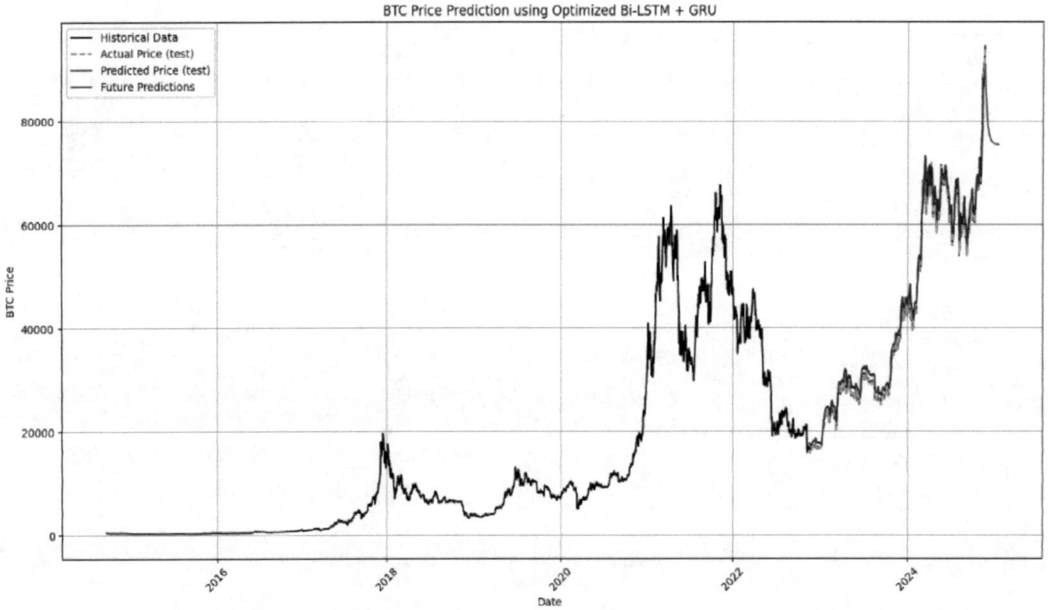

Figure 4. Actual price BTC vs predicted price BTC via Bi-LSTM-GRU

5. CONCLUSION

Cryptocurrencies have emerged as a fast-growing area of business today, and diverse communities are interested in their involvement. Similarly, for all currencies, the prediction of cryptocurrencies is a complex and challenging task. Many studies have referred to different methods, such as machine learning and reinforcement learning. This paper discusses deep learning models. We compare the GRU, BiLSTM and a hybrid model. Our results are promising, and the hybrid model provides accurate predictions for both the GRU and Bi-LSTM. The aim of this paper is to improve bitcoin price prediction with a lower error rate.

6. PERSPECTIVES

Several factors affect cryptocurrency price prediction; at a later time, we analyse the impact of the determinants on our dataset and adjust the framework to suit all cryptocurrencies.

ACRONYMS

Monero	**XMR**
Bitcoin	**BTC**
Tether	**USDT**
Solana	**SOL**
Binance Coin	**BNB**
Ripple	**XRP**
Doge coin	**DOGE**
Litecoin	**LTC**
Ethereum	**ETH**
ADA	**Cardano**
RMSE	**Root mean square error**
MAPE	**Mean absolute percentage error**
LSTM	**Long short term memory**
GRU	**Gated recurrent unit**
Bi-LSTM	**Bidirectional LSTM**
RF	**Random Forest**
ML	**Machine learning**
SVR	**Support Vector Regression**
LR	**Linear regression**
SANN	**Stacked Artificial Neural Network**
ANN	**Artificial Neural Network**
SVM	**Support Vector Machines**

REFERENCES

Awoke, T., Rout, M., Mohanty, L., & Satapathy, S. C. (2020). Bitcoin price prediction and analysis using deep learning models. In Communication Software and Networks: Proceedings of INDIA 2019 (pp. 631-640). Singapore: Springer Singapore.

Hamayel, M. J., & Owda, A. Y. (2021). A novel cryptocurrency price prediction model using GRU, LSTM and bi-LSTM machine learning algorithms. *Ai*, *2*(4), 477-496.

Hansun, S., Wicaksana, A., & Khaliq, A. Q. (2022). Multivariate cryptocurrency prediction: comparative analysis of three recurrent neural networks approaches. *Journal of Big Data*, *9*(1), 50.

Jakubik, J., Nazemi, A., Geyer-Schulz, A., & Fabozzi, F. J. (2023). Incorporating financial news for forecasting Bitcoin prices based on long short-term memory networks. *Quantitative Finance*, *23*(2), 335-349.

Khedr, A. M., Arif, I., El-Bannany, M., Alhashmi, S. M., & Sreedharan, M. (2021). Cryptocurrency price prediction using traditional statistical and machine-learning techniques: A survey. *Intelligent Systems in Accounting, Finance and Management*, *28*(1), 3-34.

Kwak, G. H., Park, C. W., Ahn, H. Y., Na, S. I., Lee, K. D., & Park, N. W. (2020). Potential of bidirectional long short-term memory networks for crop classification with multitemporal remote sensing images. *Korean Journal of Remote Sensing*, *36*(4), 515-525.

Modi, P. D., Arshi, K., Kunz, P. J., & Zoubir, A. M. (2023, June). Data-driven Deep Learning Approach for Bitcoin Price Forecasting. In 2023 24th International Conference on Digital Signal Processing (DSP) (pp. 1-4). IEEE.

Mudassir, M., Bennbaia, S., Unal, D., & Hammoudeh, M. (2020). Time-series forecasting of Bitcoin prices using high-dimensional features: a machine learning approach. *Neural computing and applications*, 1-15.

Nakamoto, S. (2008). Bitcoin: A peer-to-peer electronic cash system.

Nithyakani, P., Tom, R. J., Gupta, P., Shanthini, A., John, V. M., & Sharma, V. (2021, January). Prediction of bitcoin price via the Bi-LSTM network. In 2021 International Conference on Computer Communication and Informatics (ICCCI) (pp. 1-5). IEEE.

Patel, M. M., Tanwar, S., Gupta, R., & Kumar, N. (2020). A deep learning-based cryptocurrency price prediction scheme for financial institutions. *Journal of information security and applications*, 55, 102583.

Rafi, M., Hameed, S., Sohail, I., Aliasghar, M., Aziz, A., & Mirza, Q. A. K. (2023). Enhancing cryptocurrency price forecasting accuracy: A feature selection and weighting approach with bidirectional LSTM and trend-preserving model bias correction. IEEE Access.

Raju, R., & Ramlal, N. P. (2023, August). Dual deep learning model for electricity price forecasting: Bi-LSTM and GRU fusion. In Proceedings of the 2023 Fifteenth International Conference on Contemporary Computing (pp. 13-17).

Su, Y., & Kuo, C. C. J. (2019). On extended long short-term memory and dependent bidirectional recurrent neural network. *Neurocomputing*, 356, 151-161.

Tanwar, S., Patel, N. P., Patel, S. N., Patel, J. R., Sharma, G., & Davidson, I. E. (2021). Deep learning-based cryptocurrency price prediction scheme with interdependent relations. IEEE Access, 9, 138633-138646.

Wang, J., Feng, K., & Qiao, G. (2024). A hybrid deep learning model for Bitcoin price prediction: data decomposition and feature selection. *Applied Economics*, *56*(53), 6890-6905.

Zhao, R., Wang, D., Yan, R., Mao, K., Shen, F., & Wang, J. (2017). Machine health monitoring using local feature-based gated recurrent unit networks. IEEE Transactions on Industrial Electronics, 65(2), 1539-1548.

RISK-BASED CYBER THREAT MODELING FOR PREVENTING APT ATTACKS: A CYBERSECURITY METHOD PROPOSAL

Abinel Santiago Cerqueira Junior[1], Carlos Hideo Arima[1], Napoleão Verardi Galegale[1],
Marília Macorin de Azevedo[1], Marcelo Duduchi Feitosa[1] and Leandro Lima Raineri[2]
[1]*Centro Estadual De Educação Tecnológica Paula Souza (CEETEPS), Brazil*
[2]*Serviço Nacional de Aprendizagem Comercial (SENAC), Brazil*

ABSTRACT

This paper presents the *Modelling Cyber Threats using Risk-Based approach* (MCT-RB), developed to model Advanced Persistent Threat (APT) cyber threats with a focus on public organizations. The advancement of digital transformation and the increasing dependence on digital public services have significantly expanded the surface exposed to sophisticated cyber threats. In this context, MCT-RB proposes a risk-based approach that integrates automated, manual, graphical, and formal methods to identify vulnerabilities, model threats, and support risk management. The research was conducted using the Design Science Research (DSR) methodology and was applied in a Brazilian public IT company. The method was validated through a critical business process using the Mitre ATT&CK knowledge base, the Cyber Kill Chain, and CVSS v3. Results showed that MCT-RB enables structured analysis of the Tactics, Techniques, and Procedures (TTPs) used by APT groups such as APT 29, highlighting exploitable vulnerabilities and allowing the proposal of specific controls. Internal and external experts evaluated the method positively, emphasizing its clarity, applicability, and contribution to strengthening the Information Security Management System (ISMS). As a contribution, MCT-RB offers a novel, practical, and adaptable framework for preventing APT attacks in a real context and can be extended to private organizations or hybrid public-private environments. Future studies should expand the empirical base for multi-cases scenarios and explore its application across various organizational contexts.

KEYWORDS

APT, Threat Modeling, Cybersecurity, Risk Management, Digital Public Services

1. INTRODUCTION

Technological advancements, including applications of machine learning (Martins et al., 2022, 2023), big data (Iwata et al., 2024), sustainable data centers (Azevedo et al., 2024), and high-performance software development (Camargo et al., 2024), have enabled organizations to develop products and services aligned with market demands, driving significant changes in business models through digital transformation. This evolution has impacted how we interact with consumers and suppliers and is also influenced by privacy and data protection regulations (Boggini, 2024), such as the General Data Protection Regulation (GDPR) in the European Union and Brazil's General Data Protection Law (LGPD), which governs the protection of personal data in Brazil (European Union, 2016; Brasil, Law No. 13.709, 2018; Moşteanu, 2020; Feliciano-Cestero et al., 2023).

Digital transformation in public administration enables services to be delivered to citizens through applications and online platforms. In Brazil, the gov.br portal centralizes digital interactions with the federal government and is regulated by Decree No. 9.756 of 2019, which provides detailed guidelines on the implementation and unification of digital service channels for the Brazilian government (Brazil, 2019).

Given the relevance and scope of a digital service, it is essential that each public organization has the minimum conditions necessary to identify and manage cybersecurity risks in public services available on the internet (Paul & Zhang, 2021).

As a result of these regulations, organizations must strengthen information security with appropriate policies (Galegale et al., 2017) to meet legal requirements (Wylde et al., 2022; Boggini, 2024). Given the rise in cyberattacks and data breaches, threat modeling stands out as a strategy to continuously improve security and manage cyber risks (Moşteanu, 2020; Yokoyama & Arima, 2022; Cerqueira Junior & Arima, 2023).

Cyber risk is a dynamic category that constantly evolves, representing exposure to threats, events, or circumstances in the digital environment and a key priority for organization in risk management (Eling & Wirfs, 2019; Lee, 2021). Furthermore, it has significantly matured over time (Eling & Wirfs, 2019; NIST, 2024). Among cyber threats, Advanced Persistent Threats (APTs) are particularly noteworthy due to their potential impact and the fact that they are carried out by specialized groups seeking to compromise the confidentiality, integrity, and availability of information or critical infrastructure (Tatam et al., 2021).

Considering the extensive reach and exposure of digital public services on the internet, cyber risk in public organizations must be managed diligently and can be treated and managed with known international references like an ISO security standard (Culot, Nassimbeni, Podrecca, & Sartor, 2021; Folorunso, Mohammed, Wada & Samuel, 2024). Based on this, and considering cybersecurity in governments (Fusi, Jung & Welch, 2025), the research question for this study is defined as: How can a newly proposed method, based on a risk-oriented threat modeling approach, be used to prevent complex APT cyberattacks in a Brazilian public organization?

To answer this research question, the general objective of the study is to develop a specific threat modeling method for the analysis and prevention of APT cyberattacks in digital public services, and to validate this method by applying it in a Brazilian public organization within a specific business process. Regarding the structure of the paper, Section 2 presents the theoretical framework and key concepts related to threat modeling, risk management, and the cyberattack lifecycle. Section 3 provides background information on APTs and the applied method, while Section 4 presents the proposed cybersecurity method. Finally, Section 5 offers considerations on the theoretical implications and academic contributions of this study.

2. THEORETICAL FRAMEWORK

Cyber risk is a type of risk that must be managed by organizations, as its potential impact can cause financial losses, reputational damage, and other negative consequences to any type of institution, as well as raise concerns among individuals regarding privacy and information security (Iso, 2022; Nist, 2024).

To manage cyber risks and mitigate negative consequences such as data breaches and reputational damage, organizations can use specific references that help understand, assess, and plan actions to reduce risks to acceptable levels (Culot, Nassimbeni, Podrecca, & Sartor, 2021). Among the main approaches are ISO/IEC 27005 and the NIST Cybersecurity Framework, which provide guidelines applicable to various types of organizations (Nist, 2024; Iso, 2022).

Given the presented context, it is noted that cyber risk management is a continuous and iterative process that must be carried out by organizations to reduce any impact or negative consequences of a threat. Thus, risk identification and analysis are expected to be conducted with a better understanding of which cyber events and threats may impact information security within the technology domain (Paul & Zhang, 2021; Nist, 2024).

To support decision-making in risk management (Yokoyama & Arima, 2022), it can be stated that threat modeling is a process directly related to risk management (Lallie, Debattista, & Bal, 2020; Cerqueira Junior & Arima, 2023). To understand threats, available methods for threat evaluation can be classified as formal, graphical, automated, or manual (Xiong & Lagerström, 2019; Tatam et al., 2021).

Formal methods use mathematical models, while graphical ones visually represent threats through flows or tables. Automated methods perform tests using automated security tools, and manual methods involve non-automated analysis. These methods include the Common Vulnerability Scoring System (CVSS) (Mell, Scarfone & Romanosky, 2007), Exploit Prediction Scoring System (EPSS) (Jacobs et al. 2021; First, 2025), Likely Exploited Vulnerabilities (LEV) (Mell & Spring, 2025), attack trees (Schneier, 1999), attack surfaces (Cloudflare, 2023), and the Mitre ATT&CK knowledge base for information on Tactics, Techniques, and Procedures (TTPs) used by APTs (Xiong & Lagerström, 2019; Lallie, Debattista & Bal, 2020; Mitre, 2025).

The attack surface visually maps threat vectors, and the attack tree presents paths that a threat may follow to achieve a specific objective (Alhebaishi et al., 2017). For advanced threats that may cause various negative impacts on an organization, the application of cyber threat modeling methods allows a description of how a threat may succeed in a cyberattack. In the case of APTs, it is relevant to describe and analyze TTPs to characterize their behavior (Delgado, 2018; Tatam et al., 2021).

To describe the life cycle of a cyberattack, including APTs, after the publication of the Cyber Kill Chain method in 2011, cyberattacks started being more assertively mapped to describe their life cycle and the main stages of a cyberattack in more. The seven stages described in Cyber Kill Chain are Reconnaissance, Weaponization, Delivery, Exploitation, Installation, Command and Control and Actions on Objectives detail (Hutchins et al., 2011; Chen, Desmet & Huygens, 2014; Singh et al., 2019).

It is noteworthy that the six stages mapped by the Cyber Kill Chain allow for the observation of behaviors and actions that can be executed by a highly skilled threat, such as an APT. Therefore, considering the goal of preventing this type of attack, it is relevant to map and analyze the life cycle of a cyberattack to develop effective cybersecurity defense strategies.

In this context, to strengthen information security (Moşteanu, 2020), reduce security risks in legacy government systems (Pang & Tanriverdi, 2022), and avoid negative impacts such as service unavailability or even the destruction of sensitive data (Moşteanu, 2020), the management aspects that organizations should evaluate include cybersecurity strategies, standardized processes, compliance with applicable laws and regulations, support from top leadership, and specialized resources in cybersecurity (Yusif & Hafeez-Baig, 2021).

3. BACKGROUND INFORMATION AND METHODS

An APT can be defined as a type of cyberattack conducted by specialized groups with the resources, tools, and technological infrastructure to launch targeted attacks with specific objectives (Chen, Desmet, & Huygens, 2014; Tatam et al., 2021). According to Singh et al. (2019) and Tatam et al. (2021), in the context of information security, the term APT derives from the following characteristics:

- Advanced: This type of threat is considered advanced, especially due to the high number of available resources (infrastructure and financial capability), its high technical ability to bypass security controls (firewalls, among others), and the ability to remain inside organizations and extract confidential data without detection.
- Persistent: Compared to other threats, such as hacktivists and attackers lacking specialized knowledge and cybersecurity experience, an APT attack is characterized by its persistence, meaning it may last weeks or months until its objective is achieved.
- Threat: Given these characteristics, an APT attack is considered a cyber threat.

The research methodology adopted in this study was Design Science Research (DSR). This is a research method that aims to solve problems through the construction and application of an artifact, which can be represented by a construct, method, model, or instantiation. The choice of this method is justified by its applicability in information systems that use technological resources (Peffers, Tuunanen, Rothenberger, & Chatterjee, 2007; Dresch et al., 2015; Hevner, Vom Brocke, & Maedche, 2019).

To provide a better understanding of the adopted methodology, Table 1 presents the steps, methods, and tools used in the research.

Table 1. Methodology Steps

Steps	Procedures
Problem Identification	Formulation of the research question; systematic literature review; participant observation
Definition of Expected Results	Individual meetings with personnel involved; internal research in organizational documentation
Design and Development	Document and environmental analysis; action research; participant observation; method construction; individual pre-tests with internal experts
Demonstration	Execution of the developed method and presentation of results
Evaluation	Individual interviews with participants; Descriptive evaluation
Communication	Publication of articles in conferences and journals

4. PROPOSED METHODOLOGY

The research results were divided into four parts: method construction, method execution, demonstration of results, and expert evaluation of the method for modeling cyber threats.

4.1 Method Construction

The method developed was named Modelling Cyber Threats using Risk-Based approach (MCT-RB), specifically designed to model cyber threats of the APT type using a risk-based approach. MCT-RB contains four approaches for threat modeling: automated, manual, graphical, and formal.

The automated approach of MCT-RB uses cybersecurity tools to perform automated tests that identify vulnerabilities. The manual approach relies on analyses and research in cybersecurity knowledge bases and frameworks by the operational security team.

The graphical approach of MCT-RB utilizes the attack surface and attack tree, which are visual representations of the malicious actions a cyber threat might take in a given system. These graphical methods provide visibility into a specific threat.

Lastly, the formal approach uses established and widely applied information security metrics (in this study, CVSSv3 was used for this purpose).

MCT-RB can be used cyclically and adapted according to the organizational structure of a public institution. It is understood that, beyond public organizations, the method can be adapted for private companies as needed.

Figure 1 illustrates the MCT-RB through a cycle with three distinct stages: Cybersecurity Assessment, Threat Modeling, and Risk Management.

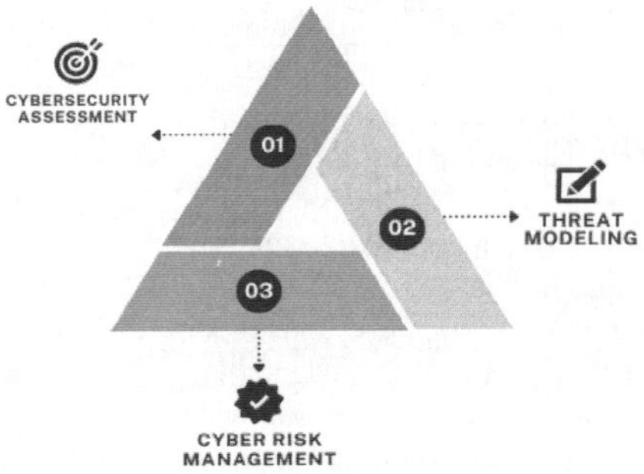

Figure 1. Modelling Cyber Threats using Risk-Based approach (MCT-RB) Stages

In the MCT-RB, the first stage is a cybersecurity assessment, which consists of automated or manual security testing of a system, application, or infrastructure to identify weaknesses and potential vulnerabilities; the second stage is threat modeling, aims to analyze what type of threat might be capable of exploiting vulnerabilities in the assessed system; and the third stage is risk management seeks to provide an executive overview of the level of cyber risk exposure of a system to a previously evaluated threat.

4.2 Method Execution

This research was developed with the support of a Brazilian public company that provides system development and IT processing services to several public agencies in Brazil. The company was selected due to having a robust information security area and agreeing to support the research, while requesting anonymity. The following are the results of applying the MCT-RB method at the company.

4.2.1 A Cybersecurity Assessment

The cybersecurity assessment enabled the identification and classification of vulnerabilities based on their severity using the CVSS scale. In the studied organization, the severity level (critical, high, medium, or low) is used to define the cyber risk level of each vulnerability. Table 2 lists all identified vulnerabilities.

Table 2. List of Identified Vulnerabilities

Vulnerabilities (CVSS)	Description
Open Ports (No CVSS)	Some open service ports unknown to the operational security team were identified on the servers that support the product. CVSS does not apply in this case
Outdated Web Application Server (CVSS 10.0)	The web application servers hosting the product website are outdated and no longer supported by the vendor
Outdated Operating System (CVSS 10.0)	Some servers were found to be running outdated operating systems that are no longer vendor-supported
Outdated and Insecure Services (CVSS 5.4)	SMB and FTP services identified during vulnerability analysis are currently considered outdated and insecure
Insecure Encryption (CVSS 4.6)	The ciphers and the version of the SSL/TLS protocol used in internal servers are considered insecure

4.2.2 Threat Modeling

The objective of the APT threat in the studied company is to obtain confidential data from a digital public service. To verify the applicability of modeling, APT 29 was selected. Table 3 presents the tactics, techniques, and procedures (TTPs) that can be executed by APT 29 based on the previously identified vulnerabilities (Mitre, 2025).

Table 3. TTPSs mapped

APT	Tactics	Techniques	Procedures
APT 29	Recognition	T1595: Active Scanning: Vulnerability Scanning	The APT29 group scans systems on the internet to identify vulnerabilities that can be exploited.
	Initial access	T1190: Exploit Public-Facing Application	The threat attempts to exploit weaknesses in internet-accessible systems to gain access to internal networks.
	Initial access	T1113: External Remote Services	The threat collects information about the network, such as IPs and TCP ports, and identifies the technologies available for access on the internet.
	Execution	T1059: Command and Scripting Interpreter	After gaining initial access, the threat uses programs from the system itself to execute malicious commands, such as viruses.
	Exfiltration	T1048: Exfiltration Over Alternative Protocol	Adversaries exfiltrate stolen data from the target system to the APT's system via a specific network protocol.

To better understand, if the attack is successful, APT 29 may gain full access to the database of the digital public service to export or copy data. This type of information is relevant for better cyber risk management within an organization. After evaluating threats, the attack surface was assessed. It is important to note that a set of attack vectors can be used by APT (see Figure 2).

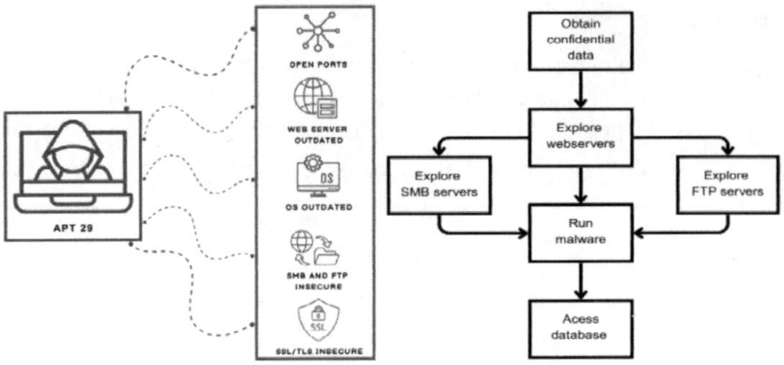

Figure 2. Attack surface and tree for APT29

4.2.3 Cyber Risk Management

Regarding cyber risk management, the company has implemented a management process integrated into its ISMS (Information Security Management System), allowing for the identification of cyber risk events, their causes, effects, and risk categories based on the company's internal corporate risk definitions.

To mitigate and respond to identified cyber risk at an acceptable risk, the company has nine security controls aligned with MITRE Framework mitigation strategies for enterprises and key cybersecurity operational processes to protect the evaluated system (Mitre, 2025). These include vulnerability scanning and management, network segmentation, IPS (Intrusion Prevention System), Multi-Factor Authentication (MFA), Web Application Firewall (WAF), network firewalls, limiting network access to resources, filtering network traffic in routers and switches, disabling or removing unnecessary features or programs, antivirus/antimalware solutions, and exploit protection. It was found that each available control is properly designed, formalized, and executed by the responsible departments.

A qualitative and quantitative analysis was conducted based on the information from previous steps, considering the controls already applied and available for use by the company. At the end of the evaluation, it was found that the residual risk is low, indicating an acceptable level of cyber risk according to the company's internal definitions. Thus, the threat modeling method developed in this research is concluded.

4.3 Evaluation

The evaluation of the developed method applied to a digital public service was conducted through individual interviews with six internal and six external experts from the organization.

The interviews were guided by three questions with the respective sources used:

1. Considering that APT cyberattacks are promoted by highly organized and experienced groups and the security measures that are currently adopted in your organization, how can the method presented to model threats protect a system hosted in your organization? (Tatam *et al.*, 2021)
2. In your opinion, what security controls are necessary for APT prevention? (ISO 27001, 2022; NIST, 2024)
3. Can the method presented be formalized in any cybersecurity process in your organization? If so, which processes? (ISO 27001, 2022; NIST, 2024)

Regarding how the method can protect a system hosted in the organization, experts agreed that the visibility of threats provided by the proposed method allows for more accurate risk analysis and integration into the organization's ISMS. As for the necessary security controls to prevent APTs, experts highlighted the use of technologies such as network firewall, WAF, database firewall, IPS, SIEM, encryption, and proxy for servers. Concerning the last question, all experts agreed that the method can be formalized into existing cybersecurity processes. In summary, all external experts agreed that the proposed method can help Brazilian public organizations take preventive actions in information security. Key characteristics such as clarity, objectivity, and functionalities related to cyber risk management were emphasized throughout the interviews.

5. FINAL CONSIDERATIONS

This research aimed to present a specific threat modeling method for the analysis and prevention of APT cyberattacks in a Brazilian public organization. The application of a specific method enables greater visibility of threats, allowing preventive actions and cyberattack strategies to be adequately executed by operational teams. A key contribution of this paper is the applicability of the proposed methodology in a real-world cybersecurity context, involving a government digital service maintained by a public IT company, using a combination of threat modeling techniques applied for APT cyberattacks, supported by consistent metrics and frameworks such as CVSS and Mitre Framework.

However, it is evident that the results achieved do not yet have a sufficient empirical basis to be representative for considering quantitative benchmarking, comparative analysis, or definitive threat modeling in the analysis and prevention of cyberattacks using automated risk scoring models and simulated attack scenarios, such as red team exercises or penetration testing. Therefore, further case studies and even statistical validations will be necessary.

As a final reflection, the following future research opportunities and improvements can be identified: (i) application of the method to a set of digital services in organizations from different market segments and a broader validation through multi-case studies; and (ii) application in new public and can be extended to private organizations or hybrid public-private environments aimed at its enhancement and continuous improvement.

REFERENCES

Alhebaishi, N., et al. (2017). Threat modeling for cloud data center infrastructures. In Foundations and Practice of Security: 9th International Symposium, FPS 2016, Québec City, QC, Canada, October 24-25, 2016, Revised Selected Papers 9 (pp. 302-319). Springer International Publishing.

Azevedo, M. M., Galegale, N. V. & Matthes, R. P. (2024). Green IT and Datacenter: a Study of Environmental Management Indicators. *Revista de Gestão Social e Ambiental*, 18(1), e07740-e07740.

Boggini, C. (2024). Reporting cybersecurity to stakeholders: a review of CSRD and the EU cyber legal framework. *Computer Law & Security Review*, 53, 105987.

Brasil. (2019). Decreto nº 9.756, de 11 de abril de 2019. Institui o portal único 'gov.br' e estabelece as regras para a unificação dos canais digitais do governo federal.

Brasil. (2018). Lei nº 13.709, de 14 de agosto de 2018. *Lei Geral de Proteção de Dados* (LGPD).

Camargo, K. G. A. & Galegale, N. V. (2024). Aumento da maturidade de equipes SCRUM de desenvolvimento de software. *RISTI - Revista Ibérica de Sistemas e Tecnologias de Informação*, (54), p. 22-38.

Cerqueira Junior, A. S., & Arima, C. H. (2023). Modelagem de ameaças: Um estudo sobre sua aplicação na transformação digital sob a perspectiva do risco. *Revista de Gestão e Secretariado*, 14(1), 1158-1169.

Chen, P., Desmet, L., & Huygens, C. (2014). A study on advanced persistent threats. In Communications and Multimedia Security: 15th IFIP TC 6/TC 11 International Conference, CMS 2014, Aveiro, Portugal, September 25-26, 2014. Proceedings 15 (pp. 63-72). Springer Berlin Heidelberg.

Cloudflare. (2023, September 18). O que é um vetor de ataque? Cloudflare. https://www.cloudflare.com/pt-br/learning/security/glossary/attack-vector/

Culot, G., Nassimbeni, G., Podrecca, M., & Sartor, M. (2021). The ISO/IEC 27001 information security management standard: literature review and theory-based research agenda. *The TQM Journal*, 33(7), 76-105.

Delgado, P. (2018). Developing an adaptive threat hunting solution: The elasticsearch stack [Master's thesis, Universidad Politécnica de Valencia].

Dresch, A., et al. (2015). *Pesquisa científica de design*. Publicação Internacional Springer.

Eling, M., & Wirfs, J. (2019). What are the actual costs of cyber risk events? *European Journal of Operational Research*, *272*(3), 1109-1119.

European Union. (2016). Regulation (EU) 2016/679 of the European Parliament and of the Council of 27 April 2016 on the protection of natural persons with regard to the processing of personal data and on the free movement of such data (General Data Protection Regulation - GDPR). Official Journal of the European Union. Retrieved from https://eur-lex.europa.eu/eli/reg/2016/679/oj.

Feliciano-Cestero, M. M., et al. (2023). Is digital transformation threatened? A systematic literature review of the factors influencing firms' digital transformation and internationalization. *Journal of Business Research*, *157*, 113546.

FIRST. (2025). Exploit Prediction Scoring System (EPSS). FIRST. https://www.first.org/epss/

Folorunso, A., Mohammed, V., Wada, I., & Samuel, B. (2024). The impact of ISO security standards on enhancing cybersecurity posture in organizations. *World Journal of Advanced Research and Reviews*, *24*(1), 2582-2595.

Fusi, F., Jung, H., & Welch, E. (2025). Technological vulnerability and knowledge of cyber-incidents: Threats to innovativeness in local governments?. *Public Management Review*, *27*(3), 545-571.

Galegale, N. V., Fontes, E.L.G. & Galegale, B. P. (2017). Uma contribuição para a segurança da informação: um estudo de casos múltiplos com organizações brasileiras. *Perspectivas em Ciência da Informação*, v.*22*, n.3, p.75-97.

Hevner, A., Vom Brocke, J., & Maedche, A. (2019). Roles of digital innovation in design science research. *Business & Information Systems Engineering*, *61*, 3-8.

Iwata, C., Galegale, N. V., Ito, M., Azevedo, M. M., Feitosa, M. D. & Arima, C. H. (2024). Data Cleaning in Big Data: A systematic literature review. In Proceedings of the IADIS. ISBN (Book): 978-989-8704-60-3, p. 75-82

International Organization for Standardization. (2022). ISO/IEC 27005:2022 - Information security risk management. https://www.iso.org/standard/80585.html.

Jacobs, J., Romanosky, S., Edwards, B., Adjerid, I., & Roytman, M. (2021). Exploit prediction scoring system (epss). *Digital Threats: Research and Practice*, *2*(3), 1-17.

Lallie, H. S., Debattista, K., & Bal, J. (2020). A review of attack graph and attack tree visual syntax in cyber security. *Computer Science Review*, *35*, 100219.

Lee, I. (2021). Cybersecurity: Risk management framework and investment cost analysis. Business Horizons, 64(5), 659-671.

Martins, E. & Galegale, N. V. (2022). Retail sales forecasting information systems: comparison between traditional methods and machine learning algorithms. In Proceedings of the 2022 IADIS, p. 30-38.

Martins, E. & Galegale, N. V. (2023). Machine learning: A bibliometric analysis. *International Journal of Innovation*, *11*(3), p. 1-37.

Mell, P., Scarfone, K., & Romanosky, S. (2007). Common vulnerability scoring system. *IEEE Security & Privacy*, *4*(6), 85-89.

Mell, P., & Spring, J. M. (2025). Likely Exploited Vulnerabilities, A Proposed Metric for Vulnerability Exploitation Probability.

MITRE. (2025). MITRE ATT&CK™ framework. MITRE. https://attack.mitre.org/.

Moşteanu, N. R. (2020). Challenges for organizational structure and design as a result of digitalization and cybersecurity. *The Business & Management Review*, *11*(1), 278-286.

National Institute of Standards and Technology (NIST). (2024). The NIST Cybersecurity Framework 2.0.

Paul, J. A., & Zhang, M. (2021). Decision support model for cybersecurity risk planning: A two-stage stochastic programming framework featuring firms, government, and attacker. *European Journal of Operational Research*, 291(1), 349-364.

Pang, M. S., & Tanriverdi, H. (2022). Strategic roles of IT modernization and cloud migration in reducing cybersecurity risks of organizations: The case of US federal government. *The journal of strategic information systems*, *31*(1), 101707.

Peffers, K., Tuunanen, T., Rothenberger, M. A., & Chatterjee, S. (2007). A design science research methodology for information systems research. *Journal of Management Information Systems*, *24*(3), 45-77.

Schneier, B. (1999, December). Attack trees. Schneier on Security. https://www.schneier.com/academic/archives/1999/12/attack_trees.html

Singh, S., et al. (2019). A comprehensive study on APT attacks and. countermeasures for future networks and communications: Challenges and solutions. *The Journal of Supercomputing*, *75*, 4543-4574. https://doi.org/10.1016/j.cose.2019.07.001.

Tatam, M., et al. (2021). A review of threat modelling approaches for APT-style attacks. *Heliyon*, *7*(1), e05969. https://doi.org/10.1016/j.heliyon.2021.e05969.

Wylde, V., Rawindaran, N., Lawrence, J., Balasubramanian, R., Prakash, E., Jayal, A., ... & Platts, J. (2022). Cybersecurity, data privacy and blockchain: A review. *SN computer science*, *3*(2), 127.

Xiong, W., & Lagerström, R. (2019). Threat modeling–A systematic literature review. *Computers & security*, *84*, 53-69. https://doi.org/10.1016/j.cose.2019.03.010

Yokoyama, R., & Arima, C. H. (2022). Modelagem de ameaça, análise de risco e suas aplicações na literatura. *International Journal of Development Research*, *12*(4), 55049-55055.

Yusif, S., & Hafeez-Baig, A. (2021). A conceptual model for cybersecurity governance. *Journal of Applied Security Research*, 16(4), 490-513.

INTRODUCING A PHYSIOLOGICAL WELLNESS INDEX (PWI) FOR HEALTH AND WELL-BEING

Ravishankar Sharma[1], Dhanjoo N. Ghista[2], Edmund Evangelista[1], Kapil Kumar Meena[3], Ashish Thakur[3] and Syed M. Salman Bukhari[4]

[1]*College of Technological Innovation, Zayed University, Abu Dhabi, UAE*
[2]*CEIDE (Center for Inclusive Digital Enterprise), New Zealand*
[3]*Indian Institute of Technology, Kharagpur, India*
[4]*Capital University of Science and Technology, Islamabad, Pakistan*

ABSTRACT

The rising prevalence of stress-related disorders and chronic health conditions calls for comprehensive metrics that extend beyond isolated physiological indicators. The Physiological Wellness Index (PWI) presents an innovative, integrative solution by combining three key metrics: Heart Rate Variability (HRV), Breathing Efficacy (BrE), and Galvanic Skin Response (GSR). HRV reflects autonomic nervous system function and stress resilience; BrE assesses respiratory efficiency vital for oxygen delivery and metabolic health; GSR captures emotional and physiological arousal via sympathetic nervous system activity. These indicators are synthesized through a weighted formula to produce a dynamic wellness score. By capturing variations across restful, active, and distressed physiological states, PWI enables early health risk detection, supports personalized interventions, and informs clinical decision-making. Leveraging real-time sensor integration and advanced signal processing, PWI serves as a pivotal tool in preventive healthcare, chronic disease management, and stress monitoring. As a holistic wellness metric, it marks a significant advancement within the Internet of Medical Things (IoMT) landscape.

KEYWORDS

Physiological Wellness Index, Health Assessment, Heart Rate Variability, Breathing Efficacy, Electrodermal Activity, Wellness Monitoring

1. INTRODUCTION

As stress-related health conditions and chronic illnesses continue to rise globally, there is a pressing need for metrics that capture both physiological and psychological resilience. The Physiological Wellness Index (PWI) is an innovative and comprehensive metric for evaluating an individual's health status by integrating multiple physiological indicators into a single, interpretable score. The PWI addresses this challenge by synthesizing three key physiological components: Heart Rate Variability (HRV), Breathing Efficacy (BrE), and Galvanic Skin Response (GSR).

In a recent empirical study, Zhang et al. (2025) investigated health professionals' attitudes and utilization of digital health technologies. They reported that such studies are limited and, more concerning, the use of clinical health tech faced barriers such as "affordability, digital literacy, and potential negative effects on service users' mental health." Over-the-counter, easy-to-use IoMT devices and apps may offer solutions to some of these challenges, especially when paired with integrative tools like the PWI.

HRV, a robust marker of autonomic nervous system function, reflects the balance between sympathetic and parasympathetic activity and is closely linked to cardiovascular health, stress adaptability, and overall physiological resilience (Braboszcz & Miranda, 2023). BrE includes measures such as respiratory rate, tidal volume, and oxygen saturation, providing critical insights into respiratory efficiency and metabolic processes essential for sustaining physical performance and vitality (Braboszcz & Miranda, 2023). GSR captures variations in skin conductance influenced by sweat gland activity and sympathetic nervous system activation, serving as a dynamic indicator of emotional arousal and stress (Rojas, 2023). Together, these components create a nuanced framework for assessing wellness.

Using a weighted formula, the PWI integrates these physiological markers to offer a multidimensional perspective on health, transcending traditional single-parameter evaluations. This composite index not only identifies baseline wellness but also tracks transitions between restful, active, and distressed states, providing actionable insights for healthcare practitioners, wellness programs, and individuals. Its potential applications span preventive healthcare, chronic disease management, stress monitoring, and personalized wellness interventions, positioning PWI as a transformative tool in the evolving Internet of Medical Things (IoMT) landscape (Braboszcz & Miranda, 2023).

2. COMPONENTS OF THE PHYSIOLOGICAL WELLNESS INDEX (PWI)

The PWI is a composite metric integrating multiple physiological indicators that reflect key aspects of wellness. This section is a terse review of the mechanisms and applications of each component, emphasizing how they collectively contribute to a comprehensive assessment of an individual's physiological state. Details of the metrics and their efficacy in determining wellness may be found in the online annex to this article.

2.1 Heart Rate Variability (HRV)

Mechanism: HRV measures variations in the time period between consecutive heartbeats, regulated by the autonomic nervous system (ANS). A higher HRV indicates better adaptability to stress, reflecting a balanced interplay between the sympathetic and parasympathetic branches of the ANS (Shaffer & Ginsberg, 2017). Conversely, low HRV is associated with elevated stress levels, autonomic dysfunction, and potential health concerns, including cardiovascular disease and chronic stress (Ross et al., 2016).

Applications: HRV is a widely used, noninvasive biomarker for monitoring physiological resilience and stress. It provides insights into lifestyle factors such as sleep quality, physical activity, and mental well-being (Braboszcz & Miranda, 2023). Continuous HRV monitoring enables individuals and healthcare providers to identify stressors and implement targeted interventions to improve resilience and cardiovascular health.

2.2 Breathing Efficacy (BrE)

Measurement: BrE assesses respiratory function through metrics such as respiratory rate, tidal volume, and minute ventilation, offering a detailed view of oxygen delivery and metabolic processes (Courtney, 2011).

Significance: Efficient breathing ensures optimal tissue oxygenation, essential for energy production and metabolic health. Reduced BrE may reflect inefficiencies caused by brain stem dysfunction, low cardiac fitness, or conditions like asthma and COPD (Rojas, 2023). Monitoring BrE supports fitness training and early detection of respiratory issues, enabling proactive management.

2.3 Galvanic Skin Response (GSR) / Electrodermal Activity (EDA)

Measurement: GSR, or Electrodermal Activity (EDA), measures changes in skin conductance driven by sweat gland activity, regulated by the sympathetic nervous system (Posada-Quintero & Chon, 2020). These changes are closely tied to emotional arousal and physiological stress.

Significance: Elevated GSR levels indicate increased arousal or stress, while lower levels suggest relaxation (Braboszcz & Miranda, 2023). Longitudinal GSR tracking provides valuable insights into emotional regulation and stress management. As a noninvasive biomarker, GSR is widely applicable in therapeutic and wellness contexts, including anxiety assessment.

3. FORMULA AND WORKING EXAMPLE

The PWI provides a complete measure of physiological well-being by integrating multiple key indicators. To ensure a robust assessment, the PWI is computed using a weighted formula that synthesizes these physiological metrics:

$$PWI = \frac{(w_1 \times HRV_{score} + w_2 \times BrE_{score} + w_3 \times GSR_{score})}{(w_1 + w_2 + w_3)}$$

Where w_1, w_2, and w_3 are weight coefficients assigned to HRV, BrE, and GSR, respectively. These weights coefficients are dynamically determined based on statistical analysis, clinical validation, and empirical studies to reflect their relative contributions to overall wellness (Courtney, 2011; Posada-Quintero & Chon, 2020; Ross et al., 2016). To show the structured computational workflow of PWI, **Figure 1** visually captures the transformation of raw physiological data into actionable wellness classifications. The framework consists of four primary stages:

- **Input Stage:** Data collection from wearable devices, capturing HRV, BrE, and GSR signals in real-time.
- **Processing Stage:** Feature extraction and signal processing, including noise removal, normalization, and data scaling for consistency.
- **Computation Stage:** Application of the weighted formula to derive the PWI score, which dynamically adjusts based on physiological significance.
- **Output Stage:** Classification of wellness states into Restful, Active, or Distressed categories, facilitating real-time health monitoring and proactive interventions.

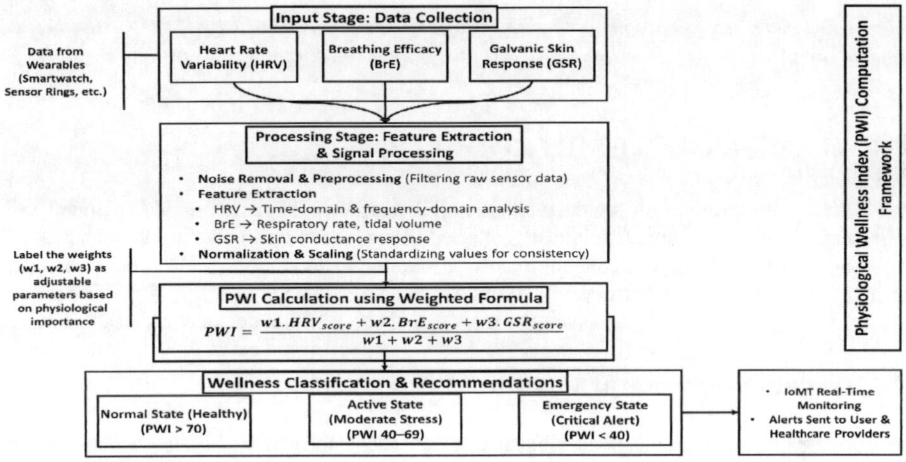

Figure 1. Computational Workflow of the PWI. This framework illustrates the integration of HRV, BrE, and GSR metrics through signal processing, weighted computation, and classification into wellness states

This structured approach ensures that the PWI effectively captures real-time physiological variations, enabling its application in wellness monitoring, chronic disease management, and personalized health interventions. The following section further explores how different physiological states influence PWI calculations and their practical applications.

3.1 PWI Calculation Across Physiological States

3.1.1 Restful State

In the **restful state**, the individual is at rest or experiencing minimal stress, with weights ranging from 1 to 14.9 to reflect physiological stability. HRV scores above 50 ms (e.g., RMSSD or LF/HF ratio) typically indicate healthy autonomic function, influenced by age and fitness level (Shaffer & Ginsberg, 2017). Breathing is characterized by 12–20 balanced breaths per minute, adequate tidal volume, and oxygen saturation levels above 95% (Courtney, 2011). EDA values typically range between 0.5 and 1.5 μS, with occasional transient increases due to mild stress (Posada-Quintero & Chon, 2020). A PWI score between 24–26.5 represents this stable physiological condition.

3.1.2 Active State

The **active state** reflects moderate-to-intense physical activity, where weights range from 15 to 29.9 to capture increased energy demands. HRV typically falls below 30 ms due to heightened sympathetic activity and reduced parasympathetic tone (Shaffer & Ginsberg, 2017). Breathing patterns include a higher respiratory rate, reduced tidal volume, and occasionally reduced oxygen saturation, indicating inefficient oxygen delivery (Courtney, 2011). EDA values exceeding 1.5 μS signify elevated arousal and physiological stress (Posada-Quintero & Chon, 2020). A corresponding PWI score generally lies between 27–29. Individual responses may vary based on physical fitness and stress tolerance.

3.1.3 Distressed State

In the **distressed state**, representing critical health crises or extreme stress, weights are elevated between 30 and 44.9. HRV becomes extremely low, indicating severe autonomic dysfunction and heightened stress (Ross et al., 2016). Breathing patterns show increased respiratory rate, reduced tidal volume, and low Peak Expiratory Flow Rate (PEFR), indicating respiratory distress (Courtney, 2011). EDA values often exceed 3.0 μS, marking extreme sympathetic arousal (Posada-Quintero & Chon, 2020). A PWI score greater than 29 is indicative of this critical state, often necessitating immediate medical intervention.

Note: *PWI scores across all states are influenced by individual variations such as age, baseline health, and chronic conditions. Weight assignments may be adapted accordingly for accurate representation.*

4. PWI ASSESSMENT METHODOLOGY

The PWI integrates three key physiological metrics, EDA, HRV, and BrE, to provide a comprehensive wellness assessment. These metrics are continuously collected via advanced wearable devices such as electronic rings, smartphones, and sensor arrays, enabling real-time monitoring of responses including heart rate, respiratory rate, and skin conductance (Courtney, 2011; Posada-Quintero & Chon, 2020; Shaffer & Ginsberg, 2017). This approach leverages modern sensor technologies to ensure accurate and personalized health evaluations.

4.1 Calculation Framework and Data Integration

The PWI calculation is grounded in clinical research and empirical studies, particularly those addressing chronic illness management and physiological stress responses (Ross et al., 2016). It combines HRV, BrE, and EDA using weighted contributions that reflect each metric's relative impact on overall wellness. These weights are derived through statistical analysis, clinical validation, and empirical modeling to ensure reliability across diverse populations (Braboszcz & Miranda, 2023).

Weight assignment for the PWI formula (w_1, w_2, w_3) follows a structured, three-tiered validation process. First, descriptive statistical analysis was conducted on physiological data from wearable devices. This data was normalized and segmented into three health states—restful, active, and distressed. Mean values and standard deviations across these segments provided empirical evidence for estimating each metric's influence on wellness.

Second, clinical heuristics from existing literature guided the relative scaling of each parameter. Prior studies emphasize HRV's role in autonomic regulation, BrE's link to oxygenation efficiency, and EDA's sensitivity to stress reactivity. Finally, iterative tuning through time-series validation tested trial weight configurations on daily physiological data. This ensured PWI scores accurately reflected transitions between physiological states, such as from rest to exertion or during acute stress.

This multi-layered approach ensures the weights align with physiological theory while demonstrating empirical robustness across individuals and usage scenarios. Future improvements may include dynamic weighting through deep and unsupervised machine learning to further personalize PWI computation.

4.2 Weight Assumptions for Different States

To account for physiological variability across health states, the PWI assigns specific weight ranges to its components. In the restful state, representing calm and stable conditions, weights w_1, w_2, and w_3 range from 1 to 14.9, aligning with baseline wellness. The active state, associated with moderate physical activity or mild stress, uses weights between 15 and 29.9 to capture elevated physiological demands. In contrast, the distressed state, reflecting critical health conditions, is defined by weights ranging from 30 to 44.9 to represent significant physiological disruption. These weight ranges are designed to reflect progressive shifts in wellness. For instance, increased EDA and respiratory rate alongside decreased HRV often signal a transition from a restful to an active or distressed state. Adjusting weights accordingly allows the PWI to remain sensitive to these shifts while supporting consistent classification of wellness states.

4.3 Interpretation of PWI Ranges

The PWI ranges have been categorized based on clinical validation and empirical modelling of preliminary data collected in the manner described in the Online Annex:

- **0-39 (Distressed State):** Indicates compromised health requiring urgent medical attention.
- **40-69 (Active State):** Reflects moderate health challenges, necessitating lifestyle or clinical interventions.
- **70-100 (Restful State):** Represents optimal wellness, with balanced autonomic function, cardiovascular health, and stress regulation.
- For practical application:
  - **24-26.5:** Typically corresponds to a restful state.
  - **27-29:** Indicates a active state with moderate physiological demands.
  - **>29:** Reflects a distressed state requiring immediate medical intervention.

Several physiological and external factors influence HRV, BrE, and EDA, contributing to the inter-related nature of PWI:

- **Heart Rate Variability:** Decreases with age but improves with regular physical activity, reflecting cardiovascular health and autonomic resilience.
- **Breathing Efficacy:** Relates to VO_2max and typically declines with age, but varies significantly with fitness levels and respiratory efficiency.
- **Electrodermal Activity:** Sensitive to emotional and psychological stressors, showing daily fluctuations based on individual stress levels and environmental factors.

Chronic conditions, such as cardiovascular disease, diabetes, and respiratory illnesses, also significantly affect these metrics. Persistently low HRV or reduced BrE may indicate underlying health concerns, while elevated EDA often corresponds with chronic stress or pain. Therefore, PWI calculations are calibrated to individual baselines to ensure accurate and meaningful wellness assessments.

Individuals who regularly practice yoga and meditation often display unique physiological adaptations, including lower resting heart and breathing rates, reduced stress reactivity, and faster recovery after physical or emotional exertion. These patterns suggest greater autonomic resilience and emotional regulation. Consequently, conventional interpretations of HRV and BrE may not fully capture the wellness states of such individuals.

In these cases, the PWI should be adapted to personalized baselines, especially in populations with advanced stress-regulation capabilities. This underscores the need for adaptive or population-specific PWI models and supports the development of complementary indices such as the Meditation Effectiveness Index (MEFI), discussed in a forthcoming article, for mindfulness-focused applications.

4.4 Key Dataset Factors

The dataset used for PWI calculation highlights several critical trends and considerations. First, weight optimization is performed by applying trial-and-error methods on extrapolated data to minimize ambiguity in wellness scoring. Second, range consistency is maintained, with PWI values remaining within specified limits and varying slightly depending on clinically derived weights. Third, data modeling based on clinical and research sources offers valuable insights into physiological variability across different health conditions and populations. Finally, clinical interpretation of PWI values aligns with established references for critical physiological states, including respiration, heart rate, oxygen saturation, EDA activity, HRV, and BrE. This methodological framework ensures the PWI's robustness and adaptability for diverse healthcare applications, supporting proactive wellness monitoring and improved clinical outcomes. This methodological framework enhances the robustness and adaptability of the PWI, supporting proactive wellness monitoring and improved clinical decision-making across diverse healthcare settings. The dataset used for this empirical study may be found in the Online Annex.

5. ANALYSIS OF IOMT DATA

To investigate physiological responses to stress, we analyzed EDA, PRV, and RR metrics collected from wearable devices used by subjects across different days. They were either staff or students at Zayed University who consented (in accordance with ZU's IRB approval) to using a medical grade IoMT device for a period of a month. As they went about their daily activities, they reported any exceptional activities or how well they felt at regular intervals. For brevity, we present two representative cases, March 01 (acute stress event) and March 03 (baseline day). Additional multi-day observations and visualizations are available on GitHub as the Online Annex to this paper.

5.1 Data Observations and Analytics

5.1.1 March 01 Observations

The raw EDA data shows a pronounced peak at approximately 06:00, indicating heightened arousal or a significant stress event. This is accompanied by a concurrent drop in PRV and an increase in RR, aligning with a classic fight-or-flight response. Interpolated data smooths noise and highlights the synchronization of these signals during the episode.

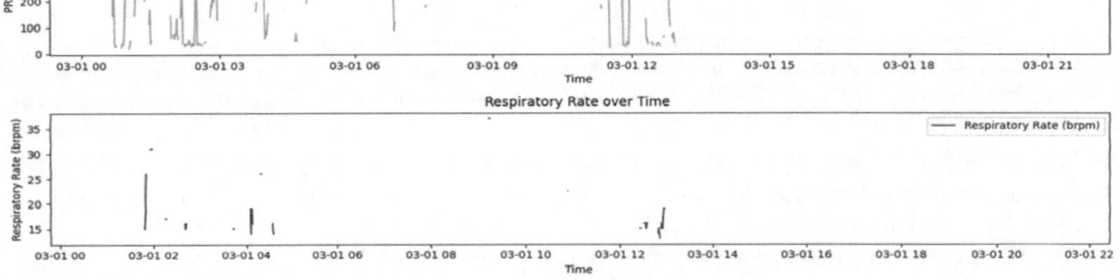

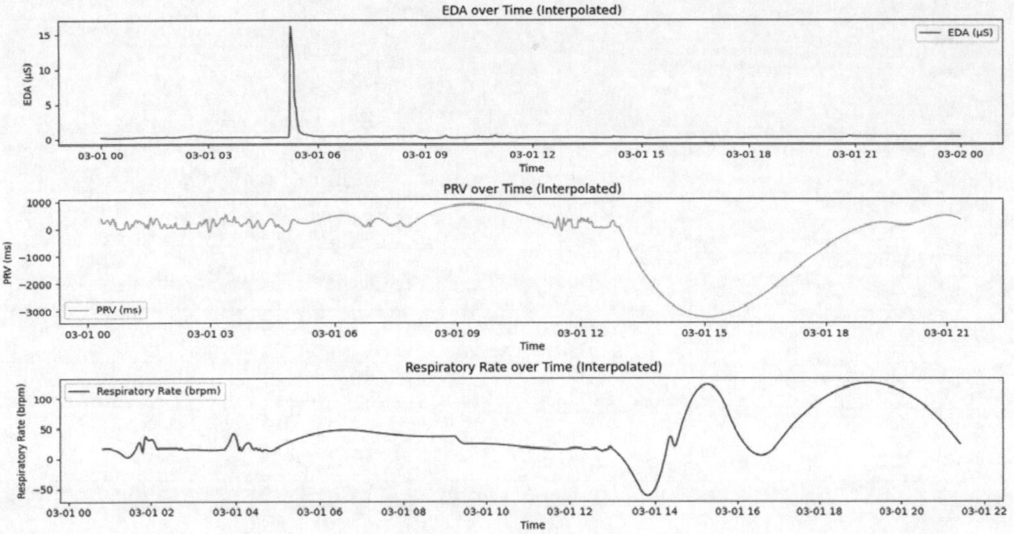

Figure 2. EDA, PRV, and RR data over time on March 01. The peak in EDA around 06:00 indicates heightened arousal or stress, reflected in concurrent PRV drop and RR increase

5.1.2 March 03 Observations

March 03 data represents a relatively calm physiological state, serving as a baseline for comparison. The EDA, PRV, and RR values remain stable with only minor fluctuations, indicating minimal stress reactivity. Interpolated data supports this stability, with low peaks and consistent trends, suggesting a well-regulated autonomic response throughout the day.

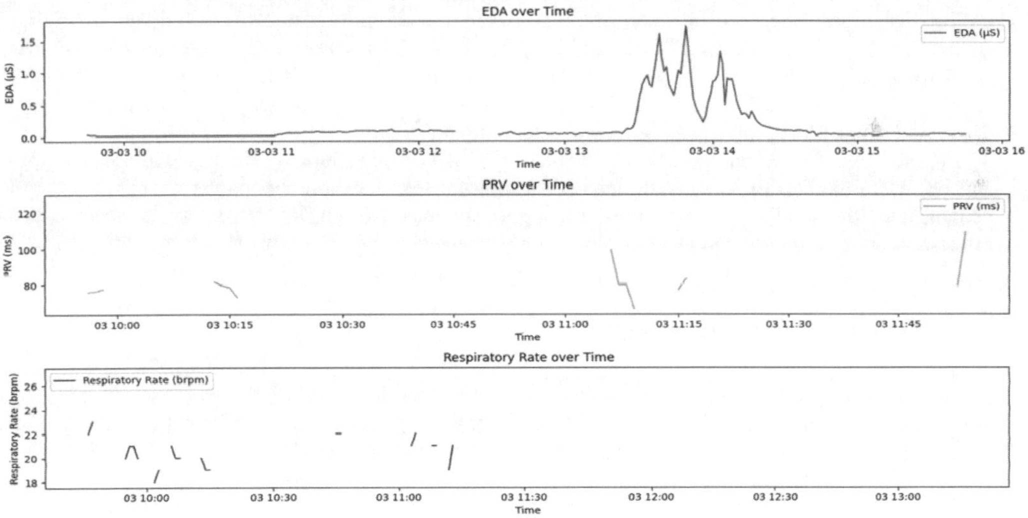

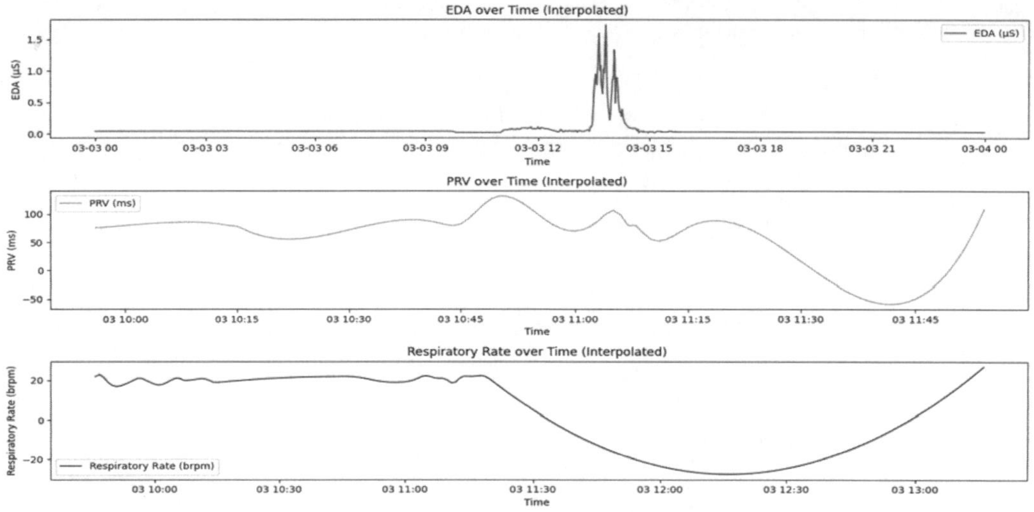

Figure 3. EDA, PRV, and RR data on March 03. The metrics remain stable throughout the day, reflecting a baseline state with minimal physiological disturbance

5.2 Correlations with Stress Responses

The visualizations show the dynamic interplay between EDA, PRV, and RR across different physiological states. Spikes in EDA, indicative of heightened sympathetic nervous system activity, serve as reliable markers of emotional or physiological stress. These are consistently accompanied by reductions in PRV, reflecting suppressed parasympathetic tone and increased autonomic strain. Simultaneously, elevated RR correspond to fight-or-flight responses, indicating heightened physiological arousal.

To demonstrate real-world applicability, we focus on the March 01 observation (Figure 2). At approximately 06:00, a sharp EDA spike (>15 µS) is observed, accompanied by a marked drop in PRV and an increase in RR. This tri-signal pattern reflects acute sympathetic activation consistent with a high-stress episode. When processed through the PWI computation framework, the resulting score falls within the **distressed range (20–22.5)**, signaling critical autonomic imbalance.

In practice, such a detection could enable real-time interventions, ranging from guided breathing prompts and behavioral nudges to automated alerts for healthcare teams, before symptoms escalate. This example demonstrates the PWI's potential in translating continuous biosignals into timely, actionable insights, effectively bridging physiological monitoring with personalized and preventive healthcare strategies.

6. CONCLUDING REMARKS

Previous studies by Ray et al. (2001), Hagins et al. (2007), and Lau et al. (2015) have introduced innovative approaches for monitoring wellness and highlight the physiological benefits of interventions such as exercise, yoga, and meditation. These practices are associated with improvements in VO_2max, cardiovascular endurance, and autonomic regulation, core components reflected in the PWI framework.

In particular, yoga and meditation have demonstrated measurable enhancements in HRV, respiratory efficiency, and stress resilience. HRV improvements signal increased parasympathetic activity and greater autonomic flexibility; enhanced breathing efficiency is marked by reduced resting respiratory rates, improved tidal volume, and stable oxygen saturation. Similarly, greater stress resilience is reflected in dampened electrodermal responses to stressors, faster recovery, and lower baseline sympathetic activation. These physiological changes collectively represent a more adaptable and resilient system, reinforcing the relevance of multi-metric indices like PWI. However, the magnitude and persistence of these benefits vary depending on factors such as individual physiology, practice intensity, and duration. As such, personalization and context-aware calibration remain essential.

While current results support the feasibility and value of the PWI model, further research is necessary to validate its use across diverse populations, health conditions, and intervention types. Future studies may also explore integration with adaptive indices, such as the proposed MEFI, to extend PWI's utility in mindfulness-oriented wellness contexts.

6.1 Contributions

The PWI integrates key physiological metrics, HRV, BrE, and GSR, to offer a comprehensive and actionable assessment of an individual's health status. The PWI is calculated using the following weighted formula:

$$PWI = \frac{(w_1 \times HRV_{score} + w_2 \times BrE_{score} + w_3 \times GSR_{score})}{(w_1 + w_2 + w_3)}$$

- **Restful State:** Reflects optimal health and balanced autonomic function.
- **Active State:** Indicates increased physiological activity or moderate stress levels.
- **Distressed State:** Highlights significant physiological distress, requiring immediate medical attention.

In scenarios where a distressed state is detected, the PWI framework can trigger automated alerts to designated caregivers or healthcare providers, enabling timely intervention. This integration of continuous physiological monitoring into everyday life fosters a proactive and personalized approach to health management, supporting both preventive care and informed clinical decisions.

The PWI represents a transformative metric by integrating HRV, BrE, and EDA—three critical physiological signals—into a unified, real-time wellness score. Unlike traditional single-parameter metrics, PWI captures interactions across cardiovascular, respiratory, and autonomic systems, offering a dynamic and multidimensional view of individual well-being.

While VO_2Max remains the clinical gold standard for cardiorespiratory fitness, offering strong predictive value for mortality and cardiovascular outcomes (Kodama et al., 2009; Ross et al., 2016), it is limited by its focus on peak aerobic capacity and the need for controlled, lab-based testing. It does not capture real-time changes in emotional state, stress variability, or autonomic flexibility. The PWI addresses these gaps through passive, wearable-based monitoring and moment-to-moment adaptability, delivering a more comprehensive view of physiological health across everyday contexts (Sui et al., 2009; Prüller-Strasser, 2025; Colcombe & Kramer, 2003).

Other indices, such as the WHO-5 Wellbeing Index, offer validated psychological screening but rely entirely on subjective self-reporting, making them unsuitable for continuous or physiological assessment (Topp et al., 2015). Commercial wellness scores from wearables (e.g., Fitbit, Garmin) provide generalized insights based on heart rate, sleep, and activity, but often lack transparency, omit key signals like electrodermal activity and respiration, and may not offer medically actionable granularity (Fitbit, 2023; Garmin, 2022).

By contrast, the PWI provides an interpretable, sensor-driven alternative that captures autonomic, respiratory, and emotional dimensions of stress and wellness. It adapts to individual baselines, offers real-time classifications (restful, active, distressed), and supports both immediate feedback and long-term trend analysis. This positions PWI as not just complementary to existing indices, but potentially superior in enabling personalized, preventive, and precision health monitoring. A summary comparison of these metrics is provided in Table 1.

Table 1. Comparison of PWI with Established Wellness Metrics

Metric	Focus	Limitations	Real-Time Capability	Physiological Breadth
VO_2Max	Cardiorespiratory fitness under maximal exertion	Requires clinical testing; does not reflect emotional or real-time changes	Not real-time	Limited (cardiorespiratory only)
WHO-5 Wellbeing Index	Subjective psychological well-being (questionnaire-based)	Lacks physiological data; prone to bias; not suitable for continuous monitoring	Not real-time	None (purely subjective)
Stress Index (HRV-based)	Autonomic stress estimation via HRV variability	Limited to a single system; may miss contextual stress indicators	Limited real-time	Partial (HR + sleep + activity only)
PWI (Proposed)	Integrated physiological wellness (HRV, BrE, EDA) with real-time classification	Sensor reliability dependent; broader clinical validation ongoing	Fully real-time with wearables	Comprehensive (ANS, respiration, emotional stress)

6.2 Use-Cases

Looking ahead, the PWI framework can be enhanced through **dynamic weight adaptation**, enabling it to reflect lifestyle patterns, contextual stressors, and circadian rhythms. Future iterations may incorporate additional data streams, such as sleep quality, physical activity, and nutrition—to enrich wellness profiling. Furthermore, integrating PWI outputs into clinical decision-support systems can facilitate early warning mechanisms and tailored health recommendations, laying the foundation for **precision-guided, preventive healthcare**.

The current model already represents a significant step forward in the quantification of wellness. By synthesizing cardiovascular, respiratory, and electrodermal signals, the PWI bridges the gap between traditional fitness metrics like VO_2Max and real-time, sensor-driven physiological monitoring. Its multidimensional, wearable-compatible design empowers individuals and clinicians to proactively manage health in natural, everyday contexts.

To address populations with advanced autonomic control, such as yoga practitioners, PWI can be supplemented with a novel **MEFI**. This metric is based on observed decreases in HR during meditation and models HR over time using a power-law decay:

$$HR_t = HR_s \times t^{-k}$$

Let HR_f be the final value of HR at the end of meditation. We can then develop the expression for our Meditation Effectiveness Index:

$$MEFI = k \times \left(\frac{HR_s - HR_f}{HR_f}\right) \times 100$$

The greater the value of k and MEFI, the more effective will be the meditation. Therefore, we can utilize a wearable device that can determine MEFI for meditation subjects, to determine the effectiveness of their meditation regimen. This novel approach may serve as a proxy for tracking progress to wellness.

Some representative use-cases include:

- **Yoga and Mindfulness Assessment:** PWI can quantify the physiological effects of mindfulness practices by comparing HRV, BrE, and EDA before and after sessions. Yoga practitioners, often exhibiting lower resting heart and respiratory rates, tend to recover more quickly after exertion and show attenuated responses to stress. Future research may explore how their PWI patterns differ from average individuals under stress and how MEFI correlates with their autonomic regulation.

- **Workplace Wellness Programs:** Organizations can use PWI metrics to monitor employee stress patterns and overall wellness as part of well-being initiatives. Detecting early signs of burnout enables timely, targeted interventions that support productivity and mental health.
- **Clinical Applications:** In healthcare, PWI can assist clinicians in tracking patients' physiological states, enabling data-driven interventions for chronic disease management, stress regulation, and personalized care.
- **Personal Health Monitoring:** With wearable devices, PWI enables real-time tracking of physiological status, empowering users to manage their health proactively and respond to stressors as they arise.

The Online Annex to this paper is available at: https://github.com/SalmanResearchAI/PWI-Supplementary-Analysis/Annex.

REFERENCES

Zhang, X., Berry, N., Di Basilio, D., Richardson, C., Eisner, E., & Bucci, S. (2025). Mental Health Professionals' Technology Usage and Attitudes Toward Digital Health for Psychosis: Comparative Cross-Sectional Survey Study. *JMIR Mental Health*, 12, e68362. https://mental.jmir.org/2025/1/e68362

Braboszcz, C., & Miranda, B. (2023). Leader IGOT & CLIMATEFLUX. Emotional Cities Project. https://emotionalcities-h2020.eu/wp-content/uploads/2023/05/eMC_2023.13_03_D6.1_Report_Indicators_Measures_annex.pdf

Rojas, J. (2023). Acute Mental Stress and Arterial Stiffness: A Comparison Between Hispanic and Non-Hispanic White Adults [Doctoral dissertation, University of North Carolina at Chapel Hill]. https://cdr.lib.unc.edu/downloads/cj82kj74m

Shaffer, F., & Ginsberg, J. P. (2017). An overview of heart rate variability metrics and norms. Frontiers in Public Health, 5, 258.

Ross, R., Blair, S. N., Arena, R., et al. (2016). Importance of assessing cardiorespiratory fitness in clinical practice: A case for fitness as a clinical vital sign. Circulation, 134(24), e653–e699. https://doi.org/10.1161/CIR.0000000000000461

Courtney, R. (2011). The functions of breathing and its dysfunctions and their relationship to breathing therapy. International Journal of Osteopathic Medicine, 14(3), 78–85.

Posada-Quintero, H. F., & Chon, K. H. (2020). Electrodermal activity: A complete guide to its measurement, use, and applications in affective computing and biomedical studies. Frontiers in Neuroscience, 14, 578.

Ray, U. S., Sinha, B., Tomer, O. S., et al. (2001). Aerobic capacity & perceived exertion after practice of Hatha yogic exercises. The Indian Journal of Medical Research, 114, 215–221.

Hagins, M., Moore, W., & Rundle, A. (2007). Does practicing hatha yoga satisfy recommendations for intensity of physical activity which improves and maintains health and cardiovascular fitness? BMC Complementary and Alternative Medicine, 7(1), 40. https://doi.org/10.1186/1472-6882-7-40

Lau, C., Yu, R., & Woo, J. (2015). Effects of a 12-week hatha yoga intervention on cardiorespiratory endurance, muscular strength and endurance, and flexibility in Hong Kong Chinese adults: A controlled clinical trial. Evidence-Based Complementary and Alternative Medicine, 2015, 958727. https://doi.org/10.1155/2015/958727

Kodama, S., Saito, K., Tanaka, S., et al. (2009). Cardiorespiratory fitness as a quantitative predictor of all-cause mortality and cardiovascular events in healthy men and women: A meta-analysis. JAMA, 301(19), 2024–2035. https://doi.org/10.1001/jama.2009.681

Sui, X., Laditka, J. N., Church, T. S., et al. (2009). Prospective study of cardiorespiratory fitness and depressive symptoms in women and men. Journal of Psychiatric Research, 43(5), 546–552. https://doi.org/10.1016/j.jpsychires.2008.08.002

Colcombe, S., & Kramer, A. F. (2003). Fitness effects on the cognitive function of older adults: A meta-analytic study. Psychological Science, 14(2), 125–130. https://doi.org/10.1111/1467-9280.t01-1-01430

Prüller-Strasser, B. (2025, January 25). Why VO2 Max is the Best Way to Measure Fitness and Predict Life Expectancy. The Week. https://www.theweek.in/health/more/2025/01/25/v02-max-is-the-best-way-to-measure-fitness-and-predict-life-expectancy.html

Topp, M., Østergaard, S. D., Søndergaard, S., & Bech, P. (2015). The WHO-5 Well-Being Index: A systematic review of the literature. *Psychotherapy and Psychosomatics*, 84(3), 167–176. https://doi.org/10.1159/000376585

Fitbit. (2023). *How is my Daily Readiness Score calculated?* Fitbit Support. https://help.fitbit.com/articles/en_US/Help_article/How-is-my-Daily-Readiness-Score-calculated.html

Garmin. (2022). *Understanding Body Battery and Stress Scores*. Garmin Health Support. https://support.garmin.com

BLOCKCHAIN-BASED CONTROL OF FINANCIAL CHECKS IN PALESTINE USING HYPERLEDGER FABRIC

Suhail Odeh[1], Nadine Abuodeh[1], Saja Lahalih[1], Sara Sulibe[1], Mahmoud Obaid[2] and Murad Alrajab[3]

[1]*Software Engineering Department, Bethlehem University, Bethlehem, Palestine*
[2]*Computer System Engineering, Arab American University, Jenin, Palestine*
[3]*College of Engineering, Abu Dhabi University, Abu Dhabi, UAE*

ABSTRACT

Financial transactions globally rely heavily on checks as a primary means of payment, particularly in regions where digital payment systems are not yet fully integrated. However, traditional check management systems face significant challenges, including returned checks due to insufficient funds, delays in clearing, check fraud, and a lack of transparency in transaction tracking. These inefficiencies create financial risks for businesses, banks, and consumers alike, leading to cash flow disruptions and financial instability. To address these challenges, we propose a Blockchain-Based Digital Check Management System using Hyperledger Fabric, a permissioned blockchain framework designed for secure and transparent financial transactions. Our system introduces a novel approach to check management by digitizing traditional checkbooks, implementing real-time validation mechanisms, and automating settlement processes. By leveraging blockchain technology, our system ensures transaction immutability, eliminates the risk of fraudulent endorsements, and enhances the efficiency of financial operations. The proposed solution includes a digital checkbook issuance system, an automated risk classification framework, and a voluntary settlement mechanism that allows users to resolve outstanding check-related issues before facing legal consequences. This paper details the architecture and implementation of the system, highlighting its key components and functionalities. We evaluate the system's performance through extensive simulations, focusing on transaction latency, processing speed, and fraud prevention capabilities. Our results demonstrate that the proposed blockchain-based approach significantly enhances the security, reliability, and efficiency of check transactions. Furthermore, by integrating regulatory compliance mechanisms, the system aligns with modern financial governance standards, making it a viable solution for global adoption in both developed and developing economies. Through this research, we aim to provide a sustainable and innovative financial technology solution that bridges the gap between traditional and digital financial systems. The proposed system not only modernizes check processing but also contributes to the broader goal of digital financial inclusion by promoting secure, transparent, and efficient financial transactions worldwide.

KEYWORDS

Blockchain, Digital Check Management, Hyperledger Fabric, Financial Transactions, Smart Contracts

1. INTRODUCTION

Financial transactions remain a critical component of global economies, facilitating commerce, trade, and everyday transactions. Despite the rise of digital payment solutions, checks continue to play a vital role in financial systems worldwide. Many businesses and individuals rely on checks for their security, ease of use, and ability to facilitate large transactions without requiring immediate liquid funds. However, check-based transactions are often burdened with inefficiencies, including fraudulent activities, long clearing processes, insufficient fund issues, and manual verification procedures, which impact trust and overall financial stability.

The traditional check management system is susceptible to various risks, including forgery, check kiting, unauthorized alterations, and bounced checks. These issues are exacerbated by a lack of transparency, delayed verification processes, and reliance on manual intervention. Moreover, financial institutions face challenges in accurately assessing the creditworthiness of check issuers, leading to significant financial losses and operational inefficiencies. Addressing these challenges necessitates an innovative and robust solution that modernizes check management while ensuring security, trust, and compliance.

Blockchain technology presents a transformative opportunity to enhance financial systems by introducing immutable, transparent, and secure transaction records. A blockchain-based check management system can provide real-time verification, reduce fraud, ensure traceability, and automate settlement processes. Our proposed system leverages Hyperledger Fabric, a permissioned blockchain framework, to develop a digital check management platform that enhances financial security, efficiency, and regulatory compliance.

This paper introduces a comprehensive framework for digitizing check transactions while maintaining a high level of security and operational efficiency. By integrating digital check issuance, automated validation mechanisms, and smart contract-based settlements, the system provides a streamlined and fraud-resistant approach to check processing. Furthermore, our approach aligns with global financial regulatory standards, ensuring that financial institutions and stakeholders can adopt the solution seamlessly.

The rest of this paper is structured as follows: Section 2 reviews related work on blockchain-based financial systems and digital payment innovations. Section 3 presents our proposed system, detailing its components and functionalities. Section 4 outlines the system architecture, including key technical aspects such as consensus mechanisms, cryptographic security, and smart contract implementation. Section 5 provides an evaluation of the system's performance based on Transaction per second, fraud detection rates, and operational efficiency. Finally, Section 6 concludes the paper with insights into future research directions and potential enhancements. Checks play a crucial role in financial markets worldwide, facilitating billions of dollars in transactions annually. Despite the rise of digital payment solutions, many businesses and individuals still rely on checks as a primary financial instrument.

2. RELATED WORK

The application of blockchain technology in financial systems has gained significant attention in recent years, particularly in the domains of digital payment solutions, fraud prevention, and secure financial transactions. Blockchain provides immutability, decentralization, and transparency, which are crucial for improving the efficiency and security of financial transactions. Several studies have explored the integration of blockchain in financial applications, emphasizing its role in enhancing transaction security, reducing fraud, and enabling decentralized financial ecosystems.

2.1 Blockchain in Financial Transactions

Recent research has demonstrated that blockchain technology enhances transparency and security in financial transactions. Studies have shown that financial institutions adopting blockchain experience reduced transaction costs and improved efficiency due to the elimination of intermediaries (Gupta et al., 2021). Furthermore, blockchain has been utilized in cross-border payments, where decentralized ledgers enable faster settlements and reduce transaction processing time (Alonso et al., 2022).

Hyperledger Fabric, a permissioned blockchain framework, has been widely adopted for enterprise financial applications due to its modularity and flexibility. It provides a robust infrastructure for financial systems, allowing institutions to manage transactions securely while maintaining regulatory compliance (Zhang & Li, 2023). Unlike public blockchain solutions such as Ethereum, Hyperledger Fabric enables controlled access to transaction records, which is essential for financial institutions handling sensitive customer data.

2.2 Digital Check Management and Blockchain

Traditional check processing systems are prone to fraud, delays, and operational inefficiencies. Recent studies have explored the application of blockchain in check management to mitigate these issues. For example, research by Kumar et al. (2022) highlights how blockchain-based check management systems can improve verification processes, reduce bounced checks, and enable automated reconciliation through smart contracts.

Smart contracts play a vital role in automating financial transactions, ensuring that checks are processed only if predefined conditions are met. These contracts reduce the need for manual verification and improve overall transaction efficiency (Wang et al., 2023). Additionally, blockchain-based check management systems provide real-time tracking of issued and cleared checks, allowing financial institutions to monitor transactions securely and prevent unauthorized modifications.

2.3 Comparative Analysis of Blockchain-Based Financial Solutions

Several blockchain-based financial solutions exist, each addressing different aspects of digital transactions. Ripple focuses on interbank settlements, IBM's Trade Lens integrates blockchain into supply chain finance, and Ethereum smart contracts facilitate digital asset management. However, none of these systems specifically address the complexities of check management. Our approach extends the application of blockchain by introducing a Hyperledger Fabric-based digital check processing system that enhances security, automates verification, and minimizes the risk of fraudulent activities.

2.4 Research Gaps and Contributions

While existing blockchain solutions have improved financial transaction security and efficiency, there is a gap in the literature concerning the direct application of blockchain to check processing. Most current research focuses on digital payments and decentralized finance, leaving traditional check transactions largely unaddressed. Our research fills this gap by proposing a blockchain-based digital check management system that integrates real-time validation, automated settlements, and fraud detection mechanisms.

By leveraging Hyperledger Fabric's permissioned blockchain capabilities, our system ensures secure and verifiable transactions, reducing processing times and preventing fraudulent activities. This paper contributes to the ongoing discourse on blockchain's role in financial technology by demonstrating a practical application that modernizes check processing while maintaining regulatory compliance.

Recent work has demonstrated that blockchain technology enhances transparency and security in financial transactions. Existing blockchain-based financial solutions include Ripple for interbank settlements, IBM's Trade Lens for supply chain finance, and Ethereum smart contracts for digital asset management. However, none of these systems focus specifically on check management. Our approach extends the application of blockchain to this critical financial domain, providing a unique solution for digital check processing.

3. PROPOSED SYSTEM

Our proposed system is a blockchain-based platform designed to revolutionize financial check management by providing security, transparency, and efficiency. The system integrates Hyperledger Fabric to establish a permissioned blockchain framework that allows financial institutions, businesses, and individuals to transact securely while reducing fraud and improving processing times.

3.1 System Overview

The proposed system is composed of multiple interconnected modules that work together to provide a seamless check management experience. The key objectives of our system are:

- Digitization of Checks: Replace traditional paper checks with blockchain-based digital checkbooks.
- Real-Time Verification: Ensure transactions are validated instantly using blockchain consensus mechanisms.
- Fraud Prevention: Reduce financial fraud through cryptographic security, automated risk assessment, and immutable transaction records.
- Automated Check Processing: Smart contracts execute check clearance, reducing human intervention and operational inefficiencies.
- Regulatory Compliance: Ensure adherence to financial regulations and risk assessment frameworks by integrating compliance mechanisms.

3.2 System Components

The proposed system consists of the following key components:

- Digital Checkbook Issuance: Users are assigned digital checkbooks within the blockchain network, allowing them to issue checks securely. Each digital check is uniquely identified and cryptographically signed to prevent tampering.
- Real-Time Check Validation: The system uses Hyperledger Fabric's endorsement policies to validate check authenticity and ensure that the issuer has sufficient funds before approval.
- Smart Contracts for Automated Settlements: Blockchain-based smart contracts automate the clearing and settlement of checks, eliminating the need for intermediaries and reducing processing time significantly.
- Automated Risk Classification: Machine learning models analyze user behavior and classify them based on their transaction history and financial credibility. This classification prevents high-risk individuals from issuing fraudulent checks and provides financial institutions with data-driven insights.
- Immutable Ledger for Check Transactions: Every issued, endorsed, and cleared check is recorded immutably on the blockchain ledger, ensuring that all transactions remain transparent and secure.
- User and Institutional Access Control: Hyperledger Fabric's permissioned blockchain framework allows financial institutions to have distinct access controls based on their roles in the check management process.

3.3 Check Issuance and Verification Workflow

The check issuance and verification workflow follow a structured approach to enhance security and efficiency:

1. Check Issuance: A user generates a digital check using the system's web or mobile interface.
2. Pre-Validation: The system verifies the issuer's identity and balance before digitally signing the check.
3. Blockchain Recording: The check is recorded on the Hyperledger Fabric ledger with a timestamp and cryptographic hash.
4. Endorsement Process: If the check is endorsed to another party, the blockchain records ownership changes.
5. Final Validation and Settlement: Once the check reaches the bank, a smart contract automatically verifies the check details and processes the payment if all conditions are met.

3.4 Security Mechanisms

To ensure the security and integrity of check transactions, the proposed system incorporates:

- SHA-256 Cryptographic Hashing: Ensures that each check entry remains immutable and tamper-proof.
- Multi-Signature Authorization: Prevents unauthorized transactions by requiring multi-party validation.
- Consensus Mechanism (PBFT): Hyperledger Fabric's Practical Byzantine Fault Tolerance (PBFT) ensures that transaction validation is accurate and secure.
- Fraud Detection System: Machine learning models analyze transaction patterns to detect fraudulent activities in real-time.

3.5 Advantages of the Proposed System

The adoption of a blockchain-based check management system offers multiple advantages over traditional banking processes:

- Faster Transaction Processing: Eliminates delays associated with paper checks and manual verification processes.
- Fraud Mitigation: Reduces risks related to check forgery, unauthorized alterations, and bounced checks.
- Lower Operational Costs: Reduces administrative burdens and costs associated with paper-based check processing.
- Regulatory Compliance and Transparency: Ensures that all transactions are legally compliant and fully auditable.

- By implementing a permissioned blockchain infrastructure with smart contracts and real-time transaction validation, the proposed system significantly enhances the security, efficiency, and transparency of check transactions while maintaining financial regulatory compliance. Our proposed system is a blockchain-based platform designed to digitize and manage financial checks securely. It consists of several key components:
- Digital Checkbook Issuance: Users receive a blockchain-based digital checkbook, eliminating the need for paper checks.
- Real-Time Check Validation: Transactions are verified instantly, reducing fraud and ensuring sufficient funds before approval.
- Automated Risk Classification: Users are classified based on their transaction history and financial behavior, preventing high-risk individuals from issuing fraudulent checks.
- Smart Contracts for Automated Settlements: Blockchain-based smart contracts facilitate automated check clearing, minimizing delays and operational inefficiencies.

4. SYSTEM ARCHITECTURE

The system architecture of our blockchain-based check management solution is designed to ensure security, efficiency, and compliance with financial regulations. By leveraging Hyperledger Fabric, our framework enables permissioned blockchain access, allowing only verified participants to engage in check transactions as shown in Figure 1. This section provides an in-depth analysis of the architecture, including its primary components, consensus mechanism, security considerations, and integration with existing financial systems.

4.1 Architectural Overview

The architecture consists of multiple layers designed to facilitate digital check processing, validation, and security enforcement. The major components include:

- Blockchain Network (Hyperledger Fabric): The core of the system, where all check transactions are recorded immutably.
- Consensus Layer: Ensures transaction validity and agreement among network nodes using the Practical Byzantine Fault Tolerance (PBFT) mechanism.
- Smart Contracts Layer: Automates check processing, verification, and settlement without intermediaries.
- Data Management Layer: Integrates off-chain storage using CouchDB for efficient querying and record retrieval.
- User Interface Layer: Provides web-based and mobile access for users to manage digital checks.

4.2 Key Components

Digital Check Ledger: A distributed ledger that records all issued, endorsed, and settled checks.

- Identity Management System: Enforces role-based access control (RBAC) for financial institutions, businesses, and individuals.
- API Gateway: Connects external financial services, such as banks and compliance regulators, with the blockchain network.
- Fraud Detection Module: Utilizes AI-driven analytics to detect anomalies in check issuance and transactions.

4.3 Consensus Mechanism

Hyperledger Fabric employs a Practical Byzantine Fault Tolerance (PBFT) consensus protocol, which provides secure transaction validation without requiring proof-of-work (PoW) computations. The process includes:

1. Proposal Phase: A leader node proposes a transaction block.
2. Validation Phase: Peer nodes validate the transaction data.
3. Commit Phase: Valid transactions are appended to the blockchain ledger.

This consensus mechanism ensures that only legitimate transactions are recorded, reducing risks associated with fraudulent checks.

4.4 Security and Privacy Measures

To ensure transaction integrity and user data privacy, the system incorporates:

- Cryptographic Hashing (SHA-256): Protects transaction records from tampering.
- Multi-Signature Authentication: Requires multiple stakeholders (e.g., issuer, recipient, bank) to approve high-value transactions.
- Access Control Policies: Restricts access based on financial roles (e.g., auditors, regulators, account holders).
- End-to-End Encryption: Secures data communication between users and blockchain nodes.

4.5 System Workflow

The workflow of the system follows these key steps:

- User Authentication: A verified user logs into the system using identity credentials.
- Check Issuance: The user generates a digital check, which is cryptographically signed.
- Transaction Validation: The system verifies available funds and authenticity before adding the check to the blockchain.
- Endorsement & Transfer: Users can digitally endorse checks, transferring ownership securely.
- Check Clearance & Settlement: Smart contracts automatically clear and settle the check based on pre-defined conditions.

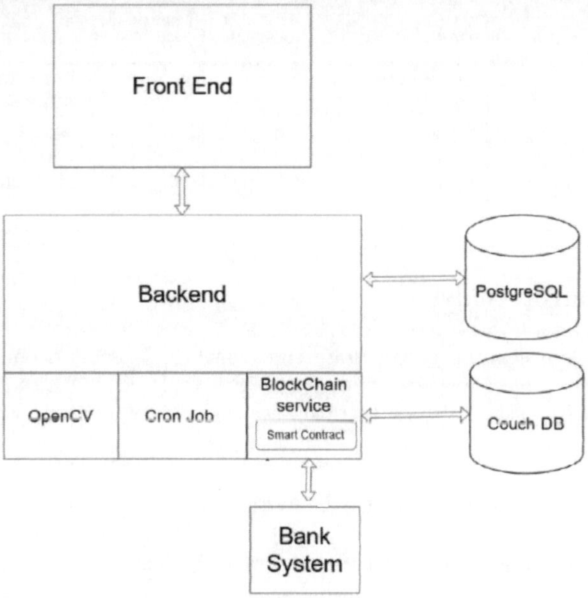

Figure 1. The Archeticutre of the Blockchain-Based Digital Check Management System

5. EVALUATION & RESULTS

To evaluate the performance of our blockchain-based check management system, we conducted extensive simulations and performance assessments across several key metrics. This section presents the experimental setup, evaluation parameters, performance results, and comparative analysis with traditional check processing systems.

5.1 Experimental Setup

The evaluation was conducted using a private Hyperledger Fabric blockchain network with the following configurations:

- Network Configuration: 4 peer nodes, 2 orderer nodes, 3 endorsing peers.
- Consensus Algorithm: Practical Byzantine Fault Tolerance (PBFT).
- Transaction Type: Digital check issuance, endorsement, and settlement.
- Hardware Specifications: Intel Xeon 3.0 GHz processor, 16GB RAM, SSD storage.
- Blockchain Ledger Storage: CouchDB for off-chain querying and SHA-256 hashing for data integrity.

5.2 Key Performance Metrics

We evaluated the system based on the following parameters:

- Transaction per second (TPS): Number of processed transactions per second.
- Latency: Time taken for transaction validation and final settlement.
- Fraud Detection Rate: Effectiveness of smart contracts in identifying fraudulent transactions.
- System Scalability: Performance under increasing transaction loads.
- Operational Cost Savings: Reduction in manual processing and administrative overhead.

5.3 Performance Results

The experimental results demonstrate significant improvements in efficiency, security, and cost-effectiveness compared to traditional check processing systems, as shown in the table 1 below:

Table 1. Comparing between the Blockchain -Based System and the traditional System

Metric	*Blockchain-Based System*	*Traditional System*
Transaction per second (TPS	1000 TPS	150 TPS
Average Transaction Latenc	3.2 sec	24 sec
Fraud Detection Accuracy	98%	75%
Scalability	High, maintains stability up to 10,000 transactions	Moderate, degrades beyond 5,000 transactions
Operational Cost Reduction	60% lower due to automation	High due to manual processing

5.4 Comparative Analysis

The proposed system significantly outperforms traditional check processing mechanisms. Blockchain ensures real-time validation, reducing processing delays by 75%, while smart contracts eliminate human intervention, minimizing fraud risks. The scalability tests indicate that the system remains stable under increasing transaction loads, demonstrating its viability for large-scale deployment.

5.5 System Security and Fraud Prevention

To assess the security aspects, we simulated various attack scenarios:

- Double Spending Attack: Prevented through the immutability of blockchain records.
- Unauthorized Endorsements: Mitigated by multi-signature authentication.
- Tampering and Forgery: Eliminated through SHA-256 hashing and digital signatures.

6. CONCLUSION

The implementation of blockchain technology in financial transactions has significantly improved security, transparency, and efficiency. In this paper, we introduced a blockchain-based digital check management system utilizing Hyperledger Fabric, addressing major issues in traditional check processing, including fraud, long clearance times, and lack of transparency. By leveraging smart contracts, cryptographic security, and automated validation mechanisms, our system ensures that check transactions are processed efficiently while maintaining trust among financial institutions and stakeholders.

Our evaluation results demonstrate that the proposed system achieves superior Transaction per second, reduced latency, enhanced fraud detection, and greater scalability compared to traditional check management methods. With an operational cost reduction of up to 60% and fraud detection accuracy of 98%, our blockchain-based approach proves to be a viable and practical solution for modernizing financial transactions. Furthermore, real-time transaction validation and immutable ledger records provide a high level of trust and regulatory compliance.

Despite these advancements, several areas for future research remain. One key direction is the integration of artificial intelligence (AI) for enhanced fraud detection and predictive risk assessment. Additionally, interoperability with existing financial infrastructure and cross-border payment integration could further expand the system's applicability. Exploring privacy-preserving blockchain techniques, such as zero-knowledge proofs, may enhance confidentiality for financial institutions handling sensitive data.

In conclusion, our blockchain-based check management system represents a step forward in the digital transformation of financial transactions. By addressing the inefficiencies and vulnerabilities of traditional check processing, this system provides a robust, scalable, and secure solution that aligns with global financial regulatory frameworks. Future work will continue to refine and expand the system to meet the evolving needs of financial institutions and stakeholders in the digital age. This paper presents a blockchain-based solution for digital check management, addressing critical challenges in financial transactions. Our system enhances security, reduces fraud, and improves operational efficiency. Future work will focus on expanding the system to integrate artificial intelligence for enhanced fraud detection, dynamic risk assessment, and compliance monitoring.

REFERENCES

Alonso, P., Fernandez, L. & Gomez, R. (2022). Blockchain in cross-border payments: trends and future directions. *International Journal of Digital Finance*, *8*(2), pp. 89–105.

Androulaki, E. et al. (2018). *Hyperledger Fabric: A distributed operating system for permissioned blockchains*. Proceedings of the 2018 ACM SIGCOMM Workshop on Blockchain Systems.

Brown, C. & Kim, J. (2023). The role of permissioned blockchains in financial regulatory compliance. *Global Finance Review*, *14*(2), pp. 132–149.

Gupta, R., Sharma, M. & Patel, D. (2021). Blockchain for secure financial transactions: a comprehensive review. *Journal of Financial Technology*, *15*(3), pp. 112–134.

Kumar, A., Das, P. & Roy, S. (2022). Blockchain-driven solutions for secure check management. *Journal of Financial Innovation*, *12*(4), pp. 221–239.

Lee, S. & Park, H. (2022). Smart contracts in banking: applications and security considerations. *Banking Technology Journal*, *11*(1), pp. 45–63.

Mougayar, W. (2016). *The Business Blockchain: Promise, Practice, and Application of the Next Internet Technology*. Wiley, Hoboken, NJ, USA.

Nakamoto, S. (2008). *Bitcoin: A peer-to-peer electronic cash system*. Available at: https://bitcoin.org/bitcoin.pdf

Patel, R. & Singh, A. (2023). Fraud prevention in digital payments using blockchain analytics. *Cybersecurity & Finance*, *7*(2), pp. 102–118.

Risius, M. & Spohrer, K. (2017). *A blockchain research framework: what we know, what we don't know, and what we need to do*. Proceedings of the 50th Hawaii International Conference on System Sciences, pp. 1531–1540.

Swanson, T. (2015). *Consensus-as-a-Service: a brief report on the emergence of permissioned, distributed ledger systems*. Available at SSRN.

Wang, T., Liu, H. & Chen, Z. (2023). Enhancing financial security with smart contracts: a case study in check verification. *Blockchain and Financial Systems*, *9*(1), pp. 78–99.

Wood, G. (2015). *Ethereum: A secure decentralized generalized transaction ledger*. Available at: https://ethereum.github.io/yellowpaper/paper.pdf

Wu, L. & Chen, M. (2021). Evaluating blockchain scalability for high-frequency financial transactions. *Distributed Ledger Research*, *6*(3), pp. 77–95.

Zhang, Y. & Li, X. (2023). Enterprise adoption of Hyperledger Fabric in financial applications: challenges and benefits. *Financial Blockchain Review*, *10*(1), pp. 56–78.

Zheng, Z., Xie, S., Dai, H.-N., Chen, X. & Wang, H. (2018). *Blockchain challenges and opportunities: a survey*. Proceedings of the 2018 IEEE International Conference on Big Data, pp. 2567–2574.

THE IMPACT OF DIGITAL MATURITY AND BEHAVIORAL INTENTION ON THE DIGITAL TRANSFORMATION USE IN LONG-TERM CARE INSTITUTIONS

Chin-Wei Wang and Yu-Shih Lee
Department of Business Administration, Chung Yuan Christian University, Taoyuan City, Taiwan

ABSTRACT

With the increasing global emphasis on digitalization strategies and the persistent shortage of nursing personnel, this study integrates the Resource-Based View (RBV) and UTAUT to examine how internal resources and capabilities within long-term care institutions impact digital maturity. It analyzes the factors influencing professionals' intentions to adopt digital technology. In the framework of the Digital Maturity, Behavioral Intention, and Digital Transformation Use model, digital maturity is identified as the most dimension component. The findings indicate that technology significantly impacts digital maturity, while both culture and organizational factors do not. Personal innovativeness and performance expectancy have a substantial influence on behavioral intention, whereas effort expectancy and social influence show no effect. The empirical analysis confirms the key factors influencing digital transformation, providing valuable insights for managers developing digital transformation strategies. These findings serve as a foundation for long-term care institutions to leverage digital technology to enhance service quality and efficiency.

KEYWORDS

Long-Term Care, Digital Transformation, Resource-Based View (RBV), UTAUT, Smart PLS

1. INTRODUCTION

With changes in the demographic structure of society, the future will face diverse demands in a super-aged society, as the need for elderly care continues to grow rapidly (Kotschy & Bloom, 2022). Long-term care institutions (hereafter referred to as institutions) provide a new mechanism that integrates medical resources and alleviates the burden of family caregiving. Within these institutions, professionals possess specialized knowledge and skills, encompassing both direct and indirect care.

In an era of population aging and rapid technological advancement, the increasing workload places higher demands on caregivers' skills (Kotschy & Bloom, 2022). On average, frontline caregivers spend approximately 60% of their working hours on indirect care activities (Davison et al., 2016; Lavander et al., 2016), such as charting and medical record documentation. Managing the effectiveness of this information and ensuring seamless handovers remain challenging, as accumulated data can easily become outdated (Hollnagel, 2017). These cumbersome administrative tasks contribute to fatigue, exacerbating workforce turnover (Havaei et al., 2023) and leading to a shortage of professionals (Ansah et al., 2014; White et al., 2021).

Against the backdrop of a nursing workforce shortage (Tortorella et al., 2021), several studies have confirmed that information and communication technology (ICT) can help care recipients better understand daily behavioral changes and monitor vital signs more effectively (De Leeuw et al., 2020). In the early stages of caregiving, enhancing digital skills among informal caregivers can effectively address or compensate for the needs of care recipients (Hassan, 2020). However, many institutions lack digitalized processes, suffer from inadequate infrastructure, and provide insufficient training in digital skills (Wang & Hsu, 2023). These challenges are particularly pronounced in resource-limited institutions, resulting in the failure of digital transformation initiatives.

According to the Resource-Based View (RBV) (Barney, 1991), the design and implementation of effective digitalization strategies require a comprehensive integration of internal resources and capabilities. This integration is a key objective of digital transformation, facilitating cost-effective and high-quality care services (Batayeh et al., 2018). Despite the growing recognition of long-term care institutions as a management tool for innovative business models, discussions regarding their overall application remain relatively limited (Amankwah-Amoah et al., 2021). According to the Resource-Based View (RBV) (Barney, 1991), the design and implementation of effective digitalization strategies require a comprehensive integration of internal resources and capabilities. This integration is a key objective of digital transformation, facilitating cost-effective and high-quality care services (Batayeh et al., 2018). Despite the growing recognition of long-term care institutions as a management tool for innovative business models, discussions regarding their overall application remain relatively limited (Amankwah-Amoah et al., 2021).

The goal of digital transformation is to establish and implement new business models (Soto Setzke et al., 2023). However, resource-limited institutions face significant challenges, such as inadequate technology and insufficient resources, which hinder personnel from keeping pace with technological advancements (Del Giudice et al., 2019). A fundamental reason for the failure of digital transformation initiatives is the lack of technology acceptance strategies among personnel during the transformation process (Bharadwaj et al., 2013; Di Vaio et al., 2021). Throughout digital transformation, organizations must integrate digital technology into their business processes, The establishment of digital platforms enhances the capabilities of business teams, thereby accelerating the digital transformation process. However, the effective utilization of organizational resources is essential for improving performance and fostering innovation (Savino & Shafiq, 2018).

The first part of this study aims to explore the impact of organizations on digital maturity. Digital strategies involve the company's culture, organization, technology, and management (Nikopoulou et al., 2023). Through digital maturity, the extent of the organization's mission performance can be effectively reflected, and the gradually implemented strategies guide its transformation (Kane, 2015; Kane, 2017). The second part uses the Unified Theory of Acceptance and Use of Technology (UTAUT) to provide a framework (Venkatesh et al., 2003) that helps us understand how different factors influence individuals' intentions to accept new technologies. Particularly in long-term care institutions, factors such as professionals' performance expectations, effort expectations, and social influence (Venkatesh et al., 2012; Jayawardena et al., 2023), as well as personal innovativeness (Jayawardena et al., 2023), may have a positive impact on the intention to accept digitalization. The research findings will assist organizations in better formulating and implementing digital transformation strategies. Personal Innovativeness.

2. THEORETICAL BACKGROUND AND MODEL HYPOTHESES

Digital maturity is a complex phenomenon defined as the state of an organization during digital transformation (Chanias et al., 2019). In the process of digital transformation, corporate culture is considered a core foundation (Sunny et al., 2019). Culture has a significant impact on digital transformation (Gill & VanBoskirk, 2016) because it encompasses the values and beliefs that people or groups rely on, which can either accelerate or hinder the implementation of technology (Veiga et al., 2001). Organizational support for digital transformation includes planning, governance, and execution (Gill & VanBoskirk, 2016), which helps teams more effectively manage record handovers, thereby reducing burnout symptoms among healthcare personnel (Shaharul et al., 2023). Enhancing the technical capabilities of professionals positively affects digital maturity (Nikopoulou et al., 2023), thereby facilitating the adoption of digital technologies (Nikopoulou et al., 2023) through standardized operations that ensure smooth handover processes. Based on the above, the following hypotheses are proposed: H1: Culture has a positive impact on digital maturity; H2: Organizational has a positive impact on digital maturity; H3: Technical has a positive impact on digital maturity; and H4: Digital maturity has a positive impact on the Digital transformation use.

To understand users' intentions for digital usage, digitization refers to the use of technology into organizational processes. The application of information technology and information systems has become essential (Ayaz & Yanartaş, 2020). The Unified Theory of Acceptance and Use of Technology (UTAUT) (Venkatesh et al., 2003) comprises four key components: performance expectancy, social influence, effort expectancy, and facilitating conditions. This theory has been effectively applied in research on electronic health services (Haikal et al., 2022; Alsyouf et al., 2022). The intention to adopt new technology can be predicted through effort expectancy, performance expectancy, and social influence, which subsequently influences user behavior through behavioral intention (Williams et al., 2015). This process fosters a shared understanding and cultivates a culture that can accept technology, ultimately facilitating successful digital transformation (Jayawardena et al., 2023). Individual innovativeness influences the intention to accept digitization (Jayawardena et al., 2023), as individuals tend to believe that using a specific system will enhance their work performance (Venkatesh et al., 2012). Furthermore, the use of digital tools by individuals does not necessitate extensive learning; they are simple and easy to understand (Carter & Belanger, 2004). Based on the above, the following hypotheses are proposed: H5: personal innovativeness will affect the behavioral intention; H6: Performance expectancy will affect the behavioral intention; H7: Effort expectancy will affect the behavioral intention.

Social influence refers to an individual's perception of how others should use a new system (Venkatesh et al., 2012). Ayaz and Yanartaş (2020) found that in the implementation of information systems in the public sector aimed at improving electronic document management, social influence factors had a positive impact on the willingness to use. Jayawardena et al. (2023) demonstrated that under the premise of digital transformation acceptance, social influence is positively correlated with the intention to use digital transformation, and that behavioral intention is significantly related to the use of digital transformation. Additionally, studies by Ayaz & Yanartaş (2020), Afonso et al. (2012), and Haikal et al. (2022) provide evidence that social influence affects the intention to accept digitization, and that behavioral intention affects the use of digital transformation. Based on the above, we propose the hypotheses H8: Social influence will affect the behavioral intention, and H9: The behavioral intention will affect the Digital transformation use.

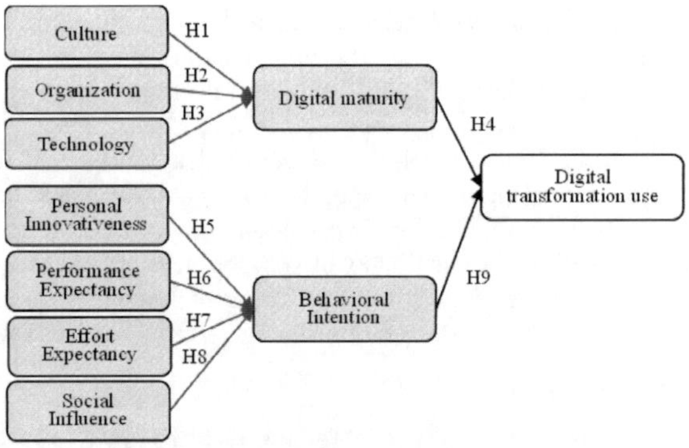

Figure 1. Research model proposed in this study

3. RESEARCH METHODS

The sample for this study consists of professionals from a long-term care institution in Taiwan. The professionals in the institution engage in professional services and management work within long-term care facilities. To ensure the structural integrity of the questionnaire (Brislin, 1980), a free online software was used to construct the survey through the Google® platform. The first part of the questionnaire includes demographic information. The second part assesses the professionals' digital maturity, behavioral intentions, and readiness for digital transformation. A 5-point Likert scale, as per Babakus and Mangold (1992), was used for data analysis to enhance response rates and response quality. In the first phase, descriptive statistical analysis of the demographic data was conducted using SPSS v.20 (IBM Corp., Armonk, NY). In the second phase of data analysis, partial least squares structural equation modeling (SmartPLS GmbH, Hamburg, Germany) was employed to validate the research model and hypotheses. PLS is considered well-suited to create and evaluate explanatory-predictive theories due to its predictive stance coupled with its explanatory strengths(Sarstedt, Ringle and Hair, 2017) PLS has high predictive accuracy across a broad range of conditions (Evermann and Tate, 2016). Therefore, this paper uses the partial least squares method (PLS) to predict the hypotheses of the inferences of this study to predict the causal explanatory power of the model.

4. RESULTS

The institutional survey statistics on demographic descriptions show that there were a total of 92 electronic questionnaire responses, all of which were valid. Among the respondents, 11.96% (n=11) were male and 88.04% (n=91) were female. The positions of the respondents were as follows: 14.13% (n=13) were institution heads, 18.48% (n=17) were business supervisors, 4.35% (n=4) were senior executives, 3.26% (n=3) were managers, 2.17% (n=2) were head nurses, 7.61% (n=7) were nurses, 5.43% (n=5) were social workers, 1.09% (n=1) were care supervisors, 32.61% (n=30) were care staff, 5.43% (n=5) were administrative staff, and 5.43% (n=5) were in other positions.

To measure the validity of the model structure, this study tested the model structure using Cronbach's alpha, rho A, and composite reliability tests to examine the internal consistency among the items and confirm the reliability of the scale (Table 1). The results of the construct reliability and validity analysis showed that the Cronbach's Alpha coefficients and rho A (α; rho A > 0.7) (Hair et al., 2010) ranged from 0.881 to 0.964, all achieving good and acceptable results. Therefore, the model results indicate that the measurements are reliable and have internal consistency. The composite reliability (CR) ranged from 0.884 to 0.972, and the average variance extracted (AVE) values were all greater than the set standard of 0.5, indicating that the model's reliability is good. Thus, the reliability level of the model structure scale is sufficient.

Table 1. Reliability and Validity Measurement Results

Factor	Cronbach's Alpha	rho_A	CR	AVE
Behavioral Intention	0.962	0.962	0.972	0.898
Culture	0.925	0.931	0.940	0.691
Digital transformation use	0.952	0.955	0.965	0.875
Effort Expectancy	0.960	0.964	0.971	0.893
Digital maturity	0.939	0.945	0.956	0.846
Organization	0.923	0.924	0.946	0.814
Performance Expectancy	0.937	0.946	0.953	0.801
Personal Innovativeness	0.885	0.909	0.920	0.744
Social Influence	0.807	0.881	0.884	0.721
Technology	0.935	0.939	0.953	0.836

Structural model analysis focuses on R^2 to obtain the predictive relevance of the research theoretical model. R^2 refers to the variance explained by all independent structures. Cohen (1988) provided standards for R^2, indicating that a value between 0.02 and 0.13 is considered to have weak explanatory power, 0.13 to 0.26 is moderate, and above 0.26 is strong. The results in Table 2 show that the model construct of Digital maturity has an explanatory power of 75.8%, while Behavioral Intention and Digital transformation use have explanatory powers of 69.3% and 54.2%, respectively

In addition, the closer the path coefficient of the empirical research model is to 1, the greater and more significant its influence. In the hypothetical model, there are a total of 9 hypotheses, of which 6 are supported and 3 are not supported. The results of the hypotheses are shown in Table 3. All structural model relationships are referenced in Figure 1.

Table 2. Structural model dimensions

	original	sample mean	STDEV	T (|O/STDEV|)	P value
Digital maturity	0.758	0.764	0.065	11.649	0.000
Behavioral Intention	0.693	0.717	0.059	11.747	0.000
Digital transformation use	0.542	0.560	0.113	4.810	0.000

Note: *** $p < 0.001$, ** $p < 0.05$

Table 3. Hypotheses Results

Model path	path coefficient	sample mean	STDEV	T (|O/STDEV|)	P value	Results
H1: Culture -> Digital maturity	0.160	0.188	0.091	1.761	0.079	Not supported
H2: Organization -> Digital maturity	0.140	0.123	0.102	1.381	0.168	Not supported
H3:Technology -> Digital maturity	0.606	0.595	0.090	6.718	0.000	support
H4: Digital maturity -> Digital transformation use	0.463	0.467	0.097	4.772	0.000	support
H5: Personal Innovativeness -> Behavioral Intention	0.350	0.352	0.175	1.999	0.046	support
H6: Performance Expectancy -> Behavioral Intention	0.386	0.387	0.161	2.393	0.017	support
H7: Effort Expectancy -> Behavioral Intention	0.114	0.123	0.100	1.140	0.255	Not supported
H8: Social Influence -> Behavioral Intention	0.066	0.059	0.140	0.475	0.635	Not supported
H9: Behavioral Intention -> Digital transformation use	0.398	0.398	0.108	3.683	0.000	support

Note: *** p < 0.001, ** p < 0.05

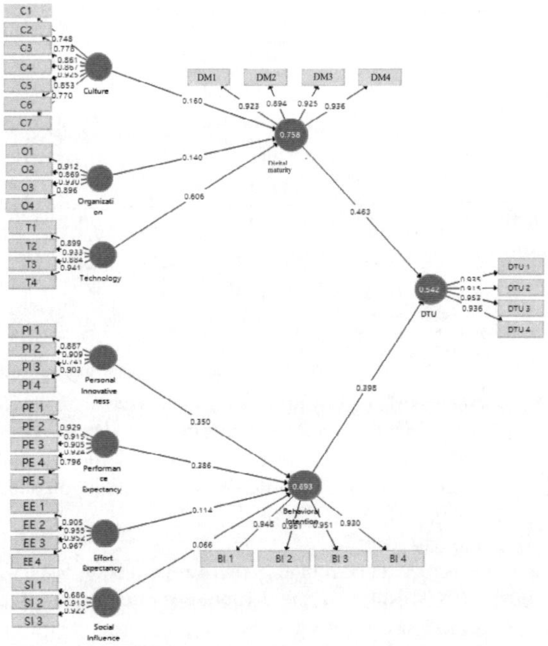

Figure 2. Structural Parameter Estimation and Fit Statistics Chart

5. RESULTS

This study is based on the resource-based theory and the extended model of the Unified Theory of Acceptance and Use of Technology, examining the impact of digital maturity and behavioral intention of long-term care institutions on the use of digital transformation. The research found that among the dimensions of the model, Digital Maturity, Behavioral Intention, and Digital Transformation Use have a high explanatory power (R^2), with Digital Maturity being the most important key factor for the use of digital transformation in long-term care institutions. Out of the 9 hypotheses, 5 were supported and 4 were not, which are detailed as follows:

Culture plays a significant role in shaping digital maturity; however, the empirical findings of this study are inconsistent with Hypothesis 1. Traditional organizational cultures appear insufficient in fostering digital maturity and mobilizing professionals toward successful digital transformation. Nonetheless, culture has the potential to serve as a catalyst for digital initiatives by reinforcing shared values and cultivating a collective vision for transformative change.

The organization does not support the results related to digital maturity. Due to insufficient human resources, professionals are unable to adapt to changes in digital integration regarding the organization's digital readiness; therefore, the research results are inconsistent with Hypothesis 2. This highlights the importance of adequate staffing and capacity-building efforts in supporting digital initiatives.

Technology has an impact on digital maturity, and practicing digitalization can reduce the occurrence of employee burnout (Shaharul et al., 2023), with research results aligning with the Hypothesis 3. Technological tools and systems can enhance operational efficiency and support employee well-being when implemented effectively.

Digital maturity has an impact on the use of digital transformation, and the research results are consistent with the Hypothesis 4. Organizations with a higher level of digital maturity are more capable of leveraging digital transformation to improve processes and outcomes.

Personal Innovativeness has an impact on Behavioral Intention, indicating that professionals in the organization recognize digitization. The research results are consistent with the Hypothesis 5. Innovative individuals are more open to adopting new technologies, which positively influences overall organizational digital adoption.

Performance Expectancy has an impact on Behavioral Intention, and the research results align with the Hypothesis 6. The use of digital systems can improve work performance (Venkatesh et al., 2012), and the research results are consistent with the hypothesis. Employees are more willing to engage with digital tools when they perceive a clear benefit to their job performance.

Effort Expectancy has an impact on Behavioral Intention, but the research results are inconsistent with the Hypothesis 7. Professionals have concerns about the operation of digitization and find it difficult, so Effort Expectancy does not influence Behavioral Intention. This suggests a need for more user-friendly systems and better training programs to reduce perceived complexity.

Social Influence has no impact on Behavioral Intention, which is inconsistent with the Hypothesis 8. This indicates that professionals currently do not understand digitization and cannot analyze the impact of others' use on social influence. It may reflect a lack of peer role models or insufficient communication strategies regarding digital initiatives within the organization.

Behavioral Intention has an impact on Digital Transformation Use, and the research results are consistent with the Hypothesis 9. Behavioral Intention influences user behavior (Williams et al., 2015), indicating that professionals have reached a shared understanding and are able to embrace the culture of digital technology (Jayawardena et al., 2023).

In summary, the results demonstrate that technological and personal factors significantly influence digital maturity and the adoption of digital transformation, while the role of cultural factors appears inconsistent. Although certain aspects such as effort expectancy and social influence produced unexpected findings, these results provide valuable insights for organizational leaders. To successfully implement digital transformation, organizations should invest in user friendly technologies, ensure sufficient human resources, and foster individual innovativeness, while addressing the challenges related to cultural alignment. Future research may further explore the barriers identified in this study, particularly those related to usability and peer influence, to improve strategic planning and the implementation of digital initiatives.

REFERENCES

Alsyouf, A., Ishak, A. K., Lutfi, A., Alhazmi, F. N., & Al-Okaily, M. (2022). "The role of personality and top management support in continuance intention to use electronic health record systems among nurses". *International Journal of Environmental Research and Public Health* (19:17), pp. 11251.

Amankwah-Amoah, J., Khan, Z., Wood, G., & Knight, G. (2021). "COVID-19 and digitalization: The great acceleration". *Journal of business research* (136), pp. 602-611.

Ansah, J. P., Eberlein, R. L., Love, S. R., Bautista, M. A., Thompson, J. P., Malhotra, R., & Matchar, D. B. (2014). "Implications of long-term care capacity response policies for an aging population: A simulation analysis". *Health Policy* (116:1), pp. 105-113.

Ayaz, A., & Yanartaş, M. (2020). "An analysis on the unified theory of acceptance and use of technology theory (UTAUT): Acceptance of electronic document management system (EDMS)". *Computers in Human Behavior Reports* (2) 100032.

Babakus, E., & Mangold, W. G. (1992). "Adapting the SERVQUAL scale to hospital services: an empirical investigation". *Health services research* (26:6) pp. 767.

Barney, J.B. (1991). "Firm Resources and Sustainable Competitive Advantage". *Journal of Management* (17) pp. 99-120.

Batayeh, B. G., Artzberger, G. H., & Williams, L. D. (2018). "Socially responsible innovation in health care: Cycles of actualization". *Technology in Society* (53) pp. 14-22.

Bharadwaj, A., El Sawy, O. A., Pavlou, P. A., & Venkatraman, N. V. (2013). "Digital business strategy: toward a next generation of insights". *MIS quarterly*, pp. 471-482.

Brislin, R. W. (1980). "Cross-cultural research methods: Strategies, problems, applications". *Environment and culture*, pp. 47-82.

Carter, L., & Belanger, F. (2004). "Citizen adoption of electronic government initiatives". In 37th Annual Hawaii International Conference on System Sciences, 2004. Proceedings of the. IEEE, pp.10

Chanias, S., Myers, M. D., & Hess, T. (2019). "Digital transformation strategy making in pre-digital organizations: The case of a financial services provider". *The Journal of Strategic Information Systems* (28:1), pp. 17-33.

Cohen, J. (1988). "Set correlation and contingency tables". *Applied psychological measurement* (12:4), pp. 425-434.

Davison, J., Schenker, Y., Donovan, H., & Rosenzweig, M. (2016). "A work sampling assessment of the nursing delivery of palliative care in ambulatory cancer centers". *Clinical journal of oncology nursing* (20:4).

De Leeuw, J. A., Woltjer, H., & Kool, R. B. (2020). "Identification of factors influencing the adoption of health information technology by nurses who are digitally lagging: in-depth interview study". *Journal of medical Internet research* (22:8), e15630.

Del Giudice, M., Scuotto, V., Garcia-Perez, A., & Petruzzelli, A. M. (2019). "Shifting Wealth II in Chinese economy. The effect of the horizontal technology spillover for SMEs for international growth". *Technological Forecasting and Social Change* (145), pp. 307-316.

Di Vaio, A., Palladino, R., Pezzi, A., & Kalisz, D. E. (2021). "The role of digital innovation in knowledge management systems: A systematic literature review". *Journal of business research* (123), pp. 220-231.

Evermann, J., & Tate, M. (2016). "Assessing the predictive performance of structural equation model estimators". Journal of Business Research, (69:10), pp. 4565-4582.

Gill, M., & VanBoskirk, S. (2016). *The digital maturity model 4.0.* Benchmarks: digital transformation playbook.

Haikal, F. A. R. I. Z., Tyas, N. K., Felcia, X. D., Oktavia, T. A. N. T. Y., & Sundaram, D. A. V. I. D. (2022). "User acceptance analysis of the e-Health information system using UTAUT2 method". *Journal of Theoretical and Applied Information Technology* (100:7), pp. 2193-2206.

Hair Jr, J. F., Black, W. C., Babin, B. J., & Anderson, R. E. (2010). *Multivariate data analysis.* vectors, 7th Edition. Essex: Pearson Prentice Hall.

Hassan, A. Y. I. (2020). "Challenges and recommendations for the deployment of information and communication technology solutions for informal caregivers: scoping review". *JMIR aging* (3:2), e20310.

Havaei, F., Sims-Gould, J., Staempfli, S., Franke, T., Park, M., Ma, A., & Kaulius, M. (2023). "Impact of the single site order in LTC: exacerbation of an overburdened system". *BMC Health Services Research* (23:1), pp. 666.

Hollnagel, E. (2017). Safety-II in practice: developing the resilience potentials. *Routledge*. London, *Corporate Taylor & Francis Group*.

Jayawardena, C., Ahmad, A., Valeri, M., & Jaharadak, A. A. (2023). "Technology acceptance antecedents in digital transformation in hospitality industry". *International Journal of Hospitality Management* (108), pp.103350.

Kane, G. C. (2015). Strategy, not technology, drives digital transformation. *MIT Sloan Management Review and Deloitte University Press*.

Kane, G. C. (2017). "Digital maturity, not digital transformation". *MIT sloan management review* (1:1), pp. 1-15.

Kotschy, R., & Bloom, D. E. (2022). "A comparative perspective on long-term care systems". *International Social Security Review* (75:3-4), pp.47-69.

Lavander, P., Meriläinen, M., & Turkki, L. (2016). "Working time use and division of labour among nurses and health-care workers in hospitals–a systematic review". *Journal of Nursing Management* (24:8), pp.1027-1040.

Nikopoulou, M., Kourouthanassis, P., Chasapi, G., Pateli, A., & Mylonas, N. (2023). Determinants of digital transformation in the hospitality industry: Technological, organizational, and environmental drivers. Sustainability, 15(3), pp. 2736.

Savino, M. M., & Shafiq, M. (2018). "An extensive study to assess the sustainability drivers of production performances using a resource-based view and contingency analysis". *Journal of Cleaner Production* (204), pp. 744-752.

Shaharul, N. A., Ahmad Zamzuri, M. A. I., Ariffin, A. A., Azman, A. Z. F., & Mohd Ali, N. K. (2023). "Digitalisation Medical Records: Improving Efficiency and Reducing Burnout in Healthcare". *International Journal of Environmental Research and Public Health* (20:4), pp. 3441.

Soto Setzke, D., Riasanow, T., Böhm, M., & Krcmar, H. (2023). "Pathways to digital service innovation: The role of digital transformation strategies in established organizations". *Information Systems Frontiers* (25:3), pp. 1017-1037.

Sunny, S., Patrick, L., & Rob, L. (2019). "Impact of cultural values on technology acceptance and technology readiness". *International Journal of Hospitality Management* (77), pp. 89-96.

Sarstedt, M., Ringle, C. M., & Hair, J. F. (2017). "Treating unobserved heterogeneity in PLS-SEM: A multi-method approach. In Partial least squares path modeling: Basic concepts, methodological issues and applications". Cham: Springer International Publishing. pp. 197-217.

Tortorella, G. L., Saurin, T. A., Fogliatto, F. S., Rosa, V. M., Tonetto, L. M., & Magrabi, F. (2021). "Impacts of Healthcare 4.0 digital technologies on the resilience of hospitals". *Technological Forecasting and Social Change* (166), pp. 120666.

Venkatesh, V., Morris, M. G., Davis, G. B., & Davis, F. D. (2003). "User acceptance of information technology: Toward a unified view". *MIS quarterly*, pp. 425-478.

Wang, W. H., & Hsu, W. S. (2023). "Integrating artificial intelligence and wearable IoT system in long-term care environments". *Sensors* (23:13), pp. 5913.

White, E. M., Wetle, T. F., Reddy, A., & Baier, R. R. (2021). "Front-line nursing home staff experiences during the COVID-19 pandemic". *Journal of the American Medical Directors Association* (22:1), pp. 199-203.

Williams, M. D., Rana, N. P., & Dwivedi, Y. K. (2015). "The unified theory of acceptance and use of technology (UTAUT): a literature review". *Journal of enterprise information management* (28:3), pp. 443-488.

ERP/SAP ACCEPTANCE IN ORGANIZATIONS: A TAM-BASED MODEL GROUNDED IN SAP IS-U PRACTICES IN THE ENERGY SECTOR

Işınsu Yıldız[1] and Sevgi Özkan Yıldırım[2]

[1]*Enerjisa Enerji*
YDA Center, Kızılırmak, Dumlupınar Blv. A-5 Blok No:24, 06530 Çankaya/Ankara, Turkey
[2]*Middle East Technical University*
Üniversiteler, METU Campus, 06800 Çankaya/Ankara, Turkey

ABSTRACT

Many organizations manage their business processes through ERP systems. Manual processes have been reduced to nearly zero, and ERP systems, as central platforms, have become increasingly prominent. SAP, the most widely used ERP system in the world, is the software most frequently preferred by companies due to the comprehensive digital solutions it offers across different sectors. Studies on the acceptance and adoption processes of this technology show that simply installing an ERP/SAP system does not guarantee positive outcomes for the company. Within the scope of the study, 23 articles were analyzed through a systematic literature review, and a technology acceptance model was proposed based on a professional experience with SAP systems at Enerjisa Enerji, a major energy company in Turkey. The reviewed studies indicate that active research on this topic continues in both developing and developed countries. Another conclusion drawn from the literature is that the external factors have mostly focused on technical infrastructure and training. However, factors related to the psychological and emotional characteristics of individuals in the acceptance process appear to be largely overlooked. In this context, the study integrated a total of 15 external factors under three categories—Emotional/Psychological Characteristics, Continuous Learning and Support-Based Characteristics, and Technical and Business Compatibility Characteristics — within the framework of the Technology Acceptance Model (TAM).

KEYWORDS

ERP; SAP, Technology Acceptance, Adaptation, User Adoption, User Acceptance

1. INTRODUCTION

In today's world, technology offers a solution at every point that makes our lives easier. With these solutions, technology provides comfort in personal life and also makes business processes more efficient in professional life. It is crucial for companies to follow and integrate these technological developments in order to improve their operational processes and reduce their costs. Today, ERP (Enterprise Resource Planning) systems, which are essential technologies that enable business processes to be more efficient by being managed from a single center, are widely used in many companies. SAP, the most common software of ERP, is also an enterprise resource planning software preferred by many corporate companies (Al Jafari & Nair, 2018). According to Albarghouthi, Qi, Wang, and Abbad (2020), business processes carried out with SAP can respond more quickly to potential changes by being managed from a single center. This situation closely affects the company's decision-making mechanism and ensures that decision-making processes are better managed. SAP offers different solutions for each sector. For example, the modules offered by SAP in the IS-U (Industry Solution for Utilities) system offered to the energy, gas, and water sectors are sector-based point-to-point modules such as Billing, CRM (Customer Relationship Management), and FICA (Financial Contract Accounting) for the main processes carried out in this sector, while this situation differs as SAP IS-H for the health sector and SAP IS-Media for the media sector (Al-Jabri & Roztocki, 2015). Since ERP/SAP systems are processes that digitalize business processes in an organization due to their structures, the currently carried out manual processes are minimized at this stage. The perspectives and perceptions of employees and managers in the organization towards this technology during this process shape the adoption and acceptance of the technology.

This study aims to categorize external factors in the model based on the Technology Acceptance Model (TAM) by combining the studies in the existing literature in this field with professional experience and by performing factor analysis in the acceptance of ERP/SAP systems. Figure 1 shows the frequency of models used over the years.

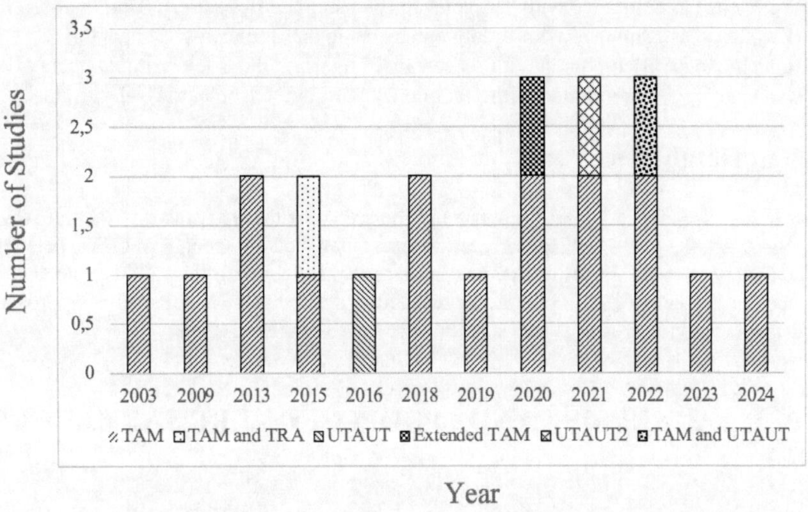

Figure 1. Year/number of studies and types of acceptance models distribution

The widespread use of TAM can be attributed to the complex structure of SAP/ERP systems and the fact that it simplifies users' perception. TAM makes the acceptance process more understandable with two fundamental determinants: perceived usefulness and perceived ease of use (Bueno & Salmeron, 2008). These determinants are especially crucial for user groups who are encountering SAP ERP for the first time or are relatively new to it. Furthermore, TAM is a comprehensive and easily adaptable model that has been applied across various sectors (Billyan & Irawan, 2021). Its extended versions, TAM2 and TAM3, offer more detailed analytical capabilities. This versatility has contributed to its widespread adoption and the confidence it inspires among researchers and practitioners. In light of these findings, the main contribution of this study lies in the development of a new model within the TAM framework. This model will incorporate external factors that have been largely overlooked—specifically those related to emotional characteristics, continuous learning, and technical compatibility. These factors will be explicitly categorized, addressing gaps in previous studies where such factors were either ignored or grouped under more general and abstract headings in the literature.

2. SEARCH METHODOLOGY

This study systematically examined the literature on SAP/ERP adoption and used the review procedure steps while conducting a comprehensive literature review to fill the gaps in the literature. Within the scope of the steps in this procedure, results are obtained by examining and analyzing the databases.

2.1 Determining the Search Criteria

Before conducting research in the relevant databases, it is necessary to conduct research with the right keywords to find the right studies. The limitations determined within the scope of this study are as follows:

- Search using specified keywords
- Time limit: review of studies between 2003 and 2024
- Including conferences, journals, and published master's theses

For this purpose, before conducting database research within the scope of this study, the keywords "SAP," "ERP systems," "acceptance," "adoption," and "ERP technology" are determined (Calisir, Gumussoy, & Bayram, 2009). When the keywords are combined, a total of 6 combinations are obtained as follows;

- "SAP" is combined with "acceptance" by using the Boolean AND operator.
- "SAP" is combined with "adoption" by using the Boolean AND operator.
- "ERP systems" is combined with "acceptance" by using the Boolean AND operator.
- "ERP systems" is combined with "adoption" by using the Boolean AND operator.
- "ERP technology" is combined with "acceptance" by using the Boolean AND operator.
- "ERP technology" is combined with "adoption" by using the Boolean AND operator.

2.2 Search in Databases

Studies are searched in Science Direct, Scopus, and journal website databases that include a wide range of study types. Since studies on SAP/ERP topics are also published in special websites belonging to some international information technology management conferences and journals, journal website databases are also preferred. Since the content of the studies to be selected is desired to have scientifically strong and reliable content, database selection is crucial at this stage.

3. FACTOR ANALYSIS AND PROPOSED ERP/SAP ACCEPTANCE MODEL

When the study examined technology acceptance studies conducted specifically for SAP/ERP systems, the most frequently used factors are perceived usefulness and perceived ease of use, subjective norm, consultant support (Lee, Lee, Olson, & Chung, 2010), top management support, computer self-efficacy (Shih & Huang, 2009), compatibility (Lee et al., 2010), ERP system functionality (Daneshgadeh, 2013), organizational culture (Lee et al., 2010), business process fit (Shih & Huang, 2009), ERP support, and ERP training. Most of the researches aim to expand theories around the determinants of perceived usefulness and perceived ease of use by taking them as references. Examining the determinants of perceived usefulness and perceived ease of use, which Davis (1989) mentioned within the scope of TAM, from a more multifaceted perspective will provide a reference for the user acceptance process and the integration of technological developments into organizations and future model designs. Although the TAM is a model that is a reference for many studies with its main determinants, it has become essential to include additional factors that affect the main determinants in the model and user usage intention in order to evaluate the models from a more comprehensive perspective. Adding a new perspective to these additional factors, Venkatesh et al. (2000) grouped additional factors that will affect perceived usefulness (PU) and perceived ease of use (PEOU) under four determinants. These are individual differences, system characteristics, social influence, and facilitating conditions. The effect of external factors on user acceptance is categorized under the headings of organizational-process characteristics, system and technological characteristics, personal characteristics, and information literacy by expanding the TAM model. Calisir et al. (2009) analyzed that personal characteristics and information literacy have a strong and positive effect on perceived ease of use, considering that each title contains different character factors. It was emphasized that the selection of factors affecting user acceptance has a great effect in reaching accurate and reliable results in studies. Mitra (2022), used factor grouping to integrate external factors into the TAM model used in the acceptance of ERP systems under three headings. These are perceived compatibility with information literacy (PCIL), organizational-process characteristics (OPC), and system and technological characteristics (STC). As a result, it was concluded that the three factor headings defined have a strong effect on usage intention. It was predicted that the external factors under the headings in the study would provide a strategy in shaping ERP usage intention, and as a result, it was emphasized that the perceived ease of use and job compatibility of the factors have a strong effect on usage intention. The reason for grouping external factors in the study is to evaluate the factors that arise from more than one different reason, which will be effective in the process of users adopting a new technology as a whole. Grouping external factors within themselves provides a multi-faceted perspective and allows for accurate analyses to be made regarding the technology acceptance process. The factors affecting users' technology adoption may be related to different factors such as organizational culture, psychology, or education/support. In this context, it is essential to group the factors in order to obtain a clearer picture while integrating multiple factors that will be categorized under this umbrella as user usage intention, perceived ease of use, and perceived usefulness of the model. When the models in the literature are examined, it is observed that most of the models established based on TAM focus on cognitive factors such as perceived ease of use and usefulness. Although the emotional and psychological characteristics of users play a significant role in the acceptance of SAP/ERP technologies, it has been observed that these factors are often overlooked or grouped under abstract and general categories rather than clearly defined conceptual headings. These factors include fear of technology, fear of losing a job, computer anxiety (Shih & Huang, 2009), trust, computer self-efficacy (Shih & Huang, 2009), subjective norm (Chauhan & Jaiswal, 2016), and organizational culture (Albarghouthi, Qi, Wang, & Abbad, 2020), which significantly affect the acceptance and adoption process of the user. These factors will be included in the model, taking into consideration the necessity of this study. In addition to psychological factors, another important factor affecting the user adoption process is continuous learning and support based characteristics. Factors related to this topic are often neglected and not prioritized. Since SAP/ERP systems are complex in nature, they require the necessary support, training, and knowledge sharing. These factors positively affect the user's learning and adoption process. For this reason, this study will include the factors consultant support/mentorship (Lee, Lee, Olson, & Chung, 2010), top management support (Calisir, Gumussoy, & Bayram, 2009), continuous training availability, and user support system. Thus, users will be made compatible with the system integration and will be able to learn the technology more effectively. Technical and business compatibility characteristics mention the relevance of the technical infrastructure and business process compliance of SAP/ERP technology mentioned in this study with the user acceptance process. In this study, the factors related to this title are determined as interoperability with business processes and external systems, system performance (Raval & Modi, 2021), customization, and ease of use design (Amoako-Gyampah & Salam, 2003).

Emotional/Psychological Characteristics include factors that indicate the effects of users' psychological reflections or behaviors on their usage intentions when using ERP/SAP systems:

- **Fear of technology:** Fear of technology encompasses anxiety and discomfort caused by uncertainties about the functionality and complexity of unknown technologies. Along with the innovations that technology brings, factors such as privacy concerns that affect decision-making mechanisms also contribute to this factor.
- **Fear of losing the job:** Fear of losing one's job is a significant barrier to technology acceptance. The possibility that technology may automate current jobs and replace people brings about concerns about this fear.
- **Computer anxiety:** Computer anxiety is the feeling of stress and discomfort that people who are not familiar with digital tools or technologies experience when they encounter a new technological development (Shih & Huang, 2009), This situation prevents interaction between the new technology and the user, making the acceptance process difficult for users.
- **Trust:** Trust is a critical factor in the process of users adopting a new technology. Having transparent policies regarding the privacy of personal information and data belonging to the new technology, in other words, presenting the reliability of that technology to the person, plays a significant role in the process of adopting a technology.
- **Computer self-efficacy:** Computer self-efficacy indicates the intrinsic competence of individuals with relevant technology (Zabukovsek & Bobek, 2013). Individuals with higher competence will accelerate the learning and adoption process by triggering the user's curiosity about technology, which serves as a motivating factor in the acceptance of a new technology.
- **Subjective norm:** Subjective norm is the effect of social pressure on a person's decision to adopt technology. This effect can create different emotional states, such as adapting to the technology to be adopted, rejecting it, or being in a dilemma during the decision-making process of the person. In short, it is a factor that has a strong effect on the adopter's behavior (Shih & Huang, 2009).
- **Organizational culture:** Corporate culture, together with the vision or perspective that it already has for its employees, is effective in the process of an individual adopting a technology. For example, if an organization carries out its values in terms of being innovation-focused or open to change and innovation, and shapes the employee's mindset in this direction, this situation will be a factor that accelerates the process of employees adopting technology. In addition, by integrating this factor into

the model, a mindset focused on collaborative teamwork will be presented, which will enable the individual to feel more comfortable in the process of adopting technology (Albarghouthi, Qi, Wang, & Abbad, 2020).

Continuous Learning and Support Based Characteristics include the training and mentoring that will be given to the user during the acceptance process, which will affect the motivation of the users towards continuous learning and future adoption:

- **Consultant Support/Mentorship:** Consultant support/mentorship, together with the support from consultants or mentors who have expert knowledge in the field, creates continuous learning opportunities and ensures that users feel supported in the technology adoption process, thus enabling them to experience a faster adoption process (Lee, Lee, Olson, & Chung, 2010). In addition, this process will also be effective in the process of learning new technologies with the mentorships that individuals will receive, contributing to the development of necessary skills.
- **Top Management Support:** The support provided by top management plays a crucial role in the technology acceptance process of users. When evaluated from a financial perspective, the support provided to users—such as time, budget, and training—will pave the way for a faster and more sustained learning process. On the other hand, moral support and encouragement can motivate employees and positively influences their attitudes and confidence toward new technology (Calisir, Gumussoy, & Bayram, 2009).
- **Continuous Training Availability:** The user acceptance process of technology requires providing regular learning opportunities to help users in order to manage ongoing updates and newly introduced know-how more efficiently. Continuous training availability enhances the effectiveness of the acceptance process by promoting long term engagement.
- **User Support System:** Facilitating the acceptance process of users and having a user support system that is accessible in the easiest and most practical way for their own learning processes positively affects the acceptance process. Solutions such as user manuals, FAQs, and help desks prepared from the beginning to the end of the process, to be included in this system, will allow users to receive real-time help and encourage them to use technology in an accelerated way.

Technical and Business Compatibility Characteristics are factors that include the effects of the technical performance of the system on user acceptance and usage intention:

- **Interoperability with Business Processes and External Systems:** When new technology is integrated with existing business processes and external platforms within the company, operational efficiency increases, and users will be more motivated and willing to adopt it.
- **System performance:** System performance has an important place in terms of reliability and efficiency in technology acceptance within the scope of technical and business compliance-based features. A system that provides data and flows consistently, with interruptions at a minimum, will exhibit high performance by increasing reliability. In a world where business processes do not interrupt, efficiency and productivity increase, and this situation becomes a reason for user acceptance.
- **Customization:** Technology can affect the technology acceptance process with its own standard structures and business processes with their own unique structures (Davis, 1989). At this stage, customization is a factor that comes into play when the unique business processes mentioned can be integrated into the new technology, that is, adapted. Where there is customization, there is flexibility; where there is flexibility, there is the ability to adapt existing business processes and changing business needs. Being part of systems, that users can personalize positively affects acceptance processes by increasing feelings of comfort and enthusiasm.
- **Ease of Use Design:** ERP/SAP systems have a very large structure with multiple modules and features. Although this situation seems beneficial in general, as it can be tailored according to the needs of companies and offers various business solutions, if the required solutions are not provided, it will cause unwanted confusion for the user. A structure aligned with the business needs, combined with an interface and ease of use designs do not create confusion for the user. It also reduces user resistance to the acceptance process and allows them to interact, which is reflected positively in the adoption processes (Damar, 2018).

This study expands the model by including multi-faceted external factor groups, divided into specific groups within the TAM model, for the initial adoption and acceptance process of ERP/SAP usage, which is still needed in the real world. This model is developed in line with the literature review and factor analysis conducted in the study. The area in the framed section indicates the original model of TAM. The three groups included from outside also cover the factors suggested in this study. Since the study focuses on the first use, the model also includes behavioral intention and actual usage determinants. In this context, the original TAM model's factors and hypotheses incorporated into the proposed model are illustrated in Figure 2.

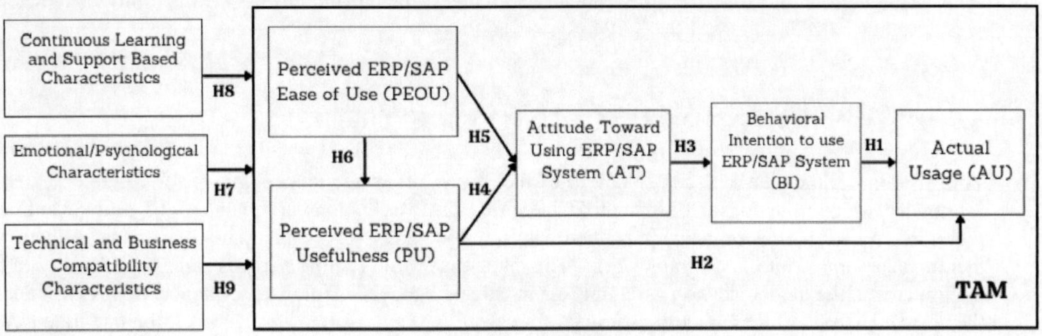

Figure 2. The proposed model

Actual Usage (AU): It represents the actual usage behavior of a user using the ERP/SAP system, at the end of the model, with the effect of the Behavioral Intention to use the ERP/SAP System (BI) and the Attitude Towards Using the ERP/SAP System (AT) factors (Martínez, 2023).

Behavioral Intention to Use ERP/SAP System (BI): Behavioral Intention to Use ERP/SAP System (BI) indicates the user's closeness to a decision to use a technology as the adoption process approaches, their intention to use the system (Chauhan & Jaiswal, 2016).

- **H1:** Behavioral intention to use ERP/SAP System has a direct positive impact on Actual Usage.

Attitude Towards Using ERP/SAP System (AT): This determinant represents the psychological attitude of the user towards the new technology. It is affected by PEOU and PU in the model.

- **H3:** Attitude Toward Using ERP/SAP System (AT) has a direct positive impact on Behavioral Intention to use ERP/SAP System (BI).

Perceived ERP/SAP Usefulness (PU): Davis (1989) defined this determinant as the degree to which an individual believes that using a particular system will improve job performance. In the TAM model, these determinant influences both Perceived Usefulness, Actual Usage, and Behavioral Intention in the acceptance process of SAP/ERP systems.

- **H2:** Perceived ERP/SAP Usefulness (PU) has a direct positive impact on Actual Usage.

- **H4:** Perceived ERP/SAP Usefulness (PU) has a direct positive impact on Attitude Towards Using ERP/SAP System (AT).

Perceived ERP/SAP Ease of Use (PEOU): PEOU refers to the ease with which a user adopts new technology when using the system (Calisir, Gumussoy, & Bayram, 2009). A high level of this determinant positively influences the level of acceptance.

- **H5:** Perceived ERP/SAP Ease of Use (PEOU) has a direct positive impact on Perceived ERP/SAP Usefulness (PU).

- **H6:** Perceived ERP/SAP Ease of Use (PEOU) has a direct positive impact on Attitude Towards Using ERP/SAP System (AT).

Additional Hypotheses:

- **H7:** A group of external factors categorized under emotional/psychological characteristics significantly influences ERP/SAP system usage.

- **H8:** A group of external factors categorized under continuous learning and support based characteristics significantly influences ERP/SAP system usage.

- **H9:** A group of external factors categorized under technical and business compatibility characteristics significantly influences ERP/SAP system usage.

4. DISCUSSION AND CONCLUSION

This section outlines the key contributions of the study, offers recommendations for future research, and acknowledges its limitations within the domain of ERP/SAP technology acceptance. The study examined the literature on ERP/SAP acceptance published between 2003 and 2024, with a particular focus on the external factors incorporated into TAM frameworks. The main motivation for this analysis is the belief that each factor integrated into the model plays an essential role in enhancing the technology acceptance processes. Therefore, the correct analysis of these factors is crucial for selecting the most relevant factors to be integrated into the new model proposed in this study. Upon review, it was found that factors related to psychological/emotional and continuous learning characteristics remain underexplored. To bridge this gap, new external factors such as fear of technology, computer anxiety, computer self-efficacy, user support system, consultant support/mentorship, and continuous training availability are proposed to guide future research. While incorporating these factors, the factors related to technical and business compatibility characteristics are also considered and not neglected. Future studies should examine ERP/SAP systems in real-world scenarios either during initial adoption or at the maturity stage using methodologies that reflect their actual usage in operational processes will yield more realistic results. Thus, external factors to be integrated into the models can be selected in a more precise way. Moreover, the external factors proposed in this study may be further developed or extended in subsequent studies. Finally, their impact on key acceptance determinants such as actual usage and usage intention can be analyzed with various analytical models and statistical methods.

ACKNOWLEDGEMENT

I would like to take this opportunity to express my sincere gratitude to my tutor and supervisor Prof. Dr. Sevgi Özkan Yıldırım, for her continuous support, guidance, encouragement and enthusiasm throughout all stages of this project. It has been both an honor and a pleasure to work with her.
I would also like to extend my heartfelt thanks to my family and friends for their unwavering support.
2025, 19 May, Işınsu Yildiz

REFERENCES

Al Jafari, A. A., & Nair, S. S. K. (2018, August). ERP implementation in the oil and gas sector: A case study in Sultanate of Oman. In Proceedings of the 7th International Conference on Reliability, Infocom Technologies and Optimization (pp. 848–854). IEEE.

Al-Jabri, I., & Roztocki, N. (2015). Adoption of ERP systems: Does information transparency matter? *Telematics and Informatics, 32,* 300–310.

Albarghouthi, M., Qi, B., Wang, T. C., & Abbad, M. (2020). ERP adoption and acceptance in Saudi Arabia higher education: A conceptual model development. *International Journal of Emerging Technologies in Learning, 15(15),* 110–120.

Amoako-Gyampah, K., & Salam, A. F. (2004). An extension of the technology acceptance model in an ERP implementation environment., *Information & Management, 41(6),* 731–745.

Billyan, B. F., & Irawan, M. I. (2021). Analysis of technology acceptance of enterprise resource planning (ERP) system in the regional office of PT. XYZ throughout Indonesia. Journal of Physics: Conference Series, 1844(1), Article 012008

Bueno, S., & Salmeron, J. (2008). TAM-based success modeling in ERP. *Interacting with Computers*, *20(6),* 515–523.

Calisir, F., Gumussoy, C. A., & Bayram, A. (2009). Predicting the behavioural intention to use enterprise resource planning systems—An exploratory extension of the technology acceptance model. *Management Research News, 32(7),* 597–613.

Chauhan, S., & Jaiswal, M. (2016). Determinants of acceptance of ERP software training in business schools: Empirical investigation using UTAUT model. *The International Journal of Management Education, 14*, 248–262.

Damar, S. (2018). "An empirical evaluation of a modified technology acceptance model for SAP ERP systems", *Engineering Management Journal, 34(2), 201–216.*

Daneshgadeh, S. (2013). Proposing a research model for internet banking usage based on a literature review. *In Proceedings of the 8th Iberian Conference on Information Systems and Technologies (CISTI).*

Davis, F. D. (1989). Perceived usefulness, perceived ease of use, and user acceptance of information technology. *MIS Quarterly, 13(3),* 319–340.

Lee, D. H., Lee, S. M., Olson, D. L., & Chung, S. H. (2010). The effect of organizational support on ERP implementation. *Industrial Management & Data Systems, 110(1-2),* 269–283.

Martínez, E. C., Astudillo-Rodríguez, C., Chica-Contreras, G., & Vásquez-Aguilera, A. (2023). Technology acceptance model of ERP software in small business: A systematic literature review. Enfoque UTE, 14(1), 46–61.

Raval, H., & Modi, N. (2021). Modeling a framework for improving a performance on an SAP-enterprise ERP. *International Journal of Computer Engineering and Technology (IJCET), 12(3),* 84–94.

Shih, Y. Y., & Huang, S. S. (2009). The actual usage of ERP systems: An extended technology acceptance perspective. Journal of Research and Practice in Information Technology, 41(3), 263–276.

Zabukovsek, S. S., & Bobek, S. (2013). TAM-based external factors related to ERP solutions acceptance in organizations. *International Journal of Information Systems and Project Management, 1(4),* 25–38.

PROTECTION MOTIVATION THEORY (PMT) AS A DRIVING FORCE FOR CYBERSECURITY AWARENESS

Namosha Veerasamy and Thulani Mashiane
Council for Scientific and Industrial Research (CSIR), South Africa

ABSTRACT

Despite the use of various technical controls and technologies, a pivotal weakness in Information Communication Technology (ICT) security remains the human element. Cybersecurity awareness training can be used to influence and change behaviour towards the adoption of secure cyber practices. It is imperative to reduce cybersecurity risks through awareness and cybersecurity training to influence safer behaviour. Various behaviour and motivation theories exist, which attempt to explain how behaviour can be influenced. This paper focuses on the benefits of Protection Motivation Theory in the delivery of security awareness topics.

Examples of stakeholders that can be involved in cyber security awareness training are mapped onto the protection motivation theory. This helps to show how PMT can be used in different user environments to effectively communicate cybersecurity awareness at the correct level. This paper proposes the usefulness of applying PMT to the cyber security awareness domain to create a culture of cybersecurity awareness and promote cybersecurity education and awareness.

KEYWORDS

Information Communication Technology (ICT), Cybersecurity Awareness, Psychological Behaviour Theory, Protection Motivation Theory (PMT)

1. INTRODUCTION

Psychology behavioural theories are a collection of theories that were developed to understand how people make decisions in performing a certain behaviour (Zachrisson & Boks, 2012). The origin of this domain is credited to B.F. Skinner (1961), a behaviourist Psychologist (Holland & Skinner, 1961). One of Skinner's contributions to the field is Operant Conditioning. Operant conditioning occurs when a reward or punishment is associated with a behaviour (Holland & Skinner, 1961). In cybersecurity, rewarding or punishing a user can be seen as applying operant conditioning. Through the progression of research, more theories of behaviour were developed under the domain of behaviourism. Other theories that have emerged are the Theory of Planned Behaviour, Social Cognitive Theory, and Protection Motivation Theory. '

The Theory of Planned Behaviour evaluates the influence of an individual's attitude, social norms, and perceived behavioural control on their intention to perform a behaviour (Ajzen, 2011). Social Cognitive Theory (SCT) considers learning as an internal cognitive process that may or may not be shown in immediate behavioral change (Bandura, 2001). Bandura (1986) conceptualised that human behaviour is a constant interaction between environmental determinates, personal determinates, and behavioural determinants (Bandura, 2001).

Another class of psychology theories that focus on an individual's behavior are motivation theories. Motivation is the inner or exterior push that drives goal-orientated behavior (Reeve, 2013). The inner push is formally referred to as intrinsic motivation, and the exterior motivation is referred to as external motivation. Internal motivations are the inner reasons for performing behaviour. These can include curiosity, morals, values, and ideas. External motivations are the external reasons for behaviour. These can include money, promotion, and social pressure (Reeve, 2013).

Motivation theories differ from behavioural theories in that behaviour theories focus on variables that influence an individual's behaviour whereas motivation theories focus on the variables that regulate the intensity of which the behaviour is carried out.

The Protection Motivation Theory (PMT) is a theory stemming from the health domain. The Health Belief Model suggests that health behaviour is influenced by four types of cognition: perceived susceptibility (perception the risk of health threat), perceived severity (the strength of the threat), the perceived benefits, and barriers (negative consequences) of the protective/recommended behaviour (Prentice-Dunn & Rogers, 1986; Rosenstock, 1974).). PMT generally describes a strategy to motivate people to take a particular action, endorse a particular policy, or buy a particular product by arousing fear. (Rogers & Mewborn, 1976). PMT explains why people engage in unhealthy practices and offers suggestions for changing these behaviors. The PMT suggests that individuals protect themselves based on considering these factors; perceived severity of the situation, perceived probability of the situation occurring, the confidence in the preventative behaviour, and the perceived self-efficacy level to administer the preventative behaviour (Boer & Seydel, 1996). Computer-mediated communication will lead us toward a new community: global, local, and everything in between (Jones, 1995). When applied to the cybersecurity space, PMT can be used a vital mechanism in order to develop preventative behaviour and also reinforce confidence in positive conduct. This paper looks the underlying theory and also provides examples on the effect and use of PMT in the cybersecurity domain.

The structure of the paper is as follows: Section 2 provides an overview of the main concepts of PMT. Section 2 covers PMT as a driving force for security awareness through a mapping of PMT onto cybersecurity awareness areas. Section 4 further unpacks the application of PMT in the cybersecurity space by covering a discussion on specific target groups with examples on effects in self-efficacy and response efficacy. The paper is concluded in Section 4.

2. INTRODUCTION TO PMT AS A DRIVING FORCE FOR SECURITY AWARENESS

Some motivation theories such as Hierarchy or Needs, Self-Determination Theory, and Equity Theory address the usefulness of intrinsic and extrinsic rewards. The focus of this paper, however, is the usefulness of Protection Motivation Theory in the promotion of cybersecurity awareness and the development of a cybersecurity culture.

Protection motivation theory (PMT) is a widely used framework to understand responses to triggers that appraise individuals of a potential threat (Shillair, 2020). These triggers include fear messages that encourage individuals to take protective measures or refrain from activities that may harm themselves or others.

To influence cyber security awareness, the development of a cyber culture would encourage stronger cybersecurity behavior. Education plays a critical role in cultivating a culture of secure behavior amongst Internet users (Kortjan & von Solms, 2014). There is an inadequate security culture in society (Kritzinger & Padayachee, 2013). Protection Motivation Theory can be used as a significant tool in the development of cybersecurity awareness programs and campaigns that can help establish a cybersecurity culture. The goal is to impact behaviour in general and not just create short-term changes (possibly resulting from a temporary reward or scare tactic).

An important aspect of information security education and training is to create awareness of the psychological, social, and ICT risks that exist in the digital domain. A fundamental challenge lies in creating awareness of these risks.

Underpinning Protection Motivation Theory is the concept of fear. Fear can also be a powerful influence strategy in cybersecurity awareness campaigns. However, fearful threats alone may not lead to good cybersecurity practices. Fear as a motivating force must be utilized with skill to influence and shape behavior.

Cybersecurity awareness can help reduce the risk profile of an organization by empowering users with the skills and knowledge to protect themselves. An effective program can be critical to modifying user behaviour. It is important to differentiate between awareness, training and education to understand how the concepts link and support each other.

Awareness is used to stimulate, motivate and remind an audience what is expected of them (Peltier, 2007). Awareness is the general reinforcement of good security practices so that individuals can identify a potential ICT security concern and react appropriately.

Training, the process teaches a skill or the use of a tool (Peltier, 2007).A good awareness foundation will help in the development of skills during training. Security basics and literacy contribute to establishing fundamentals of security awareness. Training does not necessarily result in a formal degree from a higher education institution, but it does empower users with essential knowledge about cybersecurity awareness.

Education- specialised, in-depth schooling required to support the tools or as a career development processes (Peltier, 2007). Education is more comprehensive than training and requires the integration of various skills and competencies with the goal of producing IT security specialists and professionals.

Learning is a continuous process- it begins with basic awareness, can be enhanced with training, and then moves into the domain of education.

This section covered the fundamental principles of PMT. The next section will look at PMT as a driving force for cybersecurity awareness.

3. PMT AS A DRIVING FORCE FOR SECURITY AWARENESS

The role of PMT with respect to the aspects of Training, Education and Awareness is mapped onto these three continuum aspects in Figure 1 (adapted from NIST Special Publication 800-50(Wilson & Hash, 2003)). It also indicates the role of PMT at each level.

The users of an IT system are not simply operators of the technology. They can also be managers, peers, role models, parents, and teachers. An overall awareness of the basics of security can help promote a security culture. Weaknesses or failure to comply with policies and good practices can result in system compromise, data theft, information loss, application failure and various other negative consequences. Not being aware of emerging cyber threats, such as cyber bullying, social engineering, phishing, and other exploits, can affect personal and business activities. Information security awareness spans our entire lives, both private and business, and thus it is imperative to provide training that focusses on critical topics of interest.

The basics of security can help IT users understand the basics of secure utilization of systems. Users must be aware of the impact of spreading malware (even unintentionally), the effect of clicking on phishing scams, and the overall impact of not complying with policies and standards in the business environment.

At higher levels of responsibility, come ICT users with functional roles. Among their responsibilities is the secure management of systems and networks. Being directly responsible for the prevention, detection and reaction to cyber threats, these ICT users need to be trained with the fundamental concepts of system protection and safety. Failure to secure systems and networks can result in direct breaches of security which can affect the organisation.

Overall, governance, compliance and risk management sit at higher levels of management. Failure to address these aspects in a company's cybersecurity strategy will result in unregulated systems and networks.

At each level, the instrumental role of PMT changes slightly depending on the overall goal. PMT serves as a driving force for security awareness because it drives the need for good practices (at each level of responsibility and influence). At higher managerial levels, PMT is important to ensure good governance, compliance, and risk management. At the functional level, PMT drives security awareness to ensure that systems and networks can be managed and overall to provide for the protection, detection and reaction to threats. PMT is applicable to all users of ICT to ensure proper use of systems and applications. All users should be concerned about spreading malware, falling for scams, violating policies and standards, and the consequences of following poor security practices.

A critical part of security awareness training is the selection of topics. Based on the different target audiences, material can be designed to link to the appropriate application PMT. Messages tend to be more persuasive when there is a match between the cognitive, affective, or motivational characteristics of the recipient and the content of the message formulation (Bada & Sasse 2019). The authors are involved in several cybersecurity awareness training campaigns. Based on current experience and interactions with trainees, positive responses were received when the trainers' provided examples of various scams, exploits and threats. The centre of this approach is the use of Protection Motivation Theory and the appropriate use of fear. Case usage that conveys the implications of falling victims to attacks can aptly communicate the themes of cybersecurity awareness without causing excessive fear that paralyses behaviour. Trainees are able to personally identify with the provided examples and thus are able to apply the knowledge of the example in their own situation without feeling too scared to act or engage. During training sessions, trainees often participate with responses from their own situations. Trainers do not engage in simple prescriptive behaviour by describing rules and policies of an organisation. Instead, a more applied approach is taken in which the theory of good cyber behaviour is merged with various real-life examples. Bulgurcu et al. (2010) suggested that security professionals design their information security awareness programmes to reinforce beliefs about safety and vulnerability.

The PMT suggests that individuals protect themselves based on considering these factors; perceived severity of the situation, perceived probability of the situation occurring, the confidence in the preventative behaviour, and the perceived self-efficacy level to administer the preventative behaviour (Bulgurcu et al., 2010) (Elaborated on in Figure **1**).

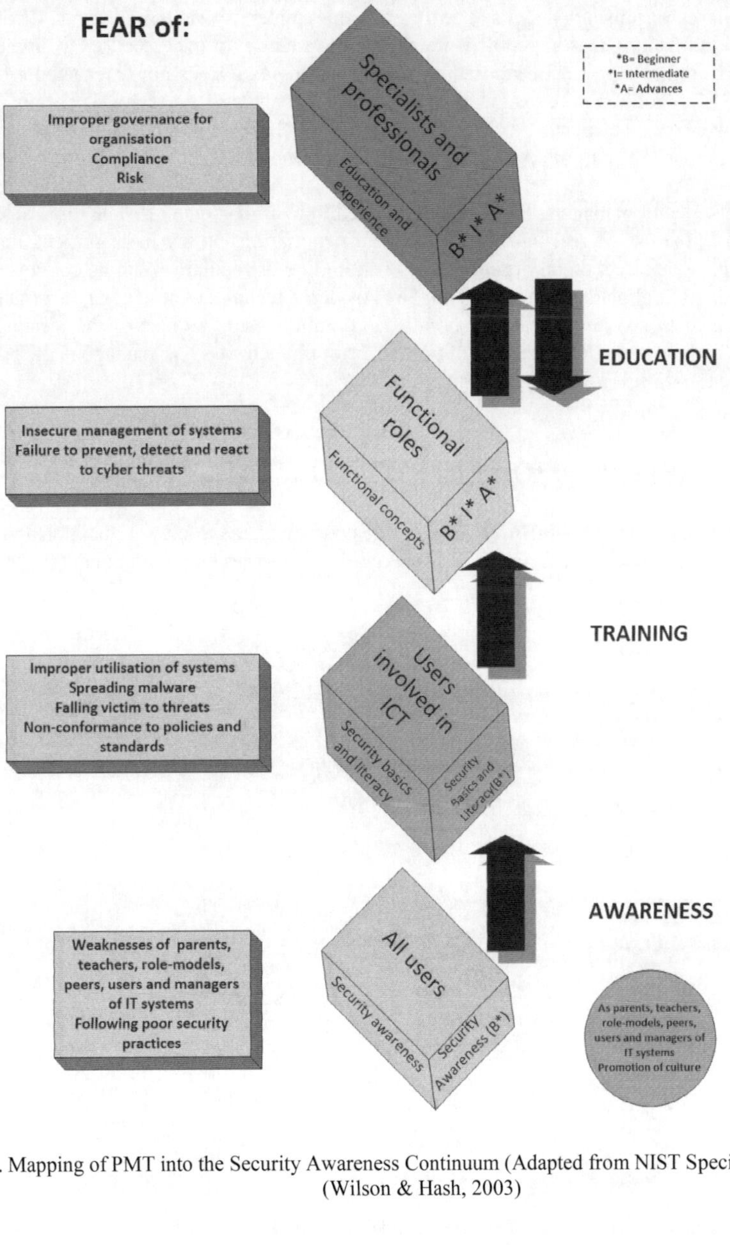

Figure 1. Mapping of PMT into the Security Awareness Continuum (Adapted from NIST Special Publication 800-50 (Wilson & Hash, 2003)

PMT went beyond stating that the perceptions of threat severity, vulnerability, response cost, response efficacy, and self-efficacy drive behaviour change, but it captured the complexity of motivation by explaining the effects of two cognitive appraisal processes (coping appraisals and threat appraisals) (Floyd, Prentice-Dunn & Rogers, 2000).).

With regard to cybersecurity awareness, the techniques that are used to apply this model can be as follows: Provide statistics about the number of people falling victim to phishing scams, explain the consequences of clicking on phishing emails, describe the various indicative signs which can be checked, and advise to ignore such emails if they do not seem legitimate. Describing the practical application of cyber vulnerabilities and threats fits into PMT, as it demonstrates the likelihood of the threat occurring, the effect of the threat manifesting, and empowers trainees with the knowledge and skills to prevent the threat, demonstrating to users that it is possible to prevent phishing attacks once they are able to identify the telltale signs. Chang and Coppel highlight the idea that invoking fear in people is not an effective tactic for cybersecurity awareness campaigns (2020). Fear can be used as a powerful motivating factor, as long as it does not deter people from using the technology itself. Risks should not be exaggerated but rather conveyed in everyday scenarios. This promotes self-efficacy of preventive mechanisms, as concepts become much easier to understand and apply. Relatable material should be prepared as part of security awareness programmes and not just a list of company rules and regulations.

For functional users and managers, PMT can be applied in a similar manner. The topic selection may be slightly different, but the use of real instances of system penetration, policy infringement, and governance failure can be related. The effect on an organisation's bottom line or reputation can be conveyed to executive level trainees. If higher-level management does not have in-depth technical knowledge, information regarding the frequency and effect of system breaches should be communicated. As part of the training programme, discussions should be held about the necessity of policies, compliance, and risk management. This will help to build a strategy to defend itself against cyber threats.

4. FURTHER APPLICATION OF PMT TO CYBERSECURITY

The previous section covered a mapping of PMT onto the constructs of Training, Education and Awareness.

In general, a summary of how PMT can increase overall cyber awareness among users is shown in Figure **2**.

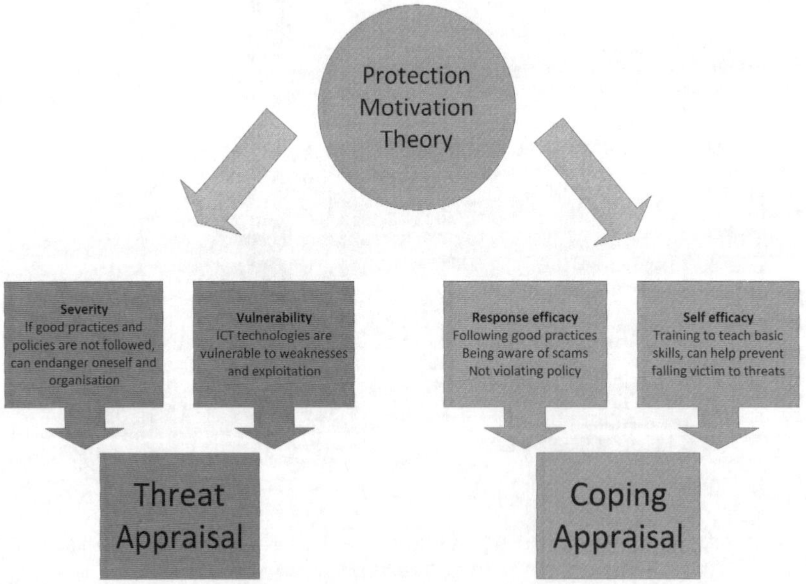

Figure 2. Summary of protection motivation theory and how it can drive cyber awareness (Own compilation)

To elaborate on Figure **2**, Table 1 shows a few more examples of how PMT is applicable to security awareness. However, the key is not just to communicate the severity and vulnerability, but to show the practicality of the response efficacy and how users can develop a high level of self- efficacy to react and respond to cyber threats. An ideal way to convey this information is through the use of practical examples that show the consequences of the threat. This can have a greater impact on users as it shows the real effects and methodologies used by attackers rather than simply lecturing about the 'dos and donts' in an organisation. Examples and statistics help illustrate severity, vulnerability, and response efficacies. This may also allow users to develop their own self-efficacy. Empowering users with practical tips does not have to be tedious. Instead, innovative use of technologies can be quite beneficial. Games, videos, quizzes, and learning factories can also be used to reinforce good cyber behaviour. Serious games provide a fun, enjoyable educational environment where the participants learn theory and concepts in cybersecurity and put them into practice through the game (Hart, Margheri, Paci & Sassone, 2020). Learning factories facilitate action- and practice-based training and learning by compelling the learners to think and apply themselves rather than doing or acting only (Veerasamy, Mkhwanazi & Dawood. 2023).

Table 1. Target and how elements of PMT can drive security awareness (Own compilation)

Topic	**Target**	**Severity**	**Vulnerability**	**Response Efficacy**	**Self-Efficacy**	**Example**
Governance	Specialists and professionals	Organisation cannot afford no to have a proper governance framework as it will open itself u to a host of threats.	Humans can make critical mistakes when operating ICTs. Technology is vulnerable to many threats and risks.	Cybersecurity Policies Security awareness programme Risk strategies Technical Controls	Ability to develop the leadership of the organisation. Actively involved in the cybersecurity strategy Creation of a security awarenes programme	Statistics of loss of revenue from cybercrime Downtime data Loss of availability of services
Compliance	Specialists and professionals	Non-compliant organisations can face prosecution for failure to address laws. Appropriate policies and standards should be followed.	The absence of policies puts an organisation at risk Failure to follow laws can compromise data and systems.	Development of controls and policies to ensure compliance Ensure compliance with necessary laws and regulations.	Implement the necessary policie and technical controls.	Legal consequences o failure to meet legislative requirements
Threat prevention	Functional role	Without protection, systems can be compromised.	Unpatched systems can be hacked and open up for exploitation.	Regular updates and patches should be performed.	System administration to activate updates and patching.	Statistics on the number of intrusions and data breaches & Ransomware
Phishing	All users	Users may click on phishing emails and disclose information.	Phishing emails are sent to users in an effort to trick them into clicking on malicious links.	How to spot a phishing email (looking at heade information, hovering over links, strange requests, urgency etc.).	Ability to inspect emails before making the decision to click on links and requests.	Show actual phishing email examples.
Internet Banking	All users	Users may click on a fake bankin web site or app and disclose thei bank login credentials.	If credentials are disclosed, it cou lead to a loss of money.	Navigate to URL directly instead o links Ensure that you are on the correc site before	Once trained, know how to go the legitimate bank website and app	Show fake website exampl

Topic	Target	Severity	Vulnerability	Response Efficacy	Self-Efficacy	Example
				entering credentials. Safety of App Installation		
Cyber-bullying	All users	People are cyber bullied as a result of insults, harassment, and negative comments. Strong impact or children	Social media provides the ability to harass, embarrass, and stalk a person digitally.	Not accepting friend requests from unknown contacts. Avoid online flaming wars Refrain from posting too much personal information. Be careful of wh you engage with digitally.	Every user has the ability to limi the amount of content they post and with whom they engage to prevent being cyber-bullied.	Show examples of the impact of cyber bullying.

5. CONCLUSION

This paper looks at Protection Motivation Theory as a driving force for cybersecurity awareness training. The generation of fear can be carried out in a strategic manner so as not to cause panic or a paralysed response. Cautionary messages, indications of implications, advice on how to identify signs of potential exploits, and warnings can help cyber users better protect themselves and adjust their behavior to ensure compliance. The use of effective examples can have a longer lasting impression on users than just the instructions to impose practices. Awareness of basic security threats like cyberbullying, malware, social networking dangers, phishing, credit card theft, and various other scams will not only be of assistance in the workplace but also in their interaction with family, friends, and technology at home. Through a directed and example-based approach to security awareness training, participants can be taught to assess threats and develop effective coping strategies to empower them and prevent falling victim to cyber threats.

REFERENCES

Ajzen, I., (2011). *The theory of planned behaviour: Reactions and reflections*. Psychology & health, 26(9), pp.1113-1127.

Bada, M. & Sasse, A., Nurse J., July (2019). Cyber Security Awareness Campaigns Why do they fail to change behaviour?, s.l.: Global Cyber Security Capacity Centre, https://doi.org/10.48550/arXiv.1901.02672.

Bandura, Albert. (2001). Social cognitive theory of mass communication. *Media psychology*, 3(3), pp. 265-299.

Boer, H. and Seydel, E.R., (1996). *Protection motivation theory. In Predicting health behaviour: Research and practice with social cognition models. eds. Mark Conner and Paul Norman (pp. 95-120).* Open University Press.

Bulgurcu, B., Cavusoglu, H. & Benbasat, I., (2010). Compliance with information security policy: an empirical study of rationality-based beliefs and awareness of information security. *MIS quarterly*, 34(3), pp. 523-548.

Chang LYC, Coppel N, (2020), Building cyber security awareness in a developing country: Lessons from Myanmar, *Computers & Security*, Volume 97.

Floyd, D.L., Prentice-Dunn, S. and Rogers, R.W., (2000). A meta-analysis of research on protection motivation theory. *Journal of Applied Social Psychology*, 30(2), pp.407-429.

Hart S, Margheri A, Paci F, Sassone V, (2020), Riskio: A Serious Game for Cyber Security Awareness and Education, *Computers & Security*, Volume 95.

Holland, James G, & Skinner, Burrhus, Frederic. (1961). *The Analysis of Behavior A program for self-instruction*. McGraw-Hill.

Jones, S. G., (1995). *Computer-Mediated Communication and Community*. California, USA: Sage Publications.

Kortjan, N. & von Solms, R., (2014). A conceptual framework for cyber-security awareness and. South African Computer Journal, July(52), pp. 29-40.

Kritzinger, E., and Padayachee, K., (2013), September. The development of an e-safety awareness culture within the South African context. *In 2013 Africon* (pp. 1-5). IEEE.

Kunc, Norman. (1992). *The need to belong: Rediscovering Maslow's hierarchy of needs.*

Maslow, Abraham, & Lewis, KJ. (1987). *Maslow's hierarchy of needs*. Salenger Incorporated, 14, 987.

Peltier, T., (2007). Implementing an Information Security Awareness Program. Information Systems *Security*, Issue May/June 2005, pp. 37-49.

Prentice-Dunn, S. & Rogers, R.W. (1986). Protection Motivation Theory and preventive health: beyond the Health Belief Model. *Health Education Research*, 1 (3),pp. 153-161.

Reeve, J., (2013). *Extrinsic rewards and inner motivation. In Handbook of classroom management* (pp. 655-674). Routledge.

Rogers, Ronald W, & Mewborn, Ronald C. (1976). Fear appeals and attitude change: effects of a threat's noxiousness, probability of occurrence, and the efficacy of coping responses. *Journal of personality and social psychology*, 34(1), pp. 54.

Rosenstock, I.M. (1974). Historical Origins of the Health Belief Model. Health Education Monographs, 2 (4), pp. 328-335.

Shillair, R., (2020). *Protection motivation theory. The International Encyclopedia of Media Psychology*, pp.1-3.

Veerasamy, N., Mkhwanazi, T., and Dawood, Z., (2023), March. Towards the usefulness of learning factories in the cybersecurity domain. *In International Conference on Cyber Warfare and Security* 18(1), pp. 412-419. Academic Conferences International Limited.

Wilson, M. & Hash, J., (2003). Building an Information Technology Security Awareness and Training Program, s.l.: National Institute of Standards and Technology (NIST).

Zachrisson, Johannes, & Boks, Casper. (2012). Exploring behavioural psychology to support design for sustainable behaviour research. *Journal of Design Research* 14, 10(1-2), pp. 50-66.

SONIFICATION IN INFORMATION SECURITY: STUDIES AND PATENTS

Nadezhda Abbas[1], Claudio Ruff[1], Marcelo Ruiz[1], Eduard Bondarev[1] and Vishnevsky Andrey[2]
[1]*Cybersecurity Research Center, Universidad Bernardo O'Higgins, UBO*
Santiago, Chile
[2]*Bauman Moscow State Technical University*
Moscow, Russia

ABSTRACT

This review is devoted to the systematization of scientific articles on sonification in the domain of information security. Sonification is a scientific field dedicated to the representation of data using non-speech sound. Sonification methods are used in medicine, aviation, complex systems management, business analytics, seismography, assistive technologies for the visually impaired, astronomy, encode complex data structures using various types of voicing. Research trends summarized here reveal the key forms and semantics of sound used in auditory displays of information security applications. This review systematizes methods of sonification of information security solutions to help the developers of assistive technologies.

KEYWORDS

Auditory Display, Sound Icons, Earcons, Music, Assistive Technologies, Cybersecurity

1. INTRODUCTION

Information security relates to data analysis tasks, monitoring and defense mechanisms development. The most widely applications in information security field are command line utilities which process various types of texts which characterize anomalies in system behavior. Optionally security scanners provide the ability to visualize the data using plots, diagrams and graphs. The non-visual data representation in form of sounds is rarely used in practice, but is valuable option for visually impaired users of information security tools. People with healthy eyesight potentially can have the advantage of using sonification in critical situations when they perform several visual tasks simultaneously and the visual channel is overloaded.

This review is devoted to the systematization of scientific articles on sonification in the domain of information security and covers scientific articles and patents published since late 1990s to middle 2020s. As a result of this research, trends in the auditory display development and their causes were revealed in case of information security area within whole range of information technologies.

2. MATERIALS AND METHODS

We have used well-known online libraries of scientific publications (Google Scholar, SpringerLink etc.) and popular patent search services (Yandex patents, Google patents etc.) to find all articles, reports, books, and invention disclosures related to non-verbal audio representation of data in information security tasks. The topic is very specific so we have analyzed papers for a large range of publication dates since late 90th. The keywords used for search were related to sonification: earcons, auditory icons, sonification, auditory displays, vocalization, speech synthesis and connected with information security: cybersecurity, hacking attacks, network monitoring, malware, vulnerabilities, phishing, software security testing.

3. TERMINOLOGY AND CATEGORIES OF SONIFICATION

De Campo defines three types of sonification by the way sound is activated: *discrete*, *continuous*, and *interactive* (De Campo, 2007). Discrete sonification encodes each data item with a separate audio object. Continuous sonification operates with data as a continuous process. With interactive sonification, the user has a wide range of tools to modify a sound object in the process of sound synthesis.

In the case of *direct* sonification, the time-varying data directly affect the parameters of the sound presented to the user. One of the methods of direct sonification is approximation of the sound characteristics to the contour of the data that are being mapped to sound. *Parametric* sonification is a continuous sonification in which the information process is mapped to the timbral space. When direct sonification is used, the user's experience with the sound is directly influenced by the time-varying data.

In terms of semantics, sonification methods are divided into two polar directions: *sound icons* and *earcons* (Worrall, 2019). Sound icons are characterized by certain stable associations. Contrary *earcons* are sounds which do not provoke evident associations in user's mind but are combined in structured scheme to be learned during the training. In order to correctly interpret the earcons, the user must be familiar with the appropriate thesaurus. Earcons have the advantage of being able to create a symbolic basis that is consistent with musical harmony and melody. To qualify as sound icons, they must have an existing cultural or other connection between the symbol and its definition.

Features used in musical sonification can be divided into the next levels: pitch (mode, harmony, timbres, registers, tonality, melody); rhythmic patterns; compositional side (the musical process as a whole); performance interpretation (articulation, strokes, and performing intonation). Musical sounds make up melody and harmony, which interacting with each other, form metro-rhythmic patterns and are formed into musical images. Lazutina has shown that symbols in music can be individual sounds, their melodic, harmonic, timbre, and dynamic combinations, as well as strictly differentiated musical images (Lazutina, 2009).

4. SEMANTICS-BASED SONIFICATOIN METHODS

PEEP is a vocalized tool created by Gilfix to monitor computer networks (Gilfix & Couch, 2000). When comparing the noises, they hear with the sounds of a network that is typically operating and learning its sounds, PEEP enables the user to identify anomalies in the network. PEEP continually vocalizes the network state (average network load) with discrete sonification of security incidents (like email spam). The PEEP's creators assert that it can be used to identify typical network issues, such as heavy traffic.

To monitor computer networks, Seoud studied the sonification of security incidents using piano sheet music recordings and audio icons (El Seoud, et al., 2008). Brute-force assaults, port scanning, and attacks on the authentication protocols were all connected with sound recordings. Studies revealed that users found it easier to recall sound symbols that feature animal voices than those that contain notes.

Ballora et al. (Ballora & Hall, 2010) (Ballora, et al., 2011) (Ballora, et al., 2010)presented a technique for sonification of computer network states to identify anomalies in the network. Certain forms of network activity, such as accessing non-standard network ports, were assigned different noises to indicate them. The suggested auditory display expresses many network properties to provide a "soundscape". Raw network traffic is sold as an input, and the system processes it to create sound pictures that allow the operator to identify network threats audibly.

With the use of musical samples, Anna Wolf vocalized the network activity events. The suggested approach involves first analyzing the network traffic using a network monitor like Wireshark, and then voice-coding the observed network events using a user-defined mapping to recorded music. Specifically, it was suggested that some elements of the user interface would be sung by musical snippets from "Peter and the Wolf," a symphonic fairy tale by Sergei Prokofiev (Wolf & Fiebrink, 2013).

Vickers suggested using sounds similar to those found in rural areas to simulate the characteristics of network traffic (Vickers, 2011) (Vickers, et al., 2017) (Vickers, et al., 2014). Several sound recordings of a stream that flows and rain are processed to alter their amplitude, phase, and spectral properties based on the number of network packets received and sent. The administrator built the system with the ability to identify security and performance abnormalities, namely, identifying denial-of-service assaults on audio. The authors claim that because the aural landscape created by the sounds of nature is more aesthetically beautiful and possibly less taxing on the operator.

Hildebrandt conducted experiments to investigate the viability of employing sonification in decision-making related to technological process monitoring. In the experiment, a set of participants used graphical and audio user interfaces to assess the network event records. Continuous, real-time monitoring of technical processes was achieved through the application of sonification. Sounds that are frequently heard in real life and that the operator is familiar with are better perceived than artificial audio signals. Perhaps as a result of the use of alternative imaging in control groups, participants using the multimodal system produced higher results (Hildebrandt, et al., 2014).

Sarah Lenzi and her coauthors have developed more informative audio interfaces to cyber threat defenses by displaying a hierarchical ordering of indicators of network attacks on a system of natural sounds of nature (Lenzi, et al., 2019) (Lenzi, et al., 2020). The developed sound display complements the graphical interface and is designed for employees of Information Security Incident Response Centers (SOC). Continuous sonification methods also voice anomalies to provide real-time monitoring. A method is proposed to automatically create a taxonomy of attack indicators to group signs of anomalies within a semantic hierarchy (ontology). Hierarchical sounds allow the user to adjust the scale of the data presentation. It is assumed that the designed auditory display retains both sufficient detail and the ability to generalize and, therefore, maintains the accuracy of the user's reactions. The semantic hierarchy of sounds is based on pitch, timbre, and rhythm. The state of the network is represented by the sounds of the forest in different weather conditions, the recordings of birdsong, and the chirping of insects. Birds, insects and the wind that blows through trees are assigned to different segments of the network infrastructure, and changes in weather, rain, and thunder express the detected anomalies. According to the authors, such a sound system allows you to scale the auditory display to more developed network infrastructures. Experiments with their auditory display of cyber threat detection tool have been carried out successfully at water pumping stations.

Lutz developed and developed a vocalized process for detecting covert web tracking. The presence of surveillance of an Internet user is announced when network connections to web tracking servers appear. A voice in the audio interface says the name of the company whose servers are involved in spying on the user. A total of 12 people participated in the experimental test of the proposed approach, confirming the hypothesis of increasing awareness and users of web tracking by ear (Lutz, et al., 2019). In the course of further research, the mechanism to verify and trust user-generated passwords was vocalized with JavaScript to play sounds on web browsers (Lutz, et al., 2020).

Datta has also vocalized web browser messages about phishing threats, malware download notifications, and warnings about errors in the fill-out of web forms. On average, 58% of the participants correctly remembered the signals from the sound interface, and 73% of the participants were able to correctly identify the threat expressed by it (Datta, et al., 2021).

Jones investigated the applicability of sonification to cyber threat notification by asking students how they perceived the potential damage from hacker attacks (Jones, et al., 2022). Common computer attacks were grouped based on the responses of participants in the experiment, with the aim of developing a more user-friendly scheme to encode cyber threats using sounds.

Sound user interfaces for anti-malware and network attack detection tasks can be based on musical recordings (Vishnevsky & Abbas, 2023). It requires some basic knowledge of musical fragments, but the sound scheme can be enough scalable for typical information security tasks.

Studies on user fatigue resulting from memorization of speech, earcons, and sound icons have been carried out on different auditory displays, for example by Lei (Lei, et al., 2022). Throughout the trial, it became evident that sound icons outperformed earcons in terms of subject accuracy and reaction time when it came to verbal activities and visual image memorization.

5. SONIFICATION METHODS BASED ON THE FORM OF SOUND

Brewster used discrete sonification to express the user's interaction with a mobile device (Brewster & Cryer, 1999). The touchscreen's virtual buttons were assigned to several earcons. With this method, the proportion of users that correctly input four-character passwords might be increased.

Kimoto wrote the sound-user-interface application Stetho, which speaks network events that are obtained from the Linux network monitor command's output. When regular expressions are triggered, Stetho uses virtual musical instruments (MIDI) to synthesize sounds and vocalize the status of the network. They were able to determine the condition of the computer network by ear during tests involving system administrators and Stetho (Kimoto & Ohno, 2002).

Malandrino has created Nemos, a monitoring system with auditory display that connects network events to virtual musical instrument MIDI tracks. Nemos offers concurrent network monitoring of various subnets, displaying the subnet's entire condition as a single music stream. Nemos is intended to track several audio channels to indicate system load, printer print queue, and network performance (Malandrino, et al., 2003). The intrusion detection system also uses sonification of the network data transfer rate created by Brown (Brown, et al., 2009).

Gopinath wrote the JListen software, which speaks out against network attacks picked up by the Snort network monitor, a popular cross-platform tool for defense against network attacks (Gopinath, 2004). JListen users have demonstrated in experiments that they are capable of detecting network attack indicators. Sonification reduced the amount of time it took test subjects to identify false positives, but music education and musical knowledge had no discernible effect on their ability to use the system to detect intrusions.

To simplify network monitoring, Papadopoulos created the Cyberseer sound display, which speaks of network security incidents and enhances its visuals (Papadopoulos, et al., 2004). The user can view events from the network intrusion detection system and the network traffic log displayed by the program. The efficacy of Cyberseer has not been tested experimentally by the authors.

A multimodal network threat protection system that can identify DoS attacks and port scans has been published by Qi et al. (Qi, et al., 2007). The suggested sonification technique is intended to identify these two types of attack audibly. The system is fed raw, unprocessed network data as input.

Giot wrote a program called InteNtion, which synthesizes the sounds of virtual musical instruments (MIDI) based on network traffic data (Giot & Courbe, 2012). The network activity of the network as a whole is synchronized. The system is designed for the system and the network administrator and is potentially useful for detecting network attacks.

De Butts vocalized events from network access logs. Security analysts who work on computer network security are the target audience for his audio-user interface application (deButts, 2014).

Mancuso et al. experimentally tested the effectiveness of sonification of network packets received during cyber operations at a US Air Force base (Mancuso, et al., 2015). Participants in the experiment analyzed network traffic by triggering the signature using a graphical interface or using a graphical interface, complemented by a sound display. The visual interface has been made similar to the popular network traffic analysis program Wireshark. The experiment showed that the method of sounding IP addresses with musical instrument notes and adjusting the volume according to the size of the network packet does not increase the accuracy of the responses of the subjects working with the proposed multimodal system.

Worrall developed NetSon, a multimodal program for sonification and visualization of network data. In the proposed sonification method, musical sounds are mapped to network traffic. The program has been successfully tested in a relatively large corporate network (Worrall, 2015).

Axon investigated the possibility of using sonification in the work of information security incident response centers (Axon & Nurse, 2017) (Axon, et al., 2020) (Axon, et al., 2016) (Axon, et al., 2018) (Axon, et al., 2019) (Axon, et al., 2019). The advantage of using sonification in critical situations where the operator performs several visual tasks at the same time and the visual channel is overloaded has been shown. A standardized procedure for experimental verification is proposed to demonstrate the effectiveness of sonification in real-world conditions. The researchers also developed and tested their sonification method on real data, trying to encode the maximum amount of data in synthesized musical notes. The focus of the study is on encoding as much data as possible in a musical signal.

In Namin's work, experiments on the ergonomics of sound user interfaces were considered (Siami Namin, et al., 2016), using examples of sonification means to detect network attacks. As a key indicator of ergonomics, fatigue indicators of the user of the sound interface were chosen, which are calculated depending on the algorithm to voicing the data.

Egorova proposed a method for sonification of computer networks using graph models (Egorova, et al., 2016). The developed software package simulates dynamic processes in complex networks and provides the operator with the ability to control numerical parameters in real time.

Markhotin created a method of sonification designed to monitor wireless networks using the fuzzy logic apparatus (Markhotin, 2016). The proposed approach to the use of fuzzy logic in sonification systems can be applied to the development of applications for which it is difficult to formalize the correspondence of input data to output sound signals, as well as the complex organization of timbre space.

Debashi investigated the prospects of using network traffic sonification to ensure the security of computer networks. Experiments have shown that humans are more accurate at detecting network attacks (including denial-of-service attacks and network requests from infected devices) by hearing using sonification analysis tools than automated anomaly detection systems based on machine learning (Debashi & Vickers, 2018).

As shown in Figure 1, Falk and Dykstra experimentally tested the effectiveness of musical sonification of information security events associated with attempts to authorize a user on the corporate network (Falk & Dykstra, 2019). The frequency of synthesized music is 80 beats per minute, or 1.33 beats per second. According to the calculations of the authors of the method, this music transmitted 22.66 bits of information per second.

Figure 1. Sonification of a continuous data signal where the differences in the input signal are encoded into the volume of the notes, source: Falk & Dykstra, 2019

Polaczyk suggested that baroque music should be used to describe the characteristics of network traffic associated with the distribution of malicious files on the network, as shown in Figure 2 (Polaczyk, et al., 2021). Especially for the experiment, the composer composed melodies to play the harp. The experiment has shown that listeners can successfully identify both sound images of data played on the live harp and the computer-synthesized sound of the same melodies. Participants without a musical background were able to accurately answer questions about the data they listened to, but the results improved significantly when a visualization was added. The rhythm of the melody was 60 beats per minute. The easiest thing for the participants was to identify the first and last notes of the melody.

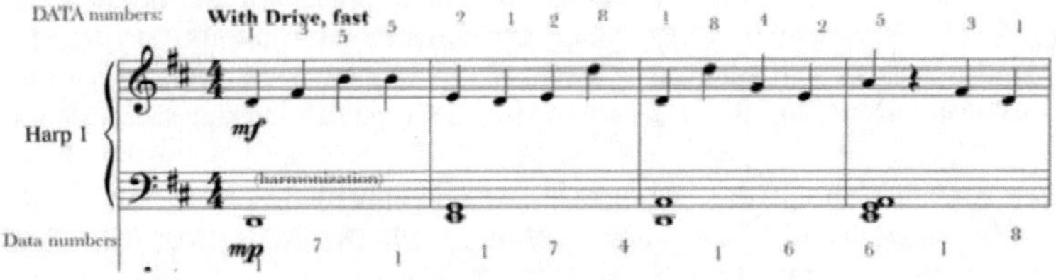

Figure 2. Example of pitch-based sonification of the malware distribution via network

6. SONIFICATION TRENDS AND EVALUATION

Table 1 lists the quality evaluations of the sonification methods published by the authors of the articles in this review. If the researchers published several different experimental estimates of the quality of sonification, we took the smallest and highest of them and placed them in a table as a range of values. As it could be seen from the table above the accuracy level could reach 100%. Table 2 summarizes the key features of proposed sonification approaches in chronological order of corresponding publications.

Table 1. Sonification quality metrics

Author, year of publication	Accuracy	Precision	Recall
Mancuso, 2015	24 – 47%	Not Calculated	Not Calculated
Debashi, 2018	94.29%	89.19%	100%
Axon, 2019	25 – 96%	100%	60% – 100 %
Datta, 2021	4% – 96%	Not Calculated	Not Calculated
Polaczyk, 2021	5% – 100%	Not Calculated	Not Calculated

We have copied all the names of the signs of computer attacks from the above-mentioned scientific articles and formed them into a word cloud on the left side of Figure 3. The names of the sonification methods, characteristics of sound waves, and sound sources that have been mentioned in scientific publications are listed on the right side of Figure 3. The larger the size of the word in the cloud in the figure, the more articles in this review mentioned a sign of a computer attack or a sonification method.

Figure 3. Computer Attack Feature Cloud (left) and Sonification Cloud (right)

Table 2. Evolution of sonification methods

Author, year of publication	Form	Semantics	Key feature
Gilfix & Couch, 2000	No	Yes	Natural noises
De Campo, 2007	Yes	No	Parametric sonification
Ballora & Hall, 2010	No	Yes	Soundscapes
Vickers, 2011	No	Yes	Aural landscape
Hildebrandt, 2014	No	Yes	Real life sounds
Worrall, 2019	No	Yes	Musical sounds
Axon, 2018	Yes	No	Synthesized musical notes
Falk & Dykstra, 2019	Yes	No	Music synthesis
Lenzi, et al., 2020	No	Yes	Ontology of natural sounds
Polaczyk, 2021	Yes	No	Baroque music usage
Datta, 2021	No	Yes	Web messages

7. PATENTS REVIEW

The first registered invention of Childs vocalizes the streams of the data by means of music. It is assumed that the source data may have numerous parameters. Algorithmically computed input characteristics are used to define the properties of the output sequence of musical sounds. In the case of financial transactions, the pitch of the musical tone is compared in an evenly tempered scale. Sounds are generated based on the parameters of dynamic changes in the market, for example, currency fluctuations, stock prices, etc. (Childs & Tomic, 2006). The second patent of invention by Childs in the field of data sonification describes a way to represent complex data, such as financial market data, using musical notes. The invention illustrates a scheme for continuous real-time sonification of financial data. In the proposed sonification method, the sound signal generator converts the input data into sound parameters based on user-defined configuration files (Childs, et al., 2009).

Invention patented by Plott is intended to automatically convert multidimensional data into musical sounds and simultaneously present the same data in the form of animated graphics. The system groups the data into subsets according to user-defined rules and matches the grouped objects with musical notes (Plott, et al., 2015).

The application of sonification in the field of cybersecurity includes the invention of a method to encode network anomalies using the sounds of rustling leaves, burning fireworks, birdsong, chirping crickets, whistling wind and bell ringing. Voiced events are aggregated by the type of firewall action (allow/deny/alert/drop/reset). IP-addresses and network ports are checked for the presence in blacklists (Kuzmin, 2019). Second patented sonification method by Kuzmin is designed to improve the efficiency and response to cybersecurity events in computer networks by vocalization of cybersecurity events including: type of network protocol, IP addresses, connection times, and firewall responses. The volume of sound expresses the number of connections and the deviation from the average is expressed by timbre and pitch (Kuzmin, 2019). Third patent of Kuzmin describes the principle of anomalies sonification in the corporate networks. The sound environment is formed from the protocol of the observed network interaction. The rustle of leaves represents TCP network connections, the sound of sea waves represents UDP connections, and the whistling of the wind indicates ICPM communication (Kuzmin, 2019).

A sonification method of the signs of computer attacks based on the analysis of network traffic has been patented. Multiple acoustic signals can be combined (stacked on top of each other) for joint analysis. The detection of anomalies is supposed to be based on digital signal processing methods. Among the features of network events, Horstmeyer mentions the time of network connections, the source and destination address, the number of bytes and network packets transmitted, and the type of network protocol (Horstmeyer, et al., 2020).

Computer attack detection system patented by Abbas includes a module for collecting data and clustering user behavior in web applications, and a machine learning module that dynamically changes the audio representation of input data. An interactive auditory display allows the operator to select the number of notes in the chords to identify and block suspicious activity (Abbas, 2022).

8. CONCLUSION

The number of practical applications of audio interfaces is growing, and the effectiveness of sonification methods depends on the context and scenarios of the user's work. With the special capabilities of sound, it has been shown to be effective in monitoring processes in real time. In information security area the development of sonification methods is focused on increasing the amount of information in audio messages and on improving the ergonomics of auditory displays. The interpretability of audio signals remains the greatest challenge when scaling an audio message system to encoded input. Most of the reviewed articles in this summary focus on the characteristics of the shape of sound which help to express the form of the data. But the listed experimental studies show that this kind of data representation is not always well understood by the users of auditory displays. Selected and structured collections of sound icons which user is familiar with are better perceived than synthetic audio signals in terms of user reaction accuracy and time. The further research of automatic selection of well-known sounds and making sonification schemes from them looks promising.

REFERENCES

Abbas, N. Y. et al., (2022). A sonified computer attack detection system: patent. DE202022103738U1 Germany.

Axon, L. et al., (2020). Data presentation in security operations centres: exploring the potential for sonification to enhance existing practice. *Journal of Cybersecurity,* Volume 6, p. tyaa004.

Axon, L., Creese, S., Goldsmith, M. & Nurse, J., (2016). Reflecting on the use of sonification for network monitoring.

Axon, L., Goldsmith, M. & Creese, S., (2018). Sonification mappings: estimating effectiveness, polarities and scaling in an online experiment. *Journal of the Audio Engineering Society,* Volume 66, p. 1016–1032.

Axon, L., Happa, J., Goldsmith, M. & Creese, S., (2019). Hearing attacks in network data: an effectiveness study. *Computers & Security,* Volume 83, p. 367–388.

Axon, L. et al., (2019). Sonification to support the monitoring tasks of security operations centres. *IEEE Transactions on Dependable and Secure Computing,* Volume 18, p. 1227–1244.

Axon, L. & Nurse, J., (2017). A Formalised Approach to Designing Sonification Systems for Network- Security Monitoring. *International Journal on Advances in Security.*

Ballora, M., Giacobe, N. A. & Hall, D. L., (2011). *Songs of cyberspace: an update on sonifications of network traffic to support situational awareness.* s.l., s.n., p. 202–207.

Ballora, M. & Hall, D. L., (2010). *Do you see what I hear: experiments in multi-channel sound and 3D visualization for network monitoring?.* s.l., s.n., p. 143–149.

Ballora, M., Panulla, B., Gourley, M. & Hall, D. L., (2010). *Preliminary steps in sonifying web log data.*, p. 83–87.

Brewster, S. A. & Cryer, P. G., (1999). *Maximising screen-space on mobile computing devices.* s.l., s.n., p. 224–225.

Brown, A. et al., (2009). *Poster: Towards music-assisted intrusion detection.* s.l., s.n.

Childs, E. P., Perkins, J. C. & Brooks, J. G., (2009). System and method for musical sonification of data: patent US7511213.

Childs, E. P. & Tomic, S., (2006). System and method for musical sonification of data parameters in a data stream: patent. US7135635.

Datta, P., Namin, A. S., Jones, K. S. & Hewett, R., (2021). Warning users about cyber threats through sounds. *SN Applied Sciences,* Volume 3, p. 1–21.

De Campo, A., (2007). *Toward a data sonification design space map.* s.l., s.n., p. 342–347.

Debashi, M. & Vickers, P., (2018). Sonification of network traffic flow for monitoring and situational awareness. *PloS one,* Volume 13, p. e0195948.

deButts, B., (2014). Network access log visualization & sonification. *Student Project, Tufts University, Medford, USA.*

Egorova, A. N., Osypenko, I. N. & Rogozinsky, G. G., (2016). Software complex for sonification of complex networks and systems. *IoT and 5G,* pp. 51-55.

El Seoud, S. et al., (2008). Auditory display as a tool for teaching network intrusion detection. *International Journal of Emerging Technologies in Learning (iJET),* Volume 3, p. 59–62.

Falk, C. & Dykstra, J., (2019). *Sonification with music for cybersecurity situational awareness.* s.l., s.n., p. 50–55.

Gilfix, M. & Couch, A., (2000). *Peep (the network auralizer): Monitoring your network with sound.* s.l., s.n.

Giot, R. & Courbe, Y., (2012). *Intention–interactive network sonification.* s.l., s.n., p. 235–236.

Gopinath, M., (2004). Auralization of intrusion detection system using Jlisten. *Development,* Volume 22, p. 3.

Hildebrandt, T., Hermann, T. & Rinderle-Ma, S., (2014). *A sonification system for process monitoring as secondary task.* s.l., s.n., p. 191–196.

Horstmeyer, N. S., Horn, D. B. & Shanbhag, S., (2020). Detecting cyber-attacks with sonification. United States patent US 20190253441A1. *Cisco Technology Inc, assignee..*

Jones, K. S. et al., (2022). Grouping and determining perceived severity of cyber-Attack consequences: gaining information needed to sonify cyber-attacks. *Journal on Multimodal User Interfaces,* Volume 16, p. 399–412.

Kimoto, M. & Ohno, H., (2002). *Design and implementation of stetho: Network sonificiation system.* s.l., s.n.

Kuzmin, A. M., (2019). Method and system for cybersecurity events sonification based on analysis of actions of network protection means: patent RU2724984C1.

Kuzmin, A. M., (2019). Method and system for sonification events of cybersecurity: patent WO2021045639A1.

Kuzmin, A. M., (2019). Method and system for sonification of cyber-security events based on analysis of network connection protocols: patent RU2723458C1.

Lazutina, T. V., (2009). *Onto-gnoseological and axiological foundations language of music.* s.l., s.n.

Lei, Z., Ma, S., Li, H. & Yang, Z., (2022). The impact of different types of auditory warnings on working memory. *Frontiers in Psychology,* Volume 13, p. 780657.

Lenzi, S. et al., (2019). *Disclosing cyber-attacks on water distribution systems. An experimental approach to the sonification of threats and anomalous data..* s.l., s.n., p. 125–132.

Lenzi, S., Terenghi, G. & Moreno-Fernandez-de-Leceta, A., (2020). A design-driven sonification process for supporting expert users in real-time anomaly detection: Towards applied guidelines. *EAI Endorsed Transactions on Creative Technologies,* Volume 7, p. e4–e4.

Lutz, O. H.-M., Kroger, J. L., Schneiderbauer, M. & Hauswirth, M., (2019). Surfing in sound: Sonification of hidden web tracking.

Lutz, O. H.-M. et al., (2020). *That password doesn't sound right: interactive password strength sonification.*, p. 206–213.

Malandrino, D. et al., (2003). *Nemos: Network monitoring with sound.* s.l., s.n., p. 251–254.

Mancuso, V. F. et al., (2015). Augmenting cyber defender performance and workload through sonified displays. *Procedia Manufacturing,* Volume 3, p. 5214–5221.

Markhotin, A. A., (2016). Fuzzy mapping in data sonification system of wireless sensor network. *Scientific and Technical Journal of Information Technologies, Mechanics and Optics,* 16(6), pp. 1073-1077.

Papadopoulos, C., Kyriakakis, C., Sawchuk, A. & He, X., (2004). *Cyberseer: 3d audio-visual immersion for network security and management.* s.l., s.n., p. 90–98.

Plott, C. R., Hirschhorn, M. J. & Hsingyang, L. E., (2015). Systems and methods for musical sonification and visualization of data: patent US9190042.

Polaczyk, J., Croft, K. & Cai, Y., (2021). *Compositional sonification of cybersecurity data in a baroque style.* s.l., s.n., p. 304–312.

Qi, L. et al., (2007). *Toward sound-assisted intrusion detection systems.* s.l., s.n., p. 1634–1645.

Siami Namin, A., Hewett, R., Jones, K. S. & Pogrund, R., (2016). *Sonifying internet security threats*, p. 2306–2313.

Vickers, P., (2011). Sonification for process monitoring.

Vickers, P., Laing, C., Debashi, M. & Fairfax, T., (2014). Sonification aesthetics and listening for network situational awareness. *arXiv preprint arXiv:1409.5282.*

Vickers, P., Laing, C. & Fairfax, T., (2017). Sonification of a network's self-organized criticality for real-time situational awareness. *Displays,* Volume 47, p. 12–24.

Vishnevsky, A. S. & Abbas, N. Y., (2023). *Application of Sonification Method in Teaching Information Security.* In: Rocha, Á., Ferrás, C., Ibarra, W. (eds) Information Technology and Systems. ICITS 2023. Lecture Notes in Networks and Systems, vol 692., Springer, Cham. https://doi.org/10.1007/978-3-031-33261-6_41.

Wolf, K. & Fiebrink, R., (2013). *SonNet: A Code Interface for Sonifying Computer Network Data..* s.l., s.n., p. 503–506.

Worrall, D., (2015). *Realtime sonification and visualisation of network metadata.* s.l., s.n.

Worrall, D., (2019). Sonification Design. *Cham: Springer.*

DEVELOPMENT OF PUBLIC WARNING SYSTEMS

Øyvind Heimset Larsen, Anna Maria Urbaniak-Brekke and Ivar Petter Grøtte
Western Norway Research Institute, Norway

ABSTRACT

Research shows that Digital Audio Broadcasting warning systems are effective in Norwegian rural settings when implementing specific audio parameters and message strategies. Five studies directly address the development and testing of public warning systems. The problem to be solved is to find a method with accompanying products and services to be able to alert and evacuate the population/public regardless of nationality in a range of different events. Research question: Uncover user needs and validate components and the fully integrated system. Field tests in a Norwegian rural school in Selje, and in municipal centres of Sykkylven and Hellesylt, showed that a Digital Audio Broadcasting system works well when short, repeated, and multilingual audio messages are used; reducing audio volume from 75% to 50% improved clarity despite wind and noise. An avalanche warning service spanning 21 regions in Norway and Svalbard received positive user feedback when messages offered detailed, comprehensible information. An observational study of wildlife warning systems at 29 railway sites in Norway and Sweden recorded an 88% response rate to human voice alerts. A literature review on medicine overdose warning systems noted that integration with existing monitoring infrastructure promotes rapid alerting, and a case study across 26 Norwegian municipalities revealed how risk and vulnerability analyses guide system adaptation to local conditions.These studies show that public warning systems based on digital broadcasting and related technologies can be designed to meet varied emergency scenarios. Adjustments in signal delivery and tailored message strategies are essential for success across different environments and risk profiles.

KEYWORDS

User Involvement, Public Warning Systems, Digital Audio Broadcasting

1. INTRODUCTION

The main task of public warning technologies is to inform people about danger, make evacuation easier, and guide them to a safer place (Bean and Botterell, 2019; Toyoda and Kanegae, 2014). An increasing number of new technologies is being developed, having the potential to improve existing warning systems. One of them is an innovative, DAB-based system developed by a Norwegian company called Paneda, together with its partner-companies of regional and national range. Digital Audio Broadcasting (DAB) is designed for delivery of high-quality digital audio programs and data services for mobile, portable and fixed reception from terrestrial transmitters in the Very High Frequency (VHF) frequency bands (WorldDAB, n.d.). And furthermore, using DAB makes it possible to 'take over' audio equipment, interrupt other broadcasting, and send a message or trigger specialised equipment (visual, sound, text, etc.) that will warn people about a threat (e.g., natural disasters or terror attack). However, this new technology needs structured user testing and evaluation before introduction to a broader market. That is why a research project called Public Warning System (PWS) has been conducted and is about to finish now in 2025, to test this new system's ability to inform different societal groups about dangerous events. Western Norway Research Institute has had the responsibility of conducting tests and evaluation to assure the usability of the new technology (Vestlandsforsking, 2020, Urbaniak-Brekke et al, 2022).

This paper's main goal is to compare lessons learnt from the DAB project in Western Norway with other identified relevant Scandinavian studies. The comparison will include and present selected results of applying a user involvement method to test and evaluate the new Norwegian DAB warning system.

2. METHOD

In the DAB research project, the authors use an action research approach, where researchers are participants in the development and their conclusions are grounded in this action research (Greenwood and Levin, 2007). The use of case studies is a key element as "the study of the particularity and complexity of a single case, coming to understand its activity within important circumstances" (Stake, 1995, p. xi). The three selected studies are single cases where one, with their consent, investigates specific local communities. According to Yin (1981, pp. 98–99) the strength of the case study is that it both covers a contemporary phenomenon and its context. Findings are from a select few single cases, but we claim that these findings also can be a "force of example" (Flyvbjerg, 2006) for other communities of the same nature (rural, school environments) facing similar challenges related to emergencies and population evacuation. The DAB project was carried out in accordance with the Norwegian Research Ethics Act, which is a Norwegian law intended to ensure that research is conducted according to recognized research ethical standards. To compare lessons learnt from the DAB project in Western Norway with other identified relevant Scandinavian studies we conducted a literature review supported by the AI tool Elicit (https://elicit.com/). We then selected relevant cases and then also supported our meta-analysis with Elicit.

2.1 Screening

The authors screened papers that met these criteria:

- **Warning System Type**: Does the study examine public warning systems or emergency notification systems, including but not limited to DAB-based or digital radio network technologies?
- **Community Setting**: Does the study focus on or include small communities or rural areas (rather than exclusively urban metropolitan areas)?
- **Implementation Evidence**: Does the study include practical field testing, experimental studies, or real-world implementation data (rather than purely theoretical models)?
- **Performance Evaluation**: Does the study evaluate system effectiveness, performance metrics, or evacuation outcomes?
- **Hazard Scope**: Does the study examine warning systems capable of addressing multiple types of hazards or threats?
- **Community Feedback**: Does the study include community response, user feedback, or public inter- action with the warning system?
- **System Integration**: Does the study address integration with emergency response operations or emergency response centers?
- **Data Type**: Does the study present empirical data or practical testing results rather than purely theoretical or conceptual discussion?

We considered all screening questions together and made a holistic judgement about whether to screen in each paper.

2.2 Data Extraction

We asked the large language model to extract each data column below from each paper. We gave the model the extraction instructions shown below for each column.

- **Study Design Type**:
  Identify the primary research design used in the study. Look in the methods section for explicit description of study design. Possible categories include:
- Field test/pilot study, Case study, Observational study, Intervention study, Mixed methods study

If multiple design types are used, list them in order of prominence. If unclear, note "design not clearly specified". Specific to this review's context of public warning systems, pay special attention to whether the study involves:

- System testing, User involvement, Technology evaluation

- **Research Methods and Data Collection Approaches**:
  List all research methods used for data collection. Look in methods section and identify specific techniques such as:
- Qualitative interviews, Observation, User surveys, System testing, Technical verification, Dialogue workshops

For each method, if possible, note:

- Number of participants/respondents, Duration of data collection, Specific focus or purpose of the method

If multiple methods were used, describe how they were integrated or triangulated.

- **Public Warning System Technology Details**:
  Describe the specific warning system technology being studied:
- Technology platform (e.g., DAB network), Communication modes (audio, text, visual), Geographical coverage, Technical specifications

Look in methods, results, and discussion sections. Extract specific technical details about system design, implementation, and performance.

If multiple system configurations were tested, describe each variant and its specific characteristics.

- **Testing Scenarios and Contexts**:
  Identify and describe:
- Geographic locations of testing
- Types of emergency scenarios simulated
- Specific local conditions considered

Look in methods and results sections. Note details about:

- Urban vs rural settings
- Types of potential emergencies (natural disasters, terror threats)
- Specific environmental or infrastructural challenges

If multiple scenarios were tested, list them with brief descriptions.

- **Key Performance and Effectiveness Findings**:
  Extract primary findings related to warning system performance:
- Effectiveness of communication
- User comprehension rates
- Technical reliability
- Areas requiring improvement

Look in the results and discussion sections. Prioritize quantitative metrics if available, but also include qualitative insights. Note specific performance indicators such as:

- Message clarity, Sound quality, Coverage effectiveness, User satisfaction levels

If multiple findings exist, rank them by significance or prominence in the study.

3. RESULTS

3.1 Characteristics of Included Studies

Table 1. Characteristics of included studies

Study focus	Study	Geographic Context	Warning System Type	Testing Methodology	Full text retrieved
Testing Public Warning System at School, 2022	Testing a new Digital Audio Broadcasting (DAB) public warning system	Rural school setting in Norway	DAB-based public warning system	Field test/pilot study; Case study	No
Borge and Muller, 2023	Overdose warning systems	Not specified (literature review)	Overdose warning systems	Scoping review of existing literature	Yes

Study focus	Study	Geographic Context	Warning System Type	Testing Methodology	Full text retrieved
Engeset et al., 2018	Avalanche warning communication	Norway and Svalbard	National Avalanche Warning Service	Web-based user survey; Expert panel evaluation	Yes
Njå and Vastveit, 2016	Risk and vulnerability analyses in municipalities	26 municipalities across Norway	General emergency preparedness systems	Case study; Qualitative interviews; Document analysis	Yes
Seiler et al., 2022	Wildlife warning systems for railways	29 railway sites in Sweden and Norway	Acoustic wildlife warning systems	Intervention study; Field test/pilot study; Observational study	Yes

The studies we analyzed covered five different warning systems, each focusing on a unique area:

1. Digital Audio Broadcasting (DAB)-based public warning system
2. Overdose warning system
3. Avalanche warning system
4. General emergency preparedness system
5. Wildlife warning system for railways (acoustic)

Regarding geographic context:

- 4 studies were conducted in Norway
- 1 study included both Norway and Sweden
- We didn't find specific geographic information for 1 study (literature review)

We found a variety of methodologies used across the studies, including field tests, case studies, literature reviews, surveys, and interviews.

3.2 Thematic Analysis

3.2.1 Technical Implementation and Performance

Table 2. Technical Implementation and Performance

Theme	Key Findings	Implementation Challenges	Success Factors
DAB network effectiveness	No mention found	No mention found	No mention found
System coverage and reliability	Avalanche warning system covers Norway and Svalbard with 21 regional warnings; Wildlife warning systems tested at 29 railway sites	Technical limitations in mounting speakers on trains for wildlife warning systems	Broad coverage of avalanche warning system; Timely alerts (within 4 hours) for overdose warning systems
Integration with existing infrastructure	Overdose warning systems may not require new infrastructure, but can link existing monitoring and harm reduction systems	Challenges in implementing risk-based management principles in municipalities	Potential for integrating existing systems in overdose warnings

Key Findings:

1. Limited information on DAB network effectiveness
2. Avalanche warning systems: 21 regional warnings covering Norway and Svalbard
3. Wildlife warning systems: Tested at 29 railway sites
4. Overdose warning systems: Potential integration with existing systems

Implementation Challenges:

1. Technical limitations for wildlife warning systems on trains
2. Challenges in implementing risk-based management in municipalities

Success Factors:
1. Broad coverage of avalanche warning system
2. Timely alerts for overdose warning systems
3. Potential for integrating existing systems in overdose warnings

3.2.2 User Response and System Effectiveness

Table 3. User Response and System Effectiveness

Theme	Key Findings	Implementation Challenges	Success Factors
Public reception and understanding	Avalanche warning service generally found useful by users	Effectiveness varies with user competency and scenario complexity	Detailed information improves comprehension, especially at lower danger levels
Response time and behavior	Wildlife warning systems elicit high response rates (88% for human voice)	No mention found for human response	Clear and recognizable signals (e.g., human voice) in wildlife warning systems
Communication clarity	Importance of clear, informative, and repeated messages emphasized in DAB system testing	Environmental factors like wind and noise can interfere with audio messages	Short, clear messages; Repetition of messages; Use of multiple languages

Key findings:
1. Avalanche warning services: Generally useful to users
2. Wildlife warning systems: High response rates (88%) for human voice signals
3. DAB system: Emphasis on clear, informative, repeated messages

Implementation challenges:
1. Effectiveness varies with user competency and scenario complexity
2. Environmental factors (wind, noise) interfere with audio messages

Success factors:
1. Detailed information improves comprehension
2. Clear, recognizable signals (e.g., human voice)
3. Short, clear messages with repetition and multiple languages

3.2.3 Testing and Validation Methods

Table 4. Testing and Validation Methods

Theme	Key Findings	Implementation Challenges	Success Factors
Field test outcomes	DAB system functions well in most tested locations; Wildlife warning systems show high effectiveness	Need for adjustments to cover all areas effectively in DAB system; Technical limitations in wildlife warning system implementation	Reduction of sound volume from 75% to 50% improved effectiveness in DAB system
User involvement approaches	Web-based surveys used for avalanche warning system evaluation; User involvement method applied in DAB system testing	Potential for self-selection bias in web-based surveys	Inclusion of both expert and general user perspectives in avalanche warning system evaluation
System adjustments and improvements	Need for adaptation to different scenarios and local conditions identified across studies	Challenges in implementing risk-based management principles in municipalities	Iterative testing and adjustment process evident in wildlife warning system development

Key findings:
1. DAB system: Functions well in most tested locations
2. Wildlife warning systems: High effectiveness reported
3. User involvement: Web-based surveys and user involvement methods used
4. Adaptation needs: Identified across studies for different scenarios and local conditions

Implementation challenges:
1. DAB system: Adjustments needed for effective coverage
2. Wildlife warning systems: Technical limitations in implementation
3. Web-based surveys: Potential self-selection bias
4. Municipalities: Challenges in implementing risk-based management principles

Success factors:
1. DAB system: Reduced sound volume (75% to 50%) improved effectiveness
2. Avalanche warning system: Inclusion of expert and general user perspectives
3. Wildlife warning system: Iterative testing and adjustment process

3.3 Cross-Context Analysis

3.3.1 Geographic and Demographic Factors

The studies covered diverse geographic contexts, from rural school settings to national-level systems in Norway and Sweden:

- DAB-based public warning system: Tested in a rural school environment in Norway
- Avalanche warning system: Covers all of Norway and Svalbard
- Wildlife warning systems: Tested at multiple railway sites across Sweden and Norway
- Municipal risk and vulnerability analyses: Covered 26 municipalities across Norway

3.3.2 System Adaptability

System adaptability across studies:

- DAB-based system: Adjustments needed for effective coverage and local adaptation
- Avalanche warning system: Effectiveness varied with scenario complexity
- Both systems indicated a need for adaptable communication strategies

Technical adjustments:

- DAB system: Reducing sound volume from 75% to 50% improved effectiveness
- Wildlife warning systems: Different acoustic signals tested, with human voice proving most effective

Integration capabilities:

- Overdose warning system: Potential to integrate with existing monitoring and harm reduction infrastructure

These findings highlight various approaches to system adaptability, including technical adjustments, integration capabilities, and the need for context-specific adaptations across different warning system types and geographic settings.

4. DISCUSSION

The review of warning systems in Norway reveals several important patterns and challenges across different domains. Digital platforms have emerged as a key component of modern warning systems, with evidence of successful implementation in avalanche warning services (Johnsen, 2013). The exploration of DAB-based warning systems represents an innovative approach to public alerting (Urbaniak-Brekke, et al., 2022), though effectiveness data remains limited.

A significant challenge identified across studies is the integration of warning systems into existing municipal operations. Research indicates that municipalities struggle with implementing risk and vulnerability analyses due to competence gaps and resource constraints (Njå and Vastveit, 2016). This suggests that technical solutions alone may be insufficient without adequate organizational capacity and support.

The evaluation of warning system effectiveness presents particular challenges, as demonstrated in the overdose warning system study (Borge and Muller, 2023). The difficulty in isolating the impact of warning systems from other preventive measures highlights the need for more robust evaluation methodologies.

User engagement emerges as a crucial factor, with evidence supporting the value of public participation in both system development (Urbaniak-Brekke, et al., 2022) and data collection (Johnsen, 2013). This suggests that future warning system implementations should prioritize user involvement and public education components.

5. CONCLUSIONS

The findings from this review highlight both the potential and challenges of warning systems in Norway. While digital platforms and new technologies offer promising solutions (Johnsen, 2013), successful implementation requires addressing fundamental challenges in competence, resources, and system integration (Njå and Vastveit, 2016).

Several key recommendations emerge from this analysis:

- Integration of existing systems should be prioritized over creating new infrastructure
- Investment in competence development and training is crucial for effective implementation
- User involvement should be incorporated throughout system development and deployment

Future research should focus on:

- Developing robust methodologies for evaluating warning system effectiveness
- Investigating ways to better integrate warning systems with municipal operations
- Exploring opportunities for cross-system coordination and standardization

Limitations of this review include the small number of studies examined and their varied geographical scopes and methodological approaches. Additionally, the limited availability of effectiveness data suggests a need for more comprehensive evaluation studies in this field.

It is important to predict and avoid dangerous situations, so that there is as little need as possible for the evacuation. Emergencies occur, especially when it comes to natural disasters in some areas (e.g. the risk of avalanches and tsunami waves in parts of Norway), and the warning will then have an essential role in evacuating and securing life of citizens. The national warning system in Norway today, based mainly on alarm sirens and mobile phone networks, should be supported by the innovative DAB equipment and other new technologies, making it more robust and resilient to potential threats setting human health and life in danger. DAB is also built on a separate infrastructure, digital broadcast, not the mobile network, and will be operational even if the local mobile network is not working due to failure in local power supply or other elements in the mobile infrastructure.

Our analysis of selected studies show that public warning systems based on digital broadcasting and related technologies can be designed to meet varied emergency scenarios. Adjustments in signal delivery and tailored message strategies are essential for success across different environments and risk profiles.

REFERENCES

Bean, H., Botterell, A. (2019). *Mobile technology and the transformation of public alert and warning*. First edition. Praeger Security International, Santa Barbara, California.

Borge, T. C., Muller, A. E. (2023). Overdosevarslingssystemer – en kartleggingsoversikt med maskinlæring. *Nordic Studies on Alcohol and Drugs, 40*(5):443-462. https://doi.org/10.1177/14550725221143180

Eide, D., Ljunggren, E. (2018). *Testing som metode i innovasjonsprosesser. Et verktøyhefte med eksempler fra opplevelsesbasert reiseliv*. Rapport.

Engeset, R., Pfuhl, G., Landrø, M., Mannberg, A., & Hetland, A. (2018). Communicating Public Avalanche Warnings – What Works? *Natural Hazards and Earth System Sciences*, 2018.

Flyvbjerg, B. (2006). Five Misunderstandings About Case-Study Research. *Qual. Inq. 12*, 219–245. https://doi.org/10.1177/1077800405284363

Greenwood, D., Levin, M. (2007). *Introduction to Action Research*. SAGE Publications, Inc., Thousand Oaks, California. https://doi.org/10.4135/9781412984614

Johnsen, E. (2013). Modern forms of communicating avalanche danger - A Norwegian case. *Environmental Science, Geography.* https://www.semanticscholar.org/paper/Modern-forms-of-communicating-avalanche-danger-A-Johnsen/66b4ef5a185251939958aa9829f9d023c8d23dad

Njå, O., Vastveit, K. R. (2016). *Norske kommuners planlegging, gjennomføring og bruk av risiko- og sårbarhetsanalyse i forbindelse med samfunnssikkerhetsarbeidet.* Rapport nr. 59, Univeersity of Stavanger. https://ebooks.uis.no/index.php/USPS/catalog/book/164

Seiler, A., Winsvold, A., Olsson, M., Eilertsen, S.,& Berndt, C. (2022). *VILTVARNING: Test Av Nya Tekniska Åtgärder För Att Minska Antalet Viltpåkörningar På Järnväg*. Rapport. https://doi.org/10.54612/a.7pbjcv25mc

Stake, R.E. (1995). *The art of case study research*. Sage Publications, Thousand Oaks.

Tiril C. Borge, and Ashley E. Muller. (2023). Overdosevarslingssystemer – En Kartleggingsoversikt Med Maskin- læring. *The Naturalist*, 2023.

Urbaniak-Brekke, A.M., Larsen, Ø.H., & Grøtte, I.P. (2022). Testing public warning system at school with user involvement - case study from a rural community. *Proceedings of the 15th International Conference on ICT, Society and Human Beings (ICT 2022)*.

Vestlandsforsking. (2020). *Public Warning System (PWS)*.https://www.vestforsk.no/en/project/public-warning-system-pws.

WorldDAB. (n.d.). *DAB+ emergency broadcasting and warnings*. https://www.worlddab.org/dab/emergency-warning.

Yin, R.K. (1981). The Case Study as a Serious Research Strategy. *Knowledge 3*, 97–114. https://doi.org/10.1177/107554708100300106

BEHAVIORAL FINANCE: A RECOMMENDER SYSTEM FOR PERSONALIZED INVESTMENT STRATEGIES BASED ON SURVEY DATA

Asefeh Asemi[1] and Mahdi Houshangi[1,2]
[1]*Corvinus University of Budapest*
Budapest 1093, Fovam Ter 8, Hungary
[2]*Czech University of Life Sciences*
1093 Budapest, Fovam Ter 8, Hungary & Praha 6, Prague, Czech Republic

ABSTRACT

This research introduces a novel framework for an investment recommender system that leverages Generative AI to analyze investor behavior and provide personalized recommendations. The system utilizes a Combined Adaptive Neuro-Fuzzy Inference System (CANFIS) to predict optimal investment strategies based on a range of investor characteristics, including demographics, decision-making patterns, personality traits, financial situation, and past experiences. The integration of K-Means and Self-Organizing Maps (SOM) for data clustering enhances prediction accuracy compared to using K-Means alone. By applying XAI to survey data, the system uncovers hidden patterns in investor behavior and adapts its recommendations according to expert and investor feedback, allowing flexibility in dynamic market environments. With an average testing error of 0.75675, the system demonstrates high accuracy and can provide predictions even when data is incomplete. This adaptability makes it suitable for personalized investment guidance, helping investors make more informed decisions aligned with their unique profiles. The research emphasizes the system's ability to handle large volumes of categorized data and improve decision-making through AI-driven insights. It contributes to the field of behavioral finance by offering a human-centric and adaptable solution for personalized investment services, showcasing the potential of AI to transform financial advisory systems.

KEYWORDS

Neuro-Fuzzy Inference System, Investment Recommender System, Personalized Investment Strategies, Financial Decision Support

1. INTRODUCTION

Investment decision-making is complex, especially for individual investors, due to diverse financial goals, risk tolerances, and the abundance of investment options. Traditional one-size-fits-all investment recommendations are often inadequate. As a solution, this research proposes a personalized Investment Recommender System using an Adaptive Neuro-Fuzzy Inference System (ANFIS), integrated with K-Means and Self-Organizing Maps (SOM). The system aims to provide customized investment advice by analyzing multiple factors, including demographics, decision-making behaviors, personality traits, financial status, experience, and managerial attributes. It incorporates expert knowledge and investor feedback to improve accuracy and adapt to changing conditions. The research focuses on developing a novel framework that: Personalizes investment strategies using neuro-fuzzy logic, Identifies key factors affecting recommender performance, integrates user feedback for ongoing improvement, Compares its effectiveness against traditional recommendation methods. Ultimately, the goal is to enhance investment outcomes for individual investors by offering a smart, adaptable, and data-driven decision support tool.

2. LITERATURE REVIEW

Traditional investment recommender systems lack personalization, adaptability to market dynamics, and user feedback integration. ANFIS addresses these gaps by modeling complex investor behaviors through a hybrid of neural networks and fuzzy logic. Its ability to incorporate diverse traits and evolving data makes it a robust tool for personalized financial recommendations, outperforming static models. One study by (Abraham et al., 2022) explore the use of a GA and random forest to predict stock trends, while (Aggarwal & Reddy, 2014) examine data clustering algorithms and their applications in stock prediction. Aksar and colleagues examine the relationship between cash holding and investment efficiency for financially distressed firms, and the moderating effect of corporate governance (Aksar et al., 2022). A study investigates the role of creative accounting in increasing the marketing of shares and profits in the Iraqi stock exchange (AL-Khafaji et al., 2022), and Andajani examines customer experience management in retailing (Andajani, 2015). Asemi and Ko propose a novel combined business recommender system model using customer investment service feedback (Asemi & Ko, 2025, Asemi & Ko, 2021), furthermore, a study applies an ANFIS to evaluate dysarthric automatic speech recognition systems (Asemi et al., 2019). Benkraiem et al. investigate the impact of economic policy uncertainty, investor protection, and excess cash on stock value in a cross-country comparison (Benkraiem et al., 2023). Birim et al. use an ANFIS-PSO method to estimate the return rate of blockchain financial products (Birim et al., 2022), and Chatterjee et al. propose an NLP and LSTM-based stock prediction and recommender system for KOSDAQ and KOSPI (Chatterjee et al., 2021). Chen reviews investment products (Chen, J., 2020), and Chen et al. study user perception of sentiment-integrated critiquing in recommender systems (L. Chen et al., 2019). Chen et al. propose a cluster-based mutual fund classification and price prediction system using machine learning for Robo-advisors (X. Chen et al., 2021), and D'lima and Khan use ANN and ANFIS to predict FOREX rates (D'lima & Khan, 2016). Davies et al. implement a type-2 fuzzy logic-based prediction system for the Nigerian stock exchange (Davies et al., 2022), and Ezhilarasi and Sashi Rekha propose a secure recommendation application for environment crops using big data analytics with a fuzzy framework (Ezhilarasi & Sashi Rekha, 2020). Faridniya and Faridnia provide a model for allocating resources and choosing investment types using Data Envelopment Analysis (Faridniya & Faridnia, 2019). Garbade discusses the differences between AI, machine learning, and deep learning (Garbade, 2021), and Gong and Li study the investment value and opportunity of renewable energies under the carbon trading system (Gong & Li, 2016). Halloumis examines the chain of the money cycle (Halloumis, 2022), and Han et al. provide an overview of data mining concepts and techniques (Han et al., 2012). Hernández et al. propose an investment recommender multi-agent system in financial technology (Hernández et al., 2019), and Huang et al. investigate neural network models for stock selection based on fundamental analysis (Huang et al., 2019). These studies provide a comprehensive examination of various aspects of stock prediction and investment efficiency, utilizing a range of methods and techniques including machine learning, artificial intelligence, and data analysis. Also, the literature suggests that NFS have the potential to provide personalized investment recommendations to individual investors and overcome the limitations of traditional recommender systems. However, more research is needed to further explore the use of NFS in investment decision-making and to evaluate their performance in comparison to traditional methods.

3. METHODOLOGY

The proposed ANFIS-based investment recommender system is a hybrid intelligent model that combines neural networks and fuzzy logic to deliver personalized investment recommendations. It utilizes a diverse dataset from Mendeley, encompassing investor demographics, decision-making factors, personality traits, financial conditions, experiences, and managerial traits. The system preprocesses this data, removing inconsistencies and normalizing formats—before using clustering techniques (via JMP) to organize input data for training. It is trained through both supervised and unsupervised learning, evaluated using performance metrics like accuracy and precision, and continuously improved through user feedback. This adaptive and data-driven approach allows the system to offer accurate, personalized, and evolving investment advice to individual investors.

4. PROPOSED SYSTEM FRAMEWORK & EXPERIMENTAL RESULTS

The proposed framework, illustrated in Figure 1, outlines a comprehensive and adaptive Investment Recommender System that integrates multiple intelligent components across three core layers: data collection, data analysis, and decision-making.

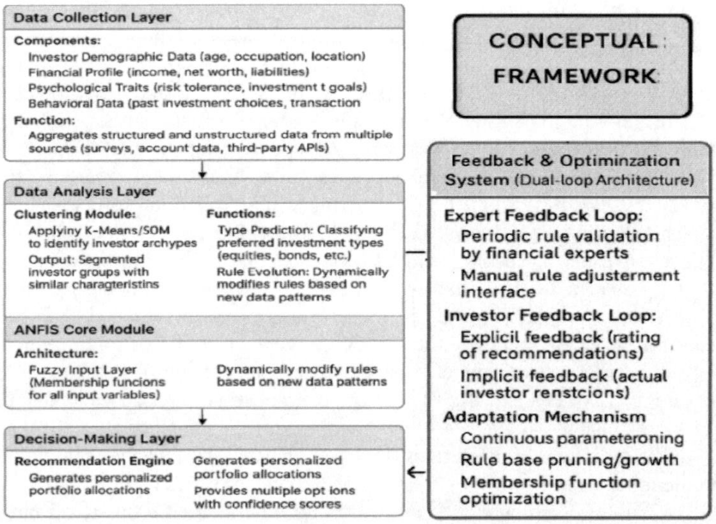

Figure 1. A framework of the combined Investment Recommender system

4.1 Clustering Investment-Type Output

To develop the ANFIS system, the output was defined as the investment type/product. This output was chosen based on the research objectives and was determined using four questions in the questionnaire (pages 24-27). The data collected included four variables with 1542 respondents. Question 24 asked about the investment products used by the potential investors, with five options available: listed stock, mutual fund, voluntary pension fund, government securities, and other financial products. Respondents were able to select multiple options, resulting in 31 categories being created based on the multiple choices. Question 25 asked if the respondents had made any stock market investments in the last 3 years, with options of "Yes" or "No." Question 26 asked if the respondents regularly monitored or followed the performance of their stock investments, with options of "Yes" or "No." Question 27 asked if the respondents had any government bond investments, with options of "Yes" or "No." These questions and data were used as a sample to propose the system, and companies can adapt the questions based on their objectives. K-Means clustering, implemented in JMP, was used to group 1,542 investment-type records into three clusters, optimized via the Cubic Cluster Criterion (CCC). Dimensionality reduction revealed key variance components, with principal components aiding cluster visualization. To validate scalability, simulated data (n=10,000) confirmed the method's robustness for large datasets, supporting its integration into ANFIS for accurate investment-type prediction. A new data table was constructed with the simulated investment-type data, utilizing the estimated mixing probabilities, means, and standard deviations for each cluster obtained from the clustering process. This table was used to analyze the performance of the clustering method and its ability to accurately group the data into distinct clusters.

4.2 Inputs for the Combined Recommender ANFIS

In proposing the system, six categories of data were used as inputs for the ANFIS including "respondents' demographics," "key factors in investment decision-making by respondents," "personality traits, knowledge and ability of the respondents," "respondent's experiences," "respondents' financial situation," and "managerial traits of the respondents." Table 1 shows the different inputs used in the ANFIS system, as well as a brief description of each input. JMP software was utilized to cluster each category of data and create inputs for the ANFIS system by utilizing K-Means and SOM methods. As per JMP documentation (2023), SOM is a technique developed by Kohonen (Kohonen, 1990) and further extended by several other neural network enthusiasts and statisticians. In this study, the combined method of K-Means and SOM was used for clustering demographic data, as it was found that this method resulted in better outcomes compared to using K-Means alone.

Table 1. Brief description of inputs for Combined ANFIS

Inputs	Description
Demographics	Age, Gender, Education level, Income, Occupation
Decision-making Factors	Risk tolerance, Goals, Time horizon, Investment knowledge
Personality Traits	Extraversion, Agreeableness, Conscientiousness, Neuroticism, Openness
Experiences	Investment history, Financial literacy
Financial Situation	Net worth, Debt, Savings
Managerial Traits	Leadership, Decision-making, Strategic thinking

SOM, an unsupervised ANN-based clustering method, map high-dimensional data onto a 2D grid for better visualization. Combined with K-Means in JMP, SOM refines cluster centers iteratively via expectation-maximization. The optimal number of clusters is determined using the Cubic Clustering Criterion (CCC), ensuring compact and well-separated clusters. The performance of the CCC is evaluated by Monte Carlo methods (Chow et al., 2003). In the initial step of clustering data for inputs of the ANFIS, six sets of data from 1542 respondents were imported into JMP software. Each set consisted of four columns containing various information, such as respondents' demographics, key factors in investment decision-making, personality traits, experiences, financial situation, and managerial traits. The data was then prepared for clustering using the K-Means and SOM methods in JMP. The rows were grouped into a specific number of clusters based on numeric variables, such as safety, excess money, computational awareness, investment fund, saving factors, and accounting knowledge. The number of clusters was determined using the CCC in JMP. The next steps of the process are explained in the following sections.

4.2.1 Clustering Input Demographics Data

Demographic data—based on variables like age, gender, education, and income—was clustered into three groups using a combined K-Means and SOM approach in JMP. Despite some feature overlapping, SOM enabled clearer differentiation. A parallel coordinate plot visualized cluster patterns, and validation with simulated data confirmed the method's effectiveness for large-scale demographic segmentation. Demographic data were simulated with 10,000 samples and clustered into three groups using K-Means in JMP, guided by the CCC. The clusters included 1,999, 3,126, and 4,875 observations, respectively. Cluster characteristics were detailed through means and standard deviations, confirming clear segmentation and successful application of the iterative clustering process in 19 steps.

4.2.2 Clustering Input Decision Key Factors Data

Decision key factor data were clustered into three groups using K-Means in JMP over 8 steps, resulting in cluster sizes of 449, 712, and 343. Principal component biplots (PC1–PC2, PC1–PC3, PC1–PC4) showed partial overlap between clusters. A simulation with 10,000 samples validated the method across 18 steps, yielding clusters of 2,323, 3,328, and 4,349. Means and standard deviations were calculated for each group to characterize cluster properties.

4.2.3 Clustering Input Personality Traits Data

Personality traits were clustered using K-Means and SOM, resulting in three clusters (370, 637, 471). The results show that regression lines and confidence intervals. A simulated dataset (n=10,000) validated the clustering, yielding three clusters (1238, 7436, 1326) after 18 steps.

4.2.4 Clustering Input Experiences Data

Experiences data was clustered using K-Means and SOM, yielding three clusters (514, 669, 320). The results show the clustering results. The scatterplot matrix displays relationships between variables within the clusters, with confidence ellipses indicating the uncertainty around the mean. Simulations at a scale of 10,000 optimized the clusters.

4.2.5 Clustering Input Financial Data

K-Means and SOM clustered financial data into three groups (309, 807, 421). The results show relationships between variables. Simulations (n=10,000) validated the clustering, resulting in three clusters (1544, 4866, 3590).

4.2.6 Clustering Input Managerial Traits Data

K-Means and SOM clustered "managerial traits" into three groups (289, 767, 461). Simulated managerial traits data (n=10,000) was used to evaluate clustering performance. The results show the cluster mixing probabilities, means, and standard deviations. K-Means clustering resulted in three clusters (3895, 4215, 1890) after 41 steps.

5. PROPOSING THE COMBINED ANFIS

CANFIS uses "IF_THEN" rules based on MFs, with six inputs and one output, each having three triangular MFs. MATLAB's fuzzy logic toolbox was used for data processing, involving six steps. The FIS, named CANFIS, contains 1542 data points. Trained with a hybrid method (3 epochs, error ~0.76), the network has 1503 nodes, 729 linear, 54 nonlinear, and 783 total parameters, using 729 fuzzy rules. The EM algorithm-based training completed in the second epoch (RMSE 0.756752). Testing results are with average error 0.75675. The Sugeno-type "CANFISRules" (version 2.0) utilizes product, probabilistic sum, and weighted average methods. Six inputs (range [0, 3]) have three triangular MFs each, and the output (range [0, 3]) has 729 constant MFs. There are 729 accessible rules and 101 plot points, adjustable based on feedback. Figure 2 illustrates the CANFIS model structure with inputs, MFs, layers, and output for investment type selection, using demographics, decision-making factors, personality traits, experiences, financial situations, and managerial traits as inputs.

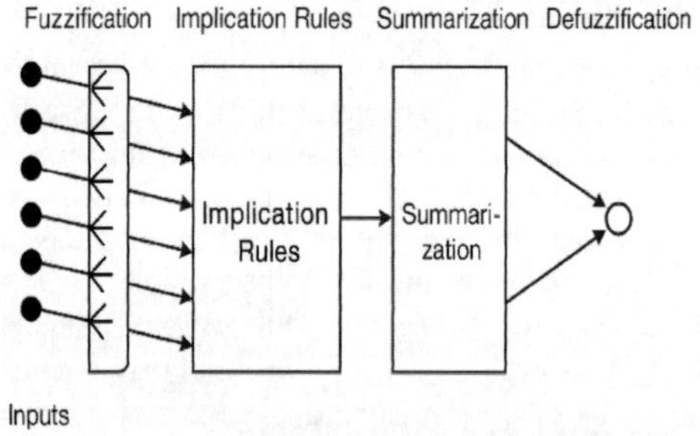

Figure 2. CANFIS Model Structure

The MFs are used to assign a degree of membership to each input, which allows the system to handle the uncertainty and vagueness of the data. The model shows the different layers of the ANFIS, which include fuzzification, implication rules, normalization, defuzzification, and integration. Fuzzification is the process of converting crisp inputs into fuzzy sets. Implication rules are used to link the inputs to the output. Normalization is the process of adjusting the output to ensure that it falls within a specific range. Defuzzification is the process of converting the fuzzy output into a crisp value. Integration or aggregated output membership function is the final step of the ANFIS, where the output is produced, and it's a recommendation to the investors to select an investment type based on the clusters.

6. INCORPORATION OF EXPERT KNOWLEDGE AND INVESTORS' FEEDBACK

Incorporating expert knowledge and investor feedback is crucial for the Combined Investment Recommender system. It allows tailoring the system to specific needs by adding, changing, or deleting ANFIS-generated rules. Expert knowledge improves accuracy with additional market insights, while investor feedback aligns recommendations with preferences. This iterative process updates the system, enhancing transparency, understandability, and reliability. Addressing ethical concerns, it ensures socially responsible decisions through inclusive feedback mechanisms.

7. DISCUSSION

CANFIS was proposed to predict investment using investor data (demographics, decision-making factors, etc.). The study aimed to improve prediction accuracy by clustering data with K-Means and SOM in JMP, which proved more effective than K-Means alone. SOM maps data to a 2D space for visualization. The clustering process involved the EM algorithm and CCC for cluster number selection. Clustered data was then used as input for the ANFIS system. Evaluation using RMSE and average testing error showed improved accuracy with clustered inputs. The system generated 729 rules and had a 0.75675 average testing error.

Table 2. Innovations of the Proposed Combined System

Innovation	Description
Combination of K-Means and SOM	The proposed system utilizes a combination of K-Means and SOM for clustering data, which results in better outcomes compared to using K-Means alone.
Multi-Criteria Decision Making	The proposed system uses six different criteria to predict investment type, including demographics, decision-making factors, personality traits, experiences, financial situation, and managerial traits.
Flexible and Adaptive	The proposed system is flexible and can be adjusted based on experts' and investors' feedback, making it more adaptable to changing market conditions.
High-performance	The proposed system has been tested and showed a high performance in terms of accuracy, with an average testing error of 0.75675.
Comprehensive Output	The proposed system provides a comprehensive output as a recommendation to the investors to select an investment type based on the clusters.
Working with Incomplete Data	The proposed system can work with incomplete data and still provide accurate predictions.
Potential Investors	The proposed system can be used by potential investors to make more informed investment decisions based on their characteristics and experience.
Clustering for Input and Output	The proposed system utilizes clustering for both input and output data, which allows for the handling of a high number of categorized data and increases accuracy. Clustering allows the system to group similar data points, making it easier to analyze and make predictions based on that data. This improves the overall performance and accuracy of the system.

Previous studies have also utilized ANFIS for investment prediction, such as the work by Wang et al. (2022) which proposed an ANFIS model for stock market prediction, and the research by Huang et al. (2019) which used ANFIS for predicting stock prices of real estate investment trusts. However, these studies have not specifically focused on predicting the investment type based on a combination of inputs including demographic, decision key factors, personality traits, experiences, and financial and managerial traits as this study does. Additionally, the research by Birim et al. (2022) proposed an ANFIS-based model for stock price prediction, and they used a GA to optimize the system's parameters. This research also provides a similar approach to this study, but they only focused on stock price prediction, and not on investment type prediction. According to a study conducted by Chen (2020) and Sulistiyo & Mahpudin, (2020), they proposed an ANFIS-based approach to predict the investment type of investors by considering the investor's demographic characteristics, investment behavior, and investment preferences. The study found that the ANFIS-based approach had better performance compared to traditional methods such as decision trees and logistic regression. Similarly, a study by Sharma et al. (2022) proposed a hybrid system that combines ANFIS and particle swarm optimization (PSO) for predicting investment type. The study found that the hybrid system had better performance compared to ANFIS alone and other traditional methods such as support vector machines and artificial neural networks. A study by Kim et al. Abraham et al. (2022) proposed a hybrid system that combines ANFIS and GA for predicting investment type. This research contributes by using CANFIS and clustering to improve prediction accuracy (729 rules, 0.75675 testing error). Limitations include sample size and lack of dynamic market consideration. Future research should explore larger samples, advanced clustering, real-world data, and comparisons with other models like ANNs and SVMs. Table 2 shows the innovations of the Proposed Combined System.

8. CONCLUSION

This research proposed a CANFIS-based recommender system to predict investment types based on investor characteristics. The system used six data categories, clustered with K-Means and SOM in JMP. The ANFIS model, developed from the clustered data, included MFs, layers, and an output for investment recommendations. Evaluation showed strong performance (0.75675 average testing error) and generated 729 rules. The system assists investors and experts in making informed investment decisions.

REFERENCES

Abraham, R., Samad, M. E., Bakhach, A. M., El-Chaarani, H., Sardouk, A., Nemar, S. E., & Jaber, D. (2022). Forecasting a Stock Trend Using Genetic Algorithm and Random Forest. *Journal of Risk and Financial Management*, *15*(5), Article 5. https://doi.org/10.3390/jrfm15050188

Aggarwal. Ch.C. & Reddy, Ch.K. (2014). *Data Clustering: Algorithms and Applications*. CRC Press, Taylor & Francis Group. http://charuaggarwal.net/clusterbook.pdf

Aksar, M., Hassan, S., Kayani, M. B., Khan, S., & Ahmed, T. (2022). Cash holding and investment efficiency nexus for financially distressed firms: The moderating role of corporate governance. *Management Science Letters*, *12*(1), 67–74. https://doi.org/10.5267/j.msl.2021.7.001

AL-Khafaji, A. A. K., Mustangs, R. F., & Alsaalim, F. H. A. J. (2022). The role of creative accounting in increasing the marketing of shares and their profits in the Iraqi stock exchange. *Periodicals of Engineering and Natural Sciences*, *10*(2), 323–335. Scopus. https://doi.org/10.21533/pen.v10i2.2886

Andajani, E. (2015). Understanding Customer Experience Management in Retailing. *Procedia - Social and Behavioral Sciences*, *211*, 629–633. https://doi.org/10.1016/j.sbspro.2015.11.082

Asemi, A. (2023). *Data for "Customizing Investment Recommendations Using ANFIS and Potential Investor's Financial Situation in Retail Banking"—Mendeley Data*. https://data.mendeley.com/drafts/n2j64ktpc6

Asemi, A. (2023). Data for "Investment Intelligence: A Combined Neuro-Fuzzy Inference-Based Recommender System for Personalized Investment Strategies." 1. https://doi.org/10.17632/fh2zsdmrdz.1

Asemi, A., Asemi, A., & Kő, A. (2024). A model for investment type recommender system based on the potential investors using investors and experts feedback with ANFIS and MNN. Journal of Big Data, 11(1), 128. https://doi.org/10.1186/s40537-024-00965-y

Asemi, A., & Ko, A. (2021). A Novel Combined Business Recommender System model Using Customer Investment Service Feedback. 34th Bled conference Digital Support from Crisis to Progressive Change: Conference Proceedings, 223–237. https://doi.org/10.18690/978-961-286-485-9.17

Asemi, A., Salim, S. S. B., Shahamiri, S. R., Asemi, A., & Houshangi, N. (2019). Adaptive neuro-fuzzy inference system for evaluating dysarthric automatic speech recognition (ASR) systems. SOFT COMPUTING, 23, 3529–3544. https://doi.org/10.1007/s00500-018-3013-4

Benkraiem, R., Gaaya, S., Lakhal, F., & Lakhal, N. (2023). Economic policy uncertainty, investor protection, and the value of excess cash: A cross-country comparison. Finance Research Letters, 52, 103572. https://doi.org/10.1016/j.frl.2022.103572

Birim, Ş. Ö., Sönmez, F. E., & Liman, Y. S. (2022). Estimating Return Rate of Blockchain Financial Product by ANFIS-PSO Method. Lecture Notes in Networks and Systems, 504 LNNS, 802–809. Scopus. https://doi.org/10.1007/978-3-031-09173-5_92

Chatterjee, I., Gwan, J., Kim, Y. J., Lee, M. S., & Cho, M. (2021). An NLP and LSTM-Based Stock Prediction and Recommender System for KOSDAQ and KOSPI. In M. Singh, D. K. Kang, J. H. Lee, U. S. Tiwary, D. Singh, & W. Y. Chung (Eds.), Intelligent Human Computer Interaction, Pt I (Vol. 12615, pp. 403–413). Springer International Publishing Ag. https://doi.org/10.1007/978-3-030-68449-5_40

Chen, J. (2020). Investment Product. Reviewed by Godon Scott, Investopedia.Com. https://www.investopedia.com/terms/i/investment-product.asp

Chen, L., Yan, D., & Wang, F. (2019). User perception of sentiment-integrated critiquing in recommender systems. International Journal of Human-Computer Studies, 121, 4–20. https://doi.org/10.1016/j.ijhcs.2017.09.005

Chen, X., Ye, S., & Huang, C. (2021). Cluster-Based Mutual Fund Classification and Price Prediction Using Machine Learning for Robo-Advisors. Computational Intelligence and Neuroscience, 2021, e4984265. https://doi.org/10.1155/2021/4984265

Chow, J. C. L., Wong, E., Chen, J. Z., & Van Dyk, J. (2003). Comparison of dose calculation algorithms with Monte Carlo methods for photon arcs. Medical Physics, 30(10), 2686–2694. https://doi.org/10.1118/1.1601331

Davies, I. N., Ene, D., Cookey, I. B., & Lenu, G. F. (n.d.). Implementation of a Type-2 Fuzzy Logic-Based Prediction System for the Nigerian Stock Exchange.

D'lima, N., & Khan, S. (2016). FOREX rate prediction using ANN and ANFIS Conference. https://www.semanticscholar.org/paper/FOREX-rate-prediction-using-ANN-and-ANFIS-D%27lima-Khan/6817d1cc9f7ac35cf28404f0e17e358b54fa16d1

Ezhilarasi, T. P., & Sashi Rekha, K. (2020). Secure recommendation application for environment crop using big data analytics with the fuzzy framework. Journal of Green Engineering, 10(4), 1799–1815. Scopus.

Faridniya, A., & Faridnia, M. (2019). Providing a model for allocating resources and choosing investment type using Data Envelopment Analysis (DEA) (Case Study: Social Security Organization). Journal of Advanced Pharmacy Education & Research, 9(S2), 112–124. https://japer.in/storage/models/article/et0pIWClvo41b1Rk0kK0g25dwiwg85RgsRsGFGDgP80KldRAN33ipHhEd1Rc/providing-a-model-for-allocating-resources-and-choosing-investment-type-using-data-envelopment-ana.pdf

Garbade, D. M. J. (2021, April 19). Clearing the Confusion: AI vs Machine Learning vs Deep Learning Differences. Medium. https://towardsdatascience.com/clearing-the-confusion-ai-vs-machine-learning-vs-deep-learning-differences-fce69b21d5eb

Gong, P., & Li, X. (2016). Study on the investment value and investment opportunity of renewable energies under the carbon trading system. Chinese Journal of Population Resources and Environment, 14(4), 271–281. https://doi.org/10.1080/10042857.2016.1258796

Halloumis, C. (2022). Chain of cycle of money (SSRN Scholarly Paper No. 4073947). https://papers.ssrn.com/abstract=4073947

Han, J., Kamber, M., & Pei, J. (2012). Data Mining: Concepts and Techniques (3rd ed.). Elsevier. https://myweb.sabanciuniv.edu/rdehkharghani/files/2016/02/The-Morgan-Kaufmann-Series-in-Data-Management-Systems-Jiawei-Han-Micheline-Kamber-Jian-Pei-Data-Mining.-Concepts-and-Techniques-3rd-Edition-Morgan-Kaufmann-2011.pdf

Hernández, E., Sittón, I., Rodríguez, S., Gil, A. B., & García, R. J. (2019). An Investment Recommender Multi-agent System in Financial Technology. Advances in Intelligent Systems and Computing, 771, 3–10. Scopus. https://doi.org/10.1007/978-3-319-94120-2_1

Huang, Y., Capretz, L. F., & Ho, D. (2019). Neural Network Models for Stock Selection Based on Fundamental Analysis. 2019 IEEE Canadian Conference of Electrical and Computer Engineering (CCECE), 1–4. https://doi.org/10.1109/CCECE.2019.8861550

JMP Documentation. (2023). Data Analysis Software. https://www.jmp.com/en_us/software/data-analysis-software.html

Kérdőív. (n.d.). Retrieved January 23, 2023, from http://www.portfolio.hu/befektetesi-kerdoiv/

Kohonen, Teuvo. (1990). The Self-Organizing Map. Proceedings of the IEEE, 78(9). https://sci2s.ugr.es/keel/pdf/algorithm/articulo/1990-Kohonen-PIEEE.pdf

Sharma, S., Rana, V., & Malhotra, M. (2022). Automatic recommendation system based on hybrid filtering algorithm. *Education and Information Technologies*, *27*(2), 1523–1538. https://doi.org/10.1007/s10639-021-10643-8

Sulistiyo, H., & Mahpudin, E. (2020). Demographic analysis for the selection of an investment type for amateur golfers. In *Advances in Business, Management, and Entrepreneurship*. CRC Press.

Wang, X., Chen, Y., Jin, J., & Zhang, B. (2022). Fuzzy-clustering and fuzzy network-based interpretable fuzzy model for prediction. *Scientific Reports*, *12*(1), Article 1. https://doi.org/10.1038/s41598-022-20015-y

THE CHARACTERISTICS OF AGENDA SETTING ON ONLINE MEDIA IN MONGOLIA

Bolormaa Battsogt[1] and Dagiimaa Davaadorj[2]

[1]*Ph.D, Media Consultant, Media Council of Mongolia*

[2]*Professor in Department of Journalism and Media Technology, University of the Humanities*

Ulaanbaatar, Mongolia

ABSTRACT

The agenda-setting function of the media is based on the hypothesis that issues they emphasize "media agenda" become important issues for people "public agenda". Until now, research on agenda-setting functions has focused primarily on mass media, such as newspapers and television. However, in recent years, while the influence of mass media on public opinion has declined, the influence of Internet media has increased. Therefore, the purpose of this paper is to clarify the characteristics of media agendas in local online media by comparing them with local newspapers. The session 2 presents the basic research results, such as the status of news distribution and publications on local online media. Then the study shows the extent to which political articles published on the front pages of local newspapers, and we examine the degree of congruence between issues therein. Then, we clarify the distribution and publication status of political-related detailed reports published in each newspaper affiliated with local online media. We also examine the status of attribute agendas on local online media. The final session summarizes the overall discussion, discusses the possible effects of media agenda characteristics on local online media, and states the challenges of this research.

KEYWORDS

Local Online Media, Local Newspapers, Agenda-setting, Local Citizen

1. INTRODUCTION

In recent years, while the influence of mass media on public opinion has declined, the influence of Internet media has increased. Since the early 2000s, as the number of Internet media users has increased, the influence of Internet media on public opinion has also increased to a point that cannot be ignored. The level of influence has surpassed that of newspapers and television, particularly among young people. Furthermore, with the rapid changes in the media contact environment, research on the influence of Internet media on public opinion and political knowledge has been actively conducted in recent years. Many researchers have indicated that the use of Internet news increases political knowledge and interest. Additionally, the influence of Internet media extends to various aspects, the most important of which is its influence on Cabinet approval ratings and public opinion during elections. Conversely, people obtain news information about major incidents and accidents, as well as major political and economic news, from newspapers, television, and other media. Newspapers and Internet media may have different agenda-setting functions. The agenda-setting function of the media is based on the hypothesis that the issues they emphasize (media agenda) become important issues for people (public agenda). Until now, research on agenda-setting functions has focused primarily on mass media, such as newspapers and television. Many studies have been conducted on the differences in the news information disseminated by national and local newspapers. Based on these considerations, this study addresses the characteristics of news content in local online media from the perspective of agenda-setting functions by comparing them to those of local newspapers.

2. DIVERSE DEFINITIONS AND PROBLEMS OF THE FRAME CONCEPT

Nelson and Willey (2001) have classified the term "frame" in political communication research into four types. The first, "collective action frame," is proposed by sociologists. It concerns strategies for mobilizing support in social movements (Gamson 1992). The second is "decision frames"; psychologists have shown that by subtly changing the wording of tasks used in experiments, the judgments of experimental participants can be significantly changed (Tversky and Kahneman 1981) because human judgment is influenced not by objective facts but by their interpretation. The third type, "news frame," relates to how news media frame messages, and the fourth type relates to the perspective from which a particular issue is reported. The third and fourth news frames are closely related to the framing effect of the media. A typical example of a news frame is the "game" or "substantive" frame in election and political reporting. Such frames include the content frame (Patterson 1980), strategic versus issue frame (Cappella and Jamieson 1997), and episode versus theme frame in social reporting (Iyengar 1994). The studies state that news frames stem from media coverage practices and commercial needs and can be found across a specific genre of reporting. News frames specialize in specific issues, such as abortion, and frame carriers include policymakers, interest group spokespersons, and think tank researchers rather than the media. The research of Nelson and Willey (2001) belongs to the fourth lineage, although the media include editorials, commentaries, and analyses. In some cases, people actively participate in framing issues through articles.

Regarding framing effects, research on the third news frame has the following limitations. First, by relying on approximately binary frames, oversimplifying the portrayal of the news is a possible risk. The danger of oversimplifying the portrayal of the news involves the effect formation process and if the receiver perceives it using a frame that corresponds to that of the media. In many cases, news frames are directly linked to follow-on effects (e.g., perceived responsibility for social issues), thereby bypassing the actual issue. Conversely, research on the fourth issue frame highlights the difficulty in generalizing the role of the media in reporting on issues. Constructing an issue frame model that is "universal" is important; several attempts have been made to do so. Newman have provided an example with the five-item "utilitarianism," "conflict," "feelings of helplessness," "human influence," and "morality" frame model proposed by Neuman et al. (1992). Newman conducted in-depth interviews with over 40 citizens from 1987 to 1988 and determined how five public issues (apartheid, the Star Wars Initiative, the 1987 stock market crash, and drug abuse) were interpreted. We identified several central frames that appeared when interpreting an issue. However, even within a relatively prominent set of frames, questions remain regarding systematicity and comprehensiveness.

3. RESEARCH PERSPECTIVE: "ISSUE-BASED" AND "ATTRIBUTE-BASED"

Various viewpoints have been presented in research on agenda-setting functions. However, herein, we divide the media agenda into two categories "issue-based" and "attribute-based issues" and investigate the state of news coverage for each.

The agenda-setting hypotheses include first-level agenda-setting (issue-based agenda-setting) and second-level agenda-setting (attribute-based agenda-setting) with the corresponding media agendas for each. In first-level agenda-setting, economic issues and political reform become public agenda items depending on the degree of emphasis (prominence) in the media. Attribute agendas in second-level agenda-setting refer to issues located below the issue agenda. For example, when economic issues are on the agenda, other aspects are included, such as "employment" and "pension issues." Thus, we have an attribute agenda, and, like the issue agenda, it becomes a public agenda depending on the degree of emphasis from the media (Takeshita 2008, 213). Furthermore, this emphasis on attribute issues is not only related to people's cognition; it can also influence their opinions and attitudes. McCombs (2014, 134) argues that "the various aspects of an issue that the media present – and that is the media's attribution agenda – shape our views and opinions about that issue." This agenda-setting function in which attribute agendas influence opinions and attitudes is also called "emotional attribute-based agenda setting" (Takeshita 2008, 277). The agenda-setting function, traditionally discussed regarding its influence on cognition, includes its influence on opinions and attitudes. Ishikawa's (2004) research is well-known for examining the influence of media coverage on attitudes. Ishikawa investigated the tone of three local newspapers and the opinions of their subscribers regarding constitutional amendments, arguing that the tone of the newspapers to which they subscribed influenced their opinions. Ishikawa called this outcome "parroting." Saito et al. (2014), who elaborated on Ishikawa's research, found that when readers were highly interested in the nuclear power issue, a relationship was observed between the tone of the newspaper to which they subscribed and their attitudes, even after controlling for reader attributes.

Newspaper articles consist of the main story and detailed information (side articles that convey the background of the news and voices of those involved, as well as the essential causes and social impact). They can be broadly divided into two categories. The content of the main story is the same in all newspapers; however, the tone is different, and detailed reports are included. Generally, for big news published on the front page of a newspaper, the main story is published on the first page, followed by detailed information in the general and social sections. Thus, the main story on the front page is the issue topic, which is related to the recognition of the issue, and detailed information, such as the comprehensive section, is the attribute topic, which influences opinions and attitudes. Regarding research related to this point, Ogawa (2001) conducted an experimental survey in Japan and found that news that conveys specific advantages and disadvantages of an event is better than news that only conveys the facts of the event. Reports indicate that this approach increases interest in each subject. Although differences in interests and opinions exist, the idea and direction of attribute-based agenda-setting are consistent in that detailed information has a significant impact.

Based on the above research, in this study, we investigate the media agenda on two levels: issue and attribute agendas. Thereafter, we determine if a quantitative difference between online media and local newspapers can be identified regarding the coverage of controversial news and what differences exist between online media and local newspapers in reporting news that can be considered attribute topics.

4. ANALYSIS OF NEWS CONTENT

Four local online media outlets and newspapers were surveyed. Various studies have shown that it is the most popular online media platform, surpassing newspaper news sites. In 2021, 24 local newspapers were published in Mongolia. We selected two newspapers published every 10–14 days and two monthly newspapers (Table 1). The survey was conducted in January 2022. The number of topics to be investigated did not require a survey lasting several days. Sufficient comparison could not be made possibly because the analysis target was anticipated to be considerably large, making a detailed analysis difficult.

Table 1. The selected local newspaper

Province	Umnugovi	Selenge	Sukhbaatar	Bulgan
Name of newspaper	"Goviin medee"	"Selengiin Medee"	"Sykhbaatariin Ungu"	"Bulganii Medee"
Year of establishment	1945	2002	2014	2003
Price per issue	1000	2500	800	1000
Total Sales (2020)	6000	-	18000	24000
Number of issues per month	1	1	3	2
Number of pages	12	4	4	4

In this section, based on the results of a survey of the front-page articles in four national newspapers and the "main" articles in local online media platforms, we will examine the degree of congruence in the contentious agendas of the two. From this section onward, the analyzed articles will be limited to those related to politics. This is because the articles that appear on the front pages of newspapers cover a wide range of topics, including economics and society, in addition to politics, and it is complicated to research all of them. Agenda-setting research often focuses on politically related topics because such topics significantly impact public opinion. Therefore, our analysis is limited to articles related to politics; in this survey, we include all news related to central government politics. Consequently, the subjects of the analysis included the administration and diplomacy of the government and central ministries, legislation in the Diet, trends of politicians, and court cases related to the country.

Here, we will compare and examine the extent to which political articles published on the front page of newspapers are published in the "main" section. When published in the "main" section, the name of the media is listed. The "Local online media headlines" column lists the headlines published in the "main" section. In the "Number of articles published" and "Total number of articles published" columns, the number of articles published in the "Main" section and the total number of articles published are recorded.

First, looking at the coverage status of local online media by topic, including cases where articles distributed by media other than newspapers were published, many of the topics that appeared on the front page of newspapers were published in the "main" section. We observed that the three articles that the four newspapers published on their front pages were published in the "main" category. The 10 articles published on the front page of a few newspapers were listed as "main", except for "marine plastic waste." Of the 17 articles that only one newspaper published on the front page, nine were published in the "main" section. In this way, the more newspapers a topic appears on the front page of, the more likely the topic is to be published in the "main" section.

Second, in local online media, the number of articles published is an indicator of the degree of emphasis on an issue. Therefore, we compared the number of front-page publications and the number of "main" articles; however, we found no relationship between the two. For example, the "forced sterilization verdict" was published on the front page of the morning editions of four newspapers and was listed as a "main" article five times. It cannot be said that the numerous publications have a clear relationship with the number of "main" publications. Considering these details, while there are some discrepancies between newspapers and local online media, the majority of political topics that appear on the front pages of multiple newspapers also appear on the "Main" page. It can be said that the main controversial topics in newspapers are also covered by local online media.

We have examined the status of coverage of topics published on the front page of newspapers in "main" local online media. However, in addition to the articles published on the front page of newspapers, the "main" section also contains many political news items. Unless this factor is considered, it cannot be said that the degree of congruence between the issues at stake in newspapers and local online media is sufficiently clear. Therefore, we will examine the publication status of "unique" political news in local online media, that is, it is not published on the front page of newspapers. The total number of "original" news articles and the total number of articles published is 28, which becomes 23 after excluding late-night articles. Conversely, as shown previously, the number of articles published on the front page of the newspaper and in the "Main" section (hereinafter referred to as "Page 1 = Main" articles) was 49, which decreased to 44 after excluding late-night articles. Comparing "original" articles and "Page 1 = main" articles, the latter exceeds the number of "original" articles by almost twice. From this alone, it appears that local online media accorded the same importance to the newspaper's front-page stories as the newspaper did.

The publication status of the "Page 1 = main" article was almost the same as that of the "original" articles. This trend is the same for each topic. As shown previously, the total number of articles posted regarding "forced sterilization sentence" was 5, and that of the most "original" item, "Remarks on war" by a lawmaker, was 6, which was almost the same number of articles posted. Furthermore, when comparing news published in the "main" category, the position of the headline can help determine the degree of emphasis in local online media.

On the "Main" screen, eight headings are displayed vertically; thus, the higher the headings, the more emphasized they are. Comparing "Page 1 = Main" articles and "Original" articles, the number of "Page 1 = Main" articles exceeds the number of "Original" articles in the first heading; however, the number of "Original" articles in the second heading exceeds the number of "Page 1 = Main" articles. However, overall, "front page = main" articles tend to be published in higher positions. This point is also the same when comparing "forced sterilization verdict" and "lawmaker's 'war' remarks,"' which had almost the same total number of articles posted above. Thus, the "original" articles and "Page 1 = main" articles had almost the same number of publications. However, regarding the position of the headline, there was a tendency for "Page 1 = main" articles to be given slightly higher overall importance than the "original" articles.

This section examines political topics in newspapers and their local online media by comparing front pages with "mainstream" media. First, the main political topics that appeared on the front pages of newspapers were also published in local online media. Conversely, articles that did not appear on the front pages of newspapers were ranked slightly less important but appeared in similar numbers in the local online media. Thus, local online media published more controversial topics than newspapers, including articles that newspapers had not published on their front pages. Consequently, issues in local online media are more dispersed and less emphasized than those in newspapers.

5. ANALYSIS OF INFORMATION RECEIVED BY LOCAL CITIZENS

The survey included 238 citizens from 17 provinces in four regions of the country (except Ulaanbaatar). Google Forms were used for the survey. Local citizens such as teachers, doctors, herders, students, and students living in the main city of the economic zone, the provincial center, were randomly selected, and their opinions were obtained. In the "Regional Development Concept" approved by the Parliament in 2001, the territory of Mongolia was divided into five economic zones. Although an economic zone is not a strict administrative or territorial boundary, the main idea of the development concept is to establish economic zoning in Mongolia through which the regional economy is based on a unified and independent system of regional, urban, and rural development. It represents the formation of social complexes. In Mongolia, four economic zones have been established: western, eastern, central, and eastern. Ulaanbaatar has been developed according to the standards of independent regions. The general schedule of the provinces belonging to each economic zone has been set, and the schedule has been flexibly changed according to the current development situation.

Based on the concept of regional development, the research sample was classified into western, eastern, central, and eastern regions because this relates to how the current socioeconomic environment of citizens is related to receiving information. The sample structure of the participants regarding age was as follows: 22% were aged under 24 years, 27% were aged 25–34 years, 25% were aged 35–44 years, 13% were aged 45–54 years, and 17% were aged 55 years or older. For sex, 46% of the participants were male, and 54% were female.

Considering the local news offering information to local citizens by type, regardless of region, citizens typically obtain information using electronic platforms, such as news sites and Facebook pages (37%–47%), and television (28%–36%) (Figure 1). According to one survey, television was the most common source of information for citizens until 2013. Thereafter, the situation changed, and electronic platforms assumed a leading position. The use of electronic platforms has increased not only in Ulaanbaatar but also in rural areas, and it has been selectively used by local people, regardless of the infrastructure and industrial development of the region. People under the age of 34 years receive more information from news sites and social media. However, television is also important for people aged over 35 years. Additionally, people over the age of 45 years are more likely to use traditional media, such as newspapers and FM radio, as sources of information.

Given the increase in the number of television channels and the wide technical possibilities of receiving and transmitting not only broadcasts but also cable channels, citizens can now watch approximately 15–80 channels on television. Approximately 80% of the respondents answered that they watched local television, which was capable of meeting the needs of citizens. People over 45 years old watched it regularly, while those under 35 years answered that they "watch it occasionally because they change the channel by chance" or "because other family members watch it." The programs with the most views were mainly news programs, local portrait programs, and feature films, without distinguishing between the central and western regions. However, over 35-year-olds prioritized watching the news and regularly watched local social and event news and specially prepared programs.

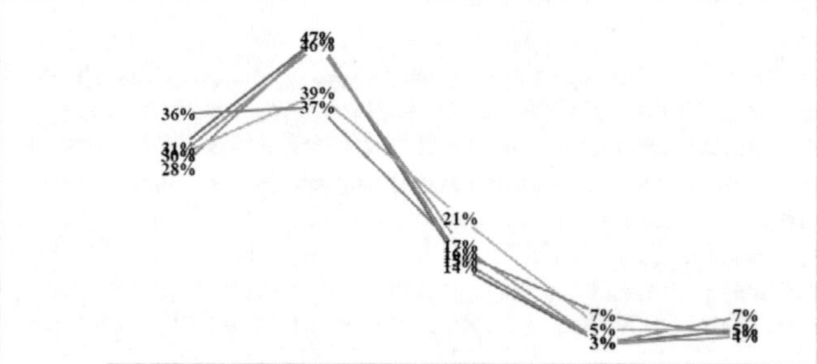

	TV	Online Platform	Newspaper	Radio	Other
~24	31%	47%	14%	3%	5%
25-34	28%	47%	15%	3%	7%
35-44	30%	46%	17%	3%	4%
45-54	30%	39%	21%	5%	5%
54~	36%	37%	16%	7%	4%

Figure 1. The local news offering information to local citizens by type

Additionally, less than 10% of the residents who watched their province's television on an online platform answered that they went to Facebook to view weather reports and advertisements. According to the responses stating that local television is not broadcast in the province, it can only be viewed in the center of the province, it is possible to improve the digital technology innovation of the Internet through free access to cable channels such as "DDesh TV" and "Univision" in the future. Citizens also responded that "it is good that they do not broadcast information such as black PR and election ads on local television." "They receive daily information regularly." It is important to perform the function of reporting, rather than watching television, as a watchdog.

As previously mentioned, the use of newspapers and magazines has been steadily declining since 2013, not only in the local area but also in Ulaanbaatar. Local newspapers have reduced their publication frequency; half of all newspapers (11 newspapers) are now published every 10–14 days. Less than 20% of the total age group reads newspapers; those under 25 in the central region do not read newspapers at all, while those over 35 in the western region read the most. People who read local newspapers reported that most of the news was about local events. Further, they said that they only read the paper by chance, rather than reading the newspaper on purpose: "I read it when I come across it" and "I often read it when ordered at the workplace."

The local FM radio was the least used media, with less than 1% of the total sample responding that they listened to it. However, people with low and middle levels of education were more likely to listen to the radio than people with a higher education level, and those aged 44 years and older predominantly listened to it. Most citizens who listen to the radio in one way or another answered that they "listen more during the day" and "listen a lot in the car." We received information about the types of programs they mainly listened to, such as the weather and other social topics. They also listened to music programs. There were no significant regional differences in the types of programs received from radio stations.

We studied how the local people classified local newspapers and the kind of information they expected from them (Figure 2). The citizens answered that they wanted to know more about sensational news on the unethical actions of the government and economic influencers of their province from news sites and electronic platforms, such as Facebook pages; however, they wanted to read news about the government, public organizations, and parties from newspapers. The citizens had high expectations of quality social news from local television and radio. Electronic platforms such as local news sites and Facebook pages can become media for citizens and help them read, watch, and wait for further information by monitoring the actions and decisions of the government, nongovernmental organizations (NGOs), and social institutions serving the public.

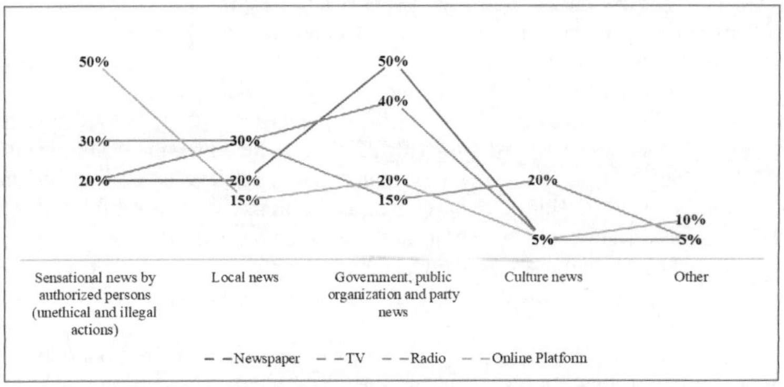

Figure 2. Citizens' expectations regarding access to local media

Up to this point, the differences between the types of local newspapers and the type of information received by local citizens are very similar to those presented in the studies of Press Institute (2021) which analyzed the national average. This is because the study sample included people with higher education, who could be considered to have a high level of media education. However, an important feature of local newspapers is that they cover all layers of the population, including viewers and readers, which should significantly impact the direction of information in the local newspapers. In Mongolia, the population includes herders, government employees, private sector workers, students of provinces, and people with higher and lower education, and a medium that serves the needs of all these social classes is required.

Therefore, based on the questionnaire responses of 43 citizens with low education levels in this area, television was the most commonly used medium. Approximately 86% of the respondents said that they watch local television because of "DDesh TV." As for television transmission, "DDesh TV" can transmit more than 130 domestic and foreign channels by satellite to all provinces, the center of Soum, and remote rural pastoral households. Rural herding households purchase televisions and antennas to match their analog receiver packages. Presently, it is possible to watch local TV channels of provinces other than Khovd, Bayan-Olgii, and Sukhbaatar provinces on "DDesh TV," which indicates that the source of information has been supported. As mentioned in the previous research on the content of news information by local newspaper, there is much to be developed in the content of television news (Battsogt 2023). In the future, it will be necessary to improve the quality of television by considering not only the provincial center but also the citizens of Soum as receivers, reflecting on the direction of information, increasing the type of information, and improving the quality of the information.

6. CONCLUSION

In this study, we compared news posted on websites with news printed in newspapers from the perspectives of issue-based issues and attribute-based issues. Two findings were obtained.

First, many political news items were posted on the homepage of the website, these items corresponding to newspaper front-page articles. However, these news items have not been reported to the public. Resultantly, compared with newspapers, the relationship between the issue topics and their recognition was dispersed on websites; therefore, the degree of emphasis on each issue was relatively weak. Second, many of the articles distributed by newspaper companies to their websites were the same as their physical articles. The websites offered substantially less detailed information, which could influence the opinions and attitudes of readers as an attribute topic. Compared with newspapers, websites have far less information that can be used to determine what the current issue is (issue-based) and why it is an issue (attribute issues).

Although the survey period was only one month, the results obtained were somewhat generalizable. If the media agenda on a website has the above characteristics, how will the public agenda be affected by this? Examining this requires a survey of website users, which is beyond the scope of this study. Here, we present a hypothetical statement referring to the findings of previous research.

As shown in this article, the homepage of a website contains more political news than the front page of a newspaper. Kobayashi (2011) points out that the use of internet news increases "political knowledge"; however, the abundance of such news in internet media may also be related.

However, it is possible that "political knowledge" may negatively affect "political interest." Related to this point, Kobayashi (2011) shows that "soft knowledge," such as the scandals of politicians, negatively affects voter turnout among young people. In the news examined in this article, the "war" remark made by a lawmaker is an example of soft knowledge. This news was not reported on the front page of the newspaper; however, the website posted it under "Main" on the homepage. In other words, when opportunities to increase soft knowledge through online media increase, political cynicism among young people may also increase.

Additionally, mass media is said to adopt "strategic neutrality" (Ikeda 2010, 277). However, mass media is not neutral, and the opinions presented in the news vary. The tone of the argument is more pronounced in detailed reports than in the main articles; however, as we have clarified in this article, most of the articles distributed and posted on websites are the main articles. Resultantly, the news published on websites will be more neutral than that published in mass media. Similar to mass media, websites may also adopt "strategic neutrality" to make them acceptable to numerous users. Websites may intentionally avoid publishing detailed information.

The above has provided various possibilities for the relationship between news and readers. Yet, if most individuals are exposed to news from a specific website article, their attitudes might not be affected; however, they also may not be able to express their opinions. If individuals read only one article, they will not understand what type of political and social issues are included in the news, what type of relationship it has with them, or if they have a conflict of interest. Even if political knowledge increases, the number of people who do not have political opinions may increase because of the use of Internet media.

In any case, the characteristics of the media agenda on websites shown in this paper suggest that the influence of Internet media on public opinion cannot be underestimated. As Ishikawa (2004) has argued, the parroting created by newspaper subscriptions is not desirable, nor is the apathy created by websites. Saito et al. (2014) discussed how newspapers could manipulate public opinion, and the same possibility exists in Internet media, such as websites.

Finally, we will address the problems and limitations of this study and discuss issues that can be addressed in future Internet media research. Initially, we were unable to examine only one point in this survey because many news sites contain only basic facts. Additionally, although newspapers were the subject of comparison in this survey, comparisons with television and other Internet media are important. According to Ishido (2018), LINE news, which is often used by young people, is softer than that from websites and has a different media agenda. More Internet media users are also accessing smart news (ICT Research Institute 2018), and various Internet media must be studied in the future.

Investigating the influence of Internet media is important. As discussed at the beginning of this article, a great deal of research has been conducted on this topic. However, it is equally and urgently important to analyze the Internet media and clarify the factors causing its influence.

REFERENCES

Battsogt, B. (2023). *The Study on the Development of Local Media in Mongolia,* Ulaanbaatar: Soyombo Printing.

Cappella, Joseph N., and Kathleen J., (1997). *Spiral of cynicism: The press and the public good.* Oxford University Press.

Gamson, William A. (1992). *Talking politics*. Cambridge university press,

ICT Research Institute. (2018). "2018 Mobile News App Market Trend Survey." ICT Research Institute Website. Accessed November 2, 2019. https://ictr.co.jp/report/20180509.html.

Ikeda, K. (2010). "Mass Media and the Internet." In *Social Psychology*, edited by Kenichi Ikeda, Jo Karasawa, Eriko Kudo, and Yukiko Muramoto, 267–289. Yuhikaku.

Ishido, A. (2018). "A Study on Line News' Reporting: A Comparison with Yahoo! News and Mass Media." *Seikei Humanities Research* (26), 97–120.

Ishikawa, O. (2004). *The Crisis Caused by Parroting: A Theory Cultivated by the Media*. Liberta Publishing.

Iyengar, Sh. (1994). *Is Anyone Responsible? How television frames political issues*. University of Chicago Press.

Kobayashi, T. (2011). "Political Knowledge Brought by Internet News." *New Information* 99: 10–18.

McCombs, M. (2014). *Setting the Agenda: Mass Media and Public Opinion*. 2nd ed. Cambridge: Polity Press.

Nelson, T. E., and Willey, E. A. (2001). Issue Frames That Strike a Value Balance: A Political Psychology Perspective. In *Framing Public Life,* edited by S. D. Reese, O. H. Gandy, JR., and A. E. Grant, 245–266. Mahwah, NJ: Lawrence Erlbaum Associates.

Neuman, W. R., Just, M. R., and Crigler, A. N. (1992). *Common Knowledge*. Chicago: University of Chicago Press.

Ogawa, T. (2001). "Framing and Agenda Setting Function: A Comparative Study Between "Objective Fragmentary Information" and "Influential Forecast Information"." *Keio Communication Review* 23: 71–86.

Patterson, T. E. (1980). *The Mass Media Election*. New York: Praeger.

Press Institute, (2021). *Mongolian Media-Today*, Ulaanbaatar: Press Institute

Saito, S., Takeshita, T., and Inaba, T. (2014). "Does the Tone of Newspapers Affect Readers' Attitudes? Using the Nuclear Power Plant Issue as an Example." *Society and Research* 13: 58–69.

Takeshita, T. (2008). "Agenda-Setting Function of the Media." Tokyo: Gakubunsha.

Tversky, A., and Kahneman, D. (1981). The Framing of Decisions and the Psychology of Choice. *Science* 211: 453–458.

THE APPLICATION AND CHALLENGES OF TECHNOLOGICAL INTERVENTION IN HOME REHABILITATION FOR STROKE PATIENTS

Ching-Yu Liao[1] and Ju-Joan Wong[2]
[1]*National Yunlin University of Science and Technology, Industrial Design, Taiwan*
[2]*National Yunlin University of Science and Technology, Graduate School of Design, Director, Taiwan*

ABSTRACT

According to the American Heart Association (2024), stroke affects approximately 12 million new patients globally each year, resulting in the loss of 143 million healthy life years. In Taiwan, stroke is the second leading cause of death. To improve acute post-stroke care, Taiwan's Ministry of Health and Welfare launched the Post-Acute Care Program for Cerebrovascular Disease (PAC-CVD) in 2014. However, current rehabilitation faces several challenges, including fragmented tracking of patient progress across hospitals and limitations in home-based rehabilitation. Advances in IoT-based medical technologies, such as telemedicine and wearable exoskeleton devices, demonstrate significant potential for digital assistive solutions. This study identifies rehabilitation challenges based on stroke patients' experiences and outlines user requirements for future assistive technology design. The findings underscore the importance of medical care, family support, and patient autonomy in stroke recovery, offering critical insights for IoT-based assistive technologies to improve patient rehabilitation outcomes and quality of life.

KEYWORDS

Stroke, User Experience, Rehabilitation, Assistive Devices, Technology

1. INTRODUCTION

Approximately 12 million new stroke cases occur globally each year, resulting in the loss of 143 million healthy life years. According to the American Heart Association (2024), around 10% of these cases occur in individuals aged 18 to 50, indicating a rising trend among younger individuals. In Taiwan, stroke is the second leading cause of death. To reduce the burden on families and society, Taiwan's Ministry of Health and Welfare launched the Post-Acute Care for Cerebrovascular Disease (PAC-CVD) program in 2014, aiming to enhance rehabilitation efficiency during the critical subacute recovery period.

Despite being a pivotal recovery phase, subacute rehabilitation often faces constraints due to limited healthcare resources, hindering patients' access to high-quality services following discharge. Current rehabilitation devices heavily depend on professional healthcare personnel and lack precise data support, resulting in suboptimal outcomes.

Digital health technologies and the Internet of Medical Things (IoMT), including telemedicine and wearable exoskeletons like the ReStore soft exosuit, present promising directions for remote rehabilitation and data monitoring. However, significant challenges remain in effectively addressing patients' needs and improving their rehabilitation experiences.

This study investigates both intrinsic and extrinsic factors influencing patient motivation to better identify user requirements and provide stable support within the current healthcare system. By examining the rehabilitation experiences of Taiwanese stroke patients, this study aims to (1) identify needs and challenges in both traditional and technology-assisted rehabilitation and (2) propose relevant technological design guidelines.

By integrating data analytics and personalized rehabilitation strategies, this study seeks to enhance recovery outcomes and quality of life. User feedback will be used to assess the strengths and limitations of assistive technologies, establishing an evidence-based foundation for future rehabilitation device development and implementation.

2. LITERATURE REVIEW

This paper examines recent policies, technological innovations, and systemic constraints affecting stroke care, as well as current technological applications in rehabilitation.

2.1 System and Limitations of the Stroke PAC Program

Stroke, caused by blocked or ruptured blood vessels leading to brain hypoxia, remains a major global health issue. Stroke care and rehabilitation typically occur in three stages: acute (stabilization of vital signs), subacute (considered the "golden period," emphasizing neural repair and restoration of daily function), and chronic (long-term maintenance). Early rehabilitation following stabilization helps prevent joint stiffness and muscle atrophy (Liu et al., 2019).

Table 1. Medical Options for Post-Stroke Rehabilitation (illustrated by the author)

	Post-Acute Care Program for Stroke (PAC)	**Former Rehabilitation Division Rehabilitation**	**Outpatient Rehabilitation**
Care Facilities	Neighborhood/area hospitals	Hospital of your choice	Institutions Rehabilitation Clinics
Length of stay	3-6 weeks maximum, up to 12 weeks if necessary with health insurance approval.	6 months inpatient rehabilitation 28 days in each hospital	No hospitalization required
Suitable patients	Moderate to moderately severe	moderately severe	Mild
Rehabilitation Strength	High Intensity (2-5 times per day)	Average strength (1-3 times per day)	Depending on the patient's wish
Referral Methods	Personal Manager Arrangement	Arrangement by our Rehabilitation Department Arrangement by family members	daily round trip
Disadvantages	1. Family Support Needed 2. Patient Screening Required 3. No PAC Post-Closure	1. Longer Hospital Stay 2. Hospital Stay Window 3. Self-Managed Referrals 4. Nursing Care Costs 5. Monthly Team Change	1. Travel 2. FatigueInsufficient 3. RehabReliance on Willpower

Taiwan's traditional rehabilitation model under the national health insurance system allows stroke patients to stay in hospitals for up to 28 days per session within a six-month period. Once this limit is reached, families must arrange transfers to other facilities, leading to care interruptions and additional burdens. To address these issues, Taiwan initiated the PAC-CVD program in 2014, which offers intensive rehabilitation (3–12 weeks, 5–6 days per week, up to five daily sessions) with case managers coordinating activities such as gait and balance training, aiming to enhance efficiency and reduce readmissions (National Health Insurance Administration, 2020).

The PAC program employs standardized tools such as the Barthel Index and Berg Balance Scale. While these tools simplify assessments, they tend to favor patients with mild to moderate cases, leaving those with severe conditions dependent on costly private care. Patients in remote areas encounter additional challenges due to limited transportation and resources, while ineffective communication among rehabilitation facilities further impacts overall efficiency (Lee et al., 2018).

Rehabilitation plans largely depend on therapists' expertise and typically involve treadmill and balance training (Rand & Eng, 2012). However, the administrative burden of completing evaluation scales reduces therapist efficiency, and the lack of professional guidance for home-based rehabilitation further limits the outcomes. Family stress and patients' emotional distress also hinder recovery, highlighting the need for integrated medical and social support (Chang, 2016; Liu et al., 2019).

2.2 Technology-Driven Advances in Rehabilitation

In recent years, technology has increasingly been integrated into stroke rehabilitation. Taiwan's FREE Walk exoskeleton, developed by Fourier Intelligence, uses computer control to assist patients with step length, walking speed, and leg lift (Hou et al., 2024). Studies have shown that it improves lower limb strength and endurance, even in patients with minimal muscle power. However, it still requires trainer assistance and has a limited impact on neural activation (Lee et al., 2023).

Japan's HAL (Hybrid Assistive Limb), developed by Cyberdyne, emphasizes voluntary intention. It detects brain signals and converts them into motion, significantly improving walking time in non-ambulatory patients when paired with a suspension system (Nakajima et al., 2021; Tsai et al., 2022).Technology also supports remote rehabilitation. Pressure-sensing insoles transmit gait data to the cloud for real-time monitoring (Hsu et al., 2023). ReWalk's ReStore Exo-Suit assists ankle movement using cable-driven actuators and sensors, providing precise feedback to correct gait (Awad et al., 2020). Earlier wearable devices tracked fall risk and daily activity levels, promoting exercise habits during the early stages of rehabilitation (Giansanti et al., 2009). Although basic, these tools are flexible and easy to install, making them suitable for home use in low-resource settings.

Despite notable progress, challenges remain. High costs, complex setups, and learning curves affect accessibility. Technologies have evolved from passive support to motion simulation, intention sensing, and remote monitoring. However, human assistance remains essential for effective outcomes.

2.3 User Experience of Stroke Patients

A key challenge for stroke patients is maintaining motivation for continuous training. Marchal-Crespo and Reinkensmeyer (2009) noted that excessive robotic assistance may reduce voluntary effort and hinder neuroplasticity—a concept referred to as the "Slacking Hypothesis." They suggest adaptive support based on user performance through assistive, challenging, or task-oriented strategies.

Maharjan et al. (2024) examined virtual coaching systems incorporating auditory and visual feedback, which enhanced users' motivation, sense of control, and personalization. Participants reported reduced anxiety compared to traditional gym environments. Both studies emphasized that adaptive control and real-time feedback can increase user engagement, which aligns with this study's user-centered design approach.

Pan and Hur (2017) developed a wrist sensor that translates posture deviations into tactile cues, enabling balance correction without visual input, thus demonstrating the potential of multisensory feedback. However, adoption remains limited. Yetisen et al. (2018) found that a third of wearable users discontinued use within six months due to novelty loss and usability challenges, highlighting the need for improved long-term adherence strategies. Eng et al. (2003) proposed community-based group training involving daily functional tasks, which improved rehabilitation acceptance, confidence, and adherence. Maceira-Elvira et al. (2019) combined IMU and EMG sensors to collect precise movement data, enabling therapists to develop personalized recovery plans.

This study explores not only motivation and training modes but also how design can enhance usability and adherence. Despite the potential of the IoMT for remote monitoring and data analysis, widespread adoption remains constrained by connectivity and ecosystem limitations. Without a stable user experience, sustained engagement and positive rehabilitation outcomes are difficult to achieve.

3. RESEARCH METHODOLOGY

This study aims to explore the needs of stroke patients in Taiwan and examine how assistive technologies can be integrated into traditional rehabilitation, with a focus on user experience and specific requirements. This section outlines the methods used for data collection and analysis.

3.1 Research Methodology

This study adopts a qualitative research approach, employing semi-structured in-depth interviews and participant observation to examine stroke patients' experiences and attitudes toward assistive technologies during rehabilitation. The interviews explored patients' rehabilitation trajectories, sources of motivation, and perceptions of technology use, complemented by field observations to capture non-verbal interactions and environmental influences on patient behavior. The research emphasizes the dynamic interaction between individuals, physical settings, and technological tools, focusing on the interpretation of social realities rather than relying solely on quantitative data.

3.2 Sampling Strategy, Participants and Ethical Considerations

Purposeful sampling was used to recruit stroke patients in the subacute or chronic rehabilitation phase, diagnosed with either ischemic or hemorrhagic stroke. Participants were recruited through stroke support forums and rehabilitation centers. Only mild to moderate cases were included to ensure clear communication and reliable data collection (Patton, 2002). Snowball sampling was also applied. As shown in Table 2, eight stroke patients with diverse rehabilitation experiences were interviewed, covering cases from mild to severe, with the time since onset ranging from three months to 18 years. Their rehabilitation experiences included inpatient, home-based, outpatient, and alternative traditional rehabilitation settings. Each interview lasted between 1 and 2.5 hours. Theoretical sampling was used to refine data collection until theoretical saturation was achieved.

This study did not involve invasive procedures or the collection of sensitive personal information. The interview content focused on participants' reflections on their rehabilitation experiences and the use of assistive devices. Therefore, it did not require institutional ethical review. All participants signed informed consent forms prior to the interviews and agreed to audio recording and data usage, ensuring transparency and ethical integrity throughout the research process.

Table 2. List of interviewees (The ages in the table are the actual ages at the time of the stroke.)

ID	Location	Age	Stroke Year	Course	Severity	Main Earner	Policy	Post-Discharge	Outcome
S01	Hsinchu	37	2007	18 yrs	Mild	Yes	None	Home rehab	Independent work, normal speech
S02	Taichung	74	2024/10	3 months	Mild	No	Self-paid bed OP rehab	Original hospital, acupuncture, park exercise	Slow walking/speech, needs help bathing
S03	Kaohsiung	43	2017/12	8 yrs	Severe	Yes	Old system	Caregiver, acupuncture, massag	Needs assistance walking, joint stiffness
S04	Yunlin	45	2008	17 yrs	Moderate	Yes	OP rehab	Acupuncture, rehab clinic, home	Normal work/walking/ speech, limb numbness
S05	Taichung	69	2020/7	5 yrs	Severe	Yes	Old system	Original hospital, gy training	Needs help walking, left side is numb,and fatigue
S06	Chiayi	50	2015/1	10 yrs	Moderate	Yes	PAC self-paid	Original hospital, biking, hiking	Independent walking, normal speech, slow response
S07	Taichung	54	2020/4	5 yrs	Moderate	Yes	Self-paid OP rehab	Original hospital	Independent walking, normal speech, dizziness
S08	Chiayi	45	2014/9, 2024/4	11 yrs	Severe / Mild	Yes	PAC self-paid	Office	Independent walking, joint stiffness, slow speech

3.3 Data Coding and Analysis

This study adopted grounded theory to identify patterns within patients' rehabilitation experiences. The coding process consisted of three stages:

(1) **Open coding** – identifying themes from interviews and observations;
(2) **Axial coding** – establishing relationships among categories; and

(3) **Selective coding** – constructing a final theoretical framework based on core concepts (Corbin & Strauss, 2014).

Using ATLAS.ti, researchers systematically analyzed qualitative data to ensure that the findings reflect the needs, challenges, and attitudes of stroke patients toward assistive technologies in the context of rehabilitation in Taiwan.

4. RESULTS

4.1 Uncertainty in the Rehabilitation Process

Post-stroke recovery is influenced by medical professionals, personal motivation, and available resources. Interviews with several patients revealed that physicians' initial diagnoses and prognoses significantly impacted their confidence. S03 expressed frustration over a diagnosis indicating no possibility of full recovery, while S07 described feelings of helplessness due to pessimistic remarks from the doctor. In contrast, S02, S06, and S08 found motivation through clear rehabilitation goals and optimistic assessments provided by their physicians. S05, S06, and S08 also mentioned that the Barthel Index often reduced their subjective feelings and real-life needs to a mere "functional score," resulting in a sense of alienation from their actual rehabilitation goals and contributing to a fragmented recovery process.

Basic hospital-based rehabilitation programs were frequently perceived as insufficient. S03 criticized the standardized rehabilitation system and sought alternative solutions, such as training her caregiver in foreign caregiving methods. Although her doctor emphasized the importance of early physical activity during the golden recovery phase, her physical limitations prevented significant progress, leading to emotional distress. As a result, she explored other rehabilitation environments and found that a lack of hospital resources hindered her treatment. Similarly, S07 and S05 reported dissatisfaction with hospital rehabilitation programs but chose to remain at the same hospital for continuity of care, which ultimately delayed their rehabilitation progress.

These examples confirm that the quality of rehabilitation is greatly influenced by the availability of medical resources, staffing levels, and the duration of treatment, resulting in variability across hospitals that significantly impacts patient motivation (Chang, 2016; Liu et al., 2019).

4.2 Personalized Rehabilitation Trajectories

Stroke patients often choose rehabilitation methods based on their individual conditions and daily needs. Some integrate traditional Chinese and Western medicine, while others prefer personal training equipment or alternative recovery environments. Medical centers and clinics typically offer similar rehabilitation facilities. Participants such as S01, S02, S04, S06, S07, and S08 followed therapy plans designed by professional therapists. S01 focused on strength training but preferred to exercise independently. S05 supplemented clinical sessions with self-funded weight training. After years of rehabilitation, S06 sought a sense of achievement through activities such as mountain climbing, swimming, and cycling.

S01 chose home-based rehabilitation due to family responsibilities, using grip balls, dumbbells, and resistance bands, and maintained daily walking routines to regain stamina. S02 walked for extended periods and participated in household chores to maintain basic activity levels. In contrast, S03, who had been bedridden during the early stages, relied more heavily on caregiver assistance. Over time, she gradually regained mobility through acupuncture, massage therapy, and rehabilitation exercises. Meanwhile, S04 treated rehabilitation as a long-term challenge, incorporating weight and balance training at home. After ten years of effort, he achieved approximately 90% recovery and integrated exercise into his daily routine.

All eight cases emphasized the importance of self-driven effort and personalized goal-setting in the rehabilitation process. As Marchal-Crespo et al. (2009) suggested, strategically planned training toward specific goals enhances motivation. Four participants opted for structured inpatient rehabilitation to reduce external risks, while others adapted to their environmental needs through home-based, autonomous, or integrated approaches. Adjusting rehabilitation methods based on available resources and convenience helped improve recovery outcomes and goal attainment.

4.3 Perceptions Toward Assistive Technologies

Researchers introduced participants to the operational principles of exoskeleton robots and their potential application in Taiwan's rehabilitation medicine. S03 remarked, "Machines are not as smart as people; they don't understand your body. You have to rely on your own efforts, not let the machine do the work for you." She believed machines cannot address individual needs, emphasizing that effective rehabilitation relies on personal engagement and human support rather than technology alone. She also cited a peer who, despite using hyaluronic acid injections and assistive devices, remained unable to walk. This further reinforced her skepticism regarding the effectiveness of lightweight assistive tools and her belief that only persistent effort leads to meaningful recovery.

When asked whether she would want a device to monitor her recovery progress, S03 responded, "You know whether you're improving—you don't need a machine to tell you that your muscles are shrinking or your blood vessels are blocked." She insisted that recovery is best understood through subjective experience rather than external validation. Similarly, S02 also emphasized the importance of personal perception, expressing satisfaction with his current recovery and indicating that technological intervention was unnecessary.

S06 had briefly used an exoskeleton and acknowledged its potential to assist with standing. However, he dismissed the idea that it could replicate natural walking as "a fantasy." He found data charts and feedback mechanisms more valuable than the training equipment itself. S07 shared a similar view, stating that it felt like the machine was walking for him rather than activating his thigh muscles, highlighting a disconnect between user experience and exoskeleton design.

In contrast, S04 expressed positive expectations toward assistive technologies. He stated, "I want to know my rehab progress, but doctors don't provide that information. If there's a device that can monitor and improve numbness, that would be really convenient." He hoped for technology that could deliver real-time feedback for targeted rehabilitation and accurate assessments.

Although previous studies have demonstrated that exoskeletons can improve gait and lower limb strength in stroke patients (Lee et al., 2023; Hou et al., 2024) and support motor simulation in the short term, most participants in this study (e.g., S03, S06, S07) expressed skepticism or limited acceptance. They emphasized that technology cannot replace personal effort and professional human guidance. These views are consistent with the "Slacking Hypothesis" proposed by Marchal-Crespo and Reinkensmeyer (2009), which suggests that excessive reliance on assistive devices may reduce patient initiative and hinder neuroplasticity.

Interview data highlight the importance of considering psychological engagement, motivational triggers, and contextual fit in the implementation of rehabilitation technology. Such technology should support rather than dominate the rehabilitation process. Its design should focus on adaptive feedback, reduced dependency, and enhanced user control.

4.4 Family Support in Stroke Rehabilitation

Six participants experienced a stroke during their prime working years, and their recovery was closely linked to the preservation of their family systems. In most cases, five of these individuals demonstrated greater initiative during rehabilitation. However, S03 encountered more significant challenges due to limited family support, which negatively affected both emotional well-being and motivation. This highlights the critical role of family in the rehabilitation process. Patients such as S02, S06, and S08 reported relatively stable family finances post-stroke and shared a common goal of returning to work. With sufficient manpower and economic resources within the family unit, these patients were able to adopt more flexible strategies for managing their condition.

For example, S02 received both logistical and emotional support from his children, who took turns driving him to therapy sessions. He felt a strong responsibility to meet his family's expectations, which helped him persevere through difficult phases of recovery. Despite initially lacking personal motivation, this support enabled steady progress, highlighting the importance of family involvement. Similarly, S06 was motivated by his role as a caregiver for his elderly parents, which reinforced his commitment to rehabilitation. S04, constrained by limited household resources, engaged in home rehabilitation with assistance from his spouse during the early stages. Driven by a desire for independence, he aimed to return to work and restore self-sufficiency.

In contrast, S03 struggled emotionally. Although he relied on caregivers, he resented the resulting sense of dependency. During interviews, he expressed frustration over his family's limited involvement and compared his situation unfavorably to neighbors with stronger family support. This left him feeling neglected and demotivated. His story illustrates how the presence—or absence—of family support can directly influence rehabilitation outcomes.

Ultimately, successful rehabilitation depends not only on individual effort but also on sustained support from both family and healthcare professionals. These factors contribute to a more holistic recovery, encompassing both physical and emotional dimensions. The findings clearly show that emotional and practical support from family members plays a crucial role in motivating patients throughout the rehabilitation process.

5. CONCLUSION

This study interviewed eight stroke patients to examine the complex challenges they face during rehabilitation, including interactions with healthcare systems, family support, personal motivation, and attitudes toward assistive technologies. Although Taiwan's current health insurance system offers some rehabilitation support, patients frequently reported gaps between policy provisions and actual needs. These gaps often lead to inconsistent services, interruptions, and delays—particularly among patients living in rural or resource-limited settings.

While exoskeletons and wearable technologies are regarded as promising innovations in rehabilitation, participant responses varied. Some emphasized the importance of personal effort and human guidance, expressing skepticism about overreliance on machines. Others welcomed the quantitative feedback and real-time monitoring to improve recovery precision. These findings suggest that psychological acceptance, usability, and integration into daily routines should be prioritized in the design and promotion of rehabilitation technologies. The assumption that "technology equals outcome" should be avoided. The data also highlighted that family support serves not only as a source of practical assistance but as a key emotional pillar sustaining motivation during rehabilitation. When family members are actively involved and express clear expectations, patients tend to engage more proactively and perceive a return to everyday life and employment as attainable goals. Conversely, the absence of emotional support may turn rehabilitation into a passive process, increase psychological distress, and impede functional recovery.

In IoMT-related research, Maceira-Elvira (2019) emphasized the importance of motivation and social reintegration in the design of wearable devices n using IMU (Inertial Measurement Units) and EMG (Electromyography) monitoring technologies. This aligns with Eng's (2003) community-based group training approach, which incorporates functional and familiar movements (e.g., standing up) in rehabilitation planning, thereby promoting both physical and emotional recovery.

In conclusion, the effective advancement of stroke rehabilitation depends on the integration of three core factors: accessible institutional support, sustained family involvement, and the patient’s own agency and willingness to recover. The role of IoMT technologies should evolve from providing basic assistance to offering personalization, motivation-driven, and context-sensitive support.

ACKNOWLEDGEMENT

This research was supported by the National Science and Technology Council, Republic of China, Taiwan, under project number NSTC 113-2410-H-224-014.

REFERENCES

Abiteboul, S. et al., (2000). *Data on the Web: From Relations to Semistructured Data and XML*. Morgan Kaufmann Publishers, San Francisco, USA.

Awad, L.N. et al., (2020). The ReWalk ReStore™ soft robotic exosuit: a multi-site clinical trial of the safety, reliability, and feasibility of exosuit-augmented post-stroke gait rehabilitation. *Journal of NeuroEngineering and Rehabilitation*, 17(1), p. 80. https://doi.org/10.1186/s12984-020-00702-5

Chang, K.W., (2016). Effects of physical therapy intervention on post-acute stroke patients. *Southern Taiwan Medical Journal*.

Corbin, J. and Strauss, A., (2014). *Basics of qualitative research: Techniques and procedures for developing grounded theory*. Sage Publications, Thousand Oaks, USA.

Eng, J.J. et al., (2003). A community-based group exercise program for persons with chronic stroke. *Medicine & Science in Sports & Exercise*, 35(8), pp.1271–1278. https://doi.org/10.1249/01.mss.0000079079.58477.0b

Giansanti, D. et al., (2009). Toward the design of a wearable system for fall-risk detection in telerehabilitation. *Telemedicine and e-Health*, 15(3), pp.296–299. https://doi.org/10.1089/tmj.2008.0106

Giansanti, D. et al., (2009). Toward the integration of novel wearable step-counters in gait telerehabilitation after stroke. *Telemedicine and e-Health*, 15(1), pp.105–111. https://doi.org/10.1089/tmj.2008.0051

Hou, H.F., Chang, Y.L. and Tsai, C.H., (2024). The short-term effect of an exoskeleton training for non-ambulatory patients with subacute stroke: A case report [Abstract]. *Physical Therapy*, 49(2), p. 125. https://doi.org/10.6215/fjpt.202406.P20

Hsu, T.H. et al., (2023). Effect of wearable exoskeleton on post-stroke gait: A systematic review and meta-analysis. *Annals of Physical and Rehabilitation Medicine*, 66(1), p.101674. https://doi.org/10.1016/j.rehab.2022.101674

Lee, M.C. et al., (2018). Comparison of the system of home-based rehabilitation between Taiwan and Japan: Experience of the Taipei City Hospital and the Saku Medical Care Institutions in Nagano. *Physical Therapy*, 43(3), pp. 193–202. https://doi.org/10.6215/fjpt.201809_43(3).0001

Lee, Y.H. et al., (2023). Therapeutic effects of robotic-exoskeleton-assisted gait rehabilitation and predictive factors of significant improvements in stroke patients: A randomized controlled trial. *Bioengineering*, 10(5), p. 585. https://doi.org/10.3390/bioengineering10050585

Liu, C.C., Lin, P.Y. and Tseng, S.F., (2019). Outpatient nursing experience of changes in family dynamics following a first-time stroke: A case study. *Cheng Ching Medical Journal*, 15, pp.58–66.

Maceira-Elvira, P. et al., (2019). Wearable technology in stroke rehabilitation: Towards improved diagnosis and treatment of upper-limb motor impairment. *Journal of NeuroEngineering and Rehabilitation*, 16(1). https://doi.org/10.1186/s12984-019-0612-y

Maharjan, R. et al., (2024). Exploring user engagement with real-time verbal feedback from an exoskeleton-based virtual exercise coach. *Digital Health*, 10. https://doi.org/10.1177/20552076241302652

Marchal-Crespo, L. and Reinkensmeyer, D.J., (2009). Review of control strategies for robotic movement training after neurologic injury. *Journal of NeuroEngineering and Rehabilitation*, 6(1), p.20. https://doi.org/10.1186/1743-0003-6-20

Nakajima, T. et al., (2021). Cybernic treatment with wearable cyborg Hybrid Assistive Limb (HAL) improves ambulatory function in patients with slowly progressive rare neuromuscular diseases: A multicentre, randomised, controlled crossover trial for efficacy and safety (NCY-3001). *Orphanet Journal of Rare Diseases*, 16(1). https://doi.org/10.1186/s13023-021-01928-9

National Health Insurance Administration, Ministry of Health and Welfare, (2020). *Integrated post-acute care program for stroke (marked version)*. Document No. 1090004503. https://www.nhi.gov.tw/ch/cp-5499-734a5-2898-1.html

Pan, Y.T. and Hur, P., (2017). Interactive balance rehabilitation tool with wearable skin stretch device. *Proceedings of the 2017 26th IEEE International Symposium on Robot and Human Interactive Communication (RO-MAN)*. Lisbon, Portugal, pp.761–766.

Patton, M.Q., (2002). *Qualitative research & evaluation methods*. SAGE Publications, Thousand Oaks, USA. https://books.google.com.tw/books?id=FjBw2oi8El4C

Rand, D. and Eng, J.J., (2012). Disparity between functional recovery and daily use of the upper and lower extremities during subacute stroke rehabilitation. *Neurorehabilitation and Neural Repair*, 26(1), pp. 76–84. https://doi.org/10.1177/1545968311408918

Tsai, M.H. et al., (2022). The short-term effect of a hybrid assistive lower limb exoskeleton training in a patient with subacute stroke: Case report [Abstract]. *Physical Therapy*, 47(2), p.143. https://doi.org/10.6215/fjpt.202206.P27

Yetisen, A.K. et al., (2018). Wearables in medicine. *Advanced Materials*, 30(33), p. 1706910. https://doi.org/10.1002/adma.201706910

Short Papers

ARE ONLINE COMMUNICATIONS AN EFFECTIVE TOOL IN TOURISM DESTINATION MARKETING?

Carmen-María Hervás-Cortina, Irene Gil-Saura and Maria Eugenia Ruiz-Molina
Universitat de Valencia, Spain

ABSTRACT

The objective of this research is to assess the impact of online communications, user-generated and destination-generated communications, on e-reputation of the tourism destination and the tourist intention to communicate online about his perceptions about the destination. From the data obtained on 300 tourists of small tourism destinations, a structural equations model is tested through Partial Least Squares technique. The results show that destination-generated online communications positively influence e-reputation and tourist electronic word-of-mouth intention. Besides, in contrast to previous research, user-generated online communications do neither influence e-reputation or tourist electronic word-of-mouth intention. The study allows to conclude the vital role of destination management organizations in promoting the tourism destination, specifically in small and lesser-known destinations.

KEYWORDS

User-Generated Online Communications, Destination-Generated Online Communications, Tourism Destination E-Reputation, Tourist Intention to Communicate Online

1. INTRODUCTION

In recent decades, following the emergence of digitalisation, it is essential for companies and organizations, both public and private, to build two-way relationships with consumers on digital media in order to encourage interaction. In particular, online (social media) communications generated by tourist organisations or destinations are considered essential promotional tools as they allow interaction with consumers/tourists and influence their perceptions (Stojanovic, 2022; Schivinski and Dabrowski, 2016).

After digitalization, it is important to reconsider the concept of reputation as e-reputation (online) as analysing the brand's reputation on the Internet it is considered a tool to make visible the wide intangible economy, even measurable through online reputation indicators (Elmurngi and Gherbi, 2020). Previous research has underscored the pivotal role of digital marketing initiatives undertaken by organizations, particularly in local and rural tourism destinations, in promoting regional development and economic growth (Zvaigzne *et al.*, 2023). In this context, tourism organizations actively utilize smart devices to construct and sustain their e-reputation, digital image, and brand identity by enabling the dissemination and co-creation of tourism-related content through destination-focused social media platforms (Graziano and Albanese, 2020).

Historically, the content and image of a destination were predominantly controlled by the Destination Management Organization (DMO), making the role of tourism organizations in constructing, promoting, and maintaining the destination's image essential—an influence that continues to be relevant today (Stepchenkova and Zhan, 2013). In the current digital era, the quantitative characteristics of social media accounts managed by tourism organizations, along with the destination's contributions on these platforms, are regarded as important tools for destination marketing (Hruška and Pásková, 2018). Nonetheless, recent studies have increasingly emphasized the importance of electronic word-of-mouth (eWOM), or user-generated content, in shaping destination perception (e.g., Baber and Baber, 2023). However, the influence of eWOM on online communication intention is not always significant. For example, Gharib *et al.* (2019) found that eWOM intention affects opinion passing but not opinion giving, while other components of eWOM—such as perceived usefulness—do not significantly impact users' intentions to share content (Anh *et al.,* 2019). Moreover, Martín-Delgado *et al.* (2020) highlight that rural and small-scale destinations often exhibit a weak online reputation, as reflected by limited user-generated content. Similarly, user opinions may not accurately represent organisational perspectives and may even be fictitious. Therefore, as Platov *et al.* (2020) argue, it is crucial to consider the authenticity of posts and comments generated by the destination itself in order to obtain a comprehensive understanding of its online reputation. In this context, and in line with previous research on destinations (e.g., Stojanovic *et al.,* 2022), this paper focuses on distinguishing between destination-generated content (DGC) and user-generated content (UGC).

In addition, the recent economic crises have dramatically increased public deficit, so that public spending devoted to the promotion of tourist destinations should be optimized, offering managers of tourism destinations some guidance on how to invest their marketing budget in the most efficient way to attract tourists to these destinations. In this way, the identification of the most effective strategy to promote the tourism destination emerges as a priority for DMO, especially for small and lesser-known destinations in which online DGC seems to be more influential than online UGC, as other authors such as Martín-Delgado *et al.* (2020) acknowledge.

This study aims to examine how different types of online content, namely user-generated content (UGC) and destination-generated content (DGC), influence the e-reputation of tourism destinations and affect tourists' willingness to share their experiences online. By doing so, it seeks to assist Destination Management Organizations (DMOs) in identifying the most effective strategies for destination promotion. From a theoretical perspective, the research contributes to the extension of the Stimulus-Organism-Response (SOR) model (Mehrabian and Russell, 1974) within the field of destination marketing. It does so by emphasizing the influential role of DGC in building e-reputation and fostering eWOM, while also drawing comparisons with UGC and recognizing its limitations—particularly in the case of smaller or lesser-known destinations.

As previously noted, empirical evidence regarding the distinct impact of online destination-generated content (DGC) and user-generated content (UGC) on e-reputation and eWOM intention remains limited, particularly in the context of small or lesser-known destinations. Therefore, based on the literature review conducted, the present study aims at testing the following hypotheses:

H1. Destination-generated (DG) online communications have a positive and significant effect on e-Reputation.

H2. User-generated (UG) online communications have a positive and significant effect on e-Reputation.

H3. Destination-generated (DG) online communications have a positive and significant effect on tourist intention to communicate online (eWOM).

H4. User-generated (UG) online communications have a positive and significant effect on tourist intention to communicate online (eWOM).

H5. Tourism destination e-Reputation has a positive and significant effect on the tourist intention to communicate online (eWOM).

2. METHODOLOGY

To achieve the proposed objective, quantitative research is proposed through an ad hoc structured questionnaire with closed-ended questions. The survey was administrated (using QR code) to tourists at the exit of the tourist offices they have visited. Sampling is carried out for convenience as only some tourist offices from various locations in the Valencian Community, in Spain, have agreed to collaborate with the study: Benicàssim, Sagunt, Gandia, Canet d'en Berenguer, Castelló de la Plana, Altura, Riba-roja de Túria, Segorbe, and other nearby cities and towns. Data collection was carried out during May and June 2024, and between December 2024 and January 2025, obtaining a total of 300 valid questionnaires.

The items to measure the variables analysed have been extracted from various scales used in the marketing literature, and have been adapted to the specifications of the context and objective of the present study. Specifically, to measure online user-generated content, the scale has been adapted from Yadav *et al.* (2022) and Schivinski and Dabrowski (2016). The scale proposed by Schivinski and Dabrowski (2016) has been used to measure online destination-generated content. Finally, e-Reputation has been evaluated through the scale proposed by Baber and Baber (2023) and electronic word-of-mouth scale have been adapted from the authors Cheung *et al.* (2021) and Afshardoost and Eshaghi (2020)[1]. All the items in the questionnaire were measured with a 7-point Likert scale (1 = strongly disagree; 7 = strongly agree) and considered as reflective indicators.

[1] For the sake of brevity, the items are not included in the paper, but are available from the authors upon request.

Regarding the profile of the tourists, the majority are women (67.7%), more than half (52.3%) work as employees and around 70% have completed university studies. Regarding the reason for travel, 88% travel for holidays and 53.3% travel between 2 and 4 times a year.

3. RESULTS

Firstly, we carry out an Exploratory Factor Analysis (Principal Components Analysis) to observe how the items of the scales used are grouped in different factors: online destination-generated content (online DGC) (4 items); online user-generated content (online UGC) (13 items); electronic word-of-mouth (eWOM) intention (4 items); and e-reputation (10 items). Next, we use PLS-SEM statistical technique to check the validity and reliability of the measurement instrument, calculating a PLS algorithm. The results obtained from Cronbach's alpha and the composite reliability are satisfactory, exceeding the threshold of 0.7 (Churchill, 1979; Chin, 1998). Regarding the average variance extracted (AVE), all the factors of the structural model present values higher than 0.5, which means each construct explains at least 50% of the variance of the assigned indicators (Fornell and Larcker, 1981). Therefore, the results obtained allow us to confirm the reliability and convergent validity of the structural model measurement instrument. Furthermore, the analysis of discriminant validity using the criterion put forward by Fornell and Larcker (1981) allow us to confirm the discriminant validity of the constructs included in the model.

After confirming the reliability and validity of the measurement instrument in this study, we analyze the proposed structural model. A complete bootstrapping procedure with 5,000 subsamples was conducted (Ringle *et al.,* 2015). The results of the structural model estimation are presented in Figure 1.

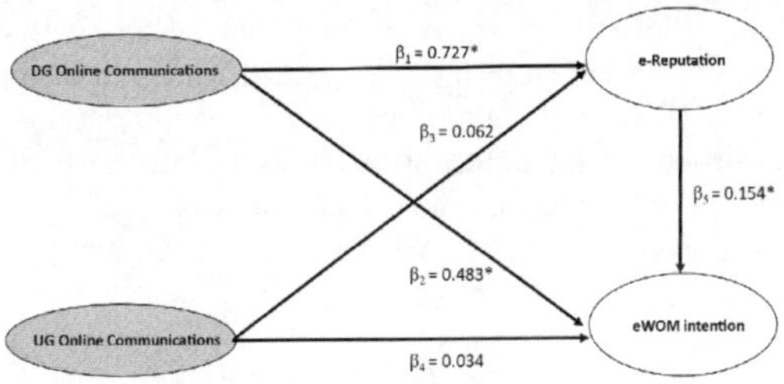

e-Reputation: R2=0.562; Q2=0.555; eWOM intention: R2=0.382; Q2=0.359
*Statistically significant at *p<0.05.
Source: Authors' proposal.

Figure 1. Estimation of causal relationships

Based on the PLS-SEM analysis of the structural relationships in this study, the hypotheses formulated with online destination-generated content (DGC) (H1, H2) can be accepted as well as the one between e-Reputation and eWOM intention (H5). Specifically, the relationships DGC-online reputation (H1) and DGC-eWOM intention (H3) demonstrates a positive and significant effect respectively (β_1=0.727, $p<0.01$; β_2=0.483, $p<0.01$). Similarly, the third hypothesis, which examines the relationship e-Reputation-eWOM intention (H5), is also supported, as the results indicate a positive and significant effect (β5 = 0.154, $p<0.05$). In contrast, user-generated online communications do not seem to be relevant to explain either e-reputation or tourist eWOM intention. The mediation analysis results reveal that DGC has a statistically significant indirect effect on eWOM intention through e-reputation (β = 0.112, t = 1.966, p = 0.049), while UGC did not have a significant indirect effect on eWOM intention via e-reputation (β = 0.009, t = 1.273, p = 0.203).

4. CONCLUSION

Taking as a reference the Stimulus-Organism-Response model, the present study confirms that in low-awareness contexts, the stimulus (DGC) takes on a heightened role in shaping the organism (perception/e-reputation), which in turn creates a response (eWOM). In contrast, user-generated content (UGC) appears to have a comparatively weaker influence on both variables, diverging from the results reported in previous research. Thus, even though it contradicts other studies previously mentioned, it offers to academia a deeper insight into how digital strategies must be tailored to context, particularly for small or lesser-known tourism destinations, in which UGC is limited and also, this limited UGC could be untrustworthy (Martín-Delgado *et al.*, 2020; Platov *et al.*, 2020). In addition, the findings reveal that building trust and positive e-reputation in lesser-known destination is not organic, it must be engineered by DMOs. Thus, tourism organisations need digital marketing recommendations to enhance and control the destination's online reputation and eWOM. For instance, integrating AI-driven tourism technologies for content generation and analysis (using social media analytics tools) and content optimization (using SEO or Search Engine Optimization), as suggested by Altin *et al.* (2023). Furthermore, AI-powered chatbots can personalise in real-time the tourist experience in tourism destination digital platforms and compile customised interests from users/tourists (Palahan and Arunthari, 2024). As UGC it is not as significant as DGC, small municipalities could also stimulate buzz using AI tools to identify micro-influencers or creators of online content taking into account the DMOs target segment/s to increase eWOM (Han and Zhang, 2024).

Notwithstanding, the study has a number of limitations that, in some cases, offer opportunities for future research. Firstly, the available sample is limited. Furthermore, by using a QR code as a method of accessing the questionnaire, the subjects in the older age group may be underrepresented. Moreover, convenience sampling has been carried out, that is, only certain tourist offices in the Valencian Community took part and not all of them have a high number of visits, so there could be varying degrees of development regarding DGC. Another limitation of the study is that, for recently arrived tourists in lesser-known destinations, the references shaping their image are primarily those received at the destination itself. However, in well-established destinations, the image may have been formed over years from various inputs.

Regarding future lines of research, additional variables and relationships should be incorporated into the model, for instance constructs related to the characteristics of the posts generated by the destination, variables such as the intention to visit or interactive effects between UGC and DGC. Additionally, future research should focus on analysing DGC applying AI techniques such as Social Listening with Web Scraping. Last, the findings obtained should be validated by broader geographic testing, as well as longitudinal analysis.

ACKNOWLEDGEMENT

This research has been developed within the framework of the project Grant PID2020-112660RB-I00 funded by MCIN/AEI/10.13039/501100011033, the consolidated research group AICO/2021/144 and CIAICO/2023/069 funded by the Conselleria d'Innovació, Universitats, Ciència i Societat Digital of the Generalitat Valenciana. It has been additionally supported by the Conselleria d'Educació, Cultura, Universitats i Ocupació of the Generalitat Valenciana, with co-financing from the European Social Fund Plus (ESF+).

REFERENCES

Afshardoost, M. and Eshaghi, M. S. (2020). Destination image and tourist behavioural intentions: A meta-analysis. *Tourism management*, *81*, p.104154. https://doi.org/10.1016/j.tourman.2020.104154

Altin, C.O., Dogan, M. T. and Kozak, S. N. (2023). The effectiveness of search engine optimization practices in promoting Turkey's tourism destinations. A case study of tourism destinations in Istanbul city. *Journal of Hospitality and Tourism Management*, *6*(2), pp.11-21. https://doi.org/10.53819/81018102t4137

Anh, T., Hanh, P., Cam, L., Van, K. and Dinh, L. (2019). A study of the factors affecting the content created by international travellers in Vietnam. *Management Science Letters*, *9*(12), pp.2051-2062. https://doi.org/10.5267/j.msl.2019.7.001

Baber, R. and Baber, P. (2023). Influence of social media marketing efforts, e-reputation and destination image on intention to visit among tourists: application of SOR model. *Journal of Hospitality and Tourism Insights*, *6*(5), pp. 2298-2316. https://doi.org/10.1108/JHTI-06-2022-0270

Cheung, M. L., Ting, H., Cheah, J. H. and Sharipudin, M. N. S. (2021). Examining the role of social media-based destination brand community in evoking tourists' emotions and intention to co-create and visit. *Journal of Product & Brand Management*, *30*(1), pp.28-43. https://doi.org/10.1108/JPBM-09-2019-2554

Chin, W. W. (1998). The partial least squares approach to structural equation modeling. *Modern methods for business research*, *295*(2), pp.295-336. https://doi.org/10.4324/9781410604385-10

Churchill Jr, G.A. (1979). A paradigm for developing better measures of marketing constructs. *Journal of marketing research*, *16*(1), pp.64-73. https://doi.org/10.1177/002224377901600110

Elmurngi, E. I. and Gherbi, A. (2020). Building sentiment analysis model and compute reputation scores in e-commerce environment using machine learning techniques. *International Journal of Organizational and Collective Intelligence (IJOCI)*, *10*(1), pp.32-62. https://doi.org/10.4018/IJOCI.2020010103

Fornell, C. and Larcker, D. F. (1981). Evaluating structural equation models with unobservable variables and measurement error. *Journal of marketing research*, *18*(1), pp. 39-50. https://doi.org/10.1177/002224378101800104

Gharib, R.K., Garcia-Perez, A., Dibb, S. and Iskoujina, Z. (2019). Trust and reciprocity effect on electronic word-of-mouth in online review communities. *Journal of Enterprise Information Management*, *33*(1), pp. 120-138. https://doi.org/10.1108/JEIM-03-2019-0079

Graziano, T. and Albanese, V. E. (2020). Online place branding for natural heritage: Institutional strategies and users' perceptions of Mount Etna (Italy). *Heritage*, *3*(4), pp. 1539-1558. https://doi.org/10.3390/heritage3040085

Han, W. and Zhang, T. (2024). Can residents engage potential tourists as 'micro'and 'nano'influencers?. *Current Issues in Tourism*, *27*(20), pp. 3249-3265. https://doi.org/10.1080/13683500.2023.2260062

Hruška, J. and Pásková, M. (2018). How do the national tourism organizations use the social media?. https://doi.org/10.15240/tul/001/2018-4-015

Martín-Delgado, L. M., Sánchez-Martín, J. M. and Rengifo-Gallego, J. I. (2020). An Analysis of Online Reputation Indicators by Means of Geostatistical Techniques—The Case of Rural Accommodation in Extremadura, Spain. *ISPRS International Journal of Geo-Information*, *9*(4), p.208. https://doi.org/10.3390/ijgi9040208

Mehrabian, A. and Russell, J. A. (1974). *An approach to environmental psychology*. the MIT Press.

Palahan, S. and Arunthari, S. (2024). April. Innovating Tourism: Personalized Recommendations through AI. In *Proceedings of the 2024 2nd Asia Conference on Computer Vision, Image Processing and Pattern Recognition* (pp. 1-5). https://doi.org/10.1145/3663976.366399

Platov, A.V., Litvinova, O.I. and Troitskaya, N.G. (2020), May. The Structure of the Online Reputation Analysis in Tourism. In *2nd International Scientific and Practical Conference "Modern Management Trends and the Digital Economy: from Regional Development to Global Economic Growth" (MTDE 2020)* (pp. 813-816). Atlantis Press. https://doi.org/10.2991/aebmr.k.200502.132

Ringle, C. M., Wende, S. and Becker, J. M. (2015). *SmartPLS 3*. SmartPLS. GmbH. http://www.Smartpls.Com.

Schivinski, B. and Dabrowski, D. (2016). The effect of social media communication on consumer perceptions of brands. *Journal of Marketing Communications*, *22*(2), pp. 189-214. https://doi.org/10.1080/13527266.2013.871323

Stepchenkova, S. and Zhan, F. (2013). Visual destination images of Peru: Comparative content analysis of DMO and user-generated photography. *Tourism management*, *36*, pp. 590-601. https://doi.org/10.1016/j.tourman.2012.08.006

Stojanovic, I., Andreu, L. and Curras-Perez, R. (2022). Social media communication and destination brand equity. *Journal of Hospitality and Tourism Technology*, *13*(4), pp. 650-666. https://doi.org/10.1108/JHTT-11-2020-0302

Yadav, N., Verma, S. and Chikhalkar, R.D. (2022). eWOM, destination preference and consumer involvement–a stimulus-organism-response (SOR) lens. *Tourism Review*, *77*(4), pp.1135-1152. https://doi.org/10.1108/TR-10-2020-0506

Zvaigzne, A., Mietule, I., Kotane, I., Sprudzane, S. and Bartkute-Norkuniene, V. (2023). Digital innovations in tourism: the perceptions of stakeholders. *Worldwide Hospitality and Tourism Themes*, *15*(5), pp. 528-537. https://doi.org/10.1108/WHATT-06-2023-0080

MATCHING INTERORGANIZATIONAL SYSTEM OWNERSHIP AND DEPENDENCE TO MAXIMIZE FIRM PERFORMANCE

Philippe Marchildon and Pierre Hadaya
Université du Québec à Montréal (UQAM)
École des sciences de la gestion (ESG)
Department of Analytics, Operations, and Information Technologies
315, Ste. Catherine East St.
Room DS-3933 (3rd Floor)
Montreal (Quebec), Canada, H2X 1L7

ABSTRACT

This study explores how organizational performance in dyadic business relationships can be enhanced by aligning interorganizational system (IOS) ownership structures with the level of dependence between firms. Drawing on Resource Dependence Theory, we propose that IOS benefits are not equally distributed but contingent on the power dynamics within the relationship. Specifically, powerful firms can reap benefits by owning and controlling the IOS, thereby increasing their partner's dependence. Conversely, dependent firms can derive performance gains by adopting their partner's IOS, leveraging integration mechanisms to formalize the relationship and offset power imbalances. We thus hypothesize that a strategic match between IOS ownership structure and organizational dependence leads to improved performance outcomes. As we plan to test this hypothesis by collecting data from purchasing professionals by means of a field survey, we hope to fill important gaps in the IOS and governance literatures by providing a sound decision-making framework for firms seeking to optimize their IOS strategy in dyadic relationships.

KEYWORDS

Dyadic Relationships, Interorganizational Systems (IOS), IOS Ownership Structure, Power Asymmetry, Alignment, Resource Dependency Theory

1. INTRODUCTION

After almost four decades of research, there is a consensus in the literature that interorganizational systems (IOS) – defined in broad terms as information systems (IS) that facilitate the exchange of products, services and information between firms (Johnston and Vitale, 1988) – can provide significant benefits to organizations (Robey et *al.*, 2008). Early works on IOS suggest that the benefits stemming from these systems are distributed unevenly and skewed in favor of the supply chain leader that owns and champions the IOS (Riggins and Mukhopadyay, 1994; Srinivasan et *al.*, 1994). However, more recently, a handful of studies have shown that organizations with less bargaining power can also realize significant gains by adopting the IOS owned by network leaders (Lee et *al.*, 1999; Subramani, 2004). While these novel findings seem to contradict previous results, we suggest that they complement them. What they seem to indicate is that reaping IOS benefits in dyadic relationships is contingent upon matching the IOS ownership structure (i.e., who has financial responsibility and determines the rules and mechanisms of the IOS) to the power dynamic characterizing the relationship.

Unfortunately, while intuitive, this assumption has yet to be validated with empirical results. Indeed, although IOS ownership structure has been shown to influence IOS usage (Shi *et al.*, 2010), its impact on the sharing of IOS benefits remained understudied, leaving key gaps in the IOS and governance literatures (Mukhopadyay and Bouwman, 2019; Roehrich *et al.*, 2020). This study thus hypothesizes that an organization involved in a dyadic relationship can improve its performance by matching the ownership structure of the IOS with its level of dependence on its business counterpart. To do so, we draw upon the resource dependency theory (RDT) to provide theoretical arguments that explain how both the dominant organization that owns the IOS and the dependent firm that adopts it can both reap IOS benefits and hypothesize that a match between IOS ownership structure and organizational dependence leads to improved performance outcomes. In addition, we present the data collection and data analysis strategies we intend to use to test this hypothesis and, ultimately, provide a sound decision-making framework for firms seeking to optimize their IOS strategy in dyadic relationships.

2. THEORETICAL BACKGROUND

According to RDT, the core and purpose of an organization is determined by the activities it controls (Pfeffer and Salancik, 1978). To complete their activities, organizations must, in turn, rely on valuable resources present in their environment. The reliance on these resources creates a procurement problem which is exacerbated by the fact that no organization has full control over the resources it requires (Pfeffer and Salancik, 1978). This obliges organizations to transact with one another and creates interdependencies amongst them (Tillquist *et al.*, 2002). The exchanges that ensue are not always balanced since the parties involved often give an unequal importance to the exchanges (Casciaro and Piskorski, 2005). In such situations of asymmetric dependence between trading partners, the less dependent organization can influence the actions of its counterpart to its own advantage whereas the dependent organization must often comply (Casciaro and Piskorski, 2005). Dependence thus measures the extent to which an organization's decision making should consider the demands of external partners (Pfeffer and Salancik, 1978).

Three factors must be weighted to assess an organization's level of dependence on its business counterpart. First, the extent to which it requires the other party's resource to continue its operations and survive (i.e., importance of the resource). Second, the extent to which the organization from which the resource will be acquired has discretion over the resource allocation and usage (i.e., discretion over the resource). Third, the extent to which there are few alternatives or other organizations from which the resource can be obtained (i.e., presence of alternatives) (Pfeffer and Salancik, 1978).

In addition, RDT suggests that a powerful organization should gain control over resources that (1) minimize its dependence and (2) maximize the dependence of others (Ulrich and Barney, 1984). In doing so, a powerful organization will change the proprietorship of key resources to its advantage to be able to strengthen its hold over its business counterparts. On the opposite side, RDT proposes that a dependent organization dealing with imposed demands can take three types of actions: comply, evade, or alter the demands of its business counterpart (Pfeffer and Salancik, 1978). To alter demands, a dependent organization can rely on one of two strategies (Pfeffer and Salancik, 1978; Tillquist *et al.*, 2002). The first approach entails adopting an ownership alteration strategy that eliminates interdependency through the acquisition of the needed external resource. The second approach entails adopting a quasi-hierarchical strategy that does not involve a change in ownership, but rather the creation of a quasi-hierarchical relationship to more formally govern the interfirm relationship. In pursuing this second strategy, the dependent organization will shift the nature of the relationship with its counterpart from an arm's length to an integrated one. Therefore, increasing its external partner's stake in the relationship and alleviating power asymmetries so it may secure its access to critical resources.

3. RESEARCH HYPOTHESIS

As mentioned previously, the IOS literature presents two contrasting views on how IOS benefits are shared between participating firms. The first takes the perspective of an independent organization that pursues an acquisition strategy by owning the IOS and deriving benefits by imposing its demands on others. Indeed, owning the IOS allows the independent firm to improve its bargaining power and more easily impose its demands on its trading partner. For instance, by dictating the functioning of the IOS (Webster, 1995), controlling access to data (Clemons and Row, 1993) and/or shifting activities and costs to them (Iacovou et al. 1995; Riggins and Mukhopadhyay 1994).

The second view takes the perspective of a dependent organization that, by adopting the IOS owned by its partner, pursues a quasi-hierarchical strategy to reap benefits by formalizing the relationship with its partner. Indeed, relying on an IOS to support a dyadic relationship implies the setup of integration mechanisms that change the nature of the relationship from an arm's length to a more integrated stance. Therefore, allowing the dependent organization to alter demands and retain a bigger proportion of IOS benefits (Lee *et al.*, 1999; Subramani, 2004). Amongst the various integration mechanisms that can change the nature of a business relationship (see Barki and Pinsonneault, 2005), we note that an IOS enables the following: 1) standardizing work (i.e., common and clearly specified procedures and tasks), 2) standardizing output (i.e., clearly specified results or output of work), 3) standardizing skills and knowledge (i.e., standardized training and expertise), 4) standardizing norms (i.e., establishment of common values, beliefs, and expectations), 5), joint planning (i.e., establishment of schedules governing activities of different units), and 6) mutual adjustment (i.e., people or units adapting to each other during their work processes) (Hill *et al.*, 2009; Lee *et al.*, 1999; Nakayama 2003; Srinivasan et al., 1994; Subramani, 2004; Vijayasathy and Robey, 1997). In addition, a handful of case studies have highlighted that a mismatch between the IOS ownership structure and the context of dependence can reduce the benefits for one or the two parties involved in an IOS initiative.

With their study of Wholesale Corp., a retail purchasing organization in the Netherlands, and Superstore Corp., one of its suppliers, Boonstra and de Vries (2005) illustrate the importance of matching the IOS ownership model to the level of dependence of one partner over its counterpart. Indeed, Wholesale Corp. overestimated its influence over Superstore Corp. and chose an IOS ownership model that didn't reflect the actual balance of power between both firms. In addition, because it had better alternatives, Superstore Corp opted for minimal participation in the IOS, resulting in limited or no benefits for either party.

The partnership between Procter and Gamble (P&G) and Wal-Mart also illustrates how IOS ownership structure alignment with relational dependence can affect outcomes. At the beginning of their partnership, P&G could not leverage its own complicated IOS and would not adopt Wal-Mart's efficient IOS to support the relationship (Grean and Shaw, 2002). Later, once both sides recognized the importance of information technology to support their exchanges, the partners jointly developed an IOS that enabled both parties to reap significant benefits ever since (Grean and Shaw, 2002). Hence, in accordance with RDT's tenets and evidence from the IOS literature, we state the following research hypothesis:

Hypothesis 1: By matching the IOS ownership structure to its level of dependence on its business counterpart an organization will improve its performance.

4. METHODOLOGY

The unit of analysis of this study is the business relationship between a customer and one of its suppliers. As integrating information from both customers and suppliers has not often been attempted because of prohibitive research costs and low response rates associated with matched respondent pairs, we will adopt the perspective of the customer and collect data from purchasing professionals via a field survey. Specifically, members of the American Purchasing Society (APS), which has over 50 000 members worldwide, will be targeted. We chose purchasing professional for two reasons. First, specialists in this boundary role have significant knowledge about customer-supplier relationships in their firms (Philips and Bagozzi, 1986). Second, purchasing professionals possess Campbell's (1955) criteria for effective key informants: informedness and ability to communicate with a researcher. Based on MacKenzie et al.'s (2011) recommendations, who suggest that we need between three and ten times the number of respondents as there are items in a questionnaire and given the expected operationalization of our constructs, a sample of at least 250 respondents is required for our study. In addition, we intend to collect data from medium to large North American firms involved in the retail, high tech manufacturing, automotive, healthcare, finance and logistics industries since their level of IOS adoption is high and because firms involved in these industries have developed integrated supply chains and strong business partnerships to fulfill market demands (Fortune Business Insights, 2025).

The survey instrument will include measures specifically developed for the purpose of this study as well as measures drawn and/or adapted from the literature. Since existing scales of dependence do not account for the three dimensions identified by Pfeffer and Salancik (1978), scales for each of these dimensions will be developed by following the three-stage approach proposed by Moore and Benbasat (1991). First, a preliminary pool of items that appear to fit each construct definitions will be generated by identifying and leveraging items from existing scales as well as by drawing inspiration from the relevant literature to create additional items. Second, experts, who have experience in software development and have already collaborated on several co-development projects, will be asked to sort the various items into construct categories. Third, a pilot test of our new scales as well as the overall survey instrument will be conducted to confirm their validity. Traditional measures and thresholds will be followed to ensure convergent validity (i.e., average variance extracted item weights should be significant and exceed 0.70, composite construct reliability should be greater than 0.80, average variance extracted should exceed or be above 0.50, Cronbach's alpha above 0.70) and discriminant validity (i.e., the square root of AVE for each construct should exceed all correlations between that and other constructs) will be followed (Fornell and Larcker, 1981) In addition, the customer's level of dependence upon its supplier will be conceptualized as a second order aggregate construct comprised of these three dimensions (Law *et al*., 1998). The remaining constructs (i.e., IOS ownership structure and organizational performance) will be adapted from the literature.

A two-phase analytical procedure will be employed to analyze our data and test our research hypothesis. During phase one, a principal component analysis (PCA) and a confirmatory factor analysis will be performed to assess the internal consistency and convergent validity of the three dimensions of dependence as well as the IOS ownership and performance constructs. To ensure that the dimensions/constructs are distinct, discriminant validity between constructs will also be examined. In addition, tests will be performed to assess nonresponse and common method biases (i.e., Harman's single factor test and Lindell and Whitney's (2001) marker variable technique). Finally, structural equation modeling (SEM) will be used to ensure that the customer's dependence construct is indeed a second order aggregate construct. During phase two, two approaches will be used to assess the match between the IOS ownership structure and the customer's level of dependence upon its supplier: an analysis of variance approach and a deviation score approach (Bergeron et al., 2001; Venkatraman, 1989).

5. CONCLUSION

This study hypothesizes that organizational performance in dyadic business relationships can be enhanced by aligning IOS ownership structure with the level of dependence between firms. In addition to proposing a novel theoretical and conceptual framework, we also detail a research methodology that should help us reconcile the two seemingly opposite views of how IOS benefits are shared between participating firms. In doing so, we hope to fill important gaps in the IOS and governance literatures and to provide a sound decision-making framework for firms seeking to optimize their IOS strategy in dyadic relationships.

REFERENCES

Bales R.R., et al., (2004). The Development of Supply Chain Management within the Aerospace Manufacturing Sector. *Supply Chain Management: An International Journal*, Vol. 9, No. 3, pp. 250-255.

Barki, H. and Pinsonneault, A. (2005). A Model of Organizational Integration, Implementation Effort, and Performance. *Organization science,* Vol. 16, No. 2, pp. 165-179.

Bergeron, F. et al (2001). Fit in Strategic Information Technology Management Research: An Empirical Comparison of Perspectives. *Omega,* Vol. 29, No. 2, pp. 125-142.

Boonstra, A. and De Vries, J. (2005). Analyzing Inter-Organizational Information Systems from a Power and Interest Perspective. *International Journal of Information Management,* Vol. 25, No. 6, pp. 485-501.

Campbell, D.T. (1955). The informant in quantitative research. *American Journal of Sociology*, Vol. 60, No. 4, pp. 339-342.

Casciaro, T. and Piskorski, M.J. (2005). Power Imbalance, Mutual Dependence, and Constraint Absorption: A Closer Look at Resource Dependence Theory. *Administrative Science Quarterly,* Vol. 50, No. 2, pp. 167-199.

Clemons, E.K. and Row, M.C. (1993). Limits to Interfirm Coordination through Information Technology: Results of a Field Study in Consumer Packaged Goods Distribution. *Journal of Management Information Systems,* Vol. 10, No. 1, pp. 73-95.

Fornell, C. and Larcker, D. (1981). Structural equation models with unobservable variables and measurement error. *Journal of Marketing Research*, Vol. 18, No. 1, pp. 39-50.

Fortune Business Insights (2025). Electronic Data Interchange (EDI) Software Market Size, Share & Industry Analysis, By Type (In-house, Outsourcing, and Hybrid), By Deployment (Cloud and On-premises), By Industry (Healthcare, Automotive, Financial Services, High Tech/Manufacturing, Retail, Logistics, and Others), and Regional Forecast, 2025-2032, FBI103690, Fortune Business Insights.

Grean, M. and Shaw, M.J. (2002). Supply-Chain Partnership Between P&G and Wal-Mart. In E-Business Management: Integration of Web Technologies with Business Model, M.J. Shaw (ed.), New York: Kluwer Academic Publishers, pp. 1-21.

Iacovou, C.L. et al. (1995). Electronic Data Interchange and Small Organizations: Adoption and Impact of Technology. *MIS Quarterly,* Vol. 19, No. 4, pp. 465-485.

Johnston, H.R. and Vitale, M.R. (1988). Creating Competitive Advantages with Interorganizational Information Systems. *MIS Quarterly,* Vol. 12, No, 2, pp. 153-165.

Law, K.S. et al. (1998), Toward a Taxonomy of Multidimensional Constructs. *Academy of Management Review,* Vol. 23, No. 4, pp. 741–755.

Lee, H.G. et al. (1999). Research Report: Can EDI Benefit Adopters?. *Information Systems Research,* Vol. 10, No. 2, pp. 186-95.

Lindell, M.K. and Whitney, D.J. (2001). Accounting for common method variance in cross-sectional research designs. *Journal of Applied Psychology*, Vol. 86, No. 1, pp. 114-121.

Moore, G.C. and Benbasat, I. (1991). Development of an Instrument to Measure the Perception of Adopting an Information Technology Innovation. *Information Systems Research,* Vol. 2, No. 3, pp. 192-222.

Mukhopadyay, S. and Bouwman, H. (2019). Orchestration and governance in digital platform ecosystems: a literature review and trends. *Digital policity, regulation and governance*, Vol. 21, No. 4, pp. 329-351.

Pfeffer, J. and Salancik, G.R. (1978). *The External Control of Organizations: A Resource Dependence Perspective*, Harper and Row, New York, NY.

Phillips, L.W. and Bagozzi, R.P. (1986). On Measuring the Organizational Properties of Distribution Channels: Methodological Issues in the Use of Key Informants. *Research in Marketing,* Vol. 8, No. 1, pp. 313-369.

Riggins, F. and Mukhopadhyay, T. (1994). Interdependent Benefits from Interorganizational Systems: Opportunities for Business Partner Engineering. *Journal of Management Information Systems,* Vol. 11, No. 2, pp. 37-57.

Robey, D. et al. (2008). Theoretical Foundations of Empirical Research on Interorganizational Systems: Assessing Past Contributions and Guiding Future Directions. *Journal of the Association for Information Systems,* Vol. 9, No. 9, pp. 497-518.

Roehrich, J.K. et al. (2020). Inter-organizational governance: a review, conceptualisation and extension. *Production planning & control*, Vol. 31, No. 6, pp. 453-469.

Shi, Z. et al. (2008). Exploring the impact of interdependent relationships on IOS use: the roles of governance mechanisms. *Journal of Computer Information Systems*, Vol. 50, No. 3, pp. 50-62.

Srinivasan, K. et al. (1994). Impact of Electronic Data Interchange Technology on JIT Shipments. *Management Science,* Vol. 40, No. 10, pp. 1291-1304.

Subramani, M. (2004). How Do Supplier Benefit from Information Technology Use in Supply Chain Relationships?. *MIS Quarterly,* Vol. 28, No. 1, pp. 45-73.

Tillquist, J. et al. (2002). A Representational Scheme for Analyzing Information Technology and Organizational Dependency. *MIS Quarterly,* Vol. 26, No. 2, pp. 91-118.

Ulrich, D. and Barney, J.B. (1984). Perspectives in Organizations: Resource Dependence, Efficiency, and Population. *Academy of Management Review,* Vol. 9, No. 3, pp. 471-481.

Venkatraman, N. (1989). Strategic Orientation of Business Enterprises: The Construct, Dimensionality, and Measurement. *Management Science,* Vol. 35, No. 8, pp. 942-963.

Webster, J. (1995). Networks of Collaboration or Conflict? Electronic Data Interchange and Power in the Supply Chain. *Journal of Strategic Information Systems,* Vol. 4, No. 1, pp. 31-42.

BARRIERS TO AI PERSONALISATION IN BEAUTY SECTOR SMES IN DEVELOPING ECONOMIES

Yanjun Chen and Xinwen Zhang
Birmingham City University, UK

ABSTRACT

This paper investigates the barriers to adopting AI-powered personalisation tools by small and medium-sized enterprises (SMEs) in the beauty service sector across developing economies. Despite the transformative potential of artificial intelligence technologies, such as augmented reality (AR) try-ons, virtual skincare advisors, and algorithmic recommendation systems, SMEs in identity-sensitive, resource-constrained contexts face challenges such as infrastructural gaps, limited digital skills, trust deficits, and cultural misalignment. Drawing on the Technology Acceptance Model (TAM) and the Stimulus–Organism–Response (S-O-R) model, this study employs a convergent mixed-methods approach to examine how psychological, technological, and socio-cultural factors interact to influence AI adoption behaviours. The conceptual framework incorporates emotional and ethical tensions inherent in deploying AI within personalised beauty services, particularly in mobile-first markets such as China. By proposing a culturally embedded and operationally grounded implementation model tailored to SME realities, this research contributes to the discourse on inclusive digital transformation and offers practical insights for AI integration in emerging service economies.

KEYWORDS

AI Adoption, Beauty Industry SMEs, Technology Acceptance Model (TAM), Stimulus-Organism-Response (S-O-R) Model, Culturally Embedded Digital Transformation, Emotional and Ethical Design in AI, Ai Adoption

1. INTRODUCTION AND RESEARCH PROBLEM

1.1 Introduction

Artificial intelligence (AI) technologies are redefining the landscape of service personalisation, particularly in industries where consumer expectations, identity expression, and experiential engagement are central. In the beauty service sector, AI tools such as augmented reality (AR) try-ons, intelligent skincare diagnostics, and algorithmic recommendation systems are transforming how services are designed and delivered (Dwivedi et al., 2021). These innovations are increasingly embraced by digital-native consumers across developing economies, who demand hyper-personalised, tech-integrated service journeys (Abrokwah-Larbi & Awuku-Larbi, 2023; Schwaeke et al., 2025). Despite this rising demand, AI adoption among small and medium-sized enterprises (SMEs) operating in these markets remains fragmented and uneven. SMEs, which dominate the service economy in many developing countries, often struggle to translate consumer enthusiasm into effective AI deployment. This paradox reflects a complex interplay of infrastructural limitations, digital literacy gaps, and concerns surrounding implementation risks, organisational change, and ethical design (Lemos et al., 2022; Chatterjee et al., 2022). Moreover, emotional resistance, symbolic dissonance, and trust deficits exacerbate the challenge in sectors like beauty, where AI tools directly mediate deeply personal and culturally embedded experiences.

While much of the existing AI adoption research focuses on large firms in technologically advanced economies, SMEs in developing economies confront unique conditions. These include poor integration capacity, funding limits, and AI tools that misalign with local expectations (Schwaeke et al., 2025). Even when AI solutions are available, their interface design and algorithmic logic often fail to reflect diverse aesthetic standards or socio-cultural realities, creating mismatches between service providers and their clients. This paper responds to these challenges by examining the barriers to AI personalisation tool adoption in beauty-focused SMEs across developing economies. Building on the Technology Acceptance Model (TAM) and the Stimulus–Organism–Response (S-O-R) framework, the study explores both functional and emotional factors shaping SME adoption intent. By situating the investigation within resource-constrained, identity-sensitive service environments, it contributes to the growing body of research on inclusive digital transformation, proposing a conceptual model that balances rational evaluation with culturally and emotionally grounded user response.

1.2 Problem Statement

Despite growing enthusiasm for AI-driven personalisation among consumers in service sectors, small and medium-sized enterprises (SMEs) across developing economies remain slow to adopt these tools in practice. This disparity is most evident in beauty and wellness industries, where experience is personal, emotional, and culturally shaped. While digital technologies promise to enhance service efficiency, scalability, and emotional resonance, their implementation within SMEs is often hindered by structural limitations, organisational ambivalence, and contextual misalignments (Albats et al., 2020; Schwaeke et al., 2025). Research largely focuses on large firms in developed economies, leaving a gap in understanding SME behaviour in resource-constrained markets (Giuggioli & Pellegrini, 2023; Lemos et al., 2022). Frameworks largely emphasise rational, functionality-based criteria such as ease of use and performance expectancy. However, such models often fail to account for symbolic resistance, aesthetic misfit, emotional detachment, or trust erosion, factors which are critical(Chatterjee et al., 2022; Schillaci et al., 2024).

Further compounding the issue is the scarcity of localised, SME-specific research in emerging markets that interrogates the confluence of cultural norms, organisational capability, and technological maturity. Studies by Schwaeke et al. (2025) and Albats et al. (2020) underscore that SMEs often encounter eight interrelated challenges during AI implementation, ranging from infrastructure gaps and skill shortages to misaligned expectations from external stakeholders and regulatory uncertainty. These challenges are not merely operational but strategic, as SMEs are simultaneously navigating risk, reputation, and customer intimacy in adopting technologies often designed with large-firm logic. Consequently, there remains a pressing need for a more inclusive conceptual framework that captures not only functional but also emotional, symbolic, and organisational inhibitors of AI personalisation tool adoption.

2. LITERATURE REVIEW AND THEORETICAL FRAMEWORK

2.1 Summary of the Literature

The recent scholarship has increasingly acknowledged the strategic importance of artificial intelligence (AI) in enabling personalised services across industries, particularly in digitally maturing service sectors such as beauty, wellness, and creative retail. Tools such as augmented reality (AR) try-ons, AI-enabled diagnostics, and automated recommendation systems are transforming how consumers interact with brands and how service firms position their offerings (Winarto and Wisesa, 2024). While consumers in emerging markets demonstrate strong digital enthusiasm, the corresponding level of AI adoption among small and medium-sized enterprises (SMEs) remains limited and fragmented (Lada et al., 2023; Pu et al., 2024). This paradox is pronounced in services shaped by emotion and cultural codes. Much of the foundational research in this area draws upon the Technology Acceptance Model (TAM), which foregrounds perceived usefulness and ease of use as key determinants of behavioural intention (Davis, 1989). However, its explanatory power is constrained in emotionally sensitive contexts. Extensions via the Stimulus–Organism–Response (S-O-R) model help account for affective variables such as trust, aesthetic resonance, and symbolic meaning in user-AI interaction (Butt et al., 2021; Schillaci et al., 2024). For instance, in identity-sensitive services like beauty or healthcare, emotionally incongruent AI experiences can trigger aesthetic anxiety, reduce user satisfaction, and hinder continued engagement—even if the tools function well on a technical level (Fatima et al., 2024; Chang et al., 2022).

On the enabler side, internal organisational capabilities such as digital skills, absorptive capacity, and adaptive leadership significantly influence AI uptake (Lemos et al., 2022; Giuggioli and Pellegrini, 2023). SMEs that exhibit higher digital maturity and openness to change are better positioned to align AI tools with customer experience goals. Moreover, the design quality of AI interfaces—including features like anthropomorphism, perceived empathy, and interactional coherence—has emerged as a decisive adoption driver (Hu and Sun, 2023; Luo et al., 2019). Such attributes enhance user trust, foster rapport, and convert transactional encounters into relational experiences (Xu and Zhao, 2023). However, a wide range of barriers remains unresolved. Schwaeke et al. (2025) identify eight adoption challenge categories among SMEs in developing economies, including infrastructural gaps, regulatory ambiguity, and leadership inertia. In service contexts, emotional disconnection, lack of conversational realism, and symbolic misalignment between AI output and customer identity norms often lead to disengagement (Fatima et al., 2024; Chang et al., 2022). Further, concerns around data privacy, trustworthiness, and limited behavioural realism have also been reported as inhibitors of chatbot adoption (Chang et al., 2022; Luo et al., 2019).

2.2 Identified Theories and Conceptual Models

Two theoretical frameworks are central to this study: the Technology Acceptance Model (TAM) and the Stimulus–Organism–Response (S-O-R) model. These frameworks offer complementary lenses—TAM provides a rationalist, utility-driven perspective on technology acceptance behaviour, while S-O-R introduces a psychological and emotionally grounded framework suited to identity-sensitive service interactions. Their integration allows for a multidimensional understanding of AI adoption in emotionally rich, culturally embedded service environments typical of SMEs in developing economies. The Technology Acceptance Model (TAM), introduced by Davis (1989), posits that two primary beliefs, perceived usefulness and perceived ease of use, shape a user's attitude toward adopting new technology. However, TAM has also faced criticism for its limited treatment of affective, cultural, and symbolic dimensions (Bagozzi, 2007). In services that intersect with identity and emotion, such as AI-mediated beauty consultation or personalised skincare recommendations, decision-making is often shaped by symbolic trust, emotional congruence, and brand aesthetics—factors that exceed TAM's original scope (Butt et al., 2021; Chang et al., 2022).

To address these limitations, the Stimulus–Organism–Response (S-O-R) model (Mehrabian and Russell, 1974) is introduced as a complementary framework. S-O-R conceptualises stimuli (e.g. AI interfaces, chatbot interactions) as external inputs that generate organismic responses (emotions such as trust, alienation, satisfaction), which in turn produce behavioural outputs (adoption, avoidance, engagement). This model has proven effective in contexts where digital interfaces carry emotional and cultural weight, including healthcare (Fatima et al., 2024), tourism (Hu and Sun, 2023), and retail innovation (Xu and Zhao, 2023). Its affective structure is especially relevant for SMEs offering personalised services, where emotional resonance and symbolic legitimacy often determine user engagement. While frameworks such as the Technology–Organisation–Environment (TOE) or UTAUT are valuable for system-level adoption analysis, they are often better suited to large, process-driven enterprises. By contrast, this study focuses on SMEs in developing economies where AI interfaces interact directly with end-users in emotionally salient ways. The integration of TAM and S-O-R enables a more user-centred, emotionally aware, and contextually sensitive model of AI adoption, capable of capturing both rational assessments and symbolic-friction effects.

Recent research also emphasises the role of organisational readiness and stakeholder alignment in shaping AI adoption at the SME level. For example, Schwaeke et al. (2025) which identify barriers related to institutional fragility, leadership inertia, and regulatory ambiguity, factors that compound emotional or symbolic resistance to AI, even when perceived utility is high. So the TAM–S-O-R model serves as an integrated lens through which to investigate both behavioural intent and emotional resistance in AI personalisation adoption. It is well-suited to SMEs in developing economies, where digital immaturity, cultural factors, and resource limits intersect.

2.3 Applications of Theories in Industry Contexts

The Technology acceptance model (TAM) and the Stimulus–Organism–Response (S-O-R) model have been widely used in various fields to investigate the adoption patterns of digital technologies. In the retail industry, TAM has played an important role in assessing user perceptions of AI tools such as chatbots, virtual assistants, and product recommendation systems, especially in terms of perceived ease of use and functional effectiveness. In healthcare, the model has been used to assess user acceptance of telemedicine platforms, often highlighting issues of trust, data privacy, and usability (Kraus et al., 2022). These applications highlight the utility of TAM in understanding adoption behaviour, where decisions to use digital technologies are shaped by rational assessments of utility and effort. At the same time, the S-O-R model has gained traction in environments where emotional and sensory triggers such as visual aesthetics, interactivity, and symbolic value are integral to user experience. However, the beauty industry offers a more emotionally and symbolically complex area for technology adoption. While TAM has been applied to examine AI-driven virtual try-ons and personalised skincare tools (Winarto & Wisesa, 2024), it often fails to capture the emotional and socio-cultural dynamics that underpin user responses. For example, emotional dissonance or alienation may be triggered when algorithmic beauty advice reinforces Eurocentric or hegemonic beauty norms that fail to reflect the diversity of users, especially in non-Western markets such as China (Georgievskaya et al., 2023). At the same time, studies by Polisetty et al. (2024) and Pu et al. (2024) highlight the centrality of trust, familiarity, and intuitive design in shaping AI adoption factors for small businesses, closely aligning with TAM's emphasis on perceived ease of use and utility.

2.4 Research Gaps

The literature reveals several key gaps that this study seeks to address:

- Under-representation of SMEs in AI research: Most empirical studies continue to focus on large, digitally mature enterprises, overlooking how SMEs, particularly those in emerging economies, navigate AI adoption amid infrastructural limitations, skill gaps, and market volatility. Arroyabe et al. (2024) argue that internal capabilities such as digital proficiency and innovation readiness are more critical than external support in determining successful outcomes, a view reinforced by Schwaeke et al. (2025), who not only underscore leadership adaptability but also identify eight interlinked categories of SME-specific adoption constraints—including regulatory ambiguity, digital ecosystem fragmentation, and cultural inertia—which are especially relevant in under-researched sectors such as beauty and wellness.
- Neglect of socio-cultural and emotional dimensions: While the TAM framework explains adoption through perceived usefulness and ease of use, it insufficiently accounts for affective and symbolic barriers, particularly in emotionally sensitive sectors like beauty. Schillaci et al. (2024) demonstrate that user perceptions of AI are shaped by emotional congruence, gender-role expectations, and anthropomorphic design features, which can affect trust and adoption even when technical functionality is strong.
- Lack of context-specific research in developing economics' beauty sector for example China: limited academic work has explored how local consumer norms, mobile-first behaviours, and algorithmic personalisation affect SME service innovation.
- Ethical and representational issues remain disconnected from adoption models: While existing literature highlights problems such as algorithmic bias and aesthetic exclusion, these are rarely linked to practical SME-level adoption decisions. While conceptual critiques of algorithmic bias and aesthetic exclusion exist (Georgievskaya et al., 2023), few studies examine how such ethical misalignments translate into actual hesitation or resistance among beauty service SMEs.

By adopting an integrated TAM–S-O-R framework, this study aims to approach enables a more inclusive view of digital transformation in identity-sensitive SME services across developing economies.

3. RESEARCH CONCEPTUAL MODEL

This study adopts an integrated conceptual model that combines the Technology Acceptance Model (TAM) and the Stimulus–Organism–Response (S-O-R) framework to investigate the adoption of AI-powered personalisation tools by small and medium-sized enterprises (SMEs) in the beauty and service sectors across developing economies. The hybrid model addresses limitations in existing adoption literature by incorporating both cognitive-functional factors and affective-symbolic variables that influence technology use in emotionally sensitive, culturally embedded service contexts. The Technology Acceptance Model (TAM) (Davis, 1989) provides the rational core of the model, positing that perceived usefulness (PU) and perceived ease of use (PEOU) shape users' attitudes toward a technology, which in turn influence their intention to adopt it. This framework has been widely validated across sectors including healthcare, education, and retail (Venkatesh and

Davis, 2000). However, TAM has been critiqued for assuming that adoption is purely rational and underemphasising the affective, symbolic, and trust-based factors that frequently arise in AI-mediated experiences (Bagozzi, 2007; Chang et al., 2022).

To address this gap, the model integrates the Stimulus–Organism–Response (S-O-R) framework (Mehrabian and Russell, 1974), which conceptualises AI technologies as external stimuli (e.g., chatbot interface, AR try-on), that influence organismic states (e.g., trust, emotional alignment, aesthetic satisfaction), and ultimately shape response behaviours (e.g., adoption, resistance, disengagement). This framework has proven highly relevant in emotionally charged domains such as healthcare (Fatima et al., 2024), tourism (Hu and Sun, 2023), and personalised retail (Schillaci et al., 2024), where users react not only to functionality but also to the emotional and cultural compatibility of AI interactions. In this study's model, TAM variables represent the cognitive-evaluative path, while S-O-R variables represent the emotional-affective path. For example, an SME may perceive a virtual skincare recommender as useful (PU) and intuitive (PEOU), but adoption could still fail if customers experience symbolic dissonance, lack emotional trust in the AI interface, or perceive the chatbot as culturally inappropriate (Chang et al., 2022; Fatima et al., 2024). The model therefore includes affective mediators such as perceived empathy, emotional congruence, and anthropomorphic rapport—factors that have been shown to influence trust and continued engagement with AI (Hu and Sun, 2023). Additionally, adoption decisions within SMEs are not made in a vacuum. Research has shown that organisational readiness, leadership support, and stakeholder expectations also moderate technology implementation outcomes (Albats et al., 2020; Schwaeke et al., 2025). While these organisational variables are not explicitly modelled here, they form part of the contextual layer that explains why affective and symbolic triggers—often treated as peripheral—become central in emotionally driven service environments. The resulting TAM–S-O-R conceptual model thus captures the dual logic of AI adoption: the rational evaluation of functionality, and the affective evaluation of symbolic and emotional congruence. This hybrid lens provides a more inclusive, empirically grounded framework to understand AI adoption behaviour in under-resourced SMEs operating in service sectors where customer experience is both intimate and identity-laden.

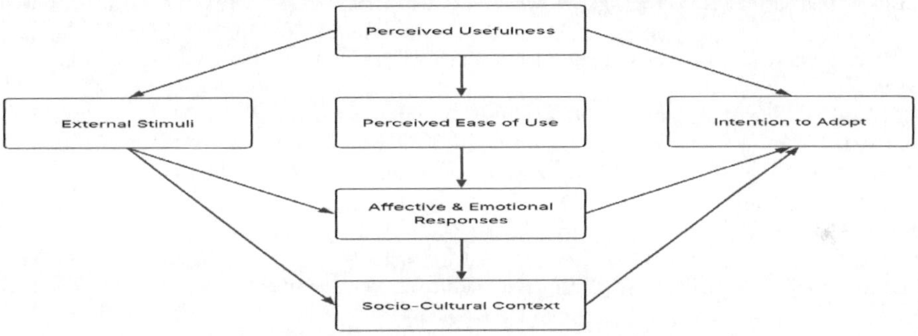

Figure 1. Research Conceptual Model (Author, 2025)

REFERENCES

Albats, E., Alexander, A., Mahdad, M., Miller, K. and Post, G. (2020). Stakeholder management in SME open innovation: interdependences and strategic actions. *Journal of Business Research*, *119*, pp. 291-301.

Abrokwah-Larbi, K. and Awuku-Larbi, Y. (2023). The impact of artificial intelligence in marketing on the performance of business organizations: evidence from SMEs in an emerging economy. *Journal of Entrepreneurship in Emerging Economies*, 16(4), pp. 1090-1117.

Arroyabe, M.F., Arranz, C.F., De Arroyabe, I.F. and de Arroyabe, J.C.F. (2024). Analyzing AI adoption in European SMEs: A study of digital capabilities, innovation, and external environment. *Technology in Society*, 79, p.102733.

Bagozzi, R. P. (2007). The legacy of the technology acceptance model and a proposal for a paradigm shift. *Journal of the Association for Information Systems*, *8*(4), 244–254.

Butt, A., Ahmad, H., Muzaffar, A., Ali, F. and Shafique, N. (2021). WOW, the make-up AR app is impressive: A comparative study between China and South Korea. *Journal of Services Marketing*, 36(1), pp. 73-88.

Chatterjee, S., Chaudhuri, R., Vrontis, D. and Basile, G. (2022). Digital transformation and entrepreneurship process in SMEs of India: a moderating role of adoption of AI-CRM capability and strategic planning. *Journal of Strategy and Management*, 15(3), pp.416-433.

Chang, I.C., Shih, Y.S. and Kuo, K.M. (2022). Why would you use medical chatbots? interview and survey. *International Journal of Medical Informatics*, 165, p.104827.

Davis, F. D. (1989). Perceived usefulness, perceived ease of use, and user acceptance of information technology. *MIS Quarterly*, *13*(3), 319–340. https://doi.org/10.2307/249008

Dwivedi, Y. K., Hughes, D. L., Ismagilova, E., Aarts, G., Coombs, C., Crick, T., ... & Williams, M. D. (2023). Artificial intelligence (AI): Multidisciplinary perspectives on emerging challenges, opportunities, and agenda for research, practice and policy. *International Journal of Information Management*, *70*, 102641. https://doi.org/10.1016/j.ijinfomgt.2022.102641

Fatima, J.K., Khan, M.I., Bahmannia, S., Chatrath, S.K., Dale, N.F. and Johns, R. (2024). Rapport with a chatbot? The underlying role of anthropomorphism in socio-cognitive perceptions of rapport and e-word of mouth. *Journal of Retailing and Consumer Services*, *77*, p.103666.

Georgievskaya, Y., Natarajan, V., & Achanta, R. (2023). The coded body: Algorithmic beauty standards and representation in AI-generated skincare diagnostics. *AI & Society*, *38*(1), 121–136. https://doi.org/10.1007/s00146-022-01464-z

Giuggioli, G. and Pellegrini, M.M. (2023). Artificial intelligence as an enabler for entrepreneurs: a systematic literature review and an agenda for future research. *International Journal of Entrepreneurial Behavior & Research*, *29*(4), pp. 816-837.

Hu, Y. and Sun, Y. (2023). Understanding the joint effects of internal and external anthropomorphic cues of intelligent customer service bot on user satisfaction. *Data and Information Management*, *7*(3), p.100047.

Kraus, S., Schiavone, F., Pluzhnikova, A., & Invernizzi, A. C. (2022). Digital transformation in SMEs: A systematic literature review and future research directions. *Journal of Small Business Management*, *60*(1), 1–37. https://doi.org/10.1080/00472778.2021.1955123

Lada, S., Chekima, B., Karim, M.R.A., Fabeil, N.F., Ayub, M.S., Amirul, S.M., Ansar, R., Bouteraa, M., Fook, L.M. and Zaki, H.O. (2023). Determining factors related to artificial intelligence (AI) adoption among Malaysia's small and medium-sized businesses. *Journal of Open Innovation: Technology, Market, and Complexity*, *9*(4), p.100144.

Lemos, S.I., Ferreira, F.A., Zopounidis, C., Galariotis, E. and Ferreira, N.C. (2022). Artificial intelligence and change management in small and medium-sized enterprises: an analysis of dynamics within adaptation initiatives. *Annals of Operations Research*, pp. 1-27.

Luo, X., Tong, S., Fang, Z., & Qu, Z. (2019). Machines versus humans: The impact of AI chatbot disclosure on customer purchases. *SSRN Electronic Journal*. https://doi.org/10.2139/ssrn.3435635

Mehrabian, A., & Russell, J. A. (1974). An approach to environmental psychology. MIT Press.

Polisetty, A., Chakraborty, D., Kar, A.K. and Pahari, S. (2024). What determines AI adoption in companies? Mixed-method evidence. *Journal of Computer Information Systems*, *64*(3), pp. 370-387.

Pu, L., Radics, R.I., Umar, M. and Quan, Z. (2024). Investigating How Chinese E-Commerce SMEs Would Adopt AI Live-Streaming via a Dual Analysis: Trendy and Transformative. *Journal of Organizational and End User Computing (JOEUC)*, 36(1), pp. 1-22.

Seitz, L. (2024). Artificial empathy in healthcare chatbots: Does it feel authentic?. *Computers in Human Behavior: Artificial Humans*, *2*(1), p. 100067.

Schwaeke, J., Peters, A., Kanbach, D.K., Kraus, S. and Jones, P. (2025). The new normal: The status quo of AI adoption in SMEs. *Journal of small business management*, 63(3), pp. 1297-1331.

Schillaci, C.E., De Cosmo, L.M., Piper, L., Nicotra, M. and Guido, G. (2024). Anthropomorphic chatbots' for future healthcare services: Effects of personality, gender, and roles on source credibility, user satisfaction, and intention to use. *Technological Forecasting and Social Change*, 199, p. 123025.

Sharma, A., & Sheth, J. (2022). Resurgence of small businesses through AI-based personalisation in emerging markets. *Journal of Business Research*, *145*, 163–174. https://doi.org/10.1016/j.jbusres.2022.02.024

Venkatesh, V., & Davis, F. D. (2000). A theoretical extension of the technology acceptance model: Four longitudinal field studies. *Management Science*, *46*(2), 186–204. https://doi.org/10.1287/mnsc.46.2.186.11926

Winarto, D. A., & Wisesa, H. A. (2024). Exploring AI adoption in the beauty industry: A consumer-centric perspective on augmented reality try-on experiences. *Computers in Human Behavior Reports*, *9*, 100204. https://doi.org/10.1016/j.chbr.2024.100204

Xu, Y., Niu, N. and Zhao, Z. (2023). Dissecting the mixed effects of human-customer service chatbot interaction on customer satisfaction: An explanation from temporal and conversational cues. *Journal of Retailing and Consumer Services*, *74*, p. 103417.

FROM ALGORITHM DESIGN TO ALGORITHMIC BIAS: IDENTIFYING DISCRIMINATORY RISKS IN INNOVATION MANAGEMENT

Federico Mertoli[1], Carmela E. Schillaci[1], Luigi Piper[2], Marco Benvenuto[2], Elisa R. Ferrari[3] and Gianluigi Guido[2]
[1]*Dept of Economics and Business, University of Catania, Italy*
[2]*Dept of Economic Science, University of Salento, Italy*
[3]*Dept of Economic and Legal Sciences, University of Kore, Italy*

ABSTRACT

The growing integration of Generative Artificial Intelligence into managerial processes has enhanced decision-making, data interpretation, and operational efficiency. However, alongside these benefits, algorithmic bias has emerged as a critical concern, particularly when AI systems inadvertently reinforce existing social inequalities. This study investigates how such biases are introduced during the algorithm design, a phase where technical and personal assumptions become embedded in AI systems. Through a systematic literature review, four key areas of bias emergence are identified: gendered anthropomorphism, proxy variable selection, dataset composition and labeling, and lack of human oversight in algorithm selection. The findings emphasize that mitigating algorithmic bias requires inclusive design, diverse teams, and strong oversight, aligning AI systems development with ethical principles and regulatory standards.

KEYWORDS

Generative Artificial Intelligence, Algorithmic Bias, Algorithm Design, Discrimination

1. INTRODUCTION

In recent years, Artificial Intelligence (AI) has become increasingly pervasive across industries, transforming business models, operations, and decision-making (Guan *et al.*, 2022; Li *et al.*, 2023). Among its most disruptive developments is *Generative AI*, a branch of AI that creates original content—such as text, code, or images—by identifying patterns in large datasets (Felicetti *et al.*, 2024; Gupta, 2024). In managerial contexts, it has been integrated into systems that enhance strategic and operational decisions by improving efficiency, data interpretation, and task automation (Dakhel *et al.*, 2023; Fu *et al.*, 2023; Nguyen and Nadi, 2022).

However, the adoption of these systems raises critical concerns about fairness, transparency, and unintended consequences (Obreja *et al.*, 2024; Sen *et al.*, 2020). One of the most pressing is *algorithmic bias*—the tendency of AI systems to replicate and amplify social inequalities. These biases often originate in the early stages of algorithm design (D'Alessandro *et al.*, 2017; Hofeditz *et al.*, 2022), where engineers make foundational choices about models, architectures, activation functions, and parameters (Weisz *et al.*, 2024).

While existing literature has explored algorithmic bias in applied domains such as healthcare (Ostherr, 2022), recruitment (Soleimani *et al.*, 2022), and legal services (Bhavani & Thuraisingam, 2022), less attention has been paid to how these biases emerge during design. Much research focuses on downstream effects, neglecting the upstream decisions that shape system behavior. As a result, a conceptual and practical gap persists regarding how designers—consciously or not—embed cultural norms and assumptions into algorithms. This study addresses that gap by investigating how bias is introduced during algorithm design in managerial AI systems. Through a systematic literature review, key design choices are identified that reinforce discriminatory dynamics, along with their implications for digital leadership and AI governance.

2. METHODOLOGY

To explore the aim of the paper, a systematic literature review was conducted, adopting a qualitative approach grounded in the methodological framework developed by Tranfield *et al.* (2003). The review unfolded through a multi-phase process, beginning with the identification of conceptual gaps in the existing literature and the development of a structured research protocol. This initial stage involved clarifying the relevance of the review, delineating its scope, drafting a research plan, and defining the methodological guidelines to inform the entire process.

During the initial phase, the research question was formally defined, along with the criteria for inclusion and exclusion of studies. The search strategy was constructed in accordance with established best practices for systematic reviews, particularly those outlined by Davies & Crombie (1998). To refine the search terminology, a focus group was organized involving eight experts, equally drawn from the fields of marketing, management, and informatics. The experts were identified based on disciplinary background and research experience in AI, digital transformation, marketing, management, and informatics. Each participant was asked to independently generate a list of terms related to the intersection of ageing and technology. The terms were then compared and aggregated. A simple consensus strategy was applied, ranking keywords based on frequency and perceived relevance across disciplines. The four highest-ranking keywords—Artificial Intelligence, Bias, Discrimination, and Data—were selected to formulate the final query used in the search protocol.

The literature search was conducted using Scopus, selected for its comprehensive indexing and advanced filtering capabilities (Franceschet, 2010). The initial search returned a corpus of 575 documents, which were screened by title and abstract for relevance. After a full-text review and removal of duplicates or conceptually redundant studies, 127 articles were retained for inclusion in the final analysis. The selected documents were then subjected to systematic coding and analysis. A structured reading grid was applied to each study to extract key information, including research focus, methodological approach, analytical techniques, and typology (qualitative, quantitative, or theoretical). The coding was initially piloted on a small subset of papers to ensure consistency between reviewers, and then extended to the entire dataset. This process enabled a thematically coherent synthesis aligned with the objectives of the review.

In the final stage of the review, each article was carefully examined to assess its consistency with the research objectives. Additionally, bibliographic cross-referencing was used to identify further relevant sources, which were then assessed for inclusion. Contributions that did not meet the established content criteria were excluded. The remaining literature was analyzed using the structured synthesis methodology outlined by Bal and Nijkamp (2001), which ensured coherence in the aggregation and interpretation of findings.

3. RESULTS AND DISCUSSIONS

The systematic literature review revealed that algorithmic bias in AI systems originates from multiple, interrelated choices made during the design phase. The findings were organized into four primary areas where bias tends to emerge.

3.1 Gendered Anthropomorphism and Role Assignments

Several studies have shown that the anthropomorphization of AI systems—through the use of human-like voices, names, and conversational patterns—can reinforce stereotypical social roles. In particular, the systematic assignment of female voices and servile language to virtual assistants tends to reflect and perpetuate traditional gender expectations, symbolically encoding existing power hierarchies into digital interfaces (Manasi *et al.*, 2022; Mileti *et al.*, 2025; Schillaci *et al.*, 2024).

This phenomenon is not merely cosmetic: it highlights how design decisions shaped by interactional logic can have norm-reinforcing effects, especially when adopted uncritically across platforms. These design defaults risk turning AI into a vehicle for normalizing unequal representations, rather than challenging them. A related example is provided by Zhao *et al.* (2017), who demonstrated that semantic visual labeling systems frequently associated women with domestic activities. This suggests that biases are not confined to language but also rooted in visual data and algorithmic categorization—amplifying the systemic nature of the problem.

3.2 Proxy Variables and Model Objective Misalignment

A recurring source of bias in algorithm design stems from the use of proxy variables and the definition of model objectives. Although such proxies are often selected for reasons of data availability or computational efficiency, they may inadequately represent the real-world phenomena they aim to model, resulting in unintended discriminatory effects. A well-known example is offered by Obermeyer *et al.* (2019), who analyzed a healthcare algorithm used to allocate medical resources. The system relied on past healthcare spending as a proxy for medical need, but since historically underserved populations had lower access to care, the model systematically underestimated the needs of Black patients—thereby reinforcing existing racial disparities.

This misalignment highlights a broader issue: even when models perform well according to technical metrics like efficiency or accuracy, they may nonetheless replicate structural inequalities if their foundational variables encode social bias. Similar concerns arise in natural language processing and word embedding models. Bolukbasi *et al.* (2016) showed that embeddings trained on large corpora—such as Google News—tend to reflect and amplify gender stereotypes. For instance, the vector analogy between "man" and "computer programmer" mirrored that between "woman" and "homemaker." These biases, far from being neutral artifacts of language, directly shape the behavior of AI systems deployed in sensitive contexts such as recruitment, marketing, and content moderation.

3.3 Bias in Labeling Processes of the Data

Bias may also stem from the composition of training datasets and the labeling procedures used in supervised learning. Far from being neutral, labels often reflect the assumptions or biases of annotators—especially when dealing with complex phenomena like clinical outcomes or user preferences.

Agarwal *et al.* (2018) showed that labeling based on reimbursement data risks distorting the clinical picture. This highlights a critical insight: labeling is itself a normative act, and failing to acknowledge this can hardwire bias into model development. Furthermore, inconsistencies in labeling criteria—due to the lack of clear guidelines or differences between annotators—represent an epistemic vulnerability in the data pipeline. This is particularly problematic in high-stakes domains such as diagnosis or credit scoring, where ambiguity can translate into systemic discrimination (Cotter *et al.*, 2019).

3.4 Algorithm Selection and Lack of Human Oversight

Finally, algorithmic bias may result from choices made in model selection and tuning. These decisions are often guided by technical performance metrics, with limited consideration for ethical or societal dimensions. As shown by Czako *et al.* (2021), this can result in systems that are efficient but not just, amplifying pre-existing disparities.The absence of meaningful human oversight during design and calibration phases further exacerbates this issue. As Adomavicius & Yang (2022) and Laux (2024) suggest, human judgment is essential to detect, question, and mitigate emergent biases—yet is frequently sidelined in favor of automation and scalability.

4. THEORETICAL AND MANAGERIAL IMPLICATIONS

This study contributes to the theoretical discourse on algorithmic bias by reframing the design phase as a critical juncture where social inequalities can be encoded, normalized, or contested. Rather than viewing bias as a residual flaw to be addressed after deployment, the analysis emphasizes its upstream origins—emerging through variable selection, labeling practices, and implicit design assumptions. These findings call for greater managerial awareness and accountability, particularly since many decision-makers remain unaware of the risks embedded in AI systems—especially when the harms do not affect their own social group. This highlights the strategic value of building interdisciplinary and diverse teams, which are more capable of identifying and mitigating discriminatory patterns throughout the AI lifecycle.

Ensuring the ethical and responsible use of AI demands a governance perspective that goes beyond technical performance metrics and incorporates fairness, transparency, and social responsibility. In practice, this involves adopting fairness-by-design approaches, as outlined by Holstein *et al.* (2019) and Raji *et al.* (2020), which include algorithmic debiasing techniques such as adversarial training or re-weighting methods. Sensitivity audits should be conducted to assess whether proxy variables—often used due to data limitations—carry implicit social meanings or historical biases. In parallel, explainability constraints enhance transparency by revealing unintended correlations, thereby fostering stakeholder trust and enabling more effective oversight.

To institutionalize algorithmic accountability, organizations should establish cross-functional algorithm review boards. These should include not only technical experts, but also ethics officers, legal advisors, and representatives of affected stakeholder groups. As Raji *et al.* (2020) argue, such boards can serve as internal governance tools to evaluate and guide algorithmic decisions, ensuring that considerations of social impact are not overshadowed by efficiency or scale.

5. LIMITATIONS AND FUTURE RESEARCH

While this study offers a structured review of the risks associated with algorithmic bias during the design phase of AI systems, it presents some limitations that suggest directions for further inquiry. The scope of the review was necessarily shaped by the selection of databases, keywords, and inclusion criteria, potentially overlooking relevant grey literature or interdisciplinary contributions.

Moreover, the analysis remains conceptual and lacks empirical validation through fieldwork or real-world audits, limiting the generalizability of the findings. Future studies should therefore adopt qualitative and ethnographic methods to explore how bias emerges in practice within AI development contexts. Another limitation concerns the absence of a unified framework for classifying biases. Although the study identifies recurring patterns—such as anthropomorphic design, proxy misalignment, and labeling issues—terminologies across the literature remain inconsistent. Advancing this area requires greater conceptual clarity and the development of shared taxonomies.

Addressing these gaps could help move beyond diagnosis toward the creation of practical tools and governance models that support the responsible and context-sensitive deployment of AI technologies.

REFERENCES

Adomavicius, G., & Yang, M. (2022). Integrating Behavioral Economic and Technical Insight to Understand and Address Algorithmic Bias: A Human-Centric Perspective. *ACM Transactions on Management Information Systems*, Vol 13, No.3, pp 1-27. https://doi.org/10.1145/3519420

Agarwal, A et al., (2018). A reductions approach to fair classification. *International conference on machine learning*, 80, pp 60-69.

Bal, F., & Nijkamp, P. (2001). In search of valid results in a complex economic environment: The potential of meta-analysis and value transfer. *European Journal of Operational Research*, Vol. 128, No. 2, pp 364-384.

Bhavani, R. J., & Thuraisingam, S. A. (2022). Artificial intelligence and its impact on the legal fraternity. *UUM Journal of Legal Studies*, Vol. 13, No. 1, pp 129-161 https://doi.org/10.32890/uumjls2022.13.2.6

Bolukbasi, T. et al., (2016). Man is to computer programmer as woman is to homemaker? debiasing word embeddings. *Advances in neural information processing systems*, 29.

Cotter, A., Jiang, H., & Sridharan, K. (2019). Two-player games for efficient non-convex constrained optimization. *Algorithmic Learning Theory*, pp 300-332.

Czako, Z., Sebestyen, G., & Hangan, A. (2021). AutomaticAI–A hybrid approach for automatic artificial intelligence algorithm selection and hyperparameter tuning. Expert Systems with Applications, Vol. 182, p. 115225.

D'Alessandro, B., O'Neil, C., & LaGatta, T. (2017). Conscientious Classification: A Data Scientist's Guide to Discrimination-Aware Classification. *Big Data*, Vol. 5, No. 2, pp 120-134. https://doi.org/10.1089/big.2016.0048

Dakhel, A. M. et al., (2023). Github copilot ai pair programmer: Asset or liability?. *Journal of Systems and Software*, 203, 111734. https://doi.org/10.1016/j.jss.2023.111734

Davies, H. T., & Crombie, I. K. (1998). Getting to grips with systematic reviews and meta-analyses. *Hospital medicine* (London, England: 1998), Vol. 59, No. 12, pp. 955-958.

Felicetti, A. M. et al., (2024). Artificial intelligence and project management: An empirical investigation on the appropriation of generative Chatbots by project managers. *Journal of Innovation & Knowledge*, Vol. 9. No. 3, p 100545. https://doi.org/10.1016/j.jik.2024.100545.

Franceschet, M., & Costantini, A. (2010). The effect of scholar collaboration on impact and quality of academic papers. Journal of informetrics, Vol. 4, No. 4, pp 540-553.

Fu, L., Li, J., & Chen, Y. (2023). An innovative decision making method for air quality monitoring based on big data-assisted artificial intelligence technique. *Journal of Innovation & Knowledge*, Vol. 8, No. 2, p 100294. https://doi.org/10.1016/j.jik.2022.100294

Guan, H., Dong, L., & Zhao, A. (2022). Ethical Risk Factors and Mechanisms in Artificial Intelligence Decision Making. *Behavioral Sciences*, Vol. 12, No. 9, p 343 https://doi.org/10.3390/bs12090343

Gupta, V. (2024). An Empirical Evaluation of a Generative Artificial Intelligence Technology Adoption Model from Entrepreneurs' Perspectives. *Systems*, Vol. 12, No. 3, p 103. https://doi.org/10.3390/systems12030103

Hofeditz, L. et al., (2022). Applying XAI to an AI-based system for candidate management to mitigate bias and discrimination in hiring. *Electronic Markets*, Vol. 32, pp 2207-2233. https://doi.org/10.1007/s12525-022-00600-9

Holstein, K. et al. (2019). Improving fairness in machine learning systems: What do industry practitioners need?. In *Proceedings of the 2019 CHI conference on human factors in computing systems*, pp. 1-16.

Laux, J. (2024). Institutionalised distrust and human oversight of artificial intelligence: towards a democratic design of AI governance under the European Union AI Act. AI & society, Vol 39, No 6, pp 2853-2866.

Li, P. et al., (2023). How does artificial intelligence impact human resources performance. evidence from a healthcare institution in the United Arab Emirates. *Journal of Innovation & Knowledge*, Vol. 8, No. 2, p 100340. https://doi.org/10.1016/j.jik.2023.100340

Manasi, A. et al., (2022). Mirroring the bias: gender and artificial intelligence. *Gender, technology and development*, Vol 26, No 3, pp 295-305. https://doi.org/10.1080/09718524.2022.2128254

Mileti, A. et al. (2025). Tell Me How to Prompt! Healthcare Chatbots Response to Emotional Prompts for Enhanced Services. Review and Propositions. Journal of Economic Surveys.

Nguyen, N., & Nadi, S. (2022). An empirical evaluation of GitHub copilot's code suggestions. *Proceedings of the 19th International Conference on Mining Software Repositories*, pp 1-5. https://doi.org/10.1145/3524842.3528470

Obermeyer, Z. et al., (2019). Dissecting racial bias in an algorithm used to manage the health of populations. *Science*, Vol. 366, No. 6464), 447-453. https://doi.org/10.1126/science.aax2342

Obreja, D. M., Rughiniș, R., & Rosner, D. (2024). Mapping the conceptual structure of innovation in artificial intelligence research: A bibliometric analysis and systematic literature review. *Journal of Innovation & Knowledge*, Vol. 9, No. 1, p 100465. https://doi.org/10.1016/j.jik.2024.100465

Ostherr, K. (2022). Artificial intelligence and medical humanities. *Journal of Medical Humanities,* 43(2), 211-232. https://doi.org/10.1007/s10912-020-09636-4

Raji, I. D. et al. (2020). Closing the AI accountability gap: Defining an end-to-end framework for internal algorithmic auditing. In *Proceedings of the 2020 conference on fairness, accountability*, and transparency, pp. 33-44.

Schillaci, C. E. et al., (2024). Anthropomorphic chatbots' for future healthcare services: Effects of personality, gender, and roles on source credibility, user satisfaction, and intention to use. *Technological Forecasting and Social Change*, Vol. 199, No. 123025. https://doi.org/10.1016/j.techfore.2023.123025

Sen, S., Dasgupta, D. and Gupta, K.D. (2020). An empirical study on algorithmic bias, in *2020 IEEE 44th Annual Computers, Software, and Applications Conference (COMPSAC)*, IEEE, Madrid, Spain, pp 1189-1194. https://doi.org/10.1109/COMPSAC48688.2020.00-95.

Soleimani, M., Intezari, A., & Pauleen, D. J. (2022). Mitigating cognitive biases in developing AI-assisted recruitment systems: A knowledge-sharing approach. *International Journal of Knowledge Management,* Vol. 18, No. 1, pp 1-18. https://doi.org/ 10.4018/IJKM.290022

Tranfield, D., Denyer, D. & Smart, P. (2003). Towards a methodology for developing evidence informed management knowledge by means of systematic review. *British Journal of Management*, Vol. 14, No. 3, pp 207-222. https://doi.org/10.1111/1467-8551.00375

Weisz, J. D. et al., (2024, May). Design principles for generative AI applications. In Proceedings of the 2024 CHI Conference on Human Factors in Computing Systems, pp. 1-22.

Zhao, J. et al., (2017). Men also like shopping: Reducing gender bias amplification using corpus-level constraints. *arXiv preprint arXiv:1707.09457*. https://doi.org/10.48550/arXiv.1707.09457

EXAMINING CAPABILITIES IN DIGITAL SERVITIZATION: A LITERATURE REVIEW

Paulo A. Cauchick-Miguel[1,2], Brenda L. Rocha[1] and Thayla T. S. Zomer[3]
[1]*Federal University of Santa Catarina - UFSC*
Rua Eng. Agronômico Andrei Cristian Ferreira, s/n, 88040-900 Florianópolis, SC, Brazil
[2]*Pontifical Catholic University of Paraná - PUCPR*
Rua Imaculada Conceição, 1155, 80215-901 Curitiba, PR, Brazil
[3]*University of São Paulo - USP*
Av. Prof. Luciano Gualberto, n° 1380, 05508-010 São Paulo, SP, Brazil

ABSTRACT

Digitalization has changed the way services are provided, and this context demands new capabilities. However, current literature lacks a more comprehensive view of digital capabilities. In this sense, this work aims to identify and synthesize the patterns of recent literature in the field of digital servitization, with emphasis on the evaluation of emerging capabilities. Through a systematic literature review, the work analyzes capabilities, as well as a call for research aimed at the future development of digital servitization. The results reveal the main domains in which innovation and digitalization can emerge: (i) in business models, (ii) in the development of PSS; and (iii) management systems. In these domains of innovation, five capability categories stood out: (i) data driven; (ii) eco-system/technology integration; (iii) micro-service; (iv) organizational; (v) service design. Finally, the study offers perspectives for future research, for example by promoting themes that consider the need for temporal studies covering life cycles and servitization trajectories.

KEYWORDS

Digital Servitization, Digitalization, Capabilities, Digital Technologies, Product-Service System, PSS

1. INTRODUCTION

Digitalization has been transforming the services sector, reshaping the way organizations create and deliver value (Favoretto et al., 2022). The emergence of new digital technologies has prompted researchers to revisit and rethink existing research on design tools, business models, and related areas (Gaiardelli et al., 2021). Studies have highlighted cases in which specific capabilities were required to be developed within organizations, such as those related to product and service development, as well as innovation in business models (Hallstedt et al., 2020; Weking et al., 2020). Moreover, recent research underscores the importance of capabilities in navigating digital transformation effectively (Dalenogare et al., 2022). This particularly occurs in product-centric companies that transformed their business model to compete by providing services rather than product alone (Favoretto et al., 2022) in a movement called 'servitization'.

Several literature review studies (e.g., Pirola et al., 2020; Zheng et al., 2021) have explored digitalization and its associated technologies as enablers of servitization capabilities in manufacturing firms. Some studies have further emphasized the growing need for research on new capabilities essential for developing increasingly complex products and solutions. A deeper, more detailed understanding of the necessary capabilities and best practices in digital servitization remains crucial (Hallstedt et al., 2020). In this context, this study aims to identify and analyze emerging patterns in the recent literature on digital servitization, through a literature review. By doing so, this research contributes to a more comprehensive understanding of how organizations can develop and enhance their capabilities to successfully navigate digital servitization.

2. RESEARCH DESIGN

A systematic literature review was conducted in five phases (Thomé et al., 2016): (i) search query, (ii) data sourcing, (iii) screening, (iv) use of analytical tools, and (v) content analysis. The Scopus database was chosen for its extensive coverage of over 7,000 independently screened publishers. The search included keyword strings such as servitization AND digitalization, digital AND servitization, and servitization AND capabilities, yielding 878 documents. Filters were applied to include only peer-reviewed journal articles in English, reducing the count to 522 (final sample). To focus on recent trends, a time filter was set based on publication trends, as studies on this topic have surged since 2017. Qualitative screening further refined the selection by prioritizing manufacturing-focused studies and internal organizational capabilities while excluding research on customer-provider relationships and supply chain processes.

The review aimed to analyze the development of manufacturing servitization and identify future research directions. Endnote™ and Microsoft Excel™ were used for content organization. Data were structured across seven dimensions: (i) study focus, (ii) keyword statistics, (iii) presented capabilities, (iv) presented technologies, (v) innovation domains and solutions, (vi) main conclusions, and (vii) calls for future research (dimensions iv, vi, and vii were not included in this paper). A second level of categorization was applied to dimensions (iii) and (iv), but this paper specifically addresses (iii), i.e. it focuses on capabilities.

In the content analysis, studies were categorized by innovation domain (see Table 1). Capabilities were classified, grouped, and mapped to their respective studies, revealing their bidirectional relationship - acting as both inputs and outputs. Innovation domains often overlapped across capabilities, sometimes integrating both. These categories were analyzed to highlight literature gaps and inform future research.

3. GROUNDWORK RESULTS ON CAPABILITIES

Table 1 shows a classification according to the innovation domains with examples.

Table 1. Innovation domains and examples of application (partial results)

Innovation domains	Examples
Managerial systems	Fleet management system
	Ship control systems
Business model	Proactive maintenance contract for fleet management
	Cost per ton contract for grinding
	Results-based contract, depending on the network capacity used
Product-service systems (PSS)	Lifecycle services for smart engines
	Autonomous solution for underground mines
	Heavy construction equipment
	Machines and equipment for forestry solutions

Table 2 shows a codification of the capabilities, and examples that currently are the focus of studies.

Table 2. Categories of capabilities with examples (partial results)

Capability categories	Examples	References (partial)
Data driven (c1)	Workflow tool for simplifying scenario planning; Multichannel digital service delivery	Dalenogare et al. (2022); Schymanietz et al. (2022); Chen et al. (2022)
Eco-system/technology integration (c2)	AI scaling through co-evolutionary processes and feedback loops	Hallstedt et al. (2020)
Micro-service (c3)	Incremental microservice investments; Sprint-based microservice development	Sjödin et al. (2021)
Organizational (c4)	Management of production/delivery operations; Development of valuable and sustainable offers	Tronvoll et al. (2020); Benedettini (2022)
Service design (c5)	Pattern-based smart service innovation in manufacturing; Smart PSS in maritime industry	Ebel et al. (2022); Solem et al. (2022); Arioli et al. (2023)

3.1 Discussion

3.1.1 Innovation Domains: Managerial Systems; Business Model, and PSS

Impacts of digitalization on managerial systems were shown, such as the ability to streamline operations (Table 1). Digital technology has enabled managers to automate many of their processes, which has reduced the time and resources required to complete tasks in addition to the ability to collect and analyze data. For example, a business can use data to identify customer preferences, which can help them develop products and services that meet their customers' needs. Concerning business models, there has been a growing trend towards servitization as companies seek to differentiate themselves from competitors and create more sustainable business models. This has led to an increased focus on business model innovation as companies seek to develop new and innovative ways of delivering services to customers. In addition, studies have shown that digitalization has been present mostly in the development and innovation of PSS solutions.

3.1.2 Capabilities from Digital Servitization

The definition of capability can be understood as the use of resources deployed to achieve an end goal (Marcon et al., 2022). In the sample, 35 different capabilities were identified, most cited capabilities were service design, business model innovation, and data analytics. Data-driven capabilities (C1) in servitization refer to the use of data and analytics to enhance and optimize the delivery of services. Some of the examples found in recent literature are connected with the collection and integration of data (e.g. co-evolutionary processes) that will generate a database for further use of the company in the decision-making process. Another example was the capability of service personalization based on customer data (e.g. multi-channel digital service delivery), which enables innovation in service delivery with tailored service models. Thus, ecosystem integration (C2) has emerged as a capability in the domain of artificial intelligent development, specifically in the co-evolutionary process and feedback loops, exploiting interdependencies also for business model innovation.

Microservice is a term that started to appear in the past five years and needs to be explored. Micro-service (C3) in the context of digital servitization is a focused digital service functionality that does one thing and does it well. Accordingly, micro services lend themselves to a continuous delivery of increasingly more sophisticated digital servitization solutions (Sjödin et al., 2020). These micro-services are designed to work together to create a larger, more complex service offering, e.g., a company that provides a digital platform for managing industrial equipment might offer microservices for monitoring equipment performance, analyzing data, etc. Companies can improve scalability, reduce development time and costs, and offer more flexible solutions by breaking their services into smaller, modular components (Seppälä and Koskenen, 2019).

Organizational capabilities (C4) include management and functions related to the company's higher-level organization, which must adapt their methods due to the digital servitization context. Examples are knowledge sharing routines and governance mechanisms, which, while not new for companies, undergo significant changes at their core.

In the field of service design capability (C5), it is noteworthy that data-driven capabilities have emerged in recent studies, particularly within the "PSS" and "digitalization" strands. Service design is often associated with an innovative approach that incorporates machine learning. Through iterative interactions with customers, this methodology enhances the outcomes of service development.

Recent research underscores the importance of capabilities in navigating digital transformation effectively (Dalenogare et al., 2022). These capabilities also offer opportunities for strategic decisions that organizations might undertake concerning digital servitization, which can be implemented in practical business scenarios.

4. CONCLUDING REMARKS

The present study summarized and categorized the capabilities in the context of digital servitization, corroborated by recent studies in the area. As this is work in progress, this review may provide a new categorization framework to address gaps identified in previous studies. The main domains in which innovation and digitalization emerge were identified as business models, PSS development, and management systems. Within these innovation domains, five capabilities stood out, which were exemplified with examples of applicability. In capabilities, a new trend called microservices is being coined, which was explored in the context of digital servitization.

The findings of this study may contribute to the existing literature on digital servitization by offering a structured and comprehensive synthesis of emerging capabilities that facilitate the transition towards digitalized service models. While prior research has acknowledged the role of digital technologies in servitization, this study extends the discussion by identifying and categorizing five key capability domains. These categories provide a more granular understanding of how firms develop and deploy capabilities to adapt to digital servitization. Managerial implications of this study include evidence and insights into which capabilities need to be developed given the advancement in the innovation strategy along the digital servitization path. Future research will involve applying the trends identified in this literature review to an empirical study, which will substantiate the findings of this work. Although this work may exhibit bias in source selection, it nonetheless presents significant findings that can be expanded upon in subsequent studies.

ACKNOWLEDGEMENT

The authors acknowledge the funding received from CAPES (Coordination of Superior Level Staff Improvement) and CNPq (National Council for Scientific and Technological Development), both Brazilian research agencies - grants CAPES-PRINT 88887.694281/2022-00, CNPq PQ 428946/2018-6, and CNPq-Universal 310836/2020-4. Additionally, support from the Federal University of Santa Catarina for a leave of absence and resources provided by the University of Aveiro as a Visiting Professor in Portugal are recognized as well.

REFERENCES

Arioli, V. et al. (2023). A methodology for the design and engineering of smart product service systems: an application in the manufacturing sector. *Sustainability*, Vol. 15, No. 1, pp. 64.

Benedettini, O. (2022). Structuring servitization-related capabilities: A data-driven analysis. Sustainability, Vol. 14, No. 9.

Chen, M. et al. (2022). Data analytics capability and servitization: then moderate Mediation Rôle of Bricolage and Innovation Orientation. *International Journal of Operations & Production Management*, Vol. 42, No. 4, pp. 440-470.

Cong, J. et al. (2022). A machine learning-based iterative design approach to automate user satisfaction degree prediction in smart product-service system. *Computers & Industrial Engineering*, Vol. 165, pp.575-586, 107939.

Dalenogare, L.S. et al. (2022). Multichannel digital service delivery and service ecosystems: The role of data integration within Smart Product-Service Systems. *Technological Forecasting and Social Change*, Vol. 183, 121894.

Ebel, M. et al. (2022). Smart Already at Design Time-Pattern-Based Smart Service Innovation in Manufacturing. *Journal of Business Research*, Vol. 141, pp. 669-678.

Favoretto, C. et al. (2022). From servitization to digital servitization: How digitalization transforms companies' transition towards services. *Industrial Marketing Management*, Vol. 102, pp. 104–121.

Gaiardelli, P. et al. (2021). Product-service systems evolution in the era of Industry 4.0. *Service Business*, Vol. 15, No. 1, pp. 177–207.

Hallstedt, I.S. et al. (2020). The Need for New Product Development Capabilities from Digitalization, Sustainability, and Servitization Trends. *Journal of Business Research*, Vol. 121, pp.669-678.

Marcon, É. et al. (2022). Capabilities supporting digital servitization: A multi-actor perspective. *Industrial Marketing Management*, Vol. 103, pp. 97–116.

Pirola, F. et al. (2020). Digital technologies in product-service systems: a literature review and a research agenda. *Computers in Industry*, Vol. 123, pp. 1–19.

Seppälä, T. and Koskenen, K. (2019). Digital servitization: business beyond product. Cham: Springer, 2019.

Schymanietz, M. et al. (2022). Exploring Data-Driven Service Innovation – Aligning Perspectives in Research and Practice. *Journal of Business Economics*, Vol. 92, pp. 1167–1205.

Sjödin, D. et al. (2021). How AI capabilities enable business model innovation: Scaling AI through co-evolutionary processes and feedback loops. *Journal of Business Research*, Vol. 134, pp. 574–587.

Solem, B.A.A. et al. (2022). Untangling service design routines for digital servitization: empirical insights of smart PSS in maritime industry. *Sustainability*, Vol. 14, No. 11, pp. 6454.

Thomé, A.M.T. et al. (2016). Conducting systematic literature review in operations management. *Production Planning and Control*, Vol. 27, No. 5, pp. 408–420.

Tronvoll, B. et al. (2020). Transformational shifts through digital servitization. *Journal of Business Research*, Vol. 121, pp. 346-356.

Weking, J. et al. (2020). Leveraging industry 4.0 – A business model pattern framework. *International Journal of Production Economics*, Vol. 225, 107588.

REFRAMING FOOD MARKETING THROUGH A SCIENCE AND TECHNOLOGY STUDIES LENS: BRAND DEVELOPMENT AND CONSUMER BEHAVIOR IN TAIWAN'S POTATO CHIP MARKET

Wen-Jui Tan and Ju-Joan Wong
National Yunlin University of Science and Technology, Taiwan

ABSTRACT

Since Lay's entered the Taiwanese market in 1981, the sales of potato chips have steadily increased. By 2023, annual sales had surpassed NT$3.5 billion, accounting for more than half of the snack food market. Nevertheless, potato chips have long been perceived as "junk food" due to their high fat, sodium, and calorie content, which are closely linked to health issues such as obesity and diabetes. Despite this, consumers continue to find potato chips irresistible, reflecting the paradoxical nature of the product as both "unhealthy" and "popular".

Historically, marketing strategies have evolved from exaggerated advertisements in the 1980s that claimed potato chips were rich in nutrients to more recent visual and verbal tactics emphasizing natural ingredients, reduced sodium, and the absence of additives. Whether these marketing claims have genuinely altered the nature of the product—or are merely recurring superficial tactics—warrants further investigation.

This study treats potato chips as a technological artifact and adopts a Science, Technology, and Society (STS) perspective to explore how technology and design have transformed the potato from a basic food into an irresistibly tasty yet unhealthy ultra-processed product. The research integrates quantitative methods (ANOVA) with qualitative approaches, including in-depth interviews, field observations, and textual analysis, to examine how manufacturers utilize production techniques and design strategies to construct a "healthy" image of potato chips.

Findings indicate that consumer preferences for potato chips are shaped by socioeconomic background, sensory design, and everyday experiences. While consumers are influenced by packaging colors and marketing language, they also express skepticism and resistance toward health-related narratives. The study reveals how food marketing operates across multisensory and linguistic dimensions to shape consumer behavior, materialized through packaging and design. Furthermore, it questions whether these marketing tactics genuinely enhance the health attributes of the product and advocate for the development of critical thinking in consumers. Such awareness is essential for resisting misleading health claims and making dietary choices that better align with individual health needs.

KEYWORDS

Potato Chips, Food Packaging, Food Advertising, Consumer Behavior, Science and Technology Studies (STS)

1. INTRODUCTION

Since Lay's entered the Taiwanese market in 1981, the sales of potato chips have grown steadily. By 2023, the annual market value reached approximately NT$3.5 billion, accounting for over half of Taiwan's snack food sales. Meanwhile, potato chips have also been labeled as "junk food" due to their high fat, sodium, and calorie content and have been linked to health issues such as obesity, fatty liver, diabetes, and cardiovascular diseases. Yet, consumers remain highly attached to potato chips—what drives this persistent appeal?

Historically, the "health-oriented narrative" surrounding potato chips is not new. Between 1987 and 1988, the *Economic Daily News* reported that several brands had engaged in exaggerated promotional claims. For example, PoTato stated their chips were "low-calorie and nutritious, with fewer calories than the same amount of rice," while Cadina promoted their chips as rich in vitamins C, B1, E, and calcium. However, ingredient lists on the packaging revealed a different story: in addition to potatoes, chips often contained palm oil or hydrogenated vegetable oil, salt, sugar, food acids, citric acid, artificial flavoring, onion powder, and other additives potentially harmful to health—clearly contradicting the brands' health claims.

In recent years, as consumers increasingly prioritize healthy eating, brands have responded by launching products marketed as natural, healthy, and additive-free. In 2018, Lay's introduced the "natural delicious" series, using potato field imagery on the packaging and emphasizing terms such as "natural," "additive-free," and "low sodium" to construct a wholesome image. However, these visual and linguistic strategies often echo the marketing language of the 1980s, which heavily relied on vague adjectives rather than concrete nutritional information. Whether these health-centric portrayals truly reflect changes in the product's essence or are simply superficial marketing tactics remains an open question.

This study aims to explore how potato chip products construct a persuasive "healthy" image through visual design, language strategy, and cultural symbolism. It further investigates how this image is reproduced and perceived on digital platforms and mobile interfaces, shaping consumers' sensory experiences and influencing their purchasing decisions.

2. LITERATURE REVIEW - FOOD PACKAGING DESIGN AND SENSORY MANIPULATION

This study focuses on the transformation of the potato into potato chips—from a basic food to a processed product—and the role of design in that process. A review of relevant literature includes the design elements and principles applied by chip manufacturers upon entering the market, how design-translated symbols are reproduced and influence consumer behavior, and the lifestyles shaped through consumer practices.

Packaging design for potato chips is not merely a physical medium for protecting food; it also serves as a sensory interface that affects consumer behavior. Spence (2016) noted that over 90% of food brands on supermarket shelves use packaging colors to convey product information and influence consumers' taste perceptions. Piqueras-Fiszman and Spence (2011), using the case of Walkers potato chips, demonstrated that packaging color alters and interferes with consumer taste expectations and purchase intentions, revealing that color has become an internalized cue for both flavor and brand identity.

Compared to color, textual elements function as more indirect carriers of information. Visuals tend to produce stronger sensory stimulation and are more likely to capture consumer attention (Rebollar et al., 2017). However, for specific consumer groups—such as vegetarians or environmentally conscious individuals—the importance of written labels increases significantly. Research in marketing linguistics shows that negative constructions are generally harder to process than affirmative ones (García-Madariaga et al., 2018). For instance, the term "vegetarian" is more intuitive and accessible than "non-meat."

Images are the most immediate visual elements that trigger sensory responses in food packaging. Their key function is grounded in the mechanism of cross-modal associations, whereby visuals form direct neural links with gustatory stimuli, thereby intensifying the consumer's sensory experience of the product (Piqueras-Fiszman et al., 2012; Rebollar et al., 2017). Bolam et al. (2021) further observed that when consumers cannot rely solely on taste or smell to identify food characteristics, the brain integrates multisensory inputs to enhance perceptual accuracy, which is the essence of cross-modal association.

In addition, food imagery can evoke a phenomenon known as "visual hunger," which further enhances consumer appetite. Spence et al. (2015) pointed out that images of food can trigger innate eating instincts, a phenomenon rooted in humans' evolutionary sensitivity to food resources. In modern society, the food industry leverages this mechanism to influence consumer behavior and stimulate purchase intention.

Color, language, and imagery in food packaging are not merely visual elements; they function as mechanisms for shaping sensory experience and symbolic meaning. In a contemporary consumer society, consumers encounter flavors that are designed and purchase health that is imagined. Even before tasting the product, consumers anticipate its flavor and attributes based on packaging cues—color, image, and language—which serve as critical perceptual intermediaries.

3. RESEARCH METHODS

This research project adopts a mixed-methods approach, integrating both quantitative and qualitative methodologies. The quantitative component employs analysis of variance (ANOVA) to examine the relationships between consumer demographics and preferences for various attributes of potato chips in the consumer market. Based on the results of the statistical analysis, qualitative methods are applied to further investigate the underlying reasons for consumer preferences. In-depth interviews serve as the primary data collection method, targeting key informants such as food industry experts and individuals with distinctive dietary habits or flavor preferences, including those whose consumption behavior has contributed to health or body image concerns.

To comprehensively collect data on consumer preferences for potato chips, the quantitative portion of the study adopts a stratified sampling strategy, selecting participants across different gender and age groups to ensure sample representativeness and the validity of the findings. The study sample spans a diverse range of demographics—from children to older adults—allowing for a comprehensive understanding of generational differences in potato chip preferences and consumption behaviors.

During data collection, participants were asked to rate their preferences on a five-point Likert scale (1 = "least preferred," 5 = "most preferred") across five dimensions: brand, flavor, packaging color, textual description, and food texture. ANOVA was then used to analyze these ratings in relation to variables such as age, gender, BMI, education level, income, occupation, and frequency of potato chip and snack consumption.

3.1 Questionnaire Results

A total of 121 valid responses were collected for this study. The gender and age distributions of the participants were planned using stratified sampling, resulting in an approximately normal distribution. Regarding body mass index (BMI), 11.57% of the participants were classified as underweight, 47.93% as normal weight, 24.79% as overweight, and 15.70% as obese.

In terms of potato chip consumption frequency, only 0.8% reported eating them daily, 4.1% participants consumed them more than four times per week, and 44.6% participants consumed them 1 to 3 times per week—the largest group. Additionally, 29.8% participants consumed them 1 to 3 times per month, while 20.7% participants reported rarely or almost never consuming potato chips.

Regarding the frequency of consuming other snacks besides potato chips, the majority consumed them 1 to 3 times per week (41.3%), followed by 1 to 3 times per month (28.9%), daily (16.5%), more than four times per week (7.4%), and rarely or almost never (5.8%).

Table 1. Sample Demographics (n=121)

Variable	n (%)	Variable	n (%)	Variable	n (%)
Gender		**Age**		35-44	22 (18.2%)
Male	39 (32.2%)	0-14	17 (14%)	45-54	16 (13.2%)
Female	79 (65.3%)	15-24	27 (22.3%)	55-64	7 (5.8%)
Other	3 (2.5%)	25-34	22 (18.2%)	65 and above	10 (8.3%)

Further analysis of the relationship between age and potato chip consumption frequency revealed a negative correlation: younger participants tended to consume potato chips more frequently. Among participants aged 0 to 24, 29.6% consumed potato chips more than once per week. In contrast, 80% of those aged 65 and above reported rarely or never eating potato chips. Given the low level of engagement with potato chip consumption among the older age group, the interpretation of results involving this demographic should be approached with caution.

We conducted further analysis on variables with p-values < 0.05 based on the ANOVA results. In terms of flavor preference, the top three rated flavors were original, seaweed, and salted. In contrast, omelette, pork, and seafood flavors received the lowest scores. Occupational analysis showed that students tended to prefer beef and seafood flavors, while self-employed individuals showed a higher preference for pork-flavored chips. Based on the frequency of consuming snacks other than potato chips, participants who consumed snacks 1 to 3 times per week rated beef flavor highest (average = 3.40), whereas those who rarely consumed other snacks gave it the lowest rating (average = 2.00).

For packaging color preferences, yellow, orange, and green were the top three most favored colors, while blue, purple, and dark purple were rated the lowest. In particular, age had a significant effect on preferences for yellow and teal packaging. Yellow packaging received the highest rating among participants aged 45–54 (average = 4.06) and the lowest among those aged 55–64 (average = 2.71). Teal packaging was also most preferred by the 45–54 groups (average = 3.13) and least favored by the 0–14 age group (average = 1.82). In terms of occupation, students showed the lowest acceptance of purple packaging (average = 2.21). Regarding education level, participants with a master's degree expressed the highest preference for orange packaging (average = 4.00), whereas those with only a junior high school education gave the lowest ratings (average = 2.64). These differences suggest that color strategies in packaging design can be optimized according to consumer attributes such as age, education, and occupation.

In terms of textual descriptions, the most preferred phrase among participants was "crispy" (average = 4.26), followed by health-oriented terms such as "30% less fat," "no additives," and "25% less sodium." Gender differences were notable: female participants showed a stronger preference for health-related descriptors, including "30% less fat," "no additives," "natural," and "25% less sodium," while male participants tended to favor expressions such as "classic" and "thick-cut chips." Age also played a significant role. Participants aged 45–54 rated "crispy" and "−50% saturated fat" the highest, whereas those aged 65 and older showed the lowest overall preferences. Occupation and income level were additional influential variables. Both blue-collar and white-collar workers rated health-related terms more favorably than students. High-income participants expressed particularly strong preferences for the phrase "25% less sodium" (average = 4.75), suggesting that health-oriented descriptions are especially appealing to certain demographic groups.

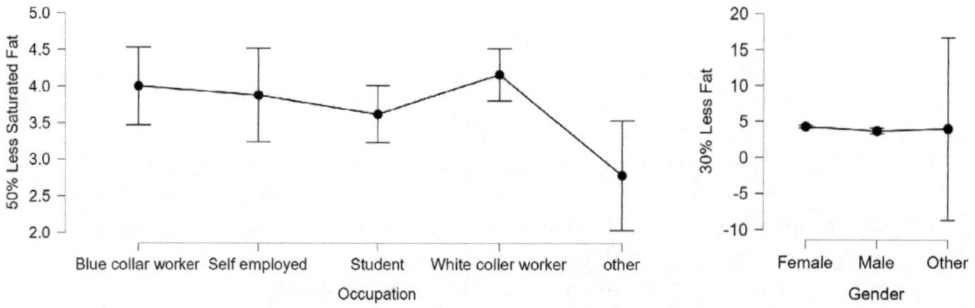

Figure 1. ANOVA results for the semantic perception of "−50% saturated fat" across occupations (left) and the semantic perception of "−30% fat" across genders (right)

In terms of textual descriptions, the most preferred phrase among participants was "crispy" (average = 4.26), followed by health-oriented terms such as "30% less fat," "no additives," and "25% less sodium." Gender differences were notable: female participants showed a stronger preference for health-related descriptors, including "30% less fat," "no additives," "natural," and "25% less sodium," while male participants tended to favor expressions such as "classic" and "thick-cut chips." Age also played a significant role. Participants aged 45–54 rated "crispy" and "−50% saturated fat" the highest, whereas those aged 65 and older showed the lowest overall preferences. Occupation and income level were additional influential variables. Both blue-collar and white-collar workers rated health-related terms more favorably than students. High-income participants expressed particularly strong preferences for the phrase "25% less sodium" (average = 4.75), suggesting that health-oriented descriptions are especially appealing to certain demographic groups.

Regarding preferences for chip texture, "thin-cut" received the highest average rating (4.00), followed by "small ridges" and "smooth saddle shape," while "large ridges" were the least preferred overall. Female participants demonstrated a significantly greater preference for thin-cut chips compared to males. Age differences were also evident: the 0–14 age group rated "thin-cut" and "small ridges" highest, whereas participants aged 65 and above generally gave lower ratings for all four texture types. Consumption frequency also played a role. Participants who consumed potato chips more frequently tended to give higher ratings for all texture types. Daily consumers rated "thin-cut," "small ridges," and "smooth saddle shape" at the maximum score of 5.00, indicating that high-frequency consumers have stronger and more distinct texture preferences.

3.2 Qualitative Research - In-Depth Interview

For the qualitative component, five key informants were selected based on their status as heavy consumers of potato chips. All interviewees demonstrated substantial familiarity with the product, strongly preferred particular flavors, and maintained distinctive dietary habits, making them suitable for in-depth exploration.

Table 2. Respondent's basic information form

Coding	Age	Occupation
Mr. Lin	**24**	**Graduate student**
Ms. Chang	**23**	**Master of Architecture student**
Ms. Liu	**47**	**Self-operated packaging industry**
Mr. Lin2	**26**	**Engineer**
Ms. Hsu	**23**	**Engineer**

Qualitative interviews revealed several visual design-related cues influencing consumers' preferences for potato chips. Ms. Hsu described her purchasing behavior, stating: *"I just recognize the color. If I see a package I haven't seen before, I'll buy it out of curiosity. I don't really check what flavor it is."* Similarly, Ms. Liu noted: *"I'm more drawn to those bold, colorful packages. They give me a sense of novelty and impact. If the packaging is dull, I just don't feel like buying it."* These insights align with the findings of Piqueras-Fiszman and Spence (2011), who suggested that packaging color significantly influences consumer choice. Some consumers may even ignore images or text on the packaging and rely solely on color as an intuitive cue, leading to the misidentification of flavors.

Ms. Chang described a specific visual effect: *"Like those typical Taiwanese street food flavors... sometimes the packaging will be kind of aggressive, like a big image of salt and pepper chicken. Then you realize, oh, it's actually potato chips—well, I guess I'll try it."* This comment suggests that using vivid food imagery as the focal point of packaging can stimulate impulse buying. When such images evoke gustatory memories through cross-modal associations, they are more likely to trigger purchasing behavior.

However, Mr. Lin offered a different perspective. Using the example of a "Taiwanese salt and pepper chicken" flavor by Lay's, he explained: *"It's not the image of the food that caught my eye—it's the temple gate motif of a Taiwanese night market."* This highlights how cultural symbols, in certain contexts, may be more compelling than literal food imagery. Thus, packaging that evokes local culture or emotional resonance can be especially powerful in attracting consumer attention.

In contrast, health-oriented textual descriptors on packaging—such as "reduced sodium" or "reduced fat"—elicited mostly negative responses from the interviewees. Among the five participants, only Ms. Liu was receptive to health-oriented design. The others generally felt that such labels evoked impressions of "blandness" and conflicted with their expectations of potato chips as flavorful, indulgent snacks. Mr. Lin plainly stated: *"As soon as I see that kind of label, I wouldn't buy it—it just looks like it has no flavor."* Ms. Hsu responded even more directly: *"I skip those. If I'm going to eat something guilty, what's the point of being healthy? There's no flavor—so what's the point of eating it? No thanks to the health stuff."*

Such responses may be explained by the fact that all interviewees were heavy potato chip consumers who viewed the product as a "guilty pleasure" snack—something expected to be rich in flavor and high in calories. Health-oriented claims were perceived as undermining the essential appeal and indulgent value of potato chips, creating a conflict between health messaging and the consumer's flavor expectations for this type of product.

4. CONCLUSION

Despite being long regarded as a "junk food" due to its high fat, sodium, and calorie content, potato chips remain the most beloved snack among Taiwanese consumers. This contradiction between consumers' awareness of health risks and their actual purchasing behaviors suggests that nutritional content alone is insufficient to explain food consumption. Potato chips are not merely a food product; they are cultural artifacts shaped by design, narrative, and sensory experience.

This study highlights how brand image, packaging color, textual language, and texture design collectively influence consumer judgment and re-encode the symbolic meaning of "potato chips" as a commodity. Field observations during interviews and questionnaire completion revealed that consumers often infer flavor based on packaging color—yellow is commonly associated with the original flavor, and green with seaweed. These associations indicate that stable cross-modal correspondences between color and taste play a vital role in visual-gustatory communication.

In terms of textual preference, women, along with both blue- and white-collar workers, showed a clear preference for health-oriented language, such as "30% less fat" or "no additives." In contrast, men tended to favor descriptors that emphasized texture and flavor, such as "thick-cut chips." Regarding texture preferences, participants who consumed chips more frequently gave significantly higher ratings to textures like "thin-cut," "small ridges," and "smooth saddle shape." This suggests that heavy consumers have heightened sensitivity to texture and distinct preferences, highlighting the importance of texture design in appealing to core consumer groups.

Interestingly, although health-related phrases received generally positive ratings in the survey, many interviewees expressed negative associations during qualitative interviews. Labels such as "reduced sodium" or "reduced fat" were often linked to a lack of flavor and decreased desire to purchase. This divergence between quantitative and qualitative findings reflects the psychological tension consumers face when balancing health consciousness with flavor expectations. It underscores the internal conflict between rational decision-making and sensory desire, suggesting that future product design should strive for a balance between the two.

In summary, consumption behavior surrounding potato chips is influenced not only by socio-economic background but also by sensory design, semantic cues, and lifestyle context. By triangulating quantitative analysis and qualitative interviews, this study reveals how packaging design shapes consumer preferences through visual, verbal, and tactile elements. The findings provide concrete empirical insights and practical directions for future food product design, branding strategies, and consumer psychology research.

ACKNOWLEDGMENTS

This research is part of a project funded by the National Science and Technology Council, Republic of China, Taiwan. (NSTC 113-2410-H-224-014).

REFERENCES

Bolam, J., Boyle, S. C., Ince, R. A., & Delis, I, (2021), *Neurocomputational mechanisms underlying cross-modal associations and their influence on perceptual decisions*. NeuroImage, 247,pp. 1-15.

García-Madariaga, J., López, M. B., Burgos, I. M., & Virto, N. R, (2018), *Do isolated packaging variables influence consumers' attention and preferences?,* Physiology & Behavior, 200, pp. 101.

Piqueras-Fiszman, B., & Spence, C, (2011), *Crossmodal correspondences in product packaging. Assessing color–flavor correspondences for potato chips (crisps).* Appetite, 57(3),pp. 753–757.

Rebollar, R., Gil, I., Lidón, I., Martín, J., Fernández, M. J., & Rivera, S, (2017), *How material, visual and verbal cues on packaging influence consumer expectations and willingness to buy: The case of crisps (potato chips) in Spain.* Food Research International, 99, pp. 243.

Spence, C., Okajima, K., Cheok, A. D., Petit, O., & Michel, C, (2015), *Eating with our eyes: From visual hunger to digital satiation.* Brain and Cognition, 110, pp. 53–63.

Spence, C., (2016). *Multisensory packaging design*. Elsevier eBooks, pp. 4–6.

AI TO SUPPORT LEVELS OF DEEP LEARNING: A COGNITIVE LOAD THEORY AND ICAP PERSPECTIVE

Robert Zheng
University of Utah, USA

ABSTRACT

The current study examined levels of deep learning in the context of AI support. Built on Chi's ICAP framework, the study looks specifically relationship between deep activities and their associated mental effort (cognitive load). It was predicted that with AI support (Chatbot), learners would show higher performance with constructive and interactive learning than with active learning. The results indicated a strong correlation between germane and content difficulty across three activities: active, constructive and interactive. The results further indicate that as learner's intrinsic load increases, their germane load increases simultaneously suggesting motivation can be solicited by the intrinsic load which can be proxied by the levels of content difficulty.

KEYWORDS

Artificial Intelligence, Cognitive Load, Deep Learning, ICAP, SDT

1. BACKGROUND

Artificial Intelligence (AI) is changing the landscape in education, transforming traditional classrooms into dynamic, data-driven learning environments. This study explores the ways in which AI engages and supports students' deep learning. Research in cognitive and affective learning illuminates the relationship between motivation and cognitive engagement in learning (Metwally et al., 2024; Ng et al., 2024). This is further supported by the research in cognitive load. According to Kalyuga (2011), germane load which represents learners' effort to learn, ebbs and flows with intrinsic load which is proxied by content difficulty. Kalyuga claims that content difficulty solicits and motivates learners to engage in new knowledge acquisition and discovery. Scholars (Chi, 2009; Chi & VanLehn, 2012) have explored the mental engagement in relation to content difficulty and levels of processing. They noted that learning activities like active, constructive and interactive differ in their engagement with learners in terms of deep processing. According to Chi et al., (2009; 2012), active learning engages learners in surface processing such as moving a manipulative or tracing a line in the text. The interactive and constructive learning, on the other hand, engage learners in deeper processing such as analyzing and synthesizing information and making predictions. Researchers (Gupta & Zheng, 2020; Zeithofer et al., 2024; Zheng et al., 2025) noticed the positive correlation between motivation (as measured by germane load), content difficulty (as measured by intrinsic load), and level of deep processing as represented by the three learning activities. It was found that germane load increased as learners engaged in different learning activities from active to constructive and to interactive learning.

Based on the literature reviewed above, the study proposed the following assumptions in the context of AI-supported learning as well as learners' engagement with different learning activities:

(1) germane load is related to motivation/interest as well as learners' cognitive engagement in learning,

(2) intrinsic and germane are positively correlated,

(3) learners' performance varies across three learning activities from active to constructive and to interactive.

2. THE STUDY

The current study examined the relationship between germane and intrinsic load and their relation to performance across three learning activities: active, constructive and interactive.

2.1 Design of Study

The study was approved by the Institutional Research Bureau (IRB). Participants signed the voluntary consent for participating in the study. They were randomly assigned to one of the three learning conditions: active, constructive, and interactive. The study material covers polar bonds and ionic bonds in organic chemistry (Figure 1).

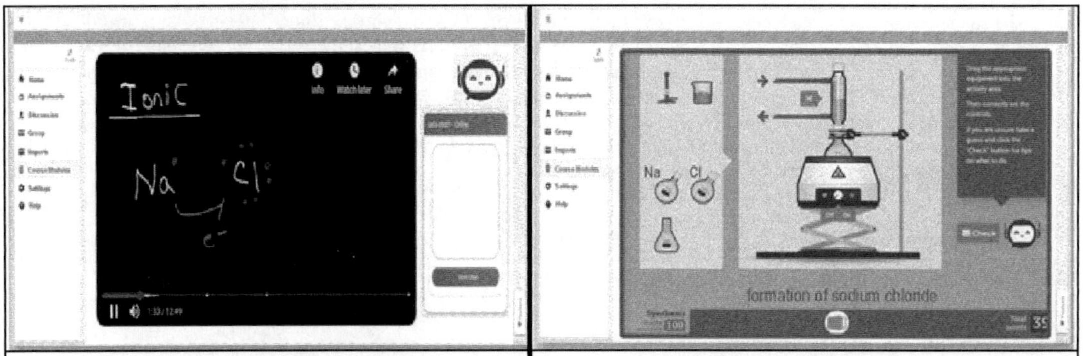

Active and Constructive Learning Conditions | Interactive Learning Condition

Figure 1. Active, Constructive and Interactive Learning with Chatbot

In *active* learning condition, the learners were introduced to the study materials and prompted to find the definition of chemical terminology with Chatbot. They were asked to record the number of terms they searched through Chatbot. In *constructive* learning condition, the learners were asked to search the terminologies using Chatbot, compare them and present what they understood, for example, the reaction between sodium and chlorine in chemical ionization (CI). In *interactive* learning condition, the learners were asked to learn through a simulation program in which they explore and discover the chemical interaction of electrostatic attraction. It is presumed that learners would experience lower intrinsic load with active learning as it simply requires search and recording actions, but would experience high intrinsic load with constructive and interactive learning as both require learners to engage in analytical and critical thinking which represent thinking at a deeper level.

2.2 Instrumentation

Cognitive load questionnaire. The self-report questionnaire consisted of 10 questions presented on an 11-point Likert-scale. Examples of questions are: "The topic covered in the video was very complex," "The instructions and/or explanations during the video were very unclear," and "The video really enhanced my understanding of the content covered." The questionnaire was adopted from Leppink et al. (2013) to measure three types of cognitive load, i.e., intrinsic, extraneous, and germane cognitive load. The instrument reported medium to high reliabilities based on the 2013 study, with three questions for intrinsic load $\alpha = 0.81$, three for extraneous load $\alpha = 0.75$, and four questions on germane load $\alpha = 0.82$. The internal consistency in the current study for the cognitive load questionnaire was $\alpha = 0.88$ for intrinsic load, $\alpha = 0.67$ for extraneous load, and $\alpha = 0.84$ for germane load, which suggests good reliability for intrinsic and germane load, but questionable reliability for extraneous load which could be explained by the different interfaces between *active/constructive* and *interactive* conditions with former as a text-based interface and the latter a simulation interface design.

Achievement test. The achievement test consists of 15 questions, of which 10 answer conceptual questions and 5 problem-solving questions. An example of conceptual question would be, "Negative ions like chlorides, bromides, and iodides involves adding ____(1)____ and ____(2)____." [Ans. (1) dilute nitric acid, (2) silver nitrate solution]. The problem-solving questions ask learners to solve or explain a particular problem in chemical reaction. An example of problem-solving question would be, "Weak acids and bases do not ionize completely. Please explain with an example the common error in assuming 100% ionization for a weak acid like HF." The total possible score a learner can attain on the achievement test is 35 points.

3. RESULTS

The study explored (1) whether there is a positive correlation among intrinsic cognitive load, germane cognitive load and student achievement scores and (2) whether intrinsic and germane cognitive load increase correspondingly with the types of learning from active to constructive, to interactive learning. The correlation analysis was performed. Results showed positive correlations among intrinsic, germane cognitive load and student achievement scores. Intrinsic cognitive load is highly correlated with germane cognitive load, $r = .955$, $p < .01$ and achievement scores $r = .828$, $p < .01$. At the same time, germane cognitive load is positively correlated with intrinsic cognitive load $r = .955$, $p < .01$ and achievement scores $r = .788$, $p < .01$. Further analysis revealed significant difference among the groups, Wilk's Lambda $\lambda = .015$, $F_{(3, 42)} = 96.127$, $p < .001$, $\eta^2 = .87$. The tests of between-subjects effects further indicate that there was significant difference among the groups (i.e., active, constructive and interactive) in terms of intrinsic load $F = 335.75$, $p < .001$, $\eta^2 = .94$, germane load $F = 729.55$, $p < .001$, $\eta^2 = .97$, and achievement $F = 49.15$, $p < .001$, $\eta^2 = .70$ (Figure 2).

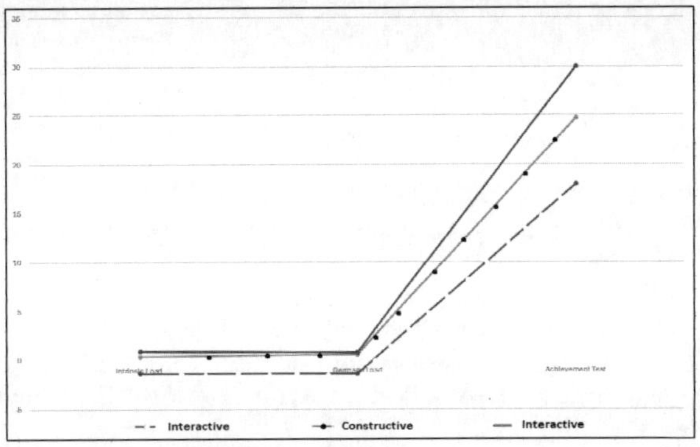

Figure 2. Intrinsic, germane cognitive load, and achievement across three learning activities

4. DISCUSSION AND CONCLUSION

The current study aimed to understand how learners' mental effort is associated with different learning activities, i.e., active, constructive and interactive when engaging in difficult content. The study also explored the relationship among germane load, intrinsic load and achievement performance.

The study showed the learners' intrinsic load is related to the learning activities. There was an increase of intrinsic load when learners engaged in learning activities from active to constructive to interactive. As the intrinsic load increases, the germane load also increases from active to constructive, but reaches a plateau after constructive learning condition (Figure 2). In the meantime, learners' achievement performance parallel with the increases of germane and intrinsic cognitive loads. This result is consistent with the literature that germane load ebbs and flows with intrinsic load in learning (Kalyuga, 2011).

There was a positive correlation between intrinsic load and achievement. With the increase of intrinsic cognitive load, the learners' performance increases across three learning activities, i.e., from active to constructive, to interactive. However, the positive correlation as we saw between intrinsic load and learning activities was partially missing pertains to germane load and learning activities. The germane load showed a positive trajectory from active to constructive learning activities. It reaches a plateau from constructive to interactive learning activities (See Figure 2). Regardless, the learners maintained a strong uptick trend in performance. Even when the germane load was below the intrinsic load at interactive learning, the learners' performance was strong. It is possible the germane load measures may not be able to capture other motivational factors which kept learners motivated during interactive learning.

In sum, the current study explored the cognitive and affective aspects that explain learners' deep processes during AI learning. The frameworks of ICAP and cognitive load theory were employed to inform the study. The results indicate positive relationship between types of cognitive load (germane and intrinsic) and learner performance across three learning conditions, i.e., active, constructive and interactive suggesting learners' cognitive processes can be significantly influenced by the types of learning activities employed, which supports Chi's ICAP learning activity theory. The study overall supports Kalyuga's theory on the positive relationship between intrinsic and germane cognitive load.

Future research should investigate the relationship between need satisfaction and cognitive engagement as measured by germane cognitive load in AI-support learning (Hypothesis 3). Further investigation should be made to examine the relationship among need satisfaction, cognitive engagement and performance (Hypothesis 4). Research on how to optimally utilizing AI tools to support learners' deep processing should be conducted in the context of activity design related to AI tools. The research should help understand (1) the cognitive functionality of AI tools, (2) the role of design activity to bring the AI tools to their fullest potential, and (3) cultural and social aspects in AI-support learning. Future research should include a wide range of population with diverse backgrounds so the findings can be generalized to a broader educational community and a large population.

REFERENCES

Chi, M. et al. (2009). Translating the ICAP theory of cognitive engagement into practice. Cognitive Science, 42, 1777-1832. Doi:10.1111/cogs.12626

Chi, M., & VanLehn, K.A. (2012). Seeing deep structure from the interactions of surface features. Educational Psychologist, 47(3), 177-188. Doi:10.1080/00461520.2012.695709

Gupta, U., & Zheng, R. (2020). Cognitive load in solving mathematics problems: Validating the role of motivation and the interaction among worked examples, task difficulty, and prior knowledge. *European Journal of STEM Education, 5*(1), 05.

Kalyuga, S. (2011). Cognitive load theory: How many types of load does it really need? Educational Psychology Review, 23(1), 1-19. Doi:10.1007/s10648-010-9150-7

Metwally, A.H.S., Huang, R., Palomino, P.T., & Yousef, A.M.F. (2024). The effect of micro gamified online homework on gameful experience, intrinsic motivation, engagement, and cognitive load. *Education and Information Technologies, 29*(18), 24489-24523. Doi:10.1007/s10639-024-12750-8

Ng, D.T.K., Chen, X., Leung, J.K.L., & Chu, S.K.W. (2024). Fostering students' AI literacy development through educational games: AI knowledge, affective and cognitive engagement. Journal of Computer Assisted Learning, 40(5), 2049-2064. Doi:10.1111/jcal.13009

Zeithofer, I., Zumbach, J., Schweppe, J. (2024). Complexity affects performance, cognitive load, and awareness. Learning & Instruction, 94, pN.PAG-N.PAG. Doi:10.1016/j.learninstruc.2024.102001

Zheng, R., Wallace, J., Soto, N., & Charles, J. (2025). Engaging Students in Deep Learning with AI: An ICAP Theory Perspective. In R. Zheng, (Ed.), *The Intersection of AI and Student Development in Learning*. IGI Global.

THE EFFECT OF ICT ON HUMAN FACTORS IN LEBANON: TRUST, SECURITY AND PRIVACY

Basima Issa
Lebanese International University – Beirut, Lebanon

ABSTRACT

The advancement of Information and Communication Technology (ICT) has reshaped human interaction, economic activities, and governance worldwide. Lebanon, with increasing ICT penetration, faces challenges related to trust, security, and privacy due to weak regulations, cyber threats, and public skepticism. This paper examines the impact of ICT adoption in Lebanon, analyzing public perception through statistical methods and graphical representation. A survey was conducted among 500 respondents from diverse demographic backgrounds, evaluating their trust in digital platforms, concerns regarding cybersecurity, and privacy awareness. Results indicate a strong correlation between ICT exposure and perceived security risks, highlighting the necessity for enhanced digital literacy and regulatory policies. Recommendations include strengthening regulations, enhancing cybersecurity infrastructure, and increasing digital literacy programs to foster a safer and more reliable ICT environment.

KEYWORDS

ICT, Security, Privacy, Lebanon, Digital Literacy, Cybersecurity

1. INTRODUCTION

The integration of ICT in everyday life has reshaped interactions, services, and societal structures. While these advancements offer numerous benefits, concerns about trust, security, and privacy have emerged. Lebanon, with its growing digital economy, faces challenges in ensuring safe ICT utilization. Moreover, ICT has become an essential part of modern life, offering communication, financial services, and data-sharing capabilities. In Lebanon, internet penetration exceeded 80% in recent years but concerns about security and data privacy persist based on the Lebanese Ministry of Telecommunications. (2023). This study aims to explore these concerns through empirical data and statistical analysis.

2. ICT IN LEBANON

Lebanon has witnessed a significant transformation in its ICT sector, with increasing internet penetration and mobile connectivity. According to government reports, internet penetration reached approximately 80% in 2023, facilitated by the expansion of fiber-optic networks and the adoption of 5G technology in select urban areas. Despite these advancements, Lebanon faces several challenges, including digital infrastructure limitations, cybersecurity threats, and regulatory gaps, the Lebanese Ministry of Telecommunications. (2023). Government initiatives, such as the Ministry of Telecommunications' digital transformation plan, aim to enhance ICT adoption and cybersecurity measures. However, political instability and economic constraints hinder the effective implementation of these policies. The private sector plays a crucial role in bridging gaps in digital services, particularly in fintech, e-commerce, and online education according to B Issa, A Saroufim, B Hussein. (2023). Public perception of ICT remains mixed, with concerns about data security and digital privacy persisting. Many users lack awareness of the best practices for online safety, underscoring the need for national digital literacy campaigns and improved cybersecurity regulations, B Issa, A Saroufim, B Hussein. (2023).

3. LITERATURE REVIEW

Trust in digital platforms is influenced by security measures, transparency, and government regulations. Studies show that weak legal frameworks lead to public skepticism in online transactions based on B Issa, A Saroufim, B Hussein. (2023). Lebanon's digital economy struggles due to inadequate consumer protection policies. Previous research highlights the complex relationship between ICT and human factors. According to Smith et al. (2021), increasing digital connectivity raises both opportunities and threats, affecting trust in technology. Similarly, Johnson & Wang (2020) emphasize the importance of cybersecurity measures in fostering user confidence. Miller et al. (2019) discuss privacy challenges associated with digital transformation. According to Al-Rifai and Omar (2018), digital policies play a crucial role in mitigating risks. Lastly, Chang et al. (2017) provide insights into the behavioral impact of ICT security breaches. In the Lebanese context and based on the Lebanese Ministry of Telecommunications. (2023), few studies have comprehensively analyzed these aspects, necessitating further exploration. Khaled and Mansour (2016) analyze cybersecurity regulations in the Middle East. Ahmed and Saleh (2015) examine digital literacy's role in trust-building. Lastly, Patel (2014) explores how evolving ICT infrastructures impact privacy concerns. In the Lebanese context, few studies have comprehensively analyzed these aspects, necessitating further exploration.

4. METHODOLOGY

A quantitative approach was employed using a structured questionnaire distributed online and in person. The survey assessed three main dimensions:

- Trust in ICT platforms
- Perceived security risks
- Privacy awareness and concerns

Data was analyzed using SPSS, employing regression analysis and correlation tests to determine relationships between ICT usage and human factors. The survey contains a sample of 500 members, divided into 300 males and 200 females diverse demographic backgrounds from university students, instructors and employees.

5. FINDINGS AND RESULTS

5.1 Trust in ICT Platforms

Survey results indicate that 62% of respondents trust online platforms for financial transactions, while 38% express concerns about data misuse (Figure 1). Regression analysis shows a positive relationship between digital literacy and trust ($R^2 = 0.67$, $p < 0.05$).

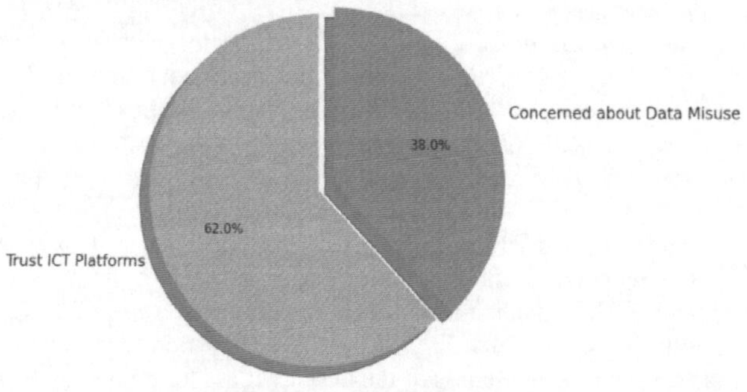

Figure 1. Trust in ICT platforms

5.2 Perceived Security Risks

Security concerns were prevalent, with 75% of respondents reporting fears of cyberattacks. Figure 2 illustrates the distribution of perceived risks, with phishing and identity theft ranking highest. Correlation analysis reveals a strong link between cybersecurity awareness and reduced fear levels ($r = -0.74$, $p < 0.01$).

Figure 2. Perceived security risk among ICT users

5.3 Privacy Awareness

Privacy remains a significant issue, as 80% of participants lack confidence in existing data protection regulations. Figure 3 presents demographic variations in privacy concerns, showing that younger individuals are more aware of digital privacy risks.

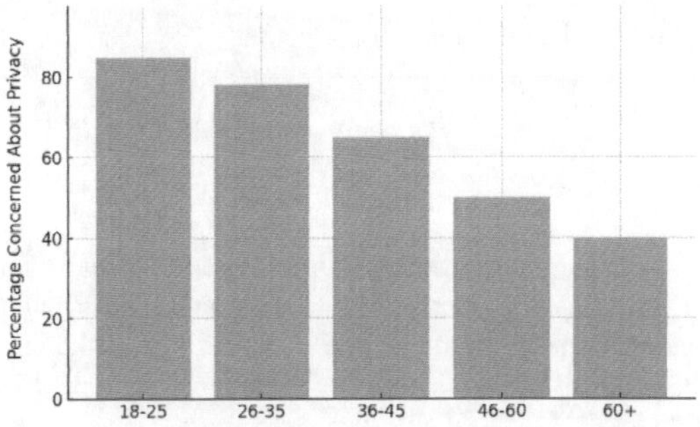

Figure 3. Age group

Findings highlight a digital trust deficit in Lebanon. Many users lack confidence in online platforms due to frequent cyber incidents and regulatory weaknesses. Moreover, cybersecurity awareness remains low, leaving individuals susceptible to threats.

The study suggests that stronger digital security frameworks and public awareness campaigns are needed to mitigate risks. Lebanon must strengthen cybersecurity laws and enforce data protection regulations to build trust.

5.4 Privacy Concerns

The Privacy Concerns Among ICT Users in Lebanon pie chart provides insights into the key concerns individuals have regarding their digital privacy. The data is based on survey responses and is divided into the following categories:

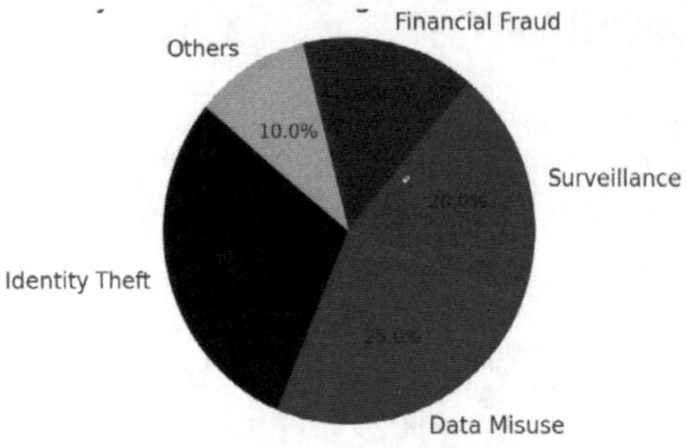

Figure 4. Privacy concerns

- **Identity Theft (30%)** – The most significant concern among respondents is the risk of identity theft. This reflects growing fears about personal information being stolen and misused, especially in financial transactions and online accounts.
- **Data Misuse (25%)** – A substantial portion of users worry about companies and institutions misusing their personal data. This includes concerns about unauthorized sharing, lack of transparency in data collection, and breaches of personal information.
- **Surveillance (20%)** – Many individuals are apprehensive about government or corporate surveillance, fearing that their online activities are being monitored without consent. This aligns with global discussions on data privacy and digital freedom.
- **Financial Fraud (15%)** – With the rise of online banking and e-commerce, cybercriminals target users for financial fraud. Respondents expressed fears about phishing scams, credit card fraud, and fraudulent online transactions.
- **Other Concerns (10%)** – This category includes worries about digital harassment, misinformation, and the spread of personal data through social media.

6. CONCLUSION

Based on the study, here is a brief summary of the key findings and corresponding recommendations:

- This study highlights the negative impact of ICT on trust, security, and privacy in Lebanon. As digital adoption grows, cybersecurity risks also increase, leading to public distrust in online services.
- Strengthening Cybersecurity Regulations – Lebanon must implement stricter data protection laws and consumer rights policies.
- Public Awareness Campaigns – Digital literacy programs should educate users on privacy measures and safe online practices.
- Stronger Security Measures by Platforms – social media and financial service providers must enforce transparent security protocols.
- Investment in Cybersecurity Infrastructure – Businesses and government entities must allocate resources to cybersecurity to protect user data.
- Findings indicate that ICT adoption in Lebanon is accompanied by significant trust, security, and privacy concerns.
- Policymakers must prioritize cybersecurity education and enforce stricter data protection laws.
- The results indicate that privacy concerns are a significant barrier to full ICT adoption, with identity theft (30%) and data misuse (25%) ranking as the top concerns. These issues, along with fears of surveillance (20%) and financial fraud (15%), indicate that Lebanese ICT users perceive substantial risks in digital interactions.

To enhance trust in ICT, Lebanese policymakers should focus on the following initiatives:

- Strengthening cybersecurity regulations to ensure consumer data protection and prevent cyber threats.

- Implementing national digital literacy programs that educate users on privacy best practices and secure online behavior.
- Increasing transparency in data collection and use, particularly in governmental and private-sector applications, to reduce fears of surveillance and data misuse.
- Encouraging financial sector security measures to build user confidence in online banking and digital transactions.
- Developing a national cybersecurity awareness campaign to educate the public about common threats and how to mitigate them.
- Enhancing collaboration between public and private sectors to establish best practices for data security and cyber threat management.
- Incentivizing businesses to adopt advanced cybersecurity measures, including encryption and multi-factor authentication, to enhance consumer trust.
- Introducing stricter enforcement of data protection laws to ensure compliance and deter cybercriminal activities.

REFERENCES

Ahmed, K., & Saleh, M. (2015). The role of digital literacy in trust-building among ICT users. Journal of Technology Adoption, 7(3), 123-138.

Al-Rifai, S., & Omar, H. (2018). Digital policies and risk mitigation in the ICT sector. Journal of Technology and Society, 10(1), 33-47.

Chang, T., Lee, R., & Kwon, H. (2017). The behavioral impact of ICT security breaches. Journal of Cybersecurity Research, 15(2), 88-103.

Issa, B., Saroufim, A., Hussein, B. (2023). Information Technology Adoption in Legislative Work: The Lebanese Parliament Model, in Atulya K. Nagar, Dharm Singh Jat, Durgesh Kumar Mishra and Amit Joshi (Eds.), Intelligent Sustainable Systems Sustainability (Selected Papers of WorldS4 2023, Volume 1), pp. 69-75. Copyright (c) Springer 2024, ISBN:978-981-99-8030-7 69-75.

Johnson, M., & Wang, X. (2020). Cybersecurity and trust in the digital age. Journal of Digital Security, 12(3), 45-60.

Khaled, N., & Mansour, R. (2016). Cybersecurity regulations in the Middle East: A comparative analysis. Journal of Information Security, 9(1), 77-94.

Lebanese Ministry of Telecommunications. (2023). ICT Development Report in Lebanon.

Miller, A., Chen, B., & Rahman, S. (2019). Privacy challenges in the era of digital transformation. International Journal of Information Management, 17(4), 201-219.

Smith, J., Brown, L., & Ahmed, R. (2021). Privacy concerns in ICT: A global perspective. International Journal of Information Systems, 18(2), 102-118.

A GENERIC PDCA BASED HOSPITAL QUALITY MANAGEMENT SYSTEM MODEL

Bassam Hussein[1], Shaza Soleiman[2], Mohamad Hajj-Hassan[3], Ahmad Kassas[2] and Amin Haj-Ali[4]
[1]*Department of Industrial Engineering, Lebanese International University, Bekaa, Lebanon*
[2]*Department of Industrial Engineering, The International University of Beirut, Beirut, Lebanon*
[3]*Department of Biomedical Engineering, Lebanese International University, Bekaa, Lebanon*
[4]*Department of Computer & Communications Engineering, Lebanese International University, Beirut, Lebanon*

ABSTRACT

The implementation of a Quality Management System (QMS) in healthcare institutions is essential for ensuring patient safety, optimizing service delivery, and maintaining high standards of care. This paper outlines a generic structured, PDCA (Plan-Do-Check-Act) model-based approach for developing and integrating a hospital QMS. The study highlights key challenges within the healthcare sector, including the frequent failure to ensure quality care and the necessity of comprehensive management systems. It further explores the benefits of a well-established QMS, such as improved efficiency, better resource allocation, and enhanced patient satisfaction. The proposed model provides a step-by-step methodology for assessment, team organization, project execution, and performance evaluation. By implementing a robust QMS, hospitals can achieve continuous improvement and sustainability in healthcare service delivery.

KEYWORDS

QMS, PDCA, Healthcare, Continuous Improvement

1. INTRODUCTION

A quality management system, based on ISO 9000 (Landau, 1996), is a standard instrument for the effective and successful management of the best organizations, all over the world. This is especially relevant in organizations that have special interest in public safety, wellbeing and welfare. This is particularly applicable and mandatory in the healthcare sector (Shaw, 2006). From both professional and ethical perspectives, ensuring safety, quality of provided care and the duty not to cause harm become paramount.

In order to successfully implement a hospital quality management system (QMS), it is important to have a good understanding of the benefits that such a system brings to the institution. Furthermore, the detailed requirements a QMS must converge to control activities from the planning (P) to the acting steps (A). Once that scope of the system is clear, a crucial step would be to perform a gap analysis and to prioritize actions to meet the standards requirements (Golden, 2018). At this point, setting up, implementing and managing the system becomes the challenge and must be done with care and in accordance with the set objectives. Finally, the roles, responsibilities and organizational interactions of the stakeholders must be captured and clarified in the system.

This paper will present a generic PDCA based hospital QMS model that may constitute an integrative framework for the development of such a system in the healthcare sector. A step-by-step approach will be outlined for easy consultation and as a practical guide for practitioner.

2. ISSUES AT STAKE

Currently, the health care sector has been perceived as harming too frequently and routinely failing to deliver its potential benefits. This has been mainly attributed to the lack of quality assurance where problems affecting many patients exist in different areas and functions of the sector.

Hospitals across the globe are constantly searching for ways to improve quality of care and promote effective quality improvement (QI) strategies.

Hospitals are in constant pursuit of a complete management system directly linked to the organizational chart, middle management, executive council, etc. It should include a system encompassing a quality improvement plan, policies and procedures, job descriptions, and other functions such as auditing services, including mock audits, and preparing the personnel for external audits. Finally, they also need training services on organizational structure, strategic planning, QMS principles and applications and quality documentation. Internal audit and self-assessment, QIP and KPI, job description, performance appraisal, competency test, EPP, patient safety and risk management are also important considerations (Shortell et al., 1998) (Ismail et al/, 2016).

3. PROPOSED SOLUTION

Research and practice have proven that a well-established QMS can benefit the organization and provide an effective mechanism for improvement, evolution and sustainability of quality initiatives and processes. One of the cornerstones of a quality organization is the concept of the customer and consultant working together for mutual benefit. In order to ensure that this relationship is effective, the customer-consultant interfacing must extend into and outside the organization beyond the immediate customers and consultants.

A QMS is defined as a set of coordinated activities to direct and control an organization in order to continually improve the effectiveness and efficiency of its performance. The main thrust of a QMS is in defining the processes, which will result in the production of quality products and services, rather than in detecting defective products or services after they have been produced.

A. QMS Implementation Benefits

A fully documented QMS will ensure that the customers' requirements are met through confidence in the ability of the organization to deliver the desired product and service consistently meeting their needs and expectations. In addition, the organization's requirements are also met both internally and externally and at an optimum cost with efficient use of the available resources including material, human, equipment, and technology and information.

As Deming states quality begins with intent, which is fixed by management (Deming, 1986). A QMS enables an organization to achieve the goals and objectives set out in its policy and strategy. It provides consistency and satisfaction in terms of methods, materials, equipment, etc. It interacts with all activities of the organization, beginning with the identification of customer requirements and ending with their satisfaction, at every transaction interface. Figure 1 depicts the benefits of QMS in terms of progress versus time.

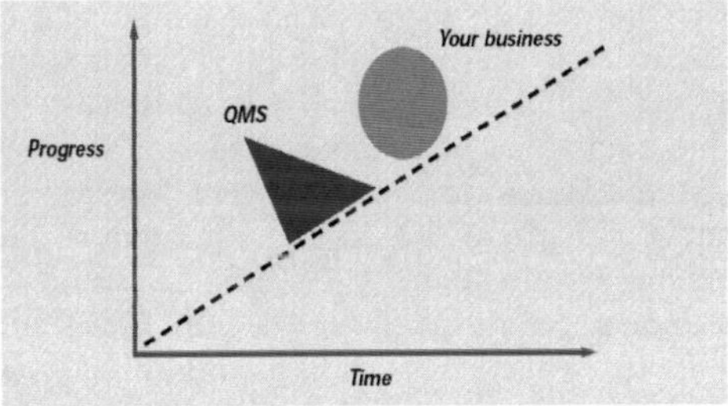

Figure 1. QMS Benefits - Progress versus Time

It is important to consider the following items when implementing a QMS: designing, building, controlling, deploying, measuring, reviewing and improving. A good QMS should set direction and meet customers' expectations, improve process control, reduce wastage, lower costs, increase market share, facilitate training, involve staff and raise morale.

QMS design must be led by senior managers to suit the needs of the organization, and this is ideally done using a framework to lead the thinking. The first important step of the QMS initiation is the decision of the top management. Design of the QMS should come from determining the organization's core processes and well-defined goals and strategies which link to the needs of stakeholders (Mourougan & Sethuraman, 2015).

Deployment and implementation are best achieved using process packages where each core process is broken down into sub-processes and described by a combination of documentation, education, training, tools, systems and metrics. Control of the QMS will depend on the size and complexity of the organization.

Measurement is carried out to determine the effectiveness and efficiency of each process towards attaining its objectives. It should include the contribution of the QMS to the organization's goals and this could be achieved by measuring the following: policy definition completeness, coverage of business, reflection of policies, deployment, usage, whether staff find the QMS helpful in their work, speed of change of the QMS and its architecture relevance to the job in hand.

Reviewing the effectiveness, efficiency and capability of a QMS is vital and the outcome of reviews should be communicated to all employees. Reviewing and monitoring should be conducted whether or not improvement activities have achieved their expected outcomes. Improvement should follow as a result of the review process, with the aim of seeking internal best practice (Nenadal, 2016). It is part of the overall improvement activities and an integral part of managing change within the organization.

Finally, the key elements of a successful strategy for quality management involve developing the right culture for quality to flourish, attracting and retaining the right people to promote quality, devising and updating the right in-house processes for quality improvement and giving staff the right tools to do the job. Special attention should be given to the 5 P's spanning across people, policies, procedures, provisions and place

B. Process Steps

A quality consultant helps clients to better identify needs that enable them to request services within the expected scope of work through a GAP analysis. Consultants must exhibit project initiation meeting activities and ensure the efficient and effective follow-up and proper evaluation of the project deliverables. In addition, they should also ensure the proper and efficient management of consultancy services and evaluate the client feedback and satisfaction:

1. **Step 1 – Preliminary Assessment:** A site visit must be performed and concluded by a detailed report to identify client needs. A general assessment form is recommended to direct consultants for better assessment of the current situation. The project manager (PM) forms a team of consultants to make the visit and perform the general assessment. Each consultant delivers a report about the findings. The PM prepares a gap analysis report about the current situation of the hospital based on consultant findings. The general manager (GM) reviews the report with PM. The chief general manager (CGM) sends the report to the client detailing the necessary actions and deliverables. These should include a wide range of forms and charts. A well-defined checklist comes in handy as an assessment tool to ensure that nothing falls in the cracks in the process (Al-Ali, 2023).
2. **Step 2 – Team Building and Organization Procedures:** The CGM assigns the team members including PM and consultants. It is mandatory to provide the team with necessary protocols, organizational charts, policies and procedures. Otherwise, it is the responsibility of the consultants to provide the clients with the necessary requirements that may include templates and job aids. A project plan/action shall be established at this stage. The CGM initiates consultancy services once the contract is signed. The CGM and the PM assign the team of consultants by referring to the list of approved consultants, based on specialty of services required by the client. CGM prepares and signs the agreement with the consultants according to standard procedure. PM and the team define project objectives and prepare project plan with baseline budget and schedule (Beer et al., 2024).
3. **Step 3 – Project Opening Meeting Policies:** PMs should explain the project plan for upper and lower management in the hospital if available, otherwise to the decision makers in the hospital. The team starts implementing the action plan immediately after the project opening meeting. The Team should know the road map of communication between consultants, PMs and the management board according to the lines of authority. PMs and the team start implementation of project plan. Visit reports are prepared by each consultant starting from the visit and submitted to PMs.
4. **Step 4 – Consultancy Evaluation and Follow-Up Policies & Procedures:** It is the responsibility of CGM to ensure that the services provided by every PM and the team of consultants are initially defined before the project begins, tracked during the project and evaluated when the project is completed. It is the responsibility of CGM to assess the number of consultants needed based on workload per service. The PM follows up on implementation and submits regular progress reports to CGM at intervals specified by both parties based on the due dates of the project plan. PM follows up on the project budget and reports regular updates to CGM. The CGM reviews and analyses all reports. The CGM and PM have regular meetings to discuss the reports. CGM arranges for field visits based on duration of projects to ensure the delivery of service according to preset project plan. PM submits regular reports to CGM summarizing progress along with follow up findings. When done, the CGM arranges for a

final site inspection to ensure proper delivery. If the inspection results are not satisfactory, the PM will report to CGM to take the necessary actions. The PM facilitates conducting customer satisfaction survey and consultant evaluation. The findings are then analyzed and reported (Kabeyi, 2019).

5. **Step 5 – Customer Satisfaction and Project Outcomes Policies**: A survey on client satisfaction and the project outcomes should be conducted at the middle and final stages of the project. Projects outcomes are evaluated according to pre-defined KPIs. When a gap is observed, the quality department initiates a root cause analysis and an action plan which clearly lists the problem and takes corrective action. A project closure ceremony will be scheduled (Ismail et al., 2016).

4. THE PROPOSED PDCA MODEL

PDCA (plan–do–check–act or plan–do–check–adjust), depicted in Figure 2, is an iterative four-step management method used for the control and continuous improvement of processes and products. It involves:

A. ***PLAN***: Establish the objectives and processes necessary to deliver results in accordance with the expected output (the target or goals). By establishing output expectations, the completeness and accuracy of the specification is also a part of the targeted improvement.

B. ***DO****:* Implement the plan, execute the process, make the product. Collect data for charting and analysis in the following "CHECK" and "ACT" steps.

C. ***CHECK****:* Study the actual results and compare against the expected results to ascertain any differences. Look for deviation in implementation from the plan and also look for the appropriateness and completeness of the plan to enable the execution, i.e., "Do". Charting data can make this much easier to see trends over several PDCA cycles and in order to convert the collected data into information. Information is what you need for the next step "ACT".

D. ***ACT****:* Request corrective actions on significant differences between actual and planned results. Analyze the differences to determine their root causes. Determine where to apply changes that will include improvement of the process or product. When a pass through these four steps does not result in the need to improve, the scope to which PDCA is applied may be refined to plan and improve with more detail in the next iteration of the cycle.

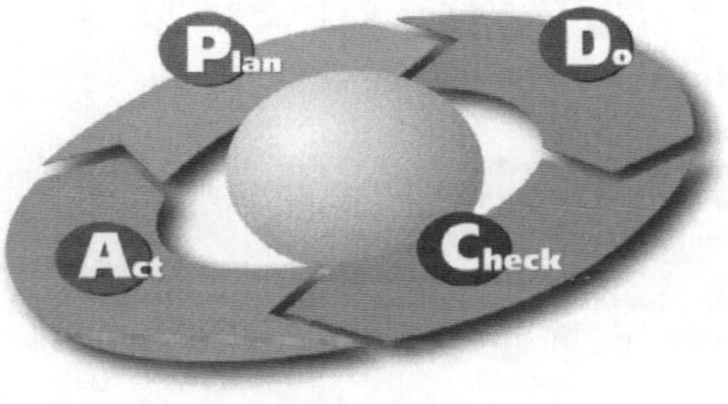

Figure 2. The PDCA Cycle

The proposed model will follow a set of well-defined steps including:

1. Supervising the change of the organizational chart to fit the quality approach (Khan et al., 2025).
2. Surveying the attribution of job descriptions for middle management by the institution.
3. Surveying/advising the institution during the appointment of middle managers.
4. Surveying/evaluating the appointment of the members of the executive council.
5. Implementing an action plan for the different committees according to accreditation standards.
6. Implementing a strategic plan (Supervision).
7. Implementing a rough action plan for building a quality system by the different departments.
8. Surveying/modifying/providing policies and procedures according to accreditation standards.
9. Helping providing job descriptions for the different positions/departments.
10. Supervising/setting a comprehensive QIP plan.
11. Training the personnel on policies and procedures and competency tests.
12. Execution of the quality system.

13. Strategic plan revision report.
14. Key performance indicators (KPI).
15. Putting in action of competency tests by the departments.
16. Employees' performance evaluation by the departments.
17. Analysis of complains, and suggestions of clients.
18. Internal and external audits.
20. Improvement plan settlement.
23. Evaluation and prevention steps.

5. CONCLUSION

A well-structured QMS is a critical component for hospitals aiming to enhance service quality, ensure compliance with standards, and improve patient outcomes. This paper has proposed a PDCA-based framework that systematically guides healthcare institutions through planning, implementation, monitoring, and continuous improvement. Effective deployment of a QMS requires strong leadership commitment, comprehensive process control, and active participation from all stakeholders. By adopting this model, healthcare institutions can foster a culture of quality, drive operational excellence, and ultimately provide safer and more efficient healthcare services. Future efforts should focus on refining QMS strategies, integrating technological advancements, and addressing evolving challenges in healthcare quality management (Abou Okdeh, 2017).

REFERENCES

Abou Okdeh, M., Hage-Diab, A., Haj-Ali, A. & Hussein, B., (2017). Concussion detection using a commercially available eye tracker. In: *2017 Fourth International Conference on Advances in Biomedical Engineering (ICABME)*, pp.1–4.

Al-Ali, M. A., (2023). A framework for effective preliminary assessment in project management. *International Journal of Project Management Studies*, 12(3), pp.45–58.

Beer, R., Qi, A. & Ríos, I., (2024). Team building and incentive schemes in collaborative projects. *SSRN Electronic Journal*, pp.1–47.

G Deming, W.E., (1986). *Out of the crisis*. Cambridge, MA: MIT Press.

olden, S. H., (2018). A gap analysis needs assessment tool to drive a care delivery and research agenda for integration of care and sharing of best practices across a health system. *Journal of Clinical and Translational Endocrinology*, 15, pp.92–99.

Ismail, S., Nehme, H., Hussein, B. & Hajj-Hassan, M., (2016). Integration of Monte Carlo simulation tool for forecasting medical equipment risks in HIQMA system. In: *2016 3rd Middle East Conference on Biomedical Engineering (MECBME)*. IEEE, pp.10–15.

Kabeyi, M. J. B., (2019). Project and program evaluation process, consultancy and terms of reference with challenges, opportunities and recommendations. *International Journal of Scientific and Research Publications (IJSRP)*, 9(12), pp.171–180.

Khan, M. F., Rashrash, M., Sawesi, S. & Anam, F., (2025). Key findings and recommendations from the American Association of Colleges of Pharmacy Curriculum Quality Survey of US pharmacy school faculty. *American Journal of Pharmaceutical Education*, March.

Landau, J.R., (1996). Implementation of ISO 9000 in the healthcare sector. *International Journal of Health Care Quality Assurance*, 9(2), pp.9–14.

Mourougan, S. & Sethuraman, K., 2015. Understanding and implementing quality management system. *IOSR Journal of Business and Management*, 17(6), pp.1–8.

Nenadal, J., (2016). Adequacy, suitability, effectiveness and efficiency of quality management systems: how to perceive and assess them? *Quality Innovation Prosperity*, 20(2), pp.39–56.

Shaw, J., (2006). The implementation of quality management systems in hospitals: a comparison between three countries. *BMC Health Services Research*, 6(50), pp.1–8.

Shortell, S. M., Bennett, J. L. & Byck, G. R., (1998). Assessing the impact of continuous quality improvement on clinical practice: what it will take to accelerate progress. *Milbank Quarterly*, 76(4), pp.593–624.

Reflection Paper

SENSORY TRANSLATION AND FRICTION IN GENERATIVE ARTIFICIAL INTELLIGENCE AND MULTI-MODAL PLATFORMS

Eun-Sung Kim
Department of Sociology, Kyung Hee University
26 Kyungheedae-ro, Dongdaemun-gu, Seoul, 02447, Korea

ABSTRACT

Generative artificial intelligence (AI) and multimodal platforms have revolutionized the political economy of AI and big data through sensory innovation. However, these phenomena lack social and political analyses. This article proposes two key concepts: sensory translation and sensory friction. Sensory translation refers to variations in data presentation within the same or across different sensory modalities. Sensory friction refers to sociotechnical challenges to sensory translation at technical, economic, and political levels. While AI-driven sensory translation strengthens surveillance capitalism by intensifying affective emotions and extracting consumer preferences through various sensory outputs, such as personalized videos, it encounters several types of sensory friction. Technical frictions reveal how multimodal platforms prioritize sight and sound over other senses. Economic frictions highlight how AI sustainability varies with different sensory modalities. Political frictions demonstrate sensory politics' impact on democracy. The conclusion emphasizes the importance of incorporating sensory approaches in social science research on AI.

KEYWORDS

Senses, Artificial Intelligence, Big Data, Friction, Surveillance Capitalism

1. INTRODUCTION

Multimodal platforms are ushering in an era of sensory innovation, with generative AI making conversion between different senses easier and more frequent than ever before. This technology enables the rapid translation of text into images, sounds, and videos, transforming digital platforms into multimodal platforms that integrate non-verbal elements such as images, sounds, voices, music, and videos. These platforms have moved beyond traditional text-based interfaces, heralding a new era where AI understands and generates content in multiple sensory formats. The free conversion of the senses and sensory diversity enabled by generative AI add complexity to power and capital formation. However, the impacts of various sensory translations on the politics and economy of digital platforms remain largely unexplored.

This study aims to investigate the reasons behind data companies' promotion of multimodal AIs, such as generative AI, and the associated sociotechnical challenges. To address these issues, it bridges the political sociology of the senses with the political sociology of big data and AI. To begin with, it proposes novel concepts, namely sensory translation and friction. Subsequently, the study examines the connection between sensory translation and surveillance capitalism, clarifying the rise of multimodal AI, such as generative AI. It further addresses the sensory friction across technical, economic, political, and institutional dimensions to understand the socio-technical challenges faced by generative AI and digital platforms. Finally, it discusses a sensory turn in social science research on AI in terms of how a political sociology of the senses provides a new lens for understanding the politics of big data and AI.

2. SENSORY TRANSLATION AND FRICTION

Sensory translation refers to the variations of modality in data presentation within the same or across different sensory dimensions. There are two types of sensory translation. Intra-sensory translation occurs within a single sensory dimension. Conversely, inter-sensory translation involves the conversion of distinct sensory modalities, such as sight, sound, smell, and touch. For generative AI, intra-sensory translation includes text-to-image, image-to-text, and image-to-3D, while intersensory translation involves text-to-audio, text-to-video, audio-to-text, and audio-to-video. Sensory friction is the sociotechnical resistance encountered during sensory translation. It encompasses socio-technical challenges that hinder the free and seamless translation of the senses. Sensory friction encompasses technological, economic, political, and institutional dimensions. The concept of sensory frictions posits that the process of sensory translation is not invariably smooth, being subject to influences such as technical infrastructure, financial considerations, and the prevailing political and institutional milieu. Even if technological advancements are able to alleviate human, technical, and economic frictions, there may still be lingering sensory frictions at the political and institutional level. The concept of sensory friction proves valuable in elucidating the role of politics, power, and capital in the context of sensation or sensory translation. It brings to light the social and political aspects of sensory experiences.

3. MULTIMODAL AI, SENSORY TRANSLATION, AND SURVEILLANCE CAPITALISM

Multimodal AIs have been linked to surveillance capitalism, a new capitalist system that accumulates capital by extracting and monitoring individuals' behavioral data in digital spaces (Zuboff, 2019). This system uses human experience as free raw material, translates it into behavioral data, and employs machine intelligence to predict future behavior. These predictive products are traded in a new type of future behavioral market, such as advertising, in which behavioral predictions are sold. A surveillance capitalist system mines users' behavioral data to predict their preferences and serve to advertise tailored to their interests. Speculations regarding a user's search behavior can reveal the individual's thoughts, feelings, and actions at a particular time or place. Advertising can be tailored based on a person's search. Zuboff (2019) argues that surveillance capitalism expands through economies of scale, scope, and behavior. Economies of scale relate to the volume of data, economies of scope relate to the variety of data, and economies of behavior relate to the coordination and inducement of individual behavior aligned with corporate interests. Sensory products enabled by multimodal AI advance the three mechanisms of surveillance capitalism.

Sensory experience is critical for shaping individual preferences and is an essential raw material for the surveillance capitalist system. Traditionally, digital platforms have extracted behavioral data by analyzing search logs or interactions, such as 'likes,' on Facebook. With Movie Gen, Meta platform allows users to create their personalized videos through generative AI. These videos hold significant value in surveillance capitalism. By uploading a photo, users receive a video. It represents the sensory translation from pictures to videos. Comparing photos and personalized videos can help meta-understand consumer desires accurately. The person realizes his dream of becoming a scientist in a video. This video reflects an individual's unrealized dreams, allowing Meta to extract users' dreams through personalized videos. These dreams are closely tied to consumer preferences and provide a more accurate indicator of consumer preferences than past methods such as Google's search logs or Meta's clicks. Understanding consumers' dreams is crucial for advertisers and merchants as it offers deep insights into what individuals truly desire.

Surveillance capitalism narrows the gap between real individuals and the algorithmic identities on digital platforms (Cheney-Lippold, 2011). On multimodal platforms, "algorithmic identities" are equipped with various sensory outputs. On the Meta website, Movie Gen introduces a personalized video: "Upload an image of yourself and transform it into a personalized video. Movie Gen's cutting-edge model lets you create personalized videos that preserve human identity and motion." According to this message, personalized videos preserve human identity, which becomes an "algorithmic identity" (Cheney-Lippold, 2011). Personalized videos enable platform algorithms to minimize the distinction between the real individual and the dividual (algorithmic identity), thereby allowing for a more precise characterization. The logic of surveillance capitalism is embedded in personalized videos as it can predict consumer preferences (Zuboff, 2019). By developing multimodal AIs, data companies create more sophisticated and versatile systems that can understand and respond to complex human inputs, thereby improving the accuracy and relevance of the services they offer.

The pictures, sounds, and videos generated by multimodal AI can produce the affective emotions–an unconscious force transmitted through the senses to our nervous system, transforming into emotions (Deleuze, 2003). Images, sounds, and videos can effectively create affective emotions, capture user attention, and enhance a platform's network effect. The multiple and diverse senses of multimodal AIs enhance user interaction and engagement with these platforms, facilitating more natural and intuitive interactions with technology. This enables users to communicate their requirements and preferences. Consequently, this increases the total data volume on the platforms, contributing to economies of scale for surveillance capitalism and enhancing algorithmic precision. Thus, the affective emotions generated by digital platforms become a source of power and capital, playing a crucial role in the attention or affective economy of platforms such as Facebook. Affective emotions serve as a significant source of capital accumulation (Lee, 2023).

Furthermore, the sensory diversity produced by multimodal AI enhances the economy of scope in surveillance capitalism. Sensory diversity is closely linked to the accuracy of AI. Qualcomm Korea states that "For AI to provide more accurate and relevant answers, large-scale multimodal models (LLMs) that can analyze voice queries, text, images, videos, and even radio frequency and sensor data are essential." The more diverse the sensory data, the more accurate the surveillance system because the system can integrate disparate sensory inputs. Platforms utilizing multiple senses, such as sound, voice, music, and video, in addition to text, can achieve more precise surveillance since sensory inputs become personal traits tracked by algorithms. This sophistication in data extraction and targeted advertising sharpens precision. Multimodality is essential to the accuracy of AI for surveillance capitalism.

Chatbots are key tools in surveillance capitalism (Zuboff, 2019), and sensory diversity is a key feature of multimodal chatbots. Imagine the difference between traditional text- and voice-based chatbots. While the former judges an individual user based on the content of the chat, the latter is able to recognize an individual by the content of the chat and by the tone of voice. In other words, the platform's algorithm can more accurately determine the interlocutor when a conversation is spoken than when it is written. Therefore, Open AI recently attempted to create a voice chatbot using Scarlett Johansson's voice. Voice-based chatbots allow for a more accurate extraction system for human behavioral data.

Fourth, multimodal platforms contribute to the behavioral economy of surveillance capitalism. Algorithms on multimodal platforms can manipulate and direct consumer behavior through sensory interactions. Sensation becomes a key resource in the creation of this "algorithmic governmentality" (Janssen & Kuk, 2016). Algorithmic governmentality means that actors govern their behavior according to the platform's algorithm. It creates an algorithmic identity and controls people's behavior (Cheney-Lippold, 2011). In this case, Algorithmic governmentality manifests itself through the sensory realm. Instead of describing products using language, algorithms can adjust and guide consumer behavior by simply matching products with personalized videos uploaded by users. It is possible to govern consumer behavior subconsciously by producing affective emotions through customized videos.

4. SENSORY FRICTION IN GENERATIVE AI AND MULTIMODAL PLATFORMS

Technological sensory frictions highlight the discrepancy between bodily and digitally mediated senses produced by AI. Furthermore, substantial technological limitations exist in replicating senses such as taste and smell in comparison to sight and hearing. The concept of economic sensory friction suggests that the sustainability of generative AIs may vary depending on the specific sensory modalities utilized, as energy consumption is likely to differ among different senses. Political sensory friction reveals the impact of sensory politics on democracy, providing new insights into democracy in the AI era. In the context of deepfake protests, sensory politics are intricately linked with both party politics (liberal democracy) and identity politics (radical democracy).

Table 1. Sensory frictions in generative AI and multimodal platforms

Concepts	Definitions	Cases
Technical sensory frictions	Lack of technical tools or infrastructure for sensory translation	The linguistic limitations of sensory translation in generative AI.
Economical sensory friction	Excessive economic costs of sensory translation	Energy costs for sensory translation in generative AI
Political sensory friction	Political backlash against the display of certain sensory data	Global women protest on deepfake technology Sensory politics in the data display of public platforms

5. CONCLUSION

This study connects the political sociology of the senses to the political sociology of AI and big data, utilizing the notions of sensory translation and friction to examine these phenomena. The notion of sensory translation elucidates the role of the senses in the proliferation of surveillance capitalism (Zuboff, 2019) and clarifies the development of multimodal platforms that incorporate nonverbal components such as images, sounds, voices, music, and video. As sensory translation becomes more seamlessly facilitated by generative AI, the senses become new raw materials for surveillance capitalism on digital platforms. Since sensation is an important part of human nature, the extraction of human sensation by platform algorithms further increases the accuracy of surveillance capitalism. The rise in sensory diversity on these platforms allows for a better understanding and prediction of user behavior, ultimately bolstering the growth of surveillance capitalism. This is achieved through a more precise characterization of users' algorithmic identities using multiple sensory modalities. In turn, algorithmic identities on multimodal platforms now possess sensory attributes. The use of AI to generate multiple sensations amplifies the production of affective emotions on these platforms. These affective emotions, as extracted by algorithms, are then transformed into capital and power. The intersection of affective politics and capitalism further compounds the effects of surveillance capitalism.

However, despite the increasing ease and frequency of sensory translation with generative AI, it still faces challenges from economic, political, and institutional frictions. This friction highlights that sensation is not solely a technical process, but is heavily influenced by social, political, and institutional factors. This sensory friction determines the direction of the sensory translation. Technical sensory friction highlights the reinforcement of a modern sensory hierarchy that prioritizes vision and sound over taste, smell, and touch within the platform society (Classen 2005). Economic sensory friction pertains to the political economy of AI, addressing debates surrounding AI extractivism and sustainability (Crawford 2024). Political sensory friction offers a novel perspective on data democracy, expanding beyond knowledge politics by linking democracy to sensory politics. Thus, political sociology of the senses can enhance and refine the social science of AI and big data.

REFERENCES

Cheney-Lippold, J. (2011). A new algorithmic identity: Soft biopolitics and the modulation of control. *Theory, Culture & Society*, Vol. 28, No.6, pp.164-181.

Classen, C. (2005). The Witch's senses: Sensory ideologies and transgressive femininities from the Renaissance to modernity. In: D. Howes, ed. *Empire of the Senses*. New York: Berg, pp.70-84.

Crawford, K. (2024). Generative AI's environmental costs are soaring — and mostly secret. *Nature*, pp.693-693.

Deleuze, G. (2003). *Francis Bacon: The Logic of Sensation*. London: Continuum.

Lee, H. (2023). *Affective Capitalism: For a Critique of the Political Economy of Affect*. Palgrave Macmillan.

Janssen, M. and Kuk, G., (2016). The challenges and limits of big data algorithms in technocratic governance. *Government Information Quarterly*, Vol.33. No.3, pp.371-377.

Zuboff, S. (2019). *The Age of Surveillance Capitalism: The fight for a human future at the new frontier of power*. New York: Public Affairs.

Posters

NAVIGATING DIGITAL TRANSFORMATION: THE ROLE OF COMPETENCY IDENTIFICATION IN TALENT MANAGEMENT STRATEGIES

Hamed Al-Abri
Petroleum Development Oman (PDO)
Muscat, Oman

ABSTRACT

In the era of digital transformation, organizations face the challenge of adapting to rapid technological changes while maintaining operational efficiency. This manuscript explores the critical role of competency identification in talent management at Petroleum Development Oman (PDO). By establishing a comprehensive corporate digital competency framework, PDO aims to align its workforce with the demands of a digital landscape. The study highlights the importance of identifying specific competencies, the roles of stakeholders in the implementation process, and the necessity of ongoing evaluation and adaptation of these competencies.

Through an examination of best practices and the internal implementation, this work underscores the need for a strategic approach to talent management that fosters a culture of continuous learning and innovation. The findings suggest that effective competency identification has the potential to enhance workforce capabilities, contributing to PDO's objectives in navigating its digital transformation journey.

KEYWORDS

Competency, Digital Transformation, Talent Management, Upskilling, Leadership

1. INTRODUCTION

The oil and gas industry is undergoing a significant transformation driven by advancements in digital technology (Bharadwaj et al., 2013). As organizations like Petroleum Development Oman (PDO) strive to enhance productivity and operational efficiency, the need for a skilled and adaptable workforce has never been more pressing. Competency identification - defining the skills, knowledge, and behaviors required for various roles – specifically for the skills that will be needed in the future has become a crucial pillar of talent management strategies, gaining even greater importance due to the evolving industry demands (Cappelli, 2008). This manuscript examines the role of competency identification in PDO's digital transformation journey, exploring how a structured approach to developing a corporate digital competency framework can empower employees and drive organizational success.

In recent years, PDO has recognized the importance of aligning its workforce capabilities with the demands of a rapidly evolving technological landscape (Collings & Mellahi, 2009). This alignment requires a deep understanding of the specific competencies that enable employees to thrive in a digital environment. By identifying and cultivating these competencies, PDO can ensure that its workforce is equipped to meet the challenges posed by digital transformation. This manuscript aims to provide a comprehensive overview of the competency identification process, the stakeholders involved, and the practical implications for PDO and similar organizations.

2. FRAMEWORK DEVELOPMENT

Developing a corporate digital competency framework involves several crucial steps, each essential for the framework's effectiveness and sustainability. This structured approach ensures that the organization identifies and nurtures the skills necessary for thriving in a digital landscape.

- **Step 1: Assessing Current Competencies:**

The first step in developing a competency framework is assessing the current competencies within the organization. This involves conducting a thorough analysis of the existing competencies for each function/discipline and the associated proficiency levels. This comprehensive data collection helps PDO create a baseline understanding of its workforce's strengths and weaknesses, serving as a foundation for future competency development.

- **Step 2: Identifying Future Competencies:**

Once current competencies are assessed, the next step is to identify the competencies required for future success. This involves analyzing industry trends, technological advancements, and the strategic goals of the organization. By understanding these future needs, PDO proactively addressed skill gaps and prepared its workforce for upcoming challenges (Garrow, 2008).

- **Step 3: Developing the Competency Framework:**

After identifying the necessary competencies, PDO developed a formal corporate competency framework. This framework includes: Segmentation of the Framework, Clear Definitions, Competency Levels., Development plans, Alignment with Organizational Goals, and Flexibility.

This structured and detailed framework serves as a roadmap for talent management and development within the organization.

- **Step 4: Implementation and Training:**

The successful implementation of the competency framework requires robust training and communication strategies. By equipping employees with the necessary tools and understanding, organizations can cultivate a culture of continuous learning and development (Edvinsson & Malone, 2001).

- **Step 5: Evaluation and Continuous Improvement:**

Finally, the competency framework should undergo regular evaluation and updates to remain effective. This includes: establishing metrics, regular feedback loops, and periodic reviews. Through this ongoing evaluation and refinement process, PDO and any other organizations can maintain a dynamic competency framework that evolves alongside the organization and its strategic objectives.

3. OVERVIEW OF THE PDO'S COMPETENCY FRAMEWORK

The Corporate Digital Competencies Framework at PDO is designed to guide the organization through the complexities of digital transformation by categorizing competencies into three distinct levels. This structured approach ensures that all employees, regardless of their role, have a clear understanding of the digital skills required to thrive in a rapidly evolving digital landscape.

- Digital Pioneers (Level 1):
  - Target Group: This level is tailored for specialized roles such as data scientists, data engineers, scrum masters, digital architects, platform engineers, and software engineers. These individuals are at the forefront of digital innovation within the organization.
- Digital Enthusiasts (Level 2):
  - Target Group: This level encompasses digital citizens across various roles within the organization. These employees may not be specialized in technology but play a critical role in supporting digital initiatives.
- Digital Literates (Level 3):
  - Target Group: This foundational level targets the entire organization, including recent graduates and new hires. It is essential for fostering a digitally competent workforce.

In summary, the Corporate Digital Competencies Framework at PDO establishes a clear pathway for developing essential digital skills across all levels of the organization. By defining distinct roles and competencies for Digital Pioneers, Digital Enthusiasts, and Digital Literates, PDO empowers its workforce to adapt to the demands of digital transformation and fosters a culture of continuous learning and innovation. This structured approach is critical for ensuring that every employee contributes to and thrives in the evolving digital landscape, ultimately driving the organization's success in its digital endeavor.

4. CONCLUSION

In conclusion, competency identification is a fundamental aspect of talent management that significantly influences the success of organizations embarking on digital transformation. For Petroleum Development Oman (PDO), establishing a comprehensive corporate digital competency framework is essential for aligning workforce capabilities with the demands of an ever-evolving technological landscape.

By systematically identifying specific competencies, engaging stakeholders at all levels, and fostering a culture of continuous learning, PDO has successfully enhanced employee performance, driven innovation, and effectively met its strategic objectives (Gladwell, 2008). The integration of soft skills, adaptability, and inclusivity within the competency framework ensures that employees are equipped with the necessary technical skills and possess the interpersonal abilities required to collaborate and thrive in a digital environment.

As the digital landscape continues to shift, the organizations should remain proactive in updating and adapting its competency framework to address emerging challenges and opportunities. This includes cultivating agile teams capable of responding swiftly to changing demands, expanding talent sources to embrace diverse perspectives, and investing in continuous learning initiatives that empower employees.

Moreover, the recommendations outlined for PDO are equally applicable to other organizations striving to succeed in the digital age. By prioritizing competency identification and development, organizations can create resilient and adaptable workforces prepared to navigate the complexities of digital transformation. Ultimately, a strategic approach to talent management that emphasizes competency identification will drive long-term success and innovation, ensuring that both PDO and similar organizations remain competitive in a rapidly changing environment. Through dedication to these principles, the organization can achieve its digital transformation goals and set a benchmark for excellence in talent management that others in the industry can emulate.

ACKNOWLEDGMENTS

The author would like to express the deepest gratitude to Petroleum Development Oman (PDO) for the unwavering support and commitment to the development of the digital competency framework. Special thanks go to the Talent Management Team, the Capability and Competency Development Team, and the Digital Transformation Team for their significant contributions and collaborative efforts in building a comprehensive competency framework.

We would also like to acknowledge the invaluable input from subject matter experts and all key stakeholders who participated in this initiative. Their dedication and insights have been instrumental in shaping a framework that aligns workforce capabilities with the demands of a rapidly evolving digital landscape.

REFERENCES

Al-Eisa, A., & Al-Mutairi, A. (2012). Antecedents of knowledge sharing willingness among employees. Journal of Knowledge Management, 16(4), 588-606.

Bharadwaj, A., El Sawy, O. A., Pavlou, P. A., & Venkatraman, N. (2013). Digital business strategy: Toward a next generation of insights. MIS quarterly, 471-482.

Cappelli, P. (2008). Talent on demand: Managing talent in an age of uncertainty. Harvard Business Press.

Collings, D. G., & Mellahi, K. (2009). Strategic talent management: A review and research agenda. Human Resource Management Review, 19(4), 304-313.

Edvinsson, L., & Malone, M. S. (2001). Intellectual capital: Realizing your company's true value by finding its hidden brainpower. Harper Business Essentials.

Garrow, V. (2008). Talent management: A strategic focus. Upper Saddle River, NJ: Pearson Education.

Gladwell, M. (2008). Outliers: The story of success. Little, Brown.

A NOVEL APPROACH TO DESIGNING PATIENT-CENTERED SERVICES FOR POSTPARTUM NURSING CENTERS: A SYSTEMS THEORY PERSPECTIVE

Li-Min Lin[1], Chih-Lung Hung[2], Te-Min Chang[3], Pei-Chen Huang[4], Yi-Cheng Chen[5] and Jen-Her Wu[6,7]

[1]Department of Nursing, Meiho University
23, Ping Kuang Rd., Pingtung 91202, Taiwan
[2]CAO, Administrative Center, E-DA Hospital
No.1, Yida Rd., Yanchao District, Kaohsiung 82445, Taiwan
[3]Department of Information Management, National Sun Yat-Sen University
70 Lien-Hai Road, Kaohsiung, 804, Taiwan
[4]Director, E-DA Bassinet Mother and Baby Care Center
No.309, Dachang 1st Rd., Kaohsiung 807, Taiwan
[5]Department of Information Science and Management Systems, National Taitung University
369, Section 2, University Road, Taitung 95092, Taiwan.
[6]Department of Information Management, National Sun Yat-Sen University
[7]Advisory Board Member, E-Da Healthcare Group
70, Lien-Hai Rd., Kaohsiung 804, Taiwan

ABSTRACT

Postpartum nursing care is shifting towards patient-centered and coordinated care. This study proposes an IT-enabled service design methodology that integrates systems theory and a patient-centered perspective to create a design roadmap and guidelines for addressing the needs of postpartum mothers. Our evaluation of 293 postpartum mothers shows that implementing this approach to designing patient-centered services can significantly enhance mothers' satisfaction during their nursing care journey. These findings provide deeper insights and guidance for practitioners designing or evaluating IT-enabled services for healthcare information systems.

KEYWORDS

Postpartum Nursing Center, Systems Theory, Patient-Centered Perspective, IT-Enabled Services, Coordinated Care

1. INTRODUCTION

Women at the postpartum period are in an urgent need to physically recover from their pre-pregnant state and, to emotionally shape their roles into “mothers” who take care of infants and establish infant-bonding relationships. This period is known to be an optimal timing of care and intervention for women to set up their long-term health and well-being. Postpartum nursing care that provides comprehensive services for women is considered an essential health-care practice for promoting maternal health after childbirth. Overwhelmingly, a growing number of women in East and Southeast Asian countries have received postpartum nursing care in a traditionally cultural manner called “doing the month” for the first 30 days postpartum to aid them in building back strength. In Taiwan, instead of staying at home, most women have elected to experience “doing the month” in the postpartum nursing centers (PNCs) that are responsible of providing such care-giving tasks as specialized meals, health education programs, and services that address the physical and emotional needs of mothers and their babies. HIT nowadays offers immense opportunities to meet patients’ needs, engage and empower patients, and lead to powerful and enduring patient experiences (Christiansen et al., 2023). Exploitations of IT-enabled services require appropriate deployment to reinforce synchronized functioning and achieve realized synergy (Nevo & Wade, 2010). Evidence shows that many nursing services delivered by PNCs neither are in proper health-care settings that match women's preferences, nor do they reach a satisfactory level for postpartum mothers (Albanese et al., 2021). Few studies have developed pragmatic roadmaps and guidelines for the implementation of effective service designs for PNCs. We therefore pose the research question: How to design patient-centered nursing services to enhance the satisfaction and experiences of postpartum mothers during their PNC journey? Our study adopts DSRM to create an IT-enabled service design methodology (ISDM) that is theoretically grounded with the SHC patient-centered perspective to align purpose, people, and performance, and with systems theory to appropriately deploy the IT-enabled services.

2. ISDM PROCESS

Firstly, gap analysis of current services is applied as an investigation of which existing IT-enabled services at the PNC meet patients' needs from a patient-centered perspective. This technique comprises involves (a) modeling current service activity with a service blueprint, (b) identifying patient-centered needs, and (c) identifying the gaps between current services and unmet patient needs as shown in Figure 1. The top section of Figure 1 presents existing IT-enabled services that meet patient-centered needs, with solid lines indicating satisfaction after careful deliberation. The middle section links to patient-centered needs. The bottom section describes gaps in the existing services or gaps with respect to meeting patient-centered needs, with dashed lines indicating a relationship. Furthermore, Step 2 involves defining objectives with respect to developing a solution on the basis of identified problems. Peffers et al. (2007) contended that objectives should be rationally derived from a specified problem and can be quantitative or qualitative. Quantitative objectives are established by defining a desirable solution that outperforms existing alternatives, and qualitative objectives are established by determining how a new solution may resolve unaddressed problems. The third step involves designing solutions to address identified gaps involving the following two activities including (a) identifying appropriate IT assets and (b) ensuring compatibility and devoting integration efforts.

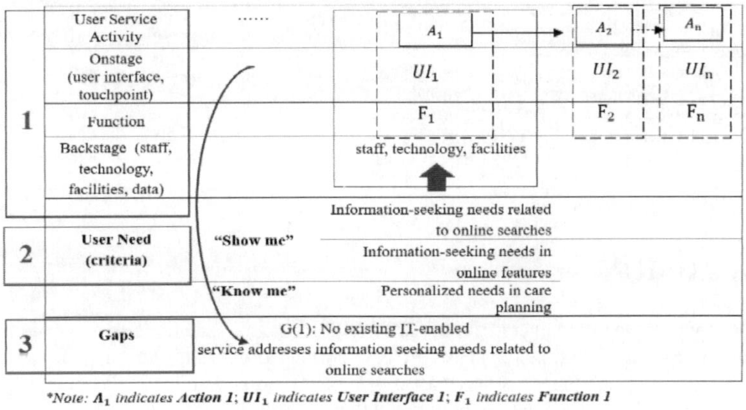

*Note: A_1 indicates **Action 1**; UI_1 indicates **User Interface 1**; F_1 indicates **Function 1***

Figure 1. Gap analysis diagram

3. ISDM INSTANTIATION AND CASE STUDY

Our research employs a case study on E-DA BASSINET PNC to instantiate the development process of ISDM. BASSINET is affiliated with E-DA Hospital in Kaohsiung, Taiwan. Part (a)-(c) in Figure 2 presents service blueprints for BASSINET's existing IT-enabled service activities for the at home, inpatient services, and outpatient feedback stages, respectively. For example, on the basis of the patient-centered needs of BASSINET, our study identified one type 2 gap in the "coordinate for me" perspective. This gap indicates the insufficient coverage of current IT-enabled services concerning BASSINET's in-facility coordinated care. It is notably observed that current backstage IT/IS resource is not capable of performing information sharing among stakeholders in a timely and accurate manner to empower participating mothers. BASSINET needs to invest additional IT assets to reinforce patient empowerment during the inpatient-services journey.

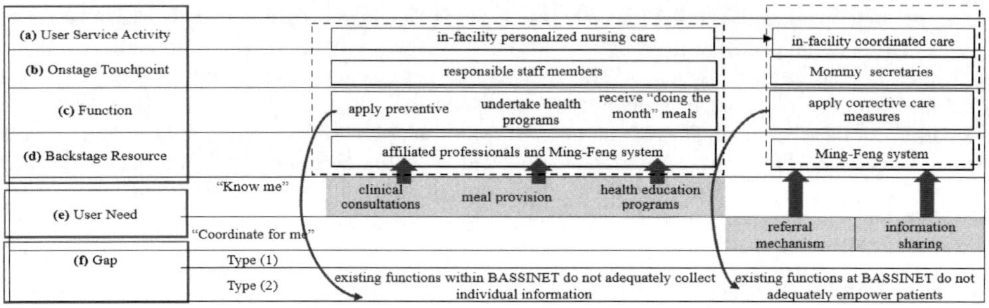

Figure 2. Service blueprint for BASSINET's coordinated care at inpatient services stage

To evaluate the Performance of the IT-enabled care services, BASSINET distributed a satisfaction survey to postpartum mothers upon their departure from the PNC. Participating mothers rated each item on a 5-point Likert scale. After we assisted BASSINET in enhancing its IT-enabled care services, the satisfaction questionnaire was substantially modified to incorporate the stages of the patient journey in PNCs. The original survey was completed by 187 mothers who stayed at and departed from BASSINET between July 2019 and December 2021. Table 1 presents the survey results.

Table 1. Survey results after service enhancement

Questionnaire item	Mean	SD	Z	Sig.
A1. I feel comfortable using the website and the Facebook fan page.	4.56	1.22	4.73	0.00**
A2. The Facebook fan page have all the functions I expect them to have.	4.24	1.18	2.09	0.02*
A3. I am satisfied with the ease of using the website and the Facebook fan page.	4.3	1.05	2.94	0.00**
A4. The contextual information of the Facebook fan page caught my attention.	4.22	1.33	1.70	0.04*
A5. I feel personally acknowledged when I contact the staff through the fan page.	4.16	1.28	1.29	0.10
A6. My personal information at home was seamlessly applied to my care plan.	4.22	1.26	1.80	0.04*
I1. I feel comfortable using the provided mode of communication.	4.24	1.22	2.03	0.02*
I2. I can receive timely responses through the provided mode of communication.	4.29	1.31	2.28	0.01*
I3. The message of the provided mode of communication is easy to understand.	4.26	1.28	2.09	0.02*
I4. I am satisfied with the services I received through the attendance system.	4.32	1.17	2.82	0.00**
I5. I am satisfied with the coordinated care I received when difficulties arose.	4.25	1.45	1.78	0.04*
O1. I believe all care services provided by BASSINET met my needs.	4.50	1.03	5.00	0.00**
O2. I am satisfied with the support from BASSINET during my journey.	4.45	1.06	4.37	0.00**
O3. I will recommend BASSINET to other prospective mothers if possible.	4.52	1.15	4.66	0.00**
O4. I enjoy the nursing care atmosphere and environment at BASSINET.	4.72	0.98	7.56	0.00**

* $p < .05$; ** $p < .01$. (H_0: $\mu > 4$)

4. CONCLUSION

This study has two key theoretical contributions. Firstly, it pioneers the development of an IT-enabled service design methodology that integrates systems theory, service blueprints, and a patient-centered perspective. Systems theory and service blueprints serve as foundational tools, systematically mapping the patient journey and pinpointing critical needs at each juncture for enhancement throughout the patient journey. Secondly, this study advances the design and development solutions based on the needs and gaps identified through the ISDM. By leveraging these insights, the ISDM serves as a structured roadmap for identifying key tasks, conducting gap analyses, and systematically designing and developing solutions tailored to enhance IT-enabled services within PNC.

REFERENCES

Albanese, A. M. et al, (2021). The Importance of Patient-Centered Research in the Promotion of Postpartum Mental Health. *Frontiers in psychiatry,* Vol. 12, 720106.

Christiansen, P. K. et al, (2023). The Development of an IT-Based Intervention to Support a Healthy Postpartum Lifestyle through Behavioral Change. *Health Informatics Journal*, Vol. 29, No. 1, 14604582231153523.

Nevo, S. and Wade, M. R., (2010). The Formation and Value of IT-Enabled Resources: Antecedents and Consequences of Synergistic Relationships. *MIS Quarterly*, Vol. 34, No. 1, pp. 163-183.

Peffers, K. et al, (2007). A Design Science Research Methodology for Information Systems Research. *Journal of Management Information Systems*, Vol. 24, No. 3, pp. 45-77.

A NEW TECHNOLOGICAL FRONTIER IN FIREPROOF UNDERWEAR FOR MOTORSPORT

Dalia Gallico
Università San Raffaele Roma, Italy

ABSTRACT

This article presents the development and testing of OMP SensorShield, a prototype of smart fireproof underwear designed for use in motorsport. The garment integrates advanced textile sensor technologies capable of real-time monitoring of the driver's physiological parameters—such as heart rate, respiration, posture, and ECG—without compromising safety, comfort, or compliance with FIA 8856-2018 standards. Developed through a collaboration between Racing Force Group, ComfTech®, and Outlast®, SensorShield combines thermoregulating, flame-resistant fabrics with wearable microelectronics and precision tailoring. Laboratory and simulator testing confirmed the feasibility of integrating biometric sensors into high-performance fireproof garments. Key challenges identified include the mechanical durability of conductive threads, washing maintenance, and sensor connection stability. The article outlines future improvements including the use of printed electronics, full wireless transmission, and advanced data analytics interfaces. The SensorShield project represents a functional innovation in motorsport safety wear, merging traditional craftsmanship with digital protection systems and paving the way for broader applications in aerospace, rescue operations, and emergency response.

KEYWORDS

Smart Textiles, Fireproof Underwear, Wearable Technology, Motorsport Safety, Physiological Monitoring, FIA Standards Compliance

1. INTRODUCTION

In the context of motorsport, driver safety represents a critical element and evolves in parallel with technological innovation. Recent episodes, such as the accident of Romain Grosjean, have highlighted the importance not only of passive protection (such as fire resistance), but also of intelligent systems capable of promptly detecting the driver's vital signs (Bianchi, 2021).

OMP SensorShield is a prototype of a fireproof underwear shirt, born from an internal idea at the company Racing Force Group. The development of the product required collaboration with two other companies: ComfTech® and Outlast®.

The shared goal was to integrate textile sensors for real-time physiological monitoring into fireproof underwear intended for automobile racing, which must fit the body like a second skin and be approved according to current FIA regulations (Bonfiglio, 2021).

The project combines tailoring and textile expertise with advanced wearable technologies, giving life to a device that protects, detects, and communicates.

2. BACKGROUND

The development of smart textiles represents one of the most fascinating revolutions in technology applied to clothing. The integration of flexible microelectronics, conductive yarns, and biometric sensors has already led to significant innovations in the sports, healthcare, and industrial sectors. (Jang &Li, 2023)

There are already commercial products used in sports, as well as devices employed for monitoring elderly people and newborns (Ferrari, 2020).

According to sources such as *ZeroUnoWeb* (ZeroUnoWeb, 2024) and *Datatex* (Datatex, 2024*),* the growing demand for smart clothing has drawn attention to fundamental aspects such as washability, energy autonomy, interoperability, and environmental sustainability. The website *Rigeneriamo Territorio* (Rigeneriamo Territorio, 2024) also highlights the value of the dialogue between traditional textile manufacturing and technological innovation, promoting the hybridization between craftsmanship and materials science.

Motorsport stands out as an ideal testing ground to trial and validate these systems, thanks to its extreme standards in terms of reliability, lightness, and thermal resistance (Stoppa &Chiolerio, 2014).

3. MATERIALS AND METODH

The OMP SensorShield prototype is made from Outlast® thermoregulating fireproof fabric, equipped with PCM (Phase Change Materials) microcapsules, which help maintain the driver's body temperature constant. This technology, originally developed for NASA, was later applied in motorsport as well. (Outlast Technologies,2022).

The garment features 5-needle closed seams and uses fireproof thread with a count of 120, as required by FIA 8856-2018 regulations. It is characterized by a mock neck, snug cuffs, and bidirectional elasticity. The manufacturing process was recently improved thanks to the introduction of more precise machinery and the presence of specialized tailors for this type of garment.

The ComfTech® textile sensors are integrated at three key points: the neck (carotid area) and the wrists (right and left). The sensors, sewn with silver conductive thread, are connected via textile tracks to a removable control unit positioned on the chest. The system is capable of detecting heart rate, respiratory rate, posture, and ECG (with the "Complete" device), transmitting the data via Bluetooth Low Energy to an application for real-time monitoring (ComfTech,2023, 2024).

The in-house tailoring department produces the garments in a partially assembled form, leaving the collar and sleeves open to allow for sensor integration. The garments are then sent to ComfTech® for technical assembly and testing, and subsequently returned for final closure and functional tests related to fit and data transmission.

4. RESULTS AND SPERIMENTATION

The SensorShield prototypes have been tested in the laboratory and on a simulator, limited to certain construction features. The checks carried out so far have concerned:

- The effectiveness of the fireproof seams
- The fit and elasticity at the sensorized points
- The integration of conductive tracks and the routing of cables within the garment's structure
- The mechanical compatibility with FIA standard suits and systems

Breathability proved to be satisfactory, and comfort was maintained even under thermal stress. However, specific tests on the detection of physiological parameters have not yet been conducted; these will be carried out in the next development phase.

At present, it was decided to begin prototyping with a shirt structurally similar to racing underwear already on the market, favoring a tailored solution over screen-printing techniques, which are already available but currently more expensive and complex to integrate at the initial stage.

Prototyping is still in the process of being completed; once finalized, procedures will be initiated for FIA homologation request and subsequent on-track tests with professional drivers. (Fédération Internationale de l'Automobile, 2018).

Table 1. "OMP SENSORSHIELD" A technical fireproof underwear shirt equipped with invisible integrated biometric sensors, intended for professional racing drivers, with FIA 8856-2018 approval. The garment detects the driver's vital parameters in real time (heart rate, body temperature, stress level) and transmits them to the box, where the team can monitor the driver's psychophysical state

Tecnology	**Way**	**Method**
Bluetooth 5.0/5.2	Bluetooth Low Energy	Direct, local, low-local wireless connection
Gateway	Collection Device	Receives Bluetooth data and transmits it to the Internet
Transmission over LTE/5G	Transmission over Cellular Network	Real-time remote data sending
WiFi Direct / Hotspot	Consumption WiFi Connection	Can work in a wider area than Bluetooth alone

5. OMP SENSORSHIELD

OMP SensorShield introduces a new approach to technical clothing for motorsport, in which safety is no longer limited to passive protection alone, but also includes active monitoring of the driver's physiological conditions. The semi-industrial approach, which combines in-house tailored production with the integration of advanced textile sensor technology, demonstrates how specialized craftsmanship can effectively collaborate with precision electronics.

However, the project presents some critical issues that have already emerged during the prototyping phase, including:

- The need for particular care during washing and maintenance of the garment
- The fragility of the conductive threads during the sewing process
- The variable reliability of the connection between the fabric and the control unit, especially in extreme or humid environments

These aspects highlight the importance of developing more robust solutions to ensure the long-term durability of the system under real operating conditions.

Future developments of the project could include:

- The adoption of printed circuits directly onto the fabric, to improve integration and reduce cable bulk
- The complete miniaturization of the control unit to increase discretion and wearing comfort
- The introduction of fully wireless transmission systems integrated into the fabric itself
- The creation of a more advanced software interface for real-time analysis and the management of physiological data history

In a broader perspective, the technology behind SensorShield can be adapted to other sectors characterized by critical operating conditions, such as alpine rescue, aerospace, civil defense, and firefighting protection.

Finally, to achieve full system validation, it will be essential to complete functional tests, initiate the FIA homologation procedure, and analyze the product's performance under real on-track conditions, with the direct involvement of professional drivers.

6. CONCLUSION

The testing of the OMP SensorShield prototype has demonstrated the feasibility of a smart, fireproof, sensor-equipped garment compliant with FIA standards, capable of monitoring the driver's physiological parameters in real time. The synergy between technical tailoring and wearable technologies represented the core of the project: the garment can be produced in-house, while sensor integration is entrusted to a qualified partner.

This solution opens new perspectives for the adoption of wearable technology in highly competitive contexts and environments with high operational risk. OMP SensorShield stands as a concrete example of functional innovation, capable of combining advanced materials, tailoring know-how, and digital safety tools.

REFERENCES

Bianchi, G., & Ceccarelli, M., (2021). Fire-resistant materials in motorsport: From regulation to application. Materials Today: Proceedings, 42, 2132–2139.

Bonfiglio, A., & De Rossi, D. (2021). Wearable Monitoring Systems. Springer.

ComfTech®. (2023). Smart textile solutions for healthcare and performance. Retrieved from https://www.comftech.com

Outlast Technologies., (2022). Thermo-regulation and PCM technology overview. Retrieved from https://www.outlast.com

ComfTech Srl., (2024). Smart Textile Solutions. https://www.comftech.com

Datatex., (2024). Tessuti smart ed elettronica indossabile. https://datatex.com

Dias, T. (Ed.)., (2015). Electronic Textiles: Smart Fabrics and Wearable Technology. Woodhead Publishing.

Fédération Internationale de l'Automobile (FIA). (2018). FIA Standard 8856-2018: Protective Clothing for Automobile Drivers.

Ferrari, V., & Franchi, F. (2020). Wearable monitoring systems for real-time physiological data in motorsports: A review. IEEE Sensors Journal, 8440–8452.

Fletcher, K., & Tham, M. (2019). Earth Logic: Fashion Action Research Plan. The J J Charitable Trust.

Jiang, Y., & Li, Y., (2023). Wearable sensors for telehealth based on emerging materials and nanotechnologies. npj Flexible Electronics.

Outlast Technologies GmbH., (2023). PCM Technology Overview. https://www.outlast.com

Rigeneriamo Territorio.,(2024). Tessuti elettronici. https://www.rigeneriamoterritorio.it

Stoppa, M., & Chiolerio, A., (2014). Wearable electronics and smart textiles: A critical review. Sensors, 14(7), 11957–11992. https://doi.org/10.3390/s140711957

ZeroUnoWeb. (2024). Smart clothing: cos'è e come funziona l'abbigliamento intelligente. https://www.zerounoweb.it

AUTHOR INDEX